THE OFFICIAL LSAT
SUPER**PREP II**™

A Publication of the Law School Admission Council,
Newtown, PA

The Law School Admission Council (LSAC) is a nonprofit corporation that provides unique, state-of-the-art admission products and services to ease the admission process for law schools and their applicants worldwide. Currently, 220 law schools in the United States, Canada, and Australia are members of the Council and benefit from LSAC's services.

LSAC fees, policies, and procedures relating to, but not limited to, test registration, test administration, test score reporting, misconduct and irregularities, Credential Assembly Service (CAS), and other matters may change without notice at any time. Up-to-date LSAC policies and procedures are available at LSAC.org.

ISBN-13: 978-0-9907186-8-0

Print number
5 4 3 2 1

TABLE OF CONTENTS

INTRODUCTION

INTRODUCTION TO THE LSAT

The LSAT is a half-day, standardized test required for admission to all ABA-approved law schools, most Canadian law schools, and many other law schools. It provides a standard measure of acquired reading and verbal reasoning skills that law schools can use as one of several factors in assessing applicants.

The test consists of five 35-minute sections of multiple-choice questions. Four of the five sections contribute to the test taker's score. These sections include one reading comprehension section, one analytical reasoning section, and two logical reasoning sections. The unscored section, commonly referred to as the variable section, typically is used to pretest new test questions or to preequate new test forms. The placement of this section in the LSAT will vary. A 35-minute writing sample is administered at the end of the test. LSAC does not score the writing sample, but copies are sent to all law schools to which you apply. The score scale for the LSAT is 120 to 180.

The LSAT is designed to measure skills considered essential for success in law school: the reading and comprehension of complex texts with accuracy and insight; the organization and management of information and the ability to draw reasonable inferences from it; the ability to think critically; and the analysis and evaluation of the reasoning and arguments of others.

For up-to-date information on LSAC's services go to our website, LSAC.org.

SCORING

Your LSAT score is based on the number of questions answered correctly (the raw score). There is no deduction for incorrect answers, and all questions count equally. In other words, there is no penalty for guessing.

Test Score Accuracy—Reliability and Standard Error of Measurement

Candidates perform at different levels on different occasions for reasons quite unrelated to the characteristics of a test itself. The accuracy of test scores is best described by the use of two related statistical terms, reliability and standard error of measurement.

Reliability is a measure of how consistently a test measures the skills being assessed. The higher the reliability coefficient for a test, the more certain we can be that test takers would get very similar scores if they took the test again. LSAC reports an internal consistency measure of reliability for every test form. Reliability can vary

from 0.00 to 1.00, and a test with no measurement error would have a reliability coefficient of 1.00 (never attained in practice). Reliability coefficients for past LSAT forms have ranged from .90 to .95, indicating a high degree of consistency for these tests. LSAC expects the reliability of the LSAT to continue to fall within the same range.

LSAC also reports the amount of measurement error associated with each test form, a concept known as the standard error of measurement (SEM). The SEM, which is usually about 2.6 points, indicates how close a test taker's observed score is likely to be to his or her true score. True scores are theoretical scores that would be obtained from perfectly reliable tests with no measurement error—scores never known in practice. Score bands, or ranges of scores that contain a test taker's true score a certain percentage of the time, can be derived using the SEM. LSAT score bands are constructed by adding and subtracting the (rounded) SEM to and from an actual LSAT score (e.g., the LSAT score, plus or minus 3 points). Scores near 120 or 180 have asymmetrical bands. Score bands constructed in this manner will contain an individual's true score approximately 68 percent of the time.

Measurement error also must be taken into account when comparing LSAT scores of two test takers. It is likely that small differences in scores are due to measurement error rather than to meaningful differences in ability. The standard error of score differences provides some guidance as to the importance of differences between two scores. The standard error of score differences is approximately 1.4 times larger than the standard error of measurement for the individual scores.

Thus, a test score should be regarded as a useful but approximate measure of a test taker's abilities as measured by the test, not as an exact determination of his or her abilities. LSAC encourages law schools to examine the range of scores within the interval that probably contains the test taker's true score (e.g., the test taker's score band) rather than solely interpret the reported score alone.

Adjustments for Variation in Test Difficulty

All test forms of the LSAT reported on the same score scale are designed to measure the same abilities, but one test form may be slightly easier or more difficult than another. The scores from different test forms are made comparable through a statistical procedure known as equating. As a result of equating, a given scaled score earned on different test forms reflects the same level of ability.

Research on the LSAT

Summaries of LSAT validity studies and other LSAT research can be found in member law school libraries and at LSAC.org.

HOW THESE PREPTESTS DIFFER FROM AN ACTUAL LSAT

These PrepTests are made up of the scored sections and writing samples from actual LSATs. These PrepTests do not contain the extra, variable section that is used to pretest new test questions of one of the three multiple-choice question types. The three multiple-choice question types may be in a different order in an actual LSAT than in these PrepTests. This is because the order of these question types is intentionally varied for each administration of the test.

THE QUESTION TYPES

The multiple-choice questions that make up most of the LSAT reflect a broad range of academic disciplines and are intended to give no advantage to candidates from a particular academic background.

The five sections of the test contain three different question types. The following material presents a general discussion of the nature of each question type and some strategies that can be used in answering them.

Analytical Reasoning Questions

Analytical reasoning questions are designed to measure the ability to understand a structure of relationships and to draw conclusions about the structure. The examinee is asked to make deductions from a set of statements, rules, or conditions that describe relationships among entities such as persons, places, things, or events. They simulate the kinds of detailed analyses of relationships that a law student must perform in solving legal problems. For example, a passage might describe four diplomats sitting around a table, following certain rules of protocol as to who can sit where. The test taker must answer questions about the implications of the given information, for example, who is sitting between diplomats X and Y.

The passage used for each group of questions describes a common relationship such as the following:

- Assignment: Two parents, P and O, and their children, R and S, must go to the dentist on four consecutive days, designated 1, 2, 3, and 4;

- Ordering: X arrived before Y but after Z;

- Grouping: A manager is trying to form a project team from seven staff members—R, S, T, U, V, W, and X. Each staff member has a particular strength—writing, planning, or facilitating;

- Spatial: A certain country contains six cities and each city is connected to at least one other city by a system of roads, some of which are one-way.

Further discussion of analytical reasoning questions, including a discussion of different varieties of these questions and strategies for answering them, can be found on pages 4–15.

Logical Reasoning Questions

Logical reasoning questions evaluate a test taker's ability to understand, analyze, criticize, and complete arguments. The arguments are contained in short passages taken from a variety of sources, including letters to the editor, speeches, advertisements, newspaper articles and editorials, informal discussions and conversations, as well as articles in the humanities, the social sciences, and the natural sciences.

Each logical reasoning question requires the examinee to read and comprehend the argument or the reasoning contained in the passage, and answer one or two questions about it. Further discussion of logical reasoning questions, including a discussion of different varieties of these questions and strategies for answering them, can be found on pages 16–41.

Reading Comprehension Questions

The purpose of reading comprehension questions is to measure your ability to read, with understanding and insight, examples of lengthy and complex materials similar to those commonly encountered in law school work. The reading comprehension section of the LSAT contains four sets of reading questions, each consisting of a selection of reading material followed by five to eight questions. The reading selection in three of the four sets consists of a single reading passage of approximately 450 words in length. The other set contains two related shorter passages. Sets with two passages are a variant of reading comprehension, called comparative reading, which was introduced into the reading comprehension section in June 2007. See page 57 for more information.

Reading selections for reading comprehension questions are drawn from subjects such as the humanities, the social sciences, the biological and physical sciences, and issues related to the law. Reading comprehension questions require you to read carefully and accurately, to determine the relationships among the various parts of the reading selection, and to draw reasonable inferences from the material in the selection. Further discussion of reading comprehension questions, including a discussion of different varieties of these questions and strategies for answering them, can be found on pages 42–57.

THE WRITING SAMPLE

On the day of the test, you will be asked to write one sample essay. LSAC does not score the writing sample, but copies are sent to all law schools to which you apply. According to a 2015 LSAC survey of 129 United States and Canadian law schools, almost all utilize the writing sample in evaluating some applications for admission. Frivolous responses or no responses to writing sample prompts have been used by law schools as grounds for rejection of applications for admission.

In developing and implementing the writing sample portion of the LSAT, LSAC has operated on the following premises: First, law schools and the legal profession value highly the ability to communicate effectively in writing. Second, it is important to encourage potential law students to develop effective writing skills. Third, a sample of an applicant's writing, produced under controlled conditions, is a potentially useful indication of that person's writing ability. Fourth, the writing sample can serve as an independent check on other writing submitted by applicants as part of the admission process. Finally, writing samples may be useful for diagnostic purposes.

You will have 35 minutes in which to plan and write an essay on the topic you receive. Read the topic and the accompanying directions carefully. You will probably find it best to spend a few minutes considering the topic and organizing your thoughts before you begin writing. In your essay, be sure to develop your ideas fully, leaving time, if possible, to review what you have written. Do not write on a topic other than the one specified. Writing on a topic of your own choice is not acceptable.

No special knowledge is required or expected for this writing exercise. Law schools are interested in the reasoning, clarity, organization, language usage, and writing mechanics displayed in your essay. How well you write is more important than how much you write. Confine your essay to the blocked, lined area on the front and back of the Writing Sample Response Sheet. Only that area will be reproduced for law schools. Be sure that your writing is legible.

The writing prompt presents a decision problem. You are asked to make a choice between two positions or courses of action. Both of the choices are defensible, and you are given criteria and facts on which to base your decision. There is no "right" or "wrong" position to take on the topic, so the quality of each test taker's response is a function not of which choice is made, but of how well or poorly the choice is supported and how well or poorly the other choice is criticized.

TAKING THE PREPTESTS UNDER SIMULATED LSAT CONDITIONS

One important way to prepare for the LSAT is to simulate the day of the test by taking a practice test under actual time constraints. This helps you to estimate the amount of time you can afford to spend on each question in a section and to determine the question types on which you may need additional practice.

Since the LSAT is a timed test, it is important to use your allotted time wisely. During the test, you may work only on the section designated by the test supervisor. You cannot devote extra time to a difficult section and make up that time on a section you find easier. In pacing yourself, and checking your answers, you should think of each section of the test as a separate minitest.

Be sure that you answer every question on the test. When you do not know the correct answer to a question, first eliminate the responses that you know are incorrect, then make your best guess among the remaining choices. Do not be afraid to guess as there is no penalty for incorrect answers.

When you take a practice test, abide by all the requirements specified in the directions and keep strictly within the specified time limits. Work without a rest period. When you take an actual test you will have only a short break—usually 10–15 minutes—after SECTION III. When taken under conditions as much like actual testing conditions as possible, a practice test provides very useful preparation for taking the LSAT.

Official directions for the four multiple-choice sections are included in these PrepTests so that you can approximate actual testing conditions as you practice.

To take a test:

- Set a timer for 35 minutes. Answer all the questions in SECTION I of a PrepTest. Stop working on that section when the 35 minutes have elapsed.

- Repeat, allowing yourself 35 minutes each for sections II, III, and IV.

- Set the timer again for 35 minutes, then prepare your response to the writing sample topic for the PrepTest.

- Refer to "Computing Your Score" for the PrepTest for instruction on evaluating your performance. An answer key is provided for that purpose.

HOW TO APPROACH ANALYTICAL REASONING QUESTIONS

In working through an Analytical Reasoning section of the LSAT, you'll want to do two things: get the answer to the questions right and use your time efficiently. In this section, you'll get advice on how to do both.

Analytical Reasoning questions test your ability to reason within a given set of circumstances. These circumstances are described in the "setup." A setup consists of sets of elements (people, places, objects, tasks, colors, days of the week, and so on) along with a list of conditions designed to impose some sort of structure, or organization, on these elements (for example, putting them into an ordered sequence from first to last, or selecting subgroups from a larger group, or pairing elements from one set with elements from another set). The different structures allowed by the setup are the "outcomes."

Consider the following setup:

> Each of five students—Hubert, Lori, Paul, Regina, and Sharon—will visit exactly one of three cities—Montreal, Toronto, or Vancouver—for the month of March, according to the following conditions:
>
> > Sharon visits a different city than Paul.
> > Hubert visits the same city as Regina.
> > Lori visits Montreal or else Toronto.
> > If Paul visits Vancouver, Hubert visits Vancouver with him.
> > Each student visits one of the cities with at least one of the other four students.[1]

This setup features two sets of elements: a set of students and a set of cities. There are five conditions that constrain how the members of these two sets are associated with each other. The kind of structure that is to be imposed on the elements is this: each student must be paired with exactly one of the cities in strict accordance with the conditions.

Note. Analytical Reasoning setups all have one crucial property in common: there is always more than one acceptable outcome. For example, in the example involving students and the cities they visit, the conditions do not work together to restrict each of the students to visiting a particular city and no other. Instead, there is more than one structure that satisfies all of the requirements of the setup.

Analytical Reasoning questions test your ability to determine what is necessary, what is possible, and what is impossible within the circumstances of the setup. Questions that you are likely to be asked, based on setups such as the one above, are questions like these:

> Which one of the following must be true for March?
> Which one of the following could be false in March?
> If Sharon visits Vancouver, which one of the following must be true for March?
> If Hubert and Sharon visit a city together, which one of the following could be true in March?

In other words, you'll need to determine what can or must happen, either in general or else in specified circumstances (such as Sharon visiting Vancouver or Hubert and Sharon visiting a city together). And now we'll look at how you go about doing this.

Figuring Out the Setup

The first thing you need to get very clear about is what exactly is supposed to happen to the elements in the setup. So first you need to recognize which parts of the setup serve only as background information.

In the example above, the five students and the three cities are the things you have to associate with one another. What happens to them makes the difference between one outcome and another. But the month of March, which is mentioned both in the original setup and in each of the questions cited, is merely background information, as is the fact that the visitors are all students. The overall setup allows for a number of different arrangements for the visits. But none of the differences is in any way related to the fact

---

[1] December 1992 LSAT, section 1, questions 1–6.

that the visits happen in March, just as none of the differences is in any way related to the fact that the visitors are students. The month could just as well have been April, and the visitors could just as well have been professors or tourists. Changing these things would not change the way the setup and the questions function.

Now, what happens to the elements in the setup? Looking at the students first, we find that each of them is to visit just one of the cities. Looking at the cities, you might at first assume that each city will be visited by at least one of the students. However, notice that there is actually nothing that says that each of the cities has to be visited. Consider the implications of the last condition. This condition essentially says that no student can visit a city alone. This means that, for all three cities to be visited by at least two students, there would have to be at least six students. In actual fact, there are only five. So we know that there cannot be student visitors in all three cities. And the first of the conditions tells us that the students cannot all visit the same city, since Sharon and Paul cannot visit the same city as each other.

So we now know, in general outline, what an acceptable outcome will look like: one of the three cities will be visited by three of the students, one of them by two, and one of them by none. This is the type of implication that can be very useful to work out as you read the conditions, even before you start to answer the questions. It underscores the importance of reading through the setup carefully in order to work through its implications and understand how it works.

HOW TO REPRESENT WHAT HAPPENS (SOME TIME-SAVING TIPS)

Because we have worked out some of the implications of the setup, we now have an idea of the basic shape of the acceptable outcomes. At this point, it might be possible for some people to figure out the answers to individual questions in their heads. Generally, however, this requires enormous powers of concentration and creates opportunities for error. For most people, trying to work these problems in their heads would be an extremely bad idea. Virtually everyone is well advised to use pencil and paper in solving Analytical Reasoning questions.

The time allotted for Analytical Reasoning questions gives you an average of less than 1½ minutes per question. Time management, therefore, is important. Since it does take time to sketch out solutions on paper, you should do whatever you can to use your time economically. Here are some time-saving tips that many people find useful:

- Abbreviate the elements by using just their initials. The elements in lists of names or places or objects will usually have different initials. When elements such as days of the week don't have different initials, be ready

to devise abbreviations that will allow you to distinguish them. (For example, in a set of questions involving days of the week, you might use "T" for "Tuesday" and "Th" for "Thursday.")

- Just as you would use initials to represent the elements, you should work with shorthand versions of the conditions. Familiarize yourself with the most common types of conditions and devise your own shorthand way of representing them. For example, one frequent kind of condition stipulates that something that happens to one member of a pair of elements also happens to the other member. In the example above, the condition saying that "Hubert visits the same city as Regina" is of this type. You might decide that your shorthand for this condition will be "H = R." And for the condition that reads, "If Paul visits Vancouver, Hubert visits Vancouver with him," you might use "if Pv then Hv" or "P(V) → H(V)."

Your shorthand versions of the conditions are the versions that you will be working with, so make sure that they correctly represent what the original conditions actually mean. The time spent in setting the conditions down in this way is more than offset by the time you'll save through the economy of working with the conditions in a form in which they can be quickly and easily taken in at a glance.

 Note. It doesn't matter whether anyone else would be able to look at your abbreviations and make sense of them. All that matters is that you yourself become fully fluent in using your abbreviations, so that you can save time when you put things down on paper. Practice doing Analytical Reasoning questions using your own abbreviations. Pick abbreviations that make sense to you. Pick abbreviations that are distinct enough that you won't mistake one for another, especially under the time pressure of taking the test.

- A quick check of the abbreviated setup conditions will sometimes show that one or more of the elements in the setup isn't mentioned in any of the conditions. Don't take this as an indication that there must be a mistake somewhere. Rather, take it at face value: those elements are not specifically constrained. You might devise a special notation for this situation. For example, you could circle those initials and include them at the bottom of your list of setup conditions. Or you might just make a shorthand list of all the elements, whether they are mentioned in the conditions or not.

- In your shorthand system, find a striking way to represent what **cannot** happen. For example, if you encounter a condition of the form "Greg cannot give the first presentation," this might be simply abbreviated as "G not 1" or even "*G(1)," where the asterisk is the symbol you use to represent "not."

- You might find it useful to represent certain conditions in more than one form. For example, you may decide that whenever you find a condition like "If Paul is selected, Raoul is also selected," you will automatically put down, as your shorthand version, both "P → R" and "not R → not P," since (as we'll see later) the two are logically equivalent and you might find it helpful to be reminded of this fact when you're answering the questions.

- You will very likely use certain elementary diagramming techniques, for example, using the elements in one set as headers and the elements in the other as entries under those headers. Try to think a bit about which diagramming techniques are effective for you. For example, in the case of the setup involving students and cities, you might diagram an outcome as follows:

M	T	V
H, R, S	L, P	

Or you might diagram it like this:

M: H, R, S
T: L, P
V:

But you might not want to end up with this diagram:

H	L	P	R	S
M	T	T	M	M

Although this last diagram presents the same information as the other two, you might well feel that it does so less usefully. For example, the last diagram does not capture the fact that one of the cities will not be visited by any of the students as graphically as the other two diagrams do. Develop strategies ahead of time that will lead you to create diagrams that you work with easily and well. There is no one way to do this, just as there is no one right way to abbreviate conditions. The only way to find out what works for you is to practice diagramming a number of setups before taking the test.

- For some questions, you might find that it is helpful to quickly write out your abbreviations for the active elements in the set—H R P L S, for example—before you begin to work out the solution. Then you can cross out each element as you satisfy yourself that you have accounted for it in the current solution. This method is especially helpful if the list of elements is too long for you to keep track of in your head or if you have already marked up your original list of elements.

ORIENTATION QUESTIONS

Most Analytical Reasoning sets begin with a question in which each answer choice represents a complete possible outcome, or sometimes just part of an outcome. The question asks you to select the answer choice that is an acceptable outcome (one that doesn't violate any part of the setup). You can think of questions of this kind as "orientation questions" since they do a good job of orienting you to the setup conditions.

For such questions, probably the most efficient approach is to take each condition in turn and check to see whether any of the answer choices violates it. As soon as you find an answer choice that violates a condition, you should eliminate that answer choice from further consideration—perhaps by crossing it out in your test booklet. When you have run through all of the setup conditions in this fashion, one answer choice will be left that you haven't crossed out: that is the correct answer.

Here's an orientation question relating to the setup in our example:

Which one of the following could be true for March?

(A) *Hubert, Lori, and Paul visit Toronto, and Regina and Sharon visit Vancouver.*
(B) *Hubert, Lori, Paul, and Regina visit Montreal, and Sharon visits Vancouver.*
(C) *Hubert, Paul, and Regina visit Toronto, and Lori and Sharon visit Montreal.*
(D) *Hubert, Regina, and Sharon visit Montreal, and Lori and Paul visit Vancouver.*
(E) *Lori, Paul, and Sharon visit Montreal, and Hubert and Regina visit Toronto.*

Let's take the setup conditions in order from first to last. First, check the first condition against each option:

Condition 1: *Sharon visits a different city than Paul.*

Condition 1 is met in (A) through (D) but violated in (E), since in (E) Sharon is scheduled to visit the same city as Paul. So you cross out (E) and do not check it any further. Now take the second condition:

Condition 2: *Hubert visits the same city as Regina.*

Condition 2 is violated in (A), since in (A) Hubert is scheduled to visit a different city than Regina. Cross out (A) and don't consider it any further. Condition 2 is not violated in (B), (C), or (D). (Remember, you don't need to check (E) since you've already ruled it out.) Proceed in the same way with the rest of the conditions:

Condition 3: *Lori visits Montreal or else Toronto.*

Condition 4: *If Paul visits Vancouver, Hubert visits Vancouver with him.*

Condition 5: *Each student visits one of the cities with at least one of the other four students.*

Condition 3 is violated in (D), since in (D) Lori is scheduled to visit Vancouver. Cross out (D). Condition 4 is violated in neither (B) nor (C), the only answer choices you are still checking. (The fact that condition 4 is violated in (D) is irrelevant at this point: you've already crossed out (D)). This leaves condition 5 to decide between (B) and (C). Condition 5 is violated in (B), since in (B) Sharon is scheduled to be the lone student visitor to Vancouver. Thus (B) gets crossed out. The only answer choice not crossed out is (C), which is consequently the correct answer. No further checking of (C) is needed. You've already checked (C) against each of the setup conditions. You are done. With this sort of question, there is no need for diagramming; all you needed to refer to was your abbreviated list of the conditions.

Another way of approaching an orientation question is to consider each answer choice in turn to see whether it violates any of the conditions. This will lead you to the correct answer relatively quickly if the correct answer is (A), and less quickly the further down the correct answer is. On balance, this is probably a less efficient way of finding the answer to orientation questions. Efficiency matters, because the more time you can save doing relatively straightforward questions such as these, the more time you have available to solve more challenging questions.

 Caution. The method of checking each condition against the answer choices is what you want to use with orientation questions. However, as we'll see below, this is generally **not** the approach you'll want to take with other types of questions. Keep in mind that your objective in answering the questions is to select the correct answer and move on to the next question, not to prove that the incorrect answer choices are wrong. (Also remember that not every set of questions includes an orientation question. When there is an orientation question, it will always be the question right after the setup.)

QUESTIONS THAT INCLUDE THE PHRASE "ANY ONE OF WHICH"

Another kind of question is concerned with complete and accurate lists of elements "any one of which" has some specific characteristic. A question of this kind might ask:

Which one of the following is a complete and accurate list of students any one of which could visit Vancouver in March?

The answer choices might be:

(A) Hubert, Lori, Regina
(B) Hubert, Regina, Sharon
(C) Paul, Regina, Sharon
(D) Hubert, Paul, Regina, Sharon
(E) Hubert, Lori, Paul, Regina, Sharon

What this question asks you to do is take each of the students in the setup and ask, "Could he/she visit Vancouver in March?" It doesn't matter whether any of the other students on the list could also visit Vancouver at the same time. You just need to ask whether there is an acceptable outcome in which the student you're considering visits Vancouver. If the answer is yes, that student needs to be included on the list, and if the answer is no, that student needs to stay off the list. If you do this systematically and correctly, the list you eventually end up with will be complete: no student who belongs on that list will have been left out. And it will be accurate: the list will not include any student who does not belong there. The correct answer is the list of all the students for whom the answer is "yes."

Sometimes the task of checking individually whether each element in the setup belongs on this list may seem daunting, but the task can often be simplified. For example, looking at the setup conditions, you notice that the third condition bars Lori from visiting Vancouver. So the two answer choices that include Lori—(A) and (E)—can immediately be crossed out.

Similarly, the second condition directly rules out (C). Condition 2 requires that Hubert visit the same city as Regina, so if we know that it is possible for one of them to visit Vancouver, it must be possible for the other to visit Vancouver too. This is what the condition requires. So (C), which includes Regina but not Hubert, is either incomplete or inaccurate.

This leaves us with (B) and (D). They both include Hubert, Regina, and Sharon. **Don't waste time checking these elements.** Since you have already determined that they are bound to be part of the correct answer, none of them will help you determine which of the remaining two answer choices is the correct one.

 Note. In general, when dealing with questions that include the phrase "any one of which" there is no point in checking an element that appears in all of the answer choices that you are still considering. It can't help you tell the correct answer from the incorrect ones.

Since the only thing that distinguishes (B) from (D) is that (D) includes Paul, the only point you need to check is whether Paul can visit Vancouver. Since he can, (B) is incomplete and thus incorrect. The correct answer is (D). In this case, when it came down to just (B) and (D), it turned out that checking one element was enough to allow you to identify the correct answer. If it had turned out that Paul could not visit Vancouver, then the correct answer would have been (B). As this case illustrates, it is generally worth your while to use time-saving strategies.

 Note. In questions that include the phrase "any one of which," if some element appears in only one of the answer choices still under consideration, check that element first. That way, if this element does belong on the list, you are done. Since any list, in order to be complete, would have to include this element, the answer choice that contains this element is the correct answer. On the other hand, if it turns out that the element doesn't belong on the list, then any remaining answer choices that include it should be crossed off.

QUESTIONS THAT ASK ABOUT WHAT MUST BE TRUE

Many Analytical Reasoning questions ask about what must be true. Something that must be true is something that is true of every single acceptable outcome. In other words, there **cannot** be an acceptable outcome in which this thing is false. But this does not mean—and this is an important point—that to find the correct answer you should somehow mechanically draw up all of the acceptable outcomes and then look through them to identify the one answer choice that these outcomes all have in common. Don't try to do this.

The reason you should avoid determining all of the acceptable outcomes is not that it will give incorrect results. If used with care and without error, it will lead you to the correct answer. The problem is that it is usually far too time-consuming.

So what should you do instead? This depends on the form of the question. Does the question ask what must be true under certain specified circumstances, or does it ask what must be true on the basis of the setup alone, no matter what the circumstances are? Let's take a look at each of these two possibilities separately.

What Must Be True Under Certain Specified Circumstances

Consider the following example:

If Sharon visits Vancouver, which one of the following must be true for March?

The answer choices are:

(A) Hubert visits Montreal.
(B) Lori visits Montreal.
(C) Paul visits Montreal.
(D) Lori visits the same city as Paul.
(E) Lori visits the same city as Regina.

In this question, we start with the supposition that Sharon visits Vancouver and then we ask if anything follows from that. In fact, something does follow. Consider the first condition, which tells us that Sharon visits a different city than Paul. From these two pieces of information, we can conclude that Paul visits either Montreal or Toronto, but not Vancouver (because Sharon visits Vancouver and Paul cannot visit the same city that she does). This is our first result, and checking this result against the answer choices, we find that we can't answer the question yet. In particular, we don't know whether (C) has to be true. We have only determined that it **can** be true.

Next, note that Paul is not the only one who visits Montreal or Toronto, but not Vancouver. The third condition tells us that this is true of Lori as well. And from the discussion in *Figuring Out the Setup* we know that only two cities will be visited by any of the students. Vancouver is one of those cities, since we are supposing that Sharon visits Vancouver. We don't know whether the other city is Montreal or Toronto. But we do know that whichever it is, it has to be the city that both Paul and Lori visit, since neither of them visits Vancouver.

Checking this second result against the answer choices, we find that we are done. Our second result guarantees the truth of answer choice (D) ("Lori visits the same city as Paul"). There is an unbroken chain of inference that takes us from the specific supposition of the question to (D). There was no need to check the other answer choices. Nor was there any need to work out even a single complete acceptable outcome. The moral of the story is: use your time wisely.

Note. A check of the incorrect answer choices, if one had been done, would have revealed a situation that is fairly typical in the case of questions about what must be true. Some of the answer choices—(B) and (C)—are things that can be true but don't have to be true, and some of them—(A) and (E)—are things that can't be true. Among the incorrect answer choices, you might encounter any combination of things that can't be true and things that can be true but don't have to be.

So what generally applicable strategies can be extracted from the way the question above was answered?

When approaching a question about what must be true under certain specified circumstances, the first thing to do is to see what inferences, if any, you can draw on the basis of the setup conditions and how they interact with the specified circumstances. Having drawn any immediately available inferences, check them against the answer choices. If, on the basis of those inferences, one of the answer choices has to be true, you're done. Remember that your objective is to select the correct answer and move on to the next question, not to prove that the incorrect answer choices are wrong.

If none of the immediately available inferences matches any of the answer choices, try to see what can be inferred from the inferences you've already made (in conjunction with the setup conditions). Check this second round of inferences against the answer choices. If any of these inferences match one of the answer choices, you're done.

This is what happened in the example above. Keep doing this until you're done.

As you work through the rest of the questions, keep trying to draw further inferences. There is a complementary strategy to pursue as you go along: Look for any answer choices that you can eliminate on the basis of inferences you have already established by working on previous questions. Cross out any incorrect answer choices that you come across in this way.

When considering "what must be true," sometimes it is possible to rule out an incorrect answer choice by constructing an acceptable outcome in which that answer choice is not true. To see how this would work, consider the example above, which asks what must be true if Sharon visits Vancouver. Suppose you were trying to rule out (B) ("Lori visits Montreal") by constructing an acceptable outcome in which (B) is false. You'd start with the following partial diagram:

$$\underline{M} \qquad \underline{T} \qquad \underline{V}$$
$$ \qquad L \qquad S$$

The starting point for the question is that Sharon visits Vancouver, so we represent this in the diagram. Now, to have an outcome in which (B) is false, Lori has to visit either Toronto or Vancouver. But Lori visiting Vancouver is ruled out by the third condition, so if Lori doesn't visit Montreal, she must visit Toronto. Since we then have Lori visiting Toronto and Sharon visiting Vancouver, the city visited by none of the students must be Montreal. This is how we established the partial diagram above.

Continue by drawing further inferences from the conditions. From the first condition we can infer that Paul has to visit Toronto. We add Paul to the diagram as follows:

$$\underline{M} \qquad \underline{T} \qquad \underline{V}$$
$$ \qquad L, P \qquad S$$

From the second condition we know that Hubert and Regina have to visit the same city. But that city can't be Toronto, because that would mean that only one person would visit Vancouver, contrary to the fifth condition. So Hubert and Regina must visit Vancouver, along with Sharon. This gives us the following outcome:

$$\underline{M} \qquad \underline{T} \qquad \underline{V}$$
$$ \qquad L, P \qquad H, R, S$$

This is an outcome in which (B) is false but that satisfies all the setup conditions plus the specific circumstance introduced in the question. So (B) does not have to be true and can thus be eliminated.

What Must Be True on the Basis of the Setup Conditions Alone

Not all of the questions that ask about what must be true ask what must be true under particular circumstances specified in the question. Some questions ask about what must be true merely on the basis of the setup.

An example of a question that asks about what must be true on the basis of the setup alone is the following:

Which one of the following must be true for March?

A correct answer would be:

Hubert visits a different city than Lori.

This follows directly from the setup conditions. Hubert cannot visit the same city as Lori, because if he did, that city would receive visits from four of the students: Hubert, Regina (who, by the second condition, visits the same city as Hubert), Lori, and either Paul or Sharon (since only two cities get visited, and Paul and Sharon cannot visit the same city, on account of the first condition). But that would mean that only one student—either Paul or Sharon—would visit one of the cities, and the fifth condition would then be violated. So we know that Hubert must visit a different city than Lori.

Questions that ask about what must be true on the basis of the setup alone have an interesting property: you can add the correct answer to what you have already inferred from the setup. Something that must be true on the basis of the setup alone is nothing but a logical consequence of how the setup conditions interact. Of course, before you use this result to help you answer other questions, you want to be very sure that the answer you selected is indeed the correct one.

Note that by contrast—and this is very important— suppositions that are introduced into individual questions, such as the supposition "if Sharon visits Vancouver" in the question discussed above, **never** carry over to any other questions. The correct answer to that question depended on the supposition, but in moving from one question to another, suppositions are not brought along. This is why it is possible for the suppositions in different questions to be inconsistent with each other.

 Note. In addition to questions about what must be true, you may encounter questions such as the following:

Which one of the following must be false? Which one of the following CANNOT be true? Each of the following could be true EXCEPT:

In all of these cases, the correct answer is something that is not true in even a single acceptable outcome. So among the incorrect answer choices you will find things that must be true as well as things that could be true.

Questions That Ask About What Could Be True

Many Analytical Reasoning questions ask about what could be true rather than about what must be true. Something that could be true is something that is true in at least one acceptable outcome, even if there are many acceptable outcomes in which it is false. This means that the incorrect answer choices are all things that **cannot** be true in any acceptable outcome.

As with questions about what must be true, some questions ask what could be true under certain specified circumstances and others ask what could be true on the basis of the setup alone.

What Could Be True Under Certain Specified Circumstances

Consider the following question:

If Regina visits Toronto, which one of the following could be true in March?

The five answer choices are:

(A) *Lori visits Toronto.*
(B) *Lori visits Vancouver.*
(C) *Paul visits Toronto.*
(D) *Paul visits Vancouver.*
(E) *Sharon visits Vancouver.*

How do you approach a question like this? A first step is to quickly check to see if any of the answer choices can be immediately ruled out as being in direct violation of one of the setup conditions. In this case, you would rule out (B) as directly violating the third condition, which requires that Lori visit either Montreal or Toronto. (There's no need to methodically go through each condition to see if any of the answer choices violate one of the conditions. That's a good strategy for orientation questions, but not usually for other questions. For non-orientation questions that ask for what can be true, just give the answer choices a quick look to see if any of them obviously violate something in the setup.)

Next, turn to the circumstance specified in the question—in this case, that Regina visits Toronto—and work from that. If Regina visits Toronto, Hubert also visits Toronto, as required by the second condition. Since by the first condition Sharon visits a different city than Paul, either Sharon or Paul will also visit Toronto, because only two cities are visited by any of the students. Toronto will thus be visited by three of the students.

So which city will be visited by just two students, Montreal or Vancouver? Since one of those two students must be Lori, it has to be Montreal; it cannot be Vancouver, because of the third condition. This means that none of the students visits Vancouver. So the answer choices specifying a visit to Vancouver (that is, (B), (D), and (E)) cannot be true. That leaves us with (A) and (C). But since we also know that Lori visits Montreal, we know that (A) cannot be true. So we know that (C) has to be the correct answer.

The approach above is to start with the setup conditions and then turn to the specific circumstance specified in the question and see what can be inferred from it in conjunction with the setup conditions. The emphasis here is not on what can be inferred to be the case, but on what **cannot** be the case, because the goal is to eliminate the incorrect answer choices and find the one that can be true. All of the incorrect answer choices must be false.

It is also possible to arrive at the correct answer by a different method. Assume that the answer choices, each in turn, are true. In four of the five cases, this assumption will lead you into a contradiction, thereby showing that the answer choice cannot be true.

Using this method to answer the question above, you would start by assuming that (A) is true. That is, you would assume that Lori visits Toronto. So Toronto would be visited by both Lori and Regina. By the second condition, if Regina visits Toronto, so does Hubert. That means that the other city visited would be visited by Paul and Sharon. But the first condition rules this out. So under the circumstance specified by the question—that Regina visits Toronto—Lori cannot visit Toronto.

Next you assume that (B) is true—namely, that Lori visits Vancouver. But this is immediately ruled out by the third condition.

You then assume that (C) is true—that Paul visits Toronto. So Toronto would be visited by Paul, Regina (as specified in the question), and Hubert (as specified by the second condition). That leaves Sharon and Lori to visit Montreal. This outcome satisfies all of the setup conditions, and is thus acceptable. Thus you know that (C) could be true, and you're done.

What Could Be True on the Basis of the Setup Conditions Alone

An example of a question that asks about what could be true on the basis of the setup alone is the following:

Which one of the following could be true for March?

The answer choices are:

(A) Hubert and Lori both visit Toronto.
(B) Paul and Sharon both visit Vancouver.
(C) Regina and Sharon both visit Montreal.
(D) Hubert visits Toronto and Paul visits Vancouver.
(E) Regina visits Montreal and Sharon visits Vancouver.

The first step, as usual, is to check if any of the answer choices can be immediately ruled out as being in direct violation of one of the setup conditions. In this case, (B) can be eliminated on those grounds, because it is in direct violation of the first condition. In addition, (D) can be eliminated as being in violation of the fourth condition.

That leaves us with (A), (C), and (E). You will have to evaluate these three answer choices one by one to see which one cannot be eliminated.

So assume that (A) is true. If Hubert and Lori both visit Toronto, then by the second condition Regina must visit Toronto as well. That leaves Paul and Sharon to visit a city together, which is ruled out by the first condition. So (A) cannot be true.

Assume, then, that (C) is true. If Regina and Sharon both visit Montreal, then by the second condition Hubert must visit Montreal as well. That leaves Paul and Lori to visit a city together, and nothing prevents them from visiting Toronto. This outcome satisfies all of the setup conditions, and is thus acceptable. Thus you know that (C) could be true, and you're done. There is no need to evaluate (E).

Note. In addition to questions about what could be true, you may encounter questions such as the following:

Which one of the following could be false?
Each of the following must be true EXCEPT:

In both of these cases, the correct answer is something that is not true in at least one acceptable outcome. Thus, all of the incorrect answer choices will be things that must be true.

You might also encounter a question that asks:

Which one of the following could be, but need not be, true?

In these cases, the correct answer is something that is true in at least one acceptable outcome but which is also false in at least one acceptable outcome. Both things that must be true and things that **cannot** be true are incorrect answer choices for this sort of question.

CONDITIONAL STATEMENTS

Often one or more of the setup conditions is in the form of a conditional statement. Conditional statements say that if something is the case, then something else is the case. For example, "If Theo is on the committee, then Vera is also on the committee." To work efficiently and effectively with Analytical Reasoning questions it is important to have a clear understanding of how to reason correctly with conditional statements and to know what errors to avoid.

Cross-reference: The topic of conditional statements is discussed from a slightly different perspective in the section on "Necessary Conditions and Sufficient Conditions" in the Guide to Logical Reasoning Questions, pages 25–27.

Conditional relationships ("conditionals") can be expressed in a variety of ways. The following are all equivalent ways of stating the same conditional:

(1) *If Theo is on the committee, then Vera is also on the committee.*
(2) *If Vera is not on the committee, then Theo is not on the committee.*
(3) *Theo is not on the committee if Vera is not on the committee.*
(4) *Theo is not on the committee unless Vera is on the committee.*
(5) *Theo is on the committee only if Vera is on the committee.*

All of these, despite the differences in their formulation, express exactly the same conditional relationship between Theo's being on the committee and Vera's being on the committee. What they all tell you is that Theo's being on the committee guarantees that Vera is on the committee. But none of them tells you that Vera's being on the committee guarantees that Theo is on the committee.

Note. The fact that all of the formulations displayed above are logically equivalent is not intuitively obvious. For most people, there is a marked difference in focus between some of these. For example, (1) seems to invite getting the facts about Theo straight first and if it turns out that Theo is on the committee, this tells you something about Vera. By contrast, (4) seems to invite finding out whether Vera is on the committee and if it turns out that she is not, this tells you that Theo is not on the committee either. Looking at things this way, it is easy to miss the underlying equivalence. But familiarity with, and automatic reliance on, this equivalence is crucial for dealing effectively with many Analytical Reasoning questions. So time that you spend now becoming thoroughly familiar with these equivalences is time well spent. Come test day, you'll be able to handle conditionals no matter how they're worded.

How does a conditional—regardless of how it happens to be formulated—work in drawing inferences? What are the kinds of additional information that, taken in conjunction with a conditional, yield proper inferences? Let's look at an example. Take the conditional "If Theo is on the committee, then Vera is on the committee." There are basically four cases to consider: 1. Theo is on the committee; 2. Theo is not on the committee; 3. Vera is on the committee; and 4. Vera is not on the committee. Each of these cases is discussed in turn below:

1. **Theo is on the committee.** If this is true, then given the conditional (in any of its formulations), it's guaranteed that Vera is also on the committee. The conditional says as much. This case is straightforward.

2. **Theo is not on the committee**. If this is true, you cannot use the conditional (regardless of how it is formulated) to derive any legitimate inferences about Vera. In particular, you **cannot** conclude that Vera is not on the committee. As far as the conditional goes, Theo's not being on the committee is consistent both with Vera's being on the committee and with her not being there. The conditional is simply silent about whether or not Vera is on the committee.

3. **Vera is on the committee.** If this is true, you cannot use the conditional (regardless of how it is formulated) to derive any legitimate inferences about Theo. In particular, you **cannot** conclude that Theo is also on the committee. In fact, we have just made this point in the discussion of point 2 above. As we said there, Theo's not being on the committee is consistent with Vera's being on the committee. In the same way, Vera's being on the committee is consistent with Theo's not being on the committee.

4. **Vera is not on the committee.** If this is true, you can use the conditional (in any of its formulations) to derive a legitimate inference about Theo. You can infer that Theo is not on the committee either. This is because if Theo were on the committee without Vera also being on the committee, then the conditional, "If Theo is on the committee, Vera must also be on the committee," would be violated. So, to sum this up, if Vera is not on the committee, the only way not to violate the conditional is for Theo not to be on the committee either.

Note. Sometimes Analytical Reasoning questions call for inferences involving more than one conditional. Suppose you're given two conditionals like the following:

If Theo in on the committee, Vera is on the committee.

If Vera is on the committee, Ralph is on the committee.

From these you can legitimately infer

If Theo is on the committee, Ralph is on the committee.

and

If Ralph is not on the committee, Theo is not on the committee.

Note that these inferences can be derived no matter how the conditionals on which they are based are formulated. So for example, from these versions:

If Vera is not on the committee, then Theo is not on the committee.

Unless Ralph is on the committee, Vera is not on the committee.

you can make the same two inferences as above:

If Theo is on the committee, Ralph is on the committee.

and

If Ralph is not on the committee, Theo is not on the committee.

WORDINGS USED IN ANALYTICAL REASONING QUESTIONS

In Analytical Reasoning questions, the language used in presenting the setup and asking the questions must be precise and unambiguous. As a result, many things are spelled out at greater length and in more detail than they would be in most other kinds of writing. For example, in a setup that talks about a group of people who will give presentations at a meeting, it will probably be stated explicitly that each person makes only one presentation and that the people give their presentations one after another. Here are some other examples:

- **at some time before/immediately before**

These expressions typically occur in place of "before" alone. This is because if you were simply told that "Smith's presentation comes before Jeng's presentation," it might be unclear whether someone else's presentation could occur between them. And so it might not be clear whether some outcome is acceptable or not. The use of phrases like "immediately before" is intended to avoid such ambiguity.

If you're told, "Smith's presentation comes **immediately before** Jeng's presentation," you know that no other presentation can occur between those two. On the other hand, if you're told, "Smith's presentation comes **at some time before** Jeng's presentation," you know that another presentation can, but doesn't have to, occur between those two. If another presentation had to occur between Smith's and Jeng's presentations, this would have to be said explicitly.

Similarly, you may be told that Smith's office is on "a higher floor" than Jeng's office (which allows for the possibility that the two offices are on adjacent floors and for the possibility that they are on nonadjacent floors), or you may be told that Smith's office is on the floor "immediately above" Jeng's office (which ensures that there are no other floors between the ones on which Smith's office and Jeng's office are located).

Or you might be told that within a row of offices, Smith's office is "the office" between Jeng's office and Robertson's office. This would tell you something different than if you were told that Smith's office is "an office" between Jeng's office and Robertson's office. In the first case, the use of the definite article "the" indicates that there is only one office between Jeng's and Robertson's offices, namely, Smith's office. In the second case, however, it is left open whether there are any offices in addition to Smith's office between those of Jeng and Robertson.

- **at least/at most/exactly**

There are times when simply being told that there must be three people on a certain committee would leave you uncertain whether this means that there can be more than three people on the committee or that there must be exactly three people on the committee. This kind of uncertainty is avoided by using precise language to talk about numbers. If the point is that three is the minimum number of committee members, you would typically be told that there must be **at least** three people on the committee. If three is the maximum number of committee members, then typically you would be told that there are **at most** three people on the committee. Otherwise, you would typically be told that there are **exactly** three people on the committee.

- **respectively/not necessarily in that order**

If you were asked to evaluate whether the statement "If Y is performed first, the songs performed second, third, and fourth could be T, X, and O," you might wonder what is meant. Does this mean (1) T, X, and O in some order or other, or does it mean (2) T second, X third, and O fourth? In Analytical Reasoning questions this potential uncertainty is avoided by saying, "If Y is performed first, the songs performed second, third, and fourth could be T, X, and O, **not necessarily in that order**," if (1) is what is meant. And by saying, "If Y is performed first, the songs performed second, third, and fourth, **respectively**, could be T, X, and O," if (2) is what is meant.

MORE POINTS TO CONSIDER

Here are several points to keep in mind. Some have been mentioned earlier and some are additional notes and tips.

- Always keep in mind that your objective is to select the correct answer, not to produce a comprehensive account of all of the logical possibilities available under the circumstances specified in the question. Arriving at the correct answer almost never requires working out all of the possible outcomes.

- As you draw inferences on the basis of how the question-specific circumstances interact with the setup conditions, keep checking the answer choices. At any point, you might be able to identify the correct answer. Or you might be able to eliminate some answer choices as incorrect. If you have succeeded in identifying the correct answer, you are done even if there are still further inferences you could draw or if there are some answer choices that you have not yet been able to eliminate. There is no need for you to prove that those answer choices are incorrect. By the same token, if you have succeeded in eliminating all but one answer choice, you are done even if you have not independently shown that the remaining answer choice is correct.

- Remember that when dealing with Analytical Reasoning questions, anything is acceptable that is not prohibited by the setup conditions or by what is implied by the setup conditions along with any circumstances specified in the question. Do not make any unwarranted assumptions, however natural they might seem. For example, if you are told that a committee must include an expert on finance and an expert on marketing, do not take it for granted that the committee's expert on finance must be a different person from the committee's expert on marketing.

- In Analytical Reasoning questions, careful and literal reading is of critical importance. Even though time management is important, it is even more important not to read too quickly. To give a specific example of the kind of problem that can arise, consider the following two statements: "F and G cannot both go on vacation during July" and "Neither F nor G can go on vacation during July." There are a number of superficial resemblances between them. However, the two are not equivalent, and mistaking one for the other would almost certainly lead to errors. If F goes on vacation in July and G does not, the first condition is not violated, but the second one is.

- Recall the earlier discussion of active elements in the setup that aren't mentioned in any of the conditions. It isn't necessary for *all* of the individual elements to be explicitly constrained by the setup conditions. If a particular element is not explicitly mentioned in the conditions, this means that the element is constrained only by what happens with the other elements. It does not mean that the set of setup conditions is incomplete or otherwise defective.

- Suppose you are asked a question like, "Which one of the following must be advertised during week 2," based on a setup involving seven products to be advertised during a four-week period. Suppose further that you determine that product H must be advertised during week 2, but that H does not appear among the answer choices. Does this mean that the question is defective? No. In this case it could be that G is also a product that must be advertised during week 2, and G is one of the answer choices. Keep in mind that there can only be one correct answer among the answer choices, but there can be more than one correct answer to the question.

- There are occasionally questions that ask about acceptable outcomes but only present partial outcomes in the answer choices. For example, the setup might be concerned with dividing a group of people into subgroups 1 and 2. The question might ask which one of the answer choices is an acceptable subgroup 1. In a case like this, if you look for violations of setup conditions only within the group that actually appears in the answer choices, you might find more than one that seems acceptable. But remember that what has to be acceptable is an outcome as a whole—the composition of **both** subgroup 1 and subgroup 2. So, even though subgroup 2 is not displayed in any of the answer choices, you still need to check it for violations of the setup conditions. That is, you would need to work out the outcome for subgroup 2 for those answer choices that you cannot otherwise eliminate as incorrect.

Recall the earlier discussion of what must be true on the basis of the setup conditions alone. It is extremely important that you keep in mind the point made there—that circumstances specified in an individual question hold for that question only. Very occasionally, a question will direct you to suppose that one of the original setup conditions were replaced with a different one. Such changes to the setup conditions also apply **only** to the question in which they are described, and never carry over to any other questions.

ARGUMENTS

What Is an Argument?

Most Logical Reasoning questions focus on arguments, which are sets of statements that present evidence and draw a conclusion on the basis of that evidence. These arguments are generally short and self-contained.

Consider this basic example:

Sarah is well-qualified, and the hiring committee is very familiar with her work. Therefore, she will probably receive a job offer.

This is a simple argument. Two pieces of evidence are presented. These are the **premises** of the argument. These premises are offered in support of the view that Sarah will probably receive a job offer. This is the **conclusion** of the argument.

Let's look at a second case:

Computer Whiz *is a well-respected magazine with a large readership, so its product endorsements carry a lot of weight in the computer electronics marketplace. The X2000 display monitor was recently endorsed by* Computer Whiz. *It is therefore likely that sales of the X2000 monitor will increase dramatically.*

In this argument, information about the magazine's reputation and large readership serves as a basis for reaching an **intermediate, or subsidiary, conclusion**: that its endorsements are very influential in the marketplace. This intermediate conclusion in conjunction with a premise that reports that the X2000 was recently endorsed by the magazine provides the grounds for the prediction of an increase in sales. This prediction is the **main, or overall, conclusion** of the argument.

Identifying the Parts of an Argument

An argument can be analyzed by identifying its various parts and the roles that those parts play. The most basic parts of an argument are premises and conclusions. As we have already seen, an argument may have one or more intermediate conclusions in addition to its overall conclusion.

Premises come in a variety of forms. Some premises are specific matters of fact, some are definitions, and others are broad principles or generalizations. What all premises have in common is that they are put forward as true without support. That is, there is no attempt within the argument to prove or justify them. In contrast, a conclusion is not simply asserted. A conclusion is presented as being justified by certain premises. Thus, the conclusion of an argument is open to the challenge that it is not adequately supported by the premises. (Premises, of course, can also be challenged, on grounds such as factual accuracy, but such challenges are not matters of logic.)

One thing to remember about premises and conclusions is that they can come in any order. Premises are presented in support of a conclusion, but this does not mean that premises always precede the conclusion. A conclusion may be at the beginning, middle, or end of an argument. Consider the following examples:

Dolores is far more skillful than Victor is at securing the kind of financial support the Volunteers for Literacy Program needs, and Dolores does not have Victor's propensity for alienating the program's most dedicated volunteers. Therefore, the Volunteers for Literacy Program would benefit if Dolores took Victor's place as director.

Dolores is far more skillful than Victor is at securing the kind of financial support the Volunteers for Literacy Program needs. Therefore, the program would benefit if Dolores took Victor's place as director, especially since Dolores does not have Victor's propensity for alienating the program's most dedicated volunteers.

The Volunteers for Literacy Program would benefit if Dolores takes Victor's place as director, since Dolores is far more skillful than Victor is at securing the kind of financial support the program needs and Dolores does not have Victor's propensity for alienating the program's most dedicated volunteers. [September 1995 LSAT, section 2, question 19]

These three examples all present the same argument. In each example, the conclusion is that the Volunteers for Literacy Program would benefit if Dolores took Victor's place as director, and this conclusion is supported by the same two premises. But each example expresses the argument in a different way, with the conclusion appearing in the final, middle, and initial position, respectively. It is important, then, to focus on the role each statement plays in the argument as a whole. Position within the argument simply doesn't matter.

Another thing to keep in mind is the presence of indicator words that mark the roles that statements play in arguments. For example, "therefore" often precedes a conclusion; it is a common conclusion indicator. So are "thus," "hence," "consequently," "it follows that," "it can be concluded that," and various others. Similarly, premises are often preceded by indicator words, the most typical being "since" and "because." However, do not rely uncritically on these indicator words. They can be misleading, especially in the case of complex arguments, which might contain one or more subarguments. There is no completely mechanical way of identifying the roles that various statements play within an argument.

It is worth noting that people, in making arguments, often do not confine themselves to presenting just the conclusion and the statements that support it. Likewise, the short arguments in Logical Reasoning questions often include statements that are neither premises nor conclusions. This includes statements that indicate the motivation for making the argument, statements that convey background information, and statements that identify the position the argument comes out against. So don't assume that everything that is not part of the argument's conclusion must be functioning as support for that conclusion.

How the Argument Goes

Once you have identified the premises and the conclusion, the next step is to get clear about exactly how the argument is meant to go; that is, how the grounds offered for the conclusion are actually supposed to bear on the conclusion. Understanding how an argument goes is a crucial step in answering many questions that appear on the LSAT. This includes questions that ask you to identify a reasoning technique used within an argument, questions that require you to match the pattern of reasoning used in two separate arguments, and of a variety of other question types.

Determining how an argument goes involves discerning how the premises are supposed to support the overall conclusion. Consider, for example, the argument presented earlier about the Volunteers for Literacy Program, which concludes that the program would benefit if Dolores took Victor's place as director. Two considerations in support of this conclusion are offered: one asserting Dolores's superiority in securing financial support and the other charging that Victor is more prone to alienating dedicated volunteers. These two considerations are both relevant to the conclusion since, all other things being equal, a

program benefits from having a director who is both better at fund-raising and less likely to alienate volunteers. Each of these considerations provides some support for the conclusion, and the support provided by one is completely independent of the support provided by the other.

In other arguments, the way in which premises support a conclusion can be much more complex. Consider this example:

The years 1917, 1937, 1956, 1968, 1979, and 1990 are all notable for the occurrence of both popular uprisings and near-maximum sunspot activity. During heavy sunspot activity, there is a sharp rise in positively charged ions in the air people breathe, and positively charged ions are known to make people anxious and irritable. Therefore, it is likely that sunspot activity has actually been a factor in triggering popular uprisings.[2]

The conclusion of this argument, signaled by "Therefore," is that it is likely that sunspot activity has been a factor in triggering popular uprisings. There are three premises. The first tells us about specific years in which both heavy sunspot activity and popular uprisings occurred. The other two are generalizations: that there is a sharp rise in positively charged ions in the air during heavy sunspot activity, and that positively charged ions make people anxious and irritable.

So how does this argument go? The first premise provides some direct support for the conclusion, but this support is very weak, circumstantial evidence. The second and third premises do not support the conclusion directly, but only in conjunction with each other. If these two premises are true, they work together to establish that sunspots are a causal factor in increased irritability. Notice that there is still no link between sunspots and popular uprisings. There is some plausibility, however, to the idea that increased irritability makes popular uprisings more likely, and the argument tacitly assumes that this is in fact so.

If we make this assumption, then we can see the connection between sunspot activity and popular uprisings. This greatly enhances the evidence that the first premise provides.

 Cross-reference: You can learn more about the role of assumptions in arguments in the discussion on pages 29–33.

2 February 1995 LSAT, section 4, question 8.

Questions About How the Argument Goes

Your test may include questions that ask you about how an argument proceeds overall, or about the logical role played by a particular part of an argument, or about the logical move one participant in a dialogue makes in responding to the other. Understanding how the relevant argument goes puts you in a position to answer these questions. Three examples are briefly discussed below.

Example 1

Red squirrels are known to make holes in the bark of sugar maple trees and to consume the trees' sap. Since sugar maple sap is essentially water with a small concentration of sugar, the squirrels almost certainly are after either water or sugar. Water is easily available from other sources in places where maple trees grow, so the squirrels would not go to the trouble of chewing holes in trees just to get water. Therefore, they are probably after the sugar.[3]

The question based on this argument is simply:

The argument proceeds by

The conclusion of this argument is quite easy to identify: red squirrels, in making holes in the bark of sugar maple trees, are probably after the sugar contained in the trees' sap. The argument arrives at this conclusion by first noting that since maple tree sap is essentially just water and sugar, the squirrels must be after either the one or the other. The argument goes on to reject the idea that it is the water that the squirrels are after, on the grounds that water is readily available for less effort where maple trees grow.

Once you have figured out how the argument goes, you're ready to check the answer choices to find the best characterization of the argument's reasoning. In this particular case, the best characterization is:

rejecting a possible alternative explanation for an observed phenomenon

This is not the only way to describe how the argument proceeds, and it may not be the description you would have given. But it is an accurate characterization and is thus the correct answer. So keep in mind when checking the answer choices that the correct answer may be just one of several acceptable ways of putting things.

Example 2

In order to determine automobile insurance premiums for a driver, insurance companies calculate various risk factors; as the risk factors increase, so does the premium. Certain factors, such as the driver's age and past accident history, play an important role in these calculations. Yet these premiums should also increase with the frequency with which a person drives. After all, a person's chance of being involved in a mishap increases in proportion to the number of times that person drives.[4]

The question based on this argument is:

The claim that insurance premiums should increase as the frequency with which a driver drives increases plays which one of the following roles in the argument?

The first step in determining how this argument goes is identifying the conclusion. To do this, find the position for which the argument offers support.

The short phrase "after all" at the beginning of the fourth sentence indicates that the statement that follows functions as a premise. This premise essentially says that the frequency with which a person drives is a factor in their risk of being involved in a traffic accident. We know from the first sentence that risk factors matter in determining a driver's automobile insurance premiums: as certain risk factors increase, the premium increases. Putting all of this together, we see that the argument is constructed to support the position stated in the third sentence: "… these premiums should also increase with the frequency with which the person drives."

So the claim that insurance premiums should increase as the frequency with which a driver drives increases is the conclusion of the argument. That is its role in the argument. The answer choice that expresses this, in some way or other, is the correct one.

Example 3

Zachary: The term "fresco" refers to paint that has been applied to wet plaster. Once dried, a fresco indelibly preserves the paint that a painter has applied in this way. Unfortunately, additions known to have been made by later painters have obscured the original fresco work done by Michelangelo in the Sistine Chapel. Therefore, in order to restore Michelangelo's Sistine Chapel paintings to the appearance that

---

[3] June 2002 LSAT, section 4, question 10.
[4] October 2002 LSAT, section 1, question 18.

Michelangelo intended them to have, everything except the original fresco work must be stripped away.

Stephen: But it was extremely common for painters of Michelangelo's era to add painted details to their own fresco work after the frescos had dried.[5]

The corresponding question is:

Stephen's response to Zachary proceeds by

Zachary tells us that Michelangelo's frescoes in the Sistine Chapel had additions made to them by later painters. On the basis of this he argues that everything except Michelangelo's original fresco work has to be stripped away if the paintings are to have the appearance Michelangelo intended them to have.

Stephen's response makes clear that for painters of Michelangelo's era, the frescoes as originally executed did not necessarily have the appearance that those painters intended them to have. So Stephen's response points to and casts doubt on an assumption of Zachary's argument. This assumption is that Michelangelo did not make additions to his own fresco work in order to give the paintings the appearance that he wanted them to have.

Turning to the answer choices, you find this statement among them:

calling into question an assumption on which Zachary's conclusion depends

This statement correctly characterizes how Stephen's response to Zachary proceeds.

A Point to Consider

- Arguments vary widely in their strength, that is, in the extent to which their conclusions are justified by their premises. In the extreme case—the case of a "deductively valid" (i.e., conclusive) argument—the truth of the conclusion is completely guaranteed by the truth of the premises. In other words, anyone who accepts those premises is thereby committed to accepting the conclusion. In most cases, however, the relationship of the premises to the conclusion is less strict: the premises provide some grounds for accepting the conclusion, but these grounds are not airtight. In other words, someone might accept all of the premises of such an argument yet still be logically justified in not accepting its conclusion.

Identifying the Main Conclusion of an Argument

Some questions present you with an argument and ask you to identify its main conclusion. In questions of this kind, the conclusion is actually drawn in the argument, but it is often stated somewhat indirectly and it is sometimes not signaled by any of the standard conclusion-indicator words such as "therefore" or "thus." To identify the conclusion, therefore, you also need to look at what the statements in the argument mean, and how they are related to each other. Look for a position that the argument as a whole is trying to establish, and rule out any statements that, either directly or indirectly, give reasons for that position. You should also eliminate statements that merely establish a context or supply background information.

An Example

Journalist: Obviously, though some animals are purely carnivorous, none would survive without plants. But the dependence is mutual. Many plant species would never have come to be had there been no animals to pollinate, fertilize, and broadcast their seeds. Also, plants' photosynthetic activity would deplete the carbon dioxide in Earth's atmosphere were it not constantly being replenished by the exhalation of animals, engine fumes, and smoke from fires, many set by human beings.[6]

The question asks:

Which one of the following most accurately expresses the main conclusion of the journalist's argument?

So, how do you tackle this question? First, read the argument through. You might immediately recognize that the argument is of a familiar sort. The argument is directed toward a position that has two sides to it: a very straightforward one that is simply asserted and a less obvious one that the argument goes to some trouble to establish. The first sentence presents the straightforward side of the position being argued for. The second sentence states the entire position. The third and fourth sentences make the case for the less obvious side of the position.

---

[5] October 2001 LSAT, section 4, question 25.
[6] October 2002 LSAT, section 4, question 3.

Suppose that after reading the argument you are not sure exactly how it goes. What do you do then? It might be helpful to go through the argument statement by statement and ask about each statement in turn, "Does this statement receive support from some other statement?" If so, the statement is either a subsidiary conclusion drawn to support the main conclusion or it is itself the main conclusion. If the statement does not receive support from anything else in the argument, ask whether it provides support for some other statement. If it does, it's a premise of the argument, and whatever statement it provides support for is either the main conclusion or a subsidiary conclusion.

In the journalist's argument, the first statement does not receive support from anything else that is said in the argument. It does, however, provide support for the second statement by establishing one side of the dependence that the second statement refers to. So the second statement is a candidate for being the main conclusion of the argument. If you go on to analyze the third and fourth statements, you'll find that neither receives any support from anything else in the argument and that each independently supports the second statement by establishing the other side of the mutual dependence. Since everything else in the argument goes toward supporting the second statement, it is clear that the second statement expresses the main conclusion of the argument.

The second statement states the main conclusion in a somewhat abbreviated way in that it doesn't spell out what is meant by "dependence." But having worked through the argument, we can recognize that the following is an accurate statement of the conclusion:

Just as animals are dependent on plants for their survival, plants are dependent on animals for theirs.

The incorrect answer choices often restate a premise or part of a premise. For example, the following incorrect answer is a partial (and inaccurate) restatement of the fourth sentence of the journalist's argument:

Human activity is part of what prevents plants from depleting the oxygen in Earth's atmosphere on which plants and animals alike depend.

Other incorrect answer choices may state something that can be inferred from statements in the argument but that is not the argument's main conclusion. Here is an example of this, based on the journalist's argument:

The chemical composition of Earth and its atmosphere depends, at least to some extent, on the existence and activities of the animals that populate Earth.

Some Points to Consider

- If there is a "thus" or "therefore" in the argument, do not assume that these words introduce the main conclusion of the argument. They often indicate a subsidiary conclusion rather than the main conclusion.

- With questions that ask you to identify the main conclusion, it is generally possible to form a fairly precise idea of what the correct answer will be like before considering the answer choices. Doing so makes it possible to select the correct answer very efficiently. You should also try to get a precise idea of the main conclusion, because some of the incorrect answer choices may be only slightly inaccurate. For example, if the actual conclusion is that something is likely to be true, an incorrect answer choice may say that it is definitely true. This choice is incorrect because it goes beyond the actual conclusion.

Matching Patterns of Reasoning in Arguments

There is another kind of question that tests your ability to determine how an argument goes. It begins with an argument and then asks you to choose one argument from among the answer choices that is most similar in its reasoning to the initial (or reference) argument. The questions themselves are worded in a variety of ways, including:

The pattern of reasoning in which of the following arguments is most similar to that in the argument above?

Which one of the following arguments is most similar in its reasoning to the argument above?

You don't need to come up with a verbal description of the pattern of reasoning in order to answer these questions. All you need is a solid intuitive grasp of the logical structure of the reference argument: what its conclusion is, and how the premises fit together to support the conclusion.

These questions are asking for a match in logical structure, that is, the way the premises fit together to support the conclusion. So do not pay any attention to similarity or dissimilarity in subject matter, or to background material that is not part of the premises or the conclusion. Nor should you concern yourself with anything about the particular way the argument is laid out, such as the order in which the premises and the conclusion are presented.

An Example

All known deposits of the mineral tanzanite are in Tanzania. Therefore, because Ashley collects only tanzanite stones, she is unlikely ever to collect a stone not originally from Tanzania.[7]

The question asks:

Which one of the following is most similar in its reasoning to the argument above?

So what is the structure of the reasoning in the reference argument? There are two premises, the one about tanzanite deposits and the one about Ashley's collecting habits. And there is a conclusion: Ashley is unlikely ever to collect a stone not originally from Tanzania. Note that the conclusion merely says that something is unlikely, not that it will definitely not happen. The conclusion is probably qualified in this way because the premise about tanzanite deposits speaks only about the known deposits of that mineral, thereby leaving open the possibility that there are undiscovered tanzanite deposits outside of Tanzania.

But also note that the argument is a fairly strong one. The premises give a reasonable basis for accepting the conclusion: if the premises are true, the only way in which Ashley would ever collect a stone that is not originally from Tanzania is if tanzanite is someday discovered outside of Tanzania or if she begins to collect some different type of stone in the future.

The next step is to check the answer choices and to find the one with the same pattern of reasoning.

So let's try this answer choice:

Frogs are the only animals known to live in the lagoon on Scrag Island. The diet of the owls on Scrag Island consists of nothing but frogs from the island. Therefore, the owls are unlikely ever to eat an animal that lives outside the lagoon.

Does this follow the same pattern of reasoning as the argument about tanzanite? The conclusion has the right shape: it says that something is unlikely ever to happen, just as the conclusion of the reference argument does. In addition, this argument, like the reference argument, has a premise that limits itself to speaking about what is known to be true, thereby leaving open the possibility of cases unlike those now known. Plus, the second premise is exclusionary in nature: where the reference argument uses "only," this argument says "nothing but." So there are a number of resemblances between important parts of the two arguments.

However, whereas the reference argument is fairly strong, this argument is seriously flawed. Notice that the two premises do not rule out the possibility there are frogs on Scrag Island that do not live in the lagoon. So there seems to be a strong possibility that the owls on Scrag Island eat frogs that aren't from the lagoon. The conclusion of this argument thus receives little or no support from the premises. If the reasoning in this argument were closely parallel to that in the reference argument, its premises would provide similarly strong support for its conclusion. So this answer choice cannot be correct.

Let's try another one of the answer choices:

The only frogs yet discovered on Scrag Island live in the lagoon. The diet of all the owls on Scrag Island consists entirely of frogs on the island, so the owls will probably never eat an animal that lives outside the lagoon.

Here, too, the conclusion has the right shape: it says that something is unlikely ever to happen. In addition, this argument has a premise that limits itself to speaking about what is known to be the case. Plus, the second premise is exclusionary in nature.

In this case, the premises provide support for the conclusion in just the same way that the premises in the reference argument do for the conclusion of that argument. This argument can be paraphrased in a way that is parallel to the reference argument: All known frogs on Scrag Island live in the lagoon. Scrag Island owls eat only frogs. It is therefore unlikely that an owl on Scrag Island will ever eat an animal that does not live in the lagoon. Thus, the pattern of reasoning in the two arguments is essentially the same.

WHAT CAN BE CONCLUDED FROM THE INFORMATION PROVIDED

Many Logical Reasoning questions test your ability to determine what is supported by a body of available evidence. These questions ask you to pick one statement that can in some way or another be inferred from the available evidence. So, in effect, you are asked to distinguish between positions that are supported by the information that you have been given and positions that

---

[7] June 2002 LSAT, section 2, question 26.

are not supported by that information. These questions come in a variety of forms.

Identifying a Position That Is Conclusively Established by Information Provided

Some questions test your ability to identify what follows logically from certain evidence or information. For these questions, you will be presented with information that provides **conclusive** support for one of the answer choices. Typical wordings for these questions include:

If the statements above are true, which one of the following must also be true?

Which one of the following logically follows from the statements above?

With these questions, you are looking for something that is **guaranteed** to be true by the information you have been given. That is, the correct answer will be a statement that **must** be true if the given information is true. Incorrect answer choices may receive some support from the information but that support will be inconclusive. In other words, an incorrect answer choice could be false even if the information provided is true.

An Example

Any sale item that is purchased can be returned for store credit but not for a refund of the purchase price. Every home appliance and every piece of gardening equipment is on sale along with selected construction tools.[8]

The question asks:

If the statements above are true, which one of the following must also be true?

Notice that the statements have a common element: they talk about sale items. This common element allows you to combine bits of information to draw conclusions. For example, since all home appliances are sale items, you could conclude that any home appliance that is purchased can be returned for store credit. Because several conclusions like this can be drawn from these statements, you cannot determine the correct answer without reading the answer choices. So you need to go through the answer choices to find one that must be true if the statements are true.

One choice reads:

No piece of gardening equipment is returnable for a refund.

We are told that every piece of gardening equipment is a sale item and sale items are **not** returnable for a refund. So it must be true that gardening equipment is not returnable for a refund. This is the correct answer choice.

For the sake of comparison, consider another answer choice:

Some construction tools are not returnable for store credit.

To rule out this answer choice, you need to see that it does not have to be true if the statements in the passage are true. It obviously doesn't have to be true for construction tools that are on sale—the statements guarantee that those construction tools are returnable for store credit. As for the rest of the construction tools, those that aren't on sale, nothing indicates that they are not returnable for store credit. Based on what the statements say, it is possible, and even likely, that these tools are returnable for store credit. The answer choice is therefore incorrect.

In this example, you were given a set of statements that do not seem to be designed to lead to any particular conclusion. It was up to you to determine the implications of those statements. In other cases, however, the information may appear to be designed to lead the reader to a specific unstated conclusion. In such cases, the correct answer could be the unstated conclusion, if it logically follows from the information provided, or it could be some other statement that logically follows from that information.

Some Points to Consider

- For some claim to logically follow from certain information, that information has to guarantee that the claim is true. It isn't enough for the information to strongly support the claim; it has to conclusively establish the claim.

- Incorrect answers to questions about what logically follows can be claims that receive some support from the information but that nevertheless **could** be false even though all of the information is correct.

---

[8] December 2001 LSAT, section 1, question 11.

- Answer choices are often incorrect because they take things one step beyond what the evidence supports. They might make claims that are too sweeping; for example, they might say "all" when the evidence supports only a "most" statement. Or where a statement about what "is likely to be" is warranted, an incorrect answer choice might say "is." Or where a statement about "all known cases" is warranted, an incorrect answer choice might say "all cases."

- Remember that a modest or limited claim can be a correct answer even if the information also supports a stronger claim. If the information supports drawing the conclusion that there will be a festival in every month, then it also supports the conclusion that there will be a festival in June.

Identifying a Position Supported by Information Provided

Some questions ask you to identify a position that is supported by a body of evidence, but not supported conclusively. These questions might be worded as follows:

Which one of the following is most strongly supported by the information above?

Which one of the following can most reasonably be concluded on the basis of the information above?

The statements above, if true, most strongly support which one of the following?

For these questions, you will generally not be presented with an argument, but merely with some pieces of information. Your task is to evaluate that information and distinguish between the answer choice that receives strong support from that information (the correct answer) and answer choices that receive no significant support (the incorrect answer choices).

An Example

Consider the following pieces of information:

People should avoid taking the antacid calcium carbonate in doses larger than half a gram, for despite its capacity to neutralize stomach acids, calcium carbonate can increase the calcium level in the blood and thus impair kidney function. Moreover, just half a

gram of it can stimulate the production of gastrin, a stomach hormone that triggers acid secretion.[9]

You are asked,

Which one of the following is most strongly supported by the information above?

With questions of this kind you shouldn't expect the correct answer to follow in a strict logical sense from the information, but you should expect the information to provide a strong justification for the correct answer. When you begin work on a question of this sort, you should note any obvious interconnections among the facts given, but there is no point in formulating a precise prediction of what the correct answer will look like. A sensible approach is to read the passage carefully, and make a mental note of any implications that you spot. Then go on to consider each answer choice in turn and determine whether that answer choice gets any support from the information you have been given.

Let's follow this approach with the question above. Reading the passage, you find that a certain antacid is described as having the obvious intended effect of neutralizing stomach acid but as also having adverse side effects if the dosage is too high. One of these adverse effects results in impaired kidney function and other results in acid secretion in the stomach.

There is a suggestion in the passage that doses exceeding half a gram are necessary for the first effect to be triggered to any serious extent. The passage also suggests that doses of half a gram or more will trigger the second effect. No other implications of this passage stand out. At this point, it is probably a good idea to consider each answer choice in turn.

One answer choice is:

Doses of calcium carbonate smaller than half a gram can reduce stomach acid more effectively than much larger doses do.

Is this choice supported by the information? The passage does give reasons as to why this might be true. It tells us that doses of half a gram or more can stimulate the production of a stomach hormone that triggers acid secretion. This hormone might counteract any extra acid-neutralization that comes from additional calcium carbonate over and above a half-gram dose; but then again it might not. Perhaps the extra calcium carbonate

[9] June 2001 LSAT, section 2, question 19.

neutralizes more stomach acid than it triggers. For this reason, this answer choice is not strongly supported by the information.

Another answer choice is:

Half a gram of calcium carbonate can causally contribute to both the secretion and the neutralization of stomach acids.

Is there support for this choice in the information provided? We have noted that at half a gram the secretion of acid in the stomach is triggered. The passage mentions the drug's "capacity to neutralize stomach acids," strongly suggesting that some acid-neutralizing effect occurs at any dosage level. So there is strong support in the passage for both parts of this answer choice.

Some Points to Consider

- In answering questions dealing with support for conclusions, base your judgment about whether or not a particular answer choice is supported strictly on the information that is explicitly provided in the passage. If the passage concerns a subject matter with which you are familiar, ignore any information you might have about the subject that goes beyond what you have been told.

- Keep in mind that the support for the correct answer does not have to involve all of the information provided. For instance, in the example about calcium carbonate, an adverse effect on the kidneys is mentioned, but this information plays no role in the support for the correct answer.

Identifying Points on Which Disputants Hold Conflicting Views

You may also encounter questions involving two speakers where the first speaker puts forward a position and the second responds to that position. You will then be asked something like:

The main point at issue between Sarah and Paul is whether

Which one of the following most accurately expresses the point at issue between Juan and Michiko?

On the basis of their statements, Winchell and Trent are committed to disagreeing over whether

An Example

Mary: Computers will make more information available to ordinary people than was ever available before, thus making it easier for them to acquire knowledge without consulting experts.

Joyce: As more knowledge became available in previous centuries, the need for specialists to synthesize and explain it to nonspecialists increased. So computers will probably create a greater dependency on experts.[10]

The question asks,

The dialogue most strongly supports the claim that Mary and Joyce disagree with each other about whether

In answering questions of this kind, you may find it useful to read the dialogue closely enough to form a clear mental picture of each person's stance and then go on to the answer choices.

Now consider this answer choice:

computers will make more information available to ordinary people

Does what Joyce and Mary say show that they disagree about this? Mary straightforwardly says that computers will make more information available to ordinary people. But what about Joyce? She predicts that computers will create a greater dependency on experts because of a historical trend of an increasing dependency on experts whenever more knowledge becomes available to ordinary people. So she seems to assume that computers will make more information become available to ordinary people. So she probably agrees with Mary on this point.

Now consider a second answer choice:

dependency on computers will increase with the increase of knowledge

Nothing either Mary or Joyce says commits either of them to a particular view on this position. This is because neither of them explicitly discusses the issue of people's

[10] December 2001 LSAT, section 3, question 4.

dependency on computers. But there is certainly no indication at all that they hold opposing views on whether dependency on computers will increase with the increase of knowledge.

Finally, consider a third answer choice:

computers will increase the need for ordinary people seeking knowledge to turn to experts

Based on what she says, Mary straightforwardly disagrees with this claim. Computers, she says, will make it easier for ordinary people to acquire knowledge without consulting experts. Joyce, on the other hand, concludes that computers will create a greater dependency on experts. The precedent from past centuries that she cites in support of this conclusion makes it clear that nonspecialists—that is, ordinary people—will depend more on experts when knowledge increases. So Mary and Joyce disagree on whether the need for ordinary people to turn to experts will be increased by computers.

Some Points to Consider

- The evidence that two speakers disagree about a particular point always comes from what they explicitly say. Sometimes there is a direct conflict between something that one of the speakers says and something that the other speaker says. The phrasing of the question indicates that you should be looking for a direct conflict when it says something straightforward like "Max and Nina disagree over whether." At other times the point of disagreement must be inferred from the explicit positions that the speakers take. The phrasing of the question will indicate that this inference needs to be made. For example, a question like "The dialogue provides the most support for the claim that Nikisha and Helen disagree over whether" does not suggest that they disagree explicitly, only that there is some evidence that they disagree.

- Do not try to derive a speaker's likely position on a topic from a psychological stereotype. It may be true that a speaker who takes a certain position would be the kind of person who would likely hold certain other positions as well, but you should not rely on this sort of association. Rely only on what a speaker explicitly says and on what can be properly inferred from that.

- The incorrect answer choices are not necessarily positions that the two speakers can be shown to agree on. In many cases, the views of at least one of the speakers on a given position cannot be determined from what has been said.

NECESSARY CONDITIONS AND SUFFICIENT CONDITIONS

Suppose you read the following statements:

You don't deserve praise for something unless you did it deliberately.

Tom deliberately left the door unlocked.

Does it follow from these statements that Tom deserves praise for leaving the door unlocked? You can probably see that this doesn't follow. The first statement says that you have to do something deliberately in order to deserve praise for doing it. It doesn't say that any time you do something deliberately you thereby deserve praise for doing it. So the mere fact that Tom did something deliberately is not enough to bring us to the conclusion that Tom deserves praise for doing it.

To put it in a slightly more technical way, the first statement expresses a **necessary condition**. Doing something deliberately is a necessary condition for deserving praise for doing it. In Logical Reasoning questions, it can be very important to recognize whether something expresses a necessary condition or whether it expresses what is called a **sufficient condition**. If the first statement had said "If you do something deliberately then you deserve praise for doing it," it would be saying that doing something deliberately is a sufficient condition for deserving praise for doing it.

 Cross-reference: Reasoning involving necessary and sufficient conditions is also covered, from a slightly different perspective, in the discussion of "Conditional Statements" in the Analytical Reasoning section, pages 12–13.

In the example above, it is fairly easy to see that the first statement expresses a necessary condition and not a sufficient condition. It would be quite strange to say that doing something deliberately is a sufficient condition for deserving praise, since saying so would imply that you deserve praise for anything you do deliberately, even if it is an immoral or criminal act. But the content of a statement doesn't always help you determine whether it expresses a necessary condition or a sufficient condition. For this reason, it pays to devote very close attention to the precise wording of any statements that express conditions. And it pays to have a clear idea in your mind about how statements that express necessary conditions function in arguments and about how statements that express sufficient conditions function in arguments.

There are many ways to express a necessary condition. The necessary condition above could have been stated just as accurately in several different ways, including:

You deserve praise for something only if you did it deliberately.

You don't deserve praise for something if you didn't do it deliberately.

To deserve praise for something, you must have done it deliberately.

If you think carefully about these statements, you should see that they all mean the same thing. And you can see that none of them says that doing something deliberately is a sufficient condition for deserving praise.

Sufficient conditions can also be expressed in several different ways:

If it rains, the sidewalks get wet.

Rain is all it takes to get the sidewalks wet.

The sidewalks get wet whenever it rains.

These statements each tell us that rain is a sufficient condition for the sidewalks getting wet. It is sufficient, because rain is all that it takes to make the sidewalks wet. But notice that these statements do not say that rain is the only thing that makes the sidewalks wet. They do not rule out the possibility that the sidewalks can get wet from melting snow or from being sprayed with a garden hose. So these statements do not express necessary conditions for wet sidewalks, only sufficient conditions.

How Necessary Conditions Work in Inferences

We've already noted one thing about basing inferences on statements that express necessary conditions, such as

N: You deserve praise for something only if you did it deliberately.

If we are also given a case that satisfies the necessary condition, such as

Tom deliberately left the door unlocked

we cannot legitimately draw an inference. Specifically, the conclusion that Tom deserves praise for leaving the door unlocked does not follow.

Statements that express necessary conditions can play a part in legitimate inferences, of course, but only in combination with the right sort of information. Suppose that in addition to statement N we are told

Tom deserves praise for leaving the door unlocked.

This allows us to conclude that Tom deliberately left the door unlocked. Since statement N says that you have to do something deliberately in order to deserve praise for doing it, Tom must have deliberately left the door unlocked if he deserves praise for what he did.

Or, suppose that in addition to statement N we are told

Tom did not leave the door unlocked deliberately.

This allows us to conclude that Tom does not deserve praise for leaving the door unlocked. This follows because statement N insists that only deliberate actions deserve praise, and because we are told clearly that Tom's action is not deliberate.

So in general, when you have a statement that expresses a necessary condition, it allows you to infer something in just two cases: (1) you can infer from knowing that the necessary condition is **not** met that the thing it is the necessary condition for does **not** occur; (2) you can infer that the necessary condition is met from knowing that the thing it is the necessary condition for occurs.

How Sufficient Conditions Work in Inferences

Statements that express sufficient conditions can also serve as a basis for inferences. Let's revisit one of the earlier statements of a sufficient condition:

S: If it rains, the sidewalks get wet.

If we are told that the sufficient condition is satisfied (i.e., told that it is raining), then we can legitimately draw the inference that the sidewalks are getting wet. This should be quite obvious.

We can also draw another conclusion from a statement of a sufficient condition, provided that we have the right sort of additional information. Suppose that in addition to statement S we are told that the sidewalks did not get wet. Since the sidewalks get wet whenever it rains, we can conclude with complete confidence that it didn't rain.

So in general, when you have a statement that expresses a sufficient condition, it allows you to infer something in just two cases: (1) if you know that the sufficient condition is met, then you can infer that the thing it is the sufficient condition for occurs; (2) you can infer that the sufficient condition is **not** met from knowing that the thing it is the sufficient condition for does **not** occur.

Though it may sometimes seem that there are other ways to draw an inference from a statement of a sufficient condition, there are none. Suppose that in addition to statement S, we are told that the sidewalks are wet. Can we legitimately conclude that it rained? No, because statement S does not rule out the possibility that something other than rain, such as melting snow, can make the sidewalks wet. Or suppose that in addition to statement S, we are told that it didn't rain. Can we legitimately conclude that the sidewalks did not get wet? Again no, and for the same reason: statement S does not rule out the possibility that something other than rain can make the sidewalks wet.

UNDERSTANDING THE IMPACT OF ADDITIONAL INFORMATION

The LSAT typically includes several questions that test your ability to see how additional facts bear on an argument. These questions may focus on facts that strengthen an argument, they may focus on facts that weaken the argument, or they may merely ask what additional information, if it were available, would be useful in evaluating the strength of the argument. Typical wordings of such questions are:

Which one of the following, if true, most strengthens the argument?

Which one of the following, if true, most weakens the argument?

In order to evaluate the argument, which one of the following would it be most useful to determine?

 Tip: When the qualifier "if true" appears in this kind of question, it tells you not to be concerned about the actual truth of the answer choices. Instead, you should consider each answer choice as though it were true. Also, consider each answer choice independently of the others, since it is not necessarily the case that the answer choices can all be true together.

Questions of this kind are based on arguments that—like most real-life arguments—have premises that provide some grounds for accepting the conclusion, but that fall short of being decisive arguments in favor of the conclusion. For an argument like this, it is possible for

additional evidence to make the argument stronger or weaker. For example, consider the following argument:

A survey of oil-refinery workers who work with MBTE, an ingredient currently used in some smog-reducing gasolines, found an alarming incidence of complaints about headaches, fatigue, and shortness of breath. Since gasoline containing MBTE will soon be widely used, we can expect an increased incidence of headaches, fatigue, and shortness of breath.[11]

The incidence of complaints about headaches, fatigue, and shortness of breath among oil-refinery employees who work with MBTE is, on the face of it, evidence for the conclusion that widespread use of gasoline containing MBTE will make headaches, fatigue, and shortness of breath more common. However, additional information could, depending on what this information is, make the argument stronger or weaker.

For example, suppose it is true that most oil-refinery workers who do not work with MBTE also have a very high incidence of headaches, fatigue, and shortness of breath. This would provide evidence that it is not MBTE but some other factor that is primarily responsible for these symptoms. But if we have evidence that something other than MBTE is causing these symptoms, then the argument provides only very weak support, if any, for its conclusion. That is, the argument's original premises, when combined with the additional information, make a much weaker case for the argument's conclusion than those premises did alone. In other words, the new information has made the argument weaker.

Of course, different additional evidence would make the argument stronger. For example, suppose that gasoline containing MBTE has already been introduced in a few metropolitan areas, and since it was first introduced, those areas have reported increased complaints about headaches, fatigue, and shortness of breath. This would provide evidence that when MBTE is used as a gasoline additive, it increases the incidence of these symptoms not just among refinery workers who work closely with it but also among the general public. So we now have evidence that is more directly relevant to the argument's conclusion. Thus, we now have a stronger case for the argument's conclusion; in other words, the new evidence has made the argument stronger.

We have seen that when new information makes an argument stronger, that information, together with the argument's original premises, makes a stronger case for the argument's conclusion than do the original premises

[11] October 2002 LSAT, section 4, question 5.

alone. There are several ways in which this could work. The additional information could eliminate an obvious weak spot in the original argument. Alternatively, there may be no obvious weak spot in the original argument; the case for the argument may simply become even stronger with the addition of the new evidence. In some cases, the additional information will be something that helps establish the argument's conclusion but only when combined with the argument's existing premises. In other cases, the new information will provide a different line of reasoning in addition to that provided by the original premises. The information that strengthens the argument about MBTE is an example of something that provides a different line of reasoning for the conclusion. In still other cases, the additional information will strengthen the argument by ruling out something that would have weakened the argument. And of course, additional information may weaken an argument in corresponding ways.

An Example

Consider this argument:

A recent study reveals that television advertising does not significantly affect children's preferences for breakfast cereals. The study compared two groups of children. One group had watched no television, and the other group had watched average amounts of television and its advertising. Both groups strongly preferred the sugary cereals heavily advertised on television.[12]

The conclusion of the argument is that television advertising does not significantly affect children's preferences for breakfast cereals. As evidence for this conclusion, the argument presents the results of a study comparing two groups of children: the study found that children in both groups—those who watched no television and those who watched average amounts of television and its advertising—strongly preferred the sugary cereals heavily advertised on television. On the face of it, the study results do seem to provide some support, although not conclusive support, for the argument's conclusion; if television advertising did significantly affect children's preferences, then we'd expect the children who watched television to have different preferences than the children who didn't watch television.

Here is the question:

Which one of the following statements, if true, most weakens the argument?

Let's consider an answer choice:

Most of the children in the group that had watched television were already familiar with the advertisements for these cereals.

Does this information weaken the argument? It suggests that even if the television advertising influenced the preferences of the children who watched television, this influence occurred some time ago. But this does not really imply anything about whether the advertising did influence the children's preferences. So the information provided by this answer choice neither strengthens nor weakens the argument.

Let's consider another answer choice:

Both groups rejected cereals low in sugar even when these cereals were heavily advertised on television.

This information may well be relevant to the argument's conclusion since it suggests that if a cereal is unappealing to children, then even a great deal of television advertising will not change the children's preferences. But this would provide additional evidence **in favor of** the argument's conclusion that television advertising does not significantly affect children's cereal preferences. So this answer choice strengthens the argument rather than weakens it.

 Tip: In questions that ask what weakens an argument, often one or more incorrect answer choices will provide evidence that strengthens the argument (or vice versa in the case of questions that ask for a strengthener). By the time you've read several answer choices, it is easy to forget what the question is asking for and pick an answer choice because it is clearly relevant—even though it's the opposite of what the question is asking for. It is important to keep the question clearly in mind in order to guard against making this kind of mistake.

---

[12] October 2002 LSAT, section 4, question 13.

Consider a third answer choice, then:

The preferences of children who do not watch television advertising are influenced by the preferences of children who watch the advertising.

How does this information affect the argument? Well, the reason originally offered for the conclusion is that the two groups of children do not differ in their preferences. But if the preferences of the children who do not watch television advertising are influenced by the preferences of those who do watch it, then the fact that the two groups do not differ in their preferences provides little, if any, reason to think that none of the children's preferences were affected by television advertising. After all, it could well be that the preferences of the children who watched television were strongly influenced by the advertising, and these children's preferences in turn strongly influenced the preferences of those who did not watch television, with the result that the two groups had the same preferences. So when combined with the additional information, the argument's original premises make a much weaker case for the argument's conclusion than they did alone. Thus, this is the correct answer.

More Points to Consider

- The additional pieces of information that weaken an argument generally do not challenge the truth of the argument's explicit premises. They are pieces of information that call into question whether the conclusion is strongly supported by those premises.

- Keep in mind that additional information may strengthen (or weaken) an argument only to a small extent or it may do so to a large extent. When the question asks for a strengthener, an answer choice will be correct even if it strengthens the argument only slightly, provided that none of the other answer choices strengthen the argument significantly. On the other hand, if one answer choice strengthens the argument a great deal, then answer choices that strengthen only slightly are incorrect. For most questions that ask for weakeners, the correct answer will weaken the argument to some extent, but the premises will still provide some support for the conclusion. However, for some of these questions, the correct answer will eliminate all or almost all of the argument's original strength.

- Beware of answer choices that are relevant to the general subject matter, but not relevant to the way the argument supports its conclusion. A weakener or strengthener must affect the support for the conclusion. For example, consider the argument about

gasoline containing MBTE. Suppose that adding MBTE to gasoline dramatically increased the price of gasoline. This information would be relevant if the argument's conclusion were broader, for example, if it concluded that gasoline containing MBTE should be widely used. Since the argument, however, is narrowly focused on whether widespread use of gasoline containing MBTE will increase the incidence of headaches, fatigue, and shortness of breath, the increased cost resulting from adding MBTE to gasoline is irrelevant and thus would neither strengthen nor weaken the argument.

- Similarly, for new information to weaken an argument, it must reduce the support that the premises provide for the conclusion. A fact may have negative connotations in the context of an argument but do nothing to weaken that argument. For example, consider the argument about television advertising and cereal preferences. Suppose that children who watch average amounts of television, unlike children who watch no television, do not get enough exercise. This would clearly be a negative aspect of watching television. But it doesn't weaken the support that the argument provides for the conclusion that television advertising does not significantly affect children's preferences for breakfast cereal.

ASSUMPTIONS

The Logical Reasoning section typically includes several questions that test your ability to identify assumptions of arguments. An assumption of an argument plays a role in establishing the conclusion. However, unlike a premise, an assumption is not something that the arguer explicitly asserts to be true; an assumption is instead just treated as true for the purposes of the argument.

Although assumptions can be stated explicitly in an argument, Logical Reasoning questions that ask about assumptions ask only about unstated assumptions. Unstated (or tacit) assumptions can figure only in arguments that are not entirely complete, that is, in arguments in which some of the things required to establish the conclusion are left unstated. There is thus at least one significant gap in such an argument.

Assumptions relate to the gaps in an argument in two different ways. An assumption is a **sufficient** one if adding it to the argument's premises would produce a conclusive argument, that is, an argument with no gaps in its support for the conclusion. An assumption is a **necessary** one if it is something that must be true in order for the argument to succeed. It is possible for an assumption to be both necessary and sufficient.

Sufficient Assumptions

Typical wordings of questions that ask you to identify sufficient assumptions are:

Which one of the following, if assumed, enables the conclusion of the argument to be properly drawn?

The conclusion follows logically from the premises if which one of the following is assumed?

An Example

Vague laws set vague limits on people's freedom, which makes it impossible for them to know for certain whether their actions are legal. Thus, under vague laws people cannot feel secure.[13]

The question you're asked about this argument is:

The conclusion follows logically if which one of the following is assumed?

In order to approach this question, you first have to identify the conclusion of the argument and the premises offered in its support. In this case, the conclusion is signaled by the conclusion indicator "thus" and reads "… under vague laws people cannot feel secure." Two considerations are explicitly presented in support of this conclusion. First, that vague laws set vague limits on people's freedom, and second, that having vague limits set on their freedom makes it impossible for people to know for certain whether their actions are legal. Note that the premises, though they tell us certain things about vague laws, make no explicit reference to whether people feel secure, and not feeling secure is what the conclusion is about. For the conclusion to follow logically, this gap has to be bridged.

At this point, you are ready to look at the answer choices. Here are two of them:

(A) *People can feel secure only if they know for certain whether their actions are legal.*

(B) *If people know for certain whether their actions are legal, they can feel secure.*

Your task is to identify the answer choice that, together with the premises you've been given, will provide conclusive support for the conclusion.

So is (A) that answer choice? The explicit premises of the argument tell you that under vague laws people cannot know for certain whether their actions are legal. (A) tells you that if people do not know for certain whether their actions are legal, they cannot feel secure. So putting the explicit premises and (A) together, you can infer that under vague laws people cannot feel secure. And this is, in fact, the conclusion of the argument. So the conclusion follows logically if (A) is assumed.

Now, let's consider why assuming (B) is not sufficient to ensure that the argument's conclusion follows logically. (B) tells us about one circumstance in which people **can** feel secure. However, the argument's conclusion will not follow logically without the right kind of information about the circumstances in which people **cannot** feel secure. (B) does not give us any such information directly. Moreover, we cannot infer such information from what (B) does tell us. After all, it's perfectly compatible with (B) that people can feel secure in some circumstances in addition to the one (B) describes. For example, perhaps people can feel secure if they know for certain that they will not be prosecuted for their actions. Thus, since (B) tells us nothing about circumstances in which people cannot feel secure, it has nothing to contribute to reaching the argument's conclusion that people cannot feel secure under vague laws.

Some Points to Consider

- In answering sufficient assumption questions, you need to find a link between the stated premises and the conclusion. Try to determine from the explicit parts of the argument what logical work that link needs to do. Finally, look among the answer choices for one that can do that logical work and that, taken along with the explicit premises, allows the conclusion to be properly inferred.

- In trying to figure out what logical work the link needs to do, don't get too specific. For example, what can be said about the logical work required of the link in the argument about vague laws analyzed above? It has to link something that has been explicitly connected with vague laws to an inability to feel secure. But there are two things like that: vague limits on people's freedom, and the impossibility of knowing for certain whether one's actions are legal. What this means is that answer choice (A) was not the only possible sufficient assumption here. An equally

---

[13] December 2001 LSAT, section 3, question 12.

acceptable sufficient assumption would have been, "People cannot feel secure if they have vague limits on their freedom." So don't approach the answer choices with too specific a view of what you're looking for.

- When trying to identify a sufficient assumption, keep in mind that the correct answer must, when added to the argument's explicit premises, result in a conclusive argument; that is, in an argument that fully establishes its conclusion (provided that the explicit premises and the added assumption are all true).

Necessary Assumptions

Typical wordings of questions that ask you to identify necessary assumptions include the following:

The argument relies on assuming which one of the following?

The argument depends on the assumption that

Which one of the following is an assumption required by the argument?

Questions about necessary assumptions refer to arguments that, while not completely spelled out, do present a comprehensible case for accepting their conclusion on the strength of evidence explicitly presented. But if you look closely at the grounds offered for the conclusion and at the conclusion itself, you find that the evidence explicitly presented falls short of establishing the conclusion. That is, there is at least one significant gap in the argument.

Example 1

Since Mayor Drabble always repays her political debts as soon as possible, she will almost certainly appoint Lee to be the new head of the arts commission. Lee has wanted that job for a long time, and Drabble owes Lee a lot for his support in the last election.[14]

As far as its explicit premises go, this argument leaves important matters unresolved. In order for the argument to show that Lee is the likely appointee, there can't be anyone else to whom Drabble has owed such a large and long-standing political debt and for whom this appointment would be adequate repayment. This idea of

there being no one ahead of Lee in line is the sort of unstated but indispensable link in the support for the conclusion that we mean when we speak of a necessary assumption of an argument.

It can readily be shown that the assumption sketched above is in fact indispensable to the argument. Suppose the situation were otherwise and there were a person to whom Mayor Drabble owed a political debt that is of longer standing than her debt to Lee, and suppose further that the appointment could reasonably be viewed as paying off that debt. In this hypothetical circumstance, the fact that Mayor Drabble always repays her political debts as soon as possible would no longer point to Lee as the likely choice for the appointment. In fact, the argument above would fail. If the argument is to succeed, there cannot be another, better-positioned candidate for the appointment. And thus the argument depends on the assumption that there isn't any better-positioned candidate.

A Test for Necessary Assumptions

Necessary assumption questions, then, require you to identify tacit assumptions. The method for testing necessary assumptions that was introduced above in analyzing Mayor Drabble's situation is quite generally applicable, and for good reason. A necessary assumption is an indispensable link in the support for the conclusion of an argument. Therefore, an argument will be ineffective if a necessary assumption is deemed to be false. This points to a useful test: to see whether an answer choice is a necessary assumption, suppose that what is stated in that answer choice is **false**. If under those circumstances the premises of the argument fail to support the conclusion, the answer choice being evaluated is a necessary assumption.

Example 2

The test for necessary assumptions can be used with the following argument:

Advertisement: Attention pond owners! Ninety-eight percent of mosquito larvae in a pond die within minutes after the pond has been treated with BTI. Yet BTI is not toxic to fish, birds, animals, plants, or beneficial insects. So by using BTI regularly to destroy their larvae, you can greatly reduce populations of pesky mosquitoes that hatch in your pond, and can do so without diminishing the

---

[14] June 1994 LSAT, section 2, question 24.

populations of fish, frogs, or beneficial insects in and around the pond.[15]

The question asks:

Which one of the following is an assumption on which the argument depends?

Before you look for a necessary assumption, you need to get clear about the structure of the argument. The conclusion is that regular applications of BTI in a pond can, without reducing populations of assorted pond life, greatly reduce the numbers of mosquitoes that emerge from the pond. The evidence is that BTI kills almost all of the mosquito larvae in the pond, but does not kill (or even harm) other pond life.

The case that the argument makes for its conclusion is straightforward. Applications of BTI, by killing mosquito larvae, prevent the adult mosquito population from being replenished, but they have no direct effect on the other populations. So the argument concludes that, of the populations under consideration, only the mosquito populations will decline.

The first answer choice reads:

The most effective way to control the numbers of mosquitoes in a given area is to destroy the mosquito larvae in that area.

Now we apply the test for necessary assumptions by asking whether the argument would fail if this answer choice were false. That is, would it fail if the destruction of mosquito larvae were not the most effective way to control the numbers of mosquitoes? Definitely not. For one thing, the argument is not concerned with mosquito control alone, but speaks to a dual purpose, that of controlling mosquitoes while leaving other creatures unaffected. So the potential existence of any mosquito-control regimen, however effective, that did not spare other pond creatures would be beside the point. For another thing, the argument merely concludes that the use of BTI works, not that it works better than all other methods. So the denial of this answer choice does not interfere with the support that the conclusion receives from the evidence presented. But if this answer choice were a necessary assumption, denying it would interfere with that support.

Now consider a second answer choice:

The fish, frogs, and beneficial insects in and around a pond-owner's pond do not depend on mosquito larvae as an important source of food.

Applying the test, we ask whether the argument would fail if this answer choice were false (that is, if these creatures did depend on mosquito larvae for food). Yes it would; after all, if the use of BTI means that fish, frogs, and so forth will be deprived of a food that is important for them (mosquito larvae), then there is no reason to conclude that these creatures will survive in undiminished numbers. So denying the answer choice under consideration would cause the argument to fail; we have found a necessary assumption.

Some Points to Consider

- As you can see from the characterization of necessary assumptions given above, they are (unstated) constituents of arguments. Whether or not the author of the argument had a particular assumption in mind is not relevant to the issue. It is important to remember that identifying necessary assumptions is a matter of logically analyzing the structure of an argument, not a matter of guessing the beliefs of the arguer.

- For the purpose of *identifying* a necessary assumption, it is not necessary or even useful to evaluate whether that assumption is actually true, or how likely it is to be true. Identifying an assumption is a matter of probing the structure of an argument and recognizing hidden parts of that structure.

- An argument may have more than one necessary assumption. For example, the argument in Example 2 ignores the fact that a small proportion of mosquito larvae in a pond are not killed by BTI. But if there is a genetic basis for their not being killed, one might imagine that regular applications of BTI in a given pond will make it more and more likely that the mosquitoes left to breed with one another will be BTI-resistant ones that will likely produce BTI-resistant offspring. This population of BTI-resistant mosquitoes might then grow, without being kept in check by further applications of BTI, contrary to the drift of the argument. So the argument also depends on assuming that the two percent of mosquito larvae not killed by an initial application of BTI do not constitute an initial breeding pool for a BTI-resistant population of mosquitoes.

---

[15] February 1994 LSAT, section 4, question 18.

An argument can thus have more than one necessary assumption. Of course, only one of them will appear among the answer choices. But the one that does appear may not be one that occurred to you when you analyzed the argument. So it is a good idea not to prejudge what the correct answer will be. Instead, keep an open mind and examine each of the answer choices in turn.

- As indicated above, an argument may have more than one gap. Any one necessary assumption will address only one such gap. Moreover, a necessary assumption will often address only some aspects of a gap. In Example 2, the gap addressed by the necessary assumption—*The fish, frogs, and beneficial insects in and around a pond-owner's pond do not depend on mosquito larvae as an important source of food*—is, broadly speaking, that BTI does not kill the fish, frogs, and beneficial insects indirectly. But food deprivation is not the only way that BTI might kill those creatures indirectly. For example, as the mosquito larvae killed by applications of BTI decay, they might harm fish, frogs, and beneficial insects.

So do not reject an answer choice as a necessary assumption merely on the grounds that the argument, even if you make that necessary assumption, is still not a strong argument.

PRINCIPLES

Some Logical Reasoning questions test your ability to apply general rules and principles and to understand their use. These questions can involve the use of principles in arguments, or they can involve applying principles to actions or states of affairs.

Principles are broad guidelines concerning what kinds of actions, judgments, policies, and so on are appropriate. Most principles spell out the range of situations to which they apply. Within that range of situations, principles often serve to justify the transition from claims about what is the case to conclusions regarding what should be done.

There are several kinds of questions involving principles. You may be given a principle and be asked which action conforms to it, or which judgment it justifies, or which argument relies on it. Alternatively, the question may present a judgment, decision, or argument and ask which principle is appealed to in making that judgment, decision, or argument. Logical Reasoning questions may also involve principles in various other

ways. For example, a question could ask which action violates a principle. You may also see Logical Reasoning questions that ask you to recognize two situations as involving the same underlying principle, where that principle is not stated.

Applying a Principle That Is Given

An Example

People who receive unsolicited advice from someone whose advantage would be served if that advice is taken should regard the proffered advice with skepticism unless there is good reason to think that their interests substantially coincide with those of the advice giver in the circumstance in question.[16]

The following question refers to this principle:

This principle, if accepted, would justify which one of the following judgments?

The correct answer is provided by the judgment that is presented below.

While shopping for a refrigerator, Ramón is approached by a salesperson who, on the basis of her personal experience, warns him against the least expensive model. However, the salesperson's commission increases with the price of the refrigerator sold, so Ramón should not reject the least expensive model on the salesperson's advice alone.

The task here is to check how well the particulars of the situation fit with the principle. Do the general terms in which the principle is expressed cover the specific circumstances of the situation?

So first you should ask, "Does someone in this situation receive unsolicited advice from someone whose advantage would be served if that advice is taken?" If the answer is "yes," then the case under consideration falls within the range of situations to which the principle applies. If the answer is "no," then the principle offers no guidance. In this situation, someone—Ramón—does receive advice. If Ramón took the advice, this would be to the advantage of the advice giver (the salesperson), because the salesperson would receive a higher commission than she would otherwise. Is the advice unsolicited? Yes, because the salesperson approached Ramón without his asking for help.

[16] December 1992 LSAT, section 4, question 19.

The next question you should ask is, "Does the situation culminate in a judgment that the advice should be regarded with skepticism?" The answer is again "yes." The judgment that Ramón should not reject the least expensive model solely on the salesperson's advice is a judgment that treats the advice given—to avoid buying the least expensive model—skeptically.

You are not quite done at this point. The principle restricts itself to situations in which the person giving the advice and the person receiving the advice do not have interests that coincide. So you need to ask one more question: "Is there reason to think that the interests of Ramón and those of the salesperson substantially coincide in this matter?" Since Ramón probably wants to spend no more than he has to and since the salesperson probably wants Ramón to spend freely, there is reason to think that in this matter their interests do **not** coincide. So the principle applies to the situation and justifies the judgment.

Identifying a Guiding Principle

In the example above, the passage contained a principle and you were asked which judgment it justified. There are also questions that present a judgment or argument in the passage and ask which principle justifies it.

An Example

Marianne is a professional chess player who hums audibly while playing her matches, thereby distracting her opponents. When ordered by chess officials to cease humming or else be disqualified from professional chess, Marianne protested the order. She argued that since she was unaware of her humming, her humming was involuntary and that therefore she should not be held responsible for it.[17]

The question that is based on this passage is:

Which one of the following principles, if valid, most helps to support Marianne's argument against the order?

To answer this question, you need to compare the specific circumstances presented in the passage with the principle presented in each answer choice. First, consider the following answer choice:

Of a player's actions, only those that are voluntary should be used as justification for disqualifying that player from professional chess.

Does this principle apply to Marianne's situation? Well, it is clear that the principle concerns which of a chess player's actions can appropriately be used as justification for disqualifying that player from professional chess. Since the argument in the passage is concerned with whether one of Marianne's actions—humming while playing—should disqualify her from professional chess, it definitely falls under the range of situations to which the principle applies.

The principle will help support Marianne's argument if it leads to a judgment that Marianne's humming while playing should not be used as justification for disqualifying her from playing. According to a subsidiary conclusion of Marianne's argument, her humming is involuntary (this is supported by the claim that she was unaware of it). The principle asserts that only voluntary actions should be used as justification for disqualifying a player from professional chess, so this principle, together with the subsidiary conclusion of Marianne's argument, leads to the judgment that Marianne's humming should not be used as justification for disqualifying her. Thus the principle does help support Marianne's argument.

For the sake of comparison, consider one of the other answer choices:

Chess players should be disqualified from professional chess matches if they regularly attempt to distract their opponents.

Does this principle apply to Marianne's situation? Yes, it apparently does since it is also about the conditions under which chess players should be disqualified from professional chess matches. So now you need to ask, does the principle establish, or help establish the conclusion that Marianne should not be disqualified for humming during matches? The answer is no. This principle just gives one condition under which a chess player should be disqualified—when that player regularly attempts to distract opponents. Since Marianne's humming is, she argues, involuntary, we can conclude that she is not trying to distract her opponents. Thus the principle does not lead to the judgment that Marianne should be disqualified for humming. But this does not mean that the principle leads to the judgment that Marianne should not be disqualified. After all, it is compatible with the principle that there are other conditions under which a player should be disqualified,

---

[17] October 1996 LSAT, section 4, question 24.

and such conditions could include humming while playing. So the principle does not lead to the conclusion that Marianne should not be disqualified from professional matches and thus does not provide any support for Marianne's argument.

 Cross-reference: Making a common reasoning error known as confusion between "sufficient conditions" and "necessary conditions" could lead one to pick this answer choice. There are many opportunities for this confusion to arise in principles questions. Further discussion of sufficient and necessary conditions, and of correct and incorrect ways of reasoning with conditions, can be found on pages 25–27.

Note that the process of finding the correct answer to a question that asks you to identify a guiding principle is basically the same as it is for a question that asks you to apply a given principle. The task is to make sure that a principle, which will be couched in general terms, fits the particulars of the situation. The only difference is that in the one case you need to check five different situations against one principle, and in the other case you need to check a single situation against five different principles. But the way you determine the best fit is the same. You check the principle for applicability, and you check to see whether the judgment, decision, recommendation, or action is in line with what the principle says.

Some Points to Consider

- Although principles always go beyond the particular case, they can vary enormously in degree of generality and abstractness. For example, the principle in the question about Ramón's refrigerator shopping is very general, applying to anyone who receives unsolicited advice. In contrast, the principle in the question about Marianne the chess player is more specific, applying only to professional chess players. And some questions have principles that can be even more specific than this. So be sure not to reject a principle as a correct answer solely because it seems to be too specific.

- When answering questions involving principles, it is always a good idea to check all of the answer choices. There is no sure way to determine whether a given answer choice provides the best fit except by considering and comparing all of the answer choices.

- Don't reject a principle as providing justification for an argument merely because it seems to do no more than spell out what the argument takes for granted. For example, someone might say, "Gerry sees very poorly without glasses. Therefore, Gerry should always wear glasses when driving." A principle justifying this judgment might be "Anyone who needs glasses to see well should always wear glasses when driving."

- Don't worry about the legitimacy of any of the principles you are presented with. Do not reject an answer because the principle involved is one that you personally would not accept.

FLAWS IN ARGUMENTS

Identifying Argument Flaws

The Logical Reasoning section includes a number of questions that ask you to identify a flaw of reasoning that has been committed in an argument. Questions of this kind are worded in a variety of ways. Here are some examples:

The reasoning in the argument is flawed because the argument

The argument commits which one of the following errors of reasoning?

The argument's reasoning is questionable because the argument fails to rule out the possibility that

The reasoning above is most vulnerable to criticism on the grounds that it

Test questions about flawed reasoning require you to recognize in what way an argument is defective in its reasoning. They will not require you to decide whether or not the argument is flawed. That judgment is already made and is expressed in the wording of the question. Your task is to recognize which one of the answer choices describes an error of reasoning that the argument makes.

When an argument is flawed, the argument exemplifies poor reasoning. This is reasoning in which the premises may appear to provide support for the conclusion but actually provide little or no real support. Poor reasoning of this sort can be detected by examining the argument itself, without considering any factual issues that aren't mentioned in the argument.

Tip: Logical Reasoning questions in the LSAT test your skills in reasoning and analysis, not what you know about any particular subject matter. Whether a premise is factually accurate is not relevant. So don't pay attention to the factual accuracy of an argument's premises. Focus instead on logical connections between the premises that the argument sets out and the conclusion that it draws.

Since the flaws that you'll be looking for are not specific to the subject matter but relate to the argument's logical structure, the characterization of those flaws can be quite general. That is to say, the flawed reasoning in an argument might be described in terms that also apply to other arguments that commit the same error of reasoning. So once you detect where a particular argument has gone wrong, you may then have to figure out which of several quite general descriptions covers the case.

Example 1

Consider the following brief exchange:

Physicist: The claim that low-temperature nuclear fusion can be achieved entirely by chemical means is based on chemical experiments in which the measurements and calculations are inaccurate.

Chemist: But your challenge is ineffectual, since you are simply jealous at the thought that chemists might have solved a problem that physicists have been unable to solve.[18]

Here is the question that is based on this exchange:

Which one of the following is the strongest criticism of the chemist's response to the physicist's challenge?

Before looking at the answer choices, briefly consider what appears to be wrong with the chemist's response. Notice that the chemist claims that the physicist's challenge is ineffectual but doesn't actually engage the substance of the physicist's challenge. Instead, the chemist accuses the physicist of professional jealousy and dismisses the physicist's challenge purely on that basis. But there is no reason to think that a challenge, even if it is fueled by jealousy, cannot be on target. So the chemist's response can rightly be criticized for "getting personal."

Now consider two of the answer choices. One of them reads,

It fails to establish that perfect accuracy of measurements and calculations is possible.

This statement is certainly true about the chemist's response. The chemist does not establish that perfect accuracy is possible. But this is not a good criticism of the chemist's response because it is entirely beside the point. Establishing that perfect accuracy is possible would have, if anything, damaged the chemist's position. So the chemist's response cannot be legitimately criticized for failing to establish this.

Another answer choice reads,

It is directed against the proponent of a claim rather than against the claim itself.

This criticism goes to the heart of what is wrong with the chemist's response. The chemist dismisses the physicist's challenge because of the physicist's alleged motives for making it and never actually discusses the merits of the challenge itself. It is directed against the person rather than against the position.

In this example, the chemist's response is clearly irrelevant to the substance of the physicist's claim. The argument that the chemist presents seems more like a rhetorical ploy than a serious argument. Many arguments are flawed in much less dramatic ways, however. They may contain only a small logical lapse that undermines the integrity of the argument, like the following two examples.

Example 2

Morris High School has introduced a policy designed to improve the working conditions of its new teachers. As a result of this policy, only one-quarter of all part-time teachers now quit during their first year. However, a third of all full-time teachers now quit during their first year. Thus, more full-time than part-time teachers at Morris now quit during their first year.[19]

Notice that the argument uses proportions to indicate the degree to which first-year teachers are quitting. It says that **one-quarter** of part-time first-year teachers quit and that **one-third** of full-time first-year teachers quit. The conclusion of the argument is not expressed in

[18] June 1995 LSAT, section 2, question 2.
[19] October 1994 LSAT, section 1, question 14.

terms of proportions, however, but in terms of a comparison between quantities: **more** full-timers than part-timers quit during their first year.

Your task is to accurately complete the following statement:

> The argument's reasoning is questionable because the argument fails to rule out the possibility that

Note that we are looking for a possibility that needs to be ruled out in order for the conclusion to be well supported. So let's consider one of the answer choices:

> before the new policy was instituted, more part-time than full-time teachers at Morris High School used to quit during their first year

How would the argument be affected by this information? It tells us something about the way things were before the new policy went into effect, but it doesn't shed much light on the effects of the new policy. And there is no way to infer anything about how many part-time and full-time teachers are quitting now, after the policy was instituted. So this information has no effect on the support for the conclusion, and there would be no reason for the argument to rule it out. Failing to rule it out, then, would not make the reasoning questionable.

Let's go on to consider another answer choice:

> Morris High School employs more new part-time teachers than new full-time teachers

So how would the argument be affected if there were more new part-time teachers than new full time teachers? If there were more new part-timers than full-timers, then one-quarter of the new part-timers could outnumber one-third of the new full-timers. So it could be true that more part-timers than full-timers quit during their first year. Since the argument concludes that more full-timers than part-timers quit in their first year, this possibility needs to be ruled out in order for the conclusion to be well supported. Thus, this choice is the correct answer.

Example 3

> If Blankenship Enterprises has to switch suppliers in the middle of a large production run, the company will not show a profit for the year. Therefore, if Blankenship Enterprises in fact turns out to show no profit for the year, it will also turn out to be true that the company had to switch suppliers during a large production run.[20]

The question asks:

> The reasoning in the argument is most vulnerable to criticism on which one of the following grounds?

This question tells you that you should be looking for a problem with the argument. When you analyze the argument, you can identify the problem if you recognize that there may well be other reasons for not showing a profit besides having to switch suppliers in the middle of a large production run. This points to a major oversight in the argument. At this point, you are ready to review the answer choices.

One answer choice says:

> The argument is a circular argument made up of an opening claim followed by a conclusion that merely paraphrases that claim.

This gives a general account of an argument flaw, but close inspection shows that the Blankenship argument does not have this flaw. That argument's conclusion says something quite different from what was said in the argument's premise. The conclusion says "If there is no profit, then there was a switch in suppliers." The premise is superficially similar, but it says "If there is a switch in suppliers, then there will be no profit." So this answer choice is not a legitimate criticism.

Another answer choice reads:

> The argument fails to establish that a condition under which a phenomenon is said to occur is the only condition under which that phenomenon occurs.

This is the correct answer. The argument could only succeed if it showed that switching suppliers in the middle of a large production run is the only condition under which the company will show no profit for the year. But the argument fails to establish this point. Note that this answer choice points out what is wrong with this particular argument using general terms that could cover many different arguments.

---

[20] December 1994 LSAT, section 2, question 26.

Cross-reference: This is an example of a common reasoning error: confusion between "sufficient conditions" and "necessary conditions." A more detailed discussion of sufficient and necessary conditions, and of correct and incorrect ways of reasoning with conditions, can be found on pages 25–27.

Some Points to Consider

- When you begin a flawed reasoning question, you should first try to get fairly clear about just where the argument goes wrong. If you have a reasonably clear sense of what is wrong with the reasoning, you can then look for the answer choice that describes the kind of error you have identified. Keep in mind that the descriptions offered may be very general—ones that could also apply to arguments very different in subject matter from the one you're considering.

- Keep in mind that for an answer to be the correct answer, it is not enough that it describe some aspect of the argument correctly. The correct answer must describe a flaw in the reasoning of the particular argument under consideration.

- When dealing with a flawed argument that contains quantitative or statistical information, always check to see that the reference groups mentioned in the argument are appropriate and consistent. An argument may, for example, present information about the percentage of primary school teachers who have degrees in education and go on to draw a conclusion about the percentage of people who receive degrees in education and go on to teach primary school. Detecting this shift in reference groups is the key to identifying the flaw in this argument. It is not unusual for argument flaws to involve subtle shifts such as this.

- Some flawed arguments involve errors in reasoning about the relationship between proportions and quantities. Example 2 is a case in point. That argument involves a shift from talk about proportions in the premises to a statement about relative quantities in the conclusion. In some other argument, there might be an illicit shift from quantities in the premises to proportions in the conclusion. So pay close attention to any shifts like these.

Matching Argument Flaws

In your test you will sometimes encounter logical reasoning questions like the following:

Which one of the following arguments is most similar in its flawed reasoning to the argument above?

It is best to approach these questions in a straightforward way. First, try to determine in what way the reasoning in the reference argument is flawed. Then go over the arguments in the answer choices until you find the one whose reasoning is flawed in just the same way.

The wording of the question tells you that the reference argument is in fact flawed in its reasoning and that at least one other argument is, too. There is no need to worry about the precise wording of that flaw: the question does not hinge on it. But you do need to get a reasonably clear idea of the kind of reasoning error committed, because you will be making a judgment about whether one of the answer choices matches that error.

For this type of question, incorrect answer choices can be of two kinds. Some present arguments that are perfectly good, so they don't contain any flaw at all, let alone one that matches the one in the reference argument. Others do present flawed arguments, but the reasoning errors in those arguments are clearly different from the one in the reference argument.

An Example

Consider the following argument:

If the majority of the residents of the apartment complex complain that their apartments are infested with ants, then the management of the complex will have to engage the services of an exterminator. But the majority of the residents of the complex indicate that their apartments are virtually free of ants. Therefore, the management of the complex will not have to engage the services of an exterminator.[21]

The question you are asked about this argument is

Which one of the following arguments contains a flawed pattern of reasoning parallel to that contained in the argument above?

This question directs us to look for a flawed **pattern** of reasoning in the reference argument and to look for an

---

[21] June 1994 LSAT, section 4, question 20.

answer choice that contains a similarly flawed pattern. This means that we should look for an argument that takes the same flawed approach to establishing its conclusion as the reference argument does, even though the two arguments might not share other characteristics, such as subject matter.

So what exactly is the flaw in the reference argument? One of the argument's premises says that under a certain condition the exterminator will have to come, and the second premise says that this condition is not met. The argument concludes that the exterminator will not have to be hired. But it is not difficult to see that something is wrong with this way of arguing: the problem is that there may be other conditions under which the exterminator has to be hired. To use a concrete example, it may also be true that if there is a rodent infestation in the apartment complex, the management has to call in an exterminator. So the fact that the condition about ants is not met is not a good enough reason for concluding that the exterminator will not have to be hired. Without offering any reasons for doing so, the argument treats one circumstance that would produce a certain result as though it were the only circumstance under which this result comes about.

The next step is to check the answer choices and to find the one that exhibits the same flawed pattern of reasoning. So let's consider the following choice:

The number of flights operated by the airlines cannot be reduced unless the airlines can collect higher airfares. But people will not pay higher airfares, so it is not the case that the number of flights will be reduced.

Is this an instance of the same flawed pattern? This argument is like the reference argument in that one of its premises asserts that under a certain condition (airlines cannot collect higher airfares) something will happen (schedules will not be cut). But this argument is unlike the reference argument in that its second premise actually meets the condition set out in the first premise. We are told that "people will not pay higher airfares," so it stands to reason that airlines cannot collect higher airfares. And thus the conclusion—that the number of flights will not be reduced—follows from these premises. So this argument does not exhibit the same pattern of flawed reasoning as the reference argument. In fact, it does not exhibit flawed reasoning at all.

Let's try another one of the answer choices:

Most employees will attend the company picnic if the entertainment committee is successful in getting a certain band to play at the picnic. But that band will be out of the country on the day of the picnic, so it is not true that most employees will attend.

Is this an instance of the pattern you are trying to match? Again, there is a conditional statement: if a certain band plays at the picnic, most employees will attend. So again, under a certain condition, something will happen. In this argument, the second premise indicates that the condition will not be met. The band, being out of the country, will certainly not play at the picnic. The argument goes on to conclude that most employees won't attend the picnic. So, as in the reference argument, this conclusion says that the thing that would happen under the original condition will not happen.

This is an exact match of the pattern of reasoning in the reference argument, hence it is an exact match of the flaw. As with the reference argument, the flaw can be illustrated concretely. Suppose, for example, that if the entertainment committee hires a certain well-known comedian to perform at the picnic, most employees will attend. This shows that the conclusion could be false even if what the argument tells us about the band is true.

Some Points to Consider

- For this type of question, there is no need to decide whether the reference argument is flawed. You are told that there is a flawed pattern of reasoning underlying the argument. It is sometimes useful, however, to determine whether or not an argument in an answer choice is flawed. If such an argument is not flawed, it cannot be the correct answer, because it will not be a relevant match for the reference argument.

- Remember that, although you need to get a reasonably clear fix on the kind of reasoning error committed in the reference argument, you do not need to come up with a precise formulation of that error. Since you are not asked to put your understanding of the reasoning error into words, all you need is a solid intuitive grasp of where the reasoning goes wrong.

- With this type of question, you look for the argument that most closely matches the reference argument in terms of its flawed reasoning. So other similarities with the reference argument, such as in the way the argument is expressed or in its subject matter, are irrelevant. Two arguments can be expressed in very different ways, or be about very different things, even though they exhibit the same pattern of reasoning.

 Cross-reference: For a more extensive discussion of this point, see "Identifying the Parts of an Argument" on pages 16–17.

EXPLANATIONS

Some of the questions in the Logical Reasoning section require you to identify a potential explanation for some state of affairs that is described to you. Broadly speaking, these questions come in two types: one in which you need to find an explanation for one particular situation, and another in which you need to explain how two seemingly conflicting elements of a given situation can both be true.

In the first sort of case, the phenomenon to be explained will merely be something that one would not ordinarily expect, the kind of thing that makes people say, "There must be an explanation for this." Imagine, for example, that it is discovered that domestic cats with purely gray coats are, on average, significantly heavier than those with multicolored coats. A fact like this calls for an explanation. The wording of a corresponding question would be along the lines of:

Which one of the following, if true, most helps to explain the difference in average weights?

In the second sort of case, the phenomenon to be explained is more complex. You are not simply presented with one fact that seems to require an explanation. Rather, you are presented with statements that appear to conflict with one another, and your task is to identify the answer choice that most helps to resolve this apparent discrepancy. That is, you are to select an answer choice that explains not just one or the other of the apparently conflicting elements but explains how they can both be true. With this sort of question, the passage might say, for example, that people spend much less time reading today than they did 50 years ago, and yet many more books are sold per year now than were sold 50 years ago. A typical wording for this sort of question is:

Which one of the following, if true, most helps to resolve the apparent discrepancy in the information given above?

Example 1

The situation that follows seems to call for an explanation. In this case, a software production company's decision to refrain from prosecuting people who illegally copy its program raises questions regarding the company's reasons.

The company that produces XYZ, a computer spreadsheet program, estimates that millions of illegally reproduced copies of XYZ are being used. If legally purchased, this number of copies would have generated millions of dollars in sales for the company, yet despite a company-wide effort to boost sales, the company has not taken available legal measures to prosecute those who have copied the program illegally.[22]

The question that is based on this situation reads as follows:

Which one of the following, if true, most helps to explain why the company has not taken available legal measures?

Incorrect answer choices such as

XYZ is very difficult to copy illegally, because a sophisticated anticopying mechanism in the program must first be disabled.

do nothing to help us understand the company's decision. They may, however, be relevant to some aspect of the situation. The answer choice above, for example, does suggest that those who do the illegal copying are knowledgeable about computers and computer software, but it doesn't throw any light on the company's decision not to prosecute.

The correct answer,

Many people who purchase a software program like XYZ are willing to purchase that program only after they have already used it.

on the other hand, does suggest a reason for the company to tolerate the use of illegal copies of its program: those copies happen to serve as effective marketing aids in many cases and lead to legal sales of the program. The company may think that it has more to lose than to gain from going to court in order to stop the illegal copying. At the very least, the correct answer tells us that there is a disadvantage for the company in stopping the illegal copying, and this helps to explain why no legal measures are taken.

---

[22] December 1994 LSAT, section 4, question 2.

Example 2

Of the five bill collectors at Apex Collection Agency, Mr. Young has the highest rate of unsuccessful collections. Yet Mr. Young is the best bill collector on the agency's staff.[23]

This situation has an air of paradox. It seems clear that a superior ability to bring a collection effort to a successful conclusion is what makes one bill collector better than another. So how can Mr. Young, who has the lowest rate of successful collections, be the best bill collector? This is the focus of the question that goes along with this situation:

Which one of the following, if true, most helps to resolve the apparent discrepancy?

Consider the following answer choice:

Mr. Young's rate of collections per year has remained fairly steady in the last few years.

This gives us information that is pertinent to Mr. Young's performance as a bill collector. But it gives us no reason to think that Mr. Young could be the best bill collector at the agency despite having the lowest collection rate. It only gives us more reason to think Mr. Young is a poor bill collector, because it allows us to infer that his collection rate has been low for years.

Now consider another choice:

Mr. Young is assigned the majority of the most difficult cases at the agency.

This gives us reason to think more highly of Mr. Young's ability as a bill collector, because it makes sense to assign the most difficult cases to Mr. Young if he is very good at collecting bills. And if his rate of success is relatively low, this is not really a surprise, because his cases tend to be more difficult. So this answer makes it clear how two facts that seemed to be difficult to reconcile with one another can in fact both be true. This resolves the apparent discrepancy in a satisfying way.

Some Points to Consider

■ The correct answers to these questions do not generally offer complete and detailed explanations. Rather, they present crucial information that plays an important part within an adequate explanation.

■ Pay close attention to what you are asked to explain. In the case of simple explanations of a particular factual matter, the wording of the question will direct you specifically to the fact to be explained. In the case of explanations that resolve an apparent conflict, however, it is generally up to you to develop a clear picture of that conflict.

■ In most cases, there is more than one way to explain a set of facts or resolve an apparent conflict. So it is generally not a good idea to work out several explanatory stories in your head before examining the answer choices. Go to the answer choices instead and, for each choice, determine whether it helps to explain or resolve the situation.

■ Note that these questions are qualified by the expression "if true." This indicates that you do not have to be concerned about the actual truth of the answer choices. Simply consider each answer choice as though it were true.

---

[23] June 1995 LSAT, section 2, question 5.

A GUIDE TO READING COMPREHENSION QUESTIONS

HOW TO APPROACH READING COMPREHENSION PASSAGES

The Reading Comprehension section is intended to assess your ability to read, with understanding and insight, passages comparable in terms of level of language and complexity to materials you are likely to have to deal with in the study of law. The passages are selected so that they can be adequately understood simply on the basis of what they say; you won't need any specialized prior knowledge to understand Reading Comprehension passages. Any technical terms that you need to understand to answer the questions are explained in the passages and all of the questions can be answered on the basis of information given in the passages.

Typically, a passage has a single main point. Sometimes the main point of a passage is to present a controversial position and either attack or defend it. Sometimes it is to examine and critique someone else's view. Sometimes it is to explain a puzzling phenomenon. Sometimes it is to give an accurate historical account of some important development. All passages will present a number of considerations that are relevant to the main point of the passage; the roles these considerations play are largely determined by the nature of that main point.

So how should you approach a Reading Comprehension passage? The single most important thing is to get clear about the main thrust of the passage: what is the passage mainly trying to get across to the reader? Occasionally, a passage will contain a particular sentence that explicitly states the main point. Even when there is such a statement, however, it does not necessarily come at the beginning of the passage; it could occur anywhere in the passage. More often, a passage will just present its position, critique, account, or explanation and rely on the reader to see where the passage is going. So what you should do as you work through a passage is read attentively, but at the same time you should be aware that it is not necessary to absorb and retain all of the descriptive detail that the author presents along the way. Try to remain focused on the main business of the passage, because the entire passage is organized around that. Without a clear sense of what the passage is about, you are likely to make mistakes about the relative significance of the various subsidiary points that the passage raises in support of its central point.

Be Aware of Paragraphs and Transition Words

Shifts in focus and perspective occur frequently in Reading Comprehension passages. A passage might shift from one concern to another, from the particular to the general, from a positive view of a topic to a negative one, or from one person to another. To get a solid grasp of how a given passage works, you must be aware of what the different ideas presented in the passage are and, more importantly, how the ideas relate to one another. A reader therefore needs to track the ideas presented by the author and the nature of the transition from one to another in order to grasp the significance, within the passage as a whole, of what is being said at any given point in the passage.

One feature of passages that can be extremely helpful in determining exactly how they work is their division into paragraphs. Paragraphs tend to have a relatively narrow focus and often play well-defined roles within the passage as a whole. So, for example, when an author switches from citing support for a position to defending the position against a challenge, the switch is typically marked by starting a new paragraph. Consequently, by asking yourself what each paragraph does you can put together a fairly accurate picture of the structure of the passage as a whole.

Still, not all shifts in focus or perspective coincide with the transition from one paragraph to the next; one or more shifts might occur within a given paragraph, or conversely, two or more paragraphs might share the same basic focus. Another useful indicator of significant shifts in Reading Comprehension passages is the use of words or phrases such as "however," "nevertheless," "on the other hand," "by contrast," "and yet," and others. If you pay close attention to these sorts of signals, they will help orient you to what the significant parts of the passage are, and they will alert you to when a significant shift in focus or perspective is taking place. Incidentally, authors often provide helpful signals of continuity as well as shifts; continuity is frequently signaled by means of words or phrases like "for example," "by the same token," "furthermore," "in the same vein," "moreover," "similarly," and others.

One final caution about understanding the author's point of view: many times authors compare competing positions or theories and ultimately endorse one position or theory over its competitors. A common technique used by authors in this type of passage is to present the ideas they ultimately intend to reject in the best light possible, at least initially. One advantage of this approach is that criticisms are much more damaging if they work against an idea that has been presented in its strongest form; another advantage is that an author who takes pains to be as fair and evenhanded as possible to his or her opponents gains greatly in credibility. But what this means for you is that it can be quite difficult to follow such passages if you do not monitor the author's stance very carefully. When the author of a passage presents an opponent's point of view in the best light possible, it can appear to the unwary reader that the author endorses a position that he or she actually rejects. All of the techniques discussed above so far in this section can help you keep oriented to where the author actually stands in passages like these.

Should You Read the Questions First?

Some of you may be wondering at this point about a commonly heard piece of advice—that you should read the questions first, and only then turn to the passage. You should, of course, feel free to try this strategy in practicing and use it if you find it helpful. It is our opinion, however, that most people will find this strategy to be unhelpful. There are several reasons for this.

First, all of the questions associated with LSAT passages fit into standard question types—questions that ask for the main point or main purpose of the passage, questions that ask what the author would agree or disagree with, questions that ask what can be inferred from the information in the passage, and so on. We will say more about these and other question types in the sections that follow; what matters here is that many of these questions, though based on very different passages, look similar from one Reading Comprehension set to the next. Through study and practice, you can familiarize yourself with the types of questions that are typically written for an LSAT passage. You will then be able to anticipate what many of the questions will look like without having to spend your valuable time reading them before you read the passage.

Of course, some of the questions that follow a given passage might not look exactly like others of the same type; some even appear to be quite unique. But even in these cases, you will probably still gain very little from reading the questions first: it takes work to remember questions as you read the passage, and your mental energy is probably better spent on simply trying to comprehend the passage. As we have discussed already, LSAT reading passages can be quite difficult, involving sophisticated ideas and complex relationships. Answering the questions correctly requires you to get a firm grasp of the big picture in the passage. If you read everything in the passage with an eye to answering questions about particular details rather than with full attention to the thrust of the passage as a whole, you can easily miss the main point of the passage, and you run the risk of failing to grasp what the author agrees and disagrees with as well. So though you might do well on the questions that ask about those details, you might very well increase your chances of getting other questions in the set wrong.

Finally, it is important to remember that in the actual testing situation you have to read four passages and answer some 27 questions in 35 minutes. Time is of the essence. You can read the questions before you read the passages, but you still have to read the questions again when you are ready to answer them (you won't remember precisely what every question asks). Assume for the sake of argument that it takes roughly five seconds to read each question without reading the responses. That adds up to more than two minutes just to read the questions in a single Reading Comprehension section. If you read them twice, you double that to more than four minutes.

HOW TO APPROACH READING COMPREHENSION QUESTIONS

After reading through the passage once, you should turn to the questions. At this point you will probably have a fairly good sense of what the passage as a whole is trying to say, how the passage is organized, and roughly where in the passage specific points are made or particular facts are mentioned. But even if you do not feel all that confident of your understanding of the passage, you should proceed to the questions anyway rather than rereading the whole passage. In most cases, the first question in a set will ask you about the main point or the main purpose of a passage. If you don't think you have a handle on the passage, you might be able to recognize the main point or purpose of the passage when you see it, and answering this first question will in turn help orient you to the passage as a whole and to the questions that follow.

Either way, you should not feel that you need to remember the passage in great detail in order to begin working on the questions. For example, a passage might talk about two theoretical accounts of the rationale for incarceration, rehabilitative and punitive, and provide detail, even important detail, about both. In reading this passage, you should try to develop a clear sense of the difference between the two accounts and a general sense of where in the passage each is discussed. But there would be no point in trying to commit all of the detail in the passage to memory. First, not everything—not even every important thing—in the passage is going to be asked about. Second, if you have a general idea of the structure of the passage and of where its key elements are located, it is easy to check on the relevant details by rereading just portions of the passage. In fact, even if you are fairly confident that you remember everything you need to answer a particular question, it usually is a good idea to confirm your answer by checking the relevant portions of the passage anyway. Only if you have absolutely no doubt about the answer to a question is it advisable to respond without consulting the passage at least briefly.

When you read the questions, you should carefully attend to how each question is worded. Many questions contain detail that is intended to direct you to the relevant information in the passage. For example, one passage in the June 2000 LSAT discussed the conflict between philosophers who subscribe to a traditional, subjective approach to studying the mind and philosophers who support a new "objectivist" approach. According to the passage, the "subjectivists" believe that the mind should be explored by means of investigating individual subjective experiences such as consciousness, pain, emotions, and the like; "objectivists" find this approach outdated, however, and they believe the study of the mind should be limited to "hard" data such as the transmission of nerve impulses in the brain. One question in this set asks,

According to the passage, subjectivists advance which one of the following claims to support their claim that objectivism is faulty? [24]

The first thing this question tells you is that the correct response will be a claim attributed in the passage to the subjectivists. Other claims in the passage are attributed to the objectivists, and the author also makes a few claims of his or her own; obviously, none of these can be the correct answer. Moreover, the question tells you that the correct answer must be the claim made by the subjectivists as part of their argument that objectivism is faulty. At this point most test takers will recall that the views of subjectivists regarding the problems with objectivism are described in the first half of the passage, and more specifically, in the second paragraph. A quick glance at that portion of the passage will enable you to identify the correct response.

In this case, the views being asked about are not the author's view, but many questions do in fact focus on what the author says, believes, or might agree with. At the same time, as we noted above, authors of passages used in the LSAT often mention other people as making claims, presenting evidence, holding beliefs, or taking positions about whatever it is that the question is asking about. Again, it is important to pay very close attention to whether a question focuses on the views or claims of the author, or those of another person or group discussed by the author.

There is one additional piece of advice that applies to all Reading Comprehension questions: in general, even if you are fairly sure you have found the correct answer, you should probably take at least a quick look at any answer choices that you have not already eliminated. Incorrect answer choices are often partially correct, and as a result incorrect choices can sometimes appear to be correct when you first read them. Sometimes, a consideration of the full set of answer choices will lead you to reject a wrong answer that you initially thought to be correct.

---

[24] June 2000 LSAT, Section 4, Question 24.

QUESTIONS ABOUT THE PASSAGE AS A WHOLE (MAIN IDEA, PRIMARY PURPOSE, OVERALL ORGANIZATION)

As we said earlier, the first question in most Reading Comprehension sets will ask you to identify the statement that best expresses the central idea, main idea, or the main point that the passage as a whole is designed to convey. These question come in three main varieties. A few will take the following form: "Which one of the following most accurately summarizes the contents of the passage?" As the question implies, you should try to identify the response that **summarizes** the passage most accurately.

The thing to remember about questions like this is that the correct response will be the one that covers the important material in the passage most completely. That is not to say that the correct answer is necessarily the longest one, but it does mean that the correct answer will be most inclusive of the major steps in the discussion in the passage. The thing to keep in mind is that for questions that ask for the best summary of the passage, the correct answer will be the most comprehensive and inclusive of the steps taken in the passage. This variant of main idea questions is fairly rare, however. We use them infrequently, and you may not encounter any when you take the test.

The second, and by far most common, variant asks you to identify the **main point**, **main idea**, or **central idea** of the passage. Rather than asking you to identify the answer that summarizes the passage the best, these questions ask you to identify the idea or point that is at the heart of the passage. The important thing to know about these questions is that they have a much narrower focus than summary questions do. To answer them correctly, you have to be able to recognize what is the most important idea that the passage is trying to establish, the idea to which all other ideas in the passage are subordinated.

The third variant offers five potential titles for the passage and asks you to identify the answer that would be the **best title**. This variant is related to the main point/main idea question inasmuch as the best title will be the one that touches most directly on the central idea or point of the passage. These questions are also relatively rare. If you come across one, focus on finding the title that contains the content you would expect to see in a standard statement of the main idea of the passage.

One important thing to know about main idea or main point questions is that an answer choice may capture something that is true about the passage is still not be the correct answer. For one thing, that answer choice may also say something that is not true about the passage, in which case it cannot be, on the whole, taken

as correctly expressing the main idea of the passage. On the other hand, an answer choice may even be accurate in its entirety in stating something said in the passage, but be about something that is only a side issue in the passage rather than the main idea of the passage.

It is also worth noting that that there is more than one way of saying what the main idea of a passage is; as a result, you may not find an answer choice that expresses the main point the way you would have put it. But if you have a good grasp of the passage, the correct answer should come closer to the way you would put it than the other responses do. What this means, however, is that the advice we mentioned earlier—namely, that you should check all the answer choices before moving on to the next question—is especially important for main point questions. As you review all the answer choices, keep in mind that each of the incorrect answer choices will either say something about the passage that is simply false or will describe something that is in the passage and might even contribute to establishing the main point but is not itself that main point. And again, the correct answer will be the only answer choice that is both entirely accurate in its statement of what is in the passage **and** on target in terms of hitting on the most important idea in the passage.

In addition to questions about the main point, which deal with the content that the passage is intended to convey, there is another kind of question that deals with the function of the passage as a whole. This kind of question asks about the way the author proceeds in developing the main idea; that is, they are questions about how the passage is structured. Such questions ask how the passage proceeds, or how the passage is organized, or what the passage is primarily meant to convey, or what the primary purpose of the passage is. For example, a passage might present a puzzling phenomenon and offer an explanation for it. Or it might contrast two opposing views and develop a case for preferring one to the other. Or it might summarize the history of a scientific dispute. The answer choices for questions of this sort won't track every twist and turn of the author's development of the main point but will instead be very broad characterizations of the way the main point is developed. So don't be concerned if the correct answer seems to contain very little detail. The incorrect answer choices will be at a similar level of generality but will clearly fail to capture how the passage as a whole is organized. An incorrect answer choice might describe something that goes on in a portion of the passage or it might not fit anything about the passage at all. In any event, though, it will not get at the main structural blueprint of the passage as a whole.

Note that questions about the structure or organization of the author's text are not all concerned with the passage as a whole. Occasionally there are questions that ask you about the organization of a single paragraph. To answer these, it is a good idea to reread the specific paragraph that the question asks about.

QUESTIONS ABOUT WHAT THE PASSAGE SAYS OR IMPLIES

For each Reading Comprehension passage, you will be asked questions about the various ideas conveyed by the passage. These questions can range from very basic and straightforward questions (what does the passage say, literally?) to more sophisticated questions (what does the author imply without saying it explicitly?) to quite complex and advanced questions (what can be inferred from evidence presented in the passage, independently of whether or not the author intended the implication?). We will discuss all of these types of questions, starting with those at the basic end of the spectrum.

Perhaps the most basic component of Reading Comprehension is simply that of grasping what the text says on a literal level, and some Reading Comprehension questions are designed to make sure that you have processed the passage accurately at this fundamental level. Questions that assess this skill might ask, "Which one of the following is stated in the passage?", "The author says which one of the following about X?", "The passage asserts which one of the following regarding X?", "According to the passage, what is true about X?", or something similar. Even though these questions are fairly straightforward, the correct answer will not be an exact word-for-word repetition of something stated in the passage; it will, however, typically consist of a very close paraphrase of some part of the passage. The idea is that you should be able to identify not the exact wording of something said in the passage, but rather the gist of it.

For example, one of the questions following a passage about muralism, a Mexican artistic movement, reads

Which one of the following does the author explicitly identify as a characteristic of Mexican mural art?

(A) Its subject matter consisted primarily of current events.
(B) It could be viewed outdoors only.
(C) It used the same techniques as are used in easel painting.
(D) It exhibited remarkable stylistic uniformity.
(E) It was intended to be viewed from more than one angle.[25]

In the passage the author asserts that the muralists' works "were designed to be viewable from many different vantage points." The correct answer is therefore (E), "It was intended to be viewed from more than one angle." Notice that the correct answer is a fairly close paraphrase of what the author had stated in the passage.

A similar example occurs after a passage that says at one point, "the lower regions of the Earth's mantle have roughly the same composition as meteorites." The question reads,

According to the passage, the lower regions of the Earth's mantle are characterized by

(A) a composition similar to that of meteorites
(B) the absence of elements found in rocks on the Earth's crust
(C) a greater stability than that of the upper regions
(D) the presence of large amounts of carbon dioxide
(E) a uniformly lower density than that of the upper regions[26]

The correct answer is (A), "a composition similar to that of meteorites." Again, the phrase "similar to" is a straightforward equivalent of "roughly the same as." Recognition of what the author says is all that is required in this question; there is no need for any significant interpretation. Questions like this one might seem unexpectedly easy, especially to test takers for whom Reading Comprehension is a relative strength. Don't be put off by how easy such questions might seem, however, and in particular, don't assume that some sort of trick must be lurking in such easy-seeming questions. Just remember that some LSAT questions are designed to test fairly basic skills, and are therefore necessarily easy.

Of course, the process of reading also typically depends on skills that are considerably more advanced than this basic skill of comprehension of the literal content of a text, and other Reading Comprehension questions are designed to test these skills. Any complex piece of writing conveys much more to the attentive reader than what it explicitly states. Authors rely on this, and without having to think about it, readers typically process texts at the level of what they convey implicitly as well as at the level of what they say explicitly. In some cases, much of what a writer leaves out and relies on the reader to supply is subject matter knowledge that the writer assumes the reader to possess. This is especially true when the writer and the intended readers are all

---

[25] December 2002 LSAT, Section 3, Question 7.
[26] June 1995, Section 1, Question 2.

thoroughly familiar with the same specialized subject matter: articles in professional journals are good examples of texts that rely on this sort of shared knowledge. It is important to note, however, that **the LSAT does not presuppose any specialized subject matter knowledge**, so none of the questions in it test this kind of specialized reading.

There are, however, many other types of information that a writer leaves out and relies on the reader to supply: things whose inclusion in the reader's comprehension of a text is supported by what the text does explicitly state. Suppose, for example, that a writer states, "The closing of the factory caused additional damage to a regional economy already experiencing high unemployment." In saying this, the writer has not explicitly said that the closing of the factory occurred before the additional damage to the regional economy, but a reader who fails to understand that the closing preceded the damage has probably failed to understand the sentence as a whole. In fact, it is probably safe to say that a reader who lacks the ability to supply such inferences cannot be said to understand what he or she reads in general.

There are a variety of Reading Comprehension questions that assess this ability. For example, you might be asked what can be inferred from a passage or from some specific portion of the passage, what the passage suggests or indicates about some particular matter addressed explicitly in the passage, or what, according to the passage, is true of some particular matter.

Other questions might ask about what a passage conveys or implies about people's beliefs—for example, "It can most reasonably be inferred that the author would agree with which one of the following statements?" or "It can be inferred from the passage that the author most clearly holds which one of the following views?" or "It can be inferred from the passage that Ellison most clearly holds which one of the following views regarding an audience's relationship to works of art?" or "Given the information in the passage, the author is LEAST likely to believe which one of the following?" In approaching such questions, you need to pay close attention to specifically whose beliefs the question asks about. The incorrect answer choices will often be beliefs held by people other than those that the question is about.

What the correct answers to all such questions have in common—whether the questions ask about beliefs or about information—is that they are justified by something that is explicitly stated in the passage. Sometimes this

may be no more than a single sentence; on the other hand, sometimes you may have to pull together information from various parts of the passage to identify the correct answer. In some cases, locating the part of the passage that justifies an inference is straightforward. In other cases, the relevant justifying information might not be where one would most naturally expect to find it. In still other cases, there is no single part of the passage that contains all the relevant justifying information.

Questions also vary widely in how closely the correct answers match the part of the passage that justifies them. Sometimes, the correct answer does not go much beyond a slight rephrasing of the explicit content of the passage. For example, one passage discusses Richard A. Posner's critique of the law-and-literature movement, a movement that advocates the use of "techniques of literary analysis for the purpose of interpreting laws and in the reciprocal use of legal analysis for interpreting literary texts." One question for this passage asks:

The passage suggests that Posner regards legal practitioners as using an approach to interpreting law that

(A) *eschews discovery of multiple meanings*
(B) *employs techniques like deconstruction*
(C) *interprets laws in light of varying community standards*
(D) *is informed by the positions of literary critics*
(E) *de-emphasizes the social relevance of the legal tradition* [27]

The correct answer is (A), "eschews discovery of multiple meanings." What the passage explicitly says is that Posner asserts that "legal interpretation is aimed at discovering a single meaning." The reasoning involved in answering this question is quite straightforward: the passage does not come right out and say that Posner believes that legal practitioners eschew discovery of multiple meanings, but on the other hand it does not take much work to see that "eschew[ing] the discovery of multiple meanings" is the flip side of "to aim at discovering a single meaning." If you can remember the relevant part of the passage or find it quickly, you will find this question and others like it to be quite easy.

Other questions involve identifying the implicit ideas underlying a particular assertion made in a passage. In such cases, the connection between what the passage says and what the correct answer says is often less direct than in the last example, though the connection may still

---

[27] December 1992 LSAT, Section 3, Question 3.

be somewhat easy to see. For example, after a passage concerning harmful bacteria that attack crops, one question reads:

It can be inferred from the passage that crop rotation can increase yields in part because

(A) moving crop plants around makes them hardier and more resistant to disease
(B) the number of Pseudomonas fluorescens bacteria in the soil usually increases when crops are rotated
(C) the roots of many crop plants produce compounds that are antagonistic to phytopathogens harmful to other crop plants
(D) the presence of phytopathogenic bacteria is responsible for the majority of plant diseases
(E) phytopathogens typically attack some plant species but find other species to be unsuitable hosts [28]

The correct answer is (E), "phytopathogens typically attack some plant species but find other species to be unsuitable hosts." The support for this answer is found in the first paragraph, where the author states:

Cultivation of a single crop on a given tract of land leads eventually to decreased yields. One reason for this is that harmful bacterial phytopathogens, organisms parasitic on plant hosts, increase in the soil surrounding plant roots. The problem can be cured by crop rotation, denying the pathogens a suitable host for a period of time.

Note that the passage says that crop rotation denies pathogens a suitable host for a period of time, but it does not provide an explanation as to why that strategy would work. It is left to the reader to fill in the gap by inferring what the relevant explanation is—namely, because crop rotation involves planting different crops in succession, and because pathogens that attack particular plants typically find other plants to be unsuitable hosts. This idea is not actually stated in the passage; it is instead an implicit assumption. In other words, this is a case in which the reader has to supply missing information in order to fully understand what the author says.

Some of you may have found that you supplied the missing information so quickly and so automatically that it hardly seemed like you drew an inference at all; as a result, you might think it odd that the question asks what

can be inferred from the passage. But do not be thrown off if filling the relevant gap required little conscious effort for you. First, what was automatic and effortless for you may in fact require conscious effort on the part of other test takers. Second, questions like this one are designed to test your skill at high-level reading, and part of what defines that skill is the ability to supply relevant presuppositions when the author relies on you to do so. In short, even if, in your subjective experience of this question, the inference was so automatic that it seemed that little or no actual reasoning was required, logically speaking, you still had to draw an inference. This is a genuine skill that this type of Reading Comprehension question is designed to test.

Of course, there are questions in which the connection between the correct answer and the part of the passage that supports it is not so close. The following question involves a relatively large inference to get from the passage to the correct answer. A second question associated with the passage on Posner and the law-and-literature movement reads:

According to the passage, Posner argues that legal analysis is not generally useful in interpreting literature because

(A) use of the law in literature is generally of a quite different nature than use of the law in legal practice
(B) law is rarely used to convey important ideas in literature
(C) lawyers do not have enough literary training to analyze literature competently
(D) legal interpretations of literature tend to focus on legal issues to the exclusion of other important elements
(E) legal interpretations are only relevant to contemporary literature [29]

The correct answer is (A), "use of the law in literature is generally of a quite different nature than use of the law in legal practice."

Here is the part of the passage that supports this answer:

Critiquing the movement's assumption that lawyers can offer special insights into literature that deals with legal matters, Posner points out that writers of literature use the law loosely to convey a particular idea, or as a metaphor for the workings of the society

---

[28] February 1993 LSAT, Section 3, Question 18.
[29] December 1992 LSAT, Section 3, Question 6.

envisioned in their fiction. Legal questions per se, about which a lawyer might instruct readers, are seldom at issue in literature.

According to Posner, therefore, lawyers can be expected to be helpful about specific technical legal questions, but detailed analysis of technical legal questions is rarely at issue when the law is invoked, as it typically is in literature, to convey an idea or serve as a metaphor. So for Posner the law as it figures in legal practice is very different from the law as it figures in literature. The correct answer, then, is justified by the text of the passage but is by no means a simple restatement of anything that is actually said there. A certain amount of interpretation is required to arrive at this answer.

Similarly, the following is an example of the more typical case of questions that ask what can be inferred from, or what is suggested by, the passage. The question asks:

It can be inferred from the passage that the author's view of Watteau's works differs most significantly from that of most late-nineteenth-century Watteau admirers in which one of the following ways?

The correct answer is:

In contrast to most late-nineteenth-century Watteau admirers, the author finds it misleading to see Watteau's work as accurately reflecting social reality.[30]

There is no statement of precisely this point anywhere in the passage. There are two points in this answer, and they have to be established separately. The first of these points is that most late-nineteenth-century Watteau admirers saw Watteau's work as accurately reflecting social reality. The clearest statement of this position comes in the first paragraph, in which we are told that nineteenth-century writers accepted as genuine the image Watteau had presented of his age (the early eighteenth century). Underscoring this point, the first paragraph ends with the statement that by 1884, the bicentenary of Watteau's birth, it was standard practice for biographers to refer to him as "the personification of the witty and amiable eighteenth century."

The second point contained in the correct answer is that the author does not see Watteau's work as accurately reflecting social reality. Watteau's work is characterized as lyrical and charming, and the century

that it portrays as witty and amiable. But the author tells us in the second paragraph that the eighteenth century's first decades, the period of Watteau's artistic activity, were "fairly calamitous ones." The author goes on to say that the year of Watteau's first Paris successes was marked by military defeat and a disastrous famine. For this question, then, justifying the correct answer requires you to identify as relevant, and then put together, various pieces of information that in the passage are interspersed among other pieces of information that have no bearing on the specific question asked.

One final comment on the general category of question we have been discussing in this section. We have been making a distinction between recognizing a paraphrase of something said in the passage and answering questions that require some interpretation or inference. But it may have occurred to some of you that this line can get quite blurry, especially if the paraphrase looks quite different from the original, or the inference seems fairly obvious. For example, think back to the question about crop rotation we discussed earlier (pages 47–48). This question asks what can be inferred from the passage, and the correct answer is indeed an inference inasmuch as it is not stated explicitly, but is rather left implicit in the relevant part of the passage. But on the other hand, the implication is not really very far from the surface of the passage; as a result, identifying it may seem unexpectedly easy to some people.

As this example shows, it can be risky to judge answer choices by whether they are easier (or harder) than you expect the correct answer to be. The important thing to remember is that, whatever form the relationship between the passage and the correct answer takes, the correct answer is always the only answer choice that is truly supported by the passage. The incorrect answer choices might appear to be right at first glance, but they will always be found on closer inspection to have something about them that is wrong. Perhaps they are not really supported by the passage, or perhaps they even contradict the passage. As with all Reading Comprehension questions, you should judge the answer choices in questions about what the passage says or implies only by whether or not they are supported by the passage.

QUESTIONS THAT REQUIRE USING CONTEXT TO REFINE MEANING (MEANING IN CONTEXT)

Another skill a good reader brings to a text is the ability to interpret words and phrases not just as a dictionary would define them, but in a more specific sense

---

[30] December 1994 LSAT, Section 3, Question 18.

identifiable from the way in which the author is using them in the particular text. In a given text, words and phrases do not appear in isolation but are embedded in the context of a narrative, an argument, an explanation, and so on. What this wider context does, among other things, is clarify ambiguous expressions, narrow the meaning of vague expressions, or supply a definition for idiosyncratic uses of an expression.

Accordingly, the Reading Comprehension section typically contains questions that test the reading skill of ascertaining the contextually appropriate meanings of words and phrases. In some cases, this task is not very involved. For example, in a passage concerned with offshore oil production, the second paragraph ends by saying:

researchers have discovered that because the swirl of its impeller separates gas out from the oil that normally accompanies it, significant reductions in head can occur as it [a centrifugal pump] operates.

One of the questions following this passage reads:

Which one of the following phrases, if substituted for the word "head" in line 47, would LEAST change the meaning of the sentence?

(A) *the flow of the crude inside the pump*
(B) *the volume of oil inside the pump*
(C) *the volume of gas inside the pump*
(D) *the speed of the impeller moving the crude*
(E) *the pressure inside of the pump* [31]

The word "head" is used here in a specialized sense not accessible to the ordinary reader. But the attentive reader of the passage at issue would have noticed that the previous paragraph ended with this sentence:

This surge in gas content causes loss of "head," or pressure inside a pump, with the result that a pump can no longer impart enough energy to transport the crude mixture through the pipeline and to the shore.

In other words, the precise sense in which the word "head" is used in this passage in connection with the operation of pumps has been explicitly clarified. Accordingly, the answer to the question that deals with the meaning of the word "head" here is "the pressure inside of the pump," or (E).

There are cases where contextual clarification is not as clear cut. Take as an example the opening sentence of the passage about the French painter Watteau:

Late-nineteenth-century books about the French artist Watteau (1684–1721) betray a curious blind spot: more than any single artist before or since, Watteau provided his age with an influential image of itself, and nineteenth-century writers accepted this image as genuine.

One of the questions about this passage reads as follows:

The phrase "curious blind spot" (lines 2–3) can best be interpreted as referring to which one of the following?

(A) *some biographers' persistent inability to appreciate what the author considers a particularly admirable quality*
(B) *certain writers' surprising lack of awareness of what the author considers an obvious discrepancy*
(C) *some writers' willful refusal to evaluate properly what the author considers a valuable source of information about the past*
(D) *an inexplicable tendency on the part of some writers to undervalue an artist whom the author considers extremely influential*
(E) *a marked bias in favor of a certain painter and a concomitant prejudice against contemporaries the author considers equally talented* [32]

The correct answer turns out to be (B), "certain writers' surprising lack of awareness of what the author considers an obvious discrepancy." You can see that the sentence in which the phrase "curious blind spot" actually appears does not provide nearly enough information to establish the correctness of this answer. No obvious discrepancy is revealed in that sentence, and also no indication that anyone was unaware of this discrepancy. All that can be inferred from the opening sentence of the passage is that the blind spot has to do with nineteenth-century writers accepting as genuine the image Watteau had provided of his age. It is not until we find, at the end of the first paragraph, a nineteenth-century description of Watteau as "the personification of the witty and amiable eighteenth century" that we can tell that the image that Watteau has provided was overwhelmingly positive. In the second paragraph we are told that "The eighteenth century's first

---

[31] February 1994 LSAT, Section 3, Question 4.
[32] December 1994 LSAT, section 3, question 17.

decades, the period of [Watteau's] artistic creativity, were fairly calamitous ones." So here the "obvious discrepancy" is finally revealed. Given its obviousness, the fact that late-nineteenth-century writers were evidently not aware of it can reasonably be seen as surprising, or "curious." Notice, however, that a phrase that is introduced in the first sentence of the passage cannot be given the fully specific sense intended for it by the author until the end of the second paragraph has been reached.

QUESTIONS ABOUT HOW THINGS THE AUTHOR SAYS FUNCTION IN CONTEXT

A skilled reader has to be able to cope with the fact that writers, even good writers, do not make explicit why they say certain things in certain places. The reader has to be able to extract the function that certain expressions, phrases, sentences, or even paragraphs have in the context of a larger piece of writing. Sometimes the writer does use conventional cues to guide the reader in how to take what is being said. Such cues, though conventional, can be quite subtle. A good reader picks up on those cues and uses them in interpreting the piece of text to which they are relevant.

An example of a textual connection not made explicit at all occurs in the following lengthy excerpt from a passage about women medical practitioners in the Middle Ages. First, a little background to place the excerpt in context: it begins with the phrase, "This common practice," which refers back to a practice discussed earlier in the same paragraph. According to the author, the typical practice among historians studying the Middle Ages is to take the term "woman medical practitioner," whenever it appears in medieval records, to mean "midwife." The relevant excerpt, then, reads:

This common practice obscures the fact that, although women were not represented on all levels of medicine equally, they were represented in a variety of specialties throughout the broad medical community. A reliable study by Wickersheimer and Jacquart documents that, of 7,647 medical practitioners in France during the twelfth through fifteenth centuries, 121 were women; of these, only 44 were identified as midwives, while the rest practiced as physicians, surgeons, apothecaries, barbers, and other healers.

There is no explicit statement in this passage of why the author chooses to cite the study by Wickersheimer and Jacquart. The sentence about that study simply

follows the one preceding it. The reader is not specifically told how to connect the information in that sentence with information presented either earlier or later. For a skilled reader, though, the connection is obvious: the study presents scholarly, documented support for a claim that is made in the preceding sentence, namely that women were represented in a variety of specialties throughout the broad medical community.

So for a question that asks:

The author refers to the study by Wickersheimer and Jacquart in order to

 (A) *demonstrate that numerous medical specialties were recognized in Western Europe during the Middle Ages*
 (B) *demonstrate that women are often underrepresented in studies of medieval medical practitioners*
 (C) *prove that midwives were officially recognized as members of the medical community during the Middle Ages*
 (D) *prove that midwives were only a part of a larger community of women medical practitioners during the Middle Ages*
 (E) *prove that the existence of the midwives can be documented in Western Europe as early as the twelfth century* [33]

the correct answer is (D),

prove that midwives were only a part of a larger community of women medical practitioners during the Middle Ages

This is so even though the author has not said anything like "As proof of this, the study by Wickersheimer and Jacquart may be cited." It is probably safe to say that a reader who does not make this connection on his or her own did not comprehend this part of the passage. For such a reader, the author's reference to the study by Wickersheimer and Jacquart will probably appear to come of out nowhere.

Now consider an example of a question that requires you to understand the way an author uses subtle cues to indicate the function of a piece of text. The passage on which the question is based reads, in part:

---

[33] June 1994 LSAT, Section 3, Question 26.

Critics have long been puzzled by the inner contradictions of major characters in John Webster's tragedies . . . The ancient Greek philosopher Aristotle implied that such contradictions are virtually essential to the tragic personality, and yet critics keep coming back to this element of inconsistency as though it were an eccentric feature of Webster's own tragic vision.

This question asks:

The author's allusion to Aristotle's view of tragedy in lines 11–13 serves which one of the following functions in the passage?

(A) *It introduces a commonly held view of Webster's tragedies that the author plans to defend.*

(B) *It supports the author's suggestion that Webster's conception of tragedy is not idiosyncratic.*

(C) *It provides an example of an approach to Webster's tragedies that the author criticizes.*

(D) *It establishes the similarity between classical and modern approaches to tragedy.*

(E) *It supports the author's assertion that Elizabethan tragedy cannot be fully understood without the help of recent scholarship.*[34]

The correct answer is (B), "It supports the author's suggestion that Webster's conception of tragedy is not idiosyncratic." The author's allusion to Aristotle's view of tragedy introduces the idea that a vision of tragedy similar to Webster's can be traced back to the ancient Greeks. So Webster's view cannot be regarded as idiosyncratic unless the critics are essentially prepared to dismiss Aristotle's view as unimportant. But what the author does is let Aristotle's view stand as authoritative by using it to portray the critics as wrongheaded. What the author says is that the critics view the element of inconsistency in Webster's characters "as though it were" eccentric. By using the phrase "as though it were" the author suggests that the critics are wrong. The author further says that the critics "keep coming back" to this element, thereby signaling a certain impatience with the stubbornness with which the critics hold on to their mistaken view. And the author says "and yet," thereby signaling that the critics hold on to their mistaken view in the face of clear evidence to the contrary, provided by Aristotle.

To understand how this type of question works, note that the author provides a variety of cues to indicate to the reader that the allusion to Aristotle is introduced to support the position, endorsed by the author, that Webster's conception of tragedy is not idiosyncratic. The cues are recognizable, but they are relatively subtle. There is no explicit statement of the author's position or of how the allusion to Aristotle bears on it.

In approaching questions about what the author's purpose is in using a certain word, phrase, or sentence, remember that, unless that word, phrase, or sentence left you puzzled, you probably already understood the author's purpose as you made your way through the passage. The process involved here is essential and often subtle, but good readers typically exercise this skill automatically and unconsciously. One conclusion to be drawn from this fact is that you should not look for far-fetched interpretations of what the author's purpose was. Most probably the purpose that you automatically supplied in the process of reading is the correct one. If you were not able to appreciate immediately what the purpose of using a particular word, phrase, or sentence was, reread the immediate context. In a well-written text, the author generally supplies all the cues you need to understand the purpose of any part of the text right around that text. An author is not likely to hide hints as to the purpose of a particular choice of word two or three paragraphs away. A close reading of the immediate context will usually reveal what the author's purpose was.

QUESTIONS THAT REQUIRE THE RECOGNITION OF ANALOGOUS PATTERNS OR FEATURES IN DIFFERENT FACTUAL SETTINGS

One way for a reader to demonstrate an understanding of a fact pattern that is presented in a text (or of the way someone has made a case for a position) is by recognizing another fact pattern (or argument) as structurally similar. Questions that test this ability are typically included in the Reading Comprehension section.

Questions of this kind will direct you to something specific in the text and ask you to find something similar to it among the answer choices. The relevant part of the passage can be characterized insightfully in general terms, and this characterization has to fit the correct answer as well. What sorts of general terms? Typically, the characterizations are of the following sorts:

- One thing is a cause of another.

- One thing is a subset of another.

- One thing is mistaken for another.

- Some type of behavior is irresponsible.

---

[34] February 1993 LSAT, Section 3, Question 10.

- Something falls short of a particular standard.

- An action has consequences that are the opposite of those intended.

These examples are given only to illustrate roughly the kind of similarity that you will typically be looking for. They are not meant to suggest that you should first try to restate what is going on in the passage in such terms. What is crucial is a clear understanding of the relevant part of the passage. You don't need an explicit formulation; in fact, attempting to come up with such an explicit formulation may be a waste of your time.

To see what is involved here, let us consider a very simple case first. The question asks,

Which one of the following is most closely analogous to the error the author believes historians make when they equate the term "woman medical practitioner" with "midwife"?

(A) *equating pear with apple*
(B) *equating science with biology*
(C) *equating supervisor with subordinate*
(D) *equating member with nonmember*
(E) *equating instructor with trainee* [35]

As we saw earlier when we considered another question from this set (pages 50–51), the author asserts that historians do in fact equate the term "woman medical practitioner," whenever they encounter it in medieval records, with "midwife." But the wording of the question further alerts us to the fact that historians who equate the two terms are committing a particular kind of error. The author's account of this error is presented in the following words: "This common practice obscures the fact that, although women were not represented on all levels of medicine equally, they were represented in a variety of specialties throughout the broad medical community." The author elaborates on this by saying that in a study of medical practitioners that included 121 women, only 44 of those women were midwives, whereas the rest practiced as physicians, surgeons, apothecaries, barbers, and other healers. So the error, stated in general terms, lies in equating a category with one of its subcategories. What you are asked to do is select the answer choice that presents the same error.

The correct answer is (B), "equating science with biology." Someone who equates science with biology

would be ignoring the fact that the category of science includes many subcategories in addition to biology. Such a person would commit an error analogous to the one that the author believes historians make.

Notice that not everything about (B) is closely analogous to the historians' equating of woman medical practitioners with midwives. For example, the terms equated in (B) refer to academic subjects and not to people. On the other hand, the terms equated in (C) and (E) do refer to people, just as do those equated by the historians. So why does the similarity in terms of people being referred to not matter? Because it is not part of what makes the historians' practice an error that they happen to be talking about people.

When you focus on finding errors analogous to the historians' error, you find that none of answer choices (A), (C), (D), and (E) make such an error. They all do make an error, and it happens to be the same kind of error in each case. They all equate two categories, neither of which includes the other, whereas the historians equate two categories, one of which—but only one of which—includes the other. What the historians get wrong is that they fail to see that not all woman medical practitioners were midwives, even though all midwives were medical practitioners. By contrast, what (A), for example, gets wrong in equating pears with apples is that it lumps together two categories, neither of which includes the other even partially.

Now let's look at a more complex example. In a passage concerned with certain interactions between the United States Bureau of Indian Affairs and the Oneida tribe of Wisconsin, we are told that the Oneida were offered a one-time lump-sum payment of $60,000 in lieu of the $0.52 annuity guaranteed in perpetuity to each member of the tribe under the Canandaigua Treaty. We are then further informed that

The offer of a lump-sum payment was unanimously opposed by the Oneida delegates, who saw that changing the terms of a treaty might jeopardize the many pending land claims based upon the treaty.

There is a question that is based on this rejection of the lump-sum offer and which reads as follows:

Which one of the following situations most closely parallels that of the Oneida delegates in refusing to accept a lump-sum payment of $60,000?

[35] June 1994 LSAT, Section 3, Question 23.

(A) A university offers a student a four-year scholarship with the stipulation that the student not accept any outside employment; the student refuses the offer and attends a different school because the amount of the scholarship would not have covered living expenses.

(B) A company seeking to reduce its payroll obligations offers an employee a large bonus if he will accept early retirement; the employee refuses because he does not want to compromise an outstanding worker's compensation suit.

(C) Parents of a teenager offer to pay her at the end of the month for performing weekly chores rather than paying her on a weekly basis; the teenager refuses because she has a number of financial obligations that she must meet early in the month.

(D) A car dealer offers a customer a $500 cash payment for buying a new car: the customer refuses because she does not want to pay taxes on the amount, and requests instead that her monthly payments be reduced by a proportionate amount.

(E) A landlord offers a tenant several months rent-free in exchange for the tenant's agreeing not to demand that her apartment be painted every two years, as is required by the lease; the tenant refuses because she would have spend her own time painting the apartment.[36]

What precisely is the situation of the Oneida delegates in refusing the lump-sum payment? It is an action (refusing the offer) that is motivated by a specific reason, namely concern that not taking that action might have undesirable legal ramifications. This is a rather broad characterization of the situation in which the Oneida delegates find themselves, but it turns out to be a description that applies equally well to the correct answer, and only to the correct answer. The correct answer is (B), "A company seeking to reduce its payroll obligations offers an employee a large bonus if he will accept early retirement; the employee refuses because he does not want to compromise an outstanding worker's compensation suit." What is parallel is the reason why an otherwise generous-seeming offer is refused.

Notice that there are some clear differences between the situation of the Oneida delegates and that of the employee. For example, in one case it is delegates refusing on behalf of a large group that would be affected by that decision, and in the other case a single individual refuses on his own behalf alone. But this difference plays no role in selecting the correct answer, even though it might be seen as a significant difference between the two situations. First, the fact that this important decision affecting the Oneida people as a whole was made by Oneida delegates, although mentioned in the passage, is not given any prominence anywhere in the passage. What the passage does focus on, in discussing the refusal of the lump-sum offer, is the reasons the delegates had for their refusal. So as the passage presents the situation, the reasons for the refusal are the central feature of the situation, and for another situation to be parallel, it would have to be parallel in this respect. Only the correct answer meets this requirement. Moreover, notice that all of the answer choices are like the correct answer in focusing on an individual, which means that it is not the case that any of the incorrect answers are more parallel to the passage even in this regard.

In fact, any scenario that is analogous or parallel to another one **has to be different** in some ways. Otherwise it would be identical to the first scenario, and not just analogous to it. So it is important to keep in mind that the correct answer to this type of question will be the one that is **most closely parallel** or **most analogous** or **most similar** to something discussed in the passage, even though it will necessarily be dissimilar in many respects.

QUESTIONS ABOUT THE AUTHOR'S ATTITUDE

Authors write things for a variety of reasons. They may just write to report, simply putting down what they take to be the facts, giving no indication of their own feelings, either positive or negative, about those facts. Or they may set down what someone else has reported as fact, without giving any indication of how that person feels about them or how they themselves feel about them. But often authors write with other purposes in mind. For example, they may write to persuade the reader of the merits of some position, in which case they typically write in such a way that the reader can tell that they have positive feelings with respect to that position. By contrast, they may write to warn the reader that a view has no merit, in which case they often make evaluative comments that allow the reader to infer what their attitude toward the matter is. Thus, one feature of a text that careful readers pay attention to is whether the author, by taking a certain tone, or by certain word choices, betrays any attitude other than bland neutrality

[36] October 1993 LSAT, Section 1, Question 13.

toward the material he or she is presenting. Also of interest is whether any of the people mentioned by the author in the passage are presented as having any particular attitude toward anything that figures in the passage. These things are potentially important in evaluating what has been read. For example, if an author's attitude is one of boundless enthusiasm, a careful reader might take what that author says with a grain of salt.

In the Reading Comprehension section, you will encounter questions that ask directly about what the author's attitude is, or the attitude of people that the author discusses. Another kind of question may ask you to consider words or phrases that appear in the passage and to identify those that indicate the attitude of the author, or of people mentioned in the passage, toward some specific thing that is discussed in the passage.

When you are dealing with a question that asks directly about attitude, you should assess the passage with an eye to whether it contains indicators of tone or evaluative terms. For example, sometimes an initially positive tone is tempered later by an expression of reservations; or an initially rather dismissive tone might be moderated later by a grudging admission of something worthwhile. The description of the author's attitude overall will reflect this and you should choose among the answer choices accordingly. An example will illustrate this point. The question reads:

The attitude of the author of the passage toward Breen and Innes's study can best be described as one of

(A) *condescending dismissal*
(B) *wholehearted acceptance*
(C) *contentious challenge*
(D) *qualified approval*
(E) *sincere puzzlement* [37]

The correct answer is (D), "qualified approval." The first reference to Breen and Innes occurs early in the passage, in the sentence

In Myne Owne Ground, T. H. Breen and Stephen Innes contribute significantly to a recent, welcome shift from a white-centered to a black-centered inquiry into the role of African Americans in the American colonial period.

The word "welcome" indicates approval, and since Breen and Innes are said to have significantly contributed to something that is welcome, the approval extends to them and their study. But this is not the only sign of the author's attitude. Much later in the passage, the author says that Breen and Innes "underemphasize much evidence that customary law, only gradually embodied in statutory law, was closing in on free African Americans well before the 1670's . . ." The verb "underemphasize" expresses a criticism of Breen and Innes' work, and so the approval indicated by "welcome" can no longer be regarded as unqualified. The correct answer, "qualified approval," does justice to both expressions of the author's attitude.

Sometimes you may be asked to identify the words or phrases in a passage that are indicative of the author's attitude toward something. A question of this sort might ask,

The author's attitude toward the "thesis" mentioned in line 56 is revealed in which one of the following pairs of words?

(A) *"biases" (line 5) and "rhetorical" (line 6)*
(B) *"wield" (line 7) and "falsification" (line 17)*
(C) *"conjectures" (line 16) and "truck with" (line 19)*
(D) *"extremism" (line 20) and "implausible" (line 24)*
(E) *"naïve" (line 35) and "errors" (line 42)* [38]

The correct answer is (D), "extremism" (line 20) and "implausible" (line 24). As the term "extremism" is used in line 20, it applies to the authors of the thesis mentioned in line 56, and thus indirectly to the thesis itself. In line 24 the author uses the term "implausible" to characterize one aspect of the thesis, its rejection of a traditional belief. Taken together, these two words reveal a strongly negative attitude on the part of the author toward the thesis at issue. By contrast, in the incorrect answer choices, at least one of the terms presented, though it may reveal an attitude of the author's, does not apply to the thesis in line 56. For example, one of the incorrect answer choices is "naïve" (line 35) and "errors" (line 42).

Both words are good candidates for indicating attitude, and both are used by the author to express an attitude. However, when you look at line 35, you discover that the author uses "naïve" to characterize a view that is an extreme opposite of the thesis at issue, and so does not express the author's attitude toward the thesis itself. Having discovered this much, you know that you can rule

---

[37] December 1994 LSAT, Section 3, Question 12.
[38] December 1992 LSAT, Section 3, Question 15.

out this answer choice, whatever it is that "errors" applies to.

QUESTIONS ABOUT THE SIGNIFICANCE OF ADDITIONAL INFORMATION

Good readers read critically. That is to say, as they read the particular case an author makes for taking a certain position, they do not just passively take in what is on the page. Rather, they evaluate the plausibility, coherence, and strength of the claims and arguments advanced by the author. As they go along, they evaluate the strength of the author's case. They may think of objections to the way an author supports a position. Alternatively, they may think of things that the author hasn't mentioned that would have strengthened the author's case. Or they may think of questions to which they don't know the answer but that would be relevant questions to raise.

The test does not require you to think up considerations that would either strengthen or undercut the case an author has made for a position, but it includes questions that require you to recognize such considerations. You will be asked to determine whether new information strengthens or weakens a particular argument made in the passage. Often, the question will use the words **strengthen** or **weaken** themselves. But questions might also use analogous expressions such as to **support**, **bolster**, or **reinforce** a given claim or position; or to **undermine**, **challenge**, or **call into question** a given claim or position.

The following is an example of how a question might be phrased that requires you to recognize a difficulty with an explanation that has been proposed:

Which one of the following, if true, would most seriously undermine the explanation proposed by the author in the third paragraph?

(A) *A number of songbird species related to the canary have a shorter life span than the canary and do not experience neurogenesis.*

(B) *The brain size of several types of airborne birds with life spans similar to those of canaries has been shown to vary according to a two-year cycle of neurogenesis.*

(C) *Several species of airborne birds similar to canaries in size are known to have brains that are substantially heavier than the canary's brain.*

(D) *Individual canaries that have larger-than-average repertoires of songs tend to have better developed muscles for flying.*

(E) *Individual canaries with smaller and lighter brains than the average tend to retain a smaller-than-average repertoire of songs.*[39]

Notice that the proviso "if true" means that you are told to treat each answer choice as if it is true, at least for the purposes of this question. You do not have to concern yourself with whether it is actually true. The explanation in the third paragraph to which the question refers is an explanation of a phenomenon called neurogenesis (the growth of new neurons) that has been observed in canaries:

A possible explanation for this continual replacement of nerve cells may have to do with the canary's relatively long life span and the requirements of flight. Its brain would have to be substantially larger and heavier than might be feasible for flying if it had to carry all the brain cells needed to process and retain all the information gathered over a lifetime.

In other words, neurogenesis is held to be explained by the hypothesized need to keep the canaries' brains small and light so that the birds can fly. This explanation would have to be abandoned, or at least greatly modified, if the correct answer, (C), were true: "Several species of airborne birds similar to canaries in size are known to have brains that are substantially heavier than the canary's brain." In other words, assuming that this answer choice is true, it seems unlikely that canaries would have any difficulty flying even if their brains were a good bit heavier than they are. In that case, the requirements of flight would not appear to be what dictates the small brain size in canaries and thus could not be invoked to explain neurogenesis, the mechanism by which canary brains are kept small.

In this example, the explanation depended on a certain supposition's being true. The additional information suggests that this supposition might well not be true. In other questions that ask about what would weaken or strengthen something in the passage, the additional information given in the correct answer might be related to the passage in other ways. For example, the additional information might suggest that something is true that would have been predicted given what the passage says, thereby strengthening the case made in the passage. Or it might tell you that something that would have been predicted given what the passage says doesn't, or isn't likely to, happen, in which case the argument advanced in the passage would be weakened. Or it might suggest that a generalization that the

---

[39] December 1994 LSAT, Section 3, Question 4.

passage relied on does not hold up in the particular case under consideration. Or it might suggest that a claim made in the passage is unlikely to be true.

What you have to keep in mind is that what you're looking for is information that has an impact on the plausibility of the position, explanation, claim, evidence, and so on that the question specifically asks you about. It is not enough that a piece of information is about something that the passage is concerned with or even about the particular thing that the question is about. The correct answer has to have a real effect on the strength of the position being asked about.

On the other hand, the correct answer does not have to conclusively establish or definitively refute the position being asked about. Given that these questions ask about what would **strengthen** or **weaken** something said in the passage, it is enough for the correct answer to increase (for **strengthen** questions) or decrease (for **weaken** questions) the likelihood that the argument or position in question is right.

Comparative Reading

Starting with the June 2007 administration, LSAC introduced a new variant of reading comprehension, called comparative reading, as one of the four sets in the LSAT reading comprehension section.

In general, comparative reading questions are similar to traditional reading comprehension questions, except that comparative reading questions are based on two shorter passages instead of one longer passage. The two passages together are of roughly the same length as one reading comprehension passage, so the total amount of reading in the reading comprehension section will remain essentially the same. A few of the questions that follow a comparative reading passage pair might concern only one of the two passages, but most will be about both passages and how they relate to each other.

Comparative reading questions reflect the nature of some important tasks in law school work, such as understanding arguments from multiple texts by applying skills of comparison, contrast, generalization, and synthesis to the texts. The purpose of comparative reading is to assess this important set of skills directly.

What Comparative Reading Looks Like

The two passages in a comparative reading set—labeled **"Passage A"** and **"Passage B"**—discuss the same topic or related topics. The topics fall into the same academic categories traditionally used in reading comprehension: humanities, natural sciences, social sciences, and issues related to the law. Like traditional reading comprehension passages, comparative reading passages are complex and generally involve argument. The two passages in a comparative reading pair are typically adapted from two different published sources written by two different authors. They are usually independent of each other, with neither author responding directly to the other.

As you read the pair of passages, it is helpful to try to determine what the central idea or main point of each passage is, and to determine how the passages relate to each other. The passages will relate to each other in various ways. In some cases, the authors of the passages will be in general agreement with each other, while in others their views will be directly opposed. Passage pairs may also exhibit more complex types of relationships: for example, one passage might articulate a set of principles, while the other passage applies those or similar principles to a particular situation.

Questions that are concerned with only one of the passages are essentially identical to traditional reading comprehension questions. Questions that address both passages test the same fundamental reading skills as traditional reading comprehension questions, but the skills are applied to two texts instead of one. You may be asked to identify a main purpose shared by both passages, a statement with which both authors would agree, or a similarity or dissimilarity in the structure of the arguments in the two passages. The following are additional examples of comparative reading questions:

- Which one of the following is the central topic of each passage?

- Both passages explicitly mention which one of the following?

- Which one of the following statements is most strongly supported by both passages?

- Which one of the following most accurately describes the attitude expressed by the author of passage B toward the overall argument in passage A?

- The relationship between passage A and passage B is most analogous to the relationship in which one of the following?

This is not a complete list of the sorts of questions you may be asked in a comparative reading set, but it illustrates the range of questions you may be asked.

INTRODUCTION TO THE EXPLANATIONS

On the following pages, you will find answers and explanations for all the questions that appear in the PrepTests A, B, and C in this book. Each question has been assigned a level of difficulty. We recommend that you read the guides on pages 4–57 before reading the explanations since some of the explanations presuppose that you have read the guides.

Level of Difficulty

The difficulty categories are based on the proportion of test takers who selected the correct answer. For each question type (Analytical Reasoning, Logical Reasoning, and Reading Comprehension), the questions for the three tests in this book are divided into five groups according to their difficulty, from 1 (easiest) to 5 (hardest). So, for example, an Analytical Reasoning question with a difficulty level of 1 is among the easiest fifth of the Analytical Reasoning questions, a Logical Reasoning question with a difficulty level of 1 is among the easiest fifth of the Logical Reasoning questions, and so on.

Organization

The explanations are divided into sets of questions corresponding to the sections of each test—first PrepTest A (December 2010 LSAT), then PrepTest B (June 2011 LSAT), and finally PrepTest C (a previously undisclosed LSAT). The explanations appear here in the same order as they appear on the test. Page numbers corresponding to the passage or question under discussion appear in italics.

General Directions for the LSAT Answer Sheet

The actual testing time for this portion of the test will be 2 hours 55 minutes. There are five sections, each with a time limit of 35 minutes. The supervisor will tell you when to begin and end each section. If you finish a section before time is called, you may check your work on that section **only;** do not turn to any other section of the test book and do not work on any other section either in the test book or on the answer sheet.

There are several different types of questions on the test, and each question type has its own directions. **Be sure you understand the directions for each question type before attempting to answer any questions in that section.**

Not everyone will finish all the questions in the time allowed. Do not hurry, but work steadily and as quickly as you can without sacrificing accuracy. You are advised to use your time effectively. If a question seems too difficult, go on to the next one and return to the difficult question after completing the section. **MARK THE BEST ANSWER YOU CAN FOR EVERY QUESTION. NO DEDUCTIONS WILL BE MADE FOR WRONG ANSWERS. YOUR SCORE WILL BE BASED ONLY ON THE NUMBER OF QUESTIONS YOU ANSWER CORRECTLY.**

ALL YOUR ANSWERS MUST BE MARKED ON THE ANSWER SHEET. Answer spaces for each question are lettered to correspond with the letters of the potential answers to each question in the test book. After you have decided which of the answers is correct, blacken the corresponding space on the answer sheet. **BE SURE THAT EACH MARK IS BLACK AND COMPLETELY FILLS THE ANSWER SPACE.** Give only one answer to each question. If you change an answer, be sure that all previous marks are **erased completely.** Since the answer sheet is machine scored, incomplete erasures may be interpreted as intended answers. **ANSWERS RECORDED IN THE TEST BOOK WILL NOT BE SCORED.**

There may be more question numbers on this answer sheet than there are questions in a section. Do not be concerned, but be certain that the section and number of the question you are answering matches the answer sheet section and question number. Additional answer spaces in any answer sheet section should be left blank. Begin your next section in the number one answer space for that section.

LSAC takes various steps to ensure that answer sheets are returned from test centers in a timely manner for processing. In the unlikely event that an answer sheet is not received, LSAC will permit the examinee either to retest at no additional fee or to receive a refund of his or her LSAT fee. **THESE REMEDIES ARE THE ONLY REMEDIES AVAILABLE IN THE UNLIKELY EVENT THAT AN ANSWER SHEET IS NOT RECEIVED BY LSAC.**

Score Cancellation

Complete this section only if you are absolutely certain you want to cancel your score. **A CANCELLATION REQUEST CANNOT BE RESCINDED. IF YOU ARE AT ALL UNCERTAIN, YOU SHOULD NOT COMPLETE THIS SECTION.**

To cancel your score from this administration, you **must:**

A. fill in both ovals here ...... ○○
AND
B. read the following statement. Then sign your name and enter the date. **YOUR SIGNATURE ALONE IS NOT SUFFICIENT FOR SCORE CANCELLATION. BOTH OVALS ABOVE MUST BE FILLED IN FOR SCANNING EQUIPMENT TO RECOGNIZE YOUR REQUEST FOR SCORE CANCELLATION.**

I certify that I wish to cancel my test score from this administration. I understand that my request is irreversible and that my score will not be sent to me or to the law schools to which I apply.

_____
Sign your name in full

_____
Date

FOR LSAC USE ONLY   ●

HOW DID YOU PREPARE FOR THE LSAT?
(Select all that apply.)

Responses to this item are voluntary and will be used for statistical research purposes only.

○ By studying the free sample questions available on LSAC's website.
○ By taking the free sample LSAT available on LSAC's website.
○ By working through official LSAT *PrepTests, ItemWise,* and/or other LSAC test prep products.
○ By using LSAT prep books or software **not** published by LSAC.
○ By attending a commercial test preparation or coaching course.
○ By attending a test preparation or coaching course offered through an undergraduate institution.
○ Self study.
○ Other preparation.
○ No preparation.

CERTIFYING STATEMENT

Please write the following statement. Sign and date.

I certify that I am the examinee whose name appears on this answer sheet and that I am here to take the LSAT for the sole purpose of being considered for admission to law school. I further certify that I will neither assist nor receive assistance from any other candidate, and I agree not to copy, retain, or transmit examination questions in any form or discuss them with any other person.

_____
_____
_____
_____
_____
_____
_____
_____
_____
_____

SIGNATURE: _____   TODAY'S DATE: ___/___/___
                                                              MONTH DAY YEAR

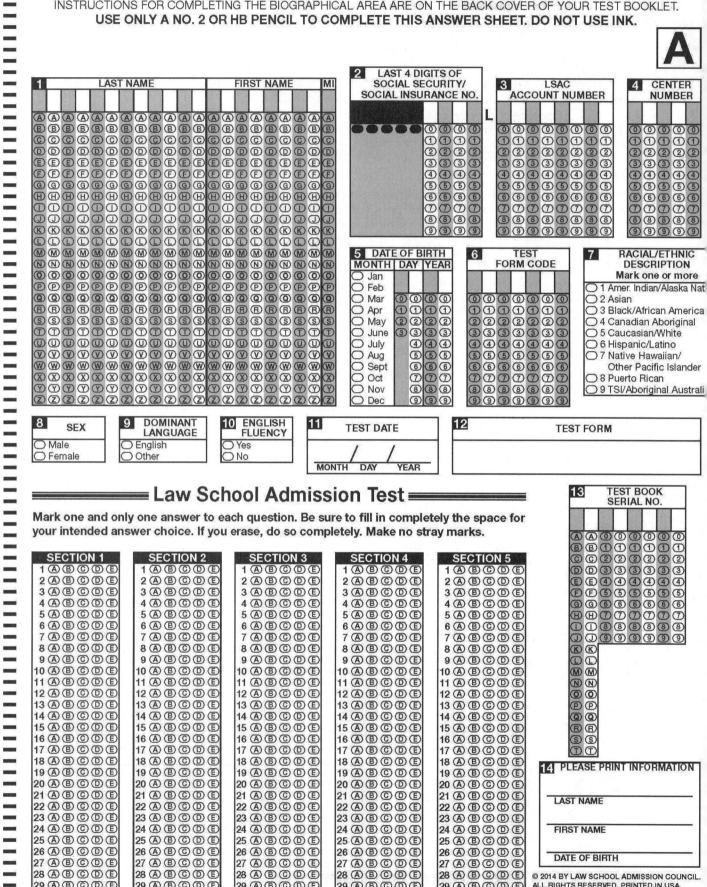

PREPTEST A, TABLE OF CONTENTS

SECTION I

Time—35 minutes

27 Questions

Directions: Each set of questions in this section is based on a single passage or a pair of passages. The questions are to be answered on the basis of what is stated or implied in the passage or pair of passages. For some of the questions, more than one of the choices could conceivably answer the question. However, you are to choose the best answer; that is, the response that most accurately and completely answers the question, and blacken the corresponding space on your answer sheet.

To study centuries-old earthquakes and the geologic faults that caused them, seismologists usually dig trenches along visible fault lines, looking for sediments that show evidence of having shifted. Using radiocarbon
(5)   dating, they measure the quantity of the radioactive isotope carbon 14 present in wood or other organic material trapped in the sediments when they shifted. Since carbon 14 occurs naturally in organic materials and decays at a constant rate, the age of organic
(10) materials can be reconstructed from the amount of the isotope remaining in them. These data can show the location and frequency of past earthquakes and provide hints about the likelihood and location of future earthquakes.
(15)   Geologists William Bull and Mark Brandon have recently developed a new method, called lichenometry, for detecting and dating past earthquakes. Bull and Brandon developed the method based on the fact that large earthquakes generate numerous simultaneous
(20) rockfalls in mountain ranges that are sensitive to seismic shaking. Instead of dating fault-line sediments, lichenometry involves measuring the size of lichens growing on the rocks exposed by these rockfalls. Lichens—symbiotic organisms consisting of a fungus
(25) and an alga—quickly colonize newly exposed rock surfaces in the wake of rockfalls, and once established they grow radially, flat against the rocks, at a slow but constant rate for as long as 1,000 years if left undisturbed. One species of North American lichen, for example,
(30) spreads outward by about 9.5 millimeters each century. Hence, the diameter of the largest lichen on a boulder provides direct evidence of when the boulder was dislodged and repositioned. If many rockfalls over a large geographic area occurred simultaneously, that
(35) pattern would imply that there had been a strong earthquake. The location of the earthquake's epicenter can then be determined by mapping these rockfalls, since they decrease in abundance as the distance from the epicenter increases.
(40)   Lichenometry has distinct advantages over radiocarbon dating. Radiocarbon dating is accurate only to within plus or minus 40 years, because the amount of the carbon 14 isotope varies naturally in the environment depending on the intensity of the radiation
(45) striking Earth's upper atmosphere. Additionally, this intensity has fluctuated greatly during the past 300 years, causing many radiocarbon datings of events during this period to be of little value. Lichenometry, Bull and Brandon claim, can accurately date an
(50) earthquake to within ten years. They note, however, that using lichenometry requires careful site selection

and accurate calibration of lichen growth rates, adding that the method is best used for earthquakes that occurred within the last 500 years. Sites must be
(55) selected to minimize the influence of snow avalanches and other disturbances that would affect normal lichen growth, and conditions like shade and wind that promote faster lichen growth must be factored in.

1. Which one of the following most accurately expresses the main idea of the passage?

(A)   Lichenometry is a new method for dating past earthquakes that has advantages over radiocarbon dating.

(B)   Despite its limitations, lichenometry has been proven to be more accurate than any other method of discerning the dates of past earthquakes.

(C)   Most seismologists today have rejected radiocarbon dating and are embracing lichenometry as the most reliable method for studying past earthquakes.

(D)   Two geologists have revolutionized the study of past earthquakes by developing lichenometry, an easily applied method of earthquake detection and dating.

(E)   Radiocarbon dating, an unreliable test used in dating past earthquakes, can finally be abandoned now that lichenometry has been developed.

2. The passage provides information that most helps to answer which one of the following questions?

(A)   How do scientists measure lichen growth rates under the varying conditions that lichens may encounter?

(B)   How do scientists determine the intensity of the radiation striking Earth's upper atmosphere?

(C)   What are some of the conditions that encourage lichens to grow at a more rapid rate than usual?

(D)   What is the approximate date of the earliest earthquake that lichenometry has been used to identify?

(E)   What are some applications of the techniques involved in radiocarbon dating other than their use in studying past earthquakes?

GO ON TO THE NEXT PAGE.

3. What is the author's primary purpose in referring to the rate of growth of a North American lichen species (lines 29–30)?

(A) to emphasize the rapidity with which lichen colonies can establish themselves on newly exposed rock surfaces

(B) to offer an example of a lichen species with one of the slowest known rates of growth

(C) to present additional evidence supporting the claim that environmental conditions can alter lichens' rate of growth

(D) to explain why lichenometry works best for dating earthquakes that occurred in the last 500 years

(E) to provide a sense of the sort of timescale on which lichen growth occurs

4. Which one of the following statements is most strongly supported by the passage?

(A) Lichenometry is less accurate than radiocarbon dating in predicting the likelihood and location of future earthquakes.

(B) Radiocarbon dating is unlikely to be helpful in dating past earthquakes that have no identifiable fault lines associated with them.

(C) Radiocarbon dating and lichenometry are currently the only viable methods of detecting and dating past earthquakes.

(D) Radiocarbon dating is more accurate than lichenometry in dating earthquakes that occurred approximately 400 years ago.

(E) The usefulness of lichenometry for dating earthquakes is limited to geographic regions where factors that disturb or accelerate lichen growth generally do not occur.

5. The primary purpose of the first paragraph in relation to the rest of the passage is to describe

(A) a well-known procedure that will then be examined on a step-by-step basis

(B) an established procedure to which a new procedure will then be compared

(C) an outdated procedure that will then be shown to be nonetheless useful in some situations

(D) a traditional procedure that will then be contrasted with other traditional procedures

(E) a popular procedure that will then be shown to have resulted in erroneous conclusions about a phenomenon

6. It can be inferred that the statements made by Bull and Brandon and reported in lines 50–58 rely on which one of the following assumptions?

(A) While lichenometry is less accurate when it is used to date earthquakes that occurred more than 500 years ago, it is still more accurate than other methods for dating such earthquakes.

(B) There is no reliable method for determining the intensity of the radiation now hitting Earth's upper atmosphere.

(C) Lichens are able to grow only on the types of rocks that are common in mountainous regions.

(D) The mountain ranges that produce the kinds of rockfalls studied in lichenometry are also subject to more frequent snowfalls and avalanches than other mountain ranges are.

(E) The extent to which conditions like shade and wind have affected the growth of existing lichen colonies can be determined.

7. The passage indicates that using radiocarbon dating to date past earthquakes may be unreliable due to

(A) the multiplicity of the types of organic matter that require analysis

(B) the variable amount of organic materials caught in shifted sediments

(C) the fact that fault lines related to past earthquakes are not always visible

(D) the fluctuations in the amount of the carbon 14 isotope in the environment over time

(E) the possibility that radiation has not always struck the upper atmosphere

8. Given the information in the passage, to which one of the following would lichenometry likely be most applicable?

(A) identifying the number of times a particular river has flooded in the past 1,000 years

(B) identifying the age of a fossilized skeleton of a mammal that lived many thousands of years ago

(C) identifying the age of an ancient beach now underwater approximately 30 kilometers off the present shore

(D) identifying the rate, in kilometers per century, at which a glacier has been receding up a mountain valley

(E) identifying local trends in annual rainfall rates in a particular valley over the past five centuries

GO ON TO THE NEXT PAGE.

While courts have long allowed custom-made medical illustrations depicting personal injury to be presented as evidence in legal cases, the issue of whether they have a legitimate place in the courtroom
(5) is surrounded by ongoing debate and misinformation. Some opponents of their general use argue that while illustrations are sometimes invaluable in presenting the physical details of a personal injury, in all cases except those involving the most unusual injuries, illustrations
(10) from medical textbooks can be adequate. Most injuries, such as fractures and whiplash, they say, are rather generic in nature—certain commonly encountered forces act on particular areas of the body in standard ways—so they can be represented by
(15) generic illustrations.

Another line of complaint stems from the belief that custom-made illustrations often misrepresent the facts in order to comply with the partisan interests of litigants. Even some lawyers appear to share a version
(20) of this view, believing that such illustrations can be used to bolster a weak case. Illustrators are sometimes approached by lawyers who, unable to find medical experts to support their clients' claims, think that they can replace expert testimony with such deceptive
(25) professional illustrations. But this is mistaken. Even if an unscrupulous illustrator could be found, such illustrations would be inadmissible as evidence in the courtroom unless a medical expert were present to testify to their accuracy.
(30) It has also been maintained that custom-made illustrations may subtly distort the issues through the use of emphasis, coloration, and other means, even if they are technically accurate. But professional medical illustrators strive for objective accuracy and avoid
(35) devices that have inflammatory potential, sometimes even eschewing the use of color. Unlike illustrations in medical textbooks, which are designed to include the extensive detail required by medical students, custom-made medical illustrations are designed to
(40) include only the information that is relevant for those deciding a case. The end user is typically a jury or a judge, for whose benefit the depiction is reduced to the details that are crucial to determining the legally relevant facts. The more complex details often found
(45) in textbooks can be deleted so as not to confuse the issue. For example, illustrations of such things as veins and arteries would only get in the way when an illustration is supposed to be used to explain the nature of a bone fracture.
(50) Custom-made medical illustrations, which are based on a plaintiff's X rays, computerized tomography scans, and medical records and reports, are especially valuable in that they provide visual representations of data whose verbal description would
(55) be very complex. Expert testimony by medical professionals often relies heavily on the use of technical terminology, which those who are not

specially trained in the field find difficult to translate mentally into visual imagery. Since, for most people,
(60) adequate understanding of physical data depends on thinking at least partly in visual terms, the clearly presented visual stimulation provided by custom-made illustrations can be quite instructive.

9. Which one of the following is most analogous to the role that, according to the author, custom-made medical illustrations play in personal injury cases?

(A) schematic drawings accompanying an engineer's oral presentation
(B) road maps used by people unfamiliar with an area so that they will not have to get verbal instructions from strangers
(C) children's drawings that psychologists use to detect wishes and anxieties not apparent in the children's behavior
(D) a reproduction of a famous painting in an art history textbook
(E) an artist's preliminary sketches for a painting

10. Based on the passage, which one of the following is the author most likely to believe about illustrations in medical textbooks?

(A) They tend to rely less on the use of color than do custom-made medical illustrations.
(B) They are inadmissible in a courtroom unless a medical expert is present to testify to their accuracy.
(C) They are in many cases drawn by the same individuals who draw custom-made medical illustrations for courtroom use.
(D) They are believed by most lawyers to be less prone than custom-made medical illustrations to misrepresent the nature of a personal injury.
(E) In many cases they are more apt to confuse jurors than are custom-made medical illustrations.

11. The passage states that a role of medical experts in relation to custom-made medical illustrations in the courtroom is to

(A) decide which custom-made medical illustrations should be admissible
(B) temper the impact of the illustrations on judges and jurors who are not medical professionals
(C) make medical illustrations understandable to judges and jurors
(D) provide opinions to attorneys as to which illustrations, if any, would be useful
(E) provide their opinions as to the accuracy of the illustrations

GO ON TO THE NEXT PAGE.

12. According to the passage, one of the ways that medical textbook illustrations differ from custom-made medical illustrations is that

(A) custom-made medical illustrations accurately represent human anatomy, whereas medical textbook illustrations do not

(B) medical textbook illustrations employ color freely, whereas custom-made medical illustrations must avoid color

(C) medical textbook illustrations are objective, while custom-made medical illustrations are subjective

(D) medical textbook illustrations are very detailed, whereas custom-made medical illustrations include only details that are relevant to the case

(E) medical textbook illustrations are readily comprehended by nonmedical audiences, whereas custom-made medical illustrations are not

13. The author's attitude toward the testimony of medical experts in personal injury cases is most accurately described as

(A) appreciation of the difficulty involved in explaining medical data to judges and jurors together with skepticism concerning the effectiveness of such testimony

(B) admiration for the experts' technical knowledge coupled with disdain for the communications skills of medical professionals

(C) acceptance of the accuracy of such testimony accompanied with awareness of the limitations of a presentation that is entirely verbal

(D) respect for the medical profession tempered by apprehension concerning the tendency of medical professionals to try to overwhelm judges and jurors with technical details

(E) respect for expert witnesses combined with intolerance of the use of technical terminology

14. The author's primary purpose in the third paragraph is to

(A) argue for a greater use of custom-made medical illustrations in court cases involving personal injury

(B) reply to a variant of the objection to custom-made medical illustrations raised in the second paragraph

(C) argue against the position that illustrations from medical textbooks are well suited for use in the courtroom

(D) discuss in greater detail why custom-made medical illustrations are controversial

(E) describe the differences between custom-made medical illustrations and illustrations from medical textbooks

GO ON TO THE NEXT PAGE.

Passage A

Because dental caries (decay) is strongly linked to consumption of the sticky, carbohydrate-rich staples of agricultural diets, prehistoric human teeth can provide clues about when a population made the transition
(5) from a hunter-gatherer diet to an agricultural one. Caries formation is influenced by several factors, including tooth structure, bacteria in the mouth, and diet. In particular, caries formation is affected by carbohydrates' texture and composition, since
(10) carbohydrates more readily stick to teeth.

Many researchers have demonstrated the link between carbohydrate consumption and caries. In North America, Leigh studied caries in archaeologically derived teeth, noting that caries rates differed between
(15) indigenous populations that primarily consumed meat (a Sioux sample showed almost no caries) and those heavily dependent on cultivated maize (a Zuni sample had 75 percent carious teeth). Leigh's findings have been frequently confirmed by other researchers, who
(20) have shown that, in general, the greater a population's dependence on agriculture is, the higher its rate of caries formation will be.

Under some circumstances, however, nonagricultural populations may exhibit relatively
(25) high caries rates. For example, early nonagricultural populations in western North America who consumed large amounts of highly processed stone-ground flour made from gathered acorns show relatively high caries frequencies. And wild plants collected by the Hopi
(30) included several species with high cariogenic potential, notably pinyon nuts and wild tubers.

Passage B

Archaeologists recovered human skeletal remains interred over a 2,000-year period in prehistoric Ban Chiang, Thailand. The site's early inhabitants
(35) appear to have had a hunter-gatherer-cultivator economy. Evidence indicates that, over time, the population became increasingly dependent on agriculture.

Research suggests that agricultural intensification
(40) results in declining human health, including dental health. Studies show that dental caries is uncommon in pre-agricultural populations. Increased caries frequency may result from increased consumption of starchy-sticky foodstuffs or from alterations in tooth wear. The
(45) wearing down of tooth crown surfaces reduces caries formation by removing fissures that can trap food particles. A reduction of fiber or grit in a diet may diminish tooth wear, thus increasing caries frequency. However, severe wear that exposes a tooth's pulp
(50) cavity may also result in caries.

The diet of Ban Chiang's inhabitants included some cultivated rice and yams from the beginning of the period represented by the recovered remains. These were part of a varied diet that also included
(55) wild plant and animal foods. Since both rice and yams are carbohydrates, increased reliance on either or both should theoretically result in increased caries frequency.

Yet comparisons of caries frequency in the Early and Late Ban Chiang Groups indicate that overall
(60) caries frequency is slightly greater in the Early Group. Tooth wear patterns do not indicate tooth wear changes between Early and Late Groups that would explain this unexpected finding. It is more likely that, although dependence on agriculture increased, the diet
(65) in the Late period remained varied enough that no single food dominated. Furthermore, there may have been a shift from sweeter carbohydrates (yams) toward rice, a less cariogenic carbohydrate.

15. Both passages are primarily concerned with examining which one of the following topics?

(A) evidence of the development of agriculture in the archaeological record

(B) the impact of agriculture on the overall health of human populations

(C) the effects of carbohydrate-rich foods on caries formation in strictly agricultural societies

(D) the archaeological evidence regarding when the first agricultural society arose

(E) the extent to which pre-agricultural populations were able to obtain carbohydrate-rich foods

16. Which one of the following distinguishes the Ban Chiang populations discussed in passage B from the populations discussed in the last paragraph of passage A?

(A) While the Ban Chiang populations consumed several highly cariogenic foods, the populations discussed in the last paragraph of passage A did not.

(B) While the Ban Chiang populations ate cultivated foods, the populations discussed in the last paragraph of passage A did not.

(C) While the Ban Chiang populations consumed a diet consisting primarily of carbohydrates, the populations discussed in the last paragraph of passage A did not.

(D) While the Ban Chiang populations exhibited very high levels of tooth wear, the populations discussed in the last paragraph of passage A did not.

(E) While the Ban Chiang populations ate certain highly processed foods, the populations discussed in the last paragraph of passage A did not.

GO ON TO THE NEXT PAGE.

17. Passage B most strongly supports which one of the following statements about fiber and grit in a diet?

   (A)   They can either limit or promote caries formation, depending on their prevalence in the diet.

   (B)   They are typically consumed in greater quantities as a population adopts agriculture.

   (C)   They have a negative effect on overall health since they have no nutritional value.

   (D)   They contribute to the formation of fissures in tooth surfaces.

   (E)   They increase the stickiness of carbohydrate-rich foods.

18. Which one of the following is mentioned in both passages as evidence tending to support the prevailing view regarding the relationship between dental caries and carbohydrate consumption?

   (A)   the effect of consuming highly processed foods on caries formation

   (B)   the relatively low incidence of caries among nonagricultural people

   (C)   the effect of fiber and grit in the diet on caries formation

   (D)   the effect of the consumption of wild foods on tooth wear

   (E)   the effect of agricultural intensification on overall human health

19. It is most likely that both authors would agree with which one of the following statements about dental caries?

   (A)   The incidence of dental caries increases predictably in populations over time.

   (B)   Dental caries is often difficult to detect in teeth recovered from archaeological sites.

   (C)   Dental caries tends to be more prevalent in populations with a hunter-gatherer diet than in populations with an agricultural diet.

   (D)   The frequency of dental caries in a population does not necessarily correspond directly to the population's degree of dependence on agriculture.

   (E)   The formation of dental caries tends to be more strongly linked to tooth wear than to the consumption of a particular kind of food.

20. Each passage suggests which one of the following about carbohydrate-rich foods?

   (A)   Varieties that are cultivated have a greater tendency to cause caries than varieties that grow wild.

   (B)   Those that require substantial processing do not play a role in hunter-gatherer diets.

   (C)   Some of them naturally have a greater tendency than others to cause caries.

   (D)   Some of them reduce caries formation because their relatively high fiber content increases tooth wear.

   (E)   The cariogenic potential of a given variety increases if it is cultivated rather than gathered in the wild.

21. The evidence from Ban Chiang discussed in passage B relates to the generalization reported in the second paragraph of passage A (lines 20–22) in which one of the following ways?

   (A)   The evidence confirms the generalization.

   (B)   The evidence tends to support the generalization.

   (C)   The evidence is irrelevant to the generalization.

   (D)   The evidence does not conform to the generalization.

   (E)   The evidence disproves the generalization.

GO ON TO THE NEXT PAGE.

Recent criticism has sought to align Sarah Orne Jewett, a notable writer of regional fiction in the nineteenth-century United States, with the domestic novelists of the previous generation. Her work does
(5) resemble the domestic novels of the 1850s in its focus on women, their domestic occupations, and their social interactions, with men relegated to the periphery. But it also differs markedly from these antecedents. The world depicted in the latter revolves around children.
(10) Young children play prominent roles in the domestic novels and the work of child rearing—the struggle to instill a mother's values in a child's character—is their chief source of drama. By contrast, children and child rearing are almost entirely absent from the world of
(15) Jewett's fiction. Even more strikingly, while the literary world of the earlier domestic novelists is insistently religious, grounded in the structures of Protestant religious belief, to turn from these writers to Jewett is to encounter an almost wholly secular world.
(20)   To the extent that these differences do not merely reflect the personal preferences of the authors, we might attribute them to such historical transformations as the migration of the rural young to cities or the increasing secularization of society. But while such
(25) factors may help to explain the differences, it can be argued that these differences ultimately reflect different conceptions of the nature and purpose of fiction. The domestic novel of the mid-nineteenth century is based on a conception of fiction as part of
(30) a continuum that also included writings devoted to piety and domestic instruction, bound together by a common goal of promoting domestic morality and religious belief. It was not uncommon for the same multipurpose book to be indistinguishably a novel, a
(35) child-rearing manual, and a tract on Christian duty. The more didactic aims are absent from Jewett's writing, which rather embodies the late nineteenth-century "high-cultural" conception of fiction as an autonomous sphere with value in and of itself.
(40)   This high-cultural aesthetic was one among several conceptions of fiction operative in the United States in the 1850s and 1860s, but it became the dominant one later in the nineteenth century and remained so for most of the twentieth. On this
(45) conception, fiction came to be seen as pure art: a work was to be viewed in isolation and valued for the formal arrangement of its elements rather than for its larger social connections or the promotion of extraliterary goods. Thus, unlike the domestic novelists, Jewett
(50) intended her works not as a means to an end but as an end in themselves. This fundamental difference should be given more weight in assessing their affinities than any superficial similarity in subject matter.

22. The passage most helps to answer which one of the following questions?

(A) Did any men write domestic novels in the 1850s?
(B) Were any widely read domestic novels written after the 1860s?
(C) How did migration to urban areas affect the development of domestic fiction in the 1850s?
(D) What is an effect that Jewett's conception of literary art had on her fiction?
(E) With what region of the United States were at least some of Jewett's writings concerned?

23. It can be inferred from the passage that the author would be most likely to view the "recent criticism" mentioned in line 1 as

(A) advocating a position that is essentially correct even though some powerful arguments can be made against it
(B) making a true claim about Jewett, but for the wrong reasons
(C) making a claim that is based on some reasonable evidence and is initially plausible but ultimately mistaken
(D) questionable, because it relies on a currently dominant literary aesthetic that takes too narrow a view of the proper goals of fiction
(E) based on speculation for which there is no reasonable support, and therefore worthy of dismissal

24. In saying that domestic fiction was based on a conception of fiction as part of a "continuum" (line 30), the author most likely means which one of the following?

(A) Domestic fiction was part of an ongoing tradition stretching back into the past.
(B) Fiction was not treated as clearly distinct from other categories of writing.
(C) Domestic fiction was often published in serial form.
(D) Fiction is constantly evolving.
(E) Domestic fiction promoted the cohesiveness and hence the continuity of society.

GO ON TO THE NEXT PAGE.

25. Which one of the following most accurately states the primary function of the passage?

    (A) It proposes and defends a radical redefinition of several historical categories of literary style.
    (B) It proposes an evaluation of a particular style of writing, of which one writer's work is cited as a paradigmatic case.
    (C) It argues for a reappraisal of a set of long-held assumptions about the historical connections among a group of writers.
    (D) It weighs the merits of two opposing conceptions of the nature of fiction.
    (E) It rejects a way of classifying a particular writer's work and defends an alternative view.

26. Which one of the following most accurately represents the structure of the second paragraph?

    (A) The author considers and rejects a number of possible explanations for a phenomenon, concluding that any attempt at explanation does violence to the unity of the phenomenon.
    (B) The author shows that two explanatory hypotheses are incompatible with each other and gives reasons for preferring one of them.
    (C) The author describes several explanatory hypotheses and argues that they are not really distinct from one another.
    (D) The author proposes two versions of a classificatory hypothesis, indicates the need for some such hypothesis, and then sets out a counterargument in preparation for rejecting that counterargument in the following paragraph.
    (E) The author mentions a number of explanatory hypotheses, gives a mildly favorable comment on them, and then advocates and elaborates another explanation that the author considers to be more fundamental.

27. The differing conceptions of fiction held by Jewett and the domestic novelists can most reasonably be taken as providing an answer to which one of the following questions?

    (A) Why was Jewett unwilling to feature children and religious themes as prominently in her works as the domestic novelists featured them in theirs?
    (B) Why did both Jewett and the domestic novelists focus primarily on rural as opposed to urban concerns?
    (C) Why was Jewett not constrained to feature children and religion as prominently in her works as domestic novelists were?
    (D) Why did both Jewett and the domestic novelists focus predominantly on women and their concerns?
    (E) Why was Jewett unable to feature children or religion as prominently in her works as the domestic novelists featured them in theirs?

S T O P

IF YOU FINISH BEFORE TIME IS CALLED, YOU MAY CHECK YOUR WORK ON THIS SECTION ONLY.
DO NOT WORK ON ANY OTHER SECTION IN THE TEST.

SECTION II
Time—35 minutes
26 Questions

Directions: The questions in this section are based on the reasoning contained in brief statements or passages. For some questions, more than one of the choices could conceivably answer the question. However, you are to choose the best answer; that is, the response that most accurately and completely answers the question. You should not make assumptions that are by commonsense standards implausible, superfluous, or incompatible with the passage. After you have chosen the best answer, blacken the corresponding space on your answer sheet.

1. In a recent study, a group of young children were taught the word "stairs" while walking up and down a flight of stairs. Later that day, when the children were shown a video of a person climbing a ladder, they all called the ladder stairs.

Which one of the following principles is best illustrated by the study described above?

(A) When young children repeatedly hear a word without seeing the object denoted by the word, they sometimes apply the word to objects not denoted by the word.

(B) Young children best learn words when they are shown how the object denoted by the word is used.

(C) The earlier in life a child encounters and uses an object, the easier it is for that child to learn how not to misuse the word denoting that object.

(D) Young children who learn a word by observing how the object denoted by that word is used sometimes apply that word to a different object that is similarly used.

(E) Young children best learn the names of objects when the objects are present at the time the children learn the words and when no other objects are simultaneously present.

2. Among people who live to the age of 100 or more, a large proportion have led "unhealthy" lives: smoking, consuming alcohol, eating fatty foods, and getting little exercise. Since such behavior often leads to shortened life spans, it is likely that exceptionally long-lived people are genetically disposed to having long lives.

Which one of the following, if true, most strengthens the argument?

(A) There is some evidence that consuming a moderate amount of alcohol can counteract the effects of eating fatty foods.

(B) Some of the exceptionally long-lived people who do not smoke or drink do eat fatty foods and get little exercise.

(C) Some of the exceptionally long-lived people who exercise regularly and avoid fatty foods do smoke or consume alcohol.

(D) Some people who do not live to the age of 100 also lead unhealthy lives.

(E) Nearly all people who live to 100 or more have siblings who are also long-lived.

3. Medications with an unpleasant taste are generally produced only in tablet, capsule, or soft-gel form. The active ingredient in medication M is a waxy substance that cannot tolerate the heat used to manufacture tablets because it has a low melting point. So, since the company developing M does not have soft-gel manufacturing technology and manufactures all its medications itself, M will most likely be produced in capsule form.

The conclusion is most strongly supported by the reasoning in the argument if which one of the following is assumed?

(A) Medication M can be produced in liquid form.
(B) Medication M has an unpleasant taste.
(C) No medication is produced in both capsule and soft-gel form.
(D) Most medications with a low melting point are produced in soft-gel form.
(E) Medications in capsule form taste less unpleasant than those in tablet or soft-gel form.

GO ON TO THE NEXT PAGE.

4. Carol Morris wants to own a majority of the shares of the city's largest newspaper, *The Daily*. The only obstacle to Morris's amassing a majority of these shares is that Azedcorp, which currently owns a majority, has steadfastly refused to sell. Industry analysts nevertheless predict that Morris will soon be the majority owner of *The Daily*.

Which one of the following, if true, provides the most support for the industry analysts' prediction?

(A) Azedcorp does not own shares of any newspaper other than *The Daily*.

(B) Morris has recently offered Azedcorp much more for its shares of *The Daily* than Azedcorp paid for them.

(C) No one other than Morris has expressed any interest in purchasing a majority of *The Daily*'s shares.

(D) Morris already owns more shares of *The Daily* than anyone except Azedcorp.

(E) Azedcorp is financially so weak that bankruptcy will probably soon force the sale of its newspaper holdings.

5. Area resident: Childhood lead poisoning has declined steadily since the 1970s, when leaded gasoline was phased out and lead paint was banned. But recent statistics indicate that 25 percent of this area's homes still contain lead paint that poses significant health hazards. Therefore, if we eliminate the lead paint in those homes, childhood lead poisoning in the area will finally be eradicated.

The area resident's argument is flawed in that it

(A) relies on statistical claims that are likely to be unreliable

(B) relies on an assumption that is tantamount to assuming that the conclusion is true

(C) fails to consider that there may be other significant sources of lead in the area's environment

(D) takes for granted that lead paint in homes can be eliminated economically

(E) takes for granted that children reside in all of the homes in the area that contain lead paint

6. Although some nutritional facts about soft drinks are listed on their labels, exact caffeine content is not. Listing exact caffeine content would make it easier to limit, but not eliminate, one's caffeine intake. If it became easier for people to limit, but not eliminate, their caffeine intake, many people would do so, which would improve their health.

If all the statements above are true, which one of the following must be true?

(A) The health of at least some people would improve if exact caffeine content were listed on soft-drink labels.

(B) Many people will be unable to limit their caffeine intake if exact caffeine content is not listed on soft-drink labels.

(C) Many people will find it difficult to eliminate their caffeine intake if they have to guess exactly how much caffeine is in their soft drinks.

(D) People who wish to eliminate, rather than simply limit, their caffeine intake would benefit if exact caffeine content were listed on soft-drink labels.

(E) The health of at least some people would worsen if everyone knew exactly how much caffeine was in their soft drinks.

7. When the famous art collector Vidmar died, a public auction of her collection, the largest privately owned, was held. "I can't possibly afford any of those works because hers is among the most valuable collections ever assembled by a single person," declared art lover MacNeil.

The flawed pattern of reasoning in which one of the following is most closely parallel to that in MacNeil's argument?

(A) Each word in the book is in French. So the whole book is in French.

(B) The city council voted unanimously to adopt the plan. So councilperson Martinez voted to adopt the plan.

(C) This paragraph is long. So the sentences that comprise it are long.

(D) The members of the company are old. So the company itself is old.

(E) The atoms comprising this molecule are elements. So the molecule itself is an element.

GO ON TO THE NEXT PAGE.

8. A leading critic of space exploration contends that it would be wrong, given current technology, to send a group of explorers to Mars, since the explorers would be unlikely to survive the trip. But that exaggerates the risk. There would be a well-engineered backup system at every stage of the long and complicated journey. A fatal catastrophe is quite unlikely at any given stage if such a backup system is in place.

The reasoning in the argument is flawed in that the argument

(A) infers that something is true of a whole merely from the fact that it is true of each of the parts

(B) infers that something cannot occur merely from the fact that it is unlikely to occur

(C) draws a conclusion about what must be the case based on evidence about what is probably the case

(D) infers that something will work merely because it could work

(E) rejects a view merely on the grounds that an inadequate argument has been made for it

9. A retrospective study is a scientific study that tries to determine the causes of subjects' present characteristics by looking for significant connections between the present characteristics of subjects and what happened to those subjects in the past, before the study began. Because retrospective studies of human subjects must use the subjects' reports about their own pasts, however, such studies cannot reliably determine the causes of human subjects' present characteristics.

Which one of the following, if assumed, enables the argument's conclusion to be properly drawn?

(A) Whether or not a study of human subjects can reliably determine the causes of those subjects' present characteristics may depend at least in part on the extent to which that study uses inaccurate reports about the subjects' pasts.

(B) A retrospective study cannot reliably determine the causes of human subjects' present characteristics unless there exist correlations between the present characteristics of the subjects and what happened to those subjects in the past.

(C) In studies of human subjects that attempt to find connections between subjects' present characteristics and what happened to those subjects in the past, the subjects' reports about their own pasts are highly susceptible to inaccuracy.

(D) If a study of human subjects uses only accurate reports about the subjects' pasts, then that study can reliably determine the causes of those subjects' present characteristics.

(E) Every scientific study in which researchers look for significant connections between the present characteristics of subjects and what happened to those subjects in the past must use the subjects' reports about their own pasts.

GO ON TO THE NEXT PAGE.

10. Gigantic passenger planes currently being developed will have enough space to hold shops and lounges in addition to passenger seating. However, the additional space will more likely be used for more passenger seating. The number of passengers flying the air-traffic system is expected to triple within 20 years, and it will be impossible for airports to accommodate enough normal-sized jet planes to carry that many passengers.

Which one of the following most accurately states the conclusion drawn in the argument?

(A) Gigantic planes currently being developed will have enough space in them to hold shops and lounges as well as passenger seating.

(B) The additional space in the gigantic planes currently being developed is more likely to be filled with passenger seating than with shops and lounges.

(C) The number of passengers flying the air-traffic system is expected to triple within 20 years.

(D) In 20 years, it will be impossible for airports to accommodate enough normal-sized planes to carry the number of passengers that are expected to be flying then.

(E) In 20 years, most airline passengers will be flying in gigantic passenger planes.

11. Scientist: To study the comparative effectiveness of two experimental medications for athlete's foot, a representative sample of people with athlete's foot were randomly assigned to one of two groups. One group received only medication M, and the other received only medication N. The only people whose athlete's foot was cured had been given medication M.

Reporter: This means, then, that if anyone in the study had athlete's foot that was not cured, that person did not receive medication M.

Which one of the following most accurately describes the reporter's error in reasoning?

(A) The reporter concludes from evidence showing only that M can cure athlete's foot that M always cures athlete's foot.

(B) The reporter illicitly draws a conclusion about the population as a whole on the basis of a study conducted only on a sample of the population.

(C) The reporter presumes, without providing justification, that medications M and N are available to people who have athlete's foot but did not participate in the study.

(D) The reporter fails to allow for the possibility that athlete's foot may be cured even if neither of the two medications studied is taken.

(E) The reporter presumes, without providing justification, that there is no sizeable subgroup of people whose athlete's foot will be cured only if they do not take medication M.

12. Paleontologist: Plesiosauromorphs were gigantic, long-necked marine reptiles that ruled the oceans during the age of the dinosaurs. Most experts believe that plesiosauromorphs lurked and quickly ambushed their prey. However, plesiosauromorphs probably hunted by chasing their prey over long distances. Plesiosauromorph fins were quite long and thin, like the wings of birds specialized for long-distance flight.

Which one of the following is an assumption on which the paleontologist's argument depends?

(A) Birds and reptiles share many physical features because they descend from common evolutionary ancestors.

(B) During the age of dinosaurs, plesiosauromorphs were the only marine reptiles that had long, thin fins.

(C) A gigantic marine animal would not be able to find enough food to meet the caloric requirements dictated by its body size if it did not hunt by chasing prey over long distances.

(D) Most marine animals that chase prey over long distances are specialized for long-distance swimming.

(E) The shape of a marine animal's fin affects the way the animal swims in the same way as the shape of a bird's wing affects the way the bird flies.

13. Buying elaborate screensavers—programs that put moving images on a computer monitor to prevent damage—can cost a company far more in employee time than it saves in electricity and monitor protection. Employees cannot resist spending time playing with screensavers that flash interesting graphics across their screens.

Which one of the following most closely conforms to the principle illustrated above?

(A) A school that chooses textbooks based on student preference may not get the most economical package.

(B) An energy-efficient insulation system may cost more up front but will ultimately save money over the life of the house.

(C) The time that it takes to have a pizza delivered may be longer than it takes to cook a complete dinner.

(D) A complicated hotel security system may cost more in customer goodwill than it saves in losses by theft.

(E) An electronic keyboard may be cheaper to buy than a piano but more expensive to repair.

GO ON TO THE NEXT PAGE.

14. Music professor: Because rap musicians can work alone in a recording studio, they need not accommodate supporting musicians' wishes. Further, learning to rap is not as formal a process as learning an instrument. Thus, rap is an extremely individualistic and nontraditional musical form.

    Music critic: But rap appeals to tradition by using bits of older songs. Besides, the themes and styles of rap have developed into a tradition. And successful rap musicians do not perform purely idiosyncratically but conform their work to the preferences of the public.

    The music critic's response to the music professor's argument

    (A) challenges it by offering evidence against one of the stated premises on which its conclusion concerning rap music is based

    (B) challenges its conclusion concerning rap music by offering certain additional observations that the music professor does not take into account in his argument

    (C) challenges the grounds on which the music professor generalizes from the particular context of rap music to the broader context of musical tradition and individuality

    (D) challenges it by offering an alternative explanation of phenomena that the music professor cites as evidence for his thesis about rap music

    (E) challenges each of a group of claims about tradition and individuality in music that the music professor gives as evidence in his argument

15. Speaker: Like many contemporary critics, Smith argues that the true meaning of an author's statements can be understood only through insight into the author's social circumstances. But this same line of analysis can be applied to Smith's own words. Thus, if she is right we should be able, at least in part, to discern from Smith's social circumstances the "true meaning" of Smith's statements. This, in turn, suggests that Smith herself is not aware of the true meaning of her own words.

    The speaker's main conclusion logically follows if which one of the following is assumed?

    (A) Insight into the intended meaning of an author's work is not as important as insight into its true meaning.

    (B) Smith lacks insight into her own social circumstances.

    (C) There is just one meaning that Smith intends her work to have.

    (D) Smith's theory about the relation of social circumstances to the understanding of meaning lacks insight.

    (E) The intended meaning of an author's work is not always good evidence of its true meaning.

16. Tissue biopsies taken on patients who have undergone throat surgery show that those who snored frequently were significantly more likely to have serious abnormalities in their throat muscles than those who snored rarely or not at all. This shows that snoring can damage the throat of the snorer.

    Which one of the following, if true, most strengthens the argument?

    (A) The study relied on the subjects' self-reporting to determine whether or not they snored frequently.

    (B) The patients' throat surgery was not undertaken to treat abnormalities in their throat muscles.

    (C) All of the test subjects were of similar age and weight and in similar states of health.

    (D) People who have undergone throat surgery are no more likely to snore than people who have not undergone throat surgery.

    (E) The abnormalities in the throat muscles discovered in the study do not cause snoring.

GO ON TO THE NEXT PAGE.

17. One should never sacrifice one's health in order to acquire money, for without health, happiness is not obtainable.

The conclusion of the argument follows logically if which one of the following is assumed?

(A) Money should be acquired only if its acquisition will not make happiness unobtainable.
(B) In order to be happy one must have either money or health.
(C) Health should be valued only as a precondition for happiness.
(D) Being wealthy is, under certain conditions, conducive to unhappiness.
(E) Health is more conducive to happiness than wealth is.

18. Vanessa: All computer code must be written by a pair of programmers working at a single workstation. This is needed to prevent programmers from writing idiosyncratic code that can be understood only by the original programmer.

Jo: Most programming projects are kept afloat by the best programmers on the team, who are typically at least 100 times more productive than the worst. Since they generally work best when they work alone, the most productive programmers must be allowed to work by themselves.

Each of the following assignments of computer programmers is consistent both with the principle expressed by Vanessa and with the principle expressed by Jo EXCEPT:

(A) Olga and Kensuke are both programmers of roughly average productivity who feel that they are more productive when working alone. They have been assigned to work together at a single workstation.
(B) John is experienced but is not among the most productive programmers on the team. He has been assigned to mentor Tyrone, a new programmer who is not yet very productive. They are to work together at a single workstation.
(C) Although not among the most productive programmers on the team, Chris is more productive than Jennifer. They have been assigned to work together at a single workstation.
(D) Yolanda is the most productive programmer on the team. She has been assigned to work with Mike, who is also very productive. They are to work together at the same workstation.
(E) Kevin and Amy both have a reputation for writing idiosyncratic code; neither is unusually productive. They have been assigned to work together at the same workstation.

19. In West Calverton, most pet stores sell exotic birds, and most of those that sell exotic birds also sell tropical fish. However, any pet store there that sells tropical fish but not exotic birds does sell gerbils; and no independently owned pet stores in West Calverton sell gerbils.

If the statements above are true, which one of the following must be true?

(A) Most pet stores in West Calverton that are not independently owned do not sell exotic birds.
(B) No pet stores in West Calverton that sell tropical fish and exotic birds sell gerbils.
(C) Some pet stores in West Calverton that sell gerbils also sell exotic birds.
(D) No independently owned pet store in West Calverton sells tropical fish but not exotic birds.
(E) Any independently owned pet store in West Calverton that does not sell tropical fish sells exotic birds.

20. Astronomer: Earlier estimates of the distances of certain stars from Earth would mean that these stars are about 1 billion years older than the universe itself, an impossible scenario. My estimates of the distances indicate that these stars are much farther away than previously thought. And the farther away the stars are, the greater their intrinsic brightness must be, given their appearance to us on Earth. So the new estimates of these stars' distances from Earth help resolve the earlier conflict between the ages of these stars and the age of the universe.

Which one of the following, if true, most helps to explain why the astronomer's estimates of the stars' distances from Earth help resolve the earlier conflict between the ages of these stars and the age of the universe?

(A) The stars are the oldest objects yet discovered in the universe.
(B) The younger the universe is, the more bright stars it is likely to have.
(C) The brighter a star is, the younger it is.
(D) How bright celestial objects appear to be depends on how far away from the observer they are.
(E) New telescopes allow astronomers to see a greater number of distant stars.

GO ON TO THE NEXT PAGE.

21. Most large nurseries sell raspberry plants primarily to commercial raspberry growers and sell only plants that are guaranteed to be disease-free. However, the shipment of raspberry plants that Johnson received from Wally's Plants carried a virus that commonly afflicts raspberries.

Which one of the following is most strongly supported by the information above?

(A) If Johnson is a commercial raspberry grower and Wally's Plants is not a large nursery, then the shipment of raspberry plants that Johnson received was probably guaranteed to be disease-free.

(B) Johnson is probably not a commercial raspberry grower if the shipment of raspberry plants that Johnson received from Wally's Plants was not entirely as it was guaranteed to be.

(C) If Johnson is not a commercial raspberry grower, then Wally's Plants is probably not a large nursery.

(D) Wally's Plants is probably not a large, well-run nursery if it sells its raspberry plants primarily to commercial raspberry growers.

(E) If Wally's Plants is a large nursery, then the raspberry plants that Johnson received in the shipment were probably not entirely as they were guaranteed to be.

22. Drug company manager: Our newest product is just not selling. One way to save it would be a new marketing campaign. This would not guarantee success, but it is one chance to save the product, so we should try it.

Which one of the following, if true, most seriously weakens the manager's argument?

(A) The drug company has invested heavily in its newest product, and losses due to this product would be harmful to the company's profits.

(B) Many new products fail whether or not they are supported by marketing campaigns.

(C) The drug company should not undertake a new marketing campaign for its newest product if the campaign has no chance to succeed.

(D) Undertaking a new marketing campaign would endanger the drug company's overall position by necessitating cutbacks in existing marketing campaigns.

(E) Consumer demand for the drug company's other products has been strong in the time since the company's newest product was introduced.

23. Consumer advocate: TMD, a pesticide used on peaches, shows no effects on human health when it is ingested in the amount present in the per capita peach consumption in this country. But while 80 percent of the population eat no peaches, others, including small children, consume much more than the national average, and thus ingest disproportionately large amounts of TMD. So even though the use of TMD on peaches poses minimal risk to most of the population, it has not been shown to be an acceptable practice.

Which one of the following principles, if valid, most helps to justify the consumer advocate's argumentation?

(A) The possibility that more data about a pesticide's health effects might reveal previously unknown risks at low doses warrants caution in assessing that pesticide's overall risks.

(B) The consequences of using a pesticide are unlikely to be acceptable when a majority of the population is likely to ingest it.

(C) Use of a pesticide is acceptable only if it is used for its intended purpose and the pesticide has been shown not to harm any portion of the population.

(D) Society has a special obligation to protect small children from pesticides unless average doses received by the population are low and have not been shown to be harmful to children's health.

(E) Measures taken to protect the population from a harm sometimes turn out to be the cause of a more serious harm to certain segments of the population.

24. Legal commentator: The goal of a recently enacted law that bans smoking in workplaces is to protect employees from secondhand smoke. But the law is written in such a way that it cannot be interpreted as ever prohibiting people from smoking in their own homes.

The statements above, if true, provide a basis for rejecting which one of the following claims?

(A) The law will be interpreted in a way that is inconsistent with the intentions of the legislators who supported it.

(B) Supporters of the law believe that it will have a significant impact on the health of many workers.

(C) The law offers no protection from secondhand smoke for people outside of their workplaces.

(D) Most people believe that smokers have a fundamental right to smoke in their own homes.

(E) The law will protect domestic workers such as housecleaners from secondhand smoke in their workplaces.

GO ON TO THE NEXT PAGE.

25. University president: Our pool of applicants has been shrinking over the past few years. One possible explanation of this unwelcome phenomenon is that we charge too little for tuition and fees. Prospective students and their parents conclude that the quality of education they would receive at this institution is not as high as that offered by institutions with higher tuition. So, if we want to increase the size of our applicant pool, we need to raise our tuition and fees.

The university president's argument requires the assumption that

(A) the proposed explanation for the decline in applications applies in this case
(B) the quality of a university education is dependent on the amount of tuition charged by the university
(C) an increase in tuition and fees at the university would guarantee a larger applicant pool
(D) there is no additional explanation for the university's shrinking applicant pool
(E) the amount charged by the university for tuition has not increased in recent years

26. Editorial: It has been suggested that private, for-profit companies should be hired to supply clean drinking water to areas of the world where it is unavailable now. But water should not be supplied by private companies. After all, clean water is essential for human health, and the purpose of a private company is to produce profit, not to promote health.

Which one of the following principles, if valid, would most help to justify the reasoning in the editorial?

(A) A private company should not be allowed to supply a commodity that is essential to human health unless that commodity is also supplied by a government agency.
(B) If something is essential for human health and private companies are unwilling or unable to supply it, then it should be supplied by a government agency.
(C) Drinking water should never be supplied by an organization that is not able to consistently supply clean, safe water.
(D) The mere fact that something actually promotes human health is not sufficient to show that its purpose is to promote health.
(E) If something is necessary for human health, then it should be provided by an organization whose primary purpose is the promotion of health.

S T O P

IF YOU FINISH BEFORE TIME IS CALLED, YOU MAY CHECK YOUR WORK ON THIS SECTION ONLY.
DO NOT WORK ON ANY OTHER SECTION IN THE TEST.

SECTION III

Time—35 minutes

23 Questions

Directions: Each group of questions in this section is based on a set of conditions. In answering some of the questions, it may be useful to draw a rough diagram. Choose the response that most accurately and completely answers each question and blacken the corresponding space on your answer sheet.

Questions 1–6

A motel operator is scheduling appointments to start up services at a new motel. Appointments for six services—gas, landscaping, power, satellite, telephone, and water—will be scheduled, one appointment per day for the next six days. The schedule for the appointments is subject to the following conditions:

The water appointment must be scheduled for an earlier day than the landscaping appointment.

The power appointment must be scheduled for an earlier day than both the gas and satellite appointments.

The appointments scheduled for the second and third days cannot be for either gas, satellite, or telephone.

The telephone appointment cannot be scheduled for the sixth day.

1. Which one of the following is an acceptable schedule of appointments, listed in order from earliest to latest?

   (A)   gas, water, power, telephone, landscaping, satellite

   (B)   power, water, landscaping, gas, satellite, telephone

   (C)   telephone, power, landscaping, gas, water, satellite

   (D)   telephone, water, power, landscaping, gas, satellite

   (E)   water, telephone, power, gas, satellite, landscaping

GO ON TO THE NEXT PAGE.

2. If neither the gas nor the satellite nor the telephone appointment is scheduled for the fourth day, which one of the following must be true?

   (A) The gas appointment is scheduled for the fifth day.
   (B) The power appointment is scheduled for the third day.
   (C) The satellite appointment is scheduled for the sixth day.
   (D) The telephone appointment is scheduled for the first day.
   (E) The water appointment is scheduled for the second day.

3. Which one of the following must be true?

   (A) The landscaping appointment is scheduled for an earlier day than the telephone appointment.
   (B) The power appointment is scheduled for an earlier day than the landscaping appointment.
   (C) The telephone appointment is scheduled for an earlier day than the gas appointment.
   (D) The telephone appointment is scheduled for an earlier day than the water appointment.
   (E) The water appointment is scheduled for an earlier day than the gas appointment.

4. Which one of the following CANNOT be the appointments scheduled for the fourth, fifth, and sixth days, listed in that order?

   (A) gas, satellite, landscaping
   (B) landscaping, satellite, gas
   (C) power, satellite, gas
   (D) telephone, satellite, gas
   (E) water, gas, landscaping

5. If neither the gas appointment nor the satellite appointment is scheduled for the sixth day, which one of the following must be true?

   (A) The gas appointment is scheduled for the fifth day.
   (B) The landscaping appointment is scheduled for the sixth day.
   (C) The power appointment is scheduled for the third day.
   (D) The telephone appointment is scheduled for the fourth day.
   (E) The water appointment is scheduled for the second day.

6. Which one of the following, if substituted for the condition that the telephone appointment cannot be scheduled for the sixth day, would have the same effect in determining the order of the appointments?

   (A) The telephone appointment must be scheduled for an earlier day than the gas appointment or the satellite appointment, or both.
   (B) The telephone appointment must be scheduled for the day immediately before either the gas appointment or the satellite appointment.
   (C) The telephone appointment must be scheduled for an earlier day than the landscaping appointment.
   (D) If the telephone appointment is not scheduled for the first day, it must be scheduled for the day immediately before the gas appointment.
   (E) Either the gas appointment or the satellite appointment must be scheduled for the sixth day.

GO ON TO THE NEXT PAGE.

Questions 7–13

An artisan has been hired to create three stained glass windows. The artisan will use exactly five colors of glass: green, orange, purple, rose, and yellow. Each color of glass will be used at least once, and each window will contain at least two different colors of glass. The windows must also conform to the following conditions:

Exactly one of the windows contains both green glass and purple glass.

Exactly two of the windows contain rose glass.

If a window contains yellow glass, then that window contains neither green glass nor orange glass.

If a window does not contain purple glass, then that window contains orange glass.

7. Which one of the following could be the color combinations of the glass in the three windows?

(A)   window 1: green, purple, rose, and orange
       window 2: rose and yellow
       window 3: green and orange

(B)   window 1: green, purple, and rose
       window 2: green, rose, and orange
       window 3: purple and yellow

(C)   window 1: green, purple, and rose
       window 2: green, purple, and orange
       window 3: purple, rose, and yellow

(D)   window 1: green, purple, and orange
       window 2: rose, orange, and yellow
       window 3: purple and rose

(E)   window 1: green, purple, and orange
       window 2: purple, rose, and yellow
       window 3: purple and orange

GO ON TO THE NEXT PAGE.

8. Which one of the following CANNOT be the complete color combination of the glass in one of the windows?

   (A) green and orange
   (B) green and purple
   (C) green and rose
   (D) purple and orange
   (E) rose and orange

9. If two of the windows are made with exactly two colors of glass each, then the complete color combination of the glass in one of those windows could be

   (A) rose and yellow
   (B) orange and rose
   (C) orange and purple
   (D) green and rose
   (E) green and orange

10. If the complete color combination of the glass in one of the windows is purple, rose, and orange, then the complete color combination of the glass in one of the other windows could be

   (A) green, orange, and rose
   (B) green, orange, and purple
   (C) orange and rose
   (D) orange and purple
   (E) green and orange

11. If orange glass is used in more of the windows than green glass, then the complete color combination of the glass in one of the windows could be

   (A) orange and purple
   (B) green, purple, and rose
   (C) green and purple
   (D) green and orange
   (E) green, orange, and rose

12. Which one of the following could be used in all three windows?

   (A) green glass
   (B) orange glass
   (C) purple glass
   (D) rose glass
   (E) yellow glass

13. If none of the windows contains both rose glass and orange glass, then the complete color combination of the glass in one of the windows must be

   (A) green and purple
   (B) green, purple, and orange
   (C) green and orange
   (D) purple and orange
   (E) purple, rose, and yellow

GO ON TO THE NEXT PAGE.

Questions 14–18

A conference on management skills consists of exactly five talks, which are held successively in the following order: Feedback, Goal Sharing, Handling People, Information Overload, and Leadership. Exactly four employees of SoftCorp—Quigley, Rivera, Spivey, and Tran—each attend exactly two of the talks. No talk is attended by more than two of the employees, who attend the talks in accordance with the following conditions:

Quigley attends neither Feedback nor Handling People.
Rivera attends neither Goal Sharing nor Handling People.
Spivey does not attend either of the talks that Tran attends.
Quigley attends the first talk Tran attends.
Spivey attends the first talk Rivera attends.

14. Which one of the following could be a complete and accurate matching of the talks to the SoftCorp employees who attend them?

(A)   Feedback: Rivera, Spivey
Goal Sharing: Quigley, Tran
Handling People: None
Information Overload: Quigley, Rivera
Leadership: Spivey, Tran

(B)   Feedback: Rivera, Spivey
Goal Sharing: Quigley, Tran
Handling People: Rivera, Tran
Information Overload: Quigley
Leadership: Spivey

(C)   Feedback: Rivera, Spivey
Goal Sharing: Quigley, Tran
Handling People: Tran
Information Overload: Quigley, Rivera
Leadership: Spivey

(D)   Feedback: Rivera, Spivey
Goal Sharing: Tran
Handling People: Tran
Information Overload: Quigley, Rivera
Leadership: Quigley, Spivey

(E)   Feedback: Spivey
Goal Sharing: Quigley, Tran
Handling People: Spivey
Information Overload: Quigley, Rivera
Leadership: Rivera, Tran

GO ON TO THE NEXT PAGE.

15. If none of the SoftCorp employees attends Handling People, then which one of the following must be true?

    (A) Rivera attends Feedback.
    (B) Rivera attends Leadership.
    (C) Spivey attends Information Overload.
    (D) Tran attends Goal Sharing.
    (E) Tran attends Information Overload.

16. Which one of the following is a complete and accurate list of the talks any one of which Rivera and Spivey could attend together?

    (A) Feedback, Information Overload, Leadership
    (B) Feedback, Goal Sharing, Information Overload
    (C) Information Overload, Leadership
    (D) Feedback, Leadership
    (E) Feedback, Information Overload

17. If Quigley is the only SoftCorp employee to attend Leadership, then which one of the following could be false?

    (A) Rivera attends Feedback.
    (B) Rivera attends Information Overload.
    (C) Spivey attends Feedback.
    (D) Spivey attends Handling People.
    (E) Tran attends Goal Sharing.

18. If Rivera is the only SoftCorp employee to attend Information Overload, then which one of the following could be false?

    (A) Quigley attends Leadership.
    (B) Rivera attends Feedback.
    (C) Spivey attends Feedback.
    (D) Tran attends Goal Sharing.
    (E) Tran attends Handling People.

GO ON TO THE NEXT PAGE.

Questions 19–23

Exactly six witnesses will testify in a trial: Mangione, Ramirez, Sanderson, Tannenbaum, Ujemori, and Wong. The witnesses will testify one by one, and each only once. The order in which the witnesses testify is subject to the following constraints:

    Sanderson must testify immediately before either Tannenbaum or Ujemori.

    Ujemori must testify earlier than both Ramirez and Wong.

    Either Tannenbaum or Wong must testify immediately before Mangione.

19. Which one of the following lists the witnesses in an order in which they could testify?

(A) Ramirez, Sanderson, Tannenbaum, Mangione, Ujemori, Wong

(B) Sanderson, Tannenbaum, Ujemori, Ramirez, Wong, Mangione

(C) Sanderson, Ujemori, Tannenbaum, Wong, Ramirez, Mangione

(D) Tannenbaum, Mangione, Ujemori, Sanderson, Ramirez, Wong

(E) Wong, Ramirez, Sanderson, Tannenbaum, Mangione, Ujemori

GO ON TO THE NEXT PAGE.

20. If Tannenbaum testifies first, then which one of the following could be true?

    (A) Ramirez testifies second.
    (B) Wong testifies third.
    (C) Sanderson testifies fourth.
    (D) Ujemori testifies fifth.
    (E) Mangione testifies sixth.

21. If Sanderson testifies fifth, then Ujemori must testify

    (A) first
    (B) second
    (C) third
    (D) fourth
    (E) sixth

22. Which one of the following pairs of witnesses CANNOT testify third and fourth, respectively?

    (A) Mangione, Tannenbaum
    (B) Ramirez, Sanderson
    (C) Sanderson, Ujemori
    (D) Tannenbaum, Ramirez
    (E) Ujemori, Wong

23. Which one of the following pairs of witnesses CANNOT testify first and second, respectively?

    (A) Sanderson, Ujemori
    (B) Tannenbaum, Mangione
    (C) Tannenbaum, Sanderson
    (D) Ujemori, Tannenbaum
    (E) Ujemori, Wong

S T O P

IF YOU FINISH BEFORE TIME IS CALLED, YOU MAY CHECK YOUR WORK ON THIS SECTION ONLY.
DO NOT WORK ON ANY OTHER SECTION IN THE TEST.

SECTION IV
Time—35 minutes

26 Questions

Directions: The questions in this section are based on the reasoning contained in brief statements or passages. For some questions, more than one of the choices could conceivably answer the question. However, you are to choose the best answer; that is, the response that most accurately and completely answers the question. You should not make assumptions that are by commonsense standards implausible, superfluous, or incompatible with the passage. After you have chosen the best answer, blacken the corresponding space on your answer sheet.

1. Marine biologist: Scientists have long wondered why the fish that live around coral reefs exhibit such brilliant colors. One suggestion is that coral reefs are colorful and, therefore, that colorful fish are camouflaged by them. Many animal species, after all, use camouflage to avoid predators. However, as regards the populations around reefs, this suggestion is mistaken. A reef stripped of its fish is quite monochromatic. Most corals, it turns out, are relatively dull browns and greens.

Which one of the following most accurately expresses the main conclusion drawn in the marine biologist's argument?

(A) One hypothesis about why fish living near coral reefs exhibit such bright colors is that the fish are camouflaged by their bright colors.

(B) The fact that many species use camouflage to avoid predators is one reason to believe that brightly colored fish living near reefs do too.

(C) The suggestion that the fish living around coral reefs exhibit bright colors because they are camouflaged by the reefs is mistaken.

(D) A reef stripped of its fish is relatively monochromatic.

(E) It turns out that the corals in a coral reef are mostly dull hues of brown and green.

2. To discover what percentage of teenagers believe in telekinesis—the psychic ability to move objects without physically touching them—a recent survey asked a representative sample of teenagers whether they agreed with the following statement: "A person's thoughts can influence the movement of physical objects." But because this statement is particularly ambiguous and is amenable to a naturalistic, uncontroversial interpretation, the survey's responses are also ambiguous.

The reasoning above conforms most closely to which one of the following general propositions?

(A) Uncontroversial statements are useless in surveys.

(B) Every statement is amenable to several interpretations.

(C) Responses to surveys are always unambiguous if the survey's questions are well phrased.

(D) Responses people give to poorly phrased questions are likely to be ambiguous.

(E) Statements about psychic phenomena can always be given naturalistic interpretations.

GO ON TO THE NEXT PAGE.

3. A recent study of perfect pitch—the ability to identify the pitch of an isolated musical note—found that a high percentage of people who have perfect pitch are related to someone else who has it. Among those without perfect pitch, the percentage was much lower. This shows that having perfect pitch is a consequence of genetic factors.

Which one of the following, if true, most strengthens the argument?

(A) People who have relatives with perfect pitch generally receive no more musical training than do others.

(B) All of the researchers conducting the study had perfect pitch.

(C) People with perfect pitch are more likely than others to choose music as a career.

(D) People with perfect pitch are more likely than others to make sure that their children receive musical training.

(E) People who have some training in music are more likely to have perfect pitch than those with no such training.

4. Paleontologists recently excavated two corresponding sets of dinosaur tracks, one left by a large grazing dinosaur and the other by a smaller predatory dinosaur. The two sets of tracks make abrupt turns repeatedly in tandem, suggesting that the predator was following the grazing dinosaur and had matched its stride. Modern predatory mammals, such as lions, usually match the stride of prey they are chasing immediately before they strike those prey. This suggests that the predatory dinosaur was chasing the grazing dinosaur and attacked immediately afterwards.

Which one of the following most accurately describes the role played in the argument by the statement that the predatory dinosaur was following the grazing dinosaur and had matched its stride?

(A) It helps establish the scientific importance of the argument's overall conclusion, but is not offered as evidence for that conclusion.

(B) It is a hypothesis that is rejected in favor of the hypothesis stated in the argument's overall conclusion.

(C) It provides the basis for an analogy used in support of the argument's overall conclusion.

(D) It is presented to counteract a possible objection to the argument's overall conclusion.

(E) It is the overall conclusion of the argument.

5. Researchers announced recently that over the past 25 years the incidence of skin cancer caused by exposure to harmful rays from the sun has continued to grow in spite of the increasingly widespread use of sunscreens. This shows that using sunscreen is unlikely to reduce a person's risk of developing such skin cancer.

Which one of the following, if true, most weakens the argument?

(A) Most people who purchase a sunscreen product will not purchase the most expensive brand available.

(B) Skin cancer generally develops among the very old as a result of sunburns experienced when very young.

(C) The development of sunscreens by pharmaceutical companies was based upon research conducted by dermatologists.

(D) People who know that they are especially susceptible to skin cancer are generally disinclined to spend a large amount of time in the sun.

(E) Those who use sunscreens most regularly are people who believe themselves to be most susceptible to skin cancer.

6. University administrator: Any proposal for a new department will not be funded if there are fewer than 50 people per year available for hire in that field and the proposed department would duplicate more than 25 percent of the material covered in one of our existing departments. The proposed Area Studies Department will duplicate more than 25 percent of the material covered in our existing Anthropology Department. However, we will fund the new department.

Which one of the following statements follows logically from the university administrator's statements?

(A) The field of Area Studies has at least 50 people per year available for hire.

(B) The proposed Area Studies Department would not duplicate more than 25 percent of the material covered in any existing department other than Anthropology.

(C) If the proposed Area Studies Department did not duplicate more than 25 percent of the material covered in Anthropology, then the new department would not be funded.

(D) The Anthropology Department duplicates more than 25 percent of the material covered in the proposed Area Studies Department.

(E) The field of Area Studies has fewer than 50 people per year available for hire.

GO ON TO THE NEXT PAGE.

7. Researcher: Over the course of three decades, we kept records of the average beak size of two populations of the same species of bird, one wild population, the other captive. During this period, the average beak size of the captive birds did not change, while the average beak size of the wild birds decreased significantly.

Which one of the following, if true, most helps to explain the researcher's findings?

(A) The small-beaked wild birds were easier to capture and measure than the large-beaked wild birds.

(B) The large-beaked wild birds were easier to capture and measure than the small-beaked wild birds.

(C) Changes in the wild birds' food supply during the study period favored the survival of small-beaked birds over large-beaked birds.

(D) The average body size of the captive birds remained the same over the study period.

(E) The researcher measured the beaks of some of the wild birds on more than one occasion.

8. Storytelling appears to be a universal aspect of both past and present cultures. Comparative study of traditional narratives from widely separated epochs and diverse cultures reveals common themes such as creation, tribal origin, mystical beings and quasi-historical figures, and common story types such as fables and tales in which animals assume human personalities.

The evidence cited above from the study of traditional narratives most supports which one of the following statements?

(A) Storytellers routinely borrow themes from other cultures.

(B) Storytellers have long understood that the narrative is a universal aspect of human culture.

(C) Certain human concerns and interests arise in all of the world's cultures.

(D) Storytelling was no less important in ancient cultures than it is in modern cultures.

(E) The best way to understand a culture is to understand what motivates its storytellers.

9. If a mother's first child is born before its due date, it is likely that her second child will be also. Jackie's second child was not born before its due date, so it is likely that Jackie's first child was not born before its due date either.

The questionable reasoning in the argument above is most similar in its reasoning to which one of the following?

(A) Artisans who finish their projects before the craft fair will probably go to the craft fair. Ben will not finish his project before the fair. So he probably will not go to the craft fair.

(B) All responsible pet owners are likely to be good with children. So anyone who is good with children is probably a responsible pet owner.

(C) If a movie is a box-office hit, it is likely that its sequel will be also. *Hawkman II*, the sequel to *Hawkman I*, was not a box-office hit, so *Hawkman I* was probably not a box-office hit.

(D) If a business is likely to fail, people will not invest in it. Pallid Starr is likely to fail, therefore no one is likely to invest in it.

(E) Tai will go sailing only if the weather is nice. The weather will be nice, thus Tai will probably go sailing.

10. Science journalist: Europa, a moon of Jupiter, is covered with ice. Data recently transmitted by a spacecraft strongly suggest that there are oceans of liquid water deep under the ice. Life as we know it could evolve only in the presence of liquid water. Hence, it is likely that at least primitive life has evolved on Europa.

The science journalist's argument is most vulnerable to criticism on the grounds that it

(A) takes for granted that if a condition would be necessary for the evolution of life as we know it, then such life could not have evolved anywhere that this condition does not hold

(B) fails to address adequately the possibility that there are conditions necessary for the evolution of life in addition to the presence of liquid water

(C) takes for granted that life is likely to be present on Europa if, but only if, life evolved on Europa

(D) overlooks the possibility that there could be unfamiliar forms of life that have evolved without the presence of liquid water

(E) takes for granted that no conditions on Europa other than the supposed presence of liquid water could have accounted for the data transmitted by the spacecraft

GO ON TO THE NEXT PAGE.

11. A bacterial species will inevitably develop greater resistance within a few years to any antibiotics used against it, unless those antibiotics eliminate that species completely. However, no single antibiotic now on the market is powerful enough to eliminate bacterial species X completely.

Which one of the following is most strongly supported by the statements above?

(A) It is unlikely that any antibiotic can be developed that will completely eliminate bacterial species X.

(B) If any antibiotic now on the market is used against bacterial species X, that species will develop greater resistance to it within a few years.

(C) The only way of completely eliminating bacterial species X is by a combination of two or more antibiotics now on the market.

(D) Bacterial species X will inevitably become more virulent in the course of time.

(E) Bacterial species X is more resistant to at least some antibiotics that have been used against it than it was before those antibiotics were used against it.

12. Political scientist: It is not uncommon for a politician to criticize his or her political opponents by claiming that their exposition of their ideas is muddled and incomprehensible. Such criticism, however, is never sincere. Political agendas promoted in a manner that cannot be understood by large numbers of people will not be realized for, as every politician knows, political mobilization requires commonality of purpose.

Which one of the following is the most accurate rendering of the political scientist's main conclusion?

(A) People who promote political agendas in an incomprehensible manner should be regarded as insincere.

(B) Sincere critics of the proponents of a political agenda should not focus their criticisms on the manner in which that agenda is promoted.

(C) The ineffectiveness of a confusingly promoted political agenda is a reason for refraining from, rather than engaging in, criticism of those who are promoting it.

(D) A politician criticizing his or her political opponents for presenting their political agendas in an incomprehensible manner is being insincere.

(E) To mobilize large numbers of people in support of a political agenda, that political agenda must be presented in such a way that it cannot be misunderstood.

13. Many symptoms of mental illnesses are affected by organic factors such as a deficiency in a compound in the brain. What is surprising, however, is the tremendous variation among different countries in the incidence of these symptoms in people with mental illnesses. This variation establishes that the organic factors that affect symptoms of mental illnesses are not distributed evenly around the globe.

The reasoning above is most vulnerable to criticism on the grounds that it

(A) does not say how many different mental illnesses are being discussed

(B) neglects the possibility that nutritional factors that contribute to deficiencies in compounds in the brain vary from culture to culture

(C) fails to consider the possibility that cultural factors significantly affect how mental illnesses manifest themselves in symptoms

(D) presumes, without providing justification, that any change in brain chemistry manifests itself as a change in mental condition

(E) presumes, without providing justification, that mental phenomena are only manifestations of physical phenomena

14. Politician: It has been proposed that the national parks in our country be managed by private companies rather than the government. A similar privatization of the telecommunications industry has benefited consumers by allowing competition among a variety of telephone companies to improve service and force down prices. Therefore, the privatization of the national parks would probably benefit park visitors as well.

Which one of the following, if true, most weakens the politician's argument?

(A) It would not be politically expedient to privatize the national parks even if doing so would, in the long run, improve service and reduce the fees charged to visitors.

(B) The privatization of the telecommunications industry has been problematic in that it has led to significantly increased unemployment and economic instability in that industry.

(C) The vast majority of people visiting the national parks are unaware of proposals to privatize the management of those parks.

(D) Privatizing the national parks would benefit a much smaller number of consumers to a much smaller extent than did the privatization of the telecommunications industry.

(E) The privatization of the national parks would produce much less competition between different companies than did the privatization of the telecommunications industry.

GO ON TO THE NEXT PAGE.

15. Jewel collectors, fearing that their eyes will be deceived by a counterfeit, will not buy a diamond unless the dealer guarantees that it is genuine. But why should a counterfeit give any less aesthetic pleasure when the naked eye cannot distinguish it from a real diamond? Both jewels should be deemed of equal value.

Which one of the following principles, if valid, most helps to justify the reasoning in the argument above?

(A) Jewel collectors should collect only those jewels that provide the most aesthetic pleasure.

(B) The value of a jewel should depend at least partly on market demand.

(C) It should not be assumed that everyone who likes diamonds receives the same degree of aesthetic pleasure from them.

(D) The value of a jewel should derive solely from the aesthetic pleasure it provides.

(E) Jewel collectors should not buy counterfeit jewels unless they are unable to distinguish counterfeit jewels from real ones.

16. All etching tools are either pin-tipped or bladed. While some bladed etching tools are used for engraving, some are not. On the other hand, all pin-tipped etching tools are used for engraving. Thus, there are more etching tools that are used for engraving than there are etching tools that are not used for engraving.

The conclusion of the argument follows logically if which one of the following is assumed?

(A) All tools used for engraving are etching tools as well.

(B) There are as many pin-tipped etching tools as there are bladed etching tools.

(C) No etching tool is both pin-tipped and bladed.

(D) The majority of bladed etching tools are not used for engraving.

(E) All etching tools that are not used for engraving are bladed.

17. A 24-year study of 1,500 adults showed that those subjects with a high intake of foods rich in beta-carotene were much less likely to die from cancer or heart disease than were those with a low intake of such foods. On the other hand, taking beta-carotene supplements for 12 years had no positive or negative effect on the health of subjects in a separate study of 20,000 adults.

Each of the following, if true, would help to resolve the apparent discrepancy between the results of the two studies EXCEPT:

(A) The human body processes the beta-carotene present in foods much more efficiently than it does beta-carotene supplements.

(B) Beta-carotene must be taken for longer than 12 years to have any cancer-preventive effects.

(C) Foods rich in beta-carotene also tend to contain other nutrients that assist in the human body's absorption of beta-carotene.

(D) In the 12-year study, half of the subjects were given beta-carotene supplements and half were given a placebo.

(E) In the 24-year study, the percentage of the subjects who had a high intake of beta-carotene-rich foods who smoked cigarettes was much smaller than the percentage of the subjects with a low intake of beta-carotene-rich foods who smoked.

GO ON TO THE NEXT PAGE.

18. If there are sentient beings on planets outside our solar system, we will not be able to determine this anytime in the near future unless some of these beings are at least as intelligent as humans. We will not be able to send spacecraft to planets outside our solar system anytime in the near future, and any sentient being on another planet capable of communicating with us anytime in the near future would have to be at least as intelligent as we are.

The argument's conclusion can be properly inferred if which one of the following is assumed?

(A) There are no sentient beings on planets in our solar system other than those on Earth.

(B) Any beings that are at least as intelligent as humans would want to communicate with sentient beings outside their own solar systems.

(C) If there is a sentient being on another planet that is as intelligent as humans are, we will not be able to send spacecraft to the being's planet anytime in the near future.

(D) If a sentient being on another planet cannot communicate with us, then the only way to detect its existence is by sending a spacecraft to its planet.

(E) Any sentient beings on planets outside our solar system that are at least as intelligent as humans would be capable of communicating with us.

19. Doctor: Medical researchers recently examined a large group of individuals who said that they had never experienced serious back pain. Half of the members of the group turned out to have bulging or slipped disks in their spines, conditions often blamed for serious back pain. Since these individuals with bulging or slipped disks evidently felt no pain from them, these conditions could not lead to serious back pain in people who do experience such pain.

The reasoning in the doctor's argument is most vulnerable to the criticism that it fails to consider which one of the following possibilities?

(A) A factor that need not be present in order for a certain effect to arise may nonetheless be sufficient to produce that effect.

(B) A factor that is not in itself sufficient to produce a certain effect may nonetheless be partly responsible for that effect in some instances.

(C) An effect that occurs in the absence of a particular phenomenon might not occur when that phenomenon is present.

(D) A characteristic found in half of a given sample of the population might not occur in half of the entire population.

(E) A factor that does not bring about a certain effect may nonetheless be more likely to be present when the effect occurs than when the effect does not occur.

20. Many workers who handled substance T in factories became seriously ill years later. We now know T caused at least some of their illnesses. Earlier ignorance of this connection does not absolve T's manufacturer of all responsibility. For had it investigated the safety of T before allowing workers to be exposed to it, many of their illnesses would have been prevented.

Which one of the following principles most helps to justify the conclusion above?

(A) Employees who are harmed by substances they handle on the job should be compensated for medical costs they incur as a result.

(B) Manufacturers should be held responsible only for the preventable consequences of their actions.

(C) Manufacturers have an obligation to inform workers of health risks of which they are aware.

(D) Whether or not an action's consequences were preventable is irrelevant to whether a manufacturer should be held responsible for those consequences.

(E) Manufacturers should be held responsible for the consequences of any of their actions that harm innocent people if those consequences were preventable.

21. It is virtually certain that the government contract for building the new highway will be awarded to either Phoenix Contracting or Cartwright Company. I have just learned that the government has decided not to award the contract to Cartwright Company. It is therefore almost inevitable that Phoenix Contracting will be awarded the contract.

The argument proceeds by

(A) concluding that it is extremely likely that an event will occur by ruling out the only probable alternative

(B) inferring, from a claim that one of two possible events will occur, that the other event will not occur

(C) refuting a claim that a particular event is inevitable by establishing the possibility of an alternative event

(D) predicting a future event on the basis of an established pattern of past events

(E) inferring a claim about the probability of a particular event from a general statistical statement

GO ON TO THE NEXT PAGE.

22. Researchers have found that children in large families—particularly the younger siblings—generally have fewer allergies than children in small families do. They hypothesize that exposure to germs during infancy makes people less likely to develop allergies.

Which one of the following, if true, most supports the researchers' hypothesis?

(A) In countries where the average number of children per family has decreased over the last century, the incidence of allergies has increased.

(B) Children in small families generally eat more kinds of very allergenic foods than children in large families do.

(C) Some allergies are life threatening, while many diseases caused by germs produce only temporary discomfort.

(D) Children whose parents have allergies have an above-average likelihood of developing allergies themselves.

(E) Children from small families who entered day care before age one were less likely to develop allergies than children from small families who entered day care later.

23. Film preservation requires transferring old movies from their original material—unstable, deteriorating nitrate film—to stable acetate film. But this is a time-consuming, expensive process, and there is no way to transfer all currently deteriorating nitrate films to acetate before they disintegrate. So some films from the earliest years of Hollywood will not be preserved.

Which one of the following is an assumption on which the argument depends?

(A) No new technology for transferring old movies from nitrate film to acetate film will ever be developed.

(B) Transferring films from nitrate to acetate is not the least expensive way of preserving them.

(C) Not many films from the earliest years of Hollywood have already been transferred to acetate.

(D) Some films from the earliest years of Hollywood currently exist solely in their original material.

(E) The least popular films from the earliest years of Hollywood are the ones most likely to be lost.

24. In a recent study of arthritis, researchers tried but failed to find any correlation between pain intensity and any of those features of the weather—humidity, temperature swings, barometric pressure—usually cited by arthritis sufferers as the cause of their increased pain. Those arthritis sufferers in the study who were convinced of the existence of such a correlation gave widely varying accounts of the time delay between the occurrence of what they believed to be the relevant feature of the weather and the increased intensity of the pain. Thus, this study _____.

Of the following, which one most logically completes the argument?

(A) indicates that the weather affects some arthritis sufferers more quickly than it does other arthritis sufferers

(B) indicates that arthritis sufferers' beliefs about the causes of the pain they feel may affect their assessment of the intensity of that pain

(C) suggests that arthritis sufferers are imagining the correlation they assert to exist

(D) suggests that some people are more susceptible to weather-induced arthritis pain than are others

(E) suggests that the scientific investigation of possible links between weather and arthritis pain is impossible

GO ON TO THE NEXT PAGE.

25. Cities with healthy economies typically have plenty of job openings. Cities with high-technology businesses also tend to have healthy economies, so those in search of jobs should move to a city with high-technology businesses.

The reasoning in which one of the following is most similar to the reasoning in the argument above?

(A) Older antiques are usually the most valuable. Antique dealers generally authenticate the age of the antiques they sell, so those collectors who want the most valuable antiques should purchase their antiques from antique dealers.

(B) Antique dealers who authenticate the age of the antiques they sell typically have plenty of antiques for sale. Since the most valuable antiques are those that have had their ages authenticated, antique collectors in search of valuable antiques should purchase their antiques from antique dealers.

(C) Antiques that have had their ages authenticated tend to be valuable. Since antique dealers generally carry antiques that have had their ages authenticated, those collectors who want antiques that are valuable should purchase their antiques from antique dealers.

(D) Many antique collectors know that antique dealers can authenticate the age of the antiques they sell. Since antiques that have had their ages authenticated are always the most valuable, most antique collectors who want antiques that are valuable tend to purchase their antiques from antique dealers.

(E) Many antiques increase in value once they have had their ages authenticated by antique dealers. Since antique dealers tend to have plenty of valuable antiques, antique collectors who prefer to purchase the most valuable antiques should purchase antiques from antique dealers.

26. Sociologist: A recent study of 5,000 individuals found, on the basis of a physical exam, that more than 25 percent of people older than 65 were malnourished, though only 12 percent of the people in this age group fell below government poverty standards. In contrast, a greater percentage of the people 65 or younger fell below poverty standards than were found in the study to be malnourished.

Each of the following, if true, helps to explain the findings of the study cited by the sociologist EXCEPT:

(A) Doctors are less likely to correctly diagnose and treat malnutrition in their patients who are over 65 than in their younger patients.

(B) People over 65 are more likely to take medications that increase their need for certain nutrients than are people 65 or younger.

(C) People over 65 are more likely to suffer from loss of appetite due to medication than are people 65 or younger.

(D) People 65 or younger are no more likely to fall below government poverty standards than are people over 65.

(E) People 65 or younger are less likely to have medical conditions that interfere with their digestion than are people over 65.

S T O P

IF YOU FINISH BEFORE TIME IS CALLED, YOU MAY CHECK YOUR WORK ON THIS SECTION ONLY.
DO NOT WORK ON ANY OTHER SECTION IN THE TEST.

Wait for the supervisor's instructions before you open the page to the topic.
Please print and sign your name and write the date in the designated spaces below.

Time: 35 Minutes

General Directions

You will have 35 minutes in which to plan and write an essay on the topic inside. Read the topic and the accompanying directions carefully. You will probably find it best to spend a few minutes considering the topic and organizing your thoughts before you begin writing. In your essay, be sure to develop your ideas fully, leaving time, if possible, to review what you have written. **Do not write on a topic other than the one specified. Writing on a topic of your own choice is not acceptable.**

No special knowledge is required or expected for this writing exercise. Law schools are interested in the reasoning, clarity, organization, language usage, and writing mechanics displayed in your essay. How well you write is more important than how much you write.

Confine your essay to the blocked, lined area on the front and back of the separate Writing Sample Response Sheet. Only that area will be reproduced for law schools. Be sure that your writing is legible.

Both this topic sheet and your response sheet must be turned over to the testing staff before you leave the room.

Topic Code	Print Your Full Name Here		
095316	Last	First	M.I.
Date	Sign Your Name Here		
/ /			

Scratch Paper
Do not write your essay in this space.

LSAT® Writing Sample Topic

Directions: The scenario presented below describes two choices, either one of which can be supported on the basis of the information given. Your essay should consider both choices and argue for one over the other, based on the two specified criteria and the facts provided. There is no "right" or "wrong" choice: a reasonable argument can be made for either.

The Wangs must arrange summer child care for their ten-year-old child. They have found two summer-long programs that are affordable and in which friends of their child would also be participating. Using the facts below, write an essay in which you argue for one program over the other based on the following two considerations:

- The Wangs want their child to enjoy activities that would add variety to the regular school experience.
- Transportation to the program must be easy for the Wangs to accommodate to their work situations.

City Summer is located at a college near Mrs. Wang's job but a considerable distance from Mr. Wang's. It offers early arrival and late pick-up times for parent convenience. Mrs. Wang has somewhat flexible work hours, but must travel overnight occasionally. City Summer offers classes in the visual arts, dance, drama, music, swimming, and gymnastics, as well as gym activities like basketball and volleyball. In addition, there are organized field trips to museums, plays, and historical sites. The program concludes with a presentation of student work from the classes.

Round Lake Camp is located 30 minutes outside the city. Bus transportation is provided to and from several city schools, one of which is next door to Mr. Wang's job. Pick-up and drop-off are at set times in the early morning and late afternoon. Mr. Wang has flexibility in his work starting time but often must work late. The camp has classes in swimming, sailing, archery, nature study, crafts, and outdoor skills. It also has regular free periods when campers can choose among outdoor activities or just explore the woods. At the end of the summer the campers have an overnight camping trip at a nearby state wilderness area.

WP-R095A

Writing Sample Response Sheet

DO NOT WRITE IN THIS SPACE

**Begin your essay in the lined area below.
Continue on the back if you need more space.**

COMPUTING YOUR SCORE

Directions:

1. Use the Answer Key on the next page to check your answers.

2. Use the Scoring Worksheet below to compute your raw score.

3. Use the Score Conversion Chart to convert your raw score into the 120–180 scale.

Scoring Worksheet

1. Enter the number of questions you answered correctly in each section.

	Number Correct
Section I	_____
Section II	_____
Section III	_____
Section IV	_____

2. Enter the sum here: _____
   This is your Raw Score.

Conversion Chart
For Converting Raw Score to the 120–180 LSAT Scaled Score
LSAT Form 0LSN85

Reported Score	Raw Score	
	Lowest	Highest
180	99	102
179	98	98
178	97	97
177	96	96
176	95	95
175	94	94
174	93	93
173	91	92
172	90	90
171	89	89
170	88	88
169	86	87
168	85	85
167	83	84
166	82	82
165	80	81
164	79	79
163	77	78
162	75	76
161	74	74
160	72	73
159	70	71
158	69	69
157	67	68
156	65	66
155	63	64
154	62	62
153	60	61
152	58	59
151	57	57
150	55	56
149	53	54
148	52	52
147	50	51
146	48	49
145	47	47
144	45	46
143	43	44
142	42	42
141	40	41
140	39	39
139	37	38
138	36	36
137	35	35
136	33	34
135	32	32
134	30	31
133	29	29
132	28	28
131	27	27
130	25	26
129	24	24
128	23	23
127	22	22
126	21	21
125	20	20
124	18	19
123	17	17
122	16	16
121	15	15
120	0	14

ANSWER KEY

SECTION I

1. A	8. D	15. A	22. D
2. C	9. A	16. B	23. C
3. E	10. E	17. A	24. B
4. B	11. E	18. B	25. E
5. B	12. D	19. D	26. E
6. E	13. C	20. C	27. C
7. D	14. B	21. D	

SECTION II

1. D	8. A	15. B	22. D
2. E	9. C	16. E	23. C
3. B	10. B	17. A	24. E
4. E	11. A	18. D	25. A
5. C	12. E	19. D	26. E
6. A	13. D	20. C	
7. C	14. B	21. E	

SECTION III

1. D	8. C	15. A	22. A
2. D	9. B	16. A	23. D
3. E	10. B	17. D	
4. E	11. A	18. E	
5. B	12. C	19. B	
6. A	13. E	20. E	
7. B	14. C	21. A	

SECTION IV

1. C	8. C	15. D	22. E
2. D	9. C	16. B	23. D
3. A	10. B	17. D	24. C
4. C	11. B	18. D	25. C
5. B	12. D	19. B	26. D
6. A	13. C	20. E	
7. C	14. E	21. A	

Questions 1–8

Synopsis: The passage is about lichenometry, a newly developed technique for detecting and dating past earthquakes. The first paragraph describes radiocarbon dating, a more established procedure for dating earthquakes. Radiocarbon dating works by measuring the quantity of carbon 14 present in organic material in sediments along fault lines. Carbon 14 occurs naturally in organic materials and decays at a constant rate, so the amount of remaining carbon 14 indicates age.

The second paragraph describes lichenometry, which works by measuring the size of lichens growing on rocks in mountain ranges. Large earthquakes cause rockfalls that expose rock surfaces. Lichens quickly colonize those newly exposed rock surfaces and then grow at a constant rate. The size of the largest lichens thus reveals when the rock surfaces were exposed. If the surfaces of many rocks in a large geographic area were exposed simultaneously, this indicates that many rock falls occurred at the same time, which in turn reveals when a large earthquake last occurred.

The third paragraph describes advantages lichenometry has over radiocarbon dating. Radiocarbon dating is accurate to only within 40 years because of variation in the amount of carbon 14 found in the environment. Lichenometry, according to its inventors, is accurate to within 10 years. Lichenometry can achieve this accuracy only with careful selection of sites where the influence of factors that disturb or accelerate lichen growth can be minimized or taken into account.

Question 1

The Correct Answer:

A   The passage is primarily about lichenometry, which is a new method for dating earthquakes. The first part of the passage is concerned with explaining lichenometry and the older method that uses radiocarbon dating. The third paragraph is dedicated to discussing the advantages of lichenometry over radiocarbon dating. So (A) accurately expresses the main idea of the passage.

The Incorrect Answer Choices:

B   Lichenometry is asserted to be more accurate than radiocarbon dating. The passage does not compare lichenometry to any other method for dating earthquakes besides radiocarbon dating, nor does it imply that it is likely to be the most accurate method among other possible methods. So (B) cannot express the main idea of the passage.

C   The passage does not provide any indication that most seismologists have embraced lichenometry. It describes lichenometry as a "new method" and the first paragraph strongly suggests that radiocarbon dating is the usual method still employed by seismologists. Thus, (C) cannot express the main idea of the passage.

D   The passage says that lichenometry has distinct advantages over radiocarbon dating. However, the passage stops far short of describing the development of lichenometry as revolutionary. Additionally, the passage does not indicate that lichenometry is easily applied. The passage specifically states that lichenometry requires careful site selection and accurate calibration of lichen growth rates; there is no reason to think that this is particularly easy. So (D) does not express the main idea of the passage.

E   The passage does not indicate that radiocarbon dating is wholly unreliable or aim to show that it can now be abandoned. Rather, it explains that a new method, lichenometry, has come along that may have some advantages over radiocarbon dating for dating earthquakes up to 500 years old. There is no suggestion that radiocarbon dating is not still the best method for dating older earthquakes. So (E) cannot express the main idea of the passage.

- *Difficulty Level: 1*

Question 2

The Correct Answer:

C The last sentence of the passage says that "conditions like shade and wind that promote faster lichen growth must be factored in." So the passage provides an answer to the question stated in (C): shade and wind are some of the conditions that encourage lichens to grow at a more rapid rate than usual.

The Incorrect Answer Choices:

A The passage indicates that snow avalanches and other disturbances, as well as shade and wind, affect lichen growth. But the passage does not provide information that indicates how scientists measure lichen growth under these or any other conditions.

B The passage does not say anything about how scientists determine the intensity of the radiation striking Earth's upper atmosphere.

D The passage says that lichenometry is **best** used for earthquakes that occurred within the last 500 years. But this fact does not entail anything about the earliest earthquake that lichenometry has actually been used to identify. The earliest earthquake that has been identified with the method could be significantly younger or older than 500 years old. So the passage does not indicate even an approximate date of the earliest earthquake that lichenometry has been used to identify.

E The passage does not discuss any applications of radiocarbon dating other than its use in studying past earthquakes.

- *Difficulty Level: 3*

Question 3

The Correct Answer:

E A reader who initially had no idea of the timescale on which lichen growth occurs might expect lichens to grow by a sizable amount each year. Given that they can grow for as long as 1,000 years, in order to be useful to seismologists, lichens would have to grow at a fairly slow rate, covering only a portion of a rock each year. So there is a need for the passage to provide a sense of the sort of timescale on which lichen growth occurs. The lichen species used as an example is presented without qualification. It is not presented as a particularly slow- or fast-growing lichen, so it can provide a sense of the sort of timescale on which lichen growth typically occurs.

The Incorrect Answer Choices:

A In the preceding sentence the passage says that lichens "quickly colonize newly exposed rock surfaces," but the sentence goes on to reference their slow rate of growth. The reference to the growth rate of a North American lichen species in the next sentence is intended to emphasize how slowly they grow once established, not how fast they can establish themselves on rocks.

B The growth rate of a North American lichen species is presented in an unqualified way—it is not put forward as an example of a fast- or slow-growing lichen. So the author's purpose in referring to the rate of growth of the lichen species is not to offer an example of a lichen species with a particularly slow rate of growth.

C The part of the passage that refers to the rate of growth of a North American lichen species does not say anything about variations in lichens' rate of growth. So the author's purpose in referring to the rate of growth of the lichen species is not to present additional evidence that environmental conditions can alter lichens' rate of growth.

D The statement about the rate of growth of a North American lichen species does not help to explain why lichenometry works best for earthquakes that occurred in the last 500 years. The discussion of the best use of lichenometry occurs much later in the passage and there is no apparent connection between this discussion and the reference to the lichen species. Furthermore, the passage indicates that lichens can grow at a constant rate for up to 1,000 years. So there's no reason to think that mentioning that a lichen has a rate of growth of 9.5 millimeters per century would show that lichenometry is best used for earthquakes that occurred in the last 500 years.

- *Difficulty Level: 2*

Question 4

The Correct Answer:

B The first paragraph of the passage describes how seismologists use radiocarbon dating to date earthquakes. The method requires the collection of sediments from trenches that they dig along fault lines. If an earthquake had no identifiable fault line associated with it, then it is not likely that seismologists would be able to collect the materials necessary to use radiocarbon dating to date the earthquake—they would not know where to dig. Information in the passage thus strongly supports (B).

The Incorrect Answer Choices:

A The passage indicates in the first paragraph that radiocarbon dating "provides hints about the likelihood and location of future earthquakes," but does not explicitly address whether lichenometry can provide such hints. It cannot be inferred from the passage that lichenometry is less accurate than radiocarbon dating in providing these hints. Moreover, it is reasonable to suppose that radiocarbon dating provides these hints by virtue of the information it yields about the age and location of past earthquakes. Given that lichenometry provides the same kind of information, it is reasonable to think that it would provide information about future earthquakes at least as accurate as the information radiocarbon dating provides. (A) is thus not strongly supported by the passage.

C The passage only discusses radiocarbon dating and lichenometry, but this does not suggest that these are the only two viable methods for detecting and dating past earthquakes. The passage does not provide the basis for inferring anything about the relative viability of other methods as compared to radiocarbon dating and lichenometry.

D The last paragraph of the passage says that radiocarbon datings of events in the last 300 years may be of "little value," suggesting that it may be viable for dating older events, for example earthquakes 400 years ago. But it also says that lichenometry is best used for dating earthquakes within the last 500 years and gives no reason to think that lichenometry is inferior to radiocarbon for dating 400-year-old earthquakes.

E The last sentence of the passage says that using lichenometry requires that sites be selected "to minimize the influence of snow avalanches and other disturbances that would affect normal lichen growth" and sites where factors that promote faster lichen growth can be "factored in." This suggests that lichenometry would be most useful for dating earthquakes in geographic regions that have sites where these factors do not occur. But the passage does not suggest that lichenometry is useful **only** for such regions. On the contrary, in saying that the influence of disturbing factors should be "minimized" and that accelerating factors should be "factored in," the passage suggests that lichenometry can still be useful even where these factors occur.

- *Difficulty Level: 5*

Question 5

The Correct Answer:

B The first paragraph of the passage describes radiocarbon dating, which is an established procedure for dating earthquakes. The remaining paragraphs describe lichenometry, a new procedure, which is compared to radiocarbon dating. So the primary purpose of the first paragraph is to describe an established procedure to which a new procedure will then be compared.

The Incorrect Answer Choices:

A The first paragraph describes radiocarbon dating, which is a well-known procedure. However, the passage does not examine radiocarbon dating on a step-by-step basis. Rather, the focus in the remaining paragraphs is lichenometry.

C The first paragraph describes radiocarbon dating, which is an established procedure. The passage goes on to discuss lichenometry, a new method for dating earthquakes, but gives no indication that lichenometry has supplanted radiocarbon dating, rendering it outdated. Nor does the passage go on to describe specific situations in which radiocarbon dating would be useful.

D The first paragraph describes radiocarbon dating, which could be considered a traditional procedure. However, the passage does not compare radiocarbon dating to any other traditional procedure. Radiocarbon dating is contrasted with lichenometry, which is described as a "new method."

E The first paragraph says that radiocarbon dating is usually used. The passage goes on to suggest that radiocarbon dating may be less accurate than lichenometry for a certain range of cases, but it does not attempt to show that radiocarbon dating has led to any particular erroneous conclusions about a phenomenon.

- *Difficulty Level: 1*

Question 6

The Correct Answer:

E The statements made by Bull and Brandon and reported in the last two sentences of the passage are about requirements for using lichenometry properly. These include the requirement that "conditions like shade and wind that promote faster lichen growth must be factored in." It would make no sense to require that these conditions be factored in if it was impossible to factor them in. So Bull and Brandon must be assuming that the extent to which conditions like shade and wind have affected the growth of existing lichen colonies can be determined.

The Incorrect Answer Choices:

A The statements in question include the claim that lichenometry is best used to date earthquakes that occurred within the last 500 years. That may suggest that the method is less reliable for dating earthquakes that occurred earlier. This further claim does not depend on the assumption that lichenometry is nevertheless more accurate than other methods of dating such earthquakes.

B Claims about whether there is a reliable method for determining the intensity of the radiation now hitting Earth's upper atmosphere are irrelevant to the statements reported in the last two sentences of the passage. Those statements are about requirements for using lichenometry properly, and the amount of radiation hitting Earth's atmosphere does not figure into lichenometry.

C Neither the statements reported in the last two sentences of the passage nor anything else in the passage relies on the assumption that lichens are able to grow **only** on the types of rocks that are common in mountainous regions. As long as lichens can grow on rocks that are common in mountainous regions, it can be possible to date earthquakes by measuring lichen growth.

D The statements reported in the last two sentences of the passage do not rely on the assumption that the mountain ranges that produce the kinds of rockfalls studied in lichenometry are subject to **more frequent** snowfalls and avalanches than other mountain ranges are. Those statements need to assume only that the mountain ranges that produce the kinds of rockfalls studied in lichenometry may be subject to snowfalls and avalanches. As long as this is the case, it can be important to minimize the influence of avalanches when measuring lichen growth.

- *Difficulty Level: 3*

Question 7

The Correct Answer:

D In the third paragraph, the passage states, "Radiocarbon dating is accurate only to within plus or minus 40 years, because the amount of the carbon 14 isotope varies naturally in the environment." This variation is due to changes in the intensity of the radiation striking the upper atmosphere, and "this intensity has fluctuated greatly during the past 300 years, causing many radiocarbon datings of events during this period to be of little value." So the unreliability of radiocarbon dating is due to fluctuations in the amount of carbon 14 in the environment over time.

The Incorrect Answer Choices:

A The passage does not mention a multiplicity of different types of organic matter, and does not indicate what such a multiplicity would have to do with the unreliability of radiocarbon dating.

B The passage makes no mention of variation in the amount of organic materials caught in shifted sediments, so it does not indicate what such a variation would have to do with the unreliability of radiocarbon dating.

C The first paragraph of the passage indicates that the method of dating earthquakes using radiocarbon dating begins by digging trenches along visible fault lines. This suggests that some fault lines may not be visible and therefore that radiocarbon dating could not be used to date the earthquakes associated with those fault lines. This fact does not suggest, however, that radiocarbon dating itself is an unreliable method for dating earthquakes, just that there may be some cases in which it is difficult or impossible to use.

E The passage says that the intensity of radiation striking the upper atmosphere has fluctuated, and this has something to do with the unreliability of radiocarbon dating. However, the passage does not indicate that this unreliability is due to the possibility of times when no radiation has struck the upper atmosphere. The passage gives no indication that such a thing is possible.

- *Difficulty Level: 1*

Question 8

The Correct Answer:

D The passage says in the second paragraph that shortly after rocks become exposed by rockfalls, lichen begins growing on them. It is reasonable to think that the same thing would happen on rocks that have been exposed by receding glaciers. One could thus estimate how much time has passed since these rocks were first exposed by measuring the lichens. Using this estimate of time, one could obtain an estimate of the rate at which the glacier has been receding. Note also that the timescale on which lichen growth occurs seems to be appropriate for identifying the similarly slow rate at which glaciers recede.

The Incorrect Answer Choices:

A It is possible that the size of lichens near a river could indicate how long ago the most recent flood was, assuming that lichens are wiped out by floods. But it is not clear how lichenometry could be used to identify the number of times the river has flooded.

B The passage does not give us any reason to think that lichens would grow on a fossilized skeleton. Moreover, the skeleton would become fossilized only by being buried for a considerable time, so even if lichens did grow on it after it was exposed, lichenometry would not give an indication of the skeleton's age. Finally, these considerations aside, the passage suggests that lichenometry is best used for dating events that occurred within the last 500 years, so it is not likely that it would be useful for dating a fossilized skeleton that is many thousands of years old.

C The passage says that lichens grow on exposed rocks; there is no reason to think that lichens grow or survive underwater. So there is no reason to think that lichenometry could be used to identify the age of an ancient beach that is now underwater.

E If lichen growth rates vary with the amount of rainfall, then it may be possible to use the size of lichens to infer the rainfall rates in a valley. This would presumably require knowing independently how old the lichens are and inferring the rainfall rates from the difference in the expected size of the lichens, given their age, from their actual size. This cannot be described as a use of lichenometry, however. Lichenometry infers the age of an event that is correlated with the exposure of rocks (e.g., an earthquake) by measuring the size of lichens growing on the rocks and factoring in the influence of environmental conditions (including, possibly, rainfall) on lichen growth. In order to be factored in, these conditions must be known quantities, not inferred from the size of the lichens themselves. (E), therefore, does not describe a situation to which lichenometry would be applicable.

- *Difficulty Level: 3*

Questions 9–14

Synopsis: The first paragraph of the passage introduces the main topic of the passage—whether custom-made medical illustrations are legitimate as evidence in legal cases. The passage says that opponents of the use of custom-made medical illustrations in court argue that custom-made illustrations are typically unnecessary because illustrations from medical textbooks are adequate.

The second paragraph describes an additional objection: custom-made illustrations may misrepresent the facts in order to support one side in a case. This objection is dismissed because custom-made illustrations are not admissible as evidence unless a medical expert testifies to their accuracy.

The third paragraph considers a variation of the objection described in the second paragraph: even if custom-made illustrations are not technically inaccurate, they may nevertheless be misleading because of the subjective use of emphasis, coloration, or the like. This objection is also dismissed, on the grounds that professional illustrators strive for objective accuracy and deliberately avoid the use of devices that could have inflammatory potential. The passage goes on to point out that professional illustrators include only information that is relevant to the case. This point is used to introduce an advantage of custom-made illustrations over those from medical textbooks: custom-made illustrations can exclude irrelevant details that would be confusing to a judge or jury.

The final paragraph presents an additional benefit of custom-made illustrations: they provide a visual representation of information that would be difficult for most people to understand if presented only verbally.

Question 9

The Correct Answer:

A According to the passage, the role played by custom-made medical illustrations in personal injury cases is to assist juries or judges in their understanding of pertinent physical data in two ways. First, they provide simplified representations of physical data (for example, of the injuries themselves) that depict only those details that are relevant to a case (third paragraph). Second, they provide visual representations of data that, when used as an accompaniment to expert medical testimony, can facilitate a judge's or jury's understanding of material that might be very difficult to understand if presented only in verbal form (last paragraph).

Analogously, a schematic drawing that accompanies an engineer's oral presentation serves to assist the audience's understanding of the information presented in two ways. First, a schematic drawing provides a simplified representation of some physical system (for example, an electronic circuit) that omits details that are not relevant to information that the schematic is intended to convey. Second, a schematic drawing can facilitate the audience's understanding of material that would, in all probability, be difficult to understand if the engineer presented that material only in verbal form.

The Incorrect Answer Choices:

B Road maps are like custom-made medical illustrations in that they assist people via visual representation. However, (B) describes road maps as playing a role in which they replace, rather than accompany, verbal descriptions. Nor is there any indication that verbal instructions would be particularly difficult to understand. Thus, the role of road maps described in (B) is distinct from that played by custom-made medical illustrations.

C A custom-made medical illustration is a simplified representation designed to convey something that is already known (i.e., the nature of an injury) to a non-expert audience (the judge or jury). In contrast, a child's drawing that is used by a psychologist to detect wishes and anxieties that are not apparent in the child's behavior is, in effect, being used as a diagnostic device. It is not something intended to simplify known information in order to present it to a new audience; it is a picture created for some other purpose (fun, or creative expression, perhaps) that is then used to reach new conclusions about matters that were not previously known.

D One could perhaps argue that the role played by a reproduction of a famous painting in an art history textbook is to assist readers in their understanding of the original work. However, by definition, a reproduction attempts to include all the details of the original. So, unlike a custom-made medical illustration, a reproduction's role is not to facilitate understanding via a simplified representation.

E An artist's preliminary sketches are like custom-made medical illustrations in that they leave out details. However, the role played by an artist's preliminary sketches is different from that of custom-made medical illustrations. Custom-made illustrations leave out details in order to facilitate understanding of the physical data the illustrations are meant to represent, whereas an artist's preliminary sketches leave out details that have not yet been fully worked out.

- *Difficulty Level: 4*

Question 10

The Correct Answer:

E In describing custom-made illustrations, the passage says that "The more complex details often found in textbooks can be deleted so as not to confuse the issue" (third paragraph). As an example, the passage points out that whereas a textbook illustration might include depictions of veins and arteries, such details would be distracting in an illustration that is used to explain a bone fracture. So the author is likely to believe that textbook illustrations are in many cases more apt to confuse jurors than are custom-made medical illustrations.

The Incorrect Answer Choices:

A The passage says that custom-made illustrations sometimes eschew the use of color, but it does not suggest that textbook illustrations ever do. So it is likely the author believes that textbook illustrations tend to rely more, not less, on color.

B The passage says that custom-made illustrations are inadmissible unless a medical expert testifies to their accuracy. But the passage does not provide any reason to think that the author believes this requirement also applies to textbook illustrations.

C The passage does not say anything to suggest that the same people draw both textbook illustrations and custom-made ones. Even if this is independently plausible, we cannot conclude based on the passage that the author is likely to believe it.

D The passage does say that some lawyers believe that custom-made illustrations often misrepresent the facts in order to bolster a litigant's case. Moreover, it is reasonable to think that these same lawyers would believe that textbook illustrations are less prone to such misrepresentations. However, the fact that some lawyers believe this does not imply that most lawyers do. So we cannot conclude based on the passage that the author is likely to believe the statement in (D).

- *Difficulty Level: 2*

Question 11

The Correct Answer:

E The passage says in the second paragraph that if a lawyer tried to use custom-made medical illustrations that misrepresented the facts, "such illustrations would be inadmissible as evidence in the courtroom unless a medical expert were present to testify to their accuracy." So a role of medical experts is to provide opinions about the accuracy of custom-made illustrations.

The Incorrect Answer Choices:

A The passage says that medical experts provide testimony regarding the accuracy of custom-made illustrations. The passage does not, however, say that a role of medical experts is to decide which medical illustrations should be admissible as evidence. The passage states "such illustrations would be inadmissible as evidence in the courtroom unless a medical expert were present to testify to their accuracy." By putting the point this way, the author indicates that while medical experts testify as to the accuracy of medical illustrations, the responsibility for decisions regarding admissibility lies elsewhere (likely with judges).

B While the third paragraph suggests that professional illustrators may attempt to lessen the inflammatory impact of medical illustrations on judges and juries by avoiding devices that have inflammatory potential, there is nothing in the passage to suggest that it is a role of medical experts to temper the impact of custom-made illustrations on judges and jurors who are not medical professionals.

C The passage does not claim that a role of medical experts is to make medical illustrations understandable to judges and juries. In fact, the last paragraph of the passage says essentially the opposite: a role of medical illustrations is to help make the information provided by medical experts understandable to judges and jurors.

D The passage does not say anything about attorneys seeking or receiving opinions about the usefulness of illustrations from medical experts.

- *Difficulty Level: 4*

Question 12

The Correct Answer:

D In the third paragraph, the passage says that illustrations in medical textbooks "are designed to include the extensive detail required by medical students." In contrast, "custom-made medical illustrations are designed to include only the information that is relevant for those deciding a case." In other words, the passage claims that a difference between textbook illustrations and custom-made ones is that the textbook illustrations are very detailed whereas the custom-made illustrations include only details relevant to the case.

The Incorrect Answer Choices:

A The passage says that illustrators who produce custom-made medical illustrations strive for objective accuracy. But nothing in the passage suggests that those who produce illustrations for textbooks do not also produce accurate ones.

B The passage does say that custom-made illustrations sometimes eschew the use of color, but it provides no indication that custom-made illustrations **must** avoid color.

C As a response to the charge that custom-made medical illustrations are subjective in that they may subtly distort the issues, the author states that "professional medical illustrators strive for objective accuracy" (second paragraph). In other words, the author is arguing that the claim that custom-made illustrations are subjective is mistaken.

E In the fourth paragraph, the passage emphasizes that custom-made illustrations are helpful to those without medical backgrounds. Textbook illustrations, on the other hand, generally include extensive detail that can be confusing to nonmedical audiences (third paragraph).

- *Difficulty Level: 1*

Question 13

The Correct Answer:

C There is nothing in the passage to suggest that the author questions the accuracy of testimony provided by medical experts. Instead, the author takes for granted the accuracy of such testimony with respect to both the accuracy of medical illustrations (second paragraph) and explanations of plaintiff injuries (last paragraph). In other words, the author accepts the accuracy of expert testimony.

The last paragraph of the passage reveals that the author is aware of the limitations of a presentation of medical information that is entirely verbal. The author says that custom-made illustrations are especially valuable because they provide visual representations of data whose verbal description would be very complex. The author further says that the technical terminology used in expert medical testimony is difficult for nonexperts to translate mentally into visual imagery and that most people can adequately understand medical information only by thinking about it in visual terms. Together these statements imply that there are serious limitations to a presentation of medical information that is entirely verbal.

The Incorrect Answer Choices:

A As discussed in the explanation of the correct answer, the author does appreciate the difficulty involved in explaining medical data to judges and jurors. However, there is no indication that the author is skeptical of the effectiveness of that testimony. On the contrary, with regard to expert testimony concerning the accuracy of custom-made illustrations, we can infer that the author thinks such testimony is very effective since the author argues in the second paragraph that it is because of such testimony that deceptive illustrations are inadmissible as evidence. With regard to expert testimony concerning plaintiff injuries, the author does suggest in the last paragraph that such testimony, if presented only verbally, may not be fully understandable to judges and jurors. But this does not necessarily mean the author is skeptical of the effectiveness of expert medical testimony generally. In fact, the author clearly believes such testimony can be quite effective if accompanied by medical illustrations.

B   In the last paragraph, the author discusses the limitations of conveying medical information entirely verbally. But the discussion concerns only the limitations of verbal communication itself; there is no indication that the difficulty stems from the communications skills of medical professionals.

D   The author says in the last paragraph that expert testimony often relies heavily on the use of technical terminology, but there is no indication that this is done in an attempt to overwhelm judges and juries. It is plausible that medical experts have become so accustomed to using technical terminology that they do so without realizing it, or that certain medical facts cannot be communicated efficiently without technical terminology.

E   The passage does say that expert witnesses make heavy use of technical terminology. However, this is stated as a neutral factual claim; there is no strong attitude expressed. In particular, the passage does not indicate that the author is intolerant of the use of technical terminology.

- *Difficulty Level: 3*

Question 14

The Correct Answer:

B   The third paragraph opens with a description of an objection to custom-made medical illustrations: they "may subtly distort the issues through the use of emphasis, coloration, and other means, even if they are technically accurate." This objection is a variant of the objection discussed in the second paragraph insofar as the central concern of both objections is the potential for custom-made medical illustrations to convey a biased version of the facts. Whereas the objection discussed in the second paragraph is concerned with the distortion of facts via factual inaccuracy, the objection discussed in the third paragraph is concerned with the distortion of facts via more subtle devices. After describing the objection, the author then offers a response to it: professional medical illustrators strive for objectivity and avoid devices with inflammatory potential as well as details that are irrelevant for those deciding a case. So the author's primary purpose in the third paragraph is to reply to a variant of the objection described in the second paragraph.

The Incorrect Answer Choices:

A   It is not the author's purpose anywhere in the passage to argue for a greater use of custom-made illustrations. Indeed, in the first paragraph, the author says that courts have long allowed their use. Instead, the passage as a whole is an effort to counter objections to the use of custom-made illustrations from those who would like to see their use in court cases curtailed.

C   In the third paragraph, the author does describe an advantage of custom-made illustrations over ones from textbooks: custom-made illustrations include only information that is relevant to the case. However, this discussion occurs in the course of a response to the objection that custom-made illustrations may be misleading; the author's goal is to defend the use of custom-made illustrations against this objection, not to argue that medical textbook illustrations are ill-suited to courtroom use.

D The beginning of the third paragraph does briefly state a reason why custom-made illustrations are controversial: some people maintain that they are misleading. But the rest of the paragraph does not provide further details about this controversy; it instead tries to dispel the controversy by arguing that custom-made illustrations are not only objectively accurate but expressly designed to suit the needs of courtroom decision makers.

E In the third paragraph, the author does describe some differences between custom-made illustrations and textbook illustrations. However, this is not the primary purpose of the paragraph. Instead, it flows naturally out of the author's response to the objection that custom-made illustration might be misleading. Part of that response is that professional illustrators avoid devices with inflammatory potential. The author then expands upon this point with the statement that unlike detailed illustrations in textbooks, custom-made illustrations are designed to include only information relevant to a case.

- *Difficulty Level: 5*

Questions 15–21

Synopsis: The two passages in this set discuss the link between agriculture and dental caries (tooth decay) found in prehistoric human teeth. Agricultural diets generally rely more heavily on carbohydrate-rich foods than do hunter-gatherer diets. Since carbohydrate-rich foods tend to produce higher rates of dental caries, one might reasonably expect there to be a correlation between a population's dependence upon agriculture and its rate of dental caries.

Passage A

In the first paragraph, the author of passage A sets out the link between dental caries in the archaeological record and the shift to agriculture, as described above. Then, in the second paragraph, the author describes a study in North America that supports the connection between carbohydrate consumption and caries. The study found that caries rates in teeth derived from indigenous populations that primarily consumed meats were lower than in those derived from populations that depended upon agriculture.

However, the author notes in the last paragraph that the correlation between dependence on agriculture and caries does not always hold. Some early nonagricultural populations in North American consumed highly processed acorn flour and had relatively high rates of caries, while the Hopi gathered pinyon nuts and wild tubers, foods with high cariogenic potential (that is, high potential to produce caries). Note: it is not stated explicitly, but the implication is that these foods had high cariogenic potential because they were rich in carbohydrates, even though they were gathered rather than cultivated.

Passage B

In passage B, the author considers archaeological evidence, in this case evidence from a 2,000-year span of the Ban Chiang culture, in Thailand. The author notes that the site's early inhabitants appear to have had a hunter-gatherer-cultivator economy, but that the archaeological evidence suggests that over time the population became increasingly dependent on agriculture.

The author then discusses the relationship between agricultural intensification and the rate of caries in a population. The author mentions the stickiness of carbohydrates, like the author of passage A, and asserts that agricultural intensification connects to declining dental health (and declining health in general). Passage B also considers the role of tooth wear on caries formation.

In the last two paragraphs of the passage, the author seeks to connect the evidence from Ban Chiang to what is known about agriculture and dental caries. Since the Ban Chiang population became increasingly dependent upon agriculture, one might expect that the rate of caries in the sample increased over time. Surprisingly, however, the evidence showed slightly higher caries frequency in the Early Group.

In the last paragraph, the author discusses possible explanations for this surprising result. The diet in the Late period may have remained sufficiently varied, the author suggests, or the Late Group's diet might have shifted away from yams (a more cariogenic carbohydrate) and toward rice (a less cariogenic carbohydrate).

Question 15

The Correct Answer:

A   Both passages are concerned with evidence of the development of agriculture in the agricultural record, and in particular with what archaeologically derived teeth can tell us about a population's dependence on agriculture. Passage A discusses evidence from studies of the dental remains of prehistoric populations in North America, and passage B discusses similar evidence from Ban Chiang, Thailand. Both authors examine the extent to which the archaeological evidence supports the generalization that the greater a population's dependence on agriculture is, the higher its level of dental caries will typically be.

The Incorrect Answer Choices:

B   The author of passage B does mention in passing that agricultural intensification results in "declining human health" (first sentence of the second paragraph), but this is a minor point in the passage. The primary concern of the passage is how the archaeological evidence from Ban Chiang relates to that culture's agricultural development. On the other hand, passage A includes no mention at all of how agriculture affects the overall health of human populations; instead, it concentrates narrowly on the relationship between agriculture, diet, and rates of dental caries. Thus, examining the impact of agriculture on the overall health of human populations cannot be said to be the primary concern of either passage.

C   The research findings presented in the two passages concern the effect of carbohydrate-rich (and other) foods on dental decay, but none of the populations discussed are identified as **strictly agricultural**. Indeed, both authors discuss the effects of carbohydrate-rich foods on caries formation in societies that are not strictly agricultural. For example, passage A mentions high caries frequencies in North American populations that ate flour processed from gathered acorns, and it also discusses the Hopi practice of consuming pinyon nuts and wild tubers. Similarly, passage B discusses caries frequencies among the inhabitants of Ban Chiang, who are described as having a varied diet that included wild plant and animal foods. Thus neither passage is primarily concerned with examining the effect of carbohydrate-rich foods on caries rates in strictly agricultural societies.

D Neither passage attempts to identify any particular population as **the first** agricultural society. Instead, both passages discuss archaeological evidence concerning diet and agriculture in certain populations without presuming that those populations were the first to have adopted agriculture. So examining the evidence regarding when the first agricultural society arose cannot be said to be the purpose of either passage.

E As noted in the synopsis of the passages, the central concern of passage A is the ability of dental remains in the archaeological record to tell us something about the transition to agriculture in prehistoric populations, not the extent to which those populations were able to obtain carbohydrate-rich foods. And the discussion in passage B is focused on a population that is **not** pre-agricultural—that of Ban Chiang. Thus neither passage is primarily concerned with examining the extent to which pre-agricultural populations were able to obtain carbohydrate-rich foods.

- *Difficulty Level: 5*

Question 16

The Correct Answer:

B The western North American populations described in the last paragraph of passage A are explicitly identified as "nonagricultural." Passage A states that these populations ate stone-ground acorn flour, pinyon nuts, wild tubers, and other species of wild plants. In other words, they consumed wild plants that they collected, not cultivated plants. In contrast, passage B states that inhabitants of Ban Chiang practiced agriculture throughout the period under discussion, and it specifically mentions that these populations ate cultivated rice and yams. Thus the populations in question are distinguished by the fact that those discussed in passage B ate cultivated foods, while those discussed in the last paragraph of passage A did not.

The Incorrect Answer Choices:

A The populations mentioned in the last paragraph of passage A are said to have eaten some highly cariogenic foods. For example, the author notes that the Hopi ate foods with high cariogenic potential like pinyon nuts and wild tubers. According to passage B, the Ban Chiang population also ate some highly cariogenic foods, such as yams. Since both populations ate highly cariogenic foods, consumption of such foods cannot be what distinguishes them.

C Both passages simply state that the populations at issue had diets that consisted of some carbohydrate-rich foods. Neither passage provides any information about what proportion of these diets consisted of carbohydrate-rich foods.

D Although tooth wear is discussed in passage B, the author does not claim that the Ban Chiang populations had very high levels of tooth wear. On the other hand, tooth wear is not even mentioned in passage A. So there is no basis for saying that tooth wear is what distinguishes populations discussed in the two passages.

E The author of passage B does not say or suggest that the Ban Chiang populations ate highly processed foods. The author of passage A, on the other hand, does point out that some western North American populations consumed large amounts of "highly processed stone-ground flour made from gathered acorns."

- *Difficulty Level: 4*

Question 17

The Correct Answer:

A In the second paragraph of passage B, the author explains how eating fiber and grit can reduce dental caries. Eating fiber and grit wears tooth surfaces down, thereby eliminating dental fissures (cracks or gaps) that can trap food particles and thus promote tooth decay. However, the author goes on to say that severe wear from fiber and grit consumption can expose a tooth's pulp cavity, which would then increase caries formation. Therefore, passage B strongly supports the statement that fiber and grit can either limit or promote caries formation, depending on their prevalence in the diet.

The Incorrect Answer Choices:

B The author of passage B does not offer any evidence suggesting that fiber and grit are typically consumed in greater quantities as a population adopts agriculture. Indeed, the passage might be suggesting the opposite—since agricultural foods are described in the second paragraph as contributing to increased caries because they are "starchy-sticky," it is plausible to think that those foods contain might contain less fiber and grit than gathered wild foods do.

C The author of passage B does mention that agricultural intensification results in declining human health, but there is no suggestion that this effect is connected in any way to fiber and grit in the diet. Moreover, the author of passage B does not refer to a lack of nutritional value in dietary fiber and grit.

D Rather than contributing to the formation of fissures, fiber and grit in the diet can **remove** a tooth's naturally occurring fissures by wearing tooth surfaces down, according to the author of passage B. And while the author also mentions that severe wear to a tooth from fiber and grit can damage teeth by exposing the pulp cavity, this kind of severe wear is clearly distinct from fissures.

E In the second sentence of the second paragraph, the author of passage B refers to starchy-sticky foodstuffs and their possible contribution to increased rates of caries formation, but the author does not make any connection between fiber and grit in the diet and the stickiness of carbohydrate-rich foods. If anything, the very description of such foods as "starchy-sticky" suggests that they might contain little in the way of fiber or grit. In any case, passage B provides no support for the statement that fiber and grit increase the stickiness of carbohydrate-rich foods.

- *Difficulty Level: 3*

Question 18

The Correct Answer:

B The prevailing view referred to in the question is that dental caries is strongly linked to the consumption of carbohydrate-rich foods (see the first sentence of passage A and the second paragraph of passage B). Both authors cite the relatively low incidence of caries among nonagricultural people (who typically do not consume much carbohydrate-rich food) as evidence that supports this view. In the middle of the second paragraph, passage A refers to a Sioux population who primarily ate meat and whose archaeological remains showed almost no caries. And in the second paragraph of passage B, the author points to research suggesting that dental caries is uncommon in pre-agricultural populations.

The Incorrect Answer Choices:

A Passage A does mention one North American population that consumed "highly processed" stone-ground acorn flour, which in turn contributed to a relatively high rate of caries. But this piece of evidence is not used to establish a link between caries and eating highly processed foods in particular; instead, it is offered as an example of a nonagricultural population that had a relatively high rate of caries because they consumed carbohydrate-rich foods. More importantly, the author of passage B offers no information at all about highly processed foods. Thus neither passage discusses the effect of highly processed foods on caries formation as evidence supporting the prevailing view (i.e., that dental caries is strongly linked to consumption of carbohydrate-rich foods).

C Information about the effects of fiber and grit in the diet on caries formation is found only in passage B. Passage A does not mention fiber and grit at all. And while the information regarding fiber and grit in passage B relates to the issue of diet and caries formation in general, it has no bearing on the prevailing view regarding the relationship between dental caries and carbohydrate consumption. Thus, neither passage discusses the effect of fiber and grit in the diet on caries formation as evidence supporting the prevailing view (i.e., that dental caries is strongly linked to consumption of carbohydrate-rich foods).

D Both passages mention populations that consumed wild foods, but neither passage draws any connection between the consumption of wild foods and tooth wear. Thus neither passage discusses the effect of the consumption of wild foods on tooth wear as evidence supporting the prevailing view (i.e., that dental caries is strongly linked to consumption of carbohydrate-rich foods).

E The author of passage B does mention that agricultural intensification results in declining human health. But this is not being offered as evidence supporting the prevailing view concerning the link between caries in particular and consumption of carbohydrate-rich foods. More importantly, the author of passage A does not say anything at all about the effects of agricultural intensification on overall human health, much less about whether such evidence might support the prevailing view. Thus, neither passage discusses the effect of agricultural intensification on overall human health as evidence supporting the prevailing view.

- *Difficulty Level: 4*

Question 19

The Correct Answer:

D Each author acknowledges that there is a correlation between a population's dependence on agriculture and its rate of dental caries (second paragraph of each passage). However, each passage ends with a discussion of evidence demonstrating that this correspondence is not absolute. In the third paragraph of passage A, the author points to early nonagricultural populations in western North America with relatively high caries levels linked to their consumption of acorn flour. Similarly, the author of passage B points to evidence that the Early Ban Chiang Group showed slightly higher caries frequency than the Late Ban Chiang Group, even though the Late Group had a greater dependence on agriculture (fourth paragraph). Thus both authors would agree that the frequency of dental caries in a population does not necessarily correspond directly to the population's degree of dependence on agriculture.

The Incorrect Answer Choices:

A There is no evidence that either author would agree that the incidence of dental caries increases over time, let alone increases **predictably** over time. Indeed, the author of passage B mentions that the Ban Chiang population showed a slight **decline** in caries over time.

B Neither passage mentions any impediments to detecting dental caries in teeth recovered from archaeological sites. Therefore, there is no evidence suggesting that either author would agree with the assertion that detecting caries in such teeth is difficult.

C Nothing the two authors relate would support the generalization that dental caries tends to be more prevalent in populations with a hunter-gatherer diet than in populations with an agricultural diet. In fact, both authors assert that the reverse is generally true (last sentence of the second paragraph in passage A; first three sentences of the second paragraph in passage B).

E Both authors cite evidence linking dental caries to the consumption of carbohydrate-rich foods. Only passage B discusses a link between dental caries and tooth wear, and the passage provides no information suggesting that the author believes caries to be linked more strongly to tooth wear than to the consumption of carbohydrates. Thus neither author would be likely to agree that caries is more strongly linked to tooth wear than to the consumption of a particular type of food.

- *Difficulty Level: 3*

Question 20

The Correct Answer:

C Both authors suggest that not all carbohydrates are alike in their ability to cause caries. In the last paragraph of passage A, the author states that "early nonagricultural populations in western North America who consumed large amounts of highly processed stone-ground flour made from acorns show relatively high caries frequencies." The author then points out that several wild plants collected by the Hopi, notably pinyon nuts and wild tubers, had "high cariogenic potential," which suggests that the latter foods had higher cariogenic potential than the acorn flour. Likewise, in passage B, the author notes that sweet carbohydrates like yams are more cariogenic than less sweet carbohydrates like rice. Thus both passages suggest that some carbohydrate-rich foods have a greater tendency than others to cause caries.

The Incorrect Answer Choices:

A Neither author supplies information suggesting that cultivated varieties have a greater tendency to cause caries than varieties that grow wild. The authors suggest that agricultural intensification typically increases caries rates because it increases the proportion of carbohydrate-rich foods in the diet, not because carbohydrate-rich foods selected for cultivation have a higher cariogenic potential than those not selected for cultivation.

B No mention of carbohydrate-rich foods that require substantial processing is made in passage B, so it cannot be said that passage B suggests anything regarding the role of such foods in the diet of any given population. On the other hand, passage A mentions early populations in western North America who ate highly processed stone-ground acorn flour, but these populations are identified as nonagricultural. So the author of passage A would be likely to **disagree** with the statement that carbohydrate-rich foods that require substantial processing played no role in hunter-gatherer diets.

D Passage A does not specifically address the role of tooth wear in caries formation, so it cannot be said that passage A suggests anything regarding this relationship. Passage B does supply some specific information about the effect of fiber and grit on tooth wear and caries formation (second paragraph), but none of the information provided identifies particular carbohydrate-rich foods as having higher fiber content, or producing greater tooth wear, than other foods. Thus there is no reason to conclude that passage B suggests that some carbohydrate-rich foods reduce caries formation by increasing tooth wear.

E Neither passage provides information suggesting that the cariogenic potential of a given variety of carbohydrate-rich food increases if it is cultivated rather than gathered in the wild.

- *Difficulty Level: 3*

Question 21

The Correct Answer:

D The question asks how the evidence from Ban Chiang relates to the generalization in the second paragraph of passage A: "in general, the greater a population's dependence on agriculture is, the higher its rate of caries formation will be."

In the first paragraph of passage B, the author says that the archaeological evidence from Ban Chiang indicates that the population became increasingly dependent on agriculture over time. In the fourth paragraph, however, the author notes that the Early Ban Chiang Group had a slightly greater caries frequency than did the Late Ban Chiang Group. So the Ban Chiang evidence reveals a situation in which a population became increasingly dependent on agriculture while simultaneously showing a slight decline in its rate of caries formation. In other words, the evidence from Ban Chiang does not conform to the generalization in passage A.

The Incorrect Answer Choices:

A The Early Ban Chiang Group is said to have a slightly higher caries frequency than the Late Ban Chiang Group, even though the evidence indicates that the latter group was more dependent on agriculture. Thus the Ban Chiang evidence does not confirm the generalization that "in general, the greater a population's dependence on agriculture is, the higher its rate of caries formation will be."

B The Early Ban Chiang Group is said to have a slightly higher caries frequency than the Late Ban Chiang Group, even though the evidence indicates that the latter group was more dependent on agriculture. Thus, the Ban Chiang evidence discussed in passage B does not tend to support the generalization that "in general, the greater a population's dependence on agriculture is, the higher its rate of caries formation will be."

C The Early Ban Chiang Group is said to have a slightly higher caries frequency than the Late Ban Chiang Group, even though the evidence indicates that the latter group was more dependent on agriculture. Thus the Ban Chiang evidence appears to be an exception to the generalization that "in general, the greater a population's dependence on agriculture is, the higher its rate of caries formation will be," and it cannot be said that an exception to a generalization is irrelevant.

E As discussed in the explanation of the correct answer, the Ban Chiang evidence does not conform to the generalization that "in general, the greater a population's dependence on agriculture is, the higher its rate of caries formation will be." However, it would be too strong to say that the Ban Chiang evidence disproves the generalization. After all, the generalization states that the correspondence holds in general, not in all cases.

- *Difficulty Level: 4*

Questions 22–27

Synopsis: The topic of the passage is the nineteenth-century fiction writer Sarah Orne Jewett. The passage states that recent criticism classifies Jewett's writing as closely aligned with that of the domestic novelists of the previous generation. The author of the passage seeks to challenge this classification, arguing that Jewett's work is significantly different than that of the domestic novelists. The passage acknowledges that Jewett's work has superficial similarities to the domestic novels but notes that it differs in that two topics that are central to the domestic novels—child-rearing and religion—are almost completely absent from Jewett's work.

The passage argues that these differences in subject matter ultimately reflect different conceptions of the nature and purpose of fiction. The domestic novels are based on a conception according to which part of the purpose of fiction is to promote domestic morality and religious belief. For domestic novels this naturally took the form of featuring child-rearing and religion prominently in the stories, as a means to fulfilling their purpose. Jewett's writing, on the other hand, is based on a "high-cultural" conception of fiction as an autonomous sphere with intrinsic value. Given this conception, Jewett did not need her fiction to promote any social goals, and thus her choice of subject matter was unconstrained. The central contention of the passage is that the fundamental difference between Jewett's conception of fiction and the domestic novelists' outweighs the kind of superficial similarities in their work noted by recent criticism.

Question 22

The Correct Answer:

D The passage states that Jewett's writing embodied the high-cultural conception of literary art, and a chief concern of the passage is identifying the effect this conception had on her fiction. The passage states that "unlike the domestic novelists, Jewett intended her works not as a means to an end but as an end in themselves" (final paragraph). The high-cultural conception accounts for the absence in Jewett's fiction of the didactic aims found in domestic fiction. Most tangibly, a central contention of the passage is that Jewett's conception of fiction is what ultimately accounts for the differences in subject matter found between her work and that of the domestic novelists. Thus, the passage clearly helps to identify an effect that Jewett's conception of literary art had on her fiction.

The Incorrect Answer Choices:

A The passage says that the subject matter of the domestic novels of the 1850s was primarily women and their concerns. However, no claim is made about the authors of these novels. The suggestion is perhaps that many, if not most, of these novels were written by women, but the passage says nothing about whether any of these novels were written by men.

B The passage discusses the domestic novels exclusively from the 1850s and provides information about their subject matter and underlying conception of fiction. However, the passage does not indicate whether any domestic novels were written in other decades. In particular, the passage does not provide information about whether any domestic novels were written, and widely read, after 1860.

C The passage mentions migration to urban areas as a factor that might help to explain the differences between the domestic novels of the 1850s and Jewett's fiction. But this is not a point about the development of domestic fiction in the 1850s. Instead it is offered as a potential explanation of why those novels differed from Jewett's fiction, which was written at a later time and, in the author's opinion, does not deserve to be characterized as domestic fiction at all.

E The passage identifies Jewett as a writer of "regional fiction" (first sentence) but does not indicate which geographical regions her writings were concerned with.

- *Difficulty Level: 3*

Question 23

The Correct Answer:

C The claim made by the recent criticism is that Jewett's work is closely aligned with the domestic novels. The passage says that Jewett's work "does resemble the domestic novels of the 1850s in its focus on women, their domestic occupations, and their social interactions" (second sentence of the first paragraph), indicating that the author does view that claim as based on some reasonable evidence and as initially plausible. However, the passage makes clear at numerous points that the author thinks the claim is ultimately mistaken. The passage says that Jewett's work "differs markedly from" the domestic novels (middle of the first paragraph). Also, "unlike the domestic novelists, Jewett intended her works not as a means to an end but as an end in themselves" (near the end of the last paragraph); the passage adds that this is a "fundamental difference" between Jewett and the domestic novelist, whereas the similarities are only "superficial" (last sentence of the passage).

The Incorrect Answer Choices:

A The claim made by the recent criticism is that Jewett's work is closely aligned with the domestic novels. As discussed in the explanation of the correct answer, it is clear that the author thinks that this is a position that, even though initially plausible, is nevertheless mistaken. For this reason, it is incorrect to say that the author regards the recent criticism as essentially correct.

B The claim made by the recent criticism is that Jewett's work is closely aligned with the domestic novels. As discussed in the explanation of the correct answer, it is clear that the author thinks that this is a position that, even though initially plausible, is nevertheless mistaken. For this reason, the author does not think the recent criticism makes a claim that is true about Jewett.

D The claim made by the recent criticism is that Jewett's work is closely aligned with the domestic novels. The author clearly regards this position as questionable, at the very least. However, in the author's opinion this is not because the recent criticism relies on a currently dominant literary aesthetic. While the passage does discuss different historical conceptions of literature, the intent was not to identify the literary aesthetic that is currently dominant or that which underlies the recent criticism under discussion. Instead, that discussion was used as a way of showing that domestic novels and Jewett's work differ in a fundamental way.

E The claim made by the recent criticism is that Jewett's work is closely aligned with the domestic novels. As discussed in the explanation of the correct answer, the author clearly does not regard this position as based on mere speculation for which there is no reasonable support. Indeed, the author points out that there is some support for the claim made by the recent criticism; the passage says that Jewett's work "does resemble the domestic novels" in some respects (second sentence of the first paragraph). While the author ultimately dismisses the recent criticism, this is only after a serious, and fairly extended, argument. No such argument would be required if the author felt that the criticism could be dismissed simply on the grounds that the view is based on mere speculation.

- *Difficulty Level: 4*

Question 24

The Correct Answer:

B The word "continuum" occurs when the passage claims that "[T]he domestic novel … is based on a conception of fiction as a part of a continuum that also included writings devoted to piety and domestic instruction, bound together by a common goal …" Here the author is placing the emphasis on the similarities that exist between these seemingly different kinds of writing. Indeed, the next sentence illustrates this point by noting that it was common for a single book to be "**indistinguishably** a novel, a child-rearing manual, and a tract on Christian duty" (emphasis added). The point is that, under this conception of fiction, there were not distinct boundaries between fiction and writings devoted to piety and domestic instruction. Thus, the author chose the word "continuum" precisely to convey the idea that fiction was not treated as clearly distinct from other categories of writing.

The Incorrect Answer Choices:

A As described in the explanation of the correct answer, the word "continuum" is used in the context of describing the way a certain conception of fiction in the mid-nineteenth century joined fiction to a broad spectrum of other writings, including writings devoted to piety and domestic instruction. There is no indication that the author had anything other than writings from this relatively limited time period in mind. So there is no suggestion that the author meant to invoke a "continuum" of works stretching back into the past.

C As described in the explanation of the correct answer, the word "continuum" is used in the context of describing the way a certain conception of fiction joined it to a broad spectrum of other writings. The passage says nothing about the form in which these writings were published. So there is nothing to suggest that the author used the word "continuum" to convey the idea that domestic fiction was often published in serial form.

D As described in the explanation of the correct answer, the word "continuum" is used in the context of describing the way a certain conception of fiction joined it to a broad spectrum of other writings. The author's point is not to emphasize the way any of these forms of writing changed over time, but rather to highlight the links between fiction and other forms. For this reason, the author clearly did not use the word "continuum" to imply anything about the way fiction evolves over time.

E As described in the explanation of the correct answer, the word "continuum" is used in the context of describing the way a certain conception of fiction joined it to a broad spectrum of other writings. There's no indication in the passage that the common goal of these writings can be described as the promotion of the cohesiveness and continuity of society. But even if that was the common goal, this is not conveyed by the use of word "continuum." As described in the explanation of the correct answer, the author's point is rather that, under a certain conception of fiction, the boundaries between different kinds of writing were often fuzzy and indistinct.

- *Difficulty Level: 5*

Question 25

The Correct Answer:

E As discussed in the "Synopsis," the passage seeks to challenge the classification of Jewett's writing as closely aligned with the domestic novels of the 1850s. The passage defends the alternate view that Jewett's work is significantly different than that of the domestic novelists, given that her work is based on a fundamentally different conception of fiction than theirs. Thus, (E) accurately states the primary function of the passage.

The Incorrect Answer Choices:

A The passage argues that Jewett's work does not belong in the same category as domestic novels, and indicates the differing conceptions of fiction underlying each. However, it is not clear that this can be described as a discussion of historical categories of literary style. Furthermore, nothing in the passage suggests that the author is intending to radically redefine any literary categories. Instead, the focus of the passage is simply on which category the work of a particular author—Jewett—belongs to. Thus, (A) cannot be the primary function of the passage.

B The passage does distinguish between two categories of writing—the domestic novels and fiction based on a high-cultural conception—but it does not say anything about the value, significance, or worth of either category, i.e., it does not evaluate them. Also, although the passage discusses Jewett's writing and claims that it is based on a high-cultural conception of fiction, the passage says nothing to indicate that Jewett's work should be considered a paradigmatic case. Thus, (B) cannot be the primary function of the passage.

C In the passage, there is no discussion, not to mention reappraisal, of any long-held assumptions about the historical connections among any writers. Instead, as described in the explanation of the correct answer, the passage is arguing against **recent** criticism that tries to connect Jewett to the domestic novelists. Thus, (C) cannot be the primary function of the passage.

D As described in the explanation of the correct answer, the passage distinguishes between two conceptions of the nature of fiction. However, the purpose of this distinction was not to discuss the relative merits of each. Instead, this distinction was drawn as a way of identifying a fundamental difference between Jewett's work and the domestic novels. Thus, (D) cannot be the primary function of the passage.

- *Difficulty Level: 4*

Question 26

The Correct Answer:

E In the first paragraph of the passage, the author describes a difference in the subject matter of the domestic novels of the 1850s and Jewett's work. In the second paragraph, the author mentions two explanatory hypotheses for this difference: migration to cities and the increasing secularization of society. The passage then gives a mildly favorable comment on them ("such factors may help to explain the differences"). The author then spends the rest of the paragraph advocating and elaborating upon another explanation: the differing conceptions of fiction that underlie Jewett's work and the domestic novels. The use of "ultimately" (second sentence) indicates that the author considers this explanation to be more fundamental. Thus, (E) most accurately represents the structure of the second paragraph.

The Incorrect Answer Choices:

A In the second paragraph, the author considers several possible explanations for the differences between the domestic novels and Jewett's fiction. However, it is incorrect to describe the author as rejecting them in favor of the idea that any attempt at explanation does violence to the unity of the phenomenon (nor is it clear what that would mean in this context). The author seems to find some merit in all of the possible explanations, and one of them (regarding the differing conceptions of fiction held by Jewett and the domestic novelists) is clearly regarded as ultimately correct by the author.

B As described in the explanation of the correct answer, the author discusses several explanatory hypotheses in the second paragraph. However, there is no indication that the author considers them to be incompatible. Indeed, the author says that the first two hypotheses mentioned (migration to cities and the increasing secularization of society) both may **help** to explain the phenomenon in question, even though the author regards a different explanation (regarding the differing conceptions of fiction held by Jewett and the domestic novelists) as most fundamental.

C As described in the explanation of the correct answer, the author discusses several explanatory hypotheses in the second paragraph. However, the author does not argue that they are not distinct from one another. In fact, the paragraph clearly indicates that, in the author's opinion, one explanation is more fundamental than the others. It would be nonsensical to argue that one explanatory hypothesis is more fundamental than others if the author regards them as not really distinct from one another.

D While the passage as a whole is concerned with the proper classification of Jewett's fiction, it is inaccurate to describe the second paragraph as proposing two versions of a classificatory hypothesis. Furthermore, the author clearly does not set out any sort of counterargument that is rejected in the following paragraph.

- *Difficulty Level: 5*

Question 27

The Correct Answer:

C The passage says that the domestic novels were based on a conception of fiction according to which novels shared a common goal with writings devoted to piety and domestic instruction: to promote domestic morality and religious belief. Thus, the subject matter in domestic novels had to enable them to achieve this goal. In effect, this constrained domestic novels to stories in which child-rearing and religion were featured prominently. Jewett's writing, on the other hand, was based on the high-cultural conception of fiction, according to which fiction was seen as pure art, "valued for the formal arrangement of its elements rather than for its larger social connections or the promotion of extraliterary goods" (middle of the last paragraph of the passage). Thus, Jewett was free to write about any topic she chose and could exclude the topics of child-rearing and religion if she wished.

The Incorrect Answer Choices:

A As discussed in the explanation of the correct answer, the conception of fiction held by Jewett left her free to choose which topics to include in her writing, and which to exclude. Any willingness or unwillingness to include a topic in her work cannot be explained by her conception of fiction.

B The passage does not say that both Jewett and the domestic novelists focused primarily on rural concerns. The passage does say that we might attribute the differences between the subject matter in Jewett's work and that in domestic novels to the migration of the rural young to cities. But insofar as this suggests anything about the focus of the writers under discussion, it suggests a difference between Jewett and the domestic novelists: Jewett, writing later, might have focused less on rural concerns. Furthermore, there is no suggestion that a writer's conception of fiction would provide any indication of whether he or she would focus primarily on rural concerns.

D The fact that both Jewett and the domestic novelists focused predominantly on women and their concerns is in no way explained by the differing conceptions of fiction they held. Indeed, the passage distinguished between their respective conceptions of fiction precisely to explain the **differences** in subject matter between Jewett's work and that of the domestic novelists.

E As discussed in the explanation of the correct answer, the conception of fiction held by Jewett left her free to choose which topics to include in her writing, and which to exclude. That conception does not imply that she was unable to feature children or religion as prominently as the domestic novelists did.

- *Difficulty Level: 4*

Question 1

Overview: The passage describes a study in which children who were taught the word "stairs" while walking up and down stairs later misapplied the word to a ladder. The question asks you to find the principle that is best illustrated by the study.

The Correct Answer:

D (D) says that children who learn a word by observing how the object denoted by the word is used sometimes apply that word to a different object that is similarly used. This is exactly what happened in the study: the children learned "stairs" by observing that people walk up stairs, and they then applied "stairs" to a ladder—a different object that is similarly used. So (D) is well illustrated by the study.

The Incorrect Answer Choices:

A (A) describes what sometimes happens when children repeatedly hear a word without seeing the object that the word refers to. In the study, however, the children did see the object that the word "stairs" refers to when they were learning the word. So the study could not illustrate (A).

B (B) makes a claim about how children best learn words. In order to illustrate such a claim, the study would need to compare the "best" method of learning words with some other methods. However, the study considered only one method of learning words, so it cannot illustrate (B).

C (C) says that it is easier for a child to learn not to misuse a word if the child uses the object denoted by the word earlier in life. But in the study, **all** the children misused the word "stairs," which was the only word they were taught in the study. So (C) cannot illustrate any claim about how it is easier for some children to learn how not to misuse a word.

E (E) makes a claim about how children best learn the names of objects. In order to illustrate such a claim, the study would need to compare the "best" method of learning the names of objects with some other methods. However, the study looks at only one method of learning the names of objects, so it cannot illustrate (E).

■ *Difficulty Level: 1*

Question 2

Overview: The passage says that a large proportion of people who live to at least 100 have led "unhealthy" lives replete with behavior that often shortens life spans. So it's unlikely that their lifestyles are responsible for their long lives. They have long lives in spite of their behavior, so there must be some compensating factor that enables them to live a long time. The passage concludes that this factor is probably a genetic disposition.

The question asks you to select the piece of information that most strengthens this argument.

The Correct Answer:

E (E) says that almost everyone who lives to at least 100 has long-lived siblings. Since siblings share many genes, this strongly suggests that being long lived has a genetic component. By providing additional information to support the conclusion that exceptionally long-lived people are genetically disposed to long lives, (E) strengthens the argument.

The Incorrect Answer Choices:

A (A) suggests that some of the behaviors thought to be unhealthy might not be so bad, since one of those behaviors, consuming alcohol, could counteract another of the behaviors, eating fatty foods. If the behaviors thought to be unhealthy are not so bad, then there would be less need for a compensating factor that explains why some people live a long time in spite of engaging in those behaviors. So if anything, (A) weakens rather than strengthens the argument.

B, C (B) and (C) each tell us that some exceptionally long-lived people do not engage in some of the behaviors that the argument associates with shortened life spans but do engage in other such behaviors. This is not at all surprising; we would not expect that people would engage in all of those behaviors or none at all. But more importantly, the facts in (B) and in (C) do nothing to strengthen the argument, because there is no way to connect those facts to the case for long lives being a result of a genetic disposition.

D The argument seeks to find out why people who live to at least 100 do so in spite of their unhealthy behaviors. The argument is not concerned with the factors that cause other people not to live to 100. So the fact that some of them engage in unhealthy behaviors is irrelevant to the argument.

- *Difficulty Level: 1*

Question 3

Overview: The first premise of the argument in the passage is that medicines with an unpleasant taste are usually produced only in tablet, capsule, or soft-gel form. The argument then basically rules out the possibility that medication M will be produced in tablet form (since M's active ingredient can't tolerate the heat used to manufacture tablets) or in soft-gel form (since the company developing M makes all its medications itself and doesn't have soft-gel manufacturing technology). The argument concludes that M will probably be produced in capsule form.

It may appear that the conclusion is already strongly supported. After all, the argument basically rules out making M in two of the three forms mentioned in the first premise and then concludes M will probably be made in the third form. Notice, however, that the first premise applies only to medications with an unpleasant taste.

The Correct Answer:

B If we assume what (B) indicates—that M has an unpleasant taste—then the first premise of the argument is applicable to M. This assumption shores up the only weakness in the argument (as described in the "Overview"), and the conclusion is very strongly supported as a result.

The Incorrect Answer Choices:

A (A) suggests that M might be produced in some form other than tablet, capsule, or soft-gel. So, assuming (A) does not help to support the conclusion that M will probably be produced in capsule form.

C As noted in the "Overview," the argument's premises already basically rule out the possibility that M will be produced in soft-gel form. Ruling out this possibility implies that M will not be produced in both capsule and soft-gel form. Thus, (C) cannot provide any further basis for the argument's conclusion beyond that already provided in the argument.

D Since the argument states that M has a low melting point, assuming (D) would provide some support for the claim that M will be produced in soft-gel form. (But this support is countered by the fact that the argument basically rules out the possibility that M will be produced in soft-gel form, as noted in the "Overview.") But since the conclusion of the argument is that M will probably be produced in **capsule** form, (D) adds no support.

E (E) presents an apparent advantage of producing medications in capsule form, but there is nothing in the argument to suggest that the manufacturer would be convinced to produce M in capsule form because medications in capsule form taste less unpleasant. In fact, the first premise of the argument suggests that the difference in taste between tablet, capsule, or soft-gel form is not very significant for manufacturers since all these forms are used on some occasions.

- *Difficulty Level: 1*

Question 4

Overview: The passage says that Morris wants to become the majority owner of *The Daily*. The only thing preventing Morris from doing this is that Azedcorp, which currently owns a majority of *The Daily*'s shares, refuses to sell. The question asks you to find the statement that provides the most support for the prediction that Morris will soon become the majority owner.

The Correct Answer:

E Morris wants to become the majority owner of *The Daily*, and, if (E) is true, the only thing preventing her from becoming the majority owner—Azedcorp's refusal to sell—will soon no longer be an obstacle. So, if (E) is true, it is probable that Morris will soon become the majority owner of *The Daily*.

The Incorrect Answer Choices:

A The prediction is only about who will be the majority owner of *The Daily*, so owning shares in any other newspaper is irrelevant.

B If Morris has recently offered Azedcorp much more for its shares of *The Daily* than Azedcorp originally paid for them, this has little bearing on whether Azedcorp will decide to sell to Morris. We don't know that this offer is much higher than any previous offers Azedcorp has received; it is even possible that Azedcorp already refused this offer. Furthermore, comparing the share price in Morris's offer to the price Azedcorp paid is not relevant: Azedcorp may have bought its shares a long time ago, and they might be worth far more now than what Morris offered to pay.

C The fact that no one other than Morris is interested in buying a majority of *The Daily*'s shares suggests that if anyone other than Azedcorp becomes the majority owner of *The Daily*, it will be Morris. But as long as Azedcorp refuses to sell, no one else will become the majority owner. (C) gives us no reason to think that Azedcorp will sell.

D Even if Morris owns the second-most shares of *The Daily*, she will not be able to own the majority as long as Azedcorp refuses to sell. (D) gives us no reason to think that Azedcorp will sell.

- *Difficulty Level: 2*

Question 5

Overview: The area resident indicates that childhood lead poisoning declined steadily since the 1970s when steps were taken to curb two sources of lead poisoning. The resident goes on to point out a lingering source of lead poisoning in the area: lead paint in homes. The resident concludes that if this lingering source of lead poisoning is eliminated, childhood lead poisoning in the area will also be eliminated. Note that the resident does not establish that lead paint in homes is the only remaining source of lead poisoning in children.

The question asks you to identify the flaw in the argument.

The Correct Answer:

C If there are significant sources of lead in the area's environment other than lead paint in homes, then there's little reason to think that eliminating lead paint in homes will eradicate childhood lead poisoning. The argument needs to consider this possibility (and rule it out) or else the inference that it draws will not be warranted.

The Incorrect Answer Choices:

A The argument relies on two statistical claims: that childhood lead poisoning has declined steadily since the 1970s and that 25 percent of homes in the area still contain lead paint that poses significant health hazards. We are given no reason to believe that either statistical claim is unreliable.

B There are two ways in which the area resident's argument could rely on assumptions. The premises the argument puts forward could rely on assumptions, and the inference from those premises to the conclusion could rely on assumptions. The premises merely assert certain facts, none of which assume that the prediction in the conclusion is true. The inference drawn in the argument merely commits it to the view that the premises provide sufficient evidence to establish the conclusion, which is not tantamount to assuming that the conclusion is true.

D (D) is relevant to the practicality of any efforts to eliminate lead paint from homes in the area, but the argument does not take for granted that lead paint in homes can be eliminated economically. The conclusion of the argument is a causal statement drawing a connection between eliminating lead paint from homes and eliminating childhood lead poisoning. If it turns out that lead paint in homes can't be eliminated (because it can't be done economically), that does not affect the truth of this causal statement.

E The argument takes for granted that children reside in **some** of the area homes that contain lead paint—otherwise eliminating lead paint from these homes would not have an effect on childhood lead poisoning. But there is no need for the argument to presuppose that children reside in **all** of the area homes that contain lead paint. That's too strong a presupposition, and it's unlikely to be true, given that a lot of homes in the area are said to contain lead paint.

- *Difficulty Level: 1*

Question 6

Overview: The passage presents several statements about soft-drink labels and caffeine intake. The question asks you to find a statement that must be true if all those statements are true.

The Correct Answer:

A The passage states that listing exact caffeine content on soft-drink labels would make it easier to limit, but not eliminate, caffeine intake and that if it became easier to limit, but not eliminate, caffeine intake, many people would do so and this would improve their health. It follows that if exact caffeine content were listed on soft-drink labels, many people would experience improvements to their health, which of course means that the health of at least some people would improve. So if the statements in the passage are true, (A) must also be true.

The Incorrect Answer Choices:

B Only one part of the passage has implications for the issue that (B) addresses: according to the passage, it will be easier to limit caffeine intake if exact caffeine content is listed on soft-drink labels. In comparison then, it will be more difficult to limit caffeine intake if exact caffeine content is not listed, but this does not imply that it will be impossible. Hence (B) does not have to be true if the statements in the passage are true.

C According to the passage, it will be more difficult for people to limit, **but not eliminate**, their caffeine intake if exact caffeine content is not listed on soft-drink labels. However, the statements in the passage do not imply anything about how difficult it will be to **eliminate** caffeine intake if people don't know exactly how much caffeine is in their soft drinks. So (C) does not have to be true if the statements in the passage are true.

D The passage indicates that if exact caffeine content were listed on soft-drink labels, it would be easier for people to limit, but not eliminate, caffeine intake. However, the passage does not indicate or imply anything about whether this would make it easier to eliminate caffeine intake. So (D) does not have to be true if the statements in the passage are true.

E As discussed in the explanation of the correct answer, the passage has implications regarding improvements to people's health that would occur if exact caffeine content were listed on soft-drink labels. But nothing in the passage implies that anyone's health would **worsen** if people knew how much caffeine was in their soft drinks.

- *Difficulty Level: 2*

Question 7

Overview: The flawed pattern of reasoning in MacNeil's argument is characterized by its inference that what is true of a group of objects taken as a whole must be true of every individual object that comprises that group. In MacNeil's case, MacNeil infers that, because Vidmar's collection, taken as a whole, is valuable, each individual painting in Vidmar's collection must be a valuable painting. The question asks you to identify the answer choice that displays this same flawed pattern of reasoning.

The Correct Answer:

C The reasoning in (C) infers that what is true of a group as a whole (the paragraph) is true of the members that comprise the group (the sentences). According to (C), because the paragraph, taken as a whole, is long, each individual sentence in that paragraph must be a long sentence. This parallels the flawed pattern of reasoning in the passage.

The Incorrect Answer Choices:

A To the extent that (A) can be understood as being about a group (the book as a whole) and members of that group (the words in that book), the reasoning in (A) reverses the pattern from the passage. In (A), the inference is from what is true of each individual member of a group (the words) to what is true of the collection as a whole (the book). Therefore (A) does not parallel MacNeil's reasoning.

B The reasoning in (B) is different from the reasoning in the passage because (B) does not simply infer that what is true of the group is true of the members of that group. (B) tells us that the city council voted to adopt the plan, but it also tells us something more—that it voted unanimously to adopt the plan. So if the vote was unanimous to adopt the plan, each council member must have voted to adopt the plan. Thus, the reasoning in (B) is not flawed. Because the pattern of reasoning is different, and not flawed, (B) is not the correct answer.

D Like (A), to the extent that a company consists of the members of that company, (D) reverses the pattern of reasoning in the passage. It infers that what is true of each of the individual members of a group (being old) is true of the group as a whole. Thus, (D) does not parallel MacNeil's pattern of reasoning.

E Like (A) and (D), (E) reverses the pattern in MacNeil's reasoning. It infers that what is true of each individual (the atoms) is true of a larger entity (the molecule) that consists of those individuals. Thus, (E) does not parallel MacNeil's pattern of reasoning.

- *Difficulty Level: 2*

Question 8

Overview: The passage claims that a critic of space exploration is exaggerating the risk when that critic contends that people traveling to Mars would be unlikely to survive the trip. So the passage is claiming that the travelers probably would survive. The evidence for this claim is that a fatal catastrophe would be quite unlikely at each stage because there would be a backup system at each stage.

The question asks you to identify why the argument's reasoning is flawed.

The Correct Answer:

A The argument infers that something is true of the whole trip to Mars (the travelers are likely to survive) merely because it is true of each part (stage) of the trip. Note that this is a very questionable type of inference to make: in general we cannot correctly infer that something is unlikely to occur during a lengthy event merely because it is unlikely to occur during each part of the event. So (A) describes why the argument's reasoning is flawed.

The Incorrect Answer Choices:

B The argument does not infer that a fatal catastrophe during a trip to Mars cannot occur, only that it probably won't occur. Moreover, this is not inferred from a claim that a fatal catastrophe is unlikely to occur on a trip to Mars; it is instead inferred from a claim that a fatal catastrophe is unlikely to occur on any given stage of that trip.

C The argument does not infer that it must be the case that travelers to Mars would survive the trip, only that they probably would survive the trip. Moreover, that inference is not based on a claim that they probably would survive the trip; it is instead based on a claim that they probably would survive any given stage of the trip.

D The argument does not infer that anything will definitely work, whether it is the backup systems or the entire trip to Mars. It only makes claims regarding the probability that things will work. Also, the argument never draws an inference from the mere possibility that something will work.

E   The view that is rejected is that travelers to Mars would be unlikely to survive the trip. The passage does not discuss any argument that has been made for this view. So the passage does not reject this view merely on the grounds that an inadequate argument has been made for it.

- *Difficulty Level: 5*

Question 9

Overview: The passage gives a definition of a retrospective study, and then it presents a premise—retrospective studies must use subjects' reports about their pasts—and draws the conclusion that retrospective studies cannot reliably determine what caused human subjects' present characteristics. Note that there's an important gap in this argument. The premise doesn't even address the issue of reliability and so it cannot, by itself, provide sufficient grounds for the conclusion that retrospective studies are unreliable.

The Correct Answer:

C   (C) says that in studies of the kind under discussion in the passage, subjects' reports about their pasts are unreliable—their reports about their pasts are highly susceptible to inaccuracy. This is exactly the sort of statement that we need to bridge the gap in the argument. According to the argument, retrospective studies must use subjects' reports about their pasts. If, as (C) says, those reports are unreliable, then the conclusion that retrospective studies cannot reliably determine the causes of the subjects' present characteristics can be properly drawn.

The Incorrect Answer Choices:

A   (A) says that the reliability of a study may depend partly on the extent to which the study uses inaccurate reports. However, unless the argument were to give us reason to believe that subjects' reports about their pasts are inaccurate, assuming (A) would not help to establish the argument's conclusion that retrospective studies are unreliable.

B   (B) says that a retrospective study cannot be reliable unless there are correlations between subjects' present characteristics and what happened to those subjects in the past. Since the premises of the argument do not say or imply anything about whether there are such correlations, assuming (B) would not help to establish that retrospective studies are not reliable.

D The conclusion of the argument is that retrospective studies of human subjects are not reliable. (D) states a condition that ensures that studies of human subjects will be reliable. If retrospective studies satisfy this condition, we can conclude that such studies are reliable. And if retrospective studies do not satisfy this condition, it remains possible that these studies are reliable. In either case, assuming (D) would not help to establish that retrospective studies are not reliable.

E The only premise stated in the argument tells us that **retrospective** studies, which look for significant connections between subjects' present characteristics and what happened to them in the past, must use subjects' reports about their pasts. (E) says something very similar: **every scientific study** that looks for significant connections between subjects' present characteristics and what happened to them in the past must use the subjects' reports about their pasts. Since the conclusion of the argument concerns only retrospective studies, (E) gives us no further basis for the argument's conclusion beyond that already provided by the existing premise.

- *Difficulty Level: 2*

Question 10

Overview: The question asks you to identify the conclusion drawn in the argument. The conclusion of the argument is the claim that the other parts of the argument are meant to support.

The first sentence of the passage states a background fact about gigantic planes under development. The second sentence asserts that the extra space in these planes is more likely to be used for passenger seating than for shops and lounges. The next sentence presents two claims that, taken together, support this assertion. Those two claims suggest that within 20 years some planes will have to carry more passengers than a normal-sized plane, so at least some of the extra space in the gigantic planes will have to be used for passenger seating.

The Correct Answer:

B (B) essentially restates the second sentence of the passage. The claim made by this sentence is the only part of the argument for which support is offered, so it is the conclusion drawn in the argument.

The Incorrect Answer Choices:

A (A) states a background fact that is presented in the argument rather than the argument's conclusion.

C (C) states one of the claims offered in support of the argument's conclusion rather than the conclusion.

D (D) states one of the claims offered in support of the argument's conclusion rather than the conclusion.

E (E) cannot be the conclusion drawn in the argument because it says something that is not even stated in the argument. The statement in (E) is not even suggested by anything that is stated in the argument.

- *Difficulty Level: 3*

Question 11

Overview: The scientist describes a study in which some people with athlete's foot were given medication M and others were given medication N. The only people whose athlete's foot was cured were given M. In other words, some (but not necessarily all) people who were given M had their athlete's foot cured, but no one who received N had their athlete's foot cured. The reporter infers from the scientist's description that if anyone in the study did not have their athlete's foot cured, then they were not given M. This is equivalent to the statement that if someone was given M, then that person's athlete's foot was cured.

The question asks you to identify the answer choice that describes the reporter's reasoning error.

The Correct Answer:

A   As discussed in the "Overview," the study found that some, but not necessarily all, people who received M had their athlete's foot cured. That is, the study provides evidence that M can cure athlete's foot but not that it always does so. The reporter inferred that if someone was given M, then that person's athlete's foot was cured—in other words, M always cured athlete's foot for anyone who received it. So the reporter inferred that M always cures athlete's foot from evidence that M can cure it.

The Incorrect Answer Choices:

B   The reporter makes a claim only about the people in the study: everyone in the study who received M had their athlete's foot cured. So the reporter does not draw any conclusion about the population as a whole.

C   The reporter makes a claim only about the people in the study: everyone in the study who received M had their athlete's foot cured. So the reporter does not presume anything about whether M and N are available to people who did not participate in the study.

D   The reporter's inference is equivalent to the claim that everyone in the study who was given M had their athlete's foot cured. This claim is consistent with the possibility that some other medications (besides M and N) cure athlete's foot and also with the possibility that athlete's foot may be cured without medication. So the reporter's inference does allow for the possibility that that athlete's foot may be cured even if neither M nor N is taken.

E   The reporter makes a claim only about the people in the study: everyone in the study who received M had their athlete's foot cured. It is consistent with that claim that there is a sizeable subgroup of people who were not in the study whose athlete's foot will be cured only if they don't take M. So the reporter does not make the presumption described in (E).

- *Difficulty Level: 2*

Question 12

Overview: The conclusion of the passage's argument is that plesiosauromorphs probably hunted by chasing their prey over long distances. The only support offered for this conclusion is that the shape of plesiosauromorph fins was very similar to the shape of the wings of birds specialized for long-distance flight. The argument suggests that long-distance flight is appropriately analogous to long-distance swimming. It then infers that, because plesiosauromorphs' fins were similar to the wings of birds specialized for long-distance flight, plesiosauromorphs were probably well suited to long-distance swimming and used this ability to hunt their prey.

The question asks you to identify an assumption on which the argument depends.

The Correct Answer:

E The argument depends on (E) being true. To see this, suppose that (E) were false, and the shape of a marine animal's fins does not affect the way the animal swims in the same way that the shape of a bird's wings affects the way the bird flies. In that case, the only premise of the argument—that the shape of plesiosauromorph fins was very similar to the shape of the wings of birds specialized for long-distance flight—would not be relevant at all to any conclusion about how plesiosauromorphs swam. Thus the argument's premise would not provide any support for the conclusion if (E) were false. This means that the argument depends on assuming (E).

The Incorrect Answer Choices:

A The one premise of the argument is about the structural similarity between plesiosauromorphs' fins and birds' wings. Whether or not this similarity is the result of a shared evolutionary history is irrelevant to whether the structural similarity provides support for the argument's conclusion. So the argument does not depend on (A).

B (B) makes a claim about the uniqueness of plesiosauromorph fins. Since the argument makes no claims about the uniqueness of plesiosauromorphs, and whether other marine animals might have also hunted prey over long distances, the information in (B) is irrelevant to the argument.

C If (C) were true, then it would provide reason to think that the conclusion of the argument is true. The support provided by (C), however, would be completely independent of the argument in the passage. (C) does not connect the premise about the similarity in shape between a bird's wings and a plesiosauromorph's fins to the conclusion that plesiosauromorphs probably hunted by chasing prey over long distances. So whatever support the argument's premise has for the conclusion is independent of the truth of (C). Thus the argument does not depend on assuming that (C) is true.

D The argument provides some reason to think that plesiosauromorphs were specialized for long-distance swimming and then concludes that plesiosauromorphs chased their prey over long distances. The argument thus needs an assumption to bridge the gap between being specialized for long-distance swimming and chasing prey over long distances. Although (D) may appear to bridge this gap, it does not really do so. (D) says that most marine animals that chase prey over long distances are specialized for long-distance swimming, but it does not establish that most marine animals that are specialized for long-distance swimming chase prey over long distances. Since (D) does not bridge this or any other gap in the argument, the argument does not depend on (D).

- *Difficulty Level: 2*

Question 13

Overview: The task here is to identify the answer choice that conforms most closely to the principle illustrated by the passage. In performing this task, it is typically useful to form at least a rough idea of the principle before looking at the answer choices. Here, the principle might be stated as follows: implementing a solution in order to reduce costs can have unintended consequences that result in additional costs that outweigh the savings.

The Correct Answer:

D   (D) comes closest to conforming to the principle sketched in the "Overview." The purpose of a hotel security system includes the reduction of costs associated with theft. But in the case described in (D), a complicated hotel security system has the unintended consequence of reducing customer goodwill, which may outweigh the savings in losses by theft.

The Incorrect Answer Choices:

A   In (A), there is no indication that choosing textbooks based on student preference is done in order to reduce costs. (A) thus could not conform to the principle illustrated by the passage.

B   (B) does not describe a case in which a solution designed to reduce costs has unintended consequences that result in additional costs that outweigh the savings. Instead, (B) describes a case in which overall savings are achieved in spite of high initial costs.

C   In (C), it is not clear that having a pizza delivered was done in order to save time (which might be considered a cost). It may have been done for any number of reasons. Thus, the fact that ordering the pizza may not save time does not mean that ordering the pizza may have unintended consequences that outweigh intended savings.

E   In the case described in (E), buying an electronic keyboard rather than a piano might reduce purchase costs but might involve greater repair costs. But there is no indication that the repair costs that result from buying an electronic keyboard rather than a piano outweigh the savings in purchase costs. So, (E) does not conform to the principle illustrated by the passage.

- *Difficulty Level: 2*

Question 14

Overview: In the passage, a professor argues that rap is extremely individualistic and nontraditional. The premises offered to support this conclusion are that rap musicians can work alone and that learning to rap is a relatively informal process. A critic responds with considerations that suggest that rap is at least somewhat traditional and not so individualistic: rap appeals to tradition by incorporating older songs; rap has developed its own tradition; and successful rappers must conform to the public's preferences.

To answer the question, you'll need to identify the best description of how the critic responds to the professor's argument.

The Correct Answer:

B   As discussed in the "Overview," the critic suggests that rap is at least somewhat traditional and not as individualistic as the professor concludes. That is, the critic challenges the professor's conclusion that rap is extremely individualistic and nontraditional. As (B) indicates, the considerations that the critic presents to support this challenge were not taken into account by the professor's argument.

The Incorrect Answer Choices:

A   The premises on which the professor's conclusion is based are that rap musicians can work alone and that learning to rap is a relatively informal process. The critic does not offer evidence against either of these premises.

C   The professor does draw a conclusion about whether rap is traditional and individualistic. However, since the professor's conclusion concerns only rap, it is not correct to say that the professor generalizes from the particular context of rap music to a broader context. Moreover, there is no indication that the critic thinks that the professor has generalized in this way. So (C) does not accurately describe the critic's response to the professor's argument.

D   The considerations that the critic presents do not offer an explanation of any phenomena, so they are clearly not offering an alternative explanation of phenomena cited by the professor.

E The claims about tradition and individuality that the professor gives as evidence are that rap musicians can work alone, that doing so means that they need not accommodate other musicians' wishes, and that learning to rap is a relatively informal process. The critic doesn't challenge any of these claims.

■ *Difficulty Level: 4*

Question 15

Overview: The speaker describes Smith's view—that the true meaning of an author's statements can be understood only through insight into the author's social circumstances—and proceeds to argue that if we assume that Smith's view is true and apply it to Smith's own words, it will lead us to the (somewhat bizarre) conclusion that Smith is not aware of the true meaning of her own statements. The speaker reaches this conclusion by drawing it from an intermediate conclusion—that if Smith's view is right, we should be able to discern the true meaning of Smith's statements from her social circumstances.

Take note of the gap between the speaker's main conclusion and the argument that leads to that conclusion. The correct answer will need to bridge that gap.

The Correct Answer:

B If (B) is assumed, then Smith will not be able to discern the true meaning of her own statements from her social circumstances, since (B) tells us that she lacks knowledge of her social circumstances. Smith's view is that the true meaning of an author's statements can be understood only through insight into the author's social circumstances. So if we are to assume that Smith's view is true, it can be inferred that Smith is not able to discern the true meaning of her own statements. This is equivalent to the speaker's main conclusion.

The Incorrect Answer Choices:

A (A) makes a claim about the relative importance of insight into intended meaning and insight into true meaning. But the speaker's argument is concerned only with Smith's insight into the true meaning of her words. So, assuming (A) cannot help to establish the main conclusion of the speaker's argument.

C (C) says that Smith intends her work to have just one meaning, but the speaker's argument doesn't touch on the subject of authors' intentions regarding the meaning of their works. No connection can be made between (C) and any part of the speaker's argument. So, assuming (C) would not help establish the speaker's main conclusion.

D In a way, the speaker seems to be suggesting that Smith's theory about the relation of social circumstances to the understanding of meaning lacks insight. But the speaker makes this suggestion by arguing that Smith's theory leads to the bizarre conclusion that Smith herself is not aware of the true meaning of her own words. And the speaker makes this argument by applying Smith's analysis to Smith's own words. To assume what (D) says—that Smith's theory lacks insight—would, if anything, undermine the speaker's argument.

E The speaker's argument makes no claims about the intended meaning of an author's work. So, assuming (E) would not affect that argument and would not help to establish the speaker's main conclusion.

- *Difficulty Level: 4*

Question 16

Overview: The argument indicates that, among patients who have had throat surgery, those who snored frequently were more likely to have abnormalities in their throat muscles than those who snored rarely or not at all. The argument then reaches a conclusion that would explain this greater likelihood of abnormalities—snoring can damage the throat. The question asks you to find the statement that most strengthens this argument.

The evidence presented in the argument is that people with a history of frequent snoring tend to also have abnormalities in their throat muscles. This is the result we would find if snoring causes abnormalities in throat muscles. It is also, however, the result we would find if abnormalities in the throat muscles cause snoring.

The Correct Answer:

E As discussed in the "Overview," the evidence that was observed is what would result not only if the argument's conclusion is true but also if abnormalities in throat muscles cause snoring. By ruling out this latter explanation of the evidence, (E) greatly increases the likelihood that the explanation presented by the conclusion is the correct one. In this way (E) greatly strengthens the argument.

The Incorrect Answer Choices:

A The subjects' self-reporting might be inaccurate; many people who snore frequently may be unaware that they do so. This could weaken the argument by calling the evidence into question, but it does not strengthen the argument.

B If we know (B) to be true, we have a more complete picture of the circumstances under which the tissue biopsies were performed, but we don't learn anything that sheds more light on the relationship between snoring and serious abnormalities in the throat muscles. Thus (B) does not strengthen the argument that snoring can cause such abnormalities.

C Differences between subjects' age, weight, and overall health would allow certain alternative explanations of the evidence presented in the passage. For example, if there were differences in age, older test subjects might have both snored more frequently and been more likely to have abnormalities in their throat muscles, in which case it might be advanced age, not snoring, that is responsible for the greater frequency of abnormalities in the throat muscles. By ruling out these other possible explanations, (C) could conceivably strengthen the argument slightly. However, the passage never tells us of any possible connection between snoring or throat damage and factors such as age, weight, and overall health. So alternative explanations of this sort are highly speculative and thus pose a much smaller threat to the argument than the alternative explanation ruled out by (E).

D (D) indicates that there is no correlation at all between having undergone throat surgery and one's likelihood of snoring. But this has little relevance to the argument in the passage, which presented evidence that was limited to a group of patients who had all undergone throat surgery. If people who have undergone throat surgery are more likely, or less likely, to snore than people who have never undergone throat surgery, it does not affect the likelihood that snoring caused throat damage for some of the patients.

- *Difficulty Level: 5*

Question 17

Overview: The conclusion of the argument in the passage is that we should never sacrifice our health to get money. The only premise given to support this conclusion is that happiness is unobtainable without health. On its own, this premise entails that if you were to sacrifice your health in order to acquire money, you would, as a result, be unable to obtain happiness. But that doesn't mean that this is a bad thing to do. Of course, most people think that obtaining happiness is more important than acquiring money, but notice that nothing stated in the argument entails this. As far as the argument is concerned, it still has not been established that obtaining happiness is more important than acquiring money.

The question asks you to identify a statement that will make the conclusion follow logically.

The Correct Answer:

A (A) says that we should acquire money only if we can do so without making happiness unobtainable. The argument's premise is that happiness is unobtainable without health. From (A) and this premise, we can infer that we should acquire money only if we can do so without sacrificing our health, i.e., we should not sacrifice our health to acquire money. So the argument's conclusion follows logically if (A) is assumed.

The Incorrect Answer Choices:

B The claim that we must have either money or health in order to be happy does not help us reach the argument's conclusion. Even if we assume that we should avoid sacrificing happiness (an assumption that is notably missing from the passage) the claim that either money or health is required for happiness would not justify the idea that we should never sacrifice one for the other. So the argument's conclusion does not follow logically if (B) is assumed.

C The claim that health should be valued only as a precondition for happiness does not help us reach the argument's conclusion. As described in the "Overview," the argument has not established whether happiness should be valued more than money. (C) does not provide any grounds for thinking that we should not choose acquiring money over health or happiness. Thus, the argument's conclusion does not follow logically if (C) is assumed.

D The claim that wealth sometimes makes one unhappy does not help us reach the argument's conclusion. As described in the "Overview," the argument has not established whether happiness should be valued more than money. (D) does not provide any grounds for thinking that we should not choose acquiring money over health or happiness. Thus, the argument's conclusion does not follow logically if (D) is assumed.

E (E) says that health is more conducive to happiness than wealth is. (E) may appear to be logically related to the argument. But the passage already told us that happiness is unobtainable without health. This means that health is necessary for happiness. Since the passage never gave us any reason to think that money might also be necessary for happiness, (E) does not add much to what we already know. More importantly, as discussed in the "Overview," the argument has not established that we should not sacrifice happiness in order to acquire money. Even if we assume that (E) is true, that does not establish that we should avoid sacrificing health in the pursuit of money. Thus, the argument does not follow logically if (E) is assumed.

- *Difficulty Level: 5*

Question 18

Overview: The passage presents two principles, along with a justification for each. Vanessa's principle is that all computer code must be written by two programmers working together. Jo's principle is that the most productive programmers must be allowed to work alone.

The question is, in effect, asking you to find the one answer choice that is inconsistent with at least one of the principles. It may seem like the two principles are almost incompatible. However, they do not apply to the same set of programmers: Vanessa's principle applies to every programmer, but Jo's principle only applies to the most productive programmers. So any answer choice that is consistent with Vanessa's principle will also be consistent with Jo's principle as long as it does not mention a programmer who is among the most productive.

The Correct Answer:

D In (D), the most productive programmer on the team is assigned to work with someone else. This violates Jo's principle, since a programmer who is among the most productive is not allowed to work alone.

The Incorrect Answer Choices:

A, E (A) and (E) are consistent with Vanessa's principle, since each assigns two programmers to work together. Both answer choices indicate that neither of these programmers is especially productive, so these answer choices are also consistent with Jo's principle.

B, C (B) and (C) are consistent with Vanessa's principle, since each assigns two programmers to work together. While both answer choices indicate that one of the programmers is more productive than the other programmer, they also indicate that neither of the two programmers is among the most productive on the team. Therefore, these answer choices are also consistent with Jo's principle.

- *Difficulty Level: 4*

Question 19

Overview: The passage presents several statements about pet stores in West Calverton. The question asks you to find a statement that must be true if all those statements are true. To answer a question like this one, it is usually helpful to note any connections between the statements in the passage and any logical inferences that can be drawn on the basis of those connections.

The Correct Answer:

D Notice that the statement "any pet store there that sells tropical fish but not exotic birds sells gerbils" has an interesting overlap with the statement "no independently owned pet stores in West Calverton sell gerbils." Both statements concern pet stores that sell gerbils. If you consider only those pet stores that sell gerbils, you'll note that they include every pet store that sells tropical fish but not exotic birds, and that they include no pet store that is independently owned. So it must be true that none of the independently owned stores are among the stores that sell tropical fish but not exotic birds, which is what (D) says.

The Incorrect Answer Choices:

A None of the statements in the passage tell you anything about the pet stores that are **not** independently owned. So they give you no basis for concluding anything about how many or what proportion of those stores do not sell exotic birds. Thus the statements do not allow you to infer the truth of (A).

B The statements in the passage's first sentence together indicate that pet stores that sell both tropical fish and exotic birds are quite common in West Calverton. But nothing in the passage presents information that bears on the question of whether those pet stores also sell gerbils. You are told that gerbils are sold by all the pet stores that sell tropical fish **but not** exotic birds, but this statement is not a basis for inferring the truth of (B).

C The only statements that bear on the question of which pet stores sell gerbils are the ones in the second sentence. The second of those statements merely rules out the independently owned stores, so it could be true that the only pet stores that sell gerbils are those that sell tropical fish **but not** exotic birds. So (C) does not have to be true.

E Since (E) is a statement about independently owned pet stores in West Calverton, any logical support for (E) in the passage would have to come through the only statement that mentions independently owned pet stores: "no independently owned pet stores in West Calverton sell gerbils." As explained in the discussion of "The Correct Answer," this statement, together with the preceding statement, does allow a logical inference. However, it doesn't allow any logical inferences about independently owned pet stores that do not sell tropical fish, and so you cannot infer the truth of (E).

■ *Difficulty Level: 5*

Question 20

Overview: The passage presents a conflict: estimates of the distances of certain stars from Earth imply that those stars are older than the universe itself. The passage then alludes to new estimates according to which those stars are much farther away than previous estimates indicate, and indicates that when stars are farther away than we thought, those stars' intrinsic brightness must be greater than we thought. Finally, the passage claims that these new estimates help to resolve the conflict presented earlier.

The question asks you to identify the answer choice that helps explain why the new estimates help resolve the conflict. Note that in order to resolve the conflict, the new estimates would have to imply that the stars are younger than previously thought or the universe is older than previously thought, or both.

The Correct Answer:

C According to the new estimates, the stars are farther away than previously thought. Also, the passage says that the farther away that stars are, the greater their intrinsic brightness. So the new estimates imply that the stars are brighter than previously thought. (C) says that the brighter a star is, the younger it is. This implies that the stars are younger than previously thought. As discussed in the "Overview," this helps resolve the conflict.

The Incorrect Answer Choices:

A If the stars in question are the oldest objects yet discovered in the universe, this doesn't tell us that they are younger than previously thought or tell us that the universe is older than previously thought. So (A) doesn't help resolve the conflict.

B Given the information in the passage, (B) doesn't let us draw any new inferences about the age of the stars in question or about the age of the universe. In particular, (B) adds nothing to suggest that the new estimates of the stars' distances from Earth imply that the stars are younger than previously thought or that the universe is older than previously thought. So (B) doesn't help explain why the new estimates resolve the conflict between the ages of the stars and the age of the universe.

D (D) states that the brightness of a celestial object depends on its distance from the observer. But the passage has already indicated that fact; it told us that when stars are discovered to be farther away, their intrinsic brightness must be greater than previously thought, given that their appearance to us on Earth is unchanging. So (D) adds nothing to what we already know from the passage.

E This fact about new telescopes has little connection to what is stated in the passage. In particular, there is no reason to believe that the number of stars that astronomers can see is relevant to either the age of the universe or the age of the stars discussed in the passage. So (E) doesn't help resolve the conflict.

- *Difficulty Level: 5*

Question 21

Overview: The passage makes the following claims: (1) most large nurseries sell raspberry plants primarily to commercial growers; (2) most large nurseries sell only plants that are guaranteed to be disease-free; (3) the raspberry plants that Johnson received from Wally's Plants were not disease-free. Your task is to find the statement that is most strongly supported by these claims.

The Correct Answer:

E If Wally's is a large nursery, then by claim (2) in the passage, Wally's probably sells only plants that are guaranteed to be disease-free. So the plants Johnson received were probably guaranteed to be disease-free. Claim (3) says that Johnson received plants that were not disease-free. So Johnson probably received plants that were not entirely as they were guaranteed to be, as (E) says.

The Incorrect Answer Choices:

A Claim (2) of the passage says that most large nurseries sell only plants that are guaranteed to be disease-free. But the passage does not say anything about nurseries that are not large. So we cannot infer anything about whether the plants that Johnson received were guaranteed to be disease-free if Wally's is not a large nursery.

B If the shipment of plants that Johnson got from Wally's was not entirely as it was guaranteed to be, then it may have been guaranteed to be disease-free or it may have had some other guarantee. Just knowing that a shipment was not as it was guaranteed to be does not tell us anything about what the guarantee was. So we cannot infer anything from the claim that the shipment was not as it was guaranteed to be. Furthermore, even if we assume that the shipment was guaranteed to be disease-free, that does not make it any more or less likely that Johnson is a commercial raspberry grower, since it is possible to guarantee plants sold to noncommercial growers. Thus (B) is not strongly supported by the information in the passage.

C Claim (1) of the passage says that most large nurseries sell raspberry plants primarily to commercial growers. A reasonable interpretation of this claim is that for most large nurseries, most of their raspberry plant customers are commercial growers. But this does not imply that most noncommercial growers buy from someone other than large nurseries since it could be that most growers are commercial growers. Therefore, we cannot infer that if Johnson is not a commercial grower, then Wally's is probably not a large nursery.

D Claim (1) of the passage says that most large nurseries sell raspberry plants primarily to commercial growers. So there would be no reason to think that Wally's is not a large nursery if it sells raspberry plants primarily to commercial growers. Moreover, the passage does not provide any criteria for judging whether a nursery is well-run. So (D) is not strongly supported by the information in the passage.

- *Difficulty Level: 5*

Question 22

Overview: The conclusion of the drug company manager's argument is that the company should try a new marketing campaign for its newest product. The argument offers two premises in support of this conclusion: that the product is just not selling, and that a new marketing campaign is one chance to save the product.

Note that the argument also indicates that a new marketing campaign would not guarantee that the product will be saved. This means that the argument takes into account the possibility of a new marketing campaign not saving the product. As a result, statements that imply merely that the product might not be saved even if the company tries a new marketing campaign do not weaken the argument.

The Correct Answer:

D If, as (D) states, undertaking a new marketing campaign would endanger the company's overall position, this would mean that undertaking the campaign would have a serious cost for the company. This cost might outweigh the benefits to the company of undertaking the campaign (including the benefit of providing the company a chance to save its newest product), in which case the company should not undertake the new campaign. Thus, (D) seriously weakens the argument by providing a reason to think that even if a new marketing campaign has the benefits cited in the argument's premises, the conclusion that the company should try the campaign might be incorrect.

The Incorrect Answer Choices:

A (A) tells us two things, neither of which weaken the argument. If the drug company has invested heavily in this product, this does not diminish the case for the new marketing campaign—such heavy investment is not a strike against the product or its prospects for success. And when we are told that losses due to this product would be harmful to the company's profits, this doesn't tell us anything we don't already know. Since this is one of the company's products, it is to be expected that any losses from this product will affect the company's bottom line.

B (B) suggests merely that the company's newest product might not be saved even if the company tries a new marketing campaign. But, as noted in the "Overview," the argument already takes this possibility into account. Hence, (B) does not weaken the argument.

C If there were reason think that a new marketing campaign would have no chance to succeed, (C) would imply that the argument's conclusion is incorrect; otherwise, (C) would have no effect on the argument. But there is no reason to think that a new marketing campaign would have no chance to succeed; in fact, the argument suggests that the campaign would have a chance to succeed. Hence, (C) has no effect on the argument.

E The fact that the company's other products are selling well does not weaken the argument, since saving the company's newest product would still be beneficial to the company.

- *Difficulty Level: 5*

Question 23

Overview: The consumer advocate concludes that the use of TMD on peaches has not been shown to be acceptable, despite posing little risk to most of the population. The advocate supports this conclusion by noting that peaches, when consumed in average quantities, contain an amount of TMD that shows no health effects when ingested. However, most people in the advocate's country do not consume average quantities of peaches: 80 percent consume none at all, while others consume peaches—and therefore TMD—in disproportionately large amounts.

You are asked to identify the principle that, if valid, most helps to justify the advocate's argumentation. The advocate's conclusion states, in part, that the use of TMD on peaches has not been shown to be acceptable. Since the advocate's support for this conclusion says nothing about what makes a practice acceptable or unacceptable, this claim requires justification.

The Correct Answer:

C (C) indicates that the use of a pesticide must satisfy two conditions in order to be acceptable: it must match the pesticide's intended purpose and must have been shown not to harm any part of the population. Although TMD shows no adverse health effects for those who consume peaches in average amounts, this fails to show that it does not harm those people who consume peaches in larger quantities. So the practice of using TMD on peaches does not meet (C)'s second condition, and thus it is not acceptable according to (C). So if (C) is a valid principle, it helps to justify the advocate's argumentation.

The Incorrect Answer Choices:

A According to (A), a pesticide's risks should be assessed cautiously given that more data might uncover new risks associated with low doses of the pesticide. But even if TMD should be assessed cautiously, that does not tell us whether or not its use on peaches is acceptable. So this principle does not help justify the advocate's argumentation.

B (B)'s principle applies only to pesticides that are likely to be ingested by most of the population. Since most people in the advocate's country eat no peaches, there is no reason to think that most of the population is likely to ingest TMD. So this principle is not applicable to TMD, and therefore cannot help justify the advocate's argumentation.

D (D)'s principle does not apply to pesticides if the average exposure across the population is low and the average exposure has not been shown to harm children's health. The available evidence suggests that TMD is such a pesticide: 80 percent of people in the advocate's country are not exposed to any TMD at all from peaches, and average doses of TMD show no health effects. So (D)'s principle does not help justify the advocate's argumentation.

E (E)'s principle concerns measures taken to protect people from harm. But the advocate does not discuss any such measures, so this principle is not relevant to the advocate's argumentation.

- *Difficulty Level: 4*

Question 24

Overview: The legal commentator provides two pieces of information regarding a recently enacted law that bans smoking in the workplace: the goal of the law is to protect employees from secondhand smoke, and the law is written in such a way that it cannot be interpreted as prohibiting people from smoking in their own homes.

The question asks you to identify the claim that can be rejected on the basis of the legal commentator's statements. It is important to keep in mind as you consider each answer choice that you are looking for a claim that is likely to be **false** if the commentator's statements are true.

The Correct Answer:

E Regardless of what the goal of the new law is, if it is written in such a way that it cannot be interpreted as prohibiting people from smoking in their own homes, then the law cannot protect employees whose workplaces are private homes. Thus, the legal commentator's statements provide a basis for rejecting the claim that the law will protect domestic workers from secondhand smoke in their workplaces.

The Incorrect Answer Choices:

A The legal commentator's statements give us no direct information about the intentions of the legislators who supported the law, but on the assumption that these legislators were in general agreement with the law's goal, the legal commentator's statements give us some indication that these legislators wanted the law to protect employees from secondhand smoke. The legal commentator's second statement suggests that the law will be interpreted in such a way that it will not protect all employees from secondhand smoke. So the legal commentator's statements provide some basis for **accepting** the claim in (A). Clearly, they provide no basis for **rejecting** the claim in (A).

B, D The legal commentator's statements are concerned solely with the law itself and specifically with the goal of the law and the way in which the law was written. These statements provide no basis for either accepting or rejecting a claim about what some group of people believes about the law or believes about certain issues pertaining to it. Thus, the legal commentator's statements do not provide a basis for rejecting either the claim in (B) or the claim in (D).

C To provide a basis for rejecting the claim in (C), the legal commentator's statements would have to give us reason to believe that the law that bans smoking in the workplace offers some protection from secondhand smoke to people outside of their workplaces. But the statements don't do this. One statement merely indicates the goal of the law—to protect **employees** from secondhand smoke. The other statement describes an exemption from the smoking ban—an instance in which the law does not offer protection from secondhand smoke to anyone. Neither statement connects the law to protection from secondhand smoke for people outside of their workplaces, so the legal commentator's statements do not provide a basis for rejecting the claim in (C).

- *Difficulty Level: 4*

Question 25

Overview: The passage says that a university's applicant pool has been shrinking. One possible explanation for this is that the university charges too little: prospective students and their parents associate low cost with poor quality and thus choose not to apply. The argument concludes that in order to enlarge its applicant pool, the university needs to charge more.

Note that the "possible explanation" is merely possible. The university president does not offer any evidence that students are actually choosing not to apply because they associate the university's low cost with poor quality. There are other possible explanations for the shrinking applicant pool, and the rationale for the recommended course of action (raising the university's tuition and fees) only applies if the university president's proposed explanation for the shrinking applicant pool is in fact the reason for the shrinking applicant pool. Otherwise the university president's argument does not support the conclusion in the passage.

Your task is to find an assumption that is required by the university president's argument.

The Correct Answer:

A   The university president's argument requires that (A) be true. To see this, suppose that (A) were false, i.e., the proposed explanation for the decline in applications does not apply. In that case, the decline in applications is not the result of an association between low cost and poor quality, but is instead the result of some other factor. In such a case, the university could enlarge its applicant pool by addressing that other factor and would not need to raise its tuition and fees. So the university president's argument would not support the conclusion if (A) were false.

The Incorrect Answer Choices:

B   The argument could still be a good one even if (B) is false (as long as the explanation offered in the passage does apply). Even if the quality of a university education is not actually dependent on the tuition charged, the explanation discussed in the passage could still explain the shrinking applicant pool as long as prospective students and their parents **believe** that cost is a good indication of quality. So the argument does not require the assumption stated in (B).

C   Even if increasing tuition and fees does not guarantee a larger applicant pool, it can still be true that a larger applicant pool cannot be achieved without increasing tuition and fees. This might be the case if there are other things that must be done in order to increase the size of the applicant pool. For example, a larger applicant pool might not be achieved unless there is an increase in tuition and fees that is combined with the right sort of marketing campaign. Thus the university president's argument still supports the conclusion even if the proposed action falls short of actually guaranteeing a larger applicant pool.

D   The argument could still be a good one even if (D) is false (as long as the explanation offered in the passage does apply). Even if there is another explanation for the shrinking applicant pool that must also be addressed before the applicant pool will grow, it is likely to be true that as long as the university president's explanation applies, the applicant pool will not grow without raising the tuition and fees. So the university president's argument supports the conclusion regardless of the truth of (D).

E   The argument does not need to assume that the university has not increased tuition in recent years. In order for the explanation discussed to apply, the tuition currently charged by the university just needs to be considered low (relative to the university's peers) by prospective applicants and their parents.

- *Difficulty Level: 5*

Question 26

Overview: From two premises, (1) that clean water is essential for human health, and (2) that the purpose of a private company is to produce profit, not to promote health, the editorial concludes that private, for-profit companies should not be hired to supply clean drinking water to parts of the world where it is now unavailable. The question asks you to identify the principle that most helps to justify this reasoning. The correct answer will be a principle that connects the purpose of an organization to a claim about whether the organization should provide something such as clean water that is essential to human health.

The Correct Answer:

E The principle in (E) makes the connection identified in the "Overview." Since clean water is essential for human health (first premise), it follows, by the principle in (E), that it should be provided by an organization whose primary purpose is the promotion of health. Since private companies are not among those organizations (second premise), it follows that clean drinking water should not be provided by private companies. Thus, the principle in (E) would justify the editorial's reasoning.

The Incorrect Answer Choices:

A From the principle in (A), it can be inferred that a private company shouldn't supply drinking water unless a government agency also does so. But the conclusion of the editorial's argument is that a private company should not provide drinking water at all, and the reasoning in support of that conclusion makes no mention of government agencies. So the principle in (A) fails to justify the editorial's reasoning.

B From the principle in (B), it can be inferred that a private company shouldn't be given the responsibility to provide drinking water if it is unwilling or unable to do so. But the argument gives no reason for us to believe that private companies are unwilling or unable to supply drinking water to places where it is unavailable. So (B) doesn't help justify the reasoning in the editorial.

C From the principle in (C), it follows that a private company shouldn't be given the responsibility to provide drinking water if it is unable to consistently supply clean, safe water. But the argument does not state—or give any basis to infer—that private companies are unable to consistently supply clean, safe water. So (C) doesn't help justify the reasoning in the editorial.

D By the principle in (D), we can't infer that a private company's purpose is to promote health just from the fact that it actually promotes health. But the second premise of the editorial's argument states that the purpose of a private company is not to promote health. The principle in (D) fails to connect this to any claim about whether a private company can be given the responsibility to provide clean drinking water, and thus fails to help justify the reasoning in the editorial's argument.

- *Difficulty Level: 2*

Questions 1–6

What the setup tells you: This group of questions concerns the ordering of six appointments, with exactly one appointment on each of six days. There are several conditions that restrict what the order of the appointments can be. Some of the appointments must be scheduled for earlier days than others, and some of the appointments cannot be scheduled for certain specific days. According to the first condition, the water appointment must be scheduled for an earlier day than the landscaping appointment:

W . . . L

According to the second condition, the power appointment must be scheduled for an earlier day than both the gas appointment and the satellite appointment:

P . . . G
P . . . S

The fourth condition specifies that the telephone appointment can't be scheduled for the sixth day. And the third condition specifies that the appointments for the second and third days can't be any of these three: the gas appointment, the satellite appointment, the telephone appointment.

Some things you can deduce right away: The first two conditions specify that the water appointment must be earlier than the landscaping appointment and that the power appointment must be earlier than both the gas appointment and the satellite appointment. Notice that since the landscaping, gas, and satellite appointments must be preceded by some other appointment, this means that none of these three appointments can be the first appointment. That leaves only the power, telephone, and water appointments as possibilities for the first appointment:[40]

1	2	3	4	5	6
P/T/W					

Notice, too, that the first two conditions tell you that neither the power appointment nor the water appointment can be the last appointment. Since the fourth condition explicitly states that the telephone appointment can't be sixth, this leaves only the gas, landscaping, and satellite appointments as possibilities for that day:

1	2	3	4	5	6
					G/L/S

You can also make a useful inference from the third condition, which tells you that on the second and third days the appointments can't be for either gas, satellite, or telephone. The only remaining possibilities for those two days are therefore landscaping, power, and water:

1	2	3	4	5	6
		L/P/W	L/P/W		

So putting all of these inferences together, you've already narrowed things down quite a bit:

1	2	3	4	5	6
P/T/W	L/P/W	L/P/W			G/L/S

Notice that from this it's clear that the gas appointment and the satellite appointment can't be any earlier than the fourth day, and the only days other than the first that are possibilities for the telephone appointment are the fourth or the fifth day.

---

[40] In this and other figures, a slash between the initials of elements indicates that these elements are alternatives. So, for example, "P/T/W" represents "power or telephone or water."

Question 1

What you should keep in mind for this question: Most sets of analytical reasoning questions begin with a question that asks for a complete acceptable outcome. You can think of this as a basic orientation-type question—one that helps you familiarize yourself with the elements you'll be asked about and the conditions that govern their order and/or arrangement. For questions of this type, the best strategy usually is to consider each of the setup conditions in turn and check to see whether the condition is satisfied in each answer choice. (Note that this strategy is usually not a good one for other types of analytical reasoning questions. Be aware that if a set of questions includes an orientation-type question, that question will always be the first one in the set of questions.)

Overview: This question asks you to select a schedule that satisfies all of the specifications of the setup. Consider each of the setup conditions in turn and eliminate any answer choices that violate that condition. Once you've eliminated an answer choice, you don't need to consider it again. When you've eliminated all but one of the answer choices, you'll have arrived at the correct answer.

The Incorrect Answer Choices:

A   The second setup condition requires that the power appointment be scheduled for an earlier day than both the gas appointment and the satellite appointment. But in (A), the gas appointment is scheduled for an earlier day than the power appointment.

B   In (B), the telephone appointment is scheduled for the sixth day, in violation of the fourth setup condition.

C   The first setup condition requires that the water appointment be scheduled for an earlier day than the landscaping appointment. But in (C), the landscaping appointment is scheduled for an earlier day than the water appointment.

E   In (E), the telephone appointment is scheduled for the second day. This violates the third setup condition, which says that the appointments scheduled for the second and third days cannot be for either gas, satellite, or telephone.

The Correct Answer:

D   Answer choice (D) is the only one that satisfies all of the setup conditions. The water appointment is scheduled for an earlier day than the landscaping appointment. The power appointment is scheduled for an earlier day than both the gas and the satellite appointments. The appointments scheduled for the second and third days are not either gas, satellite, or telephone. And the telephone appointment is not scheduled for the sixth day.

▪ *Difficulty Level: 1*

Question 2

Overview: For this question, you're asked to suppose that neither the gas, the satellite, nor the telephone appointment is scheduled for the fourth day. The third setup condition specifies that these three appointments also cannot be scheduled for the second day or the third day. In "Some things you can deduce right away," you inferred that neither the gas nor the satellite appointment can be scheduled earlier than the fourth day. That leaves only the fifth and sixth days available for those two appointments:

1	2	3	4	5	6
				G/S	G/S

Notice that now, since the telephone appointment cannot be scheduled for the second, third, or fourth days, and since you have determined that the fifth and sixth days are reserved for the gas and satellite appointments, the only available day for the telephone appointment is the first day:

1	2	3	4	5	6
T				G/S	G/S

Since this question asks you for what **must** be true, and since you've already determined that the telephone appointment must be scheduled for the first day, a good strategy to take is to skim through the available answer choices to see whether this is in fact available among the choices. If it is, then you're done and there would be no reason to consider the other answer choices.

The Correct Answer:

D   Skimming the answer choices, you find that (D) says what you've discovered has to be true: The telephone appointment is scheduled for the first day. Since this is something that must be true and the question is asking you to identify something that **must** be true, you're safe in selecting this as the answer without even considering any of the other answer choices. You should select this as your answer and move on to the next question. Rule out the other answer choices only if you have extra time.

The Incorrect Answer Choices:

A, C   In the "Overview," you saw that for this question the gas appointment has to be scheduled for either the fifth or the sixth day and the satellite appointment has to be scheduled for either the fifth or the sixth day. But since in this case none of the conditions has an effect on the relative order of the gas and satellite appointments, it doesn't matter which one of these appointments is scheduled for the fifth day and which one is scheduled for the sixth day. So you know that neither (A) nor (C) must be true. (Either one of these **could** be true, but neither one has to be true.)

B, E   Although the power appointment could be scheduled for the third day, it doesn't have to be. And although the water appointment could be scheduled for the second day, it doesn't have to be. Here's an acceptable schedule of appointments in which the power appointment is not scheduled for the third day and the water appointment is not scheduled for the second day:

1	2	3	4	5	6
T	P	W	L	G	S

- *Difficulty Level: 3*

Question 3

What you should keep in mind for this question: This type of question, where you're asked to identify what must be true based solely on what's given in the setup, might seem rather intimidating at first. But as you've already seen in "Some things you can deduce right away," there are lots of inferences that you can make right away, and these can help you draw further inferences as well.

Overview: With questions like this one, it's a good idea to skim the answer choices to see what sort of inferences you should be considering. In this case, what you're looking for is a pair of appointments where one member of the pair has to be scheduled for an earlier day than the other one.

In general, the next step in a question like this is to quickly check to see whether any of the inferences you've already made match one of the answer choices. If so, then you've found the correct answer. If not, then you'll need to make some further inferences. For this question, you probably won't find the answer right away. But here's one relevant thing that you already know from the final paragraph of "Some things you can deduce right away": The gas appointment and the satellite appointment can be scheduled only for the fourth, fifth, or sixth day.

The Incorrect Answer Choices:

A, B You can eliminate (A) by coming up with an acceptable schedule in which the landscaping appointment is **not** scheduled for an earlier day than the telephone appointment. Here's an example:

1	2	3	4	5	6
T	W	L	P	G	S

Notice that in this example it's also the case that the power appointment is **not** scheduled for an earlier day than the landscaping appointment. So (B) is eliminated, too.

C, D You can eliminate (C) by coming up with an acceptable schedule in which the telephone appointment is **not** scheduled for an earlier day than the gas appointment. Here's an example:

1	2	3	4	5	6
W	L	P	G	T	S

Notice that in this example it's also the case that the telephone appointment is **not** scheduled for an earlier day than the water appointment. So (D) is eliminated, too.

The Correct Answer:

E Can it be false that the water appointment is scheduled for an earlier day than the gas appointment? No. You know that the water appointment can't be scheduled for the sixth day, because according to the first condition it must be followed by the landscaping appointment. And you have already determined that the earliest that the gas appointment can be scheduled is for the fourth day. So in order for the gas appointment to be earlier than the water appointment, the gas appointment would need to be scheduled for the fourth day and the water appointment would need to be scheduled for the fifth day, so that the landscaping appointment could be scheduled for the sixth day, after the water appointment:

1	2	3	4	5	6
			G	W	L

But, as noted in the "Overview," the satellite appointment needs to be scheduled for the fourth, fifth, or sixth day. Since none of these days would be available, it can't be that the gas appointment is earlier than the water appointment, and so (E) is must be true.

■ *Difficulty Level: 4*

Question 4

What you should keep in mind for this question: Be sure to note that this question asks you to find what CANNOT be the appointments scheduled for the fourth, fifth, and sixth days. The correct answer will be an **unacceptable** partial schedule.

Overview: You already know that the gas appointment and the satellite appointment have to be among the appointments scheduled for the fourth, fifth, and sixth days. So a good strategy here is to first make a quick check of the answer choices to see whether any of them **don't** include both gas and satellite. If you find such an answer choice, it must be the correct answer.

The Correct Answer:

E Answer choice (E) does not include both the gas appointment and the satellite appointment, so it must be the correct answer. There's no need to rule out the other answer choices.

The Incorrect Answer Choices:

A, B, C, D Unlike the correct answer, (E), all of these answer choices include both gas and satellite. That in itself doesn't guarantee that these answer choices are incorrect, but since you've found the correct answer, there's no need to go further to rule out these choices. For our purposes here, though, let's look at examples that rule out each of these choices. Here's an example that shows that (A) is acceptable:

1	2	3	4	5	6
T	P	W	G	S	L

Here's an example that shows that (B) is acceptable:

1	2	3	4	5	6
T	P	W	L	S	G

Here's an example that shows that (C) is acceptable:

1	2	3	4	5	6
T	W	L	P	S	G

And here's an example that shows that (D) is acceptable:

1	2	3	4	5	6
P	W	L	T	S	G

▪ *Difficulty Level: 2*

Question 5

Overview: This question asks you to identify something that must be true if you suppose that neither the gas appointment nor the satellite appointment is scheduled for the sixth day. From "Some things you can deduce right away," you already know that the sixth appointment can only be gas, landscaping, or satellite. Taking into account the supposition for this question, that leaves only the landscaping appointment available for the sixth day. Since you've therefore determined that the landscaping appointment must be scheduled for the sixth day, it would be a good idea to first make a quick scan of the answer choices to see whether that is among the available choices. If it is, you've found the correct answer and don't need to consider the other answer choices.

The Correct Answer:

B As you saw in the "Overview," it must be true that the landscaping appointment is scheduled for the sixth day (since if neither the gas appointment nor the satellite appointment is scheduled for the sixth day, none of the other appointments except landscaping can be scheduled for that day).

The Incorrect Answer Choices:

A, C, E Here's an acceptable schedule in which the gas appointment is not scheduled for the fifth day, the power appointment is not scheduled for the third day, and the water appointment is not scheduled for the second day:

1	2	3	4	5	6
T	P	W	G	S	L

So, since none of these answer choices has to be true, none of them is correct.

D As you determined in "Some things you can deduce right away," the earliest that the gas appointment and the satellite appointment can be scheduled for is the fourth day. If, as the supposition of this question requires, neither the gas appointment nor the satellite appointment is scheduled for the sixth day, then one of them has to be scheduled for the fourth day and one of them has to be scheduled for the fifth day. So in this case the telephone appointment cannot be scheduled for the fourth day.

1	2	3	4	5	6
			G/S	G/S	

▪ *Difficulty Level: 2*

Question 6

Overview: In this question, you're asked to suppose that the fourth setup condition is replaced with some other condition. Your task is to select an alternative condition that would yield precisely the same outcomes as the ones available when the original condition was present.

In order to answer this kind of question, it is sometimes possible to determine fairly straightforwardly which of the answer choices is correct. And that is the case here. First ask yourself what would change if you eliminate the setup condition that says that the telephone appointment cannot be scheduled for the sixth day. The only consequence is that whereas the original setup allowed the telephone appointment to be scheduled for just the first day, the fourth day, or the fifth day, eliminating this condition also allows the telephone appointment to be scheduled for the sixth day:

1	2	3	4	5	6
T			T	T	T

Remember that in "Some things you can deduce right away" you determined that the gas appointment and the satellite appointment must be scheduled for either the fourth, fifth, or sixth day:

1	2	3	4	5	6
T			G/S/T	G/S/T	G/S/T

Notice that if there were a condition that specified that the telephone appointment must be scheduled for an earlier day than one or both of these appointments, you'd get the same effect as the original condition: It would not be possible to schedule the telephone appointment for the sixth day, and everything else would be just as it was before the original setup condition was replaced. Here is T scheduled for an earlier day than one of the appointments:

1	2	3	4	5	6
T			G/S	T	G/S

And here is T scheduled for an earlier day than both of the appointments:

1	2	3	4	5	6
T			T	G/S	G/S

The effect of the replacement condition in (A) is that T can only be scheduled for the first, fourth, or fifth day. So (A) has the same effect as the original condition and is the correct answer.

Another way to approach this kind of question is to attempt to eliminate all of the incorrect answer choices. Under this approach, you want to rule out any answer choice that does either of the following:

- rules out outcomes that the original setup condition allows

- allows outcomes that the original setup condition rules out

Let's see how this approach would enable us to eliminate answer choices (B), (C), (D), and (E).

Consider the condition presented in (B):

> The telephone appointment must be scheduled for the day immediately before either the gas appointment or the satellite appointment.

Since neither the gas appointment nor the satellite appointment can be scheduled for any day earlier than the fourth day, inclusion of this replacement condition would require that the telephone appointment be scheduled for a day no earlier than the third day. This rules out any of the outcomes in which the telephone appointment is scheduled for the first day, such as the following schedule that was allowed when the original condition was in force:

1	2	3	4	5	6
T	P	W	G	S	L

So since (B) rules out an outcome that the original condition allows, it can't be the correct answer.

Now consider the condition presented in (C):

> The telephone appointment must be scheduled for an earlier day than the landscaping appointment.

This replacement condition would rule out any outcome in which the landscaping appointment is earlier than the telephone appointment, such as the following schedule that was allowed when the original condition was in force:

1	2	3	4	5	6
P	W	L	T	S	G

Now consider (D):

> If the telephone appointment is not scheduled for the first day, it must be scheduled for the day immediately before the gas appointment.

This replacement condition would rule out originally acceptable outcomes like the one just presented above, where the telephone appointment is scheduled for the day immediately before the satellite appointment.

And now for (E):

> Either the gas appointment or the satellite appointment must be scheduled for the sixth day.

This replacement condition would rule out any of the originally acceptable outcomes in which landscaping is the appointment scheduled for the sixth day, such as the one given in the discussion of (B) above.

The Correct Answer:

A As you saw in the "Overview," this answer choice has the same effect in determining the order of the appointments as the original condition does: It allows all of the possible outcomes that were available when the original condition was in force and does not allow any outcomes that were unavailable when the original condition was in force. So this answer choice is correct.

The Incorrect Answer Choices:

B, C, D, E As you saw in the "Overview," each of these answer choices rules out outcomes that were available when the original setup condition was in force. So none of these answer choices is correct.

- *Difficulty Level: 5*

Questions 7–13

What the setup tells you: This group of questions has to do with the colors an artisan will use to create three stained glass windows. There are five colors of glass—green, orange, purple, rose, and yellow—and each of these colors must be used in at least one window. You are also told that each of the three windows must contain at least two different colors. Your task involves determining what color combinations the three windows can contain.

Three of the conditions (the first, second, and fourth) give you specific information about what colors the windows must contain. The first condition tells you that exactly one of the windows contains both purple and green. Notice that this condition does not say that one of the windows contains **only** purple and green, so it is possible that other colors might be used in this window. The second condition tells you that exactly two of the windows contain rose. And the fourth condition tells you that any window without purple must contain orange. The third condition is a restriction on how the colors can be combined. It tells you specifically that yellow cannot be combined with green or orange.

Some things you can deduce right away: From the third condition, you can deduce that the window that contains green and purple (required by the first condition) cannot also contain yellow. The effect of the fourth condition is to prohibit a window that contains neither orange nor purple, which means that each window must contain orange or purple or both orange and purple. At this point, you might want to begin summarizing information in a shorthand form. Here's one way to begin summarizing the possible color combinations for the three windows:

> **W:** green, purple (and possibly orange and/or rose, but not yellow)
>
> **W:**
>
> **W:**

- Exactly two of the windows contain rose. (Second condition)
- Each window must contain orange or purple or both. (Fourth condition)
- No window can combine yellow with green, and no window can combine yellow with orange. (Third condition)

What other conclusions can you draw from the setup and conditions? Well, notice that the third and fourth conditions together enable you to conclude that if a window contains yellow, it must also contain purple. This is because while the fourth condition tells you that each window must contain orange or purple (or both), the third condition tells you that a window **cannot** contain orange if it contains yellow. So, the only way for a window that contains yellow to satisfy the fourth condition is if that window also contains purple. Furthermore, you know that there must in fact be at least one window that contains both purple and yellow, since the setup requires that every color be used at least once. This window could also contain rose, but the third condition precludes it from containing either green or orange. Here's an updated summary of what you know so far about the possible color combinations:

W: green, purple (and possibly orange and/or rose, but not yellow)

W: purple, yellow (and possibly rose, but not green or orange)

W:

- Exactly two of the windows contain rose. (Second condition)
- Each window must contain orange or purple or both. (Fourth condition)
- If a window contains yellow, it must also contain purple. (Inference)
- No window can combine yellow with green, and no window can combine yellow with orange. (Third condition)

Finally, keep in mind that the setup requires that each color be used at least once. The above summary ensures that green, purple, rose, and yellow are used, but not orange. You might want to add something to remind yourself that at least one of the windows must contain orange. So here's the final version of what you have determined about the possible color combinations of the three windows:

W: green, purple (and possibly orange and/or rose, but not yellow)

W: purple, yellow (and possibly rose, but not green or orange)

W:

- Exactly two of the windows contain rose. (Second condition)
- At least one of the windows contains orange. (Setup)
- Each window must contain orange glass or purple or both. (Fourth condition)

If a window contains yellow, it must also contain purple. (Inference)
- No window can combine yellow with green, and no window can combine yellow with orange. (Third condition)

Note that in the interest of time you would probably want to abbreviate this information somehow. Here's one way the above information could be abbreviated:

W: GP possibly O, possibly R, not Y
W: PY possibly R, not G, not O
W:

- Exactly 2R
- At least 1O
- Each: O or P or OP
- If Y, then YP
- Not YG, not YO

Question 7

Overview: This question asks you to pick an acceptable set of color combinations for the three windows. For this kind of question, where you're asked to identify a possible complete outcome, it is generally a good strategy to consider each of the setup conditions in turn and check to see whether it is satisfied in each answer choice. If a condition is violated in an answer choice, you can eliminate that answer choice from consideration.

So, consider the first condition, which states that exactly one of the windows contains both green and purple glass. You will see that (C) violates this condition since there are two windows that contain both green and purple, whereas all of the other answer choices satisfy the condition. So you can eliminate (C) from any further consideration.

What about the second condition, which states that exactly two of the windows contain rose glass? Looking at the remaining answer choices (A), (B), (D), and (E), you can see that this condition is satisfied in (A), (B), and (D), but not in (E), where only one of the windows contains rose. So you can eliminate (E) from any further consideration.

Now consider the third condition, which states that if a window contains yellow glass, it cannot contain either green or orange glass. The remaining answer choices for consideration are (A), (B), and (D). Of these, (A) and (B) satisfy the third condition, but (D) does not, since window 2 combines yellow with orange. Thus, (D) can be eliminated from further consideration.

Finally, consider the fourth condition, which states that if a window does not contain purple glass, it must contain orange glass. There are only two answer choices left for consideration, (A) and (B). Of these, window 2 in (A) violates the fourth condition because it does not contain purple and also does not contain orange, so (A) can be eliminated from consideration.

At this point, you can safely conclude that the correct answer is (B).

The Correct Answer:

B In the "Overview," you determined by a process of elimination that (B) is the correct answer. (B) satisfies the basic setup because each of the five colors is used in at least one of the windows, and each window contains at least two colors. As for the setup conditions, (B) satisfies the first condition because window 1 contains both green and purple, and no other window contains both green and purple. (B) satisfies the second condition because windows 2 and 3, but not window 1, contain rose. (B) satisfies the third condition because the only window that contains yellow, window 3, does not also contain either green or orange. And finally, (B) satisfies the fourth condition because the only window that does not contain purple is window 2 and this window does contain orange. In other words, each window in (B) contains orange or purple or both, as the fourth condition requires.

The Incorrect Answer Choices:

A, C, D, E As demonstrated in the "Overview," each of these answer choices violates a setup condition. Answer choice (A) violates the fourth condition, answer choice (C) violates the first condition, answer choice (D) violates the third condition, and answer choice (E) violates the second condition.

- *Difficulty Level: 1*

Question 8

What you should keep in mind for this question: Be careful to note that this question is asking for a color combination that **cannot** be the color combination of one of the windows.

Overview: For this kind of question, where you're asked to identify something that cannot be true, it's generally a good idea to first glance through the answer choices to see if you can identify the correct answer based on what you already know. In this case, there is an answer choice that directly violates one of the setup conditions: answer choice (C) violates the fourth condition. No window can contain just green and rose because the fourth condition requires that any window that does not contain purple must contain orange. Therefore, (C) is the correct answer. Note that there is no need to verify that the color combinations in the other answer choices are possible combinations, though you may choose to do so if time permits.

The Correct Answer:

C As shown in the "Overview," no window can contain just green and rose, since the fourth condition says that a window must contain orange if it doesn't contain purple. So (C) is the correct answer.

The Incorrect Answer Choices:

A Answer choice (A) can be ruled out because it is possible for one of the three windows to contain just green and orange. Here's one complete outcome that satisfies all of the setup conditions and in which one of the windows contains just green and orange:

W: GO
W: GPR
W: PRY

B Answer choice (B) can be ruled out because it is possible for one of the three windows to contain just green and purple. Here's one complete outcome that satisfies all of the setup conditions and in which one of the windows contains just green and purple:

W: GP
W: OR
W: PRY

D Answer choice (D) can be ruled out because it is possible for one of the three windows to contain just purple and orange. Here's one complete outcome that satisfies all of the setup conditions and in which one of the windows contains just purple and orange:

W: PO
W: GPR
W: PRY

E Answer choice (E) can be ruled out because it is possible for one of the three windows to contain just rose and orange. Here's one complete outcome that satisfies all of the setup conditions and in which one of the windows contains just rose and orange:

W: RO
W: GPR
W: PY

- *Difficulty Level: 4*

Question 9

Overview: This question asks you to suppose that there are two windows that each contain only two colors of glass. Your task is to identify which of the answer choices is an acceptable pair of colors for one of these two windows. A good first step is to see whether any of the answer choices can be eliminated on the basis of what you know already. The first, second, and third conditions don't appear to be directly violated by any of the answer choices, but the fourth condition, which requires that each window contain orange glass or purple glass (or both), is violated by answer choices (A) and (D). So you can eliminate these two answer choices from further consideration and turn your attention to (B), (C), and (E).

When considered in isolation, the color combinations in each of these three answer choices do not appear to violate any of the setup conditions. So, in order to identify the correct answer, you will need to think about the bigger picture. That is, you need to think about whether it's possible to come up with acceptable color combinations for all three windows if one of the windows has the color combination given in the answer choice. Remember that you already know something about what a complete outcome needs to look like. You determined in "What the setup tells you" that one of the windows must contain green and purple, and another of the windows must contain purple and yellow:

W: GP possibly O, possibly R, not Y
W: PY possibly R, not G, not O

Now, this particular question asks you to suppose that two of the windows contain exactly two colors. Because there are three windows in total, you know that at least one of the windows above will be a two-colored window. Is it possible for both of the windows above to contain just two colors? No. Remember that the second condition says that exactly two windows contain rose glass, so you know that one of these windows will have to contain rose, while the other window will contain just the two colors already specified. At this point, you can deduce two things about the third window: it must be one of the two windows that contain rose and it must be one of the two windows that contain exactly two colors of glass. In other words, given the supposition for this question, any complete solution will have to conform with one of the following:

W: GPR possibly O   W: GP
W: PY   W: PRY
W: R __   W: R __

You can see from the above that in order to satisfy the supposition of this question, one of the two-colored

windows will have to contain **either** purple and yellow **or** green and purple, and the other two-colored window will have to contain rose and one other color of glass. A perusal of the remaining answer choices, (B), (C), and (E), shows that neither (C) nor (E) fits one of these characterizations. You have thus eliminated all of the answer choices except (B), which you can now safely conclude must be the correct answer.

The Correct Answer:

B   In the "Overview" you determined by a process of elimination that (B) must be the correct answer. Here's one complete outcome that verifies that this is so:

W: GP
W: PRY
W: OR

In this set of color combinations, there are two windows that contain exactly two colors, as the supposition of this question requires. The bottommost window has the color combination in answer choice (B)—orange and rose. In addition, this set of color combinations satisfies all of the setup conditions, as you can verify for yourself. Thus, (B) is the correct answer: if two of the windows contain exactly two colors of glass, then it is possible for one of these two-colored windows to contain the colors orange and rose.

The Incorrect Answer Choices:

A, D   As noted in the "Overview," neither of the color combinations in (A) and (D) can be the complete color combination for one of the windows. These color combinations—rose and yellow, green and rose—are directly ruled out by the fourth setup condition, which requires that each window contain either orange or purple or both. Thus, neither (A) nor (D) can be the correct answer.

C, E   Given the supposition that two of the windows contain exactly two colors, it is not possible for one of these windows to contain the color combinations in (C) and (E). As you saw in the "Overview," one of the two-colored windows must contain **either** purple and yellow **or** green and purple, and the other of these windows must contain rose and one other color of glass. Orange and purple, the color combination in (C), is thus not a possible color combination for one of the two-colored windows; nor is green and orange, the color combination in (E).

- *Difficulty Level: 4*

Question 10

Overview: This question asks you to suppose that the color combination of one of the windows is purple, rose, and orange, and then determine which of the answer choices could be the color combination of another of the windows.

As with most questions that ask you to identify which answer choice is possible given the supposition introduced by the question, it is usually a good idea to first glance over the answer choices to see if you can eliminate any of them based on what you already know, regardless of whether the supposition of the question holds or not. In this case, however, a quick check of the answer choices shows that none of them directly violate either the setup conditions or what you have already deduced from those conditions.

So how should you proceed? A good strategy for answering a question that introduces a supposition is to begin by considering how the question's supposition fits in with what you already know about what a possible outcome must look like. In this case, you know from the discussion in "What the setup tells you" that it will have to include one window that contains green and purple and another window that contains purple and yellow. Neither of these windows can be the window that satisfies the supposition of this question; that is, neither of these windows can be the window that contains just purple, rose, and orange glass. So you can deduce that it must be the third window in the set that contains this color combination:

> **W:** GP possibly O, possibly R, not yellow
> **W:** PY possibly R, not G, not O
> **W:** PRO

At this point your work is essentially done. All you have to do now is look for the one answer choice that is consistent with the above characterization. That answer choice is (B): green, orange, and purple.

The Incorrect Answer Choices:

A, C, E These answer choices can all be eliminated for the same reason: none of these combinations contains the color purple. Look again at the characterization of the possible color combinations of glass given in the "Overview." Notice that in any acceptable outcome, all three of the windows will contain purple. That is, if you suppose that the color combination of one of the windows is purple, rose, and orange, then you can deduce that all three of the windows must contain the color purple. This being the case, none of the color combinations in (A), (C), and (E) could be the color combination of any of the windows.

D Again, a quick look at the characterization of possible color combinations in the "Overview" shows that none of the windows can contain just orange and purple glass. Why is this so? Well, if the color combination of one of the windows is purple, rose, and orange, as this question asks you to suppose, then you know that in order for each of the five colors to be used at least once, the colors green and yellow will each have to be used in at least one of the remaining windows. The third condition says that these two colors cannot be used together. Therefore, one of the remaining two windows will have to contain green, and the other will have to contain yellow—in other words, neither of these windows can contain only orange and purple. So (D) cannot be the correct answer.

Correct Answer:

B If the color combination of one of the windows is purple, rose, and orange, then it is possible for the color combination of one of the other windows to be green, orange, and purple. Here is one complete outcome that satisfies the supposition of this question as well as all of the setup conditions:

> **W:** GOP   (Answer choice B)
> **W:** PRY
> **W:** PRO   (Supposition introduced by the question)

- *Difficulty Level: 4*

Question 11

Overview: For this question, you are asked to suppose that orange glass is used in more of the windows than green glass and then identify a possible color combination for one of the windows. A quick check of the answer choices shows that none of them appears to violate the setup conditions directly, so you can't eliminate any of the answer choices that way.

So, how should you proceed? Well, one way to approach this question is to first ask: What is the maximum number of windows that could contain orange? Could all three windows contain orange? The answer to this question is no. This is because the setup requires that each of the five colors be used in at least one window but the third condition precludes yellow from being used together with orange. So you know that there has to be at least one window that contains yellow but not orange. From this, you can deduce that the only way for the supposition of this question to be met is if exactly two of the windows contain orange and exactly one of the windows contains green.

With this in mind, let's look again at what was determined about the possible color combinations for the three windows in "What the setup tells you":

    W: GP possibly O, possibly R, not Y
    W: PY possibly R, not G, not O
    W:

It is readily apparent which window will have to be the one that contains green: it has to be the window that contains both green and purple (that is, the window that satisfies the first setup condition). So, thus far you have deduced the following: in order for this question's supposition to be satisfied, there can be only one window that contains green and that window must also contain purple glass. Notice that at this point, you can safely eliminate answer choices (D) and (E), since in each of these answer choices the color green appears but the color purple does not.

What about the remaining answer choices (A), (B), and (C)? Let's see what else can be deduced. You have deduced which window must be the only window that contains green, but what can you deduce about the two windows that must contain orange? Well, you know which window **cannot** be one of the two windows that contain orange: the window that contains yellow cannot be one of the two windows that contain orange because the third setup condition precludes orange and yellow from being used together. And from this observation you can deduce that the window that contains green and purple must also be one of the two windows that contain orange. Now notice that this inference allows you to

eliminate answer choices (B) and (C). This is because the color combinations in each of these answer choices include green but not orange, but as you have established, there can only be one window that contains green and that window must also contain both orange and purple. Thus, by a process of elimination, you can safely identify (A) as the correct answer.

The Correct Answer:

A In the "Overview," you determined by a process of elimination that (A) must be the correct answer. That the color combination in (A) is in fact a possible color combination for one of the windows, given the supposition that orange glass is used in more of the windows than green glass, is demonstrated by the following set of color combinations for the three windows:

    W: OP   (Answer choice A)
    W: PRY
    W: GOPR

As you can verify for yourself, in addition to satisfying the supposition introduced by this question, the above set of color combinations also satisfies all of the setup conditions.

The Incorrect Answer Choices:

B, C, D, E As discussed in the "Overview," the only way that the supposition of this question can be met—the only way orange glass can be used in more of the windows than green glass—is if there is exactly one window that contains green glass and that window also contains orange and purple glass. What the color combinations in (B), (C), (D), and (E) have in common is that they all include the color green, but none of them also includes both of the colors orange and purple: (B) and (C) do not include orange, and (D) and (E) do not include purple. This being the case, none of the color combinations in these answer choices is a possible color combination for one of the windows, given the supposition of this question.

■ *Difficulty Level: 5*

Question 12

Overview: For this question, you are asked to determine which one of the five colors could be used in all three of the windows. One strategy you could use to answer this question would be to go through the answer choices one by one, and see if you can come up with an acceptable outcome in which the specified color is used in all three windows. An alternative strategy would be to see if you can identify the correct answer through a process of elimination. Using this strategy, you would want to try to rule out all but one of the answer choices based on what you know already about the setup conditions and what can be deduced from those conditions. For this question, a process of elimination strategy does indeed turn out to be a good one, because as you will see below, what you know already will allow you to quickly eliminate all of the answer choices but (C).

The Incorrect Answer Choices:

A, B, E   These three answer choices can all be eliminated based on the setup requirement that each color of glass has to be used in at least one of the windows together with the third condition, which precludes yellow from being used together with either green or orange: green cannot be used in all three of the windows, since then yellow could not be used at all. Thus, (A) cannot be the correct answer. Similarly, orange cannot be used in all three of the windows, since again this would mean that yellow could not be used. Thus, (B) cannot be the correct answer. And finally, yellow cannot be used in all three of the windows, since then neither green nor orange could be used in any of the windows. Thus, (E) cannot be the correct answer.

D   Answer choice (D) can be eliminated by virtue of the second condition alone. This condition states that **exactly two** of the windows contain rose glass, thus directly precluding the possibility of rose being used in all three windows.

The Correct Answer:

C   So, by a process of elimination, you can conclude that (C) must be the correct answer choice. There's no need to verify that purple can be used in all three of the windows, though you may do so if you have time. Here's one complete outcome that satisfies the setup requirements and in which all three windows contain purple:

W: GPR
W: PRY
W: OP

- *Difficulty Level: 4*

Question 13

Overview: This question asks you to first suppose that none of the windows contains both rose and orange glass and then determine which one of the answer choices is a color combination that **must** be one of the color combinations.

In most cases, a good starting point for questions that ask what must be the case if a certain supposition holds is to see how the supposition interacts with what you have already inferred about what a complete outcome can look like. In "What the setup tells you" you deduced that any set of color combinations for the three windows must conform with the following characterization:

W: GP possibly O, possibly R, not Y
W: PY possibly R, not G, not O
W:

- Exactly 2R
- At least 1O

Now, what if, in addition to the above information, none of the windows can contain both rose and orange, as this question asks you to suppose? What can you deduce about what a possible outcome will look like? Well, the first thing to note is that since exactly two of the windows have to contain rose, and since at least one of the windows has to contain orange, you can deduce that in order to satisfy this question's supposition, exactly two of the windows will have to contain rose but not orange glass, and exactly one of the windows will have to contain orange but not rose glass. And once you've arrived at this deduction, you're almost done. This is because, according to the characterization above, there is one window that **cannot** be the window that contains orange and so must be one of the windows that contains rose.

The window that contains purple and yellow cannot be the window that contains orange because the third condition precludes both orange and green from being used together with yellow. And if this window cannot be the window that contains orange, then it must be one of the two windows that contain rose. In sum, you've deduced that if none of the windows contains both rose glass and orange glass, then the color combination of one of the windows must be purple, rose, and yellow. Thus, (E) is the correct answer choice.

The Correct Answer:

E As demonstrated in the "Overview," (E) is the correct answer choice: if none of the windows contains both rose and orange glass, then the color combination of one of the windows must be purple, rose, and yellow.

The Incorrect Answer Choices:

A, B, C For questions that ask what must be true if a certain supposition holds, you can verify that an answer choice is incorrect by showing that it is possible for the answer choice to be false while both the setup conditions and supposition are satisfied. Here's one set of color combinations for the three windows that demonstrates that none of the color combinations in (A), (B), and (C) is a color combination that one of the windows **must** have in order for this question's supposition and the setup conditions to be satisfied:

W: GPR
W: PRY
W: OP

(Note that the color combination in (A) is not a possible color combination for any of the windows, given this question's supposition. As discussed in the "Overview," in order for this question's supposition to be met, two of the windows must contain rose but not orange, and the third window must contain orange but not rose. In other words, in any acceptable outcome, each of the three windows will contain either orange or rose, but not both. Answer option (A) contains neither.)

D The following set of color combinations establishes that it is possible for both the supposition of this question and the setup conditions to be satisfied when none of the windows contains the color combination purple and orange:

W: GPR
W: PRY
W: GO

Thus, it is not the case that purple and orange must be the color combination of one of the windows if none of the windows contains both rose and orange glass. So (D) cannot be the correct answer.

- *Difficulty Level: 5*

Questions 14–18

What the setup tells you: This set of questions has to do with determining which talks at a conference on management skills each of four employees attends. There are exactly five talks—Feedback, Goal Sharing, Handling People, Information Overload, and Leadership—and they are held in that order. The setup tells you that each employee must attend exactly two talks and that each talk is attended by at most two of the employees. It might be helpful for you to note that there's no requirement that each of the talks be attended by one of these employees. Indeed, it will turn out that it is possible for there to be a talk that is attended by none of them.

The first two conditions place restrictions on which talks certain of the employees can attend. The first condition says that Quigley attends neither Feedback nor Handling People. In other words, this condition says that the only talks Quigley can attend are Goal Sharing, Information Overload, or Leadership. Similarly, the second condition says that Rivera attends neither Goal Sharing nor Handling People, which means that the only talks Rivera can attend are Feedback, Information Overload, or Leadership.

The third, fourth, and fifth conditions give you information about pairs of employees who must or cannot attend a talk together. The third condition tells you that Spivey and Tran cannot attend any of the same talks as each other. The fourth and fifth conditions tell you that Tran and Quigley must attend at least one talk together—namely, whichever of the five talks Tran attends first—and that Rivera and Spivey must attend at least one talk together—namely, whichever of the five talks Rivera attends first. When considering these last two conditions, it is important to note that the fourth condition does **not** say that the first talk Tran attends must also be the first talk Quigley attends and the fifth condition does **not** say that the first talk Rivera attends must also be the first talk Spivey attends. It is possible that the first talk Quigley attends is an earlier talk than the first talk Tran attends. In other words, it is possible that the first talk Tran attends is the second talk Quigley attends. Similarly, it is possible that the first talk Spivey attends is an earlier talk than the first talk Rivera attends. In other words, it is possible that the first talk Rivera attends is the second talk that Spivey attends.

Some things you can deduce right away: Because there are five talks and at most two employees per talk, you can deduce something about the general outline of what a complete final outcome can look like. There are two possibilities. One possibility is that four of the talks are each attended by two employees, while the remaining talk is not attended by any of the employees. The other possibility is that three of the talks are each

attended by two employees, while the remaining two talks are each attended by one. In addition, from the fourth condition you can infer that the employees at one of the talks must be Quigley and Tran. Similarly, the fifth condition allows you to infer that the employees at another one of the talks must be Rivera and Spivey.

Question 14

Overview: This question asks you to determine which answer choice represents a possible schedule for the attendance of the employees at the talks. The best strategy for answering this type of question is typically one in which you consider each setup condition in turn and eliminate any answer choices that violate that condition. When you've eliminated all but one of the answer choices, you'll have arrived at the correct answer.

So, consider first the first setup condition, which requires that Quigley attend neither Feedback nor Handling People. None of the five answer choices violates this condition, so you can turn to a consideration of the second setup condition. The second setup condition requires that Rivera attend neither Goal Sharing nor Handling People. This condition is violated in (B), where Rivera attends Handling People, so (B) can be eliminated from any further consideration.

Consider now the third setup condition, which requires that Spivey not attend either of the talks that Tran attends. This condition is violated in (A), where Spivey and Tran both attend Leadership, so (A) can be eliminated from any further consideration.

Next, consider the fourth condition, which requires that Quigley attend the first talk that Tran attends. This condition is violated in (D), where the first talk Tran attends—Goal Sharing—is not also attended by Quigley, so (D) can be eliminated from any further consideration.

And, finally, consider the fifth condition, which requires that Spivey attend the first talk that Rivera attends. This condition is violated in (E), where the first talk that Rivera attends—Information Overload—is not also attended by Spivey. Thus, you've reached a point where you've eliminated every answer choice but (C). So you can safely conclude without doing any more work that (C) is the correct answer.

The Correct Answer:

C As discussed in the "Overview," you can determine that (C) is the correct answer by a process of elimination. There is no need to verify that (C) satisfies all of the setup conditions, but if you have the time, it is relatively straightforward to do so: (C) satisfies the first and second setup conditions since Quigley attends neither Feedback nor Handling People, and Rivera attends neither Goal Sharing nor Handling People. (C) satisfies the third condition since Spivey and Tran do not attend any of the same talks as each other. (C) also satisfies the fourth condition since the first talk Tran attends (namely, Goal Sharing) is also attended by Quigley. And, finally, (C) satisfies the fifth condition since the first talk Rivera attends (namely, Feedback) is also attended by Spivey.

The Incorrect Answer Choices:

A, B, D, E As shown in the "Overview," each of these answer choices violates a condition in the setup: (A) violates the third condition, (B) violates the second condition, (D) violates the fourth condition, and (E) violates the fifth condition.

- *Difficulty Level: 2*

Question 15

Overview: This question tells you to suppose that none of the employees attends Handling People, and then asks you to determine which of the five answer choices must be true in that case. One way to approach this type of question is to see what can be deduced if the supposition in the question is true. If you can deduce that there is something that **must** be true, then you can check to see if that something is one of the five answer choices—and if it is, you're done.

So, what can be deduced if none of the employees attends Handling People? Well, you know immediately that the other four talks must be attended by two employees each.

F	G	H	I	L
_	_	none	_	_

In other words, you know that the talks Feedback, Goal Sharing, Information Overload, and Leadership are each attended by a pair of employees. Of these pairs you know, as established in "Some things you can deduce right away," that one consists of Rivera and Spivey and another consists of Quigley and Tran. What about the other two pairs? Well, since the third condition precludes Spivey and Tran from attending a talk together, you can deduce that one of the remaining pairs must be Rivera and either Spivey or Tran, and the other must be Quigley and either Spivey or Tran. That is, the pairs that go in some order in the slots above must be RS, QT, RS, and QT, or else RS, QT, RT, and QS.

What can be deduced about the order in which these pairs can be placed into the slots above? You know from the first condition that no pairing that includes Quigley can attend the first meeting (Feedback). So, this means that the first meeting must be attended by a pairing that includes R—either RS or RT. Moreover, you know that the first meeting must in fact be attended by RS, since the fourth condition requires that the first meeting attended by T must also be attended by Q. At this point, you've deduced that both R and S must attend Feedback if the supposition in the question is true. A quick check of the answer choices shows that you are done: the correct answer must be (A).

The Correct Answer:

A As demonstrated in the "Overview," if none of the employees attends Handling People, then it must be true that Rivera attends Feedback.

The Incorrect Answer Choices:

Although it is not necessary to check the remaining answer choices, you can prove to yourself that none of them is correct by showing that in each case it is possible to come up with an acceptable outcome in which the supposition in the question is true, but the statement in the answer choice is **false**. If you can come up with one, you'll have demonstrated that the statement in the answer choice is **not** something that must be true when none of the employees attends Handling People.

B The following is an acceptable outcome in which none of the employees attends Handling People and Rivera does not attend Leadership, demonstrating that it is not the case that Rivera must attend Leadership when the supposition in the question holds.

F	G	H	I	L
R, S	Q, T	none	R, T	Q, S

C The acceptable outcome above also demonstrates that it is not the case that Spivey must attend Information Overload when the supposition in the question holds.

D The following is an acceptable outcome in which none of the employees attends Handling People and Tran does not attend Goal Sharing, demonstrating that it is not the case that Tran must attend Goal Sharing when the supposition in the question holds.

F	G	H	I	L
R, S	Q, S	none	Q, T	R, T

E The following is an acceptable outcome in which none of the employees attends Handling People and Tran does not attend Information Overload, demonstrating that it is not the case that Tran must attend Information Overload when the supposition in the question holds.

F	G	H	I	L
R, S	Q, T	none	R, S	Q, T

- *Difficulty Level: 5*

Question 16

What you should keep in mind for this question: This question asks for a "complete and accurate list of the talks any one of which Rivera and Spivey could attend together." The way to construct such a list is to ask the following question for each of the five talks: Is there an acceptable outcome in which this talk is attended by both Rivera and Spivey? If the answer is yes, then that talk belongs on the list. What you need to keep in mind is that there are two different ways in which an answer choice could fail to be the correct answer choice. If an answer choice consists of a list that does not include a talk for which there is an acceptable outcome in which both Rivera and Spivey attend that talk, then that list is not a **complete** list, and the answer choice cannot be correct. On the other hand, if the answer choice consists of a list that includes a talk for which there is no acceptable outcome in which both Rivera and Spivey attend that talk, then that list is not an **accurate** list, and the answer choice cannot be correct.

Overview: Before considering each talk in turn, let's first see whether any answer choices contain direct violations of the setup conditions. This can be a fairly straightforward way of ruling out some answer choices in a question like this. The second condition prohibits Rivera from attending Goal Sharing, so any answer choice that lists Goal Sharing among the talks that can be attended by both Rivera and Spivey is incorrect. This allows you to rule out (B) right away. Now let's turn to considering each talk in turn, starting with Feedback. Is there an acceptable outcome in which Feedback is attended by both Rivera and Spivey? The answer is yes. Here is one such outcome:

F	G	H	I	L
R, S	Q, T	none	R, S	Q, T

So, a complete and accurate list of the talks that Rivera and Spivey attend together must include Feedback. (C) does not include this talk, so you can eliminate this answer choice from any further consideration.

The next talk to consider is Handling People. However, notice that none of the answer choices includes this talk, which tells you that Handling People must not be a talk that both Rivera and Spivey can attend. There's no need to verify this and you can safely go on to consider the next talk, Information Overload.

Is there an acceptable outcome in which Information Overload is attended by both Rivera and Spivey? Yes, there is. The outcome above is one such outcome. Thus, a complete and accurate list of the talks that Rivera and Spivey attend together must include Information Overload.

(D) does not include this talk, so you can eliminate this answer choice from any further consideration.

This leaves (A) and (E) as the only remaining candidates for the correct answer. Answer choice (E) contains Leadership while (A) does not, so the question to ask yourself now is whether Leadership is a talk that could be attended by both Rivera and Spivey. Here's an acceptable outcome that shows that it is:

F	G	H	I	L
R, S	Q, T	T	Q	R, S

So a complete and accurate list of the talks that Rivera and Spivey could attend together must include Leadership in addition to Feedback and Information Overload.

The Correct Answer:

A As established in the "Overview," the complete and accurate list of the talks any one of which Rivera and Spivey could attend together is: Feedback, Information Overload, and Leadership. Thus, (A) is the correct answer.

The Incorrect Answer Choices:

B The list in (B) is both inaccurate because it includes Goal Sharing and incomplete because it does not include Leadership.

C The list in (C) is incomplete because it does not include Feedback.

D The list in (D) is incomplete because it does not include Information Overload.

E The list in (E) is incomplete because it does not include Leadership.

- *Difficulty Level: 5*

Question 17

What you should keep in mind for this question: In this question, you are asked to identify the answer choice that **could be false** if a particular supposition holds. This means that the incorrect answer choices will all be statements that must be true (and so cannot be false) when that supposition holds.

Overview: This question asks you what could be false if Quigley is the only employee to attend Leadership. So let's start with that supposition and see what follows from it. You know from the second condition that Rivera can attend neither Goal Sharing nor Handling People, so with Leadership out of the running the only talks left for Rivera to attend are Feedback and Information Overload. So you can place Rivera in those positions, along with Quigley in Leadership:

F	G	H	I	L
R			R	Q alone

You can now rule out answer choices (A) and (B). Rivera **must** attend Feedback, so (A) can't be false. And Rivera **must** attend Information Overload, so (B) can't be false either. By the fifth condition, Spivey must attend the first talk attended by Rivera, which in this case is Feedback:

F	G	H	I	L
R, S			R	Q alone

Since Spivey **must** attend Feedback, (C) can't be false, and you can rule it out.

Moving on, recall that in "Some things you can deduce right away" you established that the employees at one of the talks must be Quigley and Tran. In the diagram above, the only talks that have space remaining for two employees are Goal Sharing and Handling People. However, the first condition precludes Quigley from attending Handling People, so Quigley and Tran must attend Goal Sharing:

F	G	H	I	L
R, S	Q, T		R	Q alone

Now, because Tran **must** attend Goal Sharing, (E) can't be false. Thus, you can rule out (E) too. This leaves only (D): Spivey attends Handling People. At this point, because you have ruled out the other four answer choices, you can confidently select (D) as the correct answer to this question. You don't need to demonstrate to yourself that (D) could be false. To do so when you've ruled out all four of the incorrect answer choices wouldn't be a good use of your time.

The Correct Answer:

D Answer choice (D) could be false, because Spivey need not attend Handling People if Quigley is the only one to attend Leadership. Here is an acceptable outcome in which the supposition of the question is met and in which Spivey doesn't attend Handling People:

F	G	H	I	L
R, S	Q, T	T	R, S	Q alone

The Incorrect Answer Choices:

A, B, C, E As demonstrated in the "Overview," each of these answer choices must be true when the supposition in the question holds. Because none of them can be false, none of them is the correct answer.

- *Difficulty Level: 5*

Question 18

What you should keep in mind for this question: As with the previous question, this question asks you to identify the answer choice that **could be false** if a particular supposition holds. This means that the incorrect answer choices will all be statements that must be true (and so cannot be false) when that supposition holds.

Overview: The supposition of this question is that Rivera is the only one of the employees to attend Information Overload, and you are to identify the answer choice that could be false in that case. So, what can be deduced if this supposition holds? Well, you know from "Some things you can deduce right away" that one of the talks must be attended by both Rivera and Spivey. The supposition of this question rules out Information Overload as a talk that both Rivera and Spivey attend, and you know from the second setup condition that neither Goal Sharing nor Handling People could be a talk that both Rivera and Spivey attend, so the only possibilities for the placement of Rivera and Spivey are Feedback and Leadership. First, let's consider whether it's possible given the supposition of the question for both Rivera and Spivey to attend Leadership:

F	G	H	I	L
			R alone	R, S

Looking at this diagram, we see that if Rivera and Spivey attend Leadership, then Information Overload is the first talk that Rivera attends. However, the fifth condition requires that Spivey attend the first talk that Rivera attends, but this is impossible, given the supposition of this question. So the fifth condition can't be satisfied if Rivera and Spivey attend Leadership together, which means that they must instead attend Feedback together:

F	G	H	I	L
R, S			R alone	

And if both Rivera and Spivey **must** attend Feedback when the supposition of the question holds, then neither (B) nor (C) can be a correct answer: it is impossible for either of these answers to be false when Rivera is the only employee to attend Information Overload.

Now let's turn to the placement of Quigley. The first condition limits the talks that Quigley can attend to Goal Sharing, Information Overload, and Leadership. Since Information Overload is attended by Rivera alone, the two talks attended by Quigley must therefore be Goal Sharing and Leadership:

F	G	H	I	L
R, S	Q		R alone	Q

At this point, you can rule out answer choice (A): because Quigley **must** attend Leadership, (A) cannot be false and it is thus incorrect.

Finally, let's consider whether anything can be deduced about the talks that Tran attends. The fourth condition requires that the first talk Tran attends also be attended by Quigley. Given the diagram you have worked out above, this condition can only be satisfied if the first talk Tran attends is Goal Sharing.

F	G	H	I	L
R, S	Q, T		R alone	Q

So, you've now determined that it **must** be true that Tran attends Goal Sharing when Rivera is the only employee to attend Information Overload, so you know that (D) cannot be the correct answer. This leaves (E) as the only answer choice not ruled out. So, you can safely choose (E) as the correct answer and move on to the next question.

The Correct Answer:

E It is possible for answer choice (E) to be false when Rivera is the only employee to attend Information Overload. This is demonstrated by the following acceptable outcome, in which Tran does **not** attend Handling People:

F	G	H	I	L
R, S	Q, T	S	R alone	Q, T

The Incorrect Answer Choices:

A, B, C, D As demonstrated in the "Overview," each one of these answer choices must be true. Because none of them can be false, none of them is the correct answer.

- *Difficulty Level: 5*

Questions 19–23

What the setup tells you: This group of questions is about the order in which six witnesses will testify, one at a time, during a trial. The three setup conditions tell you something about when these witnesses will testify relative to each other.

Some things you can deduce right away: The setup conditions have some consequences that you might find helpful to note before turning to the questions. For example, the first condition has implications for who can testify last (that is, sixth). Since it requires Sanderson to testify immediately before either Tannenbaum or Ramirez, it has the consequence that Sanderson can't be the last witness to testify.

One consequence of the second condition is that the latest Ujemori can testify is fourth. This is because the second condition requires that Ujemori testify before at least two of the other witnesses (namely, Ramirez and Wong). In addition, because the second condition requires Ujemori to testify earlier than both Ramirez and Wong, it has the consequence that neither Ramirez nor Wong can be the first to testify.

The third condition also has implications for who can testify first. In particular, since it requires either Tannenbaum or Wong to testify immediately before Mangione, it has the consequence that the first witness to testify can't be Mangione.

It may be helpful to summarize what you have deduced in an abbreviated form so that you can easily access this information as you work on the questions. Here is one way to do this, where numbers are used to indicate the order in which the witnesses testify:

1: cannot be M, R, or W
2:
3:
4:
5: cannot be U
6: cannot be S or U

Question 19

Overview: This question asks you to identify the ordering that is permitted by the setup conditions. As mentioned in "A Guide to Analytical Reasoning Questions," for orientation questions like this, probably the most efficient approach is to take each condition in turn and check to see whether any of the answer choices violates it. If you find that an answer choice does violate that condition, you should eliminate that answer choice from consideration—perhaps by crossing it out in your test booklet. When you have crossed out all but one answer choice, you can be confident that the remaining answer choice is the correct one.

The first condition is violated by (D), since in (D) Sanderson testifies immediately before Ramirez rather than immediately before Tannenbaum or Ujemori. So (D) can be crossed out. The other answer choices satisfy the first condition so you can go on to the second condition. Of the remaining answer choices, both (B) and (C) satisfy the second condition, but this condition is violated by both (A) and (E). In (A), Ujemori does not testify before Ramirez, and in (E), Ujemori does not testify before either Ramirez or Wong. So both (A) and (E) can be crossed out. Finally, the third condition is satisfied by (B) but violated by (C), since in (C), Ramirez (rather than Tannenbaum or Wong) testifies immediately before Mangione. So (C) can be crossed out. The correct answer is thus (B), the only one you haven't crossed out.

The Correct Answer:

As shown in the "Overview," (B) violates none of the conditions and so is a possible order in which the witnesses could testify.

The Incorrect Answer Choices:

A   In (A) Ujemori testifies later than Ramirez, in violation of the second condition.

C   In (C), neither Tannenbaum nor Wong testifies immediately before Mangione, in violation of the third condition.

D   In (D), Sanderson does not testify immediately before either Tannenbaum or Ujemori, in violation of the first condition.

E   In (E), Ujemori testifies later than both Ramirez and Wong, in violation of the second condition.

- *Difficulty Level: 1*

Question 20

Overview: This question asks you what could be true if Tannenbaum testifies first. A first step in answering this question is to see whether you can eliminate any of the answer choices based on what you already know. A quick skim of the answer choices shows that you can eliminate (D) immediately, since you determined in "Some things you can deduce right away" that Ujemori can never testify fifth. None of the remaining answer choices can be ruled out so easily. So as a next step, you might find it helpful to see what you can deduce about an ordering in which Tannenbaum testifies first.

For one thing, you know that if Tannenbaum testifies first, then Sanderson must testify immediately before Ujemori, since otherwise the first condition cannot be satisfied. You also know, as discussed in "Some things you can deduce right away," that Ujemori cannot testify later than fourth. Taking these two pieces of information together, you know that if Tannenbaum testifies first, then Sanderson and Ujemori must testify either second and third, or third and fourth. In other words, the only acceptable orderings will be ones that conform to one of the following two diagrams:

1	2	3	4	5	6
T	S	U			

1	2	3	4	5	6
T		S	U		

A good strategy at this point is to see if what you've deduced so far can help you identify the correct answer.

The Incorrect Answer Choices:

A   A check of the diagrams you came up with in the "Overview" shows that Ramirez cannot testify second when Tannenbaum testifies first. This is because if you put Ramirez in second position, there is no way the second condition, which requires that Ujemori testify earlier than Ramirez, can be satisfied.

B   You can again turn to your diagrams in the "Overview" to rule out (B). As your diagrams show, if Tannenbaum testifies first, then the third witness to testify must be either Sanderson or Ujemori.

C   This answer choice can also be ruled out by referring to your diagrams. In the "Overview" you determined that Sanderson must testify either second or third if Tannenbaum testifies first.

D In "Some things you can deduce right away," you saw that in any outcome, and hence in any outcome in which Tannenbaum testifies first, Ujemori can testify no later than fourth. Whether or not Tannenbaum testifies first, then, Ujemori can't testify fifth, which means that (D) is incorrect.

The Correct Answer:

E Since (E) is the only answer choice you haven't ruled out, you can safely conclude that it is the correct answer. There is no need to verify this. However, if you have the time, you can verify that (E) is correct by working out an ordering that satisfies all of the setup conditions and in which Tannenbaum testifies first and Mangione testifies sixth. Here's one such ordering:

1	2	3	4	5	6
T	S	U	R	W	M

- *Difficulty Level: 2*

Question 21

Overview: This question asks you to determine when Ujemori must testify if Sanderson testifies fifth. A good first step in answering this kind of question is to see what you can determine about what an acceptable outcome will look like if the supposition in the question holds. In this case, what can you determine about what an acceptable outcome will look like if Sanderson testifies fifth? Well, you know from the first setup condition that either Tannenbaum or Ujemori will have to testify sixth. But you deduced in "Some things you can deduce right away" that Ujemori can never testify sixth. So you know that one consequence of Sanderson's testifying fifth is that Tannenbaum must testify sixth:

1	2	3	4	5	6
				S	T

Now notice that given the above diagram, the only way that Ujemori could testify earlier than both Ramirez and Wong, as the second condition requires, is if Ujemori testifies first or second.

1	2	3	4	5	6
U				S	T

1	2	3	4	5	6
	U			S	T

Looking at the above possibilities, you can see that in the case where Ujemori testifies second, the third and fourth slots would have to be filled by Ramirez and Wong (in either order) so that the second condition is satisfied, leaving Mangione to fill the first position. However, as you deduced in "Some things you can deduce right away," Mangione can never testify first, given the third condition. So you can conclude that the second of the above two diagrams is impossible and that, therefore, Ujemori must testify first if Sanderson testifies fifth.

The Correct Answer:

A As you saw in the "Overview," if Sanderson testifies fifth, then Ujemori must testify first.

The Incorrect Answer Choices:

B–E In the "Overview," you've established that Ujemori must testify first if Sanderson testifies fifth. If Ujemori must testify first, then Ujemori can't testify in any other position. So, (B)-(E) are all incorrect.

- *Difficulty Level: 2*

Question 22

What you should keep in mind for this question: Be sure to note that this question asks you to find the pair of witnesses who **cannot** testify third and fourth, respectively (where "respectively" means "in the order listed in the answer choices"). This means that all of the incorrect answers will be pairs who **can** testify in these positions. Also note that the question asks you what **cannot** be true under the basic setup conditions alone. The question itself doesn't add any further constraints to those conditions.

Overview: When answering a question that asks you what **cannot** be true under the basic setup conditions alone, you'll often find that you have to go through the answer choices one by one to find the correct answer. Using this strategy, your task is to consider each answer choice in turn and determine whether it's possible to come up with a complete ordering that satisfies all of the setup conditions and in which that answer choice is true. If you can come up with such an ordering, then you'll have established that the answer choice **can** be true and eliminate it from further consideration. If you **cannot** come up with such an ordering, then you'll know that you have found the correct answer. This is a strategy you can use here and, since the correct answer choice turns out to be (A), it shouldn't be too time consuming.

To see how this strategy works, consider (A) and ask yourself the following question: Is it possible to come up with a complete ordering that satisfies all of the setup conditions and in which (A) is true? The answer is no. This is because if Mangione testifies third and Tannenbaum testifies fourth, then the third condition requires that Wong testify second, and the second condition requires that Ujemori testify first:

1	2	3	4	5	6
U	W	M	T		

But now there is no way to satisfy the first condition: Sanderson cannot testify immediately before Tannenbaum in the above ordering, nor can Sanderson testify immediately before Ujemori. Thus, (A) cannot be true and so must be the correct answer. There is no need to consider the remaining options.

As noted earlier, the strategy illustrated above can be time consuming, but it is often the only reasonable strategy to employ when tackling this kind of question. However, it can be worth your while when you encounter this type of question to first take a quick glance at the answer choices and see if there are any that look like likely candidates for being the correct answer, given what you know about the setup conditions and what can be deduced from those conditions. If you can identify such an answer choice, you may be able to save yourself a great deal of time by checking this answer choice first to see whether it is in fact the answer choice that **cannot** be true and so must be the correct answer.

In this case, for example, the question is asking for a pair of witnesses who **cannot** testify **consecutively** in the third and fourth positions. There are two setup conditions that deal specifically with the consecutive ordering of witnesses—the first and third conditions. The first condition restricts the consecutive ordering of Sanderson with respect to Tannenbaum and Ujemori, so (C), which includes two of these three witnesses, might be a likely candidate for the correct answer. The third condition restricts the consecutive ordering of Mangione with respect to Tannenbaum and Wong, so (A), which includes two of these three witnesses, might also be a likely candidate for the correct answer. As a strategy, then, you might want to consider these two answer choices first to see whether one of them is the correct answer. And as you determined above, (A) is in fact the correct answer.

The Correct Answer:

A As you saw in the "Overview," it is impossible to come up with a complete ordering that satisfies all of the setup conditions and in which (A) is true. So (A) is the correct answer.

The Incorrect Answer Choices:

B The following ordering demonstrates that it is possible to come up with a complete ordering that satisfies all of the setup conditions and in which Ramirez testifies third and Sanderson testifies fourth.

1	2	3	4	5	6
U	W	R	S	T	M

So (B) can be true and thus cannot be the correct answer.

C In the order of testimony represented in the following diagram, all of the setup conditions are satisfied and Sanderson and Ujemori testify third and fourth, respectively:

1	2	3	4	5	6
T	M	S	U	R	W

Thus, Sanderson and Ujemori can testify third and fourth, respectively, and so (C) is incorrect.

D In the order of testimony represented in the following diagram, all of the setup conditions are satisfied and Tannenbaum and Ramirez testify third and fourth, respectively:

1	2	3	4	5	6
S	U	T	R	W	M

So you can conclude that (D) is incorrect.

E The following diagram, in which all of the setup conditions are satisfied and Ujemori and Wong testify third and fourth, respectively, shows that (E) is incorrect:

1	2	3	4	5	6
S	T	U	W	M	R

- *Difficulty Level: 4*

Question 23

What you should keep in mind for this question: Like the preceding question, this question asks you what **cannot** be true under the basic setup conditions alone, without adding any further constraints to those conditions. In this case you are asked to identify a pair of witnesses who **cannot** testify first and second, respectively. This means that all of the incorrect answers will be pairs who **can** testify in these positions.

Overview: The "Overview" for Question 22 describes two strategies you can use when answering questions like this one. One strategy is to consider each of the answer choices in turn and determine whether it is possible to come up with a complete ordering that satisfies all of the setup conditions and in which that answer choice is true. If it is possible, then you will have established that the answer choice **can** be true and eliminate it from further consideration. When you've found the answer choice for which it is **not** possible to come up with a complete ordering that satisfies all of the setup conditions and in which the answer choice is true, then you are done. You will have found the correct answer—the answer choice that **cannot** be true.

The other strategy is to see if you can identify among the answer choices any that look like particularly good candidates for being the correct answer. Like Question 22, this question asks about possible consecutive orderings, so answer choices that include witnesses whose positions are constrained by the first or third setup conditions—both consecutive ordering constraints—are probably good candidates for your initial consideration. In this case, four of the answer choices meet this criterion, so it may not seem like you can save much time using this strategy: (A), (C), and (D) all include witnesses whose ordering is constrained by the first condition; (B) includes witnesses whose ordering is constrained by the third condition. However, of these four options, (A) and (B) are at least superficially consistent with the setup conditions (since in (A) Sanderson testifies immediately before Ujemori, and in (B) Tannenbaum testifies immediately before Mangione), so you might want to consider checking answer choices (C) and (D) first to see whether either of these is the correct answer.

The Correct Answer:

D It's impossible to come up with a complete ordering that satisfies all of the setup conditions and in which Ujemori testifies first and Tannenbaum testifies second. This is because the first condition requires that Sanderson testify immediately before one of these two witnesses, so there is no way for this condition to be satisfied when these witnesses are the first two witnesses to testify.

1	2	3	4	5	6
U	T				

The Incorrect Answer Choices:

A The following ordering demonstrates that it is possible to come up with a complete ordering that satisfies all of the setup conditions and in which Sanderson testifies first and Ujemori testifies second:

1	2	3	4	5	6
S	U	T	M	R	W

So (A) cannot be the correct answer.

B In the order of testimony represented in the following diagram, all of the setup conditions are satisfied and Tannenbaum and Mangione testify first and second, respectively:

1	2	3	4	5	6
T	M	S	U	R	W

Thus, Tannenbaum and Mangione can testify first and second, respectively, and (B) is incorrect.

C In the order of testimony represented in the following diagram, all of the setup conditions are satisfied and Tannenbaum and Sanderson testify first and second, respectively:

1	2	3	4	5	6
T	S	U	W	M	R

So (C) cannot be the correct answer.

E The following diagram, in which all of the setup conditions are satisfied and Ujemori and Wong testify first and second, respectively, shows that (E) is incorrect:

1	2	3	4	5	6
U	W	M	S	T	R

- *Difficulty Level: 4*

Question 1

Overview: The first sentence of the passage introduces the topic of the argument: why fish that live around coral reefs are brightly colored. The next two sentences present a suggested explanation: coral reefs are colorful and colorful fish are camouflaged by them; the fact that many species use camouflage to avoid predators is presented as providing at least some support for this explanation. But the following sentence asserts that the suggested explanation is mistaken, and the rest of the passage provides support for the claim the suggested explanation is mistaken. A coral reef without fish is monochromatic: corals themselves are usually either dull brown or green.

The question asks you to identify the main conclusion drawn in the argument. The main conclusion of the argument is the claim that the other parts of the argument are meant to establish.

The Correct Answer:

C As discussed in the "Overview," the claim that is supported by the rest of the argument is the following: the suggestion that fish living around reefs are brightly colored because they are camouflaged by the reefs is mistaken. So that is the main conclusion drawn in the argument.

The Incorrect Answer Choices:

A (A) paraphrases the second sentence of the passage, which describes the hypothesis that the argument rejects. So (A) does not express the main conclusion of the argument.

B The passage presents the claim stated in (B) as providing support for the hypothesis that colorful fish are camouflaged by reefs. So (B) does not express the main conclusion of the argument.

D (D) states some of the support offered for the main conclusion rather than the main conclusion itself.

E (E) states some of the support offered for the main conclusion rather than the main conclusion itself.

■ *Difficulty Level: 1*

Question 2

Overview: The passage describes a survey that tried to discover whether teenagers believe in telekinesis by asking about whether they agree with a certain statement. This statement, according to the passage, was ambiguous in a very particular way; it could be understood to be asking about the paranormal phenomenon intended, or it could be understood to be about something that is not paranormal. The passage then concludes that, by virtue of this ambiguity, the survey's responses to the question about whether people agreed with the statement are also ambiguous. The question asks you to identify a general proposition that this reasoning conforms to.

The Correct Answer:

D (D) says that responses to poorly phrased questions are likely to be ambiguous. According to the passage, the survey used a poorly phrased question; the survey was trying to determine whether people believe in a certain paranormal phenomenon, but the question asked about agreement with a statement that could be understood as describing something that was not paranormal. (D) implies that responses to this question are likely to be ambiguous, which is what the passage concludes. Thus the passage conforms to (D).

The Incorrect Answer Choices:

A The passage says that the statement used in the survey was ambiguous. The survey was trying to find out how many people believed in a controversial claim, but the statement the survey asked about was amenable to either a controversial or an uncontroversial interpretation. This is not the same as saying that the survey used an uncontroversial statement, and at no point does the reasoning in the passage rely on questioning the value of uncontroversial statements in surveys. Thus the reasoning in the passage does not conform to (A).

B (B) says that every statement is amenable to several interpretations, i.e., ambiguous. Reasoning that conformed to this general proposition would conclude that a particular statement is ambiguous on the grounds that all statements are ambiguous. The passage is clearly not making such an inference since it claims that there are particular features of the statement asked about by the survey that make that statement ambiguous.

C (C) says that if a survey's questions are well phrased, then responses to the survey will be unambiguous. Reasoning that conformed to this general proposition would begin with the premise that a survey's questions are well phrased and infer that the responses are not ambiguous. The passage does just the opposite: it begins with a premise that a survey's question is not well phrased and infers that the responses are ambiguous.

E Reasoning that conformed to (E) would conclude that a statement can be given a naturalistic interpretation whenever it is about a psychic phenomenon. However, the passage claims that the statement that the survey asked about is amenable to a naturalistic interpretation because it is ambiguous. The fact that the statement is about psychic phenomena never plays a part in the reasoning. Thus the reasoning in the passage doesn't conform to (E).

- *Difficulty Level: 1*

Question 3

Overview: The passage tells us that a recent study of perfect pitch found that a high percentage of people with perfect pitch are related to someone else with it. On the basis of this study, the argument draws a conclusion about why some people have perfect pitch: having perfect pitch is a result of genetic factors. The question asks you to identify additional information that most strengthens the argument.

The Correct Answer:

A It is plausible that receiving musical training would make a person more likely to have perfect pitch. So if people whose relatives have perfect pitch generally receive more musical training, then this could explain why they are more likely to have perfect pitch, even if there are no genetic factors involved. This alternative explanation would undermine the support provided by the argument for the conclusion that perfect pitch is a result of genetic factors. By ruling out a possibility that would undermine the argument, (A) thus strengthens the argument.

The Incorrect Answer Choices:

B The fact that the researchers have perfect pitch would not provide any indication of why some people have perfect pitch. And if that fact is suggestive of some sort of bias in the study, such bias would weaken the argument, not strengthen it. So (B) does not strengthen the argument that perfect pitch is a result of genetic factors.

C The fact that people with perfect pitch are more likely to choose music as a career would not provide any indication of why they have perfect pitch. So (C) does not strengthen the argument that perfect pitch is a result of genetic factors.

D If people with perfect pitch are more likely to make sure that their children get musical training, then people whose parents have perfect pitch are more likely to get musical training. It is plausible that receiving musical training would make a person more likely to have perfect pitch. So if people whose parents have perfect pitch generally receive more musical training, then this could explain why they are more likely to have perfect pitch, even if there are no genetic factors involved. That would undermine the support provided in the argument for the conclusion that perfect pitch is a result of genetic factors. So (D) weakens rather than strengthens the argument.

E By itself, the claim that people who have training in music are more likely to have perfect pitch does not affect the strength of the argument. (E) could be true because people who naturally have perfect pitch are more likely to receive musical training and it could be true because the training helps them to develop perfect pitch. So (E) does not tell us why people have perfect pitch and therefore does not strengthen the argument.

- *Difficulty Level: 1*

Question 4

Overview: The passage describes two sets of dinosaur tracks, one of a grazing dinosaur and one of a predatory dinosaur. The pattern of the tracks suggests that the predator was following the grazing dinosaur and had matched its stride. The passage then describes an analogous case, that of modern predators like lions. These modern predators usually match the stride of their prey immediately before striking the prey. On the basis of this analogy, the argument concludes that the predatory dinosaur was chasing the grazing dinosaur and attacked immediately afterward.

The question asks you to identify an accurate description of the role played in the argument by the statement that the predatory dinosaur was following the grazing dinosaur and had matched its stride.

The Correct Answer:

C As described in the "Overview," the argument uses an analogy between the behavior of a predatory dinosaur and that of modern predators to establish its conclusion. To set up this analogy, the argument establishes a fact about the predatory dinosaur—namely, that it was following the grazing dinosaur and had matched its stride. This provides the basis for the description of the analogous case; a modern predator usually matches the stride of its prey immediately before attacking. The argument concludes, by analogy, that the predatory dinosaur attacked just after matching the stride of its prey. So the claim that the predatory dinosaur was following the grazing dinosaur and had matched its stride provides the basis for an analogy that supports the argument's conclusion.

The Incorrect Answer Choices:

A As discussed in the explanation of the correct answer, the statement that the predator was following the grazing dinosaur and had matched its stride, together with an analogy with modern predators, is used to infer the argument's conclusion. Moreover, there is no sense in which this statement is helping to establish the scientific importance of the overall conclusion.

B The statement that the predator was following the grazing dinosaur and had matched its stride is not rejected by the argument. Instead, it is accepted and used, together with an analogy with modern predators, to infer the argument's conclusion.

D The passage does not discuss or suggest any potential objections to the argument's conclusion. So there is no reason to think that the statement that the predator was following the grazing dinosaur and had matched its stride is presented to counteract a possible objection.

E The argument's overall conclusion is that the predatory dinosaur was chasing the grazing dinosaur and attacked immediately afterward; this is the claim that the analogy with modern predators is used to support. So the statement that the predator was following the grazing dinosaur and had matched its stride is not the argument's overall conclusion.

- *Difficulty Level: 1*

Question 5

Overview: The passage says that over the past 25 years the incidence of skin cancer has continued to increase even though the use of sunscreen has also been increasing. This suggests that the trend of increasing incidence of skin cancer has continued despite the increased use of sunscreen. The argument concludes that using sunscreen is unlikely to reduce the risk of skin cancer.

The question asks you to identify a claim that weakens the argument. As the argument stands, its conclusion seems quite well supported. If sunscreen did reduce the risk of skin cancer, then we would expect the see the trend in the incidence of skin cancer change as sunscreen became more widely used. But over the past 25 years this has not happened, which supports the conclusion that sunscreen is unlikely to reduce the risk of skin cancer.

The Correct Answer:

B (B) says that skin cancer usually develops among the very old as a result of sunburns experienced when very young. Suppose this were true and that, for example, skin cancer typically develops among people in their 80s as result of sunburns they got as teenagers. If so, then there would be roughly a 70 year gap between sun exposure and getting skin cancer. Under this scenario, the changes in sunscreen use that have occurred over the last 25 years would not be expected to make a significant difference in the current incidence of skin cancer. And without such an expectation, the evidence cited in the passage about the incidence of skin cancer no longer supports the conclusion. Thus, (B) weakens the argument.

The Incorrect Answer Choices:

A The argument's reasoning does not make use of any claim that the most expensive sunscreen is more effective than less expensive sunscreen. So (A) does not affect the strength of the argument.

C Nothing in the argument makes reference to how sunscreen was developed, and any facts about whose research that development was based on are irrelevant to this particular argument regarding whether sunscreen reduces the risk of skin cancer. So (C) does not weaken the argument.

D The argument is based on the expectation that if sunscreen reduces the risk of skin cancer, then we would expect the trend in the incidence of skin cancer to change as sunscreen becomes more widely used. The truth of (D) is irrelevant to this expectation. (D) is a claim about a certain group of people who are generally disinclined to spend large amounts of time in the sun. But (D) does not indicate anything about their use of sunscreen, nor does it tell us anything about their incidence of skin cancer.

E The argument is based on the expectation that if sunscreen reduces the risk of skin cancer, then we would expect the trend in the incidence of skin cancer to change as sunscreen becomes more widely used. Since we don't know if the people who believe themselves to be susceptible to skin cancer are right, or if their regular use of sunscreen has had any effect on the incidence of skin cancer among them, the information in (E) does not weaken the argument in the passage.

- *Difficulty Level: 3*

Question 6

Overview: The passage says that a proposed department will not be funded if both of the following conditions are met: (1) there are fewer than 50 people per year available for hire in the field, and (2) the proposed department would duplicate more than 25 percent of the material covered in an existing department. The proposed Area Studies Department meets condition 2. Nonetheless, it will be funded.

The question asks you to identify a statement that follows logically from the statements in the passage.

The Correct Answer:

A The passage says that the Area Studies Department will be funded and that it meets condition 2. But it would not be funded if it met both conditions. It follows logically that it must not meet condition 1, i.e., there must be at least 50 people per year available for hire in the field.

The Incorrect Answer Choices:

B The passage tells us that the Area Studies Department will duplicate more than 25 percent of the material covered in the Anthropology Department, which means that Area Studies meets condition 2. But the passage gives us no reason to think that Area Studies doesn't also duplicate more than 25 percent of the material covered in another department. So (B) does not follow logically from the statements in the passage.

C If the Area Studies Department did not duplicate more than 25 percent of the material covered in the Anthropology Department, then it may or may not meet condition 2 (because it may or may not duplicate 25 percent of the material covered in some other department). In either case, Area Studies could still be funded; if it met condition 2, it could be funded as long as it did not meet condition 1. So (C) does not follow logically from the passage.

D The passage says that the Area Studies Department would duplicate more than 25 percent of the material covered in the Anthropology Department. But it does not follow that the Anthropology Department duplicates more than 25 percent of the material that would be covered by Area Studies. After all, Area Studies might cover a lot more material.

E If (E) is true, then the Area Studies Department does not meet condition 1. Since the passage tells us that Area Studies does not meet condition 2 and that a department will not be funded if it does not meet condition 1 and does not meet condition 2, this implies that Area Studies will not be funded. But the passage says that Area Studies will be funded, so (E) cannot be true if the statements in the passage are true.

- *Difficulty Level: 2*

Question 7

Overview: The passage tells you that over the course of a three-decade-long study, the average beak size of a wild population of a certain species of bird decreased while the average beak size of captive birds of that species did not change. The question asks you to identify a fact that would help to explain these results.

The Correct Answer:

C If the wild birds' food supply changed over the course of the study in a way that favored the survival of small-beaked birds, then we would expect that, over time, the proportion of small-beaked birds among the wild birds would increase. If that happened, then the average beak size among the wild birds would decrease. Since the food supply for the captive bird population was presumably unchanged, answer choice (C), if true, would help to explain the researcher's findings.

The Incorrect Answer Choices:

A If the small-beaked wild birds were easier to capture and measure, then they may have been overrepresented in the researchers' data. This would cause the researchers to believe that the average beak size of the wild population was smaller than it actually was. However, this provides no explanation of why a change was observed over the course of the study; it provides no reason to think that this distorting effect would have changed over the course of three decades. So (A) cannot help explain why the average beak size of the wild birds decreased over the course of the study.

B If the large-beaked wild birds were easier to capture and measure, then they may have been overrepresented in the researchers' data. This would cause the researchers to believe that the average beak size of the wild population was larger than it actually was. However, this provides no explanation of why a change was observed over the course of the study; it provides no reason to think that this distorting effect would have changed over the course of three decades. So (B) cannot help explain why the average beak size of the wild birds decreased over the course of the study.

D (D) says that the average body size of the captive birds stayed the same during the study period. However, this would not explain why their average beak size remained constant, nor would it explain why the average beak size of the wild birds decreased.

E If it were true that the researchers measured the beaks of some of the wild birds on more than one occasion, this might suggest that those birds that were measured repeatedly are being overrepresented in the study. But there is no way that this overrepresentation could account for the change in average beak size observed over the course of the study.

- *Difficulty Level: 1*

Question 8

Overview: The passage says that storytelling appears to be a universal aspect of culture. Additionally, a study of traditional narratives from widely varied cultures reveals common themes and story types. Your task is to identify a statement that is supported by these claims about traditional narratives.

The Correct Answer:

C The study of traditional narratives reveals common themes in stories from widely varied cultures, suggesting that there are certain human concerns and interests common to all cultures. The fact that there are common story types suggests that people in all cultures tend to find the same types of stories interesting or entertaining, thereby supporting the claim that there are interests common to all cultures.

The Incorrect Answer Choices:

A The passage says that certain themes are common in diverse cultures from widely separated epochs. While it is possible that some storytellers consciously borrowed themes from other cultures, and the borrowing of themes is one possible explanation of common themes among diverse cultures, a number of other explanations are available. And even if storytellers do borrow themes from other cultures, the passage gives no evidence that this borrowing would be a routine practice. As a result, the passage provides little support for (A).

B The passage says that storytelling appears to be a universal aspect of human culture. However, this does not mean that storytellers themselves are aware of this fact, and the passage gives us no reason to infer that storytellers are aware of this fact.

D The passage says that storytelling appears to be a universal aspect of both past and present cultures. So we may be able infer that storytelling was important to some degree in both ancient and modern cultures. However, we cannot infer anything about just how important it was in each culture. Thus, given what the passage says, it could be true that storytelling was less important in ancient cultures.

E The passage says that many themes and story types are common to diverse cultures. But this does not entail anything about how best to understand any particular culture. In fact, if anything, it suggests that storytelling is a poor way to understand what makes different cultures distinctive.

■ *Difficulty Level: 3*

Question 9

Overview: The reasoning of the argument runs as follows: (1) If a mother's first child is born early, then it is likely that her second child will be also. (2) The second child of one mother, Jackie, was not born early. Therefore, it is likely that Jackie's first child was not born early either.

The general form of the argument is this: (1) If one entity has a certain property, then another, related entity likely has that property as well. (2) In one case, the second entity does not have the property. Therefore in that same case it is likely that the first entity does not have that property either.

The question asks you to identify the answer choice containing reasoning that is most similar to the questionable reasoning in the passage. If it's not clear to you that the reasoning in the passage is questionable, note that the first claim in the passage doesn't tell us much that is relevant to cases in which a mother's second child is not born early. Note in particular that the first claim is consistent with it being likely that a second child will be born early even if the first child is **not** born early. So when we learn that Jackie's second child was not born early, this doesn't allow us to confidently conclude that her first child was not born early.

The Correct Answer:

C The argument in (C) is very similar in its reasoning to the argument in the passage. Like the argument in the passage, the argument in (C) begins with the claim that if one entity (a movie) has a certain property (being a hit), then a related entity (the movie's sequel) will probably also have that property. One particular entity of the second sort (the sequel *Hawkman II*) does not have the property (i.e., it was not a hit). The argument in (C) then concludes that a particular entity of the first sort (the original movie, *Hawkman I*) probably also does not have the property.

This argument is questionable in much the same way that the argument in the passage is questionable. The conclusion of this argument does not follow logically because it's possible that most sequels that are not hits are based on movies that were hits.

The Incorrect Answer Choices:

A The claim in (A) indicates that if someone has a certain property (finishing a project before the craft fair), then that person probably also has a second property (going to the craft fair), whereas the claim in the passage concerns whether two related things are likely to have the same property. And (A) also differs from the passage in the way that it reasons from this general claim. (A) says that a particular person does not have the one property and concludes that that person probably does not have the second property either. But the passage says that a particular person probably does not have the second property and concludes that a related person does not have the first property either. So (A) is not similar in its reasoning to the argument in the passage.

B (B) draws a highly questionable inference from one general claim (all X are likely to be Y) to a related general claim (all Y are likely to be X). The reasoning in the passage proceeds very differently. That argument begins with a general claim, adds a premise that concerns one particular case to which that general claim is applicable, and reaches a conclusion about that same case. So (B) is not at all similar in its reasoning to the argument in the passage.

D (D) is like the passage in that it begins with a general claim, adds a premise that concerns one particular case to which that general claim is applicable, and reaches a conclusion about that same case.

But the reasoning in (D) is quite different from the reasoning in the passage, as is the way in which that reasoning is questionable. To see this difference, note that the two premises in (D) allow us to validly infer that people will not invest in Pallid Starr. The reasoning in (D) is questionable because the conclusion drawn in (D)—that no one is likely to invest in Pallid Starr—is slightly different in meaning from the conclusion that can be validly inferred. The reasoning in the passage, which is outlined in the "Overview," is different in that no corresponding valid inference can be drawn from the two premises. Moreover, the reasoning in the passage is not questionable simply because the wording of the conclusion is slightly off target.

E In (E), one premise gives a necessary condition (nice weather) for an action (Tai's going sailing). Another premise affirms the necessary condition, and the conclusion of the argument is that the action will probably be undertaken. This reasoning is unlike the reasoning in the passage, which proceeds from a general claim and then moves on to consider one particular case to which that claim is applicable. The reasoning in (E) is questionable in that nice weather might be only one of several conditions that would need to be met for Tai to go sailing, but this defect in (E) bears little resemblance to what makes the argument in the passage questionable (see "Overview").

- *Difficulty Level: 1*

Question 10

Overview: The passage tells us that data transmitted by a spacecraft suggest that there is liquid water on Europa. Additionally, life as we know it could evolve only in the presence of liquid water. In other words, liquid water is a requirement for the evolution of life as we know it. The argument concludes that life has probably evolved on Europa. The question asks you to identify why the argument is vulnerable to criticism.

The Correct Answer:

B The passage presents evidence that Europa meets one of the requirements for evolution of life as we know it: liquid water. However, the passage leaves open the possibility that there could be other requirements for the evolution of life. If there are other requirements, and Europa has not met them, then it would not be reasonable to conclude that life has evolved on Europa. So the argument needs to adequately address the possibility that there are additional conditions necessary for the evolution of life, and it has not addressed this possibility at all. So the argument is vulnerable to criticism on the grounds stated in (B).

The Incorrect Answer Choices:

A The only condition that the argument suggests is necessary for the evolution of life as we know it is the presence of liquid water. The argument does not discuss any place where this condition does not hold; the only place it discusses is Europa, where the condition does hold. So the argument is not vulnerable to criticism on the grounds stated in (A).

C The argument's conclusion is only that life evolved on Europa, and the argument does not concern the issue of whether life might be present on Europa without having evolved there or whether life is currently present there. So the argument is not vulnerable to criticism on the grounds stated in (C).

D The argument says that the presence of liquid water is necessary for the evolution of life as we know it. If there is some unfamiliar form of life that could evolve without liquid water, this would not decrease the likelihood that life evolved on Europa. If anything, it would make it more likely that life evolved on Europa because it would mean that life could have evolved there without liquid water. Therefore, it is not a problem for the argument that it does not address the possibility stated in (D).

E The argument concludes only that it is likely that life evolved on Europa. This conclusion is based on a premise that data transmitted by a spacecraft strongly suggest that there is liquid water on Europa, not that the data prove that liquid water is there. Thus, the argument does not take for granted that nothing other than the presence of liquid water could have accounted for the data.

- *Difficulty Level: 2*

Question 11

Overview: The passage contains a general statement about bacterial resistance to antibiotics and a statement about a particular bacterial species, species X. Your task is to identify a statement that is strongly supported by these statements.

The Correct Answer:

B The passage says that a bacterial species will always develop greater resistance within a few years to any antibiotics used against it if those antibiotics do not completely eliminate the species. It also says that no antibiotic now on the market can completely eliminate species X. So if we use an antibiotic currently on the market against X, X will not be completely eliminated, which means that X will develop greater resistance against the antibiotic within a few years.

The Incorrect Answer Choices:

A The passage says that no single antibiotic now on the market can completely eliminate species X. This, however, does not imply anything about the likelihood of eventually developing an antibiotic that can completely eliminate X. So (A) is not strongly supported by the passage.

C The fact that no single antibiotic will eliminate species X does not imply that a combination of antibiotics now on the market would be able do so. Moreover, it remains possible that X could be eliminated by some means other than antibiotics. So the claim that the only way to eliminate X is by a combination of antibiotics is not supported by the passage.

D The passage implies that species X will inevitably develop greater resistance within a few years to antibiotics used against it if those antibiotics do not completely eliminate X. However, the passage does not indicate that any antibiotics are now being used against species X. Moreover, resistance to antibiotics is not the same thing as virulence, i.e., ability to overcome the host's own defenses. So (D) is not strongly supported by the passage.

E The passage says that a bacterial species will develop greater resistance within a few years to an antibiotic if the antibiotic does not completely eliminate the species. This suggests that this greater resistance does not develop very quickly. Since it is possible that all the antibiotics used against species X have only been used for a short time, X may not be more resistant to those antibiotics. So (E) is not strongly supported by the passage.

- *Difficulty Level: 2*

Question 12

Overview: The political scientist's argument begins by providing the background information that it is not uncommon for a politician to criticize his or her political opponents by claiming that their exposition of their ideas is muddled and incomprehensible. Next, the argument claims that such criticism is never sincere. This claim is then backed by another claim: that political agendas promoted in a manner that cannot be understood by large numbers of people will not be realized. And, in turn, this claim is supported by a premise that, according to the argument, every politician knows: that political mobilization requires commonality of purpose.

The Correct Answer:

D The main conclusion of an argument is the claim that is supported by other parts of the argument but is not itself offered as support for any other part of the argument. In the case of the political scientist's argument, the main conclusion is expressed by "Such criticism … is never sincere." As seen in the "Overview," this claim is supported by another claim that is itself supported by a premise. And it is not offered as support for any other part of the argument. By "Such criticism …" the political scientist evidently means instances in which a politician criticizes his or her political opponents by claiming that their exposition of their ideas is muddled and incomprehensible. So (D) is an accurate rendering of the political scientist's main conclusion.

The Incorrect Answer Choices:

A (A) is similar to the political scientist's main conclusion in that both claim that certain people are insincere. But whereas (A) concerns people who promote political agendas in an incomprehensible manner, the political scientist's main conclusion concerns politicians who criticize their opponents by claiming that their exposition of their ideas is muddled and incomprehensible.

B The political scientist's main conclusion says only that people who offer a certain sort of political criticism are insincere. While this conclusion might provide support for a claim like (B)—a claim about how sincere political critics **should** criticize—the political scientist never makes such a claim. So (B) is not an accurate rendering of any claim in the political scientist's argument, including its main conclusion.

C While both (C) and the political scientist's argument indicate that confusingly promoted political agendas are ineffective, the political scientist's argument indicates this only in a claim offered as support for its main conclusion, not in its main conclusion itself. Furthermore, whereas the political scientist's main conclusion concerns sincerity, (C) does not.

E The political scientist's argument does make one claim that is similar to (E): that political agendas promoted in a manner that cannot be understood by large numbers of people will not be realized. But (E) is a much more restrictive claim because it implies that presenting a political agenda in a way that is misunderstood by only a few people negatively affects that agenda. Furthermore, as seen in the "Overview," the claim made in the political scientist's argument is offered as support for another claim and hence is not the main conclusion.

- *Difficulty Level: 4*

Question 13

Overview: The passage states that organic factors, such as deficiencies in the brain's chemical compounds, affect many of the symptoms of mental illnesses. It then argues that since the prevalence of these symptoms varies among different countries, the organic factors that affect the symptoms must also vary among these countries.

The question asks you to identify an effective criticism of the reasoning in the argument. Notice that the argument does not establish that **only** organic factors affect the symptoms of mental illnesses. If something else also affects these symptoms, then a variation in that thing, rather than organic factors, might explain why the symptoms are unevenly distributed. Thus, one way to effectively criticize this argument is to identify an alternative explanation for the effects it considers.

The Correct Answer:

C   According to (C), the argument overlooks the possibility that cultural factors influence the expression of the symptoms at issue. (C) thus identifies something other than organic factors that might explain why these symptoms vary among different countries. The existence of this alternative explanation shows that the argument's conclusion might very well be false, so (C) constitutes an effective criticism of the argument's reasoning.

The Incorrect Answer Choices:

A   It is true, as (A) states, that the argument does not say how many mental illnesses are being discussed. But this is not relevant to the relationship between organic factors and the symptoms at issue, so it is not an effective criticism of the reasoning in the argument.

B   (B) indicates that the argument ignores the possibility of cultural variation in the nutritional factors that cause deficiencies in the brain's chemical compounds. But the argument has identified deficiencies in the brain's chemical compounds as organic factors, so the possibility that (B) raises is something that is entirely consistent with the conclusion of the argument. Consequently, (B) does not effectively criticize the argument's reasoning.

D   Even if the argument presumes that some changes in brain chemistry manifest as changes in mental condition, (D) goes too far in asserting that it makes this presumption for all changes in brain chemistry. The only changes in brain chemistry that the argument discusses are ones that affect the symptoms of mental illnesses, so it doesn't presume anything about any other changes.

E   According to (E), the argument presumes that mental phenomena are only manifestations of physical phenomena. But the argument merely indicates that certain mental phenomena are affected by certain physical phenomena, and this does not imply that the former are just manifestations of the latter. So the presumption identified by (E) cannot be attributed to the argument.

- *Difficulty Level: 4*

Question 14

Overview: The politician's conclusion that the privatization of the national parks would probably benefit park visitors rests on an analogy drawn between national parks and the telecommunications industry. Like any argument by analogy, the strength of this argument depends on the extent to which the two things being compared—here, national parks and the telecommunications industry—are in fact analogous in relevant respects. Any fact that reveals a critical difference between the two things being compared will significantly weaken the argument.

The Correct Answer:

E According to the politician's argument, the reason consumers benefited when the telecommunications industry was privatized was because privatization led to competition among companies. If privatization of the national parks would lead to comparatively little competition among parks, then park visitors would be significantly less likely to benefit from privatization. Thus, (E) undermines the argument that the politician puts forward.

The Incorrect Answer Choices:

A The politician's argument is concerned with the issue of whether the privatization of the national parks would benefit park visitors. (A) puts forward a consideration that has some relevance to a related question—that of whether the privatization of the national parks is politically feasible—but this question is independent of the issue of whether privatization, if it were to occur, would benefit park visitors.

B The politician's argument is concerned solely with the potential consumer benefits of privatization. The fact that the privatization of the telecommunications industry had some negative consequences for individuals associated with the industry in a capacity other than as consumers does not in any way challenge the politician's contention that privatization benefited consumers through lower prices and improved service. Thus, (B) does not weaken the politician's argument.

C Whether or not park visitors are aware of the proposal to privatize the national parks has no bearing on the question of whether or not they would in fact benefit from this action. Park visitors would not need to be aware of the proposal to receive the benefits that might come from it. Hence, (C) does not weaken the politician's argument.

D The politician's argument is not concerned with the number of consumers who would benefit as a result of the privatization of the national parks. It is concerned only with whether those consumers who use national parks—i.e., park visitors—will benefit. So, while (D) indicates that the benefits of privatizing the national parks would be more limited than were the benefits of privatizing the telecommunications industry, this fact would not weaken the politician's argument. In fact, (D) actually bolsters the politician's argument by indicating that privatizing the national parks would benefit consumers to some degree.

- *Difficulty Level: 4*

Question 15

Overview: The passage says that jewel collectors will not buy a diamond unless it is guaranteed to be genuine. The passage then asks, rhetorically, why a counterfeit diamond that is indistinguishable to the naked eye from a real one should give less aesthetic pleasure. In effect, the passage is asserting that a counterfeit gives as much pleasure as a real diamond if the naked eye cannot distinguish them. The passage then concludes that such a counterfeit and a real diamond should be considered equally valuable. Your task is to identify the principle that most helps to justify this reasoning.

The Correct Answer:

D The passage concludes that the value of real diamonds should be considered the same as the value of counterfeit diamonds that are indistinguishable to the naked eye. The passage infers this on the basis of a premise that they produce the same aesthetic pleasure. The principle expressed in (D)—namely, that the value of a jewel should derive entirely from the aesthetic pleasure it provides—helps to justify this inference, because (D), in conjunction with the argument's premise, implies the argument's conclusion.

The Incorrect Answer Choices:

A The passage makes an inference about the relative value of real diamonds and certain counterfeit diamonds on the basis of a premise about how much aesthetic pleasure is produced by each. The principle expressed in (A)—that jewel collectors should collect only those jewels that provide the most aesthetic pleasure—does nothing to help justify this inference. (A) does not imply anything about how valuable counterfeit and real diamonds should be considered—at least not without additional information that is not provided by the passage. So (A) does not help to justify the inference made in the passage.

B (B) makes a claim about market demand, a concept that was not involved in the reasoning in the passage. Without additional information about the market demand for counterfeit diamonds and real ones, or some assumption connecting market demand to aesthetic pleasure, (B) cannot help to justify the argument's reasoning.

C The passage makes an inference about the relative value of real diamonds and certain counterfeit diamonds on the basis of a premise about how much aesthetic pleasure is produced by each. (C) is a principle that only concerns the aesthetic pleasure that people get from diamonds. Specifically, (C) asserts that it should not be assumed that the degree of aesthetic pleasure provided by diamonds is the same for all people. Such a claim cannot imply anything about how valuable counterfeit and real diamonds should be considered—at least not without additional information that is not provided by the passage. So (E) does not help to justify the inference made in the passage.

E The passage makes an inference about the relative value of real diamonds and certain counterfeit diamonds on the basis of a premise about how much aesthetic pleasure is produced by each. The principle expressed in (E) concerning which jewels collectors should buy does not imply anything about how valuable counterfeit and real diamonds should be considered—at least not without additional information that is not provided by the passage. So (E) does not help to justify the inference made in the passage.

- *Difficulty Level: 1*

Question 16

Overview: The passage presents several statements about etching tools and concludes that there are more etching tools that are used for engraving than there are etching tools that are not used for engraving. Note that, as the argument stands, the conclusion does not follow logically. Suppose for the sake of argument that there are 1,000 etching tools: 400 pin-tipped ones and 600 bladed ones. The passage tells us that all 400 pin-tipped tools are used for engraving, but only some of the 600 bladed ones are. So it could be that 50 bladed tools are used for engraving. In that case, 450 etching tools would be used for engraving but the remaining 550 would not be.

Your task is to identify a statement that will make the conclusion follow logically.

The Correct Answer:

B The passage says that all etching tools are either pin-tipped or bladed. Also, some bladed etching tools, and all pin-tipped tools, are used for engraving. (B) says that there are as many pin-tipped etching tools as there are bladed ones. This means all the pin-tipped tools, which are all used for engraving, make up half of the etching tools. Of the remaining half—the bladed ones—some are used for engraving. So if (B) is true, the pin-tipped tools, together with the bladed tools used for engraving, outnumber the etching tools not used for engraving. So the conclusion follows logically if (B) is assumed.

The Incorrect Answer Choices:

A The argument's conclusion is about the proportion of etching tools that are used for engraving. (A) says that all tools used for engraving are etching tools. In other words, only etching tools are used for engraving. This won't help us determine the proportion of etching tools that are used for engraving. So the argument's conclusion still does not follow logically if (A) is assumed.

C The argument's conclusion does not follow logically even if we assume that no etching tool is both pin-tipped and bladed. We still have the problem discussed in the "Overview," namely, that there could be more bladed tools than pin-tipped ones and it could be that only a few of the bladed tools are used for engraving.

D (D) is compatible with the scenario described in the "Overview" in which the argument's conclusion is false while its premises are true. In that scenario, a majority of bladed tools (550 out of 600) are not used for engraving. So the argument's conclusion does not follow logically if (D) is assumed.

E The information in (E) follows logically from the information in the passage. The passage says that all pin-tipped etching tools are used for engraving. Since the only kinds of etching tools are pin-tipped and bladed, all the etching tools that are not used for engraving must be bladed. So (E) adds no new information to the argument, which means that assuming (E) will not make the argument any stronger.

- *Difficulty Level: 4*

Question 17

Overview: The passage describes two studies with results that seem to be at odds. In a 24-year study, subjects who ate a lot of foods that are rich in beta-carotene were less likely to die from cancer or heart disease than subjects who ate few such foods. But a 12-year study found that taking beta-carotene supplements had no effect on subjects' health.

The question asks you to select the one answer choice that would **not** help to explain why the two studies have such apparently divergent results.

The Correct Answer:

D The 12-year study found no health effects from taking beta-carotene supplements for 12 years. If half the subjects in that study took only a placebo—a substance known to have no therapeutic effect—this would not help to explain why the other half—those given beta-carotene supplements—experienced no apparent health effects. So if a placebo was used in the 12-year study, as (D) states, this would not even help to explain the 12-year study's results, let alone why the two studies have such apparently divergent results.

The Incorrect Answer Choices:

A If the body processes the beta-carotene in foods more efficiently than it does beta-carotene supplements, then this would help to explain why the 24-year study found a health effect but the 12-year study did not. Perhaps the beta-carotene had an effect on the health of the subjects in the 24-year study who consumed a lot of beta-carotene-rich foods merely because they were able to make efficient use of it, while the beta-carotene did not have an effect on the health of the subjects in the 12-year study because they could not make efficient use of it.

B If beta-carotene must be taken for longer than 12 years to have cancer-preventive effects, then this would help to explain why the 24-year study found such effects but the 12-year study did not. The 12-year study simply did not run long enough to find the positive health effects that the 24-year study found.

C If foods rich in beta-carotene also have other nutrients that help the body absorb beta-carotene, then this would help to explain why the 24-year study found positive health effects that the12-year study did not. Subjects in the 12-year study took only beta-carotene itself and their diets could well have been lacking the nutrients needed to help absorb beta-carotene. This would explain why the 12-year study found no positive health effects of beta-carotene even though the 24-year study did.

E It is well-known that cigarette smoking has adverse health effects that include increasing the risk of cancer and heart disease. Thus, the difference in smoking habits described in (E) could by itself account for why subjects in the 24-year study who had a high intake of beta-carotene-rich foods were less likely to die from cancer or heart disease. So (E) helps to explain why the two studies had such apparently divergent results.

- *Difficulty Level: 4*

Question 18

Overview: The conclusion of the argument is that, if humans are to determine in the near future that there are sentient beings on planets outside our solar system, some of those beings will have to be at least as intelligent as we are. The reasoning is that we will not be able to send spacecraft to their planets anytime in the near future to detect them up close (first premise), and they would have to be at least as intelligent as we are to be capable of communicating with us (second premise). The conclusion does not follow from the premises. For that, you would have to know that there is no other way for us to detect such beings, without using spacecraft or receiving communications from them. The question asks you to select the assumption that closes that gap.

The Correct Answer:

D Assuming (D) rules out the possibility that sentient beings on planets outside our solar system could be detected through long-distance observations from Earth in the event that they cannot communicate with us. From this and the first premise, it follows that the only way we could determine that such beings exist is if they **do** communicate with us, and by the second premise, that would require them to be at least as intelligent as we are. So the conclusion of the argument can be inferred from its premises if we assume (D).

The Incorrect Answer Choices:

A Assuming (A) settles the question of the existence of sentient beings on planets other than Earth within our solar system. But this says nothing about how we might determine whether there are sentient beings on planets outside our solar system anytime in the near future, and whether this would require them to be at least as intelligent as we are. So assuming (A) does not allow the conclusion of the argument to be properly inferred.

B Assuming (B), it follows that if there are sentient beings outside our solar system who are at least as intelligent as we are, they would want to communicate with us. But this does not support the inference that sentient beings outside our solar system would have to be at least as intelligent as we are before we could determine that they exist without sending spacecraft to their planets. In particular, it doesn't rule out that we could detect them from Earth-based observations. Thus, it doesn't close the gap in the argument's reasoning.

C Assuming (C) rules out the possibility that humans could send spacecraft in the near future to the planet of any sentient being that is as intelligent as we are. Therefore it rules out sending spacecraft to such planets outside our solar system. But (C) doesn't rule out detecting sentient beings on planets outside our solar system through Earth-based observations, even if those beings aren't as intelligent as we are. Thus, it doesn't close the gap in the reasoning of the argument.

E Assuming (E), if there are sentient beings outside our solar system that are at least as intelligent as we are, they will be capable of communicating with us. This does not allow us to infer that sentient beings outside our solar system would have to be at least as intelligent as we are if we are to determine that they exist without sending spacecraft to their planets. In particular, it doesn't rule out that we could detect them through Earth-based observations. Thus, it doesn't close the gap in the argument's reasoning.

- *Difficulty Level: 5*

Question 19

Overview: The doctor summarizes a medical study of people who had never experienced serious back pain. The study found that half of these people had bulging or slipped disks. This means that, for those people, their bulging or slipped disks are not causing serious back pain. The doctor concludes from this that bulging or slipped disks can never lead to serious back pain in people who do experience it.

But this conclusion goes beyond what is warranted by the study. The question asks you to identify a possibility that the doctor's argument fails to consider, and which calls the argument into question.

The Correct Answer:

B The study has established only that bulging and slipped disks alone are not sufficient to cause serious back pain (because a person, such as some of the participants in the study, can have bulging or slipped disks without experiencing back pain). But it is consistent with the results of the study that bulging and slipped disks are partly responsible for serious back pain for at least some people who experience such pain. That is, it could be that bulging and slipped disks, in combination with some other factor present in people who have serious back pain, do cause the pain. If this is true, then the doctor's conclusion is false. Thus, the argument is vulnerable to criticism for not considering the possibility stated by (B).

The Incorrect Answer Choices:

A (A) raises the possibility that a factor that does not have to be present for an effect to occur may still be sufficient to produce that effect. But this possibility is irrelevant to the doctor's argument. In the doctor's argument, the factor under consideration is bulging or slipped disks, and the effect is serious back pain. But (A) is not applicable to this situation, as the study has already established that bulging or slipped disks are not sufficient to produce the effect.

C (C) raises the possibility that an effect that occurs when a phenomenon is absent might not occur when the phenomenon is present. But this possibility is irrelevant to the doctor's argument. In the doctor's argument, the effect under consideration is back pain and the phenomenon is bulging or slipped disks, which means that the doctor's argument is based on situations in which the phenomenon is present but the effect does not occur. So the doctor's argument is not vulnerable to criticism for not considering (C).

D (D) raises the possibility that a characteristic found in half of a given sample might not occur in half of the entire population. But this possibility is irrelevant to the doctor's argument. The study found that bulging or slipped disks occurred in half of a sample of people without serious back pain. However, the doctor does not conclude that half of the entire population of people who do not have serious back pain have bulging or slipped disks. So the argument is not vulnerable to criticism for not considering (D).

E (E) raises the possibility that a factor that does not cause an effect may still be more likely to be present when the effect occurs than when it does not. But this possibility is irrelevant to the doctor's argument. In that argument, the factor under consideration is bulging or slipped disks, and the effect is serious back pain. The doctor has not established that bulging or slipped disks do not cause back pain. (This, in fact, is the doctor's questionable conclusion.) Nor does the doctor draw a separate conclusion about the likelihood of bulging or slipped disks being present in those with serious back pain as compared to those without serious back pain.

- *Difficulty Level: 5*

Question 20

Overview: The passage states that many workers who handled substance T became ill and that T caused at least some of these illnesses. It also states that if T's manufacturer had investigated the safety of T before allowing workers to be exposed to it, many of the workers' illnesses would have been prevented. From this, the argument concludes that T's manufacturer bears some of the responsibility for the workers' illnesses. You need to find a principle that helps to justify this conclusion.

The Correct Answer:

E The premises of the argument tell us that at least some of the illnesses of workers who handled T were consequences of the manufacturer's action of allowing workers to be exposed to T. Also, these illnesses were preventable: if the manufacturer had investigated the safety of T, those illnesses would have been prevented. (E) says that the manufacturer should be held responsible for harmful consequences that were preventable, which implies that the manufacturer should be held responsible for at least some of the illnesses caused by T. So (E) helps to justify the conclusion that the manufacturer bears some responsibility for the workers' illnesses.

The Incorrect Answer Choices:

A (A) claims that employees should be compensated, but it doesn't say who should provide this compensation. So it cannot help to justify the conclusion that the manufacturer in particular bears responsibility for the workers' illnesses.

B (B) says that manufacturers should be held responsible **only** for preventable consequences, i.e., they should not be held responsible for consequences that are not preventable. A principle that tells us only what manufacturers should not be held responsible for cannot help to justify a conclusion about what manufacturers are responsible for.

C The passage says that the manufacturer was initially unaware of the connection between T and illness. So (C), which says only that manufacturers are obligated to inform workers of health risks that they are aware of, does not help to justify the conclusion that the manufacturer bears responsibility for the workers' illnesses.

D (D) says that whether consequences were preventable is irrelevant to whether a manufacturer should be held responsible. This runs counter to the argument in the passage, which concludes that the manufacturer bears responsibility on the grounds that the adverse consequences were preventable. In order to justify the conclusion that the manufacturer bears responsibility, we need to know what **is** relevant to whether the manufacturer bears responsibility, not what is irrelevant. So (D) does not help to justify the conclusion.

■ *Difficulty Level: 2*

Question 21

Overview: The passage says that it is almost certain that a certain government contract will be awarded to either Phoenix Contracting or Cartwright Company. It then adds that the government has decided not to award the contract to Cartwright. The argument concludes that the contract will almost certainly be awarded to Phoenix. The question asks you to determine how the argument proceeds.

The Correct Answer:

A The passage says that it is almost certain that a government contract will be awarded to either Phoenix or Cartwright, which means that Cartwright is the only probable alternative to Phoenix. The argument rules out Cartwright and, on the basis of having ruled out Cartwright, concludes that it is extremely likely that Phoenix will get the contract. So (A) accurately describes how the argument proceeds.

The Incorrect Answer Choices:

B The argument infers that it is almost inevitable that Phoenix will get the contract, i.e., it infers that it is extremely likely that an event will occur. It does not infer that any event will not occur. The claim that Cartwright will not get the contract is treated as a known fact and is not inferred. So (B) does not accurately describe how the argument proceeds.

C The argument does not address any claim that an event is inevitable, nor does it appeal to the possibility of alternative events to refute anything. So (C) does not accurately describe how the argument proceeds.

D The argument does predict a future event, but it does not do so on the basis of an established pattern of past events. The passage makes no claims about any patterns of past events. So (D) does not accurately describe how the argument proceeds.

E A general statistical statement would make a claim that some proportion of events of a certain type have some feature or belong to some category. For example, "80 percent of highway contracts are awarded to Phoenix" would be a general statistical statement. Since the argument contains no such statement, (E) does not accurately describe how the argument proceeds.

- *Difficulty Level: 1*

Question 22

Overview: The passage presents a research finding that younger siblings in large families are less likely to develop allergies than are children in small families, and then presents a hypothesis meant to explain that finding. The question asks you to identify the information that, if true, would provide the most support for the hypothesis that exposure to germs during infancy makes people less likely to develop allergies.

The Correct Answer:

E When children enter day care before age one, they will probably be exposed to more germs than they otherwise would be, because of exposure to the germs of the other children in day care. (E) thus presents an instance in which children who are exposed to more germs during infancy are less likely to develop allergies than other children are. So if (E) is true, it helps to confirm the researchers' hypothesis.

Note that (E) supports the researchers' hypothesis in much the same way it is supported by the observation reported in the passage regarding younger siblings in large families. In both cases, children who are in a condition that elevates their exposure to germs as infants are found to be less likely than other children to develop allergies.

The Incorrect Answer Choices:

A The researchers' hypothesis concerns a link between exposure to germs in infancy and people's likelihood of developing allergies. While (A) might support the researchers' original finding that children from larger families were less likely to develop allergies than children from smaller families, it adds no support for the hypothesis that it is exposure to germs during infancy, rather than something else, that makes children from large families less likely to develop allergies.

B (B) tends to weaken the researchers' hypothesis rather than strengthening it. If (B) is true, it opens the possibility that the increased likelihood of children in smaller families developing allergies is due to the foods they eat, rather than their exposure to germs. In providing information that supports an alternative hypothesis, (B) undermines the researchers' hypothesis rather than supporting it.

C The information in (C) is irrelevant to the researchers' hypothesis. The researchers' hypothesis concerns a cause of developing allergies. It has nothing to do with the severity of those allergies, or how they compare with diseases caused by germs.

D At best, (D) is irrelevant to the researchers' hypothesis. Because we do not know the connection, if any, between parents who have allergies and their children's exposure to germs during infancy, we do not know how the information in (D) bears on the researchers' hypothesis. (D) might suggest that genetic factors contribute to an increased likelihood of developing allergies. But if this has any relevance to the researchers' hypothesis, it would be to reduce the support for that hypothesis by providing an alternative, genetic explanation. (D) clearly does not support the researchers' hypothesis.

- *Difficulty Level: 4*

Question 23

Overview: The conclusion of the argument is that some films from the early years of Hollywood will not be preserved (hence they will disintegrate). This conclusion is supported by the premises that film preservation requires transferring old movies from their original, unstable nitrate film to a stable acetate film, and that this process is too expensive and slow to transfer all currently deteriorating nitrate films to acetate film. Note that there is a gap between what these premises indicate and the conclusion that the argument draws. The premises strongly support the inference that some old films will likely not be preserved, but the argument's conclusion is that some films from the earliest years of Hollywood will not be preserved.

The question asks you to identify an assumption on which the argument depends.

The Correct Answer:

D The argument's conclusion is that some films from the earliest years of Hollywood **will** be lost. This certainty requires at least knowing that the film preservation process has not already been completed for some nitrate films from early Hollywood. Thus, (D) is an assumption required by the argument. If this assumption were false, it would mean none of the earliest Hollywood films exist solely on nitrate film, meaning that there would be no need to subject any of the earliest Hollywood films to the film preservation process. The two premises given would have no relevance to the conclusion that some of the earliest Hollywood films will be lost.

The Incorrect Answer Choices:

A The argument is based on the limited time available for transferring early Hollywood films from nitrate to acetate film: the transfer must be accomplished before any of these films disintegrate. However, (A) has no such time horizon. It allows for the development of a new technology at any time in the future. Moreover, (A) does not say that the new technology would make the process faster or less expensive. Since the conclusion could still be supported by the premises even if a new technology is developed at some time in the future, the argument does not depend on (A) as an assumption.

B The passage states that film preservation requires transferring films from their original material to acetate film. (B) suggests an alternative way of preserving films. However, (B) is certainly not an assumption required by the argument as it suggests that this alternative is less expensive than transferring from nitrate to acetate. If anything, (B) would tend to undermine the argument by suggesting an alternative, less expensive method. The existence of such an alternative could call into doubt the conclusion that some early Hollywood films will not be preserved.

C (C) is not an assumption on which the argument depends, since the conclusion of the argument is forward looking. The argument claims that we lack the time and money to save all the currently deteriorating films. This could hold even if many films have already been preserved. The question is how many films have yet to be preserved, not how many have already been preserved.

E The popularity of the films in question is entirely beside the point. The conclusion of the argument is that we will be not able to preserve all the early Hollywood films. It is irrelevant to this conclusion whether it is popular films or unpopular films that are lost. Because the passage has nothing to do with the popularity of the films, (E) is not an assumption on which the argument depends.

- *Difficulty Level: 5*

Question 24

Overview: The passage describes a study of arthritis in which researchers tried to find a correlation between pain intensity and the weather features that arthritis sufferers usually cite as the causes of their increased pain. The question asks you to identify a statement that logically completes the argument in the passage. To do this, you need to find a statement that fits the general thrust of the argument and can be reasonably inferred from the rest of the passage.

The Correct Answer:

C The passage says that researchers could find no correlation between pain intensity and the weather features under consideration. Nonetheless, the passage establishes that many arthritis sufferers believe such a correlation exists. This suggests that arthritis sufferers are mistaken about this correlation.

The Incorrect Answer Choices:

A While the passage does assert that arthritis sufferers report correlations with widely varying time delays between the weather and arthritis pain, the passage says that researchers could not find any such correlation. This provides reason to think that the weather does not affect arthritis sufferers at all. Thus, (A) cannot be inferred from the rest of the passage.

B (B) cannot be inferred from the passage. If anything, the passage suggests that (B) is likely false. If the arthritis sufferers' beliefs about the causes of pain affected their assessments of pain, then we would expect arthritis sufferers' reports of pain to be correlated with the supposed causes of pain, i.e., the weather features. But the passage says that researchers could find no such correlation.

D The study discussed in the passage suggests that there is no correlation between arthritis pain and certain weather features. So it supports the view that there is no weather-induced arthritis pain. Thus, (D) cannot be inferred from the rest of the passage.

E   The passage describes a scientific study that failed to find any link between arthritis pain and weather. This does not suggest that scientific investigation of possible links between weather and arthritis pain is impossible. On the contrary, it suggests that scientific investigation is possible, and in fact provides an answer to the question of whether there are such links.

- *Difficulty Level: 5*

Question 25

Overview: The premises of this argument point out a correlation between cities with high-technology businesses and cities with healthy economies and a correlation between cities with healthy economies and cities that have plenty of job openings. The argument concludes that someone searching for a job (and hence for a city with many job openings) should seek a city with high-technology businesses, taking the fact that both the presence of high-technology businesses and the presence of job openings are correlated with the presence of a healthy economy to indicate that the presence of high-technology businesses is correlated with the presence of job openings.

The question asks you to identify the answer choice that uses reasoning most similar to the reasoning in this argument.

The Correct Answer:

C   The argument in (C) follows the pattern of reasoning outlined above. Among antiques, being valuable and being carried by an antiques dealer are each correlated with having had its age authenticated. Like the argument in the passage, the argument in (C) uses this fact to conclude that someone seeking valuable antiques should act as though there is a correlation between an antique's being valuable and its being carried by an antiques dealer and should consequently seek antiques sold by antiques dealers.

The Incorrect Answer Choices:

A   The premises of the argument in (A) do not establish correlations that correspond to those in the passage's argument. To do that, the second premise would have to say that older antiques tend to be sold by antique dealers. Because the pattern in the passage of two different qualities both being correlated with a third quality is absent in (A), the reasoning in (A) does not match the reasoning in the passage.

B   The conclusion of the argument in (B), like the conclusion in the passage, is about what people who want a certain thing should do. However, the two premises in (B) do not have the pattern of two different qualities being correlated with a third quality like the premises in the passage's argument. While both premises in the passage's argument are about qualities of cities that are correlated with having healthy economies, there is no common link between the premises in (B). It's not clear how the premises in (B) are meant to support the conclusion—perhaps they're meant to work independently of each other. In any case, the argument in (B) provides little or no support for its conclusion, which is further confirmation of how it differs from the passage's argument.

D   The conclusion of the argument in (D) is about what antique collectors tend to do, and it's supported in terms of what these collectors know and facts about antiques. However, the conclusion of the argument in the passage is about what people who want a certain thing should do, regardless of what they know or what they actually do, and it is supported in terms of the way things tend to be. Because of this, the reasoning in (D) is not similar to the reasoning in the passage.

E   The conclusion of the argument in (E), like the conclusion in the passage, is about what people who want a certain thing should do. However, the two premises in (E) do not have the pattern of two different qualities being correlated with a third quality like the premises in the passage's argument. While both premises in the passage's argument are about qualities of cities that are correlated with having healthy economies, there is no common link between the premises in (E). Moreover, the premises in (E)—unlike the premises in the passage's argument—do not support their conclusion. The premises only support the conclusion that valuable antiques can be found at antiques dealers, and not the conclusion that those who want to purchase the most valuable antiques should seek them from antiques dealers.

- *Difficulty Level: 4*

Question 26

Overview: The study reported in the passage found that for people over 65 the rate of malnutrition is much higher than the poverty rate (based on government poverty standards). But for people 65 or younger the rate of malnutrition is lower than the poverty rate. While it's reasonable to presume that poverty is a contributing factor to malnutrition, the findings of the study suggest that there are other important factors as well, and that these non-poverty-related factors disproportionately affect people over 65. Such factors would help to explain the study's findings.

The task with this question is to identify the one answer choice that does **not** help to explain study's findings.

The Correct Answer:

D   (D) gives information about the poverty rates for the two groups: the poverty rate for people 65 or younger is not higher than the poverty rate for people over 65. But as far as the findings of the study are concerned, this is beside the point. To help explain the findings of the study, an answer choice needs to help account for the fact that the rate of malnutrition far exceeds the poverty rate for the one group but falls below the poverty rate for the other. (D) does nothing to explain that state of affairs.

The Incorrect Answer Choices:

A   (A) indicates that people over 65 are less likely to be correctly diagnosed and treated for malnutrition than those who are under 65. This difference in diagnosis and treatment helps to explain why the rate of malnutrition exceeds the rate of poverty for people over 65 but not for people 65 or younger, since it suggests that people over 65 are less likely to receive the treatment they need to overcome malnutrition.

B   (B) indicates that people over 65 are more likely to take medications that increase their need for certain nutrients. It's likely that some people would not meet this increased need for certain nutrients, so malnutrition is more likely to result for people taking these medications. People over 65 are thus more likely to be malnourished than people 65 or younger, who are less likely to take these medications. This helps to explain why the rate of malnutrition exceeds the rate of poverty for people over 65 but not for people 65 or younger.

C (C) indicates that those over 65 are more likely than those under 65 to suffer from loss of appetite. So they are more likely to eat too little and to be malnourished as a consequence. This difference helps to explain why the rate of malnutrition exceeds the rate of poverty for people over 65 but not for people 65 or younger.

E If people who are 65 or younger are less likely to suffer from medical conditions that interfere with their digestion, they are less likely to suffer from malnutrition because of being unable to properly digest their food. So this difference in the incidence of medical conditions that interfere with digestion helps to explain why the rate of malnutrition does not exceed the rate of poverty for people 65 or younger even though it greatly exceeds the rate of poverty for people over 65.

- *Difficulty Level: 4*

General Directions for the LSAT Answer Sheet

The actual testing time for this portion of the test will be 2 hours 55 minutes. There are five sections, each with a time limit of 35 minutes. The supervisor will tell you when to begin and end each section. If you finish a section before time is called, you may check your work on that section **only;** do not turn to any other section of the test book and do not work on any other section either in the test book or on the answer sheet.

There are several different types of questions on the test, and each question type has its own directions. **Be sure you understand the directions for each question type before attempting to answer any questions in that section.**

Not everyone will finish all the questions in the time allowed. Do not hurry, but work steadily and as quickly as you can without sacrificing accuracy. You are advised to use your time effectively. If a question seems too difficult, go on to the next one and return to the difficult question after completing the section. **MARK THE BEST ANSWER YOU CAN FOR EVERY QUESTION. NO DEDUCTIONS WILL BE MADE FOR WRONG ANSWERS. YOUR SCORE WILL BE BASED ONLY ON THE NUMBER OF QUESTIONS YOU ANSWER CORRECTLY.**

ALL YOUR ANSWERS MUST BE MARKED ON THE ANSWER SHEET. Answer spaces for each question are lettered to correspond with the letters of the potential answers to each question in the test book. After you have decided which of the answers is correct, blacken the corresponding space on the answer sheet. **BE SURE THAT EACH MARK IS BLACK AND COMPLETELY FILLS THE ANSWER SPACE.** Give only one answer to each question. If you change an answer, be sure that all previous marks are **erased completely.** Since the answer sheet is machine scored, incomplete erasures may be interpreted as intended answers. **ANSWERS RECORDED IN THE TEST BOOK WILL NOT BE SCORED.**

There may be more question numbers on this answer sheet than there are questions in a section. Do not be concerned, but be certain that the section and number of the question you are answering matches the answer sheet section and question number. Additional answer spaces in any answer sheet section should be left blank. Begin your next section in the number one answer space for that section.

LSAC takes various steps to ensure that answer sheets are returned from test centers in a timely manner for processing. In the unlikely event that an answer sheet is not received, LSAC will permit the examinee either to retest at no additional fee or to receive a refund of his or her LSAT fee. **THESE REMEDIES ARE THE ONLY REMEDIES AVAILABLE IN THE UNLIKELY EVENT THAT AN ANSWER SHEET IS NOT RECEIVED BY LSAC.**

Score Cancellation

Complete this section only if you are absolutely certain you want to cancel your score. **A CANCELLATION REQUEST CANNOT BE RESCINDED. IF YOU ARE AT ALL UNCERTAIN, YOU SHOULD NOT COMPLETE THIS SECTION.**

To cancel your score from this administration, you **must:**

A. fill in both ovals here ...... ○ ○

AND

B. read the following statement. Then sign your name and enter the date.
YOUR SIGNATURE ALONE IS NOT SUFFICIENT FOR SCORE CANCELLATION. BOTH OVALS ABOVE MUST BE FILLED IN FOR SCANNING EQUIPMENT TO RECOGNIZE YOUR REQUEST FOR SCORE CANCELLATION.

I certify that I wish to cancel my test score from this administration. I understand that my request is irreversible and that my score will not be sent to me or to the law schools to which I apply.

_____
Sign your name in full

_____
Date

FOR LSAC USE ONLY ●

HOW DID YOU PREPARE FOR THE LSAT?
(Select all that apply.)

Responses to this item are voluntary and will be used for statistical research purposes only.

○ By studying the free sample questions available on LSAC's website.
○ By taking the free sample LSAT available on LSAC's website.
○ By working through official LSAT *PrepTests*, *ItemWise*, and/or other LSAC test prep products.
○ By using LSAT prep books or software **not** published by LSAC.
○ By attending a commercial test preparation or coaching course.
○ By attending a test preparation or coaching course offered through an undergraduate institution.
○ Self study.
○ Other preparation.
○ No preparation.

CERTIFYING STATEMENT

Please write the following statement. Sign and date.

I certify that I am the examinee whose name appears on this answer sheet and that I am here to take the LSAT for the sole purpose of being considered for admission to law school. I further certify that I will neither assist nor receive assistance from any other candidate, and I agree not to copy, retain, or transmit examination questions in any form or discuss them with any other person.

_____
_____
_____
_____
_____
_____
_____
_____
_____
_____

SIGNATURE: _____ TODAY'S DATE: ___/___/___
                                                    MONTH DAY YEAR

INSTRUCTIONS FOR COMPLETING THE BIOGRAPHICAL AREA ARE ON THE BACK COVER OF YOUR TEST BOOKLET.
USE ONLY A NO. 2 OR HB PENCIL TO COMPLETE THIS ANSWER SHEET. DO NOT USE INK.

A

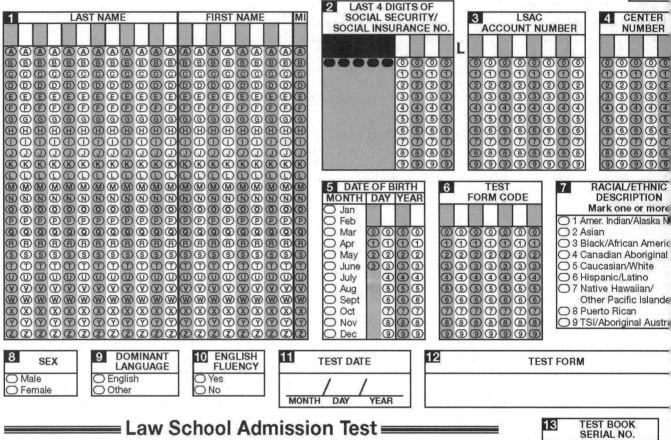

1 LAST NAME / FIRST NAME / MI

2 LAST 4 DIGITS OF SOCIAL SECURITY/ SOCIAL INSURANCE NO.

3 LSAC ACCOUNT NUMBER

4 CENTER NUMBER

5 DATE OF BIRTH — MONTH | DAY | YEAR
Jan, Feb, Mar, Apr, May, June, July, Aug, Sept, Oct, Nov, Dec

6 TEST FORM CODE

7 RACIAL/ETHNIC DESCRIPTION — Mark one or more
- 1 Amer. Indian/Alaska N
- 2 Asian
- 3 Black/African Americ
- 4 Canadian Aboriginal
- 5 Caucasian/White
- 6 Hispanic/Latino
- 7 Native Hawaiian/ Other Pacific Islande
- 8 Puerto Rican
- 9 TSI/Aboriginal Austra

8 SEX
- Male
- Female

9 DOMINANT LANGUAGE
- English
- Other

10 ENGLISH FLUENCY
- Yes
- No

11 TEST DATE — MONTH / DAY / YEAR

12 TEST FORM

Law School Admission Test

Mark one and only one answer to each question. Be sure to fill in completely the space for your intended answer choice. If you erase, do so completely. Make no stray marks.

13 TEST BOOK SERIAL NO.

SECTION 1	SECTION 2	SECTION 3	SECTION 4	SECTION 5
1 A B C D E	1 A B C D E	1 A B C D E	1 A B C D E	1 A B C D E
2 A B C D E	2 A B C D E	2 A B C D E	2 A B C D E	2 A B C D E
3 A B C D E	3 A B C D E	3 A B C D E	3 A B C D E	3 A B C D E
4 A B C D E	4 A B C D E	4 A B C D E	4 A B C D E	4 A B C D E
5 A B C D E	5 A B C D E	5 A B C D E	5 A B C D E	5 A B C D E
6 A B C D E	6 A B C D E	6 A B C D E	6 A B C D E	6 A B C D E
7 A B C D E	7 A B C D E	7 A B C D E	7 A B C D E	7 A B C D E
8 A B C D E	8 A B C D E	8 A B C D E	8 A B C D E	8 A B C D E
9 A B C D E	9 A B C D E	9 A B C D E	9 A B C D E	9 A B C D E
10 A B C D E	10 A B C D E	10 A B C D E	10 A B C D E	10 A B C D E
11 A B C D E	11 A B C D E	11 A B C D E	11 A B C D E	11 A B C D E
12 A B C D E	12 A B C D E	12 A B C D E	12 A B C D E	12 A B C D E
13 A B C D E	13 A B C D E	13 A B C D E	13 A B C D E	13 A B C D E
14 A B C D E	14 A B C D E	14 A B C D E	14 A B C D E	14 A B C D E
15 A B C D E	15 A B C D E	15 A B C D E	15 A B C D E	15 A B C D E
16 A B C D E	16 A B C D E	16 A B C D E	16 A B C D E	16 A B C D E
17 A B C D E	17 A B C D E	17 A B C D E	17 A B C D E	17 A B C D E
18 A B C D E	18 A B C D E	18 A B C D E	18 A B C D E	18 A B C D E
19 A B C D E	19 A B C D E	19 A B C D E	19 A B C D E	19 A B C D E
20 A B C D E	20 A B C D E	20 A B C D E	20 A B C D E	20 A B C D E
21 A B C D E	21 A B C D E	21 A B C D E	21 A B C D E	21 A B C D E
22 A B C D E	22 A B C D E	22 A B C D E	22 A B C D E	22 A B C D E
23 A B C D E	23 A B C D E	23 A B C D E	23 A B C D E	23 A B C D E
24 A B C D E	24 A B C D E	24 A B C D E	24 A B C D E	24 A B C D E
25 A B C D E	25 A B C D E	25 A B C D E	25 A B C D E	25 A B C D E
26 A B C D E	26 A B C D E	26 A B C D E	26 A B C D E	26 A B C D E
27 A B C D E	27 A B C D E	27 A B C D E	27 A B C D E	27 A B C D E
28 A B C D E	28 A B C D E	28 A B C D E	28 A B C D E	28 A B C D E
29 A B C D E	29 A B C D E	29 A B C D E	29 A B C D E	29 A B C D E
30 A B C D E	30 A B C D E	30 A B C D E	30 A B C D E	30 A B C D E

14 PLEASE PRINT INFORMATION

LAST NAME

FIRST NAME

DATE OF BIRTH

PREPTEST B, TABLE OF CONTENTS

SECTION I

Time—35 minutes

25 Questions

Directions: The questions in this section are based on the reasoning contained in brief statements or passages. For some questions, more than one of the choices could conceivably answer the question. However, you are to choose the best answer; that is, the response that most accurately and completely answers the question. You should not make assumptions that are by commonsense standards implausible, superfluous, or incompatible with the passage. After you have chosen the best answer, blacken the corresponding space on your answer sheet.

1. Backyard gardeners who want to increase the yields of their potato plants should try growing stinging nettles alongside the plants, since stinging nettles attract insects that kill a wide array of insect pests that damage potato plants. It is true that stinging nettles also attract aphids, and that many species of aphids are harmful to potato plants, but that fact in no way contradicts this recommendation, because _____.

   Which one of the following most logically completes the argument?

   (A) stinging nettles require little care and thus are easy to cultivate

   (B) some types of aphids are attracted to stinging nettle plants but do not damage them

   (C) the types of aphids that stinging nettles attract do not damage potato plants

   (D) insect pests typically cause less damage to potato plants than other harmful organisms do

   (E) most aphid species that are harmful to potato plants cause greater harm to other edible food plants

2. Jocko, a chimpanzee, was once given a large bunch of bananas by a zookeeper after the more dominant members of the chimpanzee's troop had wandered off. In his excitement, Jocko uttered some loud "food barks." The other chimpanzees returned and took the bananas away. The next day, Jocko was again found alone and was given a single banana. This time, however, he kept silent. The zookeeper concluded that Jocko's silence was a stratagem to keep the other chimpanzees from his food.

   Which one of the following, if true, most seriously calls into question the zookeeper's conclusion?

   (A) Chimpanzees utter food barks only when their favorite foods are available.

   (B) Chimpanzees utter food barks only when they encounter a sizable quantity of food.

   (C) Chimpanzees frequently take food from other chimpanzees merely to assert dominance.

   (D) Even when they are alone, chimpanzees often make noises that appear to be signals to other chimpanzees.

   (E) Bananas are a food for which all of the chimpanzees at the zoo show a decided preference.

3. A recent survey quizzed journalism students about the sorts of stories they themselves wished to read. A significant majority said they wanted to see stories dealing with serious governmental and political issues and had little tolerance for the present popularity of stories covering lifestyle trends and celebrity gossip. This indicates that today's trends in publishing are based on false assumptions about the interests of the public.

   Which one of the following most accurately describes a flaw in the argument's reasoning?

   (A) It takes what is more likely to be the effect of a phenomenon to be its cause.

   (B) It regards the production of an effect as incontrovertible evidence of an intention to produce that effect.

   (C) It relies on the opinions of a group unlikely to be representative of the group at issue in the conclusion.

   (D) It employs language that unfairly represents those who are likely to reject the argument's conclusion.

   (E) It treats a hypothesis as fact even though it is admittedly unsupported.

GO ON TO THE NEXT PAGE.

4. Electric bug zappers, which work by attracting insects to light, are a very effective means of ridding an area of flying insects. Despite this, most pest control experts now advise against their use, recommending instead such remedies as insect-eating birds or insecticide sprays.

Which one of the following, if true, most helps to account for the pest control experts' recommendation?

(A) Insect-eating birds will take up residence in any insect-rich area if they are provided with nesting boxes, food, and water.

(B) Bug zappers are less effective against mosquitoes, which are among the more harmful insects, than they are against other harmful insects.

(C) Bug zappers use more electricity but provide less light than do most standard outdoor light sources.

(D) Bug zappers kill many more beneficial insects and fewer harmful insects than do insect-eating birds and insecticide sprays.

(E) Developers of certain new insecticide sprays claim that their products contain no chemicals that are harmful to humans, birds, or pets.

5. Gardener: The design of Japanese gardens should display harmony with nature. Hence, rocks chosen for placement in such gardens should vary widely in appearance, since rocks found in nature also vary widely in appearance.

The gardener's argument depends on assuming which one of the following?

(A) The selection of rocks for placement in a Japanese garden should reflect every key value embodied in the design of Japanese gardens.

(B) In the selection of rocks for Japanese gardens, imitation of nature helps to achieve harmony with nature.

(C) The only criterion for selecting rocks for placement in a Japanese garden is the expression of harmony with nature.

(D) Expressing harmony with nature and being natural are the same thing.

(E) Each component of a genuine Japanese garden is varied.

6. Small experimental vacuum tubes can operate in heat that makes semiconductor components fail. Any component whose resistance to heat is greater than that of semiconductors would be preferable for use in digital circuits, but only if that component were also comparable to semiconductors in all other significant respects, such as maximum current capacity. However, vacuum tubes' maximum current capacity is presently not comparable to that of semiconductors.

If the statements above are true, which one of the following must also be true?

(A) Vacuum tubes are not now preferable to semiconductors for use in digital circuits.

(B) Once vacuum tubes and semiconductors have comparable maximum current capacity, vacuum tubes will be used in some digital circuits.

(C) The only reason that vacuum tubes are not now used in digital circuits is that vacuum tubes' maximum current capacity is too low.

(D) Semiconductors will always be preferable to vacuum tubes for use in many applications other than digital circuits.

(E) Resistance to heat is the only advantage that vacuum tubes have over semiconductors.

7. The cause of the epidemic that devastated Athens in 430 B.C. can finally be identified. Accounts of the epidemic mention the hiccups experienced by many victims, a symptom of no known disease except that caused by the recently discovered Ebola virus. Moreover, other symptoms of the disease caused by the Ebola virus are mentioned in the accounts of the Athenian epidemic.

Each of the following, if true, weakens the argument EXCEPT:

(A) Victims of the Ebola virus experience many symptoms that do not appear in any of the accounts of the Athenian epidemic.

(B) Not all of those who are victims of the Ebola virus are afflicted with hiccups.

(C) The Ebola virus's host animals did not live in Athens at the time of the Athenian epidemic.

(D) The Ebola virus is much more contagious than the disease that caused the Athenian epidemic was reported to have been.

(E) The epidemics known to have been caused by the Ebola virus are usually shorter-lived than was the Athenian epidemic.

GO ON TO THE NEXT PAGE.

8. Letter to the editor: Your article was unjustified in criticizing environmentalists for claiming that more wolves on Vancouver Island are killed by hunters than are born each year. You stated that this claim was disproven by recent studies that indicate that the total number of wolves on Vancouver Island has remained roughly constant for 20 years. But you failed to account for the fact that, fearing the extinction of this wolf population, environmentalists have been introducing new wolves into the Vancouver Island wolf population for 20 years.

Which one of the following most accurately expresses the conclusion of the argument in the letter to the editor?

(A)   Environmentalists have been successfully maintaining the wolf population on Vancouver Island for 20 years.

(B)   As many wolves on Vancouver Island are killed by hunters as are born each year.

(C)   The population of wolves on Vancouver Island should be maintained by either reducing the number killed by hunters each year or introducing new wolves into the population.

(D)   The recent studies indicating that the total number of wolves on Vancouver Island has remained roughly constant for 20 years were flawed.

(E)   The stability in the size of the Vancouver Island wolf population does not warrant the article's criticism of the environmentalists' claim.

9. Computer scientist: For several decades, the number of transistors on new computer microchips, and hence the microchips' computing speed, has doubled about every 18 months. However, from the mid-1990s into the next decade, each such doubling in a microchip's computing speed was accompanied by a doubling in the cost of producing that microchip.

Which one of the following can be properly inferred from the computer scientist's statements?

(A)   The only effective way to double the computing speed of computer microchips is to increase the number of transistors per microchip.

(B)   From the mid-1990s into the next decade, there was little if any increase in the retail cost of computers as a result of the increased number of transistors on microchips.

(C)   For the last several decades, computer engineers have focused on increasing the computing speed of computer microchips without making any attempt to control the cost of producing them.

(D)   From the mid-1990s into the next decade, a doubling in the cost of fabricating new computer microchips accompanied each doubling in the number of transistors on those microchips.

(E)   It is unlikely that engineers will ever be able to increase the computing speed of microchips without also increasing the cost of producing them.

GO ON TO THE NEXT PAGE.

10. Ms. Sandstrom's newspaper column describing a strange natural phenomenon on the Mendels' farm led many people to trespass on and extensively damage their property. Thus, Ms. Sandstrom should pay for this damage if, as the Mendels claim, she could have reasonably expected that the column would lead people to damage the Mendels' farm.

The argument's conclusion can be properly inferred if which one of the following is assumed?

(A) One should pay for any damage that one's action leads other people to cause if one could have reasonably expected that the action would lead other people to cause damage.

(B) One should pay for damage that one's action leads other people to cause only if, prior to the action, one expected that the action would lead other people to cause that damage.

(C) It is unlikely that the people who trespassed on and caused the damage to the Mendels' property would themselves pay for the damage they caused.

(D) Ms. Sandstrom knew that her column could incite trespassing that could result in damage to the Mendels' farm.

(E) The Mendels believe that Ms. Sandstrom is able to form reasonable expectations about the consequences of her actions.

11. Meyer was found by his employer to have committed scientific fraud by falsifying data. The University of Williamstown, from which Meyer held a PhD, validated this finding and subsequently investigated whether he had falsified data in his doctoral thesis, finding no evidence that he had. But the university decided to revoke Meyer's PhD anyway.

Which one of the following university policies most justifies the decision to revoke Meyer's PhD?

(A) Anyone who holds a PhD from the University of Williamstown and is found to have committed academic fraud in the course of pursuing that PhD will have the PhD revoked.

(B) No PhD program at the University of Williamstown will admit any applicant who has been determined to have committed any sort of academic fraud.

(C) Any University of Williamstown student who is found to have submitted falsified data as academic work will be dismissed from the university.

(D) Anyone who holds a PhD from the University of Williamstown and is found to have committed scientific fraud will have the PhD revoked.

(E) The University of Williamstown will not hire anyone who is under investigation for scientific fraud.

12. Aerobics instructor: Compared to many forms of exercise, kickboxing aerobics is highly risky. Overextending when kicking often leads to hip, knee, or lower-back injuries. Such overextension is very likely to occur when beginners try to match the high kicks of more skilled practitioners.

Which one of the following is most strongly supported by the aerobics instructor's statements?

(A) Skilled practitioners of kickboxing aerobics are unlikely to experience injuries from overextending while kicking.

(B) To reduce the risk of injuries, beginners at kickboxing aerobics should avoid trying to match the high kicks of more skilled practitioners.

(C) Beginners at kickboxing aerobics will not experience injuries if they avoid trying to match the high kicks of more skilled practitioners.

(D) Kickboxing aerobics is more risky than forms of aerobic exercise that do not involve high kicks.

(E) Most beginners at kickboxing aerobics experience injuries from trying to match the high kicks of more skilled practitioners.

13. A large company has been convicted of engaging in monopolistic practices. The penalty imposed on the company will probably have little if any effect on its behavior. Still, the trial was worthwhile, since it provided useful information about the company's practices. After all, this information has emboldened the company's direct competitors, alerted potential rivals, and forced the company to restrain its unfair behavior toward customers and competitors.

Which one of the following most accurately expresses the overall conclusion drawn in the argument?

(A) Even if the company had not been convicted of engaging in monopolistic practices, the trial probably would have had some effect on the company's behavior.

(B) The light shed on the company's practices by the trial has emboldened its competitors, alerted potential rivals, and forced the company to restrain its unfair behavior.

(C) The penalty imposed on the company will likely have little or no effect on its behavior.

(D) The company's trial on charges of engaging in monopolistic practices was worthwhile.

(E) The penalty imposed on the company in the trial should have been larger.

GO ON TO THE NEXT PAGE.

14. Waller: If there were really such a thing as extrasensory perception, it would generally be accepted by the public since anyone with extrasensory powers would be able to convince the general public of its existence by clearly demonstrating those powers. Indeed, anyone who was recognized to have such powers would achieve wealth and renown.

Chin: It's impossible to demonstrate anything to the satisfaction of all skeptics. So long as the cultural elite remains closed-minded to the possibility of extrasensory perception, the popular media reports, and thus public opinion, will always be biased in favor of such skeptics.

Waller's and Chin's statements commit them to disagreeing on whether

(A) extrasensory perception is a real phenomenon
(B) extrasensory perception, if it were a real phenomenon, could be demonstrated to the satisfaction of all skeptics
(C) skeptics about extrasensory perception have a weak case
(D) the failure of the general public to believe in extrasensory perception is good evidence against its existence
(E) the general public believes that extrasensory perception is a real phenomenon

15. Counselor: Hagerle sincerely apologized to the physician for lying to her. So Hagerle owes me a sincere apology as well, because Hagerle told the same lie to both of us.

Which one of the following principles, if valid, most helps to justify the counselor's reasoning?

(A) It is good to apologize for having done something wrong to a person if one is capable of doing so sincerely.
(B) If someone tells the same lie to two different people, then neither of those lied to is owed an apology unless both are.
(C) Someone is owed a sincere apology for having been lied to by a person if someone else has already received a sincere apology for the same lie from that same person.
(D) If one is capable of sincerely apologizing to someone for lying to them, then one owes that person such an apology.
(E) A person should not apologize to someone for telling a lie unless he or she can sincerely apologize to all others to whom the lie was told.

16. A survey of address changes filed with post offices and driver's license bureaus over the last ten years has established that households moving out of the city of Weston outnumbered households moving into the city two to one. Therefore, we can expect that next year's census, which counts all residents regardless of age, will show that the population of Weston has declined since the last census ten years ago.

Which one of the following, if true, most helps to strengthen the argument?

(A) Within the past decade many people both moved into the city and also moved out of it.
(B) Over the past century any census of Weston showing a population loss was followed ten years later by a census showing a population gain.
(C) Many people moving into Weston failed to notify either the post office or the driver's license bureau that they had moved to the city.
(D) Most adults moving out of Weston were parents who had children living with them, whereas most adults remaining in or moving into the city were older people who lived alone.
(E) Most people moving out of Weston were young adults who were hoping to begin a career elsewhere, whereas most adults remaining in or moving into the city had long-standing jobs in the city.

17. Psychologist: People tend to make certain cognitive errors when they predict how a given event would affect their future happiness. But people should not necessarily try to rid themselves of this tendency. After all, in a visual context, lines that are actually parallel often appear to people as if they converge. If a surgeon offered to restructure your eyes and visual cortex so that parallel lines would no longer ever appear to converge, it would not be reasonable to take the surgeon up on the offer.

The psychologist's argument does which one of the following?

(A) attempts to refute a claim that a particular event is inevitable by establishing the possibility of an alternative event
(B) attempts to undermine a theory by calling into question an assumption on which the theory is based
(C) argues that an action might not be appropriate by suggesting that a corresponding action in an analogous situation is not appropriate
(D) argues that two situations are similar by establishing that the same action would be reasonable in each situation
(E) attempts to establish a generalization and then uses that generalization to argue against a particular action

GO ON TO THE NEXT PAGE.

18. Principle: Even if an art auction house identifies the descriptions in its catalog as opinions, it is guilty of misrepresentation if such a description is a deliberate attempt to mislead bidders.

Application: Although Healy's, an art auction house, states that all descriptions in its catalog are opinions, Healy's was guilty of misrepresentation when its catalog described a vase as dating from the mid-eighteenth century when it was actually a modern reproduction.

Which one of the following, if true, most justifies the above application of the principle?

(A) An authentic work of art from the mid-eighteenth century will usually sell for at least ten times more than a modern reproduction of a similar work from that period.

(B) Although pottery that is similar to the vase is currently extremely popular among art collectors, none of the collectors who are knowledgeable about such pottery were willing to bid on the vase.

(C) The stated policy of Healy's is to describe works in its catalogs only in terms of their readily perceptible qualities and not to include any information about their age.

(D) Some Healy's staff members believe that the auction house's catalog should not contain any descriptions that have not been certified to be true by independent experts.

(E) Without consulting anyone with expertise in authenticating vases, Healy's described the vase as dating from the mid-eighteenth century merely in order to increase its auction price.

19. Anthropologist: It was formerly believed that prehistoric *Homo sapiens* ancestors of contemporary humans interbred with Neanderthals, but DNA testing of a Neanderthal's remains indicates that this is not the case. The DNA of contemporary humans is significantly different from that of the Neanderthal.

Which one of the following is an assumption required by the anthropologist's argument?

(A) At least some Neanderthals lived at the same time and in the same places as prehistoric *Homo sapiens* ancestors of contemporary humans.

(B) DNA testing of remains is significantly less reliable than DNA testing of samples from living species.

(C) The DNA of prehistoric *Homo sapiens* ancestors of contemporary humans was not significantly more similar to that of Neanderthals than is the DNA of contemporary humans.

(D) Neanderthals and prehistoric *Homo sapiens* ancestors of contemporary humans were completely isolated from each other geographically.

(E) Any similarity in the DNA of two species must be the result of interbreeding.

20. Council member: The profits of downtown businesses will increase if more consumers live in the downtown area, and a decrease in the cost of living in the downtown area will guarantee that the number of consumers living there will increase. However, the profits of downtown businesses will not increase unless downtown traffic congestion decreases.

If all the council member's statements are true, which one of the following must be true?

(A) If downtown traffic congestion decreases, the number of consumers living in the downtown area will increase.

(B) If the cost of living in the downtown area decreases, the profits of downtown businesses will increase.

(C) If downtown traffic congestion decreases, the cost of living in the downtown area will increase.

(D) If downtown traffic congestion decreases, the cost of living in the downtown area will decrease.

(E) If the profits of downtown businesses increase, the number of consumers living in the downtown area will increase.

GO ON TO THE NEXT PAGE.

21. On the Discount Phoneline, any domestic long-distance call starting between 9 A.M. and 5 P.M. costs 15 cents a minute, and any other domestic long-distance call costs 10 cents a minute. So any domestic long-distance call on the Discount Phoneline that does not cost 10 cents a minute costs 15 cents a minute.

The pattern of reasoning in which one of the following arguments is most similar to that in the argument above?

(A) If a university class involves extensive lab work, the class will be conducted in a laboratory; otherwise, it will be conducted in a normal classroom. Thus, if a university class does not involve extensive lab work, it will not be conducted in a laboratory.

(B) If a university class involves extensive lab work, the class will be conducted in a laboratory; otherwise, it will be conducted in a normal classroom. Thus, if a university class is not conducted in a normal classroom, it will involve extensive lab work.

(C) If a university class involves extensive lab work, the class will be conducted in a laboratory; otherwise, it will be conducted in a normal classroom. Thus, if a university class is conducted in a normal classroom, it will not be conducted in a laboratory.

(D) If a university class involves extensive lab work, the class will be conducted in a laboratory; otherwise, it will be conducted in a normal classroom. Thus, if a university class involves extensive lab work, it will not be conducted in a normal classroom.

(E) If a university class involves extensive lab work, the class will be conducted in a laboratory; otherwise, it will be conducted in a normal classroom. Thus, if a university class is not conducted in a normal classroom, it will be conducted in a laboratory.

22. One child pushed another child from behind, injuring the second child. The first child clearly understands the difference between right and wrong, so what was done was wrong if it was intended to injure the second child.

Which one of the following principles, if valid, most helps to justify the reasoning in the argument?

(A) An action that is intended to harm another person is wrong only if the person who performed the action understands the difference between right and wrong.

(B) It is wrong for a person who understands the difference between right and wrong to intentionally harm another person.

(C) Any act that is wrong is done with the intention of causing harm.

(D) An act that harms another person is wrong if the person who did it understands the difference between right and wrong and did not think about whether the act would injure the other person.

(E) A person who does not understand the difference between right and wrong does not bear any responsibility for harming another person.

23. Researcher: Each subject in this experiment owns one car, and was asked to estimate what proportion of all automobiles registered in the nation are the same make as the subject's car. The estimate of nearly every subject has been significantly higher than the actual national statistic for the make of that subject's car. I hypothesize that certain makes of car are more common in some regions of the nation than in other regions; obviously, that would lead many people to overestimate how common their make of car is nationally. That is precisely the result found in this experiment, so certain makes of car must indeed be more common in some areas of the nation than in others.

Which one of the following most accurately expresses a reasoning flaw in the researcher's argument?

(A) The argument fails to estimate the likelihood that most subjects in the experiment did not know the actual statistics about how common their make of car is nationwide.

(B) The argument treats a result that supports a hypothesis as a result that proves a hypothesis.

(C) The argument fails to take into account the possibility that the subject pool may come from a wide variety of geographical regions.

(D) The argument attempts to draw its main conclusion from a set of premises that are mutually contradictory.

(E) The argument applies a statistical generalization to a particular case to which it was not intended to apply.

GO ON TO THE NEXT PAGE.

24. In university towns, police issue far more parking citations during the school year than they do during the times when the students are out of town. Therefore, we know that most parking citations in university towns are issued to students.

Which one of the following is most similar in its flawed reasoning to the flawed reasoning in the argument above?

(A) We know that children buy most of the snacks at cinemas, because popcorn sales increase as the proportion of child moviegoers to adult moviegoers increases.

(B) We know that this houseplant gets more of the sunlight from the window, because it is greener than that houseplant.

(C) We know that most people who go to a university are studious because most of those people study while they attend the university.

(D) We know that consumers buy more fruit during the summer than they buy during the winter, because there are far more varieties of fruit available in the summer than in the winter.

(E) We know that most of the snacks parents buy go to other people's children, because when other people's children come to visit, parents give out more snacks than usual.

25. Counselor: Those who believe that criticism should be gentle rather than harsh should consider the following: change requires a motive, and criticism that is unpleasant provides a motive. Since harsh criticism is unpleasant, harsh criticism provides a motive. Therefore, only harsh criticism will cause the person criticized to change.

The reasoning in the counselor's argument is most vulnerable to criticism on the grounds that the argument

(A) infers that something that is sufficient to provide a motive is necessary to provide a motive

(B) fails to address the possibility that in some cases the primary goal of criticism is something other than bringing about change in the person being criticized

(C) takes for granted that everyone who is motivated to change will change

(D) confuses a motive for doing something with a motive for avoiding something

(E) takes the refutation of an argument to be sufficient to show that the argument's conclusion is false

S T O P

IF YOU FINISH BEFORE TIME IS CALLED, YOU MAY CHECK YOUR WORK ON THIS SECTION ONLY.
DO NOT WORK ON ANY OTHER SECTION IN THE TEST.

SECTION II

Time—35 minutes

23 Questions

Directions: Each group of questions in this section is based on a set of conditions. In answering some of the questions, it may be useful to draw a rough diagram. Choose the response that most accurately and completely answers each question and blacken the corresponding space on your answer sheet.

Questions 1–5

Each of seven candidates for the position of judge—Hamadi, Jefferson, Kurtz, Li, McDonnell, Ortiz, and Perkins—will be appointed to an open position on one of two courts—the appellate court or the trial court. There are three open positions on the appellate court and six open positions on the trial court, but not all of them will be filled at this time. The judicial appointments will conform to the following conditions:

  Li must be appointed to the appellate court.
  Kurtz must be appointed to the trial court.
  Hamadi cannot be appointed to the same court as Perkins.

1. Which one of the following is an acceptable set of appointments of candidates to courts?

(A)   appellate: Hamadi, Ortiz
      trial: Jefferson, Kurtz, Li, McDonnell, Perkins
(B)   appellate: Hamadi, Li, Perkins
      trial: Jefferson, Kurtz, McDonnell, Ortiz
(C)   appellate: Kurtz, Li, Perkins
      trial: Hamadi, Jefferson, McDonnell, Ortiz
(D)   appellate: Li, McDonnell, Ortiz
      trial: Hamadi, Jefferson, Kurtz, Perkins
(E)   appellate: Li, Perkins
      trial: Hamadi, Jefferson, Kurtz, McDonnell, Ortiz

GO ON TO THE NEXT PAGE.

2. Which one of the following CANNOT be true?

    (A)   Hamadi and McDonnell are both appointed to
          the appellate court.
    (B)   McDonnell and Ortiz are both appointed to the
          appellate court.
    (C)   Ortiz and Perkins are both appointed to the
          appellate court.
    (D)   Hamadi and Jefferson are both appointed to the
          trial court.
    (E)   Ortiz and Perkins are both appointed to the trial
          court.

3. Which one of the following CANNOT be true?

    (A)   Jefferson and McDonnell are both appointed to
          the appellate court.
    (B)   Jefferson and McDonnell are both appointed to
          the trial court.
    (C)   McDonnell and Ortiz are both appointed to the
          trial court.
    (D)   McDonnell and Perkins are both appointed to
          the appellate court.
    (E)   McDonnell and Perkins are both appointed to
          the trial court.

4. If Ortiz is appointed to the appellate court, which one of
    the following must be true?

    (A)   Hamadi is appointed to the appellate court.
    (B)   Jefferson is appointed to the appellate court.
    (C)   Jefferson is appointed to the trial court.
    (D)   Perkins is appointed to the appellate court.
    (E)   Perkins is appointed to the trial court.

5. Which one of the following, if substituted for the
    condition that Hamadi cannot be appointed to the same
    court as Perkins, would have the same effect on the
    appointments of the seven candidates?

    (A)   Hamadi and Perkins cannot both be appointed
          to the appellate court.
    (B)   If Hamadi is not appointed to the trial court,
          then Perkins must be.
    (C)   If Perkins is appointed to the same court as
          Jefferson, then Hamadi cannot be.
    (D)   If Hamadi is appointed to the same court as Li,
          then Perkins must be appointed to the same
          court as Kurtz.
    (E)   No three of Hamadi, Kurtz, Li, and Perkins can
          be appointed to the same court as each other.

GO ON TO THE NEXT PAGE.

Questions 6–10

Exactly six members of a skydiving team—Larue, Ohba, Pei, Treviño, Weiss, and Zacny—each dive exactly once, one at a time, from a plane, consistent with the following conditions:

Treviño dives from the plane at some time before Weiss does.

Larue dives from the plane either first or last.

Neither Weiss nor Zacny dives from the plane last.

Pei dives from the plane at some time after either Ohba or Larue but not both.

6. Which one of the following could be an accurate list of the members in the order in which they dive from the plane, from first to last?

(A)   Larue, Treviño, Ohba, Zacny, Pei, Weiss
(B)   Larue, Treviño, Pei, Zacny, Weiss, Ohba
(C)   Weiss, Ohba, Treviño, Zacny, Pei, Larue
(D)   Treviño, Weiss, Pei, Ohba, Zacny, Larue
(E)   Treviño, Weiss, Zacny, Larue, Pei, Ohba

GO ON TO THE NEXT PAGE.

7. Which one of the following must be true?

    (A) At least two of the members dive from the
         plane after Larue.
    (B) ʹ At least two of the members dive from the
         plane after Ohba.
    (C) At least two of the members dive from the
         plane after Pei.
    (D) At least two of the members dive from the
         plane after Treviño.
    (E) At least two of the members dive from the
         plane after Weiss.

8. If Larue dives from the plane last, then each of the
    following could be true EXCEPT:

    (A) Treviño dives from the plane fourth.
    (B) Weiss dives from the plane fourth.
    (C) Ohba dives from the plane fifth.
    (D) Pei dives from the plane fifth.
    (E) Zacny dives from the plane fifth.

9. If Zacny dives from the plane immediately after Weiss,
    then which one of the following must be false?

    (A) Larue dives from the plane first.
    (B) Treviño dives from the plane third.
    (C) Zacny dives from the plane third.
    (D) Pei dives from the plane fourth.
    (E) Zacny dives from the plane fourth.

10. If Treviño dives from the plane immediately after Larue,
    then each of the following could be true EXCEPT:

    (A) Ohba dives from the plane third.
    (B) Weiss dives from the plane third.
    (C) Zacny dives from the plane third.
    (D) Pei dives from the plane fourth.
    (E) Weiss dives from the plane fourth.

GO ON TO THE NEXT PAGE.

Questions 11–17

A company's six vehicles—a hatchback, a limousine, a pickup, a roadster, a sedan, and a van—are serviced during a certain week—Monday through Saturday—one vehicle per day. The following conditions must apply:

At least one of the vehicles is serviced later in the week than the hatchback.

The roadster is serviced later in the week than the van and earlier in the week than the hatchback.

Either the pickup and the van are serviced on consecutive days, or the pickup and the sedan are serviced on consecutive days, but not both.

The sedan is serviced earlier in the week than the pickup or earlier in the week than the limousine, but not both.

11. Which one of the following could be the order in which the vehicles are serviced, from Monday through Saturday?

(A) the hatchback, the pickup, the sedan, the limousine, the van, the roadster

(B) the pickup, the sedan, the van, the roadster, the hatchback, the limousine

(C) the pickup, the van, the sedan, the roadster, the limousine, the hatchback

(D) the van, the roadster, the pickup, the hatchback, the sedan, the limousine

(E) the van, the sedan, the pickup, the roadster, the hatchback, the limousine

GO ON TO THE NEXT PAGE.

12. Which one of the following CANNOT be the vehicle serviced on Thursday?

   (A) the hatchback
   (B) the limousine
   (C) the pickup
   (D) the sedan
   (E) the van

13. If neither the pickup nor the limousine is serviced on Monday, then which one of the following must be true?

   (A) The hatchback and the limousine are serviced on consecutive days.
   (B) The hatchback and the sedan are serviced on consecutive days.
   (C) The van is serviced on Monday.
   (D) The limousine is serviced on Saturday.
   (E) The pickup is serviced on Saturday.

14. If the limousine is not serviced on Saturday, then each of the following could be true EXCEPT:

   (A) The limousine is serviced on Monday.
   (B) The roadster is serviced on Tuesday.
   (C) The hatchback is serviced on Wednesday.
   (D) The roadster is serviced on Wednesday.
   (E) The sedan is serviced on Wednesday.

15. If the sedan is serviced earlier in the week than the pickup, then which one of the following could be true?

   (A) The limousine is serviced on Wednesday.
   (B) The sedan is serviced on Wednesday.
   (C) The van is serviced on Wednesday.
   (D) The hatchback is serviced on Friday.
   (E) The limousine is serviced on Saturday.

16. If the limousine is serviced on Saturday, then which one of the following must be true?

   (A) The pickup is serviced earlier in the week than the roadster.
   (B) The pickup is serviced earlier in the week than the sedan.
   (C) The sedan is serviced earlier in the week than the roadster.
   (D) The hatchback and the limousine are serviced on consecutive days.
   (E) The roadster and the hatchback are serviced on consecutive days.

17. Which one of the following could be the list of the vehicles serviced on Tuesday, Wednesday, and Friday, listed in that order?

   (A) the pickup, the hatchback, the limousine
   (B) the pickup, the roadster, the hatchback
   (C) the sedan, the limousine, the hatchback
   (D) the van, the limousine, the hatchback
   (E) the van, the roadster, the limousine

GO ON TO THE NEXT PAGE.

Questions 18–23

A street entertainer has six boxes stacked one on top of the other and numbered consecutively 1 through 6, from the lowest box up to the highest. Each box contains a single ball, and each ball is one of three colors—green, red, or white. Onlookers are to guess the color of each ball in each box, given that the following conditions hold:

There are more red balls than white balls.

There is a box containing a green ball that is lower in the stack than any box that contains a red ball.

There is a white ball in a box that is immediately below a box that contains a green ball.

18. If there are exactly two white balls, then which one of the following boxes could contain a green ball?

(A)   box 1
(B)   box 3
(C)   box 4
(D)   box 5
(E)   box 6

GO ON TO THE NEXT PAGE.

19. If there are green balls in boxes 5 and 6, then which one of the following could be true?

    (A)   There are red balls in boxes 1 and 4.
    (B)   There are red balls in boxes 2 and 4.
    (C)   There is a white ball in box 1.
    (D)   There is a white ball in box 2.
    (E)   There is a white ball in box 3.

20. The ball in which one of the following boxes must be the same color as at least one of the other balls?

    (A)   box 2
    (B)   box 3
    (C)   box 4
    (D)   box 5
    (E)   box 6

21. Which one of the following must be true?

    (A)   There is a green ball in a box that is lower than box 4.
    (B)   There is a green ball in a box that is higher than box 4.
    (C)   There is a red ball in a box that is lower than box 4.
    (D)   There is a red ball in a box that is higher than box 4.
    (E)   There is a white ball in a box that is lower than box 4.

22. If there are red balls in boxes 2 and 3, then which one of the following could be true?

    (A)   There is a red ball in box 1.
    (B)   There is a white ball in box 1.
    (C)   There is a green ball in box 4.
    (D)   There is a red ball in box 5.
    (E)   There is a white ball in box 6.

23. If boxes 2, 3, and 4 all contain balls that are the same color as each other, then which one of the following must be true?

    (A)   Exactly two of the boxes contain a green ball.
    (B)   Exactly three of the boxes contain a green ball.
    (C)   Exactly three of the boxes contain a red ball.
    (D)   Exactly one of the boxes contains a white ball.
    (E)   Exactly two of the boxes contain a white ball.

S T O P

IF YOU FINISH BEFORE TIME IS CALLED, YOU MAY CHECK YOUR WORK ON THIS SECTION ONLY.
DO NOT WORK ON ANY OTHER SECTION IN THE TEST.

SECTION III

Time—35 minutes

26 Questions

Directions: The questions in this section are based on the reasoning contained in brief statements or passages. For some questions, more than one of the choices could conceivably answer the question. However, you are to choose the best answer; that is, the response that most accurately and completely answers the question. You should not make assumptions that are by commonsense standards implausible, superfluous, or incompatible with the passage. After you have chosen the best answer, blacken the corresponding space on your answer sheet.

1. Commentator: In last week's wreck involving one of Acme Engines' older locomotives, the engineer lost control of the train when his knee accidentally struck a fuel shut-down switch. Acme claims it is not liable because it never realized that the knee-level switches were a safety hazard. When asked why it relocated knee-level switches in its newer locomotives, Acme said engineers had complained that they were simply inconvenient. However, it is unlikely that Acme would have spent the $500,000 it took to relocate switches in the newer locomotives merely because of inconvenience. Thus, Acme Engines should be held liable for last week's wreck.

The point that Acme Engines spent $500,000 relocating knee-level switches in its newer locomotives is offered in the commentator's argument as

(A) proof that the engineer is not at all responsible for the train wreck
(B) a reason for believing that the wreck would have occurred even if Acme Engines had remodeled their older locomotives
(C) an explanation of why the train wreck occurred
(D) evidence that knee-level switches are not in fact hazardous
(E) an indication that Acme Engines had been aware of the potential dangers of knee-level switches before the wreck occurred

2. Artist: Almost everyone in this country really wants to be an artist even though they may have to work other jobs to pay the rent. After all, just about everyone I know hopes to someday be able to make a living as a painter, musician, or poet even if they currently work as dishwashers or discount store clerks.

The reasoning in the artist's argument is flawed in that the argument

(A) contains a premise that presupposes the truth of the conclusion
(B) presumes that what is true of each person in a country is also true of the country's population as a whole
(C) defends a view solely on the grounds that the view is widely held
(D) bases its conclusion on a sample that is unlikely to accurately represent people in the country as a whole
(E) fails to make a needed distinction between wanting to be an artist and making a living as an artist

3. The qwerty keyboard became the standard keyboard with the invention of the typewriter and remains the standard for typing devices today. If an alternative known as the Dvorak keyboard were today's standard, typists would type significantly faster. Nevertheless, it is not practical to switch to the Dvorak keyboard because the cost to society of switching, in terms of time, money, and frustration, would be greater than the benefits that would be ultimately gained from faster typing.

The example above best illustrates which one of the following propositions?

(A) Often it is not worthwhile to move to a process that improves speed if it comes at the expense of accuracy.
(B) People usually settle on a standard because that standard is more efficient than any alternatives.
(C) People often remain with an entrenched standard rather than move to a more efficient alternative simply because they dislike change.
(D) The emotional cost associated with change is a factor that sometimes outweighs financial considerations.
(E) The fact that a standard is already in wide use can be a crucial factor in making it a more practical choice than an alternative.

GO ON TO THE NEXT PAGE.

4. Sam: Mountain lions, a protected species, are preying on bighorn sheep, another protected species. We must let nature take its course and hope the bighorns survive.

   Meli: Nonsense. We must do what we can to ensure the survival of the bighorn, even if that means limiting the mountain lion population.

   Which one of the following is a point of disagreement between Meli and Sam?

   (A) Humans should not intervene to protect bighorn sheep from mountain lions.

   (B) The preservation of a species as a whole is more important than the loss of a few individuals.

   (C) The preservation of a predatory species is easier to ensure than the preservation of the species preyed upon.

   (D) Any measures to limit the mountain lion population would likely push the species to extinction.

   (E) If the population of mountain lions is not limited, the bighorn sheep species will not survive.

5. Parent: Pushing very young children into rigorous study in an effort to make our nation more competitive does more harm than good. Curricula for these young students must address their special developmental needs, and while rigorous work in secondary school makes sense, the same approach in the early years of primary school produces only short-term gains and may cause young children to burn out on schoolwork. Using very young students as pawns in the race to make the nation economically competitive is unfair and may ultimately work against us.

   Which one of the following can be inferred from the parent's statements?

   (A) For our nation to be competitive, our secondary school curriculum must include more rigorous study than it now does.

   (B) The developmental needs of secondary school students are not now being addressed in our high schools.

   (C) Our country can be competitive only if the developmental needs of all our students can be met.

   (D) A curriculum of rigorous study does not adequately address the developmental needs of primary school students.

   (E) Unless our nation encourages more rigorous study in the early years of primary school, we cannot be economically competitive.

6. A transit company's bus drivers are evaluated by supervisors riding with each driver. Drivers complain that this affects their performance, but because the supervisor's presence affects every driver's performance, those drivers performing best with a supervisor aboard will likely also be the best drivers under normal conditions.

   Which one of the following is an assumption on which the argument depends?

   (A) There is no effective way of evaluating the bus drivers' performance without having supervisors ride with them.

   (B) The supervisors are excellent judges of a bus driver's performance.

   (C) For most bus drivers, the presence of a supervisor makes their performance slightly worse than it otherwise would be.

   (D) The bus drivers are each affected in roughly the same way and to the same extent by the presence of the supervisor.

   (E) The bus drivers themselves are able to deliver accurate assessments of their driving performance.

7. Economic growth accelerates business demand for the development of new technologies. Businesses supplying these new technologies are relatively few, while those wishing to buy them are many. Yet an acceleration of technological change can cause suppliers as well as buyers of new technologies to fail.

   Which one of the following is most strongly supported by the information above?

   (A) Businesses supplying new technologies are more likely to prosper in times of accelerated technological change than other businesses.

   (B) Businesses that supply new technologies may not always benefit from economic growth.

   (C) The development of new technologies may accelerate economic growth in general.

   (D) Businesses that adopt new technologies are most likely to prosper in a period of general economic growth.

   (E) Economic growth increases business failures.

GO ON TO THE NEXT PAGE.

8. Energy analyst: During this record-breaking heat wave, air conditioner use has overloaded the region's electrical power grid, resulting in frequent power blackouts throughout the region. For this reason, residents have been asked to cut back voluntarily on air conditioner use in their homes. But even if this request is heeded, blackouts will probably occur unless the heat wave abates.

Which one of the following, if true, most helps to resolve the apparent discrepancy in the information above?

(A) Air-conditioning is not the only significant drain on the electrical system in the area.

(B) Most air-conditioning in the region is used to cool businesses and factories.

(C) Most air-conditioning systems could be made more energy efficient by implementing simple design modifications.

(D) Residents of the region are not likely to reduce their air conditioner use voluntarily during particularly hot weather.

(E) The heat wave is expected to abate in the near future.

9. Long-term and short-term relaxation training are two common forms of treatment for individuals experiencing problematic levels of anxiety. Yet studies show that on average, regardless of which form of treatment one receives, symptoms of anxiety decrease to a normal level within the short-term-training time period. Thus, for most people the generally more expensive long-term training is unwarranted.

Which one of the following, if true, most weakens the argument?

(A) A decrease in symptoms of anxiety often occurs even with no treatment or intervention by a mental health professional.

(B) Short-term relaxation training conducted by a more experienced practitioner can be more expensive than long-term training conducted by a less experienced practitioner.

(C) Recipients of long-term training are much less likely than recipients of short-term training to have recurrences of problematic levels of anxiety.

(D) The fact that an individual thinks that a treatment will reduce his or her anxiety tends, in and of itself, to reduce the individual's anxiety.

(E) Short-term relaxation training involves the teaching of a wider variety of anxiety-combating relaxation techniques than does long-term training.

10. Editorial: Many critics of consumerism insist that advertising persuades people that they need certain consumer goods when they merely desire them. However, this accusation rests on a fuzzy distinction, that between wants and needs. In life, it is often impossible to determine whether something is merely desirable or whether it is essential to one's happiness.

Which one of the following most accurately expresses the conclusion drawn in the editorial's argument?

(A) The claim that advertising persuades people that they need things that they merely want rests on a fuzzy distinction.

(B) Many critics of consumerism insist that advertising attempts to blur people's ability to distinguish between wants and needs.

(C) There is nothing wrong with advertising that tries to persuade people that they need certain consumer goods.

(D) Many critics of consumerism fail to realize that certain things are essential to human happiness.

(E) Critics of consumerism often use fuzzy distinctions to support their claims.

11. People who browse the web for medical information often cannot discriminate between scientifically valid information and quackery. Much of the quackery is particularly appealing to readers with no medical background because it is usually written more clearly than scientific papers. Thus, people who rely on the web when attempting to diagnose their medical conditions are likely to do themselves more harm than good.

Which one of the following is an assumption the argument requires?

(A) People who browse the web for medical information typically do so in an attempt to diagnose their medical conditions.

(B) People who attempt to diagnose their medical conditions are likely to do themselves more harm than good unless they rely exclusively on scientifically valid information.

(C) People who have sufficient medical knowledge to discriminate between scientifically valid information and quackery will do themselves no harm if they rely on the web when attempting to diagnose their medical conditions.

(D) Many people who browse the web assume that information is not scientifically valid unless it is clearly written.

(E) People attempting to diagnose their medical conditions will do themselves more harm than good only if they rely on quackery instead of scientifically valid information.

GO ON TO THE NEXT PAGE.

12. When adults toss balls to very young children they generally try to toss them as slowly as possible to compensate for the children's developing coordination. But recent studies show that despite their developing coordination, children actually have an easier time catching balls that are thrown at a faster speed.

Which one of the following, if true, most helps to explain why very young children find it easier to catch balls that are thrown at a faster speed?

(A) Balls thrown at a faster speed, unlike balls thrown at a slower speed, trigger regions in the brain that control the tracking of objects for self-defense.

(B) Balls that are tossed more slowly tend to have a higher arc that makes it less likely that the ball will be obscured by the body of the adult tossing it.

(C) Adults generally find it easier to catch balls that are thrown slowly than balls that are thrown at a faster speed.

(D) Children are able to toss balls back to the adults with more accuracy when they throw fast than when they throw the ball back more slowly.

(E) There is a limit to how fast the balls can be tossed to the children before the children start to have more difficulty in catching them.

13. Like a genetic profile, a functional magnetic-resonance image (fMRI) of the brain can contain information that a patient wishes to keep private. An fMRI of a brain also contains enough information about a patient's skull to create a recognizable image of that patient's face. A genetic profile can be linked to a patient only by referring to labels or records.

The statements above, if true, most strongly support which one of the following?

(A) It is not important that medical providers apply labels to fMRIs of patients' brains.

(B) An fMRI has the potential to compromise patient privacy in circumstances in which a genetic profile would not.

(C) In most cases patients cannot be reasonably sure that the information in a genetic profile will be kept private.

(D) Most of the information contained in an fMRI of a person's brain is also contained in that person's genetic profile.

(E) Patients are more concerned about threats to privacy posed by fMRIs than they are about those posed by genetic profiles.

14. Council member: I recommend that the abandoned shoe factory be used as a municipal emergency shelter. Some council members assert that the courthouse would be a better shelter site, but they have provided no evidence of this. Thus, the shoe factory would be a better shelter site.

A questionable technique used in the council member's argument is that of

(A) asserting that a lack of evidence against a view is proof that the view is correct

(B) accepting a claim simply because advocates of an opposing claim have not adequately defended their view

(C) attacking the proponents of the courthouse rather than addressing their argument

(D) attempting to persuade its audience by appealing to their fear

(E) attacking an argument that is not held by any actual council member

15. It was misleading for James to tell the Core Curriculum Committee that the chair of the Anthropology Department had endorsed his proposal. The chair of the Anthropology Department had told James that his proposal had her endorsement, but only if the draft proposal she saw included all the recommendations James would ultimately make to the Core Curriculum Committee.

The argument relies on which one of the following assumptions?

(A) If the chair of the Anthropology Department did not endorse James's proposed recommendations, the Core Curriculum Committee would be unlikely to implement them.

(B) The chair of the Anthropology Department would have been opposed to any recommendations James proposed to the Core Curriculum Committee other than those she had seen.

(C) James thought that the Core Curriculum Committee would implement the proposed recommendations only if they believed that the recommendations had been endorsed by the chair of the Anthropology Department.

(D) James thought that the chair of the Anthropology Department would have endorsed all of the recommendations that he proposed to the Core Curriculum Committee.

(E) The draft proposal that the chair of the Anthropology Department had seen did not include all of the recommendations in James's proposal to the Core Curriculum Committee.

GO ON TO THE NEXT PAGE.

16. Travaillier Corporation has recently hired employees with experience in the bus tour industry, and its executives have also been negotiating with charter bus companies that subcontract with bus tour companies. But Travaillier has traditionally focused on serving consumers who travel primarily by air, and marketing surveys show that Travaillier's traditional consumers have not changed their vacation preferences. Therefore, Travaillier must be attempting to enlarge its consumer base by attracting new customers.

Which one of the following, if true, would most weaken the argument?

(A) In the past, Travaillier has found it very difficult to change its customers' vacation preferences.

(B) Several travel companies other than Travaillier have recently tried and failed to expand into the bus tour business.

(C) At least one of Travaillier's new employees not only has experience in the bus tour industry but has also designed air travel vacation packages.

(D) Some of Travaillier's competitors have increased profits by concentrating their attention on their customers who spend the most on vacations.

(E) The industry consultants employed by Travaillier typically recommend that companies expand by introducing their current customers to new products and services.

17. Educator: Traditional classroom education is ineffective because education in such an environment is not truly a social process and only social processes can develop students' insights. In the traditional classroom, the teacher acts from outside the group and interaction between teachers and students is rigid and artificial.

The educator's conclusion follows logically if which one of the following is assumed?

(A) Development of insight takes place only if genuine education also occurs.

(B) Classroom education is effective if the interaction between teachers and students is neither rigid nor artificial.

(C) All social processes involve interaction that is neither rigid nor artificial.

(D) Education is not effective unless it leads to the development of insight.

(E) The teacher does not act from outside the group in a nontraditional classroom.

18. The probability of avoiding heart disease is increased if one avoids fat in one's diet. Furthermore, one is less likely to eat fat if one avoids eating dairy foods. Thus the probability of maintaining good health is increased by avoiding dairy foods.

The reasoning in the argument is most vulnerable to criticism on which one of the following grounds?

(A) The argument ignores the possibility that, even though a practice may have potentially negative consequences, its elimination may also have negative consequences.

(B) The argument fails to consider the possibility that there are more ways than one of decreasing the risk of a certain type of occurrence.

(C) The argument presumes, without providing justification, that factors that carry increased risks of negative consequences ought to be eliminated.

(D) The argument fails to show that the evidence appealed to is relevant to the conclusion asserted.

(E) The argument fails to consider that what is probable will not necessarily occur.

19. Professor: One cannot frame an accurate conception of one's physical environment on the basis of a single momentary perception, since each such glimpse occurs from only one particular perspective. Similarly, any history book gives only a distorted view of the past, since it reflects the biases and prejudices of its author.

The professor's argument proceeds by

(A) attempting to show that one piece of reasoning is incorrect by comparing it with another, presumably flawed, piece of reasoning

(B) developing a case for one particular conclusion by arguing that if that conclusion were false, absurd consequences would follow

(C) making a case for the conclusion of one argument by showing that argument's resemblance to another, presumably cogent, argument

(D) arguing that because something has a certain group of characteristics, it must also have another, closely related, characteristic

(E) arguing that a type of human cognition is unreliable in one instance because it has been shown to be unreliable under similar circumstances

GO ON TO THE NEXT PAGE.

20. To date, most of the proposals that have been endorsed by the Citizens League have been passed by the city council. Thus, any future proposal that is endorsed by the Citizens League will probably be passed as well.

The pattern of reasoning in which one of the following arguments is most similar to that in the argument above?

(A) Most of the Vasani grants that have been awarded in previous years have gone to academic biologists. Thus, if most of the Vasani grants awarded next year are awarded to academics, most of these will probably be biologists.

(B) Most of the individual trees growing on the coastal islands in this area are deciduous. Therefore, most of the tree species on these islands are probably deciduous varieties.

(C) Most of the editors who have worked for the local newspaper have not been sympathetic to local farmers. Thus, if the newspaper hires someone who is sympathetic to local farmers, they will probably not be hired as an editor.

(D) Most of the entries that were received after the deadline for last year's photography contest were rejected by the judges' committee. Thus, the people whose entries were received after the deadline last year will probably send them in well before the deadline this year.

(E) Most of the stone artifacts that have been found at the archaeological site have been domestic tools. Thus, if the next artifact found at the site is made of stone, it will probably be a domestic tool.

21. Chemist: The molecules of a certain weed-killer are always present in two forms, one the mirror image of the other. One form of the molecule kills weeds, while the other has no effect on them. As a result, the effectiveness of the weed-killer in a given situation is heavily influenced by which of the two forms is more concentrated in the soil, which in turn varies widely because local soil conditions will usually favor the breakdown of one form or the other. Thus, much of the data on the effects of this weed-killer are probably misleading.

Which one of the following, if true, most strengthens the chemist's argument?

(A) In general, if the molecules of a weed-killer are always present in two forms, then it is likely that weeds are killed by one of those two forms but unaffected by the other.

(B) Almost all of the data on the effects of the weed-killer are drawn from laboratory studies in which both forms of the weed-killer's molecules are equally concentrated in the soil and equally likely to break down in that soil.

(C) Of the two forms of the weed-killer's molecules, the one that kills weeds is found in most local soil conditions to be the more concentrated form.

(D) The data on the effects of the weed-killer are drawn from studies of the weed-killer under a variety of soil conditions similar to those in which the weed-killer is normally applied.

(E) Data on the weed-killer's effects that rely solely on the examination of the effects of only one of the two forms of the weed-killer's molecules will almost certainly be misleading.

GO ON TO THE NEXT PAGE.

22. Principle: A police officer is eligible for a Mayor's Commendation if the officer has an exemplary record, but not otherwise; an officer eligible for the award who did something this year that exceeded what could be reasonably expected of a police officer should receive the award if the act saved someone's life.

Conclusion: Officer Franklin should receive a Mayor's Commendation but Officer Penn should not.

From which one of the following sets of facts can the conclusion be properly drawn using the principle?

(A) In saving a child from drowning this year, Franklin and Penn both risked their lives beyond what could be reasonably expected of a police officer. Franklin has an exemplary record but Penn does not.

(B) Both Franklin and Penn have exemplary records, and each officer saved a child from drowning earlier this year. However, in doing so, Franklin went beyond what could be reasonably expected of a police officer; Penn did not.

(C) Neither Franklin nor Penn has an exemplary record. But, in saving the life of an accident victim, Franklin went beyond what could be reasonably expected of a police officer. In the only case in which Penn saved someone's life this year, Penn was merely doing what could be reasonably expected of an officer under the circumstances.

(D) At least once this year, Franklin has saved a person's life in such a way as to exceed what could be reasonably expected of a police officer. Penn has not saved anyone's life this year.

(E) Both Franklin and Penn have exemplary records. On several occasions this year Franklin has saved people's lives, and on many occasions this year Franklin has exceeded what could be reasonably expected of a police officer. On no occasions this year has Penn saved a person's life or exceeded what could be reasonably expected of an officer.

23. Essayist: It is much less difficult to live an enjoyable life if one is able to make lifestyle choices that accord with one's personal beliefs and then see those choices accepted by others. It is possible for people to find this kind of acceptance by choosing friends and associates who share many of their personal beliefs. Thus, no one should be denied the freedom to choose the people with whom he or she will associate.

Which one of the following principles, if valid, most helps to justify the essayist's argument?

(A) No one should be denied the freedom to make lifestyle choices that accord with his or her personal beliefs.

(B) One should associate with at least some people who share many of one's personal beliefs.

(C) If having a given freedom could make it less difficult for someone to live an enjoyable life, then no one should be denied that freedom.

(D) No one whose enjoyment of life depends, at least in part, on friends and associates who share many of the same personal beliefs should be deliberately prevented from having such friends and associates.

(E) One may choose for oneself the people with whom one will associate, if doing so could make it easier to live an enjoyable life.

24. Physician: The rise in blood pressure that commonly accompanies aging often results from a calcium deficiency. This deficiency is frequently caused by a deficiency in the active form of vitamin D needed in order for the body to absorb calcium. Since the calcium in one glass of milk per day can easily make up for any underlying calcium deficiency, some older people can lower their blood pressure by drinking milk.

The physician's conclusion is properly drawn if which one of the following is assumed?

(A) There is in milk, in a form that older people can generally utilize, enough of the active form of vitamin D and any other substances needed in order for the body to absorb the calcium in that milk.

(B) Milk does not contain any substance that is likely to cause increased blood pressure in older people.

(C) Older people's drinking one glass of milk per day does not contribute to a deficiency in the active form of vitamin D needed in order for the body to absorb the calcium in that milk.

(D) People who consume high quantities of calcium together with the active form of vitamin D and any other substances needed in order for the body to absorb calcium have normal blood pressure.

(E) Anyone who has a deficiency in the active form of vitamin D also has a calcium deficiency.

GO ON TO THE NEXT PAGE.

25. Political philosopher: A just system of taxation would require each person's contribution to correspond directly to the amount the society as a whole contributes to serve that person's interests. For purposes of taxation, wealth is the most objective way to determine how well the society has served the interest of any individual. Therefore, each person should be taxed solely in proportion to her or his income.

The flawed reasoning in the political philosopher's argument is most similar to that in which one of the following?

(A) Cars should be taxed in proportion to the danger that they pose. The most reliable measure of this danger is the speed at which a car can travel. Therefore, cars should be taxed only in proportion to their ability to accelerate quickly.

(B) People should be granted autonomy in proportion to their maturity. A certain psychological test was designed to provide an objective measure of maturity. Therefore, those scoring above high school level on the test should be granted complete autonomy.

(C) Everyone should pay taxes solely in proportion to the benefits they receive from government. Many government programs provide subsidies for large corporations. Therefore, a just tax would require corporations to pay a greater share of their income in taxes than individual citizens pay.

(D) Individuals who confer large material benefits upon society should receive high incomes. Those with high incomes should pay correspondingly high taxes. Therefore, we as a society should place high taxes on activities that confer large benefits upon society.

(E) Justice requires that health care be given in proportion to each individual's need. Therefore, we need to ensure that the most seriously ill hospital patients are given the highest priority for receiving care.

26. A recent poll showed that almost half of the city's residents believe that Mayor Walker is guilty of ethics violations. Surprisingly, however, 52 percent of those surveyed judged Walker's performance as mayor to be good or excellent, which is no lower than it was before anyone accused him of ethics violations.

Which one of the following, if true, most helps to explain the surprising fact stated above?

(A) Almost all of the people who believe that Walker is guilty of ethics violations had thought, even before he was accused of those violations, that his performance as mayor was poor.

(B) In the time since Walker was accused of ethics violations, there has been an increase in the percentage of city residents who judge the performance of Walker's political opponents to be good or excellent.

(C) About a fifth of those polled did not know that Walker had been accused of ethics violations.

(D) Walker is currently up for reelection, and anticorruption groups in the city have expressed support for Walker's opponent.

(E) Walker has defended himself against the accusations by arguing that the alleged ethics violations were the result of honest mistakes by his staff members.

S T O P

IF YOU FINISH BEFORE TIME IS CALLED, YOU MAY CHECK YOUR WORK ON THIS SECTION ONLY.
DO NOT WORK ON ANY OTHER SECTION IN THE TEST.

SECTION IV

Time—35 minutes

27 Questions

Directions: Each set of questions in this section is based on a single passage or a pair of passages. The questions are to be answered on the basis of what is stated or implied in the passage or pair of passages. For some of the questions, more than one of the choices could conceivably answer the question. However, you are to choose the best answer; that is, the response that most accurately and completely answers the question, and blacken the corresponding space on your answer sheet.

In Alaska, tradition is a powerful legal concept, appearing in a wide variety of legal contexts relating to natural-resource and public-lands activities. Both state and federal laws in the United States assign
(5) privileges and exemptions to individuals engaged in "traditional" activities using otherwise off-limits land and resources. But in spite of its prevalence in statutory law, the term "tradition" is rarely defined. Instead, there seems to be a presumption that its
(10) meaning is obvious. Failure to define "tradition" clearly in written law has given rise to problematic and inconsistent legal results.

One of the most prevalent ideas associated with the term "tradition" in the law is that tradition is based
(15) on long-standing practice, where "long-standing" refers not only to the passage of time but also to the continuity and regularity of a practice. But two recent court cases involving indigenous use of sea otter pelts illustrate the problems that can arise in the application
(20) of this sense of "traditional."

The hunting of sea otters was initially prohibited by the Fur Seal Treaty of 1910. The Marine Mammal Protection Act (MMPA) of 1972 continued the prohibition, but it also included an Alaska Native
(25) exemption, which allowed takings of protected animals for use in creating authentic native articles by means of "traditional native handicrafts." The U.S. Fish and Wildlife Service (FWS) subsequently issued regulations defining authentic native articles as those
(30) "commonly produced" before 1972, when the MMPA took effect. Not covered by the exemption, according to the FWS, were items produced from sea otter pelts, because Alaska Natives had not produced such handicrafts "within living memory."
(35) In 1986, FWS agents seized articles of clothing made from sea otter pelts from Marina Katelnikoff, an Aleut. She sued, but the district court upheld the FWS regulations. Then in 1991 Katelnikoff joined a similar suit brought by Boyd Dickinson, a Tlingit from whom
(40) articles of clothing made from sea otter pelts had also been seized. After hearing testimony establishing that Alaska Natives had made many uses of sea otters before the occupation of the territory by Russia in the late 1700s, the court reconsidered what constituted a
(45) traditional item under the statute. The court now held that the FWS's regulations were based on a "strained interpretation" of the word "traditional," and that the reference to "living memory" imposed an excessively restrictive time frame. The court stated, "The fact that
(50) Alaskan natives were prevented, by circumstances beyond their control, from exercising a tradition for a

given period of time does not mean that it has been lost forever or that it has become any less a 'tradition.' It defies common sense to define 'traditional' in such
(55) a way that only those traditions that were exercised during a comparatively short period in history could qualify as 'traditional.'"

1. Which one of the following most accurately expresses the main point of the passage?

(A) Two cases involving the use of sea otter pelts by Alaska Natives illustrate the difficulties surrounding the application of the legal concept of tradition in Alaska.

(B) Two court decisions have challenged the notion that for an activity to be considered "traditional," it must be shown to be a long-standing activity that has been regularly and continually practiced.

(C) Two court cases involving the use of sea otter pelts by Alaska Natives exemplify the wave of lawsuits that are now occurring in response to changes in natural-resource and public-lands regulations.

(D) Definitions of certain legal terms long taken for granted are being reviewed in light of new evidence that has come from historical sources relating to Alaska Native culture.

(E) Alaskan state laws and U.S. federal laws are being challenged by Alaska Natives because the laws are not sufficiently sensitive to indigenous peoples' concerns.

GO ON TO THE NEXT PAGE.

2. The court in the 1991 case referred to the FWS's interpretation of the term "traditional" as "strained" (line 46) because, in the court's view, the interpretation

   (A) ignored the ways in which Alaska Natives have historically understood the term "traditional"
   (B) was not consonant with any dictionary definition of "traditional"
   (C) was inconsistent with what the term "traditional" is normally understood to mean
   (D) led the FWS to use the word "traditional" to describe a practice that should not have been described as such
   (E) failed to specify which handicrafts qualified to be designated as "traditional"

3. According to the passage, the court's decision in the 1991 case was based on which one of the following?

   (A) a narrow interpretation of the term "long-standing"
   (B) a common-sense interpretation of the phrase "within living memory"
   (C) strict adherence to the intent of FWS regulations
   (D) a new interpretation of the Fur Seal Treaty of 1910
   (E) testimony establishing certain historical facts

4. The passage most strongly suggests that the court in the 1986 case believed that "traditional" should be defined in a way that

   (A) reflects a compromise between the competing concerns surrounding the issue at hand
   (B) emphasizes the continuity and regularity of practices to which the term is applied
   (C) reflects the term's usage in everyday discourse
   (D) encourages the term's application to recently developed, as well as age-old, activities
   (E) reflects the concerns of the people engaging in what they consider to be traditional activities

5. Which one of the following is most strongly suggested by the passage?

   (A) Between 1910 and 1972, Alaska Natives were prohibited from hunting sea otters.
   (B) Traditional items made from sea otter pelts were specifically mentioned in the Alaska Native exemption of the MMPA.
   (C) In the late 1700s, Russian hunters pressured the Russian government to bar Alaska Natives from hunting sea otters.
   (D) By 1972, the sea otter population in Alaska had returned to the levels at which it had been prior to the late 1700s.
   (E) Prior to the late 1700s, sea otters were the marine animal most often hunted by Alaska Natives.

6. The author's reference to the Fur Seal Treaty (line 22) primarily serves to

   (A) establish the earliest point in time at which fur seals were considered to be on the brink of extinction
   (B) indicate that several animals in addition to sea otters were covered by various regulatory exemptions issued over the years
   (C) demonstrate that there is a well-known legal precedent for prohibiting the hunting of protected animals
   (D) suggest that the sea otter population was imperiled by Russian seal hunters and not by Alaska Natives
   (E) help explain the evolution of Alaska Natives' legal rights with respect to handicrafts defined as "traditional"

7. The ruling in the 1991 case would be most relevant as a precedent for deciding in a future case that which one of the following is a "traditional" Alaska Native handicraft?

   (A) A handicraft no longer practiced but shown by archaeological evidence to have been common among indigenous peoples several millennia ago
   (B) A handicraft that commonly involves taking the pelts of more than one species that has been designated as endangered
   (C) A handicraft that was once common but was discontinued when herd animals necessary for its practice abandoned their local habitat due to industrial development
   (D) A handicraft about which only a very few indigenous craftspeople were historically in possession of any knowledge
   (E) A handicraft about which young Alaska Natives know little because, while it was once common, few elder Alaska Natives still practice it

GO ON TO THE NEXT PAGE.

The literary development of Kate Chopin, author of *The Awakening* (1899), took her through several phases of nineteenth-century women's fiction. Born in 1850, Chopin grew up with the sentimental novels that
(5)   formed the bulk of the fiction of the mid–nineteenth century. In these works, authors employed elevated, romantic language to portray female characters whose sole concern was to establish their social positions through courtship and marriage. Later, when she
(10)   started writing her own fiction, Chopin took as her models the works of a group of women writers known as the local colorists.

After 1865, what had traditionally been regarded as "women's culture" began to dissolve as women
(15)   entered higher education, the professions, and the political world in greater numbers. The local colorists, who published stories about regional life in the 1870s and 1880s, were attracted to the new worlds opening up to women, and felt free to move within these worlds
(20)   as artists. Like anthropologists, the local colorists observed culture and character with almost scientific detachment. However, as "women's culture" continued to disappear, the local colorists began to mourn its demise by investing its images with mythic significance.
(25)   In their stories, the garden became a paradisal sanctuary; the house became an emblem of female nurturing; and the artifacts of domesticity became virtual totemic objects.

Unlike the local colorists, Chopin devoted herself
(30)   to telling stories of loneliness, isolation, and frustration. But she used the conventions of the local colorists to solve a specific narrative problem: how to deal with extreme psychological states without resorting to the excesses of the sentimental novels she read as a youth.
(35)   By reporting narrative events as if they were part of a region's "local color," Chopin could tell rather shocking or even melodramatic tales in an uninflected manner.

Chopin did not share the local colorists' growing nostalgia for the past, however, and by the 1890s she
(40)   was looking beyond them to the more ambitious models offered by a movement known as the New Women. In the form as well as the content of their work, the New Women writers pursued freedom and innovation. They modified the form of the sentimental
(45)   novel to make room for interludes of fantasy and parable, especially episodes in which women dream of an entirely different world than the one they inhabit. Instead of the crisply plotted short stories that had been the primary genre of the local colorists, the New
(50)   Women writers experimented with impressionistic methods in an effort to explore hitherto unrecorded aspects of female consciousness. In *The Awakening*, Chopin embraced this impressionistic approach more fully to produce 39 numbered sections of uneven
(55)   length unified less by their style or content than by their sustained focus on faithfully rendering the workings of the protagonist's mind.

8. Which one of the following statements most accurately summarizes the content of the passage?

(A) Although Chopin drew a great deal of the material for *The Awakening* from the concerns of the New Women, she adapted them, using the techniques of the local colorists, to recapture the atmosphere of the novels she had read in her youth.

(B) Avoiding the sentimental excesses of novels she read in her youth, and influenced first by the conventions of the local colorists and then by the innovative methods of the New Women, Chopin developed the literary style she used in *The Awakening*.

(C) With its stylistic shifts, variety of content, and attention to the internal psychology of its characters, Chopin's *The Awakening* was unlike any work of fiction written during the nineteenth century.

(D) In *The Awakening*, Chopin rebelled against the stylistic restraint of the local colorists, choosing instead to tell her story in elevated, romantic language that would more accurately convey her protagonist's loneliness and frustration.

(E) Because she felt a kinship with the subject matter but not the stylistic conventions of the local colorists, Chopin turned to the New Women as models for the style she was struggling to develop in *The Awakening*.

9. With which one of the following statements about the local colorists would Chopin have been most likely to agree?

(A) Their idealization of settings and objects formerly associated with "women's culture" was misguided.

(B) Their tendency to observe character dispassionately caused their fiction to have little emotional impact.

(C) Their chief contribution to literature lay in their status as inspiration for the New Women.

(D) Their focus on regional life prevented them from addressing the new realms opening up to women.

(E) Their conventions prevented them from portraying extreme psychological states with scientific detachment.

GO ON TO THE NEXT PAGE.

10. According to the passage, which one of the following conventions did Chopin adopt from other nineteenth-century women writers?

(A) elevated, romantic language
(B) mythic images of "women's culture"
(C) detached narrative stance
(D) strong plot lines
(E) lonely, isolated protagonists

11. As it is used by the author in line 14 of the passage, "women's culture" most probably refers to a culture that was expressed primarily through women's

(A) domestic experiences
(B) regional customs
(C) artistic productions
(D) educational achievements
(E) political activities

12. The author of the passage describes the sentimental novels of the mid–nineteenth century in lines 3–9 primarily in order to

(A) argue that Chopin's style represents an attempt to mimic these novels
(B) explain why Chopin later rejected the work of the local colorists
(C) establish the background against which Chopin's fiction developed
(D) illustrate the excesses to which Chopin believed nostalgic tendencies would lead
(E) prove that women's literature was already flourishing by the time Chopin began to write

13. The passage suggests that one of the differences between *The Awakening* and the work of the New Women was that *The Awakening*

(A) attempted to explore aspects of female consciousness
(B) described the dream world of female characters
(C) employed impressionism more consistently throughout
(D) relied more on fantasy to suggest psychological states
(E) displayed greater unity of style and content

14. The primary purpose of the passage is to

(A) educate readers of *The Awakening* about aspects of Chopin's life that are reflected in the novel
(B) discuss the relationship between Chopin's artistic development and changes in nineteenth-century women's fiction
(C) trace the evolution of nineteenth-century women's fiction using Chopin as a typical example
(D) counter a claim that Chopin's fiction was influenced by external social circumstances
(E) weigh the value of Chopin's novels and stories against those of other writers of her time

15. The work of the New Women, as it is characterized in the passage, gives the most support for which one of the following generalizations?

(A) Works of fiction written in a passionate, engaged style are more apt to effect changes in social customs than are works written in a scientific, detached style.
(B) Even writers who advocate social change can end up regretting the change once it has occurred.
(C) Changes in social customs inevitably lead to changes in literary techniques as writers attempt to make sense of the new social realities.
(D) Innovations in fictional technique grow out of writers' attempts to describe aspects of reality that have been neglected in previous works.
(E) Writers can most accurately depict extreme psychological states by using an uninflected manner.

GO ON TO THE NEXT PAGE.

Until the 1950s, most scientists believed that the geology of the ocean floor had remained essentially unchanged for many millions of years. But this idea became insupportable as new discoveries were made.
(5) First, scientists noticed that the ocean floor exhibited odd magnetic variations. Though unexpected, this was not entirely surprising, because it was known that basalt—the volcanic rock making up much of the ocean floor—contains magnetite, a strongly magnetic
(10) mineral that was already known to locally distort compass readings on land. This distortion is due to the fact that although some basalt has so-called "normal" polarity—that is, the magnetite in it has the same polarity as the earth's present magnetic field—other
(15) basalt has reversed polarity, an alignment opposite that of the present field. This occurs because in magma (molten rock), grains of magnetite—behaving like little compass needles—align themselves with the earth's magnetic field, which has reversed at various
(20) times throughout history. When magma cools to form solid basalt, the alignment of the magnetite grains is "locked in," recording the earth's polarity at the time of cooling.

As more of the ocean floor was mapped, the
(25) magnetic variations revealed recognizable patterns, particularly in the area around the other great oceanic discovery of the 1950s: the global mid-ocean ridge, an immense submarine mountain range that winds its way around the earth much like the seams of a baseball.
(30) Alternating stripes of rock with differing polarities are laid out in rows on either side of the mid-ocean ridge: one stripe with normal polarity and the next with reversed polarity. Scientists theorized that mid-ocean ridges mark structurally weak zones where the ocean
(35) floor is being pulled apart along the ridge crest. New magma from deep within the earth rises easily through these weak zones and eventually erupts along the crest of the ridges to create new oceanic crust. Over millions of years, this process, called ocean floor spreading,
(40) built the mid-ocean ridge.

This theory was supported by several lines of evidence. First, at or near the ridge crest, the rocks are very young, and they become progressively older away from the crest. Further, the youngest rocks all
(45) have normal polarity. Finally, because geophysicists had already determined the ages of continental volcanic rocks and, by measuring the magnetic orientation of these same rocks, had assigned ages to the earth's recent magnetic reversals, they were able to compare
(50) these known ages of magnetic reversals with the ocean floor's magnetic striping pattern, enabling scientists to show that, if we assume that the ocean floor moved away from the spreading center at a rate of several centimeters per year, there is a remarkable correlation
(55) between the ages of the earth's magnetic reversals and the striping pattern.

16. Which one of the following most accurately expresses the main idea of the passage?

(A) In the 1950s, scientists refined their theories concerning the process by which the ocean floor was formed many millions of years ago.

(B) The discovery of basalt's magnetic properties in the 1950s led scientists to formulate a new theory to account for the magnetic striping on the ocean floor.

(C) In the 1950s, two significant discoveries led to the transformation of scientific views about the geology of the oceans.

(D) Local distortions to compass readings are caused, scientists have discovered, by magma that rises through weak zones in the ocean floor to create new oceanic crust.

(E) The discovery of the ocean floor's magnetic variations convinced scientists of the need to map the entire ocean floor, which in turn led to the discovery of the global mid-ocean ridge.

17. The author characterizes the correlation mentioned in the last sentence of the passage as "remarkable" in order to suggest that the correlation

(A) indicates that ocean floor spreading occurs at an extremely slow rate

(B) explains the existence of the global mid-ocean ridge

(C) demonstrates that the earth's magnetic field is considerably stronger than previously believed

(D) provides strong confirmation of the ocean floor spreading theory

(E) reveals that the earth's magnetic reversals have occurred at very regular intervals

18. According to the passage, which one of the following is true of magnetite grains?

(A) In the youngest basalt, they are aligned with the earth's current polarity.

(B) In magma, most but not all of them align themselves with the earth's magnetic field.

(C) They are not found in other types of rock besides basalt.

(D) They are about the size of typical grains of sand.

(E) They are too small to be visible to the naked eye.

GO ON TO THE NEXT PAGE.

19. If the time intervals between the earth's magnetic field reversals fluctuate greatly, then, based on the passage, which one of the following is most likely to be true?

   (A) Compass readings are most likely to be distorted near the peaks of the mid-ocean ridge.

   (B) It is this fluctuation that causes the ridge to wind around the earth like the seams on a baseball.

   (C) Some of the magnetic stripes of basalt on the ocean floor are much wider than others.

   (D) Continental rock is a more reliable indicator of the earth's magnetic field reversals than is oceanic rock.

   (E) Within any given magnetic stripe on the ocean floor, the age of the basalt does not vary.

20. Which one of the following would, if true, most help to support the ocean floor spreading theory?

   (A) There are types of rock other than basalt that are known to distort compass readings.

   (B) The ages of the earth's magnetic reversals have been verified by means other than examining magnetite grains in rock.

   (C) Pieces of basalt similar to the type found on the mid-ocean ridge have been found on the continents.

   (D) Along its length, the peak of the mid-ocean ridge varies greatly in height above the ocean floor.

   (E) Basalt is the only type of volcanic rock found in portions of the ocean floor nearest to the continents.

21. Which one of the following is most strongly supported by the passage?

   (A) Submarine basalt found near the continents is likely to be some of the oldest rock on the ocean floor.

   (B) The older a sample of basalt is, the more times it has reversed its polarity.

   (C) Compass readings are more likely to become distorted at sea than on land.

   (D) The magnetic fields surrounding magnetite grains gradually weaken over millions of years on the ocean floor.

   (E) Any rock that exhibits present-day magnetic polarity was formed after the latest reversal of the earth's magnetic field.

GO ON TO THE NEXT PAGE.

Passage A

Central to the historian's profession and scholarship has been the ideal of objectivity. The assumptions upon which this ideal rests include a commitment to the reality of the past, a sharp separation
(5) between fact and value, and above all, a distinction between history and fiction.

According to this ideal, historical facts are prior to and independent of interpretation: the value of an interpretation should be judged by how well it accounts
(10) for the facts; if an interpretation is contradicted by facts, it should be abandoned. The fact that successive generations of historians have ascribed different meanings to past events does not mean, as relativist historians claim, that the events themselves lack fixed
(15) or absolute meanings.

Objective historians see their role as that of a neutral judge, one who must never become an advocate or, worse, propagandist. Their conclusions should display the judicial qualities of balance and
(20) evenhandedness. As with the judiciary, these qualities require insulation from political considerations, and avoidance of partisanship or bias. Thus objective historians must purge themselves of external loyalties; their primary allegiance is to objective historical truth
(25) and to colleagues who share a commitment to its discovery.

Passage B

The very possibility of historical scholarship as an enterprise distinct from propaganda requires of its practitioners that self-discipline that enables them to
(30) do such things as abandon wishful thinking, assimilate bad news, and discard pleasing interpretations that fail elementary tests of evidence and logic.

Yet objectivity, for the historian, should not be confused with neutrality. Objectivity is perfectly
(35) compatible with strong political commitment. The objective thinker does not value detachment as an end in itself but only as an indispensable means of achieving deeper understanding. In historical scholarship, the ideal of objectivity is most compellingly embodied in
(40) the *powerful argument*—one that reveals by its every twist and turn its respectful appreciation of the alternative arguments it rejects. Such a text attains power precisely because its author has managed to suspend momentarily his or her own perceptions so as
(45) to anticipate and take into account objections and alternative constructions—not those of straw men, but those that truly issue from the rival's position, understood as sensitively and stated as eloquently as the rival could desire. To mount a telling attack on a
(50) position, one must first inhabit it. Those so habituated to their customary intellectual abode that they cannot even explore others can never be persuasive to anyone but fellow habitués.

Such arguments are often more faithful to the
(55) complexity of historical interpretation—more faithful even to the irreducible plurality of human perspectives— than texts that abjure position-taking altogether. The powerful argument is the highest fruit of the kind of thinking I would call objective, and in it neutrality

(60) plays no part. Authentic objectivity bears no resemblance to the television newscaster's mechanical gesture of allocating the same number of seconds to both sides of a question, editorially splitting the difference between them, irrespective of their perceived merits.

22. Both passages are concerned with answering which one of the following questions?

(A) What are the most serious flaws found in recent historical scholarship?
(B) What must historians do in order to avoid bias in their scholarship?
(C) How did the ideal of objectivity first develop?
(D) Is the scholarship produced by relativist historians sound?
(E) Why do the prevailing interpretations of past events change from one era to the next?

23. Both passages identify which one of the following as a requirement for historical research?

(A) the historian's willingness to borrow methods of analysis from other disciplines when evaluating evidence
(B) the historian's willingness to employ methodologies favored by proponents of competing views when evaluating evidence
(C) the historian's willingness to relinquish favored interpretations in light of the discovery of facts inconsistent with them
(D) the historian's willingness to answer in detail all possible objections that might be made against his or her interpretation
(E) the historian's willingness to accord respectful consideration to rival interpretations

GO ON TO THE NEXT PAGE.

24. The author of passage B and the kind of objective historian described in passage A would be most likely to disagree over whether

   (A) detachment aids the historian in achieving an objective view of past events
   (B) an objective historical account can include a strong political commitment
   (C) historians today are less objective than they were previously
   (D) propaganda is an essential tool of historical scholarship
   (E) historians of different eras have arrived at differing interpretations of the same historical events

25. Which one of the following most accurately describes an attitude toward objectivity present in each passage?

   (A) Objectivity is a goal that few historians can claim to achieve.
   (B) Objectivity is essential to the practice of historical scholarship.
   (C) Objectivity cannot be achieved unless historians set aside political allegiances.
   (D) Historians are not good judges of their own objectivity.
   (E) Historians who value objectivity are becoming less common.

26. Both passages mention propaganda primarily in order to

   (A) refute a claim made by proponents of a rival approach to historical scholarship
   (B) suggest that scholars in fields other than history tend to be more biased than historians
   (C) point to a type of scholarship that has recently been discredited
   (D) identify one extreme to which historians may tend
   (E) draw contrasts with other kinds of persuasive writing

27. The argument described in passage A and the argument made by the author of passage B are both advanced by

   (A) citing historical scholarship that fails to achieve objectivity
   (B) showing how certain recent developments in historical scholarship have undermined the credibility of the profession
   (C) summarizing opposing arguments in order to point out their flaws
   (D) suggesting that historians should adopt standards used by professionals in certain other fields
   (E) identifying what are seen as obstacles to achieving objectivity

S T O P

IF YOU FINISH BEFORE TIME IS CALLED, YOU MAY CHECK YOUR WORK ON THIS SECTION ONLY.
DO NOT WORK ON ANY OTHER SECTION IN THE TEST.

**Wait for the supervisor's instructions before you open the page to the topic.
Please print and sign your name and write the date in the designated spaces below.**

Time: 35 Minutes

General Directions

You will have 35 minutes in which to plan and write an essay on the topic inside. Read the topic and the accompanying directions carefully. You will probably find it best to spend a few minutes considering the topic and organizing your thoughts before you begin writing. In your essay, be sure to develop your ideas fully, leaving time, if possible, to review what you have written. **Do not write on a topic other than the one specified. Writing on a topic of your own choice is not acceptable.**

No special knowledge is required or expected for this writing exercise. Law schools are interested in the reasoning, clarity, organization, language usage, and writing mechanics displayed in your essay. How well you write is more important than how much you write.

Confine your essay to the blocked, lined area on the front and back of the separate Writing Sample Response Sheet. Only that area will be reproduced for law schools. Be sure that your writing is legible.

Both this topic sheet and your response sheet must be turned over to the testing staff before you leave the room.

Topic Code	Print Your Full Name Here		
098123	Last	First	M.I.

Date	Sign Your Name Here
/ /	

Scratch Paper
Do not write your essay in this space.

LSAT® Writing Sample Topic

Directions: The scenario presented below describes two choices, either one of which can be supported on the basis of the information given. Your essay should consider both choices and argue for one over the other, based on the two specified criteria and the facts provided. There is no "right" or "wrong" choice: a reasonable argument can be made for either.

The biggest newspaper in a large market is deciding whether to continue to write all of its local stories in-house or to contract out much of this work off-site to local freelancers. The largest section of the newspaper is devoted to local coverage. Using the facts below, write an essay in which you argue for one choice over the other based on the following two criteria:

- The newspaper wants to maximize the quality of its local coverage.
- The newspaper wants to minimize the costs of producing local stories.

Writing all local stories in-house requires maintaining an extensive staff for this purpose. This involves expenditures for salaries, benefits, and overhead. Staff must also be reimbursed for employee business expenses associated with gathering stories. The day-to-day management of personnel frictions in a sizable staff can be challenging. Training and communicating with in-house staff is direct. This allows for the effective adoption and maintenance of strict standards. Different approaches and innovation tend to be discouraged.

Contracting out much of the responsibility for local coverage would tend to encourage different approaches and innovation. It would free up some staff time for potentially more rewarding work such as conducting in-depth investigations of local concerns. The only compensation for the freelancers contracted for local coverage would be a fixed amount for each accepted story, depending on its length after editing by in-house staff. There would be a high turnover of these freelancers. Their loyalty to the company would be relatively low. Hiring replacements would require staff time. Training and communicating with freelancers would be relatively difficult. This includes efforts to inculcate and enforce strict standards.

WP-S098A

Scratch Paper
Do not write your essay in this space.

Writing Sample Response Sheet

DO NOT WRITE IN THIS SPACE

**Begin your essay in the lined area below.
Continue on the back if you need more space.**

Directions:

1. Use the Answer Key on the next page to check your answers.

2. Use the Scoring Worksheet below to compute your raw score.

3. Use the Score Conversion Chart to convert your raw score into the 120–180 scale.

Scoring Worksheet

1. Enter the number of questions you answered correctly in each section.

	Number Correct
Section I	_____
Section II	_____
Section III	_____
Section IV	_____

2. Enter the sum here: _____
   This is your Raw Score.

Conversion Chart
For Converting Raw Score to the 120–180 LSAT Scaled Score
LSAT Form 2LSN93

Reported Score	Raw Score	
	Lowest	Highest
180	100	101
179	99	99
178	98	98
177	97	97
176	—*	—*
175	96	96
174	95	95
173	94	94
172	93	93
171	92	92
170	90	91
169	89	89
168	88	88
167	86	87
166	85	85
165	83	84
164	82	82
163	80	81
162	78	79
161	77	77
160	75	76
159	73	74
158	71	72
157	69	70
156	67	68
155	66	66
154	64	65
153	62	63
152	60	61
151	58	59
150	56	57
149	54	55
148	53	53
147	51	52
146	49	50
145	47	48
144	46	46
143	44	45
142	42	43
141	41	41
140	39	40
139	38	38
138	36	37
137	35	35
136	33	34
135	32	32
134	30	31
133	29	29
132	28	28
131	27	27
130	25	26
129	24	24
128	23	23
127	22	22
126	21	21
125	20	20
124	19	19
123	18	18
122	—*	—*
121	17	17
120	0	16

* There is no raw score that will produce this scaled score for this form.

ANSWER KEY

SECTION I

1. C	8. E	15. C	22. B
2. B	9. D	16. D	23. B
3. C	10. A	17. C	24. E
4. D	11. D	18. E	25. A
5. B	12. B	19. C	
6. A	13. D	20. B	
7. B	14. D	21. E	

SECTION II

1. E	8. C	15. A	22. C
2. B	9. D	16. B	23. D
3. A	10. A	17. B	
4. C	11. B	18. B	
5. E	12. E	19. C	
6. B	13. C	20. E	
7. D	14. E	21. A	

SECTION III

1. E	8. B	15. E	22. A
2. D	9. C	16. E	23. C
3. E	10. A	17. D	24. A
4. A	11. B	18. A	25. A
5. D	12. A	19. C	26. A
6. D	13. B	20. E	
7. B	14. B	21. B	

SECTION IV

1. A	8. B	15. D	22. B
2. C	9. A	16. C	23. C
3. E	10. C	17. D	24. B
4. B	11. A	18. A	25. B
5. A	12. C	19. C	26. D
6. E	13. C	20. B	27. E
7. C	14. B	21. A	

Question 1

Overview: The passage argues that gardeners should grow stinging nettles alongside potato plants in order to increase the yields of the potato plants, but it also considers a potential objection to this recommendation: stinging nettles attract aphids, and many aphid species harm potato plants. Your task is to find the statement that logically completes the argument by supporting the claim that the objection does not contradict the recommendation.

The Correct Answer:

C (C) indicates that none of the aphids attracted to stinging nettles damage potato plants. This shows that the objection considered in the "Overview" does not actually contradict the recommendation, because the aphid species that harm potato plants aren't attracted to stinging nettles. By reconciling that objection with the recommendation, (C) logically completes the argument.

The Incorrect Answer Choices:

A (A) indicates that stinging nettles are easy to grow, because they require little care. This is not a logical completion of the argument, because no matter how easy it is to grow stinging nettles, it wouldn't be helpful to grow them near potato plants if they attract aphids that harm those plants.

B According to (B), some aphids attracted to stinging nettles don't damage those plants. But the argument addresses the possibility that aphids damage potato plants, not stinging nettles. So (B) isn't a logical completion of the argument.

D (D) suggests that other organisms are more harmful to potato plants than aphids and other insect pests. But even if this is so, aphids might still cause significant damage to potato plants that gardeners would like to avoid. Thus, the fact that stinging nettles attract aphids could still contradict the argument's recommendation.

E (E) says that most aphid species that harm potato plants are even more harmful to other plant species. But this is not relevant to the issue that that the argument is concerned with—the yield of potato plants in a backyard garden. So (E) is not a logical completion of the argument.

- *Difficulty Level: 1*

Question 2

Overview:

The passage describes the responses of Jocko, a chimpanzee, to receiving bananas while alone. When Jocko was given a large bunch of bananas, he made loud "food barks," which caused other chimpanzees to come and take the bananas. Later, Jocko was given a single banana and kept quiet. A zookeeper concluded that Jocko kept quiet so that other chimpanzees wouldn't take the banana. You are asked to find the statement that most seriously calls this conclusion into question.

The Correct Answer:

B According to (B), chimpanzees only utter food barks when a sizable quantity of food is present. This suggests an alternative explanation for Jocko's behavior: he did not make food barks when given a single banana because one banana—unlike a large bunch of bananas—is not enough to elicit a food bark. Since (B) shows that the information in the passage is consistent with a completely different account of Jocko's behavior, the zookeeper's conclusion is called into question.

The Incorrect Answer Choices:

A (A) says that chimpanzees only make food barks when their favorite foods are present. Even if this explains why Jocko made food barks when given many bananas, it doesn't challenge the zookeeper's conclusion, because it doesn't explain why Jocko kept silent when given a single banana.

C (C) offers an explanation for the behavior of chimpanzees who take food from other chimpanzees. Since Jocko did not take any food from other chimpanzees, (C) does not call into question the zookeeper's conclusion about Jocko's behavior.

D (D) tells us that chimpanzees often make noises that appear to be signals to other chimpanzees even when no other chimpanzees are present. This is not relevant to the zookeeper's conclusion, which purports to explain why Jocko did **not** make noises when given a single banana.

E According to (E), all of the zoo's chimpanzees show a strong preference for bananas. This is entirely consistent with the zookeeper's conclusion about Jocko's behavior, since it would suggest that Jocko had a good reason to keep quiet in order to keep other chimpanzees from taking his banana.

- *Difficulty Level: 1*

Question 3

Overview: This question asks you to identify a flaw in the reasoning presented. That reasoning is based on a survey of journalism students: most of these students wanted to read stories about government and politics and disliked publishers' tendencies to print stories about lifestyle trends and celebrity gossip. The argument uses this evidence to conclude that current publishing trends are based on false assumptions about what the public wants to read.

The Correct Answer:

C The argument's conclusion is about what the general public finds interesting, but the evidence for that conclusion is only about what journalism students found interesting. Journalism students are a select group of people who are being trained in news reporting. When it comes to trends in news publishing, then, journalism students' opinions are unlikely to be representative of the general public's opinions. This is a serious flaw in the argument's reasoning.

The Incorrect Answer Choices:

A, B (A) and (B) both indicate that the argument engages in flawed causal reasoning. But the argument doesn't engage in causal reasoning or even make any explicit claims about cause and effect. Instead, the argument proceeds by presenting survey information that supposedly undermines certain assumptions held by news publishers. Thus, neither answer choice could describe a flaw in the argument's reasoning.

D (D) addresses the possibility that the argument unfairly depicts the people who are likely to oppose its conclusion. But the argument doesn't discuss any such people, so it is not vulnerable to this criticism.

E (E) says that the argument treats a hypothesis as fact while admitting that this hypothesis is unsupported. But the only part of the argument that could reasonably be considered a hypothesis is the argument's conclusion, and there is no admission that it is unsupported. So the flaw described in (E) doesn't apply to the argument.

- *Difficulty Level: 1*

Question 4

Overview: The passage indicates that even though electric bug zappers are very effective at eliminating flying insects, most pest control experts recommend against them and instead favor insect-eating birds or insecticide sprays. You are asked to find the answer choice that most helps to explain this puzzling recommendation.

The Correct Answer:

D According to (D), bug zappers kill fewer harmful insects than insect-eating birds and insecticide sprays, while also killing a greater number of beneficial insects. So birds and insecticides are better than bug zappers at eliminating just the undesirable insects. This advantage helps to explain why experts recommend birds and insecticides over bug zappers.

The Incorrect Answer Choices:

A (A) suggests that it would be reasonably easy to introduce insect-eating birds into an insect-rich area. But it might also be easy to introduce bug zappers into many of these areas. Moreover, (A) does not help to explain why, in addition to birds, experts recommend insecticides for insect control. So (A) fails to account for the experts' recommendation.

B (B) is at worst a minor shortcoming of bug zappers. It merely says that bug zappers are less effective against mosquitoes than against other harmful insects. So if bug zappers rid an area of 98 percent of other harmful insects, they might also rid it of 95 percent of mosquitoes, which would still make bug zappers a very effective means of mosquito control. And even if (B) does point out a shortcoming of bug zappers, we have no reason to think that insect-eating birds and insecticide sprays don't have this same shortcoming. So (B) fails to explain why experts recommend these methods of insect control over bug zappers.

C (C) claims that bug zappers use more electricity and provide less light than other light sources. This cannot help to explain the pest control experts' recommendation, because it offers no way to compare bug zappers to other means of insect control.

E (E) indicates that, according to their developers, certain new insecticide sprays don't harm humans, birds, or pets. Even if we accept the developers' claims, we have no reason to think that bug zappers harm these groups either. Moreover, the developers' claims don't explain why, in addition to pesticides, experts favor insect-eating birds for pest control. So (E) fails to account for the experts' recommendation.

- *Difficulty Level: 1*

Question 5

Overview: The gardener's argument concludes that the rocks chosen for placement in Japanese gardens should vary widely in appearance. Two claims support this conclusion: first, Japanese gardens should display harmony with nature, and second, rocks found in nature vary widely in appearance. You are asked to identify an assumption on which this argument depends.

The Correct Answer:

B The gardener argues that, because rocks in nature vary in appearance, rocks in Japanese gardens should also vary in appearance. This suggests that, in this respect, Japanese gardens should imitate nature. But the argument does not say that Japanese gardens should imitate nature; instead, it claims that they should display harmony with nature. In order for that claim to help support the argument's conclusion, there must be some connection between imitating nature and displaying harmony with nature. (B) provides the needed connection, so it expresses an assumption on which the gardener's argument depends.

The Incorrect Answer Choices:

A According to (A), the selection of rocks for Japanese gardens should reflect every key value embodied in those gardens' designs. But the argument is based on only one such value—that Japanese gardens should display harmony with nature. Even if this is among the key values mentioned in (A), the argument need not assume anything about whether Japanese gardens should reflect any other such values.

C The argument need not assume that the expression of harmony with nature is the only criterion that must be met by rocks selected for placement in Japanese gardens. It can allow that there are other criteria. For example, a requirement that only durable rocks should be selected would not interfere with the argument.

D The argument need not assume that expressing harmony with nature is the same thing as being natural. As long as varying the appearance of rocks in Japanese gardens helps to express harmony with nature, the argument is consistent with the possibility that expressing harmony with nature is not simply a matter of being natural.

E   (E) asserts that each component of a genuine Japanese garden is varied. But the argument only addresses the rocks chosen for placement in Japanese gardens, so it need not make any assumptions about their other components.

- *Difficulty Level: 1*

Question 6

Overview: The passage compares vacuum tubes to semiconductors, with reference to their use in digital circuits. It tells us that certain experimental vacuum tubes have higher heat resistance than semiconductors, but, as things now stand, vacuum tubes' maximum current capacity is not comparable to that of semiconductors. The passage also gives us a standard for judging whether components with high heat tolerance (such as the experimental vacuum tubes) are preferable to semiconductors: any component with higher heat resistance than semiconductors is preferable for use in digital circuits if it is also comparable to semiconductors in all other significant respects, including maximum current capacity.

You are asked to find a statement that must be true if all the statements in the passage are true.

The Correct Answer:

A   According to the standard presented in the passage, for a component with high heat tolerance to be preferable to semiconductors for use in digital circuits, it must be comparable to semiconductors in all other significant respects, including maximum current capacity. But vacuum tubes are not presently comparable to semiconductors in maximum current capacity. Given this, it must be true that vacuum tubes are not now preferable to semiconductors for use in digital circuits.

The Incorrect Answer Choices:

B   (B) implies that vacuum tubes will one day have maximum current capacity comparable to that of semiconductors, but nothing in the passage suggests that this will ever be true. So this is one way in which (B) is not guaranteed to be true if the statements in the passage are true.

We can also rule out (B) by recalling that the passage indicates that vacuum tubes would be preferable for use in digital circuits if they were comparable to semiconductors in **all** other significant respects. Even if vacuum tubes are one day comparable to semiconductors in maximum current capacity, they still might not be comparable in other significant respects, which makes it possible that vacuum tubes would not be used in any digital circuits.

C The passage says that vacuum tubes' maximum current capacity is not comparable to that of semiconductors. But it leaves open the possibility that vacuum tubes are not comparable to semiconductors in other significant respects. So the fact that vacuum tubes' maximum current capacity is too low might not be the only reason that they are not now used in digital circuits.

D The passage does not say anything about the relative advantages and disadvantages of semiconductors as compared to vacuum tubes for applications other than digital circuits. So we cannot infer that semiconductors will always be preferable to vacuum tubes for many applications other than digital circuits. We cannot even infer that they are preferable.

E The passage says that certain experimental vacuum tubes are more resistant to heat than semiconductors are. But it leaves open the possibility that vacuum tubes have other advantages over semiconductors.

- *Difficulty Level: 4*

Question 7

Overview: The argument has three premises: (1) Accounts of the 430 B.C. Athenian epidemic indicate that many victims experienced hiccups; (2) hiccups are not a symptom of any known disease except Ebola; (3) accounts of the Athenian epidemic mention other symptoms that match those of Ebola. The argument concludes that the Ebola virus was the cause of the epidemic.

You are asked to identify the one answer choice that does not weaken the argument, i.e., the answer choice that either strengthens the argument or has no effect on its strength.

The Correct Answer:

B The argument is based on accounts of the Athenian epidemic that indicate that **many** victims experienced hiccups. (B) says that **not all** victims of the Ebola virus experience hiccups, which is consistent with the accounts of the Athenian epidemic. So (B) does nothing to undermine the case for concluding that the Ebola virus was the cause of the Athenian epidemic. If anything, it strengthens that case slightly by confirming that this important observation from the accounts of the Athenian epidemic matches what would have occurred with Ebola.

The Incorrect Answer Choices:

A (A) weakens the argument by providing information that weakens the argument's third premise. The fact that certain symptoms of Ebola were mentioned in the accounts of the Athenian epidemic is not a compelling reason to think that the Ebola virus was the cause of that epidemic once we learn that many symptoms of Ebola do not appear in any accounts of the Athenian epidemic.

C If the Ebola virus's host animals did not live in Athens at the time of the epidemic, then it's hard to explain how Ebola could have infected Athenians. This makes it unlikely, or at least less likely, that the Ebola virus caused the epidemic.

D If Ebola is much more contagious than the disease that caused the Athenian epidemic was reported to have been, then the hypothesis that the Ebola virus caused the epidemic is not fully consistent with the reported facts. The accounts of the Athenian epidemic would have to be inaccurate in this respect. This means that (D) weakens the argument that the Ebola virus caused the epidemic.

E If epidemics caused by the Ebola virus are usually shorter-lived than the Athenian epidemic, then the hypothesis that the Ebola virus caused the epidemic does not explain the reported facts very well. If the Athenian epidemic was Ebola, it would have been an unusual instance of an Ebola epidemic. This reduces the likelihood that it was Ebola, and in this way (E) weakens the argument that the Ebola virus caused the epidemic.

- *Difficulty Level: 4*

Question 8

Overview: The argument in the letter objects to a criticism presented in a newspaper article. The article reportedly asserted that a claim made by environmentalists that more wolves on Vancouver Island are killed by hunters than are born each year was disproven by studies indicating that the total number of wolves has remained roughly constant for 20 years. The argument in the letter counters this assertion of disproof by presenting additional evidence: environmentalists have been introducing new wolves onto Vancouver Island for 20 years. This means that it is possible that hunters do kill more wolves than are born each year, while the additional wolves introduced by environmentalists have been keeping the population constant.

Your task is to identify the conclusion of the argument, which is the claim that all of the other parts of the argument are intended to support.

The Correct Answer:

E As outlined in the "Overview," the letter is directed toward raising a specific objection to a newspaper article and presenting evidence to support that objection. The claim in (E) basically restates that objection, which means that it is the conclusion of the argument given in the letter.

The Incorrect Answer Choices:

A The argument does claim that environmentalists have been introducing new wolves into the Vancouver Island wolf population, and the argument accepts the article's assertion that the wolf population has remained roughly constant. Together these two claims could be a basis for concluding what (A) states, but the argument never explicitly states the view in (A). Instead, the argument is set up to support a different claim, which is stated in (E). So (A) is not the conclusion of the argument.

B The argument does not directly address any claim about the number of wolves killed by hunters relative to the number born each year. It merely argues that the article has not disproven the claim that more wolves are killed by hunters than are born each year.

C (C) is a claim about what should be done. But the argument presents factual claims about what is actually happening to the wolf population and uses these to evaluate the article and the argument that it makes—it doesn't say anything about what should be done regarding the wolves on Vancouver Island. So (C) is not the conclusion of the argument.

D The argument criticizes the conclusion that the article draws from studies indicating that the total number of wolves on Vancouver Island has remained roughly constant. The argument does not, however, dispute the accuracy of those studies. So (D) does not express any claim made by the argument, which means that it could not possibly express the conclusion.

- *Difficulty Level: 4*

Question 9

Overview: The passage says that the number of transistors on new microchips, as well as the chips' computing speed, has consistently doubled every 18 months for several decades. It also indicates that for a certain period—from the mid-1990s into the next decade—each doubling of a chip's computer speed was accompanied by a doubling of the cost of production. Your task is to choose the statement that can be properly inferred from the passage.

The Correct Answer:

D We are told that for the past several decades, the number of transistors on a new microchip has doubled in lockstep with a doubling of computing speed. And we are told that over a certain part of the past several decades (the mid-1990s into the next decade), each doubling of a microchip's computing speed was accompanied by a doubling in the cost of making the microchip. It follows that within this period (the mid-1990s into the next decade) each doubling in the number of transistors on microchips was accompanied by a doubling in the cost of making those microchips, which is what (D) says.

The Incorrect Answer Choices:

A The only means discussed in the passage of doubling the speed of a microchip is increasing the number of transistors per chip. However, this does not imply that there are no other effective means of doubling the speed. So (A) cannot be inferred from the statements in the passage.

B The passage describes a situation in which increasing the number of transistors on microchips resulted in increasing the microchips' computing speed and all of this was accompanied by an increase in the cost of producing the microchip. So if computer makers used this technological improvement to produce faster computers, as seems possible or even likely, those computers would have been more expensive to produce. Inferring that there would be little if any increase in the retail cost of computers under these circumstances is unwarranted, especially when we consider that the passage gives no information about how the retail cost of computers is determined.

C The passage says that from the mid-1990s into the next decade, each doubling in a microchip's computing speed was accompanied by a doubling in the cost of producing the chip. However, we cannot infer anything from this about what the engineers tried to do. It is possible, for example, that they attempted to control the cost of producing microchips but were not successful.

E The passage says that from the mid-1990s into the next decade, engineers were unable to increase the computing speed of microchips without also increasing the cost of producing them. But we cannot infer from this that it is unlikely that engineers will ever succeed at this. It is possible that some technological breakthrough will occur that will enable engineers to increase speed without increasing cost.

- *Difficulty Level: 3*

Question 10

Overview: The argument in the passage begins with the premise that Sandstrom's column led many people to trespass on and damage the Mendels' farm. The argument concludes that if Sandstrom could have reasonably expected that the column would lead people to damage the farm, then she should pay for the damage. You are asked to identify an assumption that would enable the argument's conclusion to be properly inferred.

The Correct Answer:

A The argument claims that Sandstrom's action of writing the column led other people to cause damage to the Mendels' farm. In combination with (A), this implies that Sandstrom should pay for this damage if she could have reasonably expected that writing the column would lead people to cause damage. That is the conclusion of the argument, so (A) enables the conclusion to be properly inferred.

The Incorrect Answer Choices:

B The argument concludes that Sandstrom should pay for the damage **if** a certain condition is met. (B) limits when people should pay for damage: they should pay **only if** a certain condition is met. We don't know whether the condition in (B) actually is met, since we don't know that Sandstrom actually expected that her column would lead people to damage the farm. But even if the condition in (B) were met, assuming (B) would not enable the conclusion to be properly inferred. Since (B) limits when people should pay for damage, it can imply that a person is **not** required to pay for damage (because the condition isn't met), but it cannot imply that a person should pay.

C The fact that the trespassers will not pay for the damage establishes that someone else would need to pay for it, but it does not imply anything about who should pay. So (C) does not enable the conclusion to be properly inferred.

D Even if we assume (D), we cannot properly infer the conclusion without an additional assumption. Neither (D) nor the premises of the argument provide any link between knowing that an action could lead people to cause damage and a requirement to pay. Without such a link, there is no way to infer the conclusion of the argument.

E (E) tells us something that the Mendels believe, but their beliefs aren't relevant to the issue of whether Sandstrom should pay for the consequences that her newspaper column set in motion. Moreover, there is nothing in the passage to suggest that whether people are required to pay for damage depends on whether they can form reasonable expectations about the consequences of their actions. Clearly then, (E) does not enable the conclusion to be properly inferred.

- *Difficulty Level: 3*

Question 11

Overview: Meyer's employer found that he committed scientific fraud by falsifying data. The university where Meyer got his PhD investigated whether he had also falsified data in his doctoral thesis; despite finding no evidence that he had, they still decided to revoke his PhD. You are asked to identify the university policy that most justifies this decision.

The Correct Answer

D (D) states that anyone who has a PhD from the university and is found to have committed scientific fraud will have the PhD revoked. Meyer has a PhD from the university, and he was found to have committed scientific fraud. So this policy justifies the university's decision to revoke Meyer's PhD.

The Incorrect Answer Choices

A, C Both (A) and (C) describe policies that pertain only to fraud committed by a person while that person was a student at the university. But the passage gives no indication that Meyer committed fraud while a student at the university; instead, it says that the university found no evidence that Meyer falsified data in his doctoral thesis (which was written while Meyer was a student at the university). So there is no reason to think that either of these policies applies to Meyer's situation.

B, E The policy stated in (B) applies only to the university's admissions decisions, while that in (E) applies only to its hiring decisions. Therefore, neither policy can justify a decision to revoke a PhD.

- *Difficulty Level: 1*

Question 12

Overview: The instructor says that kickboxing aerobics is a highly risky form of exercise. The instructor also indicates that beginners who try to match skilled practitioners' high kicks are very likely to overextend and that overextension often leads to injury. Your task is to identify the answer choice that is most strongly supported by these statements.

The Correct Answer:

B The instructor indicates that overextension, which often causes injury, is very likely to occur when beginners at kickboxing aerobics attempt to match skilled practitioners' high kicks. This strongly suggests that beginners who do not attempt to match these kicks will lower their risk of overextension, and therefore also their risk of injury. It follows that to reduce their injury risk, beginners should not try to match the high kicks of skilled practitioners.

The Incorrect Answer Choices:

A According to the instructor, beginners who try to match skilled practitioners' high kicks are especially likely to experience injuries from overextending while kicking. But even if skilled practitioners are less likely than beginners to injure themselves in this way, they may still be likely to do so. Therefore, (A) is not strongly supported by the information in the passage.

C While the instructor's statements do support the claim that beginners at kickboxing aerobics are less likely to be injured if they avoid trying to match skilled practitioners' high kicks, they do not support (C)'s much stronger claim that they **will not** be injured if they avoid this practice.

D Even if kickboxing aerobics is very risky, it might still be less risky than some forms of aerobic exercise that do not involve high kicks—perhaps because these other forms of exercise involve risky movements that are not part of kickboxing aerobics. So (D) is not strongly supported by the instructor's statements.

E The instructor's statements do not support (E)'s claim that most beginners at kickboxing aerobics are injured while trying to match skilled practitioners' high kicks, since the instructor does not claim that most beginners even attempt such kicks, let alone that they are injured while doing so.

- *Difficulty Level: 2*

Question 13

Overview: The passage begins by describing the results of a trial, in which a company was convicted but the penalty that was imposed will probably have little effect on the company's behavior. Nonetheless, it is argued that the trial was worthwhile. This suggestion is backed by two claims. First, the trial provided useful information about the company's practices. Second, that information emboldened the company's competitors, alerted rivals, and restrained the company's unfair behavior. (The terms "since" and "after all" indicate relationships of support in this argument.) You are asked to identify the overall conclusion drawn in this argument.

The Correct Answer:

D (D) says that the company's trial was worthwhile. As discussed in the "Overview," this statement is supported by the claim that the trial provided useful information, together with a statement about the trial's effects. Moreover, the claim in (D) does not itself act as support for any of the other statements in the passage. Thus, this claim represents the overall conclusion drawn in the argument.

The Incorrect Answer Choices:

A According to (A), the trial would probably have affected the company's behavior even if it had not been convicted. But the argument is concerned entirely with what actually happened; it does not suggest anything about what might have happened if things had gone differently. Hence (A) is not a conclusion that the argument draws.

B As discussed in the "Overview," the claim stated by (B) is intended to support another claim in the argument. So it cannot be the argument's overall conclusion: it identifies premises of the argument.

C While the argument does state the claim indicated by (C), none of the argument's other statements are used to support that claim. So (C) does not express the overall conclusion drawn in the argument.

E The argument does not state anything about whether the penalty imposed on the company should have been larger. Since this claim plays no role in the argument, it cannot express the argument's overall conclusion.

- *Difficulty Level: 3*

Question 14

Overview: The question presents statements made by two people, Waller and Chin, and asks what they are committed to disagreeing about on the basis of those statements.

The Correct Answer:

D On the basis of the statements, Waller is committed to accepting (D). Waller's statements suggest that Waller believes that ESP does not exist and that it is not generally accepted by the public. So Waller's statement that if ESP existed, then it would be generally accepted by the public means that the failure of the general public to believe in ESP is good evidence against its existence. Chin is committed to rejecting (D). Chin's statement implies that the cultural elite and popular media reports can bias public opinion against ESP. If public opinion can be biased against ESP, the general public might not believe in ESP even though it existed. So the failure of the general public to believe in ESP does not provide good evidence against its existence.

The Incorrect Answer Choices:

A Waller says that if ESP existed, it would be generally accepted by the public. So the failure of the general public to believe in ESP commits Waller to rejecting (A). Chin, however, could also reject (A). Chin just says that public opinion will be biased against the existence of ESP as long as the cultural elite are closed-minded about its existence. But the claim that public opinion is biased against the existence of ESP does not commit Chin to accepting that ESP exists.

B Saying that it's impossible to demonstrate anything to the satisfaction of all skeptics clearly commits Chin to rejecting (B). But Waller could reject (B) as well. Waller says only that if ESP were real, it would be accepted by the general public. But acceptance by the general public does not imply acceptance by all skeptics. So Waller is not committed to the belief that ESP would be accepted by everyone.

C Waller's statements make it clear that he thinks the skeptics have a strong case. The failure of the general public to believe in ESP is good evidence against its existence. It's not clear, however, that Chin disagrees. Chin's statements just imply that public opinion is biased in favor of the skeptics. That doesn't imply anything about how strong their case actually is.

E Waller's statements strongly suggest that he believes that the public does not believe in ESP. The way Waller talks about ESP ("If there were really such a thing"), suggests that he doesn't believe that it exists. Thus, the public must not believe in it since they would believe in it if it existed. Chin's statement that public opinion is currently biased in favor of ESP skeptics suggests that Chin probably agrees with Waller in rejecting (E).

■ *Difficulty Level: 5*

Question 15

Overview: In the passage, it is argued that Hagerle owes a sincere apology to the counselor because Hagerle sincerely apologized to the physician for lying to her, and Hagerle told the same lie to the counselor. Your task is to find a principle that helps to justify the counselor's reasoning in the passage.

The Correct Answer:

C (C) says that someone is owed a sincere apology for having been lied to by a person if the following condition is met: someone else has already received a sincere apology for the same lie from that person. In the passage, the counselor points out that this condition is met. So (C), if valid, would help to justify the counselor's reasoning.

The Incorrect Answer Choices:

A (A) says that it's good to apologize if one is capable of doing so sincerely. However, we don't know whether Hagerle is capable of sincerely apologizing to the counselor. Moreover, (A) says merely that it is good to apologize. It does not say that a sincere apology is owed in such a case. So (A) does not justify the counselor's reasoning.

B (B) says that if someone tells the same lie to two people, then that person either owes an apology to both or to neither. This could help justify the inference in the passage if we knew that Hagerle owed the physician an apology. But we don't know that; we know only that Hagerle actually apologized to the physician.

D (D) says that if one is capable of sincerely apologizing to someone for lying to them, then one owes them an apology. However, we don't know whether Hagerle is capable of sincerely apologizing to the counselor. Even though Hagerle sincerely apologized to the physician for telling the same lie that was told to the counselor, something about the circumstances might make Hagerle unable to sincerely apologize to the counselor. So (D) does not help to justify the counselor's reasoning.

E In the passage it is argued that Hagerle owes a sincere apology to the counselor. (E) cannot justify this inference because (E) tells us only when people should not apologize, i.e., they should **not** apologize when they can't sincerely apologize to everyone that they told the lie to.

- *Difficulty Level: 1*

Question 16

Overview: The argument begins with the premise that a survey of address changes shows that over the last ten years twice as many households moved out of Weston as moved in. The argument concludes that the number of people living in Weston has decreased over the last ten years. You are asked to find a statement that strengthens this argument.

Notice that the premise of the argument is about how many **households** have moved into and left Weston, while the conclusion is about a change in the number of **people** living in Weston. It's important to remember that not all households are the same size.

The Correct Answer:

D (D) says that most of the households staying in or moving into Weston were single people and most of those moving out were families with children. This makes it very likely that the households moving out were, on average, larger than those moving in. Since (D) gives us more reason to think that the population has declined, it strengthens the argument.

The Incorrect Answer Choices:

A (A) says that many people moved into Weston and then out (or vice versa) within the last ten years. This does not imply anything about the total number of people who moved into Weston or out of Weston. This would have no net effect on the population of Weston in that period, so it neither strengthens the argument nor weakens it.

B (B) says that over the past century any census of Weston showing a population loss was followed ten years later by a census showing a population gain. Even if we can expect this trend to continue, we don't know what the last census showed. So (B) is not relevant to the argument since it gives us no basis for making an inference about the next census.

C The premise of the argument uses data from post offices and driver's license bureaus to establish that more households moved out of Weston than moved in. (C) says that many of the people who moved in didn't tell the post office or the driver's license bureau, suggesting that the number of households moving in was undercounted. This would make the argument's conclusion that the number of people living in Weston has decreased less likely to be true. So (C) weakens rather than strengthens the argument.

E   (E) tells us about the different career situations of those moving out of Weston and those moving in. However, those facts don't tell us anything about the sizes of the households moving into or out of Weston. Nor do they tell us anything else that would support a reasonable inference about migration into or out of Weston. So (E) has no bearing on the conclusion that the number of people living in Weston has decreased.

- *Difficulty Level: 2*

Question 17

Overview: The psychologist argues that people should not necessarily try to rid themselves of a tendency to make cognitive errors of a certain type. This conclusion is supported by a comparison to the undesirability of ridding themselves of a tendency toward a certain type of visual error. Your task is to find the answer choice that describes how this argument works.

The Correct Answer:

C   The argument does what (C) describes. It argues that an action (trying to overcome our tendency to make certain cognitive errors when making predictions about future happiness) might not be appropriate. And it argues for this by presenting a situation that is analogous in that it also concerns a tendency toward error—the error of perceiving lines that are actually parallel as if they converge. Having surgery to change our tendency to misperceive parallel lines in this situation corresponds to trying to overcome our tendency to make cognitive errors. And the argument suggests that having this surgery is not appropriate.

The Incorrect Answer Choices:

A   The argument does not claim that any particular event is inevitable. It does claim that we tend to make certain kinds of errors, but it doesn't claim that we inevitably make those errors. Even in the visual context, the argument only claims that parallel lines **often** appear to converge.

B   The only thing the argument attempts to undermine is the view that people should try to rid themselves of their tendency to make certain cognitive errors, but it's not accurate to consider this view a theory. Moreover, the argument does not refer to, much less call into question, any assumption on which this view is based, so the argument cannot be said to do what (B) describes.

D   The psychologist doesn't actually argue that the two situations (the tendency to make certain cognitive errors and the tendency to make a particular visual error) are similar. The psychologist's argument merely assumes that they are similar in certain respects. Moreover, the psychologist's argument does not try to establish that the same action would be reasonable in each situation. It asserts that the action would not be reasonable in the case of the visual error and argues that the corresponding action would not be reasonable in the case of the cognitive errors.

E The psychologist does argue against a particular action (trying to get rid of a tendency to make certain cognitive errors) but the psychologist's argument does not use a generalization to do so. Instead, it compares that particular action to a different particular action (having surgery). Hence the argument does not do what (E) describes.

- *Difficulty Level: 2*

Question 18

Overview: The passage includes a principle according to which an auction house is guilty of misrepresentation if a description in its catalog is a deliberate attempt to mislead bidders, even if the catalog identified the description as an opinion. This principle is employed to conclude that Healy's was guilty of misrepresentation when it described a vase as being from the mid-eighteenth century when it was really a modern reproduction.

You are asked to determine which additional piece of information about Healy's justifies the application of the principle. Given the information in the application, all that is required to establish its conclusion is information that indicates, or at least suggests, that Healy's description was a deliberate attempt to mislead bidders.

The Correct Answer:

E (E) says that, without consulting with any expert, Healy's described the vase as dating from the mid-eighteenth century merely in order to increase its auction price. The use of the term "merely" indicates that Healy's did not do this because they believed, or had reason to believe, that the vase was from the mid-eighteenth century. So if (E) is true, what Healy's did was clearly a deliberate attempt to mislead bidders.

The Incorrect Answer Choices:

A If (A) is true, then Healy's would have a strong motivation to mislead bidders about the age of the vase. However, the fact that Healy's had a strong motivation to mislead bidders does not imply that they actually did so. Healy's may have genuinely believed that the vase was from the mid-eighteenth century.

B (B) might suggest that the knowledgeable collectors were suspicious of the catalog's description of the vase. However, even if knowledgeable collectors could tell that the description was inaccurate, that would not imply that it was deliberately inaccurate. Healy's may have genuinely believed the description.

C If (C) is true, then Healy's description of the vase violated Healy's own stated policy. However, the principle in the passage does not imply a requirement to conform to any stated policy. So (C) does not justify the application of the principle.

D (D) implies that some of Healy's staff members would think that the catalog should not have described the vase as dating from the mid-eighteenth century. However, the principle in the passage does not say that an auction house is guilty of misrepresentation just because some staff members think that its catalog shouldn't contain a particular description. So (D) does not justify the application of the principle.

- *Difficulty Level: 4*

Question 19

Overview: The only premise of the anthropologist's argument is that the DNA of contemporary humans is significantly different from that of Neanderthals. The argument concludes that prehistoric *Homo sapiens* did not interbreed with Neanderthals. You are asked to identify an assumption required by this argument.

The Correct Answer:

C The only support offered in the argument for the conclusion that prehistoric *Homo sapiens* did not interbreed with Neanderthals is that the DNA of contemporary humans is significantly different from that of Neanderthals. But this premise supports the conclusion only by giving us reason to think that the DNA of prehistoric *Homo sapiens* is significantly different than that of Neanderthals. If (C) were not true—if the DNA of prehistoric *Homo sapiens* is a lot closer to that of Neanderthals than the DNA of contemporary humans is—then the fact that the DNA of contemporary humans is significantly different from that of Neanderthals doesn't mean much. So the argument needs to assume that (C) is true in order for the premise to support the conclusion.

The Incorrect Answer Choices:

A If the anthropologist were arguing that prehistoric *Homo sapiens* did interbreed with Neanderthals, then the argument would need to assume that they lived in roughly the same place at the same time. But this assumption has no place in the argument the anthropologist actually gives, which argues that prehistoric *Homo sapiens* did not interbreed with Neanderthals. The argument that the anthropologist gives is based entirely on the results of DNA testing and never touches on the issue of whether it was possible for Neanderthals and prehistoric *Homo sapiens* to interbreed.

B In order for the argument's premise about similarity of DNA to support the conclusion, DNA testing of Neanderthal remains has to be reasonably reliable. So (B), which says that testing of remains is significantly less reliable than testing of samples from living species, calls the argument into question. Thus, (B) is not required by the argument.

D If Neanderthals and prehistoric *Homo sapiens* were completely isolated, that would imply that the argument's conclusion is true. But the anthropologist's argument presents a completely different case for the conclusion. The case made by that argument has nothing to do with Neanderthals and prehistoric *Homo sapiens* being isolated from each other. So even if (D) is not true, the anthropologist's argument is not adversely affected.

E The argument uses evidence about differences in DNA to argue that there was no interbreeding between two species. So the argument is clearly assuming that if the DNA of two species share certain significant similarities, it is evidence of interbreeding. But that doesn't mean that the argument is assuming that **any** similarity in the DNA of two species must be the result of interbreeding. That assumption is far broader than what the anthropologist's argument assumes.

- *Difficulty Level: 4*

Question 20

Overview: The question asks what else must be true if all of the council member's statements are true. We can express the statements in a uniform if/then form as follows: (1) if more consumers live downtown, then the profits of downtown businesses will increase; (2) if the cost of living downtown decreases, then more consumers will live downtown; (3) if downtown traffic congestion does not decrease, then the profits of downtown businesses will not increase.

The Correct Answer:

B Given statements (1) and (2), (B) must be true. (2) says that if the cost of living downtown decreases, then more consumers will live downtown. (1) says that if more consumers live downtown, the profits of downtown businesses will increase. Putting these together, we get (B): if the cost of living downtown decreases, the profits of downtown businesses will increase.

The Incorrect Answer Choices:

A,C,D None of the statements in the passage tell us what will happen if downtown traffic congestion decreases. The last statement in the passage might appear to tell us what happens when downtown traffic congestion decreases, but it doesn't. It tells us that a decrease in traffic congestion is a necessary condition for an increase in the profits of downtown businesses, which is equivalent to saying that if downtown traffic congestion does not decrease, the profits of downtown businesses will not increase (which is how that statement is represented in the "Overview"). Since (A), (C), and (D) are each about what will happen if downtown traffic congestion decreases, none of those statements can be inferred.

E Statement (3) is the only one that tells us anything about what will happen if the profits of downtown businesses increase. Statement (3) is equivalent to saying that if the profits of downtown businesses do increase, then downtown traffic congestion will have decreased. But we can't use statement (3) to make any inferences about what will happen if the profits of downtown businesses increase, since none of the statements in the passage tell us what will happen if downtown traffic congestion decreases. So there is no way to use statement (3) to infer (E).

- *Difficulty Level: 5*

Question 21

Overview: The structure of the argument in the passage is quite basic. The argument has two premises that cover the entire range of possibilities for domestic long-distance phone calls on Discount Phoneline. There are those calls that start between 9 and 5, and there are all other calls. Calls of the first sort have one cost per minute—15 cents. Calls of the second sort have a different cost per minute—10 cents. The conclusion of the argument clearly follows: any phone call that doesn't cost 10 cents per minute will cost 15 cents per minute.

Your task is to choose an argument with a pattern of reasoning that is most similar to the argument in the passage. You will find that all of the answer choices are like the passage argument in that their premises cover the entire range of possibilities: there are university classes that involve extensive lab work and university classes that do not. And we are told that classes of the first sort are located in one room type (a laboratory), and that classes of the second sort are located in another room type (a normal classroom). These premises, which are expressed in the first sentence of each answer choice, are the same for all of the choices. The answer choices differ only in their conclusions, and these should be the focus of your comparisons.

The Correct Answer:

E (E) concludes that if a university class is not conducted in a normal classroom, it will be conducted in a laboratory. That is, any university class that isn't in the one location type will be in the other. This exactly matches the structure of the passage argument, which concluded that any phone call that doesn't have the one cost per minute will have the other.

The Incorrect Answer Choices:

A (A) concludes that if a university class does not involve extensive laboratory work, it will not be conducted in a laboratory. In terms of the passage argument, this would be like saying that if a domestic long-distance call does not start between 9 and 5, it will not cost 15 cents per minute. Since this is not the conclusion of the passage argument, (A) has a different pattern of reasoning.

B (B) concludes that if a university class is not conducted in a normal classroom, it will involve extensive lab work. In terms of the passage argument, this would be like saying that if a domestic long-distance call does not cost 10 cents per minute, it started between 9 and 5. Since this is not the conclusion of the passage argument, (B) has a different pattern of reasoning.

C (C) concludes that if a university class is conducted in a normal classroom, it will not be conducted in a laboratory. In terms of the passage argument, this would be like saying that if a domestic long-distance call does cost 10 cents per minute, it will not cost 15 cents per minute. This conclusion, which is obviously true on its face, is entirely different from the conclusion reached in the passage argument, so (C) has a different pattern of reasoning.

D (D) concludes that if a university class involves extensive lab work, it will not be conducted in a normal classroom. In terms of the passage argument, this would be like saying that if a domestic long-distance call starts between 9 and 5, it will not cost 10 cents per minute. Since this is not the conclusion of the passage argument, (D) has a different pattern of reasoning.

- *Difficulty Level: 5*

Question 22

Overview: The premises of the argument indicate that one child caused injury to another child and that the first child understands the difference between right and wrong. The argument concludes that pushing the second child was wrong if it was intended to cause injury. Your task is to choose the principle that most helps to justify the reasoning in this argument.

The Correct Answer:

B (B) can be rephrased as saying that if a person understands the difference between right and wrong, then it is wrong for that person to intentionally harm another person. The second premise of the argument meets (B)'s condition: the first child understands the difference between right and wrong. And so (B) allows us to conclude that it would be wrong for the first child to intentionally harm the second child. We can thus conclude that pushing the second child was wrong if it was intended to cause injury (since causing injury while intending to do so clearly constitutes intentional harm). In this way, (B) helps to justify the reasoning in the argument.

The Incorrect Answer Choices:

A The conclusion of the argument is that what the first child did was wrong if a certain condition is met: it was done with an intent to injure. (A) does not help us to reach this conclusion because it merely limits the conditions under which an action is wrong: it is wrong **only if** the person understands the difference between right and wrong. So (A) can justify a claim that an action was **not** wrong (because the person didn't understand the difference between right and wrong), but it cannot justify a claim that an action was wrong.

C The argument is trying to establish that an act was wrong if it was done with intent to injure, and (C) does not help to establish this conclusion. (C) tells us that if an act was wrong then it was intended to cause harm. (C) does not tell us that if an act was intended to cause harm then it was wrong, nor does it allow us to infer anything new from the argument's premises.

D (D) is applicable only if the person who did the action did not think about whether it would cause injury. But the premises of the argument do not indicate whether the first child thought about whether pushing the second would cause injury. So (D) could not help to justify the reasoning in the argument.

E The only way in which (E) connects to the premises of the argument is that it brings up the issue of understanding the difference between right and wrong. But the argument concerns a child who **does** understand the difference between right and wrong, and (E) is applicable only to people who **do not** understand the difference between right and wrong. So (E) could not help to justify the reasoning in the argument.

- *Difficulty Level: 4*

Question 23

Overview: The researcher's argument concerns the hypothesis that some makes of car are more common in certain parts of the country than in others. This hypothesis is based on data from an experiment: when people estimated how common their make of car was nationally, almost all of them overestimated this statistic. The researcher asserts that the hypothesis, if true, would explain this result. Since that result actually occurred, the researcher concludes that the hypothesis must be true: some makes of car are indeed more common in certain areas than in others. You are asked to pick the answer choice that most accurately expresses a reasoning flaw in this argument.

The Correct Answer:

B   Suppose, as the researcher claims, that some types of car are especially common in certain areas. Then the results of the experiment are unsurprising, since people who live in those areas will be both especially likely to own those types of cars, and especially likely to overestimate how common those cars are nationally. This shows that the actual results of the experiment are precisely those predicted by the researcher's hypothesis; therefore, these results do indeed support that hypothesis.

The researcher, however, claims that these results show that the hypothesis must be true—that is, that they prove the hypothesis. This goes too far, because those results are also predicted by other hypotheses. (For example, it may be that people tend to overestimate how common their car is because they are more likely to notice when a car is very similar to their own.) The results of the experiment support these other hypotheses just as much as the researcher's hypothesis, so these results do not prove the researcher's hypothesis.

The Incorrect Answer Choices:

A   The results of the experiment already show that most subjects did not know how common their car was nationally, so there is no need for the argument to estimate the likelihood that this is the case. Consequently, (A) does not express a flaw in the argument's reasoning.

C   If the experiment's subjects came from a wide variety of geographical regions, then the researcher's hypothesis would predict that each subject would be especially likely to own, and overestimate the frequency of, types of cars that are especially common in the geographical region where that subject lives. This possibility is entirely consistent with the results of the experiment, so failing to account for it would not constitute a flaw in the argument's reasoning.

D   (D)'s claim that the argument's premises are mutually contradictory is incorrect. There is a conflict between subjects' estimates and actual statistics regarding the frequency of certain cars, but that is not a conflict between premises of the argument. In fact, all of the argument's premises are consistent with each other.

E   The argument never discusses any particular cases, so it certainly does not misapply any statistical generalizations to such cases. Thus, the criticism described in (E) fails to apply to the argument.

- *Difficulty Level: 4*

Question 24

Overview: The argument concludes that students must receive most of the parking citations in university towns because many more citations are issued when students are in town. In general terms, it says that since something (a parking citation) is dispensed more often when a certain group (university students) is present, that thing must be dispensed mostly to members of that group.

Notice that this reasoning overlooks the possibility that **everyone**, including nonstudents, is more likely to receive a parking citation when students are in town, perhaps because increased competition for parking spots causes more people to park illegally. In general terms, the argument overlooks the possibility that a group's presence causes changes that also affect non-group members. This is a flaw in the argument's reasoning. The question asks you to identify the answer choice whose flawed reasoning is most similar to that in this argument.

The Correct Answer:

E (E), like the passage, asserts that because something (a snack) is given out more frequently when a certain group (other people's children) is present, that thing must be given mostly to members of that group. (E) is also like the passage in overlooking the possibility that the group's presence causes changes that also affect non-group members: parents may simply be more likely to give out snacks when other people's children visit, even if they give these snacks to their own children as well as the visitors. (E)'s flawed reasoning, then, is very similar to that in the passage.

The Incorrect Answer Choices:

A (A) claims that movie theaters sell more popcorn as the proportion of moviegoers who are children increases. The argument in the passage, however, does not mention proportions; it is concerned only with what happens when group members who had been absent become present. This is an important difference. And another difference between the two arguments is that (A) reaches a conclusion about who buys most of the **snacks** based on information concerning only **popcorn** sales. This weakness in the reasoning in (A) does not correspond to anything in the passage argument.

B The reasoning in (B) is flawed because that argument accepts one explanation for the houseplant's being greener without considering other possible explanations. The reasoning in the passage is flawed in that it fails to consider the possibility that a group's presence causes changes that affect non-group members. The argument in (B) is not concerned with groups, so it is not flawed in this way.

C The reasoning in (C) is flawed in that it concludes that university students have a certain property (being studious) based on a single premise indicating that they have a superficially similar property (being people who study while attending university). The reasoning in the passage has a wholly different flaw that is not present in (C): the argument in the passage fails to consider the possibility that a group's presence causes changes that affect non-group members.

D (D) concludes that consumers buy more fruit in the summer, because that is when more varieties of fruit are available. This reasoning is flawed because consumers could buy more fruit in total during the winter even if the number of varieties is limited then. The argument in the passage does not have a flaw that corresponds to this. Moreover, the argument in (D) does not exhibit the flaw in the passage argument—that of failing to consider the possibility that a group's presence causes changes that affect non-group members.

- *Difficulty Level: 5*

Question 25

Overview: The counselor's argument concludes that people who are criticized will only change if the criticism is harsh. In support of this conclusion, the counselor notes that change requires a motive, and asserts that harsh criticism provides this motive. This second assertion is supported by two additional claims: unpleasant criticism provides a motive, and harsh criticism is unpleasant. You are asked to identify the grounds on which this argument is most vulnerable to criticism.

The Correct Answer:

A The counselor's conclusion says that **only** harsh criticism will cause the person criticized to change; in other words, harsh criticism is **necessary** to effect change in that person. But the counselor's argument merely establishes that harsh criticism provides a motive to change; in other words, harsh criticism is **sufficient** for giving people a motive to change. Even if this is so, change could still be accomplished without harsh criticism (by giving praise or other rewards, for example). Thus, the counselor's reasoning is vulnerable to criticism because it infers that harsh criticism, which suffices to provide a motive, is necessary for this purpose.

The Incorrect Answer Choices:

B The only goal of criticism that the counselor's argument addresses is that of bringing about change, and so you might think that the argument is vulnerable to criticism for not addressing the possibility that, in some cases, bringing about change is not the primary goal of criticism. But the counselor is merely arguing that we "should consider" one particular argument regarding the relationship of criticism and change. Since the counselor's argument does not presume that change is the primary goal of criticism in every case, there is no need to address the possibility raised in (B).

C The argument does not take for granted that everyone who is motivated to change will change. It does say that change requires a motive; this implies that only those who are appropriately motivated will change, but that is consistent with the possibility that not all of these people will actually do so.

D The counselor asserts that harsh criticism provides a motive for doing something—namely, changing. It would not be surprising if one reason that harsh criticism provides a motive to change is that people are motivated to avoid harsh criticism. But this possibility plays no role in the argument, which does not seek to explain why harsh criticism has the effects that it does. So the argument is not vulnerable to the criticism identified in (D).

E (E) indicates that the counselor's reasoning takes the refutation of an argument to show that the conclusion of that argument is false. But the counselor's reasoning never deals with the refutation of an argument, so it is not vulnerable to this criticism.

- *Difficulty Level: 4*

Questions 1–5

What the setup tells you: This group of questions has to do with seven candidates for the position of judge. Each candidate will be appointed to one of two different courts. Your task involves determining which candidates get appointed to which courts.

The setup lays out some general restrictions on the appointments by specifying the number of open positions on each court. Since these open positions do not all have to be filled, this information serves to indicate the **maximum** number of appointments that can be made to each court. At most three candidates can be appointed to the appellate court, while at most six candidates can be appointed to the trial court.

The conditions give more specific restrictions: Li must be appointed to the appellate court; Kurtz must be appointed to the trial court; and Hamadi cannot be appointed to the same court as Perkins.

Some things you can deduce right away: Since both Hamadi and Perkins must be appointed to one court or the other, the third condition amounts to saying that Hamadi and Perkins must be appointed to different courts than each other. One of them is appointed to the appellate court, while the other is appointed to the trial court. This entails that at least two candidates (Li and one of Hamadi and Perkins) will be appointed to the appellate court, which in turn entails that at most five candidates can be appointed to the trial court.

Broadly speaking, then, there are two general forms a possible solution can take here. It could be that Li, Hamadi, and maybe a third candidate are appointed to the appellate court, while Kurtz, Perkins, and up to three others are appointed to the trial court. Alternatively, it could be that, Li, Perkins, and maybe a third candidate are appointed to the appellate court while Kurtz, Hamadi, and up to three others are appointed to the trial court. Using the candidates' initials, this can be represented in the form of a simple diagram:

appellate	trial
L	K
H/P	P/H
[at most one of J, M, O]	[two or three of J, M, O]

Question 1

Overview: This question asks you to pick an acceptable set of appointments of candidates to courts from among the five answer choices. The answer choices each represent a complete set of appointments, in that every candidate is appointed to a court. (This kind of question was described as an "Orientation Question" on pages 6–7.) An efficient way to approach this type of question is to take the conditions in turn and check the answer choices against them, eliminating any answer choice as soon as you detect a violation of a condition. There's no need to recheck an answer choice once you've eliminated it.

The first condition is that Li must be appointed to the appellate court. This condition allows you to eliminate answer choice (A), since that answer choice has Li appointed to the trial court.

The second condition is that Kurtz must be appointed to the trial court. This condition allows you to eliminate answer choice (C), since that answer choice has Kurtz appointed to the appellate court.

The third condition is that Hamadi cannot be appointed to the same court as Perkins. This condition allows you to eliminate answer choice (B) and answer choice (D). In (B), Hamadi and Perkins are both appointed to the appellate court, while in (D) they are both appointed to the trial court.

The only answer choice that has not been eliminated is (E), so that's the correct answer.

The Correct Answer:

E The "Overview" shows by process of elimination that (E) is the correct answer.

The following provides an independent demonstration that (E) is an acceptable set of judicial appointments. First, it satisfies the basic setup by not exceeding the number of open positions on each court. In (E), two candidates are appointed to the appellate court, where there were three open positions, and five candidates are appointed to the trial court, where there were six open positions. (E) doesn't violate either of the first two conditions, since Li is appointed to the appellate court and Kurtz is appointed to the trial court. Finally, (E) satisfies the third condition, since Hamadi and Perkins are appointed to different courts than each other: Hamadi is appointed to the trial court, while Perkins is appointed to the appellate court.

The Incorrect Answer Choices:

A (A) can be eliminated since it violates the first condition. Li is appointed to the trial court instead of the appellate court.

B (B) can be eliminated since it violates the third condition. Both Hamadi and Perkins are appointed to the appellate court.

C (C) can be eliminated since is violates the second condition. Kurtz is appointed to the appellate court instead of the trial court.

D (D) can be eliminated since it violates the third condition. Both Hamadi and Perkins are appointed to the trial court.

- *Difficulty Level: 1*

Question 2

Overview: This question asks you to select the answer choice that CANNOT be true. In this kind of question, the answer choices that **do not** violate the setup conditions are incorrect. The correct answer is the one that **does** violate the setup conditions in some way.

As described in "Some things you can deduce right away," the setup conditions entail that any possible solution must take the form:

appellate	trial
L	K
H/P	P/H
[at most one of J, M, O]	[two or three of J, M, O]

This table provides an easy way to check whether an answer choice violates the setup conditions. Quickly scanning the answer choices reveals that answer choice (B) is impossible. You know that at most one of McDonnell and Ortiz can be appointed to the appellate court. It cannot be true that they are both appointed to the appellate court.

The Correct Answer:

B As described in the "Overview," a quick scan of the table representing the possible solutions reveals that answer choice (B) violates the setup conditions and thus cannot be true. So (B) is the correct answer.

The Incorrect Answer Choices:

Once you've identified the correct answer there is no need to eliminate the incorrect answer choices. However, for the sake of completeness, let's see how each of the other answer choices could be true.

A Could it be true that Hamadi and McDonnell are both appointed to the appellate court? Yes, here is an acceptable set of appointments in which that is the case:

appellate	trial
L	K
H	P
M	J
	O

C Could it be true that Ortiz and Perkins are both appointed to the appellate court? Yes, here is an acceptable set of appointments in which that is the case:

appellate	trial
L	K
P	H
O	J
	M

D Could it be true that Hamadi and Jefferson are both appointed to the trial court? Yes, the same set of appointments described in the explanation of answer choice (C) above shows that this is possible.

E Could it be true that Ortiz and Perkins are both appointed to the trial court? Yes, the same set of appointments described in the explanation of answer choice (A) above shows that this is possible.

- *Difficulty Level: 1*

Question 3

Overview: This question asks you to select the answer choice that CANNOT be true. In this kind of question, the answer choices that **don't** violate the setup conditions are incorrect. The correct answer is the one that **does** violate the setup conditions in some way.

As was described in the explanation of Question 2, the table given in "Some things you can deduce right away" provides an easy way to check whether an answer choice violates the setup conditions. Quickly scanning the answer choices reveals that answer choice (A) is impossible. You know that at most one of Jefferson and McDonnell can be appointed to the appellate court. It cannot be true that they are both appointed to the appellate court.

The Correct Answer:

A As described in the "Overview," a quick scan of the table representing the possible solutions reveals that answer choice (A) violates the setup conditions and thus cannot be true. So (A) is the correct answer.

The Incorrect Answer Choices:

Once you've identified the correct answer there is no need to eliminate the incorrect answer choices. However, for the sake of completeness, let's see how each of the other answer choices could be true.

B Could it be true that Jefferson and McDonnell are both appointed to the trial court? Yes, here is an acceptable set of appointments in which that is the case:

appellate	trial
L	K
H	P
	J
	M
	O

C Could it be true that McDonnell and Ortiz are both appointed to the trial court? Yes, the same set of appointments described in the explanation of answer choice (A) above shows that this is possible.

D Could it be true that McDonnell and Perkins are both appointed to the appellate court? Yes, here is an acceptable set of appointments in which that is the case:

appellate	trial
L	K
P	H
M	J
	O

E Could it be true that McDonnell and Perkins are both appointed to the trial court? Yes, the same set of appointments described in the explanation of answer choice (A) above shows that this is possible.

- *Difficulty Level: 1*

Question 4

Overview: For this question, you're looking for something that must be true if Ortiz is appointed to the appellate court. So you can start with that supposition and then use the setup conditions to draw further inferences.

As explained in "Some things you can deduce right away," you know that the appellate court can have at most three candidates appointed to it. One of those appointments must go to Li (because of the first condition) and another must go to one or the other of Hamadi and Perkins (because of the third condition). Thus, if you suppose that Ortiz is also appointed to the appellate court, this fills all of the open positions on the appellate court. The rest of the candidates—Jefferson, Kurtz, McDonnell and whichever of Hamadi and Perkins was not appointed to the appellate court—must therefore be appointed to the trial court. To use the simple diagram from "Some things you can deduce right away," you get:

appellate	trial
L	K
H/P	P/H
O	J
	M

The Correct Answer:

C As explained in the "Overview," supposing that Ortiz is appointed to the appellate court determines that Jefferson must be appointed to the trial court. Thus, answer choice (C) is something that must be true if Ortiz is appointed to the appellate court. So (C) is the correct answer.

The Incorrect Answer Choices:

Once you've identified the correct answer there is no need to eliminate the incorrect answer choices. However, for the sake of completeness, let's see why each of the other answer choices is incorrect.

A, D, E As explained in the "Overview," supposing that Ortiz is appointed to the appellate court does not tell you which of Hamadi or Perkins must be appointed to the appellate court and which must be appointed to the trial court. All you know is that one will be appointed to the appellate court and the other will be appointed to the trial court.

B As explained in the "Overview," supposing that Ortiz is appointed to the appellate court determines that Jefferson must be appointed to the trial court. Thus, the claim that Jefferson is appointed to the appellate court is something that must be **false**.

- *Difficulty Level: 2*

Question 5

Overview: In this question, you're asked to identify a condition that could replace the third setup condition in a way that would have the same effect on the judicial appointments. Your task is to identify an alternative condition that would not change which sets of judicial appointments are deemed acceptable. That is, the alternative condition cannot rule out possibilities that were originally deemed acceptable, nor can it allow possibilities that were originally deemed unacceptable.

The Correct Answer:

E In order to answer this kind of question, it is sometimes possible to determine fairly straightforwardly which of the answer choices is correct. And that is the case here. Consider the new condition offered in (E)—namely, that no three of Hamadi, Kurtz, Li, and Perkins can be appointed to the same court as each other. You know from the first and second conditions that Li and Kurtz cannot be appointed to the same court as each other. Li must be appointed to the appellate court (first condition) and Kurtz must be appointed to the trial court (second condition). Thus, from the first and second conditions, the only way that three of Hamadi, Kurtz, Li and Perkins could be appointed to the same court as each other would be if Hamadi and Perkins were both appointed to the same court as Li (the appellate court) or to the same court as Kurtz (the trial court). By specifying that this is not allowed, the new condition offered in (E) amounts to exactly the same thing as the original third condition—namely, Hamadi cannot be appointed to the same court as Perkins.

The Incorrect Answer Choices:

Once you've identified the correct answer there is no need to eliminate the incorrect answer choices. However, for the sake of completeness, let's see why each of the other answer choices is incorrect. To do so, it will help to say a bit more about what it would take for an answer choice to fail to be correct.

You are looking for an alternative condition that would yield precisely the same possible outcomes as the original condition. So one strategy for checking whether an answer choice provides such a condition is to ask two questions:

- Does the new condition rule out possibilities that the original condition allows?
- Does the new condition allow possibilities that the original condition rules out?

If the answer to either of these questions is yes, then the new condition offered in the answer choice cannot be correct.

A To see that answer choice (A) is incorrect, consider the second bulleted question above: does the condition offered in (A) allow any possibilities that the original condition rules out? The answer is yes. By only specifying that Hamadi and Perkins cannot both be appointed to the appellate court, the condition in (A) fails to rule out the possibility that they are both appointed to the trial court. Since this possibility is ruled out by the original third condition, answer choice (A) is incorrect.

B To see that answer choice (B) is incorrect, consider the second bulleted question above: does the condition offered in (B) allow any possibilities that the original condition rules out? The answer is yes. By only offering a condition that applies if Hamadi is not appointed to the trial court, (B) says nothing about the possibility where Hamadi is appointed to the trial court. In particular, the condition offered in (B) fails to rule out the possibility that Hamadi and Perkins are both appointed to the trial court. Since this possibility is ruled out by the original third condition, answer choice (B) is incorrect.

C To see that answer choice (C) is incorrect, consider the second bulleted question above: does the condition offered in (C) allow any possibilities that the original condition rules out? The answer is yes. By only offering a condition that applies if Hamadi is appointed to the same court as Jefferson, (C) says nothing about the possibility where Hamadi is **not** appointed to the same court as Jefferson. In particular, the condition offered in (C) fails to rule out the possibility that, for example, Jefferson is appointed to the appellate court, while Hamadi and Perkins are both appointed to the trial court. Since this possibility is ruled out by the original third condition, answer choice (C) is incorrect.

D To see that answer choice (D) is incorrect, consider the second bulleted question above: does the condition offered in (D) allow any possibilities that the original condition rules out? The answer is yes. By only offering a condition that applies if Hamadi is appointed to the same court as Li, (D) says nothing about the possibility where Hamadi is **not** appointed to the same court as Li. In particular, the condition offered in (D) fails to rule out the possibility that Hamadi and Perkins are both appointed to the trial court. Since this possibility is ruled out by the original third condition, answer choice (D) is incorrect.

- *Difficulty Level: 5*

Questions 6–10

What the setup tells you: This set of questions has to do with the order in which six members of a skydiving team will dive, one after the other, from a plane. Two of the four setup conditions—the second and third—are conditions on when in the order certain team members can or must dive: the second condition tells you that Larue must dive either first or last; the third condition tells you that neither Weiss nor Zacny can dive last. The first and fourth conditions are conditions on the order in which certain team members can dive relative to other team members: the first condition tells you that Treviño must dive at some time before Weiss; the fourth condition tells you that Pei must dive at some time after Ohba or Larue, but not after both. It is worth noting that the fourth condition in effect tells you that Pei must dive at some time in between Ohba and Larue. That is, the fourth condition tells you that Pei dives either at some time after Ohba but before Larue, or at some time after Larue but before Ohba. These two possibilities could be abbreviated as follows:

Fourth condition: O … P … L or L … P … O

Some things you can deduce right away: There are a number of things you can deduce right away about the order in which the six team members can dive. For example, from the first condition you can deduce that Weiss cannot dive first (since Treviño must dive at some time before Weiss) and Treviño cannot dive last (since Weiss must dive at some time after Treviño). You might summarize this deduction as:

W can't be 1st
T can't be last

The third condition allows you to deduce something more about when Treviño can dive. This condition tells you that Weiss cannot dive last. But if Weiss cannot dive last (i.e., sixth), then you know (given the first condition) that Treviño cannot dive fifth. So the first and third conditions together allow you to deduce that the latest Treviño can dive is fourth. You might summarize this deduction as:

T no later than 4th

Another thing you can deduce from the setup conditions is that the last team member to dive must be either Larue or Ohba. You already know from the first condition that the last team member to dive cannot be Treviño. You also know from the third condition that the last diver cannot be either Weiss or Zacny. Of the remaining three team members—Larue, Ohba, and Pei—you saw above in "What the setup tells you" that the fourth condition requires that Pei dive at some time between Larue and Ohba, so you know that Pei cannot be the last diver either. So, the only team members left who could dive last are Larue and Ohba. You might summarize this as:

Last diver must be L or O

Question 6

Overview: This question asks you to identify an acceptable ordering in which the six team members could dive. For this kind of question, where you're asked to identify a possible complete outcome, it is generally a good strategy to try to find the correct answer by using a process of elimination in which you proceed by considering each of the setup conditions in turn and checking to see whether that condition is satisfied in each answer choice. If a condition is violated in an answer choice, you can eliminate that answer choice from further consideration.

So, applying that strategy here, consider the first condition, which states that Treviño dives at some time before Weiss. A glance over the five answer choices shows that all of the answer choices except (C) satisfy this condition, so you can cross out (C) and eliminate it from further consideration. Next, consider the second condition, which says that Larue dives either first or last. Again, it is readily apparent that all of the remaining answer choices except one—answer choice (E)—satisfy this condition, so you can eliminate (E) from further consideration. Moving on to the third condition, which precludes both Weiss and Zacny from diving last, you can see that this condition is violated only in (A), so (A) can be eliminated from further consideration. Finally, the fourth condition tells you that Pei must dive at some time between Larue and Ohba. This condition is violated in (D), where Pei dives before both Ohba and Larue, so (D) can be eliminated from consideration (you may notice that (A), which you've already eliminated from consideration, also violates the fourth condition). You have now eliminated all but one answer choice, answer choice (B). So you can safely conclude that (B) is the correct answer.

The Correct Answer:

B   In the "Overview," you determined by a process of elimination that the correct answer is (B). The ordering in (B) is a possible ordering because it satisfies all of the setup conditions: Treviño dives at some time before Weiss, Larue dives first, neither Weiss nor Zacny dives last, and Pei dives before Ohba but not before Larue (that is, Pei dives in between Larue and Ohba).

The Incorrect Answer Choices:

A, C, D, E As shown in the "Overview," each of these answer choices violates at least one of the conditions in the setup: (A) violates both the third and fourth conditions, (C) violates the first condition, (D) violates the fourth condition, and (E) violates the second condition.

- *Difficulty Level: 1*

Question 7

Overview: When answering a question like this one, which asks you to identify the answer choice that must be true on the basis of the setup alone, it is generally a good idea to first look over the answer choices to see if you can identify the correct answer based on what you already know. In this case, you can see that the correct answer must be (D). This is because you determined in "Some things you can deduce right away" that Treviño can dive no later than fourth. And if Treviño can dive no later than fourth, that means that at least two team members must dive after Treviño (the fifth and sixth divers). Thus, you can safely select (D) as the correct answer without even considering the other answer choices.

The Correct Answer:

D As you saw in the "Overview," it must be the case that at least two of the team members dive after Treviño. This is because, as you deduced in "Some things you can deduce right away," the latest Treviño can dive is fourth.

The Incorrect Answer Choices:

A, C The following is an acceptable ordering that demonstrates that neither (A) nor (C) must be true. In this ordering, Larue dives last, so it is not the case that at least two team members must dive after Larue; and Pei dives fifth, so it is not the case that at least two team members must dive after Pei.

$\underline{1}$	$\underline{2}$	$\underline{3}$	$\underline{4}$	$\underline{5}$	$\underline{6}$
O	T	Z	W	P	L

B, E The following is an acceptable ordering that demonstrates that neither (B) nor (E) must be true. In this ordering, Ohba dives last, so it is not the case that at least two team members must dive after Ohba; and Weiss dives fifth, so it is not the case that at least two team members must dive after Weiss.

$\underline{1}$	$\underline{2}$	$\underline{3}$	$\underline{4}$	$\underline{5}$	$\underline{6}$
L	Z	T	P	W	O

- *Difficulty Level: 2*

Question 8

What you should keep in mind for this question: Be careful to note that this question asks you identify the answer choice that **cannot** be true if Larue dives from the plane last. This means that all of the incorrect answer choices will be statements that **can** be true if Larue is the last to dive.

Overview: This question tells you to suppose that Larue dives last and then determine which of the answer choices **cannot** be true. When a question provides you with a supposition (here, the supposition that Larue dives last), it is typically a good idea to first use what you already know to see what you can determine about what an acceptable outcome will look like if that supposition holds. In this case, there isn't much you can determine about what an acceptable outcome will look like if Larue dives last. About the only thing you can determine is that if Larue dives last, then in order to satisfy the fourth condition, Ohba cannot dive fifth. This is because, as you saw in "What the setup tells you," the fourth condition requires that Pei dive at some time **between** Larue and Ohba. But note that although this is about the only thing you can deduce about an ordering in which Larue dives last, it is enough to identify (C) as the correct answer.

The Correct Answer:

C As you saw in the "Overview," if Larue dives last, then it cannot be true that Ohba dives fifth. This is because if Ohba dives fifth and Larue dives sixth (last), there is no way for the fourth condition to be satisfied; that is, there is no way that Pei can dive at some time between Larue and Ohba.

The Incorrect Answer Choices:

A Below is an acceptable ordering in which Larue dives last (the supposition of the question) and Treviño dives fourth. So, (A) cannot be the correct answer.

1	2	3	4	5	6
O	P	Z	T	W	L

B, D The acceptable ordering below demonstrates that both (B) and (D) can be true if Larue dives last: Weiss can dive fourth, and Pei can dive fifth.

1	2	3	4	5	6
O	Z	T	W	P	L

So, neither (B) nor (D) can be the correct answer.

E The following is an acceptable ordering that demonstrates that (E) cannot be the correct answer, because it demonstrates that it is possible for Zacny to dive fifth when Larue dives last.

1	2	3	4	5	6
O	T	P	W	Z	L

- *Difficulty Level: 2*

Question 9

What you should keep in mind for this question: Like the preceding question, this question asks you to identify the answer choice that **cannot** be true—that is, the answer choice that must be **false**—when the supposition introduced by the question holds. This means that all of the **incorrect** answer choices will be statements that **can** be true when this supposition holds.

Overview: This question asks you to identify the answer choice that must be false if Zacny dives immediately after Weiss. What can you determine about what an acceptable outcome will look like if Zacny dives immediately after Weiss? Well, one thing you can determine is that Weiss and Zacny cannot be the first and second divers, respectively. This is because you determined in "Some things you can deduce right away" that Weiss cannot dive first. You can also determine that Weiss and Zacny cannot be the fifth and sixth divers, respectively, because the third condition precludes Zacny from diving last. This means that if Zacny dives immediately after Weiss, then Weiss and Zacny must dive second and third, third and fourth, or fourth and fifth, respectively. You also know that in each case Treviño must dive at some time before Weiss, given the first condition. So this means that any acceptable ordering in which Zacny dives immediately after Weiss will conform with one of the following three general scenarios:

Scenario 1: 1 2 3 4 5 6
             T W Z

Scenario 2: 1 2 3 4 5 6
                    W Z
           |_T_|

Scenario 3: 1 2 3 4 5 6
                       W Z
           |___T___|

A quick glance at the answer choices at this point shows that you cannot yet identify the correct answer nor can you rule any of the answer choices out. Based on the scenarios above, it looks like the answer choices that mention Treviño, Weiss, or Zacny—namely, (B), (C), and (E)—probably can be true, but you cannot know this for sure until you've determined for each of these answer choices that you can come up with a **complete** ordering in which that answer choice is true and in which Zacny dives immediately after Weiss. Nevertheless, since it looks like (B), (C), and (E) are all answer choices that probably can be true, and since you are looking for the answer choice that must be false, you might save some time by checking answer choices (A) and (D) first to see if

you can identify one of these answer choices as being the one that must be false.

The Correct Answer:

D If Zacny dives immediately after Weiss, then it must be false that Pei dives fourth. As you saw in the "Overview," there are three general scenarios under which the supposition introduced by the question holds. Of these, only Scenario 1 has an open fourth position:

Scenario 1: 1 2 3 4 5 6
                T W Z

It is impossible, however, for Pei to fill this position. This is because, as you saw in "What the setup tells you," the fourth condition requires that Pei dive sometime in between Larue and Ohba. There is no way to complete the above scenario in such a way that this condition is satisfied and Pei dives fourth.

The Incorrect Answer Choices:

A, B Below is an acceptable ordering that establishes that both (A) and (B) can be true if Zacny dives immediately after Weiss:

1 2 3 4 5 6
L P T W Z O

In this ordering, Larue dives first, so (A) cannot be the correct answer. And Treviño dives third, so (B) also cannot be the correct answer.

C The following is an acceptable ordering that establishes that Zacny can dive third if Zacny dives immediately after Weiss:

1 2 3 4 5 6
T W Z O P L

Thus, (C) cannot be the correct answer.

E The following is an acceptable ordering that establishes that Zacny can dive fourth if Zacny dives immediately after Weiss:

1 2 3 4 5 6
O T W Z P L

Thus, (E) cannot be the correct answer.

- *Difficulty Level: 3*

Question 10

What you should keep in mind for this question: Like the previous two questions, this question asks you to identify the answer choice that **cannot** be true when the supposition introduced by the question holds. All of the **incorrect** answer choices will be statements that **can** be true in that case.

Overview: This question asks you to identify the answer choice that **cannot** be true if Treviño dives from the plane immediately after Larue. As with most questions that introduce a supposition, a good first step in answering this question is to see what you can determine about what an acceptable ordering will look like if the supposition introduced by the question is true. In this case, you know that if Treviño dives **after** Larue, then Larue cannot dive last. And if Larue cannot dive last, then you know that Ohba must dive last. This is because, as you deduced in "Some things you can deduce right away," the last diver must be either Larue or Ohba. A check of the answer choices shows that you can now identify the correct answer: if Treviño dives immediately after Larue, then it **cannot** be true that Ohba dives from the plane third. Therefore, (A) must be the correct answer.

The Correct Answer:

A   As you saw in the "Overview," if Treviño dives immediately after Larue, then it **cannot** be true that Ohba dives from the plane third. This is because if Treviño dives after Larue, then Ohba **must** dive last.

The Incorrect Answer Choices:

B, D   The following is an acceptable ordering in which Treviño dives immediately after Larue and in which Weiss dives third and Pei dives fourth, thus demonstrating that both (B) and (D) **can** be true when the supposition introduced by the question holds. Thus, neither (B) nor (D) can be the correct answer.

1	2	3	4	5	6
L	T	W	P	Z	O

C, E   The following is an acceptable ordering in which Treviño dives immediately after Larue and in which Zacny dives third and Weiss dives fourth, thus demonstrating that both (C) and (E) **can** be true when the supposition introduced by the question holds. Thus neither (C) nor (E) can be the correct answer.

1	2	3	4	5	6
L	T	Z	W	P	O

- *Difficulty Level: 2*

Questions 11–17

What the setup tells you: This group of questions has to do with the order in which six different vehicles are serviced during a single week, Monday through Saturday. Exactly one of the vehicles is serviced each day, and the task is to determine which vehicle is serviced on which day. The five setup conditions tell you something about the order in which the vehicles are serviced relative to one another. The first condition requires that at least one vehicle be serviced later than the hatchback. In effect, this means that the hatchback cannot be serviced on the last day, Saturday:

H cannot be serviced on Saturday.

The second condition tells you that the van is serviced earlier than the roadster, which in turn is serviced earlier than the hatchback. This condition can be represented as follows, with the dots indicating where other vehicles can intervene in the sequence:

V ... R ... H

The third condition tells you that the pickup is serviced consecutively with either the van or the sedan, but not with both. In other words, the third condition gives you a requirement:

PV, VP, PS, or SP

along with the following prohibition:

not SPV and not VPS

The fourth condition tells you that the sedan is serviced earlier than the pickup or earlier than the limousine, but not earlier than both of them. From this, you can infer that if the sedan is not serviced earlier than the pickup then it must be serviced at some time **after** the pickup. And if the sedan is not serviced earlier than the limousine, then it must be serviced at some time **after** the limousine. So from the fourth condition you can infer that in any acceptable outcome, the relative ordering of the limousine, the pickup, and the sedan must be either one of the following:

P ... S ... L or L ... S ... P

Some things you can deduce right away: Taken together, the first and second conditions tell you something about the days of the week on which the van, the roadster, and the hatchback can be serviced. The second condition says that the van must be serviced earlier than both the roadster and the hatchback, and

the first condition says that the hatchback must be serviced earlier than at least one other vehicle. So you can deduce that there must be at least three vehicles serviced later than the van. This means that, of the six days from Monday to Saturday, you know that the van cannot be serviced on Thursday, Friday, or Saturday. Similar inferences can be made for the roadster and the hatchback. Because the van is serviced before the roadster, you know that the roadster cannot be serviced on Monday. And because at least two vehicles are serviced after the roadster (the hatchback and at least one other vehicle), you know that the roadster also cannot be serviced on either Friday or Saturday. As for the hatchback, in order for both the van and the roadster to be serviced before the hatchback, the hatchback cannot be serviced on either Monday or Tuesday. And, as you already noted in "What the setup tells you," the hatchback also cannot be serviced on Saturday.

These observations can be summed up as follows:

The van cannot be serviced on Thursday, Friday, or Saturday.

The roadster cannot be serviced on Monday, Friday, or Saturday.

The hatchback cannot be serviced on Monday, Tuesday, or Saturday.

You can make some further inferences about which vehicles can be serviced on the first day, Monday, and on the last day, Saturday. You have just determined that neither the roadster nor the hatchback can be serviced on Monday, and earlier in "What the setup tells you," you noted that the fourth condition requires that the sedan be serviced later than at least one other vehicle (either the limousine or the pickup). So the sedan is another vehicle that can't be serviced on Monday. By process of elimination, this leaves just three vehicles that can be serviced on Monday: the limousine, the pickup, and the van. Similarly, you've already noted that the van, the roadster, and the hatchback cannot be serviced on Saturday. And because the sedan must be serviced before at least one other vehicle (either the limousine or the pickup), it cannot be serviced on Saturday either. This leaves just the limousine or the pickup for Saturday. So your inferences regarding the first and last days of the schedule are as follows:

The vehicle serviced on Monday must be the limousine, the pickup, or the van.

The vehicle serviced on Saturday must be the limousine or the pickup.

Question 11

Overview: This question asks you to identify the one answer choice that contains an acceptable schedule for the six vehicles. You will probably make the most efficient use of your time by considering the setup conditions one by one, and then eliminating as you go along any answer choices that violate that condition.

The Correct Answer:

B Answer choice (B) satisfies all the requirements of the setup. The hatchback has a vehicle serviced after it, the roadster is serviced later than the van and earlier than the hatchback, the pickup and the sedan are serviced on consecutive days (while the pickup and the van are not), and the sedan is serviced earlier in the week than the limousine (but not earlier than the pickup).

The Incorrect Answer Choices:

A The second condition requires both that the van be serviced before the roadster and that the roadster be serviced before the hatchback. In (A), the first part of this condition is satisfied but not the second part. While the van is serviced before the roadster, the roadster is not serviced before the hatchback. So (A) violates the second condition.

C The first condition requires that at least one vehicle be serviced later than the hatchback. But in (C) the hatchback is serviced on Saturday, and because Saturday is the last day of the schedule there are no vehicles serviced after the hatchback. So (C) violates the first condition.

D In (D), the pickup is serviced on Wednesday, consecutive with the roadster on Tuesday and the hatchback on Thursday. But the third condition requires that the pickup be consecutive with either the van or the sedan. Since the pickup is consecutive with neither one, (D) violates the third condition.

E The fourth condition requires that the sedan be serviced earlier than the pickup or the limousine, but not both. Answer choice (E) violates the fourth condition because in (E) the sedan is serviced earlier than both the pickup and the limousine.

- *Difficulty Level: 1*

Question 12

What you should keep in mind for this question: For this question, your task is to identify a vehicle that **cannot** be serviced on Thursday. This means that each of the incorrect answer choices will be a vehicle that **can** be serviced on Thursday.

Overview: The question asks you to identify a vehicle that can't be serviced on Thursday. Recall that in "Some things you can deduce right away" you made some inferences about particular days of the week on which certain vehicles cannot be serviced, so you should check to see whether any of those inferences can be used here. You've already determined that the van cannot be serviced on Thursday. At this point, you should quickly check the answer choices to see whether the van is included among them. The van appears in answer choice (E). So, (E) is the correct answer.

The Correct Answer:

E In "Some things you can deduce right away," you made the inference that the van can't be serviced on Thursday. The second condition requires that the van be serviced before two other vehicles—the roadster and the hatchback. The hatchback in turn must be serviced before at least one other vehicle, as required by the first condition. Because there must be at least three other vehicles serviced later than the van, you know that the van can be serviced no later than Wednesday in order to leave Thursday, Friday, and Saturday for these other vehicles. This rules out Thursday as a possibility for the van, so (E) is the correct answer.

The Incorrect Answer Choices:

A Answer choice (A) is incorrect because the hatchback **can** be serviced on Thursday. Here is an acceptable schedule in which all of the requirements of the setup are met and in which the hatchback is serviced on Thursday:

M	T	W	T	F	S
V	P	R	H	S	L

B Answer choice (B) is incorrect because the limousine **can** be serviced on Thursday. Here is an acceptable schedule in which all of the requirements of the setup are met and in which the limousine is serviced on Thursday:

M	T	W	T	F	S
V	R	H	L	S	P

C Answer choice (C) is incorrect because the pickup **can** be serviced on Thursday. Here is an acceptable schedule in which all of the requirements of the setup are met and in which the pickup is serviced on Thursday:

M	T	W	T	F	S
V	R	H	P	S	L

D Answer choice (D) is incorrect because the sedan **can** be serviced on Thursday. Here is an acceptable schedule in which all of the requirements of the setup are met and in which the sedan is serviced on Thursday:

M	T	W	T	F	S
V	R	P	S	H	L

- *Difficulty Level: 4*

Question 13

Overview: This question starts out with a supposition about Monday—it asks you to suppose that neither the pickup nor the limousine is serviced on Monday. The task here is to determine what **must** be true in that case. The incorrect answer choices will all be things that either can't be true or don't have to be true. In "Some things you can deduce right away," you discovered that there are only three vehicles that can be serviced on Monday—the limousine, the pickup, and the van. Since in this question you are supposing that neither the limousine nor the pickup is serviced on Monday, this leaves only the van for that day. Scanning the answer choices, you see that the inference you are looking for is given in answer choice (C): The van is serviced on Monday. At this point, you should choose (C) as your answer and move on.

The Correct Answer:

C In "Some things you can deduce right away," you noted that the only vehicles that can be serviced on Monday are the limousine, the pickup, and the van. The supposition of this question is that neither the limousine nor the pickup is serviced on Monday, so you can conclude that it must be the van that is serviced on Monday. Answer choice (C) is something that must be true given the supposition of the question, so it is the correct answer.

The Incorrect Answer Choices:

A Although the hatchback and the limousine could be serviced on consecutive days if neither the limousine nor the pickup is serviced on Monday, they don't have to be. Here is an acceptable schedule in which the supposition of the question is met and all the setup conditions are met, but in which the hatchback and the limousine are not serviced on consecutive days:

M	T	W	T	F	S
V	L	R	H	S	P

B   Although the hatchback and the sedan could be serviced on consecutive days if neither the limousine nor the pickup is serviced on Monday, they don't have to be. Here is an acceptable schedule in which the supposition of the question is met and all the setup conditions are met, but in which the hatchback and the sedan are not serviced on consecutive days:

M	T	W	T	F	S
V	R	H	P	S	L

D   Although the limousine could be serviced on Saturday if neither the limousine nor the pickup is serviced on Monday, it doesn't have to be. The acceptable schedule given above for (A) is one in which the supposition of the question is met and all the setup conditions are met, but in which the limousine is not serviced on Saturday.

E   Although the pickup could be serviced on Saturday if neither the limousine nor the pickup is serviced on Monday, it doesn't have to be. The acceptable schedule given above for (B) is one in which the supposition of the question is met and all the setup conditions are met, but in which the pickup is not serviced on Saturday.

- *Difficulty Level: 3*

Question 14

What you should keep in mind for this question: This question starts with the supposition that the limousine is not serviced on Saturday and then asks you to identify the one answer choice that **cannot** be true in that case. The incorrect answer choices will all be things that **can** be true if the limousine is not serviced on Saturday.

Overview: In this question, you are to suppose that the limousine is not serviced on Saturday. At the end of "Some things you can deduce right away," you made some observations about Saturday, namely, that only the limousine or the pickup can be serviced on that day. So you know that if the limousine is not serviced on Saturday, then the vehicle serviced on Saturday must be the pickup. The third condition requires that the pickup be consecutive with either the sedan or the van, so one of these will have to be serviced on Friday. In "Some things you can deduce right away," you noted that the van can't be serviced on Friday. So it must be the sedan that is serviced on Friday, consecutive with the pickup:

M	T	W	T	F	S
				S	P

At this point, with a quick scan of the answer choices you will see that (E) mentions the sedan. Answer choice (E) says that the sedan is serviced on Wednesday, which cannot be true, since Friday is the day on which the sedan must be serviced. Since (E) **cannot** be true, it is the correct answer.

The Correct Answer:

E   As discussed in the "Overview" for this question, the sedan must be serviced on Friday if the limousine is not serviced on Saturday. This answer choice, which says that the sedan is serviced on Wednesday, is the correct answer because it cannot be true.

The Incorrect Answer Choices:

A, D   Here is an acceptable schedule in which the limousine is not serviced on Saturday and the setup conditions are met, and in which the limousine is serviced on Monday and the roadster is serviced on Wednesday:

M	T	W	T	F	S
L	V	R	H	S	P

Thus, both (A) and (D) **can** be true when the limousine is not serviced on Saturday, so neither of these answer choices can be the correct answer.

B, C Here is an acceptable schedule in which the limousine is not serviced on Saturday and the setup conditions are met, and in which the roadster is serviced on Tuesday and the hatchback is serviced on Wednesday:

<u>M</u>	<u>T</u>	<u>W</u>	<u>T</u>	<u>F</u>	<u>S</u>
V	R	H	L	S	P

Thus, both (B) and (C) **can** be true when the limousine is not serviced on Saturday, so neither of these answer choices can be the correct answer.

- *Difficulty Level: 5*

Question 15

Overview: The supposition of this question is that the sedan is serviced earlier in the week than the pickup, and the task is to identify an answer choice that can be true in that case. The incorrect answer choices will all be things that cannot be true. The supposition here is about the sedan and the pickup. In "Some things you can deduce right away," you observed in connection with the fourth condition that if the sedan is serviced earlier than the pickup, then the limousine must be serviced earlier than the sedan:

L ... S ... P

And if the limousine must be serviced earlier than the sedan, then you know that the pickup must be serviced on Saturday. This is because, as you previously determined in "Some things you can deduce right away," the vehicle serviced on Saturday must be either the limousine or the pickup. But if the limousine must be serviced earlier than another vehicle, then it cannot be the vehicle serviced on Saturday, leaving the pickup as the only vehicle that can be serviced on this day:

<u>M</u>	<u>T</u>	<u>W</u>	<u>T</u>	<u>F</u>	<u>S</u>
_	_	_	_	_	P

Now, what else can you determine about what an acceptable outcome will look like if the sedan is serviced earlier in the week than the pickup? Well, you can determine that the vehicle serviced on Friday must be the sedan. This is because you know from the third condition that the pickup must be serviced consecutively with either the van or the sedan, so one of these vehicles must be the vehicle serviced on Friday. However, you also know from the first condition that the van cannot be serviced on Friday, leaving the sedan as the only vehicle that can be serviced on this day:

<u>M</u>	<u>T</u>	<u>W</u>	<u>T</u>	<u>F</u>	<u>S</u>
_	_	_	_	S	P

At this point, since you know that the sedan and the pickup must be serviced on Friday and Saturday, respectively, you can quickly scan the answer choices for any that mention the sedan, the pickup, Friday, or Saturday. Answer choice (B) mentions the sedan, answer choice (D) mentions Friday, and answer choice (E) mentions Saturday. Notice that you can rule out all three of these answer choices because each one of them contradicts what you have just established—that the sedan is serviced on Friday and the pickup is serviced on Saturday.

The Correct Answer:

A   If the sedan is serviced earlier in the week than the pickup, then it could be true that the limousine is serviced on Wednesday, as the following acceptable ordering demonstrates:

M	T	W	T	F	S
V	R	L	H	S	P

So (A) is thus the correct answer.

The Incorrect Answer Choices:

B, D, E   In the "Overview," you determined that if the sedan is serviced earlier in the week than the pickup, then the sedan must be serviced on Friday and the pickup must be serviced on Saturday. Answer choice (B) cannot be true, because it says that the sedan is serviced on Wednesday (rather than Friday). Answer choice (D) cannot be true, because it says that the hatchback (rather than the sedan) is serviced on Friday. And answer choice (E) cannot be true, because it says that the limousine (rather than the pickup) is serviced on Saturday.

C   In the "Overview," you determined that if the sedan is serviced earlier in the week than the pickup, then the sedan must be serviced on Friday and the pickup must be serviced on Saturday.

M	T	W	T	F	S
–	–	–	–	S	P

Given this, it is impossible for the van to be serviced on Wednesday. This is because the first condition requires that the van be serviced before both the roadster and hatchback, but there are not enough available days to accommodate these two vehicles after Wednesday.

■ *Difficulty Level: 5*

Question 16

Overview: The supposition of this question is that the limousine is serviced on Saturday, and the question asks you to identify the answer choice that must be true in that case. The incorrect answer choices will be things that either cannot be true or need not be true. If the limousine is serviced on Saturday, then all of the other vehicles—including the sedan—are serviced earlier than the limousine. This is important to note because, as you observed in "What the setup tells you," the fourth condition tells you that if the sedan is serviced earlier than the limousine, then the pickup must be serviced earlier than the sedan. This is what (B) says. So (B) must be true and it is the correct answer.

The Correct Answer:

B   The supposition of the question is that the limousine is serviced on Saturday. As discussed in the "Overview," if the limousine is serviced on Saturday, then the sedan must be serviced earlier than the limousine. And if the sedan is serviced earlier than the limousine, then by the fourth condition the pickup must be serviced earlier than the sedan. Answer choice (B) says that the pickup is serviced earlier than the sedan, so it is the correct answer.

The Incorrect Answer Choices:

A, C, E   The following is an acceptable outcome in which the requirements of the setup are met and the supposition of the question is met, but in which the pickup is **not** serviced earlier in the week than the roadster (contrary to (A)), the sedan is **not** serviced earlier in the week than the roadster (contrary to (C)), and the roadster and the hatchback are **not** serviced on consecutive days (contrary to (E)):

M	T	W	T	F	S
V	R	P	S	H	L

Because (A), (C), and (E) need not be true, all three are incorrect answer choices.

D The following is an acceptable outcome in which the requirements of the setup are met and the supposition of the question is met, but in which the hatchback and the limousine are **not** serviced on consecutive days (contrary to (D)):

M	T	W	T	F	S
P	V	R	H	S	L

Because (D) need not be true, it is an incorrect answer choice.

- *Difficulty Level: 4*

Question 17

What you should keep in mind for this question: This question asks you to identify an acceptable schedule for Tuesday, Wednesday, and Friday. Notice that Thursday is not included in this partial schedule, so the days in question do not represent an unbroken sequence.

Overview: As with most questions that ask you what could be true on the basis of the setup alone, a good first step is to see whether you can identify the correct answer or at least eliminate one or more incorrect answers based on what you already know. In this case, however, it is certainly not obvious that any of the answer choices can be quickly identified as either correct or incorrect. So, a reasonable approach to answering this question would be to go through the answer choices one by one until you've found the one that could be true.

You might notice, however, that four of the answer choices—(A), (C), (D), and (E)—include the limousine. One thing you know regarding the limousine is that if the limousine is not serviced on Saturday, then the pickup must be serviced on Saturday (see "Some things you can deduce right away"). So, the only way that any one of these four answer choices could be correct is if the pickup is serviced on Saturday. This observation enables you to eliminate (A) right away since in this option the pickup is serviced on Tuesday. What about answer choices (C), (D), and (E)? Consider the following partial scenarios:

	M	T	W	T	F	S
(C)	_	S	L	_	H	**P**
(D)	_	V	L	_	H	**P**
(E)	_	V	R	_	L	**P**

Looking over the above partial scenarios, you will notice that each one of them violates the third condition, which requires that the pickup be serviced consecutively with either the sedan or the van. Thus, all three of these answer choices, in addition to (A), can be ruled out, leaving answer choice (B) as the only remaining possibility.

The Correct Answer:

B Here is an acceptable outcome that demonstrates that the vehicles serviced on Tuesday, Wednesday, and Friday could be (in that order) the pickup, the roadster, and the hatchback:

M	T	W	T	F	S
V	P	R	S	H	L

The Incorrect Answer Choices:

A, C, D, E As discussed in the "Overview," none of these answer choices can be true. In each case, it is impossible to come up with an acceptable complete scenario in which the listed vehicles are serviced on Tuesday, Wednesday, and Friday.

■ *Difficulty Level: 5*

Questions 18–23

What the setup tells you: This group of questions concerns a group of onlookers trying to guess the color of each of six balls that a street entertainer has placed in six boxes stacked one on top of another. The boxes are consecutively numbered 1 to 6, from the lowest box to the highest box, and there is a single ball in each of the boxes. Each ball is either green, red, or white. Your task is to determine the possible arrangement of the balls, given three conditions. First, there are more red balls than white balls. Second, there is a green ball in a box somewhere lower in the stack than any box containing a red ball. Third, there is a white ball that is in a box immediately below a box containing a green ball.

Some things you can deduce right away: Before you consider any of the questions, there are some important things that you can deduce right away about how many balls there could possibly be of each color. Suppose there is one white ball. Since there are six balls altogether, this would leave five remaining balls. Since there are more red balls than white balls, this means that there must be no fewer than two red balls. If there are two red, that leaves three that are green. If there are three red, that leaves two that are green. And if there are four red, that leaves one that is green. (Note that there cannot be five red balls, since there must be a green ball immediately above the one white ball.)

Now suppose there are two white balls, leaving four remaining balls. Since there are more red balls than white balls, there can be no fewer than three red balls. And it turns out that the only possibility in this case is that there are exactly three red balls; otherwise, there could be no green ball and you know that there is a green ball in a box immediately above a box containing a white ball.

Notice that there can't be more than two white balls. If there were three white balls, there would be only three balls remaining. But in that case, it would be impossible to have more red balls than white balls. (And likewise, of course, having four, five, or six white balls would also violate the condition concerning the relative number of white balls and red balls.)

All of this can be summarized as follows, where W represents white, R represents red, and G represents green:

1W, 2R, 3G

1W, 3R, 2G

1W, 4R, 1G

2W, 3R, 1G

These are the only possible color distributions for the balls.

Question 18

Overview: In this question you are asked to suppose that there are exactly two white balls and to identify a box that could then contain a green ball. As you saw in "Some things you can deduce right away," if there are two white balls then there must be three red balls and only one green ball. So now you've narrowed the task to identifying where that one green ball could be. Since one of the setup conditions specifies that a white ball is in a box immediately below a green ball, you know that the one green ball must be immediately above a white ball. So right away you've eliminated answer choice (A), since the one green ball cannot be in box 1, the lowest box.

None of the available answer choices is box 2, so you don't need to check that. But could the green ball be in box 3? If the one green ball is in box 3, then there must be a white ball in the box immediately below it, box 2:[41]

1	2	3	4	5	6
–	W	G	–	–	–

Now all you need to do is determine whether there is an acceptable color distribution in which there are two white balls, one of which is in box 2, one green ball, which is on box 3, and three red balls. And in fact there is:

1	2	3	4	5	6
W	W	G	R	R	R

At this point, you've determined that answer choice (B) is correct. If you were taking the actual test, you could select this answer choice and move on to the next question. There's no need for you to examine the other answer choices.

The Correct Answer:

B As you saw in the "Overview," if there are two white balls then there can be only one green ball. That green ball can be in box 3, with a white ball in box 1 and red balls in boxes 4, 5, and 6. So the correct answer is (B).

---

[41] In the diagrams here we'll represent the stack horizontally rather than vertically. This might also be a good approach for you during the test if you come upon a similar sort of scenario.

The Incorrect Answer Choices:

A As you saw in the "Overview," since the one green ball must be immediately above a white ball, the green ball can't be in box 1. So (A) is incorrect.

C, D, E As mentioned in the "Overview" (and in "Some things you can deduce right away"), if there are exactly two white balls then there must be one green ball and three red balls. None of the three red balls can be any lower than that one green ball (to satisfy the second setup condition), and so the highest box the green ball could possibly be in is box 3. So answer choices (C), (D), and (E) are all incorrect.

- *Difficulty Level: 3*

Question 19

Overview: In this question you are asked to suppose that there are green balls in boxes 5 and 6, and in that case to identify what could be true.

1	2	3	4	5	6
–	–	–	–	G	G

In order for there to be green balls in these boxes, there must be at least two green balls. You can tell right away that there can't be exactly two green balls. If there were, there would be no way to conform to the second setup condition, which specifies that there is a box containing a green ball that is lower than any box containing a red ball. So suppose instead that there are three green balls. As you saw in "Some things you can deduce right away," in this case there would have to be one white ball and two red balls. The one white ball could be in box 4 (the box immediately below box 5, which contains a green ball), with a green ball in box 1 and red balls in boxes 2 and 3:

1	2	3	4	5	6
G	R	R	W	G	G

Alternatively, the white ball could be in a box immediately below the box containing the green ball that isn't in either box 5 or box 6. That green ball has to be in a box that is below any box containing a red ball. In order for that to be the case, the white ball would have to be in box 1 with a green ball in box 2 and red balls in boxes 3 and 4:

1	2	3	4	5	6
W	G	R	R	G	G

The Correct Answer:

C One good approach here is to quickly scan through the answer choices to see if there is a choice that clearly conforms with either of the two acceptable arrangements. Upon doing this, you can see that (C) is the correct answer: a white ball can be in box 1.

The Incorrect Answer Choices:

A, B, D, E If when you're taking the actual test you identified (C) as the correct answer, there's no reason to consider any of the other answer choices. But to be thorough here, let's take a brief look at these choices, which can all be ruled out because none of them is consistent with either of the acceptable arrangements identified in the "Overview." Answer choice (A) can be ruled out because there can't be a red ball in box 1. Answer choice (B) can be ruled out because although there's an arrangement in which there's a red ball in box 2 and there's an arrangement in which there's a red ball in box 4, there's no arrangement in which there's a red ball in both box 2 and box 4. Choices (D) and (E) can be ruled out because there can't be a white ball in either box 2 or box 3. So none of these choices is the correct answer.

- *Difficulty Level: 4*

Question 20

Overview: In this question your task is to determine which box must contain a ball that is the same color as some other ball in the stack of boxes. Because the question contains no additional supposition, it concerns all possible arrangements of the balls that conform to the information given in the setup.

   At first this might seem like a daunting task, especially if you haven't already made any deductions that are directly relevant to the question. You might find, though, that a good approach here is to try to eliminate the incorrect answer choices; the remaining choice will be the correct answer.

The Incorrect Answer Choices:

A Because this question asks what box **must** contain a ball that is the same color as some other ball, you can eliminate an answer choice if there is an acceptable arrangement for which that answer choice is false. Answer choice (A) can be eliminated because there are acceptable arrangements in which box 2 contains a ball that is not the same color as any other ball in the stack of boxes. Here's an example:

1	2	3	4	5	6
W	G	R	R	R	R

So (A) is incorrect.

B Similarly, (B) can be eliminated because there are acceptable arrangements in which box 3 contains a ball that is not the same color as any other of the balls, such as this:

1	2	3	4	5	6
W	W	G	R	R	R

So (B) is incorrect.

C Answer choice (C) can also be eliminated. Here's an example of an acceptable arrangement in which box 4 contains a ball that is not the same color as any other of the balls:

1	2	3	4	5	6
G	R	R	W	G	G

So (C) is incorrect.

D And answer choice (D) can be eliminated. Here's an example of an acceptable arrangement in which box 5 contains a ball that is not the same color as any other of the balls:

1	2	3	4	5	6
G	R	R	R	W	G

So (D) is also incorrect.

The Correct Answer:

E Since you've eliminated four of the five answer choices, the remaining answer choice must be the correct answer. If you were actually taking the test, you probably would not want to use up time in verifying that (E) is correct. For thoroughness here, though, let's check to be sure that box 6 must contain a ball that is the same color as the ball in some other box in the stack.

In "Some things you can deduce right away," you saw that there can be no fewer than two red balls, so if there is a red ball in box 6 there must be a red ball in at least one other box. Suppose there were a green ball in box 6. In that case, there would have to be a green ball in at least one other box, since there must be a green ball in a box that is lower in the stack than any box containing a red ball. Now suppose there were a white ball in box 6. In that case, there would have to be a white ball in at least one other box, since there must be a white ball in a box immediately below a box that contains a green ball. So whatever the color of the ball in box 6, there must be another box that contains a ball of that same color. Answer choice (E) is therefore correct.

- *Difficulty Level: 5*

Tip: In answering questions that ask what must be true, you can sometimes approach the question more efficiently by trying to rule out the incorrect answer choices. To use this approach, scan the answer choices quickly to see if there are any you can eliminate right away. If you can't eliminate a particular answer choice right away, don't jump to the conclusion that that has to be the right answer (since it might be that you simply haven't considered all of the relevant inferences needed to eliminate that choice). If you can't quickly eliminate an answer choice, move on to the next choice and then if you need to you can return to the skipped choice later.

Remember that if you succeed in eliminating four of the five answer choices, the remaining choice must be the right answer, so in that case you can simply choose that one remaining answer choice and you're done.

Question 21

Overview: In this question your task is to determine what **must** be true based solely on the information given in the setup. As was the case with question 20, this might initially seem rather daunting. Once again, you might find that a good approach here is to try to eliminate the incorrect answer choices; the remaining choice will be the correct answer.

The Incorrect Answer Choices:

B Must it be true that there is a green ball in a box that is higher than box 4? No, here is an acceptable arrangement in which there are no green balls higher than box 4:

1	2	3	4	5	6
W	G	G	G	R	R

Since (B) doesn't have to be true, it's not the correct answer.

C Must it be true that there is a red ball in a box that is lower than box 4? No, the acceptable arrangement we just looked at for (B) has no red balls lower than box 4, so (C) is not the correct answer.

D Must it be true that there is a red ball in a box that is higher than box 4? No, here is an acceptable arrangement in which there are no red balls higher than box 4:

1	2	3	4	5	6
W	G	R	R	G	G

Since (D) doesn't have to be true, it's not the correct answer.

E Must it be true that there is a white ball in a box that is lower than box 4? No, here is an acceptable arrangement in which there are no white balls lower than box 4:

1	2	3	4	5	6
G	R	R	R	W	G

Since (E) doesn't have to be true, it's not the correct answer.

The Correct Answer:

A Since you've eliminated four of the five answer choices, the remaining answer choice must be the correct answer. If you were actually taking the test, you probably would not want to use up time in verifying that (A) is correct. For thoroughness here, though, let's check to be sure that there must be a green ball in a box lower than box 4.

Suppose that there are no green balls in boxes 1, 2, and 3. The second setup condition specifies that there is a green ball in a lower box than any box containing a red ball. And as you saw in "Some things you can deduce right away," there can be no fewer than two red balls. So box 4 would have to contain a green ball and boxes 5 and 6 would have to contain red balls:

1	2	3	4	5	6
–	–	–	G	R	R

But then what color would the balls have to be in boxes 1, 2, and 3? You're supposing that none of them is green. And none of them can be red, since a red ball can only be in a box that is higher than a green ball. And if there are only two red balls then there can't be three white balls (to conform to the first condition). So it's impossible for there to be no green balls in boxes 1, 2, and 3. This amounts to saying that it must be true that there is a green ball in a box that is lower than box 4. So (A) is the correct answer.

- *Difficulty Level: 5*

Question 22

Overview: For this question, you are to suppose that there are red balls in boxes 2 and 3. The question asks you what could be true in that case. One thing you know right away is that box 1 must contain a green ball, since the second setup condition specifies that there is a box containing a green ball that is lower than any box containing a red ball:

1	2	3	4	5	6
G	R	R	_	_	_

You also know that there must be at least one other green ball, since the third setup condition specifies that there is a white ball that is immediately below a box containing a green ball. Thus, so far there are two possibilities:

1	2	3	4	5	6
G	R	R	W	G	_

1	2	3	4	5	6
G	R	R	_	W	G

Since there must be more red balls than white balls, the remaining ball in either of these possible arrangements can't be white. That remaining ball could be either green or red:

1	2	3	4	5	6
G	R	R	W	G	G/R

1	2	3	4	5	6
G	R	R	G/R	W	G

The Correct Answer:

C A quick scan of the answer choices reveals (C) to be the correct answer. As you saw in the "Overview," the ball in box 4 can be any of the three colors, and so it could be true that the ball in box 4 is green.

The Incorrect Answer Choices:

A, B You determined in the "Overview" that the ball in box 1 has to be green, so neither of these two answer choices is correct.

D As seen in the "Overview," the ball in box 5 can only be either green or white, so this answer choice is incorrect.

E As seen in the "Overview," the ball in box 6 can only be either green or red, so this answer choice is incorrect.

■ *Difficulty Level: 4*

Question 23

Overview: For this question, you are to suppose that boxes 2, 3, and 4 all contain balls that are the same color as each other. The question asks what must be true in that case.

You know from "Some things you can deduce right away" that there can never be more than two white balls, so the balls in boxes 2, 3, and 4 can either all be red or all be green.

In working out the solution to question 22 you saw that if there are red balls in boxes 2, 3, and 4, there must be green balls in boxes 1 and 2 and a white ball in box 5. So the only possible arrangement when boxes 2, 3, and 4 are all red is this:

1	2	3	4	5	6
G	R	R	R	W	G

Now suppose the balls in boxes 2, 3, and 4 are all green. Since there can't be more than three green balls (see "Some things you can deduce right away") and there has to be a white ball in a box immediately below a box containing a green ball, the ball in box 1 must be white. And since there must be more red balls than white balls, the two remaining balls must both be red. So the only possible arrangement when the balls in boxes 2, 3, and 4 are all green is this:

1	2	3	4	5	6
W	G	G	G	R	R

The Correct Answer:

D To find what must be true, examine the two possible arrangements that were found in the "Overview" and ask yourself what is common to both of them. Right away you can see that in both cases there is only one white ball. Scanning the answer choices, you see that this is stated in (D), and so this is the correct answer.

The Incorrect Answer Choices:

A, B It can be true that there are exactly two boxes containing green balls, but it's also possible to have exactly three boxes containing green balls. So neither (A) nor (B) is correct.

C It can be true that there are exactly three boxes that contain a red ball, but it's also possible to have exactly two boxes containing red balls. So (C) is incorrect.

E It can never be true that when the balls in boxes 2, 3, and 4 are all the same color, there are exactly two boxes that contain a white ball. So (E) is incorrect.

- *Difficulty Level: 5*

Question 1

Overview: The commentator discusses a train wreck that occurred because the engineer's knee accidentally hit a fuel shutdown switch. The locomotive manufacturer (Acme Engines) says that it's not liable because it did not realize that the knee-level switches were a safety hazard. However, Acme spent $500,000 relocating these switches in newer locomotives. Acme claims this was done merely because engineers had complained that the switches were inconvenient, but the commentator claims that it is unlikely that Acme would have spent this much money just because of inconvenience. The commentator then concludes that Acme should be held liable for the wreck. You are asked to identify the function of the statement that Acme spent $500,000 relocating knee-level switches in the commentator's argument.

The Correct Answer:

E The argument's conclusion is that Acme should be held liable for the wreck. To establish this conclusion, the argument needs to challenge Acme's claim that it did not realize the knee-level switches were a safety hazard. The argument does this by making the point that Acme spent $500,000 replacing these switches in newer locomotives. Acme gives an explanation for why they spent this money (mere convenience), but the argument dismisses this explanation as unlikely. Thus, the fact that Acme spent $500,000 relocating the switches is put forward as an indication that Acme had been aware of the dangers of these switches before the wreck occurred.

The Incorrect Answer Choices:

A The argument seeks to establish that Acme should be held liable for the wreck. To do this, it is not necessary to prove that the engineer was not at all responsible for the wreck. There can be multiple factors contributing to a wreck, and more than one party may be held liable.

B There is no indication in the argument that the wreck would still have occurred even if the older locomotives had been remodeled. In fact, given the argument, there's a strong reason to believe that, contrary to the claim made in (B), the wreck might not have occurred if Acme had remodeled the older locomotives by relocating the knee-level switches.

C The passage makes it clear that the wreck occurred because the engineer lost control of the train when his knee hit the switch. There's no need for an additional explanation, nor would any additional explanation be provided by the point that Acme spent $500,000 relocating the switches in newer locomotives.

D There is no indication in the argument that the knee-level switches in the older locomotives were not hazardous. In fact, given the argument, it seems clear that, contrary to the claim made in (D), the knee-level switches were hazardous, and that Acme was aware of this fact before the wreck occurred.

- *Difficulty Level: 1*

Question 2

Overview: The artist presents an argument generalizing from almost everyone the artist knows to draw a conclusion about almost everyone in the country. The premise of the artist's argument is that almost everyone the artist knows hopes someday to be able to make a living as an artist. The conclusion of the argument is that almost everyone in the country really wants to be an artist, even if they can't fully make a living at it. You are asked to identify a flaw in the artist's argument.

The Correct Answer:

D The only support offered for the conclusion is a statement about people that the artist knows. However, we have no reason to think that this represents people in the country as a whole; in fact, it could be that the people the artist knows include an unusually high proportion of other artists. Without further information about people the artist knows or people in the country as a whole, the sample that the conclusion is based on should not be expected to accurately represent people in the country as a whole, so the conclusion is not well supported.

The Incorrect Answer Choices:

A The argument has a single premise, which does not presuppose the truth of the conclusion. The premise is that everyone the artist knows wants someday to be able to make a living as an artist. That permits us to conclude that those people want to be artists, but it is not enough to conclude, nor does it presuppose, that most people in the country want to be artists.

B The argument seems to presume that what is true of most people the artist knows is true of most people in the country as a whole. But it does not presume anything about what is true of each person in the country. In particular, it doesn't presume that what holds true of each person in the country holds true of the country's population as a whole. Thus (B) does not characterize a flaw of the argument.

C The argument does not claim that the view it is defending is widely held. So (C) does not describe what the argument actually does and therefore cannot correctly characterize how the argument is flawed.

E The artist concludes that almost everyone in the country wants to be an artist from the premise that almost everyone the artist knows wants to be able to make a living as an artist. Although the artist thereby infers that people want to be artists from the fact that they want to make a living as artists, the argument doesn't fail to make a needed distinction here. Rather than failing to distinguish wanting to be an artist with making a living as an artist, it explicitly points out that being an artist is not the same thing as making a living as an artist.

- *Difficulty Level: 1*

Question 3

Overview: The passage says that the qwerty keyboard is the standard keyboard. If the Dvorak keyboard were the standard, typists would type faster. But the passage says that it's not practical to switch to the Dvorak keyboard because the costs of switching (time, money, and frustration) outweigh the advantages of faster typing. You are asked to identify a proposition that is illustrated by the passage.

The Correct Answer:

E The passage claims that it is not practical to replace the qwerty keyboard with the Dvorak keyboard, even though the Dvorak keyboard is claimed to be superior to the qwerty keyboard in terms of typing speed, and is not claimed to be inferior to the qwerty keyboard in any inherent way. Instead, the considerations in favor of keeping the qwerty keyboard as standard all derive from the fact that the qwerty keyboard is already in wide use—namely, there would be significant costs to switching. So the passage illustrates the proposition that the fact that a standard is already in wide use can be a crucial factor in making it a more practical choice than an alternative.

The Incorrect Answer Choices:

A The passage does not give any indication of the accuracy produced by the qwerty keyboard or the Dvorak keyboard. Thus, the situation described in the passage does not illustrate any tradeoff between speed and accuracy.

B In the situation described in the passage, people settled on a standard (the qwerty keyboard) that was less efficient in terms of typing speed than at least one of the alternatives.

C The passage says that it's not practical to switch to the Dvorak keyboard because of the costs in terms of time, money, and frustration. Some of the frustration might be the result of people disliking change, but time and money are independent of people's dislike of change. So the passage does not illustrate the proposition that people often remain with an entrenched standard just because they dislike change. Further, the passage is not directly concerned with why people do or do not remain with an entrenched standard. Rather, it is concerned with whether they should.

D The passage references an emotional cost of changing to the Dvorak keyboard (frustration) and suggests that there is a complicated mix of financial considerations at play. (The passage claims there will be a financial cost associated with switching from the qwerty keyboard, but also claims that there will be benefits, presumably including financial benefits, that would be gained by faster typing.) Thus, it is inaccurate to claim that the situation described in the passage illustrates a simple case of an emotional cost outweighing financial considerations.

- *Difficulty Level: 1*

Question 4

Overview: The dialogue is about species conservation and the fact that one protected species, mountain lions, is preying on another, bighorn sheep. Sam says that we should let nature take its course, that is, humans should not intervene to protect bighorn sheep from mountain lions. Meli says that we should do whatever is necessary to ensure the survival of the sheep, even if that means limiting the mountain lion population. Your task is to identify a statement that Sam and Meli disagree over.

The Correct Answer:

A As mentioned in the "Overview," Sam says that humans should not intervene to protect bighorn sheep from mountain lions. Meli says that we must do what we can to ensure the survival of bighorn sheep even if we have to limit the mountain lion population. So Meli clearly believes that humans should intervene to protect bighorn sheep from mountain lions if doing so will help ensure the bighorns' survival.

The Incorrect Answer Choices:

B Meli clearly thinks that limiting the mountain lion population is justified if it will help ensure the survival of the bighorn sheep species, so Meli seems committed to the principle that the preservation of a species takes precedence over the fate of a few individuals, at least as it applies to mountain lions and bighorn sheep. But it is not clear that Sam disagrees with this principle, in general or in this particular instance. Sam's opposition to human intervention to save the bighorn would not have to proceed from rejecting this principle; Sam might just think that our hands are tied by the protected species designations, or that a protected species is too fragile for us to put it at risk with our intervention.

C As explained in the discussion of (A), Sam and Meli disagree about whether humans should intervene to save bighorn sheep, not about the relative ease of saving one species over the other. Also, (C) makes a broad claim about predatory and prey species in general. Since Sam and Meli discuss only two particular species, we don't know whether they would agree about the statement in (C).

D The passage says that mountain lions are protected, but there is no indication that either Sam or Meli thinks that the species is close to extinction, or that either one of them thinks that human intervention would push mountain lions to extinction.

E Meli suggests that we might have to limit the mountain lion population in order to ensure that bighorn sheep survive. But nothing in her statement indicates that she thinks it will be necessary to do so. So it's not clear whether Meli agrees with (E). Also, it's not clear whether Sam agrees or disagrees with (E). Sam says only that we should let nature take its course while hoping the bighorns survive, which suggests that Sam thinks that they may or may not survive in that case.

- *Difficulty Level: 1*

Question 5

Overview: The parent maintains that pushing very young children into rigorous study in an effort to increase national economic competitiveness does more harm than good. The parent claims that young students need curricula that address their special developmental needs. Rigorous work in primary school produces only short-term gains and may cause young children to burn out on schoolwork. Your task is to determine what can be inferred from the parent's claims.

The Correct Answer:

D The parent claims that young students need curricula that address their special developmental needs, and suggests that rigorous work in primary school is not the kind of curriculum that will do so. In the early years of primary school, rigorous work produces only short-term gains and may lead to burnout. If this is true, then it follows that a primary school student's long-term developmental needs are not adequately addressed by a curriculum of rigorous study.

The Incorrect Answer Choices:

A The parent says that rigorous work in secondary school makes sense, but does not say anything about how much rigorous work is currently included in the secondary school curriculum. Thus, nothing can be inferred about whether this curriculum should include more rigorous study than it now does.

B The parent is concerned with the developmental needs of early primary school students. The parent suggests that rigorous work is more suited to the developmental needs of secondary school students than it is to primary school students, but does not say anything about the curriculum currently in place in secondary schools. Thus, nothing can be inferred about whether the developmental needs of secondary school students are or are not currently being addressed.

C The parent opposes one way of trying to make the nation more competitive—namely, pushing very young children into rigorous study. However, in opposing this, the parent is not committing to any claim about what conditions must be met in order for the country to be competitive. Specifically, it cannot be inferred from anything the parent says that, as (C) would have it, being able to meet the developmental needs of all of the nation's students is required in order for the nation to be competitive. It is entirely possible for the country to be competitive even if it fails to meet the developmental needs of some of its students.

E Nothing the parent says allows us to infer that the country cannot be economically competitive without encouraging rigorous study in the early years of primary school. In fact, the parent suggests that doing so may ultimately work against the country, and would thus potentially stand in the way of making the country more competitive.

- *Difficulty Level: 1*

Question 6

Overview: The argument is concerned with evaluations of bus drivers that are conducted by supervisors riding with the drivers and the issue of whether the supervisors' presence affects drivers' performance. The argument uses the premise that the supervisor's presence affects every driver's performance to conclude that those drivers who perform best with a supervisor present will probably also be the drivers who perform best in general. Your task is to identify an assumption that is required by this argument.

The Correct Answer:

D To see that (D) is a required assumption, suppose that it is false. If some drivers' performance is affected by the presence of a supervisor much more than the performance of other drivers, then we can't conclude that the drivers performing best with a supervisor aboard will likely also perform best under normal conditions. For example, suppose that Sharon is an excellent driver under normal conditions and that Betty is merely good, but that Sharon completely falls apart with a supervisor present and becomes a terrible driver, whereas Betty is only slightly affected and still drives pretty well. In such a case, the better driver under normal circumstances (Sharon) is not the better driver with a supervisor on board. Thus, in order to reach its conclusion, the argument needs to assume that the drivers are each affected roughly equally by the presence of the supervisor.

The Incorrect Answer Choices:

A The argument does not need to assume that there's no other effective way to evaluate drivers' performance besides having a supervisor ride with them. The argument concludes only that having supervisors ride with drivers does not disqualify this method from being **an** effective way to evaluate them (to the extent that the best drivers when supervisors are present are probably also the best without supervisors). It does not conclude that there's no other effective way to evaluate them.

B The argument does not need to assume that the supervisors are excellent judges of drivers' performance. The argument concludes that those drivers performing best with a supervisor aboard · will likely also drive best under normal conditions. This conclusion about the drivers' actual performance under the two conditions does not require the supervisors to be excellent judges of drivers' performance.

C The argument doesn't need to assume that the presence of a supervisor makes the performance of most bus drivers slightly worse than it would otherwise be. The argument succeeds even if the presence of a supervisor actually improves each driver's performance or makes it significantly worse. For example, if the presence of a supervisor reduces Sharon's performance from excellent to mediocre and reduces Carl's performance from mediocre to terrible, then the driver performing better with a supervisor aboard (Sharon) is also the better driver under normal conditions.

E The argument accepts the bus drivers' claim that the supervisors' presence affects their performance. But this does not mean that the drivers can deliver accurate assessments of their overall driving performance; it just means that they can tell that their performance is affected by the presence of a supervisor onboard.

- *Difficulty Level: 2*

Question 7

Overview: The passage says that economic growth accelerates demand from businesses for the development of new technologies. However, an acceleration of technological change can cause both businesses that supply new technologies and those that buy new technologies to fail. The question asks you to identify the statement that is most strongly supported by the passage.

The Correct Answer:

B The passage says that economic growth accelerates business demand for the development of new technologies. It's reasonable to assume that demand for the development of new technologies will lead to the development of new technologies, i.e., that it will lead to technological change. So, economic growth accelerates technological change. The passage also says that an acceleration of technological change can cause businesses that supply new technologies to fail. This means that economic growth can cause businesses that supply new technologies to fail. So it's clear that businesses that supply new technologies may not always benefit from economic growth.

The Incorrect Answer Choices:

A The passage says that accelerated technological change can cause some businesses supplying new technologies to fail. It does not say anything about the possibility (much less the likelihood) that such businesses can prosper during times of accelerated technological change.

C The passage implies that economic growth can accelerate the development of new technologies. But it does not say anything to indicate the reverse—namely, that the development of new technologies can accelerate economic growth.

D The passage says that accelerated technological change, which is associated with economic growth, can cause businesses that adopt new technologies to fail. It does not say anything about the possibility (much less the likelihood) that such businesses can prosper during times of economic growth.

E As discussed in the explanation of the correct answer, the passage implies that economic growth can cause some businesses of a particular kind (suppliers and buyers of new technology) to fail. But this does not imply anything about whether economic growth leads to an increase in business failures overall. Given everything stated in the passage, it is entirely possible that a lack of economic growth would cause a greater number of businesses to fail, and that economic growth thus leads to an overall reduction in business failures.

- *Difficulty Level: 1*

Question 8

Overview: The energy analyst says that during the heat wave, air conditioner use has overloaded the power grid, causing blackouts. Residents have been asked to reduce air conditioner use in their homes. However, the analyst says that even if they do this, blackouts will probably occur so long as the heat wave continues. There seems to be a discrepancy here insofar as air conditioner use is stated to be the cause of the blackouts, yet reducing air conditioner use in homes may not prevent the blackouts. You are asked to identify information that helps to resolve this discrepancy.

The Correct Answer:

B If most air conditioning is used to cool businesses and factories, then reducing air conditioner use in homes will not reduce electrical consumption that much. If air conditioner use by businesses and factories continues at its current level, the power grid might well continue to be overloaded. So (B) helps to resolve the discrepancy; it explains how reducing **home** air conditioner use can fail to eliminate the blackouts even though air conditioner use is what is overloading the power grid.

The Incorrect Answer Choices:

A Suppose there are other significant drains on the electrical system. In that case, a major reduction in electrical power use from any sector should reduce or eliminate the overload and thereby help prevent blackouts. So in particular, a reduction in air conditioner use should help prevent blackouts. It would be reasonable to expect that reducing air conditioner use to the level that is typical when there's not a heat wave should be enough to prevent blackouts even if other significant drains on the electrical system are not reduced. Yet the energy analyst asserts that it probably won't. Thus, the discrepancy remains even if there are other significant drains on the electrical system.

C The question asks us to find the best explanation for why, given that air conditioning use is what has overloaded the electrical system, a reduction in home air conditioner use will probably not reduce electricity consumption enough to prevent further blackouts if the heat wave continues. This is an apparent discrepancy between expectation and fact regarding the existing systems. Pointing out that air conditioning systems could be made more efficient with certain design modifications therefore doesn't help to resolve it.

D The energy analyst says that even if people do voluntarily reduce home air conditioner use, the blackouts will probably continue. Thus the claim that people are unlikely to voluntarily reduce home air conditioner use does not help to resolve the apparent discrepancy. To resolve the discrepancy, we need some reason to think that the blackouts will continue even if people do voluntarily reduce air conditioner use.

E We're trying to find the best explanation for why the blackouts will probably continue so long as the heat wave continues, even if people do reduce home air conditioner use. Even if the heat wave is expected to abate soon, or does abate soon, we will still have to explain that apparent discrepancy. A prediction of when the heat wave will abate doesn't help explain this discrepancy about what is going on during the heat wave.

- *Difficulty Level: 5*

Question 9

Overview: The argument discusses long-term and short-term relaxation training as treatments for anxiety. The premise of the passage's argument is that symptoms of anxiety decrease to a normal level within the short-term training time period, regardless of whether short-term or long-term training is used. The argument concludes that long-term training, which is generally more expensive, is unwarranted for most people. You are asked to identify the statement that most weakens this argument.

The Correct Answer:

C (C) says that people who get long-term training are much less likely to have recurrences. This means that long-term training has a clear advantage that becomes apparent only after the end of the short-term training period. So (C) weakens the argument, which infers that long-term training is unwarranted from the claim that short-term training is as effective as long-term training within the short-term training period.

The Incorrect Answer Choices:

A (A) suggests that for many people anxiety symptoms will decrease even without treatment. This suggests that both short-term and long-term training might be unwarranted. Thus, (A) does not weaken the argument that long-term training is unwarranted.

B The argument states that long-term training is generally more expensive than short-term training, but does not claim that it is always more expensive. As described in the "Overview," the argument regards long-term training and short-term training as equally effective. Since, in most cases, long-term training is more expensive than short-term training, the argument maintains that, in most cases, there is no warrant for choosing long-term rather than short-term training. The statement in (B) describes one condition under which short-term training might be more expensive than long-term training, but this statement does nothing to weaken the argument. The core idea put forward in the argument—why pay more for treatment that's no more effective?—is in no way weakened by (B).

D (D) says that the mere fact that a person thinks that a treatment will reduce anxiety tends to reduce anxiety. If anything, this provides a different avenue of support for the argument's conclusion. If the recipient's belief that the training is effective will make it effective, then any kind of training could be effective as long as the recipient believes that it will be. In that case, why choose the generally more expensive long-term training?

E (E) is not relevant to the argument. The argument is concerned only with the relative effectiveness of short-term and long-term training. The number or variety of techniques that they use to achieve their results do not affect the strength of the argument.

- *Difficulty Level: 1*

Question 10

Overview: The editorial says that many critics of consumerism claim that advertising persuades people that they need certain things when they really just want them. The editorial next says that this accusation rests on a fuzzy distinction between wants and needs and asserts that it's often impossible to determine whether something is just desirable or essential to happiness. The question asks you to identify the conclusion drawn in this argument.

The Correct Answer:

A The first sentence of the editorial presents an accusation that many critics of advertising make, that it persuades people that they need things that they merely desire. The rest of the editorial argues that this accusation rests on a fuzzy distinction. Note that this claim is supported by the statement in the last sentence of the editorial: the fact that it is often impossible to tell whether something is merely desirable or essential to happiness certainly provides reason to say that the distinction between wants and needs is fuzzy, and therefore that the critics' accusation against advertising rests on a fuzzy distinction between wants and needs. So (A) gives the conclusion drawn in the argument.

The Incorrect Answer Choices:

B (B) restates the first sentence of the editorial's argument. The first sentence asserts that many critics of consumerism make a certain accusation against advertisers and advertising. The rest of the editorial argues that this accusation rests on a fuzzy distinction. But nothing in the rest of the editorial is presented as supporting the claim that critics make the accusation; this claim is simply accepted as fact. So the first sentence does not express the conclusion of the argument.

C The editorial argues that a critique of advertising is based on a fuzzy distinction between wants and needs. But this does not necessarily mean that there's nothing wrong with advertising that tries to persuade people that they need certain consumer goods. It's just that whatever might be wrong with such advertising can't be that it tries to persuade people that they need things that they really just want.

D Given the editorial's points, it might be natural for the editorial writer to think that critics of consumerism fail to realize that certain things are essential to human happiness. But the argument does not anywhere state that any critics do fail to realize that. So (D) isn't a conclusion drawn in the argument.

E The argument tries to establish that one statement made by critics of consumerism rests on a fuzzy distinction. But it does not claim or suggest that critics of consumerism **often** use fuzzy distinctions to support their claims. Since (E) is not a statement made in the argument, it can't be the conclusion drawn in the argument.

- *Difficulty Level: 3*

Question 11

Overview: The argument in the passage begins with the premise that people who browse the web for medical information often can't distinguish scientifically valid information from quackery. It expands on this claim by explaining that quackery is frequently more appealing because it is more clearly written. The argument concludes that people who rely on the web when attempting to diagnose their medical conditions are likely to do themselves more harm than good. The question asks you to identify an assumption that the argument requires.

The Correct Answer:

B The argument's premises state that people who browse the web for medical information often cannot tell the difference between scientifically valid information and quackery and, in fact, are likely to be especially drawn to quackery. It follows from these premises that people who rely on the web when attempting to diagnose their medical condition will be likely to rely not only on scientifically valid information, but also on some amount of information that is quackery. However, this result alone does not establish the argument's conclusion—namely, that these people are likely to do themselves more harm than good. To establish this conclusion, we need the additional assumption that failing to rely exclusively on scientifically valid information is likely to be harmful. Thus, the argument requires the additional assumption that people who attempt to diagnose their medical conditions are likely to do themselves more harm than good unless they rely exclusively on scientifically valid information.

The Incorrect Answer Choices:

A The argument qualifies its conclusion by restricting it to people who rely on the web when attempting to diagnose their medical conditions. So the argument does not require any additional assumption about how typical such behavior is. Even if (A) were false, and most people who browse the web for medical information are not trying to diagnose their medical conditions, this would not stop the argument from drawing its conclusion about the minority of people who are attempting to diagnose their medical conditions.

C The argument drew a qualified conclusion about people relying on the web when attempting to diagnose their medical conditions—namely, that those people are likely to do themselves more harm than good. This allows that some people (perhaps those with a good deal of medical knowledge) may not do themselves any harm by relying on the web, but the argument in no way requires such an assumption. Even if (C) were false, so that even people with sufficient medical knowledge to discriminate between scientifically valid information and quackery will do themselves harm when relying on the web to diagnose their medical conditions, this would not threaten the argument's conclusion.

D The argument does not require the assumption stated in (D); it could be a strong argument even if (D) is false. Even if people don't explicitly assume that material that is not clearly written is not scientifically valid, they might just ignore such material. They might therefore tend to rely more on quackery (which the argument says is usually more clearly written).

E The argument does not need to assume that the **only** way people attempting to diagnose their medical conditions can do themselves more harm than good is by relying on quackery rather than scientifically valid information. There may be a number of possible ways such people could cause themselves harm. For example, they may rely exclusively on scientifically valid information but misunderstand or misapply that information. These possibilities do not threaten the argument's conclusion.

■ *Difficulty Level: 5*

Question 12

Overview: The argument says that adults try to toss balls slowly to young children to compensate for the child's limited coordination. But children have an easier time catching balls that are thrown faster. You are asked to identify a statement that helps to explain why this latter fact is true.

The Correct Answer:

A (A) says that balls that are thrown faster trigger regions in the brain that control the tracking of objects for self-defense. So the balls that are thrown faster would trigger these regions in the children's brains, which would help them track the balls so that they could catch them. This would explain why the children were better at catching balls that were thrown faster.

The Incorrect Answer Choices:

B (B) says that balls that are thrown slower tend to have a higher arc that makes it less likely that the ball will be obscured by the body of the person throwing it. But if slower balls are less obscured, they should be easier to catch than faster balls, not harder.

C Since (C) is about adults rather than children, it does not clearly help to explain why children have an easier time catching faster balls. Also, (C) says that adults find slower balls easier to catch, which is the opposite of what we are trying to explain in children.

D (D) says that children can throw balls more accurately when they throw fast. But we're trying to explain why children are better at catching faster balls. The fact that they are more accurate throwing fast balls doesn't seem to bear on that. So (D) has no evident relevance to what we're trying to explain.

E (E) says that there's a limit to how fast balls can be thrown before they become more difficult for children to catch. We want to explain why balls thrown faster are easier for children to catch than ones thrown slowly. It does not help to explain this to be told that extremely fast balls are harder to catch.

- *Difficulty Level: 1*

Question 13

Overview: The passage says that both a genetic profile and an fMRI can have information that a patient wants to keep private. Also, an fMRI of a brain has enough information about a patient's skull to create a recognizable image of the patient's face. In contrast, a genetic profile can be linked to a patient only by labels or records. You are asked to identify the statement that is most strongly supported by the passage.

The Correct Answer:

B The passage says that an fMRI of a brain contains enough information about a patient's skull to create a recognizable image of the patient's face, but a genetic profile can be linked to a patient only by labels or records. So an unlabeled fMRI might compromise patient privacy because someone could recognize the patient's face, but this could never happen with a genetic profile. Thus there are circumstances in which an fMRI could compromise patient privacy but a genetic profile would not.

The Incorrect Answer Choices:

A The passage does not support the idea that labeling fMRIs is not important at all. Even if labels are not absolutely necessary in order to match fMRIs to patients, it's likely that it would still be important for medical providers to apply labels to fMRIs.

C The passage says only that genetic profiles have information that patients want to keep private. It does not say anything about how great the risk is that such information won't be kept private.

D As far as the passage says, the only thing that the information in an fMRI of the brain has in common with the information in a genetic profile is that patients might want to keep both kinds of information private. But that doesn't tell us anything about how much the information overlaps.

E The passage states that both fMRIs and genetic profiles can contain information that a patient wishes to keep private. This does not tell us that patients think either form of information poses a threat to their privacy, but even if it did, the passage does not indicate anything about the relative degree of concern patients have about such threats.

- *Difficulty Level: 2*

Question 14

Overview: The council member proposes using an abandoned factory as an emergency shelter. The only premise of the council member's argument is that some other council members who think that the courthouse would be a better shelter site have not provided any evidence for that claim. The argument concludes that the factory would be a better shelter site than the courthouse. You are asked to identify a questionable technique used in the argument.

The Correct Answer:

B The argument concludes that the factory would be a better shelter site than the courthouse. The only premise offered in support of this conclusion is that the council members who think that the courthouse would be better have not provided any evidence for their view. So the argument concludes that the factory would be better simply because advocates of the opposing position have not adequately defended their view. This is questionable since the council member advocating for use of the abandoned factory likewise does not provide any evidence for his or her own view.

The Incorrect Answer Choices:

A (A) comes close to describing a questionable technique used in the argument, but it has things reversed: the council member who makes the argument in the passage asserts that a lack of evidence **for** a view (the view that the courthouse would be a better shelter site) is proof that it is **wrong**. This council member does conclude that a particular view is correct, namely, the view that the abandoned factory would be a better shelter than the courthouse. But contrary to (A), the council member does not argue for this view by asserting that it is proved correct by a lack of evidence against it.

C The council member who makes the argument does not engage in any sort of personal attack on the proponents of the courthouse. This council member just says that the courthouse proponents have not offered any evidence for their assertion.

D There's nothing in the argument to suggest that the council member who favors using the factory is appealing to fear. For example, the argument does not suggest that something terrible will happen if the factory isn't used as a shelter.

E The council member who favors using the factory does not attack any argument. Instead, this council member claims that the proponents of using the courthouse as a shelter have not even made an argument.

- *Difficulty Level: 2*

Question 15

Overview: The premise of the argument in the passage is that the Anthropology Department chair had told James that she endorsed his proposal, but only if the draft proposal she saw included all the recommendations James would ultimately make to the committee. If James's actual proposal to the committee included recommendations that were not in the draft, then the chair's endorsement is not assured. The argument concludes that it was misleading for James to tell the committee that the chair had endorsed his proposal.

Your task is to find an assumption that the argument relies on. One thing to notice is that there seems to be something missing that would justify the claim that James was somehow being misleading. Given the conditional nature of the chair's endorsement, it would only have been misleading for James to claim that the chair endorsed his proposal if the final proposal contained recommendations that were not in the draft.

The Correct Answer:

E To see that (E) is an assumption relied on by the argument, suppose that (E) is false and that the draft proposal did include all of the recommendations that wound up in the final proposal. In that case, there's no reason to think that the chair did not endorse it; she said that she would endorse the proposal as long as the draft had all of the recommendations that would be in the final proposal. So if (E) is false, there's no reason to conclude that James was misleading. Thus the argument needs to assume (E) in order to reach its conclusion.

The Incorrect Answer Choices:

A The argument does not rely on (A) since it is not concerned with whether the committee would be likely to implement James's recommendations.

B The argument does not need to assume that the chair would have opposed any recommendations other than those she had seen. The chair's endorsement was conditional on the final proposal not including any new recommendations. Even if (B) were false, and the chair would have been willing to accept some new recommendations if she had seen them, it would still be misleading for James to say that the chair had endorsed a proposal that contained new recommendations.

C If (C) were true, this could explain why James would have been motivated to tell the committee that the chair endorsed his proposal even if it wasn't true. However, the argument does not need to assume (C) in order to infer its conclusion. If the proposal James made to the committee included recommendations that were not in the draft proposal, then it was misleading for James to say that the chair endorsed his proposal. This would be true regardless of whether James thought that the committee would implement the proposed recommendations only if they believed that the chair had endorsed them.

D The argument does not need to assume that James thought that the chair would have endorsed his recommendations. If anything, there would be less reason to consider James's statement to the committee misleading if he thought that the chair would have endorsed his recommendations.

- *Difficulty Level: 2*

Question 16

Overview: One premise of the argument is that Travaillier, which has focused on air travelers, has recently hired people with experience in the bus tour industry and has been negotiating with bus companies that subcontract with bus tour providers. The argument also presents evidence that Travaillier's traditional consumers have not changed their vacation preferences. The argument concludes that Travaillier is trying to attract new customers. You are asked to identify additional information that most weakens the argument.

The Correct Answer:

E (E) says that Travaillier's consultants usually recommend that companies expand by introducing their current customers to new products and services. This suggests that Travaillier would be likely to try to expand by introducing its current customers, who travel primarily by air, to new services such as bus tours. This makes it less likely that Travaillier is trying to enlarge its consumer base by attracting new customers; it could just be trying to sell additional services to its current customers. So (E) seriously weakens the argument.

The Incorrect Answer Choices:

A (A) does not weaken the argument; instead it appears to strengthen it. If Travaillier has previously found it difficult to change its customers' vacation preferences, then it's not very likely that Travaillier would now be trying to sell bus tours to its traditional customers. Given the evidence that Travaillier is trying to get into the bus tour business, this suggests that Travaillier is trying to attract new customers.

B The fact that other travel companies have tried and failed to expand into the bus tour business does not significantly weaken the argument. For one thing, Travaillier management might believe that they can succeed where others have failed. They may have studied the mistakes made by those other companies and believe that they are more likely to succeed because they have learned what not to do. But more to the point, the fact that other travel companies have recently failed at what Travaillier is evidently trying to do has no discernible bearing on whether Travaillier is doing what it is doing in an attempt to enlarge its consumer base, or for other reasons, such as that given in (E).

C (C) does not weaken the argument. The fact that at least one of the new employees has also designed air travel vacation packages means that at least some of Travaillier's recent hiring indicates a continued focus on the company's air traveling customer base. That's not inconsistent with the possibility, indicated by Travaillier's other recent actions mentioned in the argument, that Travaillier is trying to move into the bus tour business with potentially new customers. In fact, this may support the argument's claim that Travaillier is trying to **enlarge** its consumer base, not just replace air travelers with bus travelers.

D The argument is concerned with Travaillier's business strategy. (D) does not affect the strength of the argument since we have no idea whether Travaillier has adopted or is adopting the strategy that (D) attributes to Travaillier's competitors.

- *Difficulty Level: 4*

Question 17

Overview: The educator gives an argument for the conclusion that traditional classroom education is ineffective. In support of that conclusion are two related claims about traditional education. First, the argument claims that traditional education is not a social process and only social processes can develop students' insights. Second, the argument claims that in the traditional classroom the teacher acts from outside the group and the interaction between teachers and students is rigid and artificial. You are asked to identify an assumption that will make the conclusion follow logically.

The Correct Answer:

D (D) says that education is not effective unless it leads to the development of insight. In other words, if education does not develop insight, then it is not effective. The argument claims that traditional education is not a social process and only social processes can develop students' insights, which implies that traditional education cannot develop students' insights. Together with (D), this implies the argument's conclusion: traditional education is not effective. So the conclusion follows logically if (D) is assumed.

The Incorrect Answer Choices:

A The argument does not make any claims about "genuine education," so there is no way the assumption stated in (A), together with the premises, could entail the argument's conclusion that traditional education is ineffective. Even if we equated genuine education with effective education, (A) would not guarantee that traditional education is ineffective. (A) would only ensure that the development of insight requires effective education, not that it is required for effective education.

B The passage states that in the traditional classroom, the interaction between teachers and students is rigid and artificial. (B) states that classroom education is effective if the interaction between teachers and students is neither rigid nor artificial. In other words, nonrigid and nonartificial interaction is guaranteed to produce effective education. But this does not entail the reverse. That is, (B) does not entail that rigid and artificial interaction is guaranteed to produce ineffective classroom education. Thus, even if (B) were true, it would not entail the argument's conclusion that traditional education is ineffective.

C The claim that all social processes involve interaction that is neither rigid nor artificial does not help establish the argument's conclusion. If anything, this claim establishes a connection between the educator's two claims about traditional education described in the "Overview." (C) could be the reason why traditional education, with its rigid and artificial interaction, is not truly a social process. But this does not speak to the effectiveness or ineffectiveness of traditional education. Thus, (C) does not help establish the conclusion drawn in the argument, that traditional education is ineffective.

E (E) tells us something about nontraditional classrooms. Since the argument's conclusion is about the ineffectiveness of traditional classroom education, (E) cannot help establish that conclusion.

- *Difficulty Level: 4*

Question 18

Overview: The argument begins with the premise that you can increase your chance of avoiding heart disease by avoiding fat in your diet. Moreover, you're less likely to eat fat if you avoid eating dairy. The argument concludes that you can increase your chance of maintaining good health by avoiding dairy. You are asked to identify a problem or weakness with the argument.

The Correct Answer:

A The argument's premises establish that eating dairy may have potentially negative consequences due to its stated link to the consumption of fat, and thus to heart disease. However, it is possible that dairy products are also healthful in some ways. In that case, eliminating dairy may have negative consequences, which could outweigh the negative consequences of eating dairy. So a problem with the argument is that it ignores the possibility that, even though eating dairy may have potentially negative consequences, eliminating dairy from your diet may also have negative consequences.

The Incorrect Answer Choices:

B The argument concludes that avoiding dairy increases the probability of maintaining good health. It does not conclude that avoiding dairy is the only way to maintain good health. Additionally, nothing in the argument suggests that avoiding fat in the diet is the only way to decrease the chance of heart disease or that avoiding dairy is the only way to decrease the chance of eating fat. Since the argument only claims that doing certain things will decrease the risk of certain occurrences, and not that they are the only ways to decrease that risk, it is not a problem or weakness of the argument that it fails to consider other ways of decreasing that risk.

C It is generally reasonable to try to eliminate factors that carry increased risks of negative consequences (unless there is reason to think that those factors also have good consequences or that there are substantial costs to eliminating those factors). So the argument does not need to provide justification for the claim that factors that carry increased risks of negative consequences ought to be eliminated. Therefore, its failure to provide such justification is not a weakness of the argument.

D While the evidence presented is not sufficient to establish the conclusion, it is at least relevant. The conclusion is about maintaining good health, and the first premise establishes that fat consumption is relevant to heart disease (which is in turn clearly relevant to health). The second premise establishes that consumption of dairy foods is relevant to consumption of fat.

E The argument's conclusion is that the probability of maintaining good health is increased by avoiding dairy foods. The argument does not conclude that one will necessarily maintain good health by avoiding dairy foods.

- *Difficulty Level: 4*

Question 19

Overview: The professor presents two arguments. The first argument is that since each momentary perception occurs from only one perspective, a person can't frame an accurate conception of the physical environment from just one perception. The second argument, which the professor states is similar, is that each history book reflects the biases of its author, so any one history book gives a distorted view. You are asked to identify how the overall argument (which encompasses both smaller arguments) proceeds.

The Correct Answer:

C The professor presents two arguments and clearly indicates that the second one resembles the first. The second argument might be controversial and thus in need of support; some people might believe that history can be objective. The first argument is presumptively uncontroversial. So it's reasonable to understand the overall argument as making a case for the conclusion of the second argument by showing its resemblance to the first argument, which is presumably cogent.

The Incorrect Answer Choices:

A If the professor were trying to show that one piece of reasoning is incorrect by comparing it with another flawed piece of reasoning, then the argument would need to proceed very differently than it does. The professor's overall argument would need to either use obviously flawed reasoning, indicate that the reasoning was flawed, or indicate that it is rejecting a conclusion. But it does none of these things: none of the reasoning is clearly and egregiously flawed, and the professor doesn't display a negative attitude toward either of the arguments or either of the conclusions drawn.

B If the professor were developing an argument along the lines described by (B), the argument would need to proceed very differently than it does. There would need to be some indication that the professor was supposing, for the sake of argument, that some claim was false. But there is no such indication in the argument. Furthermore, the professor does not describe any consequences as Difficulty Level: , and none of the consequences seem clearly absurd.

D The professor's overall argument draws a conclusion about one type of thing (history books) by comparing it (or more precisely, an argument about it) to something else. It does not consider only a single thing and compare its known characteristics to another, related characteristic.

E The professor's overall argument does not proceed by identifying a single type of human cognition and arguing that, since this type of cognition has been shown to be unreliable in one context, it must be unreliable in another context. The professor presents two arguments. While the first is arguably about a type of human cognition (momentary perception of one's environment) the second argument is clearly not. The second argument concerns history books. Even if we understand the second argument more broadly as being about the cognition of the history book's author, it is not the case that the conclusion of this argument follows from the unreliability of the author's momentary perceptions. Rather, the argument points to the biases and prejudices of the author as a source of unreliability.

- *Difficulty Level: 4*

Question 20

Overview: This question presents a passage with the following argument. In the past, most of the proposals endorsed by the Citizens League were passed by the city council; therefore, any future proposal endorsed by the Citizens League will probably be passed by the city council as well. The question asks you to determine which other argument has a pattern of reasoning that is most similar to the pattern of this argument.

Note that the argument generalizes from a premise about most things with a certain property that have been encountered in the past to a conclusion about anything with that property that will be encountered in the future.

The Correct Answer:

E The argument in (E) is about an archaeological site. It states that most stone artifacts found at the site in the past have been domestic tools. It concludes that if the next artifact found at the site is made of stone, then it will probably be a domestic tool. The premise of this argument is similar to that of the argument about proposals endorsed by the Citizens League, in that it makes a claim about most things with a certain property that have been encountered in the past. The conclusion is a conditional conclusion about the next artifact found at the site, that if it is stone, then it is probably a domestic tool.

On the face of it, this argument may not seem quite parallel to the pattern of reasoning of the argument about endorsed proposals, as it would if it concluded that any stone artifact found at the site in the future will probably be a domestic tool. But there is nothing special, according to the argument in (E), about the next artifact to be found at the site, as opposed to any future artifact to be found. The argument does not provide a reason to conclude anything about the very next artifact found, if it is stone, that doesn't apply equally to any other stone artifact found in the future. So the conclusion of the argument in (E) effectively amounts to the claim that any stone artifact found in the future will probably be a domestic tool. Therefore, despite superficial differences, the pattern of reasoning of the argument in (E) is very similar to that of the argument about endorsed proposals.

The Incorrect Answer Choices:

A The argument in (A) states that most of the Vasani grants awarded in previous years have gone to academic biologists. It concludes that if, in the next year, most of the grants are awarded to academics, most of these academic recipients will probably be biologists. The premise of this argument is similar to that of the argument about endorsed proposals, in that it makes a claim about most things with a certain property. For the pattern of reasoning of the argument to be similar to that of the argument about endorsed proposals, it would have to draw a conclusion close to the claim that any grants awarded next year (or in future years) will probably go to academic biologists. But the conclusion actually drawn by the argument in (A) is not at all similar to this claim. In fact, it is potentially incompatible with this claim: if the conditional supposition that most of the grants awarded next year will be awarded to academics were in fact false, the conclusion of the argument in (A) could still be true, but the claim that any grants awarded will probably go to academic biologists would be false. Thus, the pattern of reasoning of the argument in (A) diverges sharply from that of the argument about endorsed proposals, even though the two arguments have similar premises.

B The argument in (B) has a premise about individuals and draws a conclusion about a broader category, species. The argument about endorsed proposals does not draw a conclusion about a broader category on the basis of a premise about individuals. So the pattern of reasoning in (B) is not at all similar to that of the argument about endorsed proposals.

C The argument in (C) states that most editors who have worked for the local newspaper in the past were not sympathetic to local farmers. This premise is similar to that of the argument about endorsed proposals, in that it makes a claim about most things with a certain property. For its reasoning to be similar to that of the argument about endorsed proposals, the argument in (C) would have to draw a conclusion close to the claim that any editor hired in the future will probably not be sympathetic to local farmers. But instead it draws the very different conclusion that if the newspaper hires someone who is sympathetic to local farmers, that person will probably not be hired as an editor.

D The argument in (D) asserts that most entries received after the deadline for last year's contest were rejected by the judges. It concludes that the people who sent in those entries last year will probably send in their entries for this year **before** the deadline. For the argument in (D) to be similar to the endorsed proposals argument, it would have to conclude that any entry that will be received after the deadline this year will probably be rejected by the judges. So, although the premise of the argument in (D) is very similar to that of the argument about endorsed proposals, the pattern of reasoning is very different.

- *Difficulty Level: 4*

Question 21

Overview: The chemist's argument begins with the premise that the molecules of a certain weed-killer are always present in two forms, one of which kills weeds, the other of which has no effect on them. A result of this is that the effectiveness of the weed-killer is influenced by which form is more concentrated in the soil. This in turn varies a lot because local soil conditions usually favor the breakdown of one form or the other. The argument concludes that a lot of the data on the weed-killer's effects are probably misleading. You are asked to determine which statement most strengthens the argument.

The Correct Answer:

B The premises of the argument imply that the effectiveness of the weed killer varies widely because of the varying amounts of each form present in different soils. It is usually the case that one form of the weed-killer is much more concentrated than the other. (B) says that almost all of the data on the effects of the weed-killer come from lab studies where both forms are equally concentrated. This entails that much of the data is misleading because it does not concern the more typical cases where one form is much more concentrated than the other. Thus, (B) strengthens the chemist's argument.

The Incorrect Answer Choices:

A (A) makes a general claim about weed-killers whose molecules are present in two forms. The chemist's argument is about a specific weed-killer. Furthermore, the general claim made by (A) is something we already know is true of the specific weed-killer discussed by the chemist. Thus, (A) does not affect the strength of the argument.

C (C) says that the form of the weed-killer that kills weeds is more concentrated in most soils. By itself, this does not strengthen the argument because we don't know whether most of the data on the effects of the weed-killer come from an examination of this form.

D If the data on the effects of the weed-killer come from studies of the weed-killer under a variety of soil conditions similar to those where the weed-killer is normally applied, then we would expect the data to represent the actual variation in effectiveness pretty well. In other words, (D) weakens the argument; it provides reason to believe the near opposite of the argument's conclusion.

E (E) says that data on the weed-killer's effects that come from an examination of the effects of only one of the two forms will almost certainly be misleading. By itself, this does not strengthen the argument because we don't know that any of the data come from an examination of the effects of only one of the two forms.

- *Difficulty Level: 5*

Question 22

Overview: This question presents a principle and a conclusion, and asks you to identify a set of facts that, when combined with the principle, would allow the conclusion to be properly drawn. The principle has two parts: (1) if a police officer has an exemplary record, then that officer is eligible for a Mayor's Commendation, but not otherwise; (2) if an officer eligible for the award did something that exceeded what could be reasonably expected, and by that action saved a life, then the officer should receive the award. The conclusion is that Franklin should receive the award but Penn should not. In order to draw this conclusion, we must be able to infer both that Franklin should receive the award, and that Penn should not receive it.

Note that only part 1 of the principle, not part 2, can be used to definitively conclude that an officer should **not** receive the award. Part 2 says that if an eligible officer did something beyond normal expectations that saved a life, then that officer should receive the award. But part 2 does not say whether there is any other condition under which an officer can receive the award. In particular, it doesn't say whether an eligible officer could receive the award without doing something beyond normal expectations that saved a life. Part 1, on the other hand, has a "not otherwise" clause that means that only officers with exemplary records are eligible. Therefore, in order to conclude that Penn should **not** receive the award, we need facts that entail that Penn's record is not exemplary.

The Correct Answer:

A (A) says that Penn does not have an exemplary record, so part 1 of the principle entails that Penn is not eligible for the award, and thus should not receive it. (A) also says Franklin has an exemplary record, and so is eligible for the award. Moreover, Franklin did something that exceeded what could be reasonably expected and by that action saved a life. Therefore, applying part 2 of the principle, Franklin should get the award.

The Incorrect Answer Choices:

B (B) does not establish that Penn should not get the award. As discussed in the "Overview," only part 1 of the principle can be used to conclude that an officer should not get the award; the only way we can definitively conclude that an officer should not receive the award is if the officer doesn't have an exemplary record. But (B) says that Penn **does** have an exemplary record.

C (C) says that Franklin does not have an exemplary record. By part 1 of the principle, Franklin is not eligible for the award and so should not get it. Thus the conclusion cannot be drawn from the facts in (C).

D In order to establish that Franklin should get the award, we first need to establish that Franklin is eligible according to part 1 of the principle. (D) does not say that Franklin has an exemplary record, so we can't establish that Franklin is eligible. Also, (D) does not say that Penn does not have an exemplary record, so we can't conclude that Penn should not get the award.

E (E) does not establish that Franklin should get the award. It says that some of Franklin's actions have saved lives, and some of these actions have exceeded what could be reasonably expected. But it does not ensure that any of Franklin's actions that exceeded reasonable expectations were among the ones that saved lives; there may be no overlap. So we cannot use the principle to conclude that Franklin should receive the award. Furthermore, (E) does not establish that Penn should not get the award. As discussed in the "Overview," only part 1 of the principle can be used to conclude that an officer should not get the award; the only way we can definitively conclude that an officer should not receive the award is if the officer doesn't have an exemplary record. But (E) says that Penn **does** have an exemplary record.

- *Difficulty Level: 5*

Question 23

Overview: The essayist's argument begins with the premise that it's much less difficult to live an enjoyable life if you can make lifestyle choices that accord with your personal beliefs and then see those choices accepted by others. An additional premise is that it's possible to see your choices accepted by others if you choose friends and associates who share many of your personal beliefs. The argument concludes that no one should be denied the freedom to choose whom to associate with. The question asks you to identify a principle that helps to justify this argument.

The Correct Answer:

C A premise of the argument is that it's possible to see your lifestyle choices accepted by others if you choose friends and associates who share many of your personal beliefs. Thus, being able choose whom to associate with could enable you to see your lifestyle choices accepted by others. Given the first premise of the argument, this could make it much less difficult to live an enjoyable life. (C) says that if having a freedom could make it less difficult for someone to live an enjoyable life, then no one should be denied that freedom. Thus, (C) enables us to infer the argument's conclusion: no one should be denied the freedom to choose whom to associate with. (C) therefore clearly helps to justify the argument.

The Incorrect Answer Choices:

A The argument's conclusion concerns the freedom to choose whom to associate with. It's not clear how (A) could help us to infer this conclusion, since (A) concerns the freedom to make lifestyle choices that accord with their personal beliefs. It's possible that you could have the freedom to make lifestyle choices that accord with your personal beliefs even if you don't have the freedom to choose whom to associate with.

B The argument's conclusion is about allowing people to have a certain freedom. (B) is about how individuals should act (assuming they are free to act that way). There's no way to draw a conclusion about what freedoms people should be granted from a claim like (B) about how individuals should act. So (B) cannot help to justify the argument.

D The principle expressed by (D) is not strong enough to help justify the essayist's argument. The argument's conclusion is that no one should be denied the freedom to choose whom to associate with. This is a very broad conclusion, in two different ways. First, the essayist intends the conclusion to hold for **all** people, on the assumption that it is possible for people generally to find acceptance by choosing friends and associates who share their personal beliefs. Second, the essayist is advocating a freedom to actively take steps to choose one's associates. The principle in (D), by contrast, only applies to a particular range of people—namely, those whose enjoyment depends, at least in part, on friends and associates who share many of the same personal beliefs. Furthermore, (D) only claims that those people should not be deliberately prevented from having such friends and associates. That is, others should not actively take steps to prevent people from having certain friends and associates. This is not quite the same as saying people have a right to actively take steps to choose their friends and associates.

E It's not clear how (E) could help to justify the argument. (E) says that one may choose whom to associate with if doing so could make it easier to live an enjoyable life. But the conclusion of the argument is that **no one** should be denied the freedom to choose whom to associate with, even if choosing whom to associate with would not make it easier for everyone to live an enjoyable life. (Note that the passage doesn't give us any reason to think that choosing to associate with people who share your personal beliefs will make it easier to live an enjoyable life if your lifestyle choices don't accord with your personal beliefs.)

• *Difficulty Level: 5*

Question 24

Overview: The physician's argument has three premises: (1) the increased blood pressure that commonly accompanies aging often results from a calcium deficiency; (2) this calcium deficiency is frequently caused by a deficiency in the active form of vitamin D needed for absorption of calcium; and, (3) a daily glass of milk has enough calcium to make up for any calcium deficiency. The argument concludes that some older people can lower their blood pressure by drinking milk. You are asked to find an assumption that will enable the argument's conclusion to be properly drawn.

Note that the premises of the physician's argument do not ensure that the calcium in a glass of milk would be absorbed. This is pertinent since the second premise states that the calcium deficiency producing high blood pressure in many older people is frequently caused by a deficiency in the vitamin D needed to absorb calcium.

The Correct Answer:

A (A) says that milk has everything that the body of an older person needs to absorb the calcium it contains. Therefore, since milk has enough calcium to make up for any calcium deficiency, drinking milk should remedy the calcium deficiency that often produces high blood pressure in older people. We can conclude that older people who have high blood pressure due to a calcium deficiency can lower their blood pressure by drinking milk. Thus, the conclusion can be properly drawn if (A) is assumed.

The Incorrect Answer Choices:

B (B) gives us reason to believe that drinking milk is not likely to increase blood pressure. But we need some way to infer that, for older people with high blood pressure caused by a calcium deficiency, drinking milk will decrease blood pressure. As discussed in the "Overview," a statement ensuring that the calcium in milk will be absorbed would suffice to bridge that gap. The statement in (B) does nothing to bridge that gap.

C (C) states that a daily glass of milk will not contribute to or worsen a deficiency in the vitamin D required to absorb calcium. But that doesn't mean that it will help. Since a vitamin D deficiency is the only cause of calcium deficiency that is mentioned in the argument, and since (C), together with the premises, doesn't give us any reason to think that drinking milk will help remedy a vitamin D deficiency, the conclusion cannot be properly drawn even if (C) is assumed.

D (D) says that consuming high quantities of calcium together with the active form of vitamin D and other substances needed for absorption of calcium leads to normal blood pressure, from which we can conclude that it would remedy the rise in blood pressure that commonly accompanies aging. But (D) does not say that the active form of vitamin D and any other substances needed in order for the body to absorb calcium are included in a glass of milk. So (D) doesn't help us to infer that some older people can lower their blood pressure by drinking milk.

E Assuming (E), we can infer that in order to remedy the calcium deficiency that often produces a rise in blood pressure among older people, it is necessary to remedy the vitamin D deficiency that causes it. But this doesn't help us to infer that a glass of milk contains vitamin D in a form that would aid the absorption of calcium. So assuming (E) does not allow us to infer that drinking milk would help older people to counteract the rise in blood pressure that results from a calcium deficiency.

- *Difficulty Level: 5*

Question 25

Overview: The political philosopher's argument begins with the premise that in order for a system of taxation to be just, it must require that each person's contribution correspond directly to the benefit that person receives from society. The argument then states an additional premise that, for purposes of taxation, wealth is the most objective way to measure the benefit a person receives from society. The argument concludes that each person should be taxed in proportion to her or his income. You are asked to find an argument whose flawed reasoning is most similar to that in the political philosopher's argument.

It may not be immediately obvious that this reasoning is flawed. However, notice that in the course of the argument, the political philosopher moved from a claim about wealth to a claim about income. Wealth is the amount of money a person has at a specific time. Income is the amount of money that one receives over an interval of time. These are clearly different, and it is a reasoning flaw for the argument to draw a conclusion about taxing in proportion to income on the basis of a premise about wealth. We can think of income as the rate at which one accumulates wealth (ignoring expenditures). So an argument that made an inference from a claim regarding one quantity to a conclusion regarding the rate at which that quantity can be reached would contain flawed reasoning similar to that in the political philosopher's argument.

The Correct Answer:

A The argument in (A) moves from a claim about a car's speed to a conclusion about its ability to accelerate. Acceleration is the rate at which a car reaches a speed, just as income is the rate at which a person accumulates wealth. (A) is thus very similar in its flawed reasoning to the political philosopher's argument.

To spell this out, notice how closely the argument in (A) parallels that of the political philosopher. Both arguments have a premise that taxation should be proportional to the degree to which a particular condition (benefit, danger) holds. And both have another premise regarding the best (most objective, most reliable) measure (wealth, speed) of that condition. Finally, they both commit the same reasoning flaw by illegitimately drawing a conclusion that taxation should be proportional, not to that measure itself, but rather to that measure's rate of change (income, acceleration).

The Incorrect Answer Choices:

B   Like the political philosopher's argument, the argument in (B) starts with a claim that one thing should be proportional to another, and puts forward a measure of that second thing. Here, the claim is that autonomy should be granted in proportion to maturity, and that a certain psychological test was designed to measure maturity. However, unlike the philosopher's argument, (B) does not go on to draw a conclusion regarding that measure's rate of change. Instead, (B) draws a dubious conclusion regarding using a certain value of that measure as a threshold.

C   Like the political philosopher's argument, the argument in (C) starts with a premise that taxation should be proportional to something else. Here, the claim is that taxation should be proportional to the benefits received from government. However, unlike the philosopher's argument, (B) does not put forward any measure of those benefits, and thus does not commit the flaw found in the political philosopher's argument of illegitimately moving to a claim regarding a measure's rate of change. Instead, (C) uses an additional premise—namely, that large corporations receive certain benefits—to draw an unsupported conclusion—namely, that corporations should pay a greater share of their income in taxes than individuals. Since the additional premise does not establish that corporations receive greater benefits than individuals do, the argument in (C) contains a very different flaw than was found in the political philosopher's argument.

D   (D) does not contain flawed reasoning similar to that found in the political philosopher's argument. Instead of starting with some claim that one thing should be proportional to another, and then putting forward a measure of one of those things, (D) starts with two claims about what should be the case for certain individuals and then draws a dubious conclusion about placing taxes on certain activities.

E   Like the political philosopher's argument, the argument in (E) starts with a premise that one thing should be proportional to another. Here, the claim is that health care should be given in proportion to need. However, unlike the philosopher's argument, (E) does not put forward any measure of either of the things involved, and thus does not commit the flaw found in the political philosopher's argument of illegitimately moving to a claim regarding a measure's rate of change.

- *Difficulty Level: 5*

Question 26

Overview: The passage says that almost half of the city's residents believe that Mayor Walker is guilty of ethics violations. However, 52 percent of residents think his performance is good or excellent, and this is no lower than it was before he was accused of ethics violations. This is certainly surprising; one would think that being accused of ethics violations would be harmful to an elected official's reputation, particularly if almost half of the population thinks that the official is guilty. The question asks you to identify information that helps to explain why the proportion of the residents who view Walker's performance as good or excellent did not fall when the ethics allegations arose.

The Correct Answer:

A As mentioned in the "Overview," we would expect, when Walker was accused of ethics violations and almost half the city's residents came to believe that he is guilty, that many residents would downgrade their judgment of his performance to "poor," causing his overall performance ratings to fall. But that presupposes that a significant portion of the residents who came to believe he is guilty previously gave him good or excellent ratings. (A) asserts that almost everyone who thinks that Walker is guilty already thought that his performance was poor before the allegations arose. Thus, (A) takes away the grounds that would lead us to expect Walker's job performance ratings to fall when the ethics allegations arose.

The Incorrect Answer Choices:

B In light of the accusations against Walker, his opponents might look better by comparison. Thus, (B) states something that would not be surprising. But it does not help to explain why the percentage of residents who think his performance is good or excellent hasn't dropped since the accusations of ethics violations surfaced.

C The 20 percent of poll respondents who didn't know that Walker has been accused of ethics violations might be just as likely as ever to think that his performance is good or excellent. But what about the other 80 percent? Presumably fewer of them would now think that Walker's performance is good or excellent. So we still need to explain why the accusation of ethics violations hasn't reduced the number of people who think Walker's performance is good or excellent, particularly since almost half of city residents think he is guilty.

D Anticorruption groups would be likely to want to get rid of Walker and would thus be likely to support his opponent. Thus, (D) states something that would not be surprising. But (D) does not help to explain why the percentage of residents who think Walker's performance is good or excellent hasn't dropped since the accusations of ethics violations were made.

E (E) could explain why slightly over half of city residents don't believe that Walker is guilty. Nonetheless, given that almost half of city residents do think he's guilty, we need to explain why the percentage who think his performance is good or excellent hasn't dropped since the accusations of ethics violations arose. (E) does not help to explain that.

- *Difficulty Level: 5*

PREPTEST B, SECTION IV: READING COMPREHENSION

Questions 1–7

Synopsis: This passage discusses the concept of tradition and the role it has played in the application of certain United States federal laws in Alaska. The first paragraph notes that state and federal laws in the U.S. grant certain privileges and exemptions to individuals engaged in traditional activities. But the difficulty, the author says, is that "tradition" is rarely defined in the law, and this has led to problematic and inconsistent legal results.

The second paragraph states that a common idea associated with "tradition" in the law is that tradition is based on long-standing practice, where the continuity and regularity of a practice are part of what makes it long-standing. The application of this sense of "traditional" in particular has led to problems.

The final two paragraphs discuss two court cases that illustrate the passage's claim that the failure to define "tradition" has led to problems. The third paragraph describes the legal restrictions on hunting sea otters that were the subject of the cases. Hunting sea otters was first prohibited by the Fur Seal Treaty of 1910. The Marine Mammal Protection Act (MMPA) of 1972 continued this prohibition, but it also included an exemption that allowed Alaska Natives to use protected animals to create authentic native articles by means of traditional native handicrafts. The Fish and Wildlife Service (FWS) subsequently issued regulations that spelled out more specifically which native articles would be covered by the exemption. Items made from sea otter pelts were not covered, the FWS declared, because they had not been produced "within living memory."

The fourth paragraph then describes the court cases. In the first, the court upheld the FWS regulations that prohibited producing items from sea otter pelts. The second case overturned this prohibition, however. The court reconsidered what counted as traditional, holding that the FWS regulations were based on a strained interpretation of "traditional," and that the use of "living memory" as a criterion was too restrictive.

Question 1

The Correct Answer:

A As discussed in the "Synopsis," the main argument in the passage is that the failure to define "tradition" in the law has led to problematic and inconsistent legal results in Alaska. In making this argument, the passage discusses two cases involving indigenous use of sea otter pelts, stating that these cases illustrate the difficulties that can arise in the legal application of the concept of tradition. So (A), which says that two cases involving sea otter pelts illustrate the difficulties involved in applying the legal concept of tradition in Alaska, accurately expresses the main point of the passage.

The Incorrect Answer Choices:

B The last paragraph of the passage does say that the court challenged the idea that for an activity to be considered traditional it must have been regularly and continually practiced. But only one of the cases discussed in the last paragraph (the 1991 case) challenged this idea. The other case discussed in the last paragraph (the 1986 case) upheld the FWS's judgment that items made from sea otter pelts were not traditional because they had not been produced within living memory. So (B) does not accurately express anything actually said by the passage, and for that reason it cannot be the main point of the passage.

C The passage does not give us any indication that there has been a wave of lawsuits in response to changes in natural-resource and public-lands regulations. The passage discusses two cases involving indigenous use of sea otter pelts; nothing in the passage would suggest that these two were part of a "wave" of cases.

D The passage does discuss the court's review of the definition of **one** legal term, "traditional" (last paragraph). However, the passage does not discuss any concepts besides "traditional" whose definitions are being reviewed. In addition, the passage gives us no reason to think that the evidence presented in this case—testimony establishing that Alaska Natives had made many uses of sea otters before the occupation of the territory by Russia—was new evidence. This evidence may have been well known to historians, or to regulators of natural resources, before the court case. For these reasons, (D) does not accurately express the main point of the passage.

E Option (E) says that Alaska Natives are challenging "Alaskan state laws and U.S. Federal laws." But the passage does not discuss any laws of the state of Alaska that are being challenged by Alaska Natives, and it discusses only **one** U.S. federal law—the MMPA of 1972—that has been involved in a challenge by Alaska Natives. Moreover, the case in question did not actually challenge the MMPA itself. Rather, it challenged the way the FWS interpreted and enforced that law, and it sought to bring the FWS's interpretation into line with a more reasonable understanding of the law.

- *Difficulty Level: 3*

Question 2

The Correct Answer:

C According to the passage, the court held that it defies common sense to define "traditional" in the way that the FWS did (line 54). The assumption underlying this judgment is that the law should define "traditional" in a way that conforms to common sense; in other words, that "traditional" as it is used in the law should be understood to mean what the word "traditional" is normally understood to mean. So, in the court's view, the FWS's interpretation was inconsistent with what "traditional" is normally understood to mean.

The Incorrect Answer Choices:

A In the last paragraph, where the passage discusses the 1991 case, there is no mention of the ways in which Alaska Natives in particular have historically understood the word "traditional." What was at stake in the case was the way in which "traditional" was to be understood in enforcement of the law, not any specifically Alaska Native understanding of the term. Ultimately, in holding that the FWS's interpretation of "traditional" defied common sense, the court was asserting that the FWS's interpretation was inconsistent with the way that English speakers in general—not just Alaska Natives—have understood the term.

B As noted in the discussion of the correct response, the court appealed to the common sense understanding of the term "traditional" in its 1991 decision. But the last paragraph of the passage, where the 1991 case is discussed, does not suggest that in its decision the court invoked definitions found in any dictionary.

D In the 1991 case, the court ruled that the FWS failed to describe a practice—using sea otter pelts to make clothing—as traditional even though it should have been described as traditional. This is the reverse of what (D) says, i.e., that the FWS did describe a practice as traditional even though it should not have been described that way.

E The passage gives us no indication that the court thought that a problem with the FWS's interpretation of "traditional" was that it failed to specify which handicrafts qualified as traditional. Instead, the problem was that the FWS specified that at least one handicraft did **not** qualify as traditional—clothing made from sea otter pelts—and did so in a way that defied common sense.

- *Difficulty Level: 4*

Question 3

The Correct Answer:

E The passage says that the court reconsidered what constituted a traditional item "after hearing testimony establishing that Alaska Natives had made many uses of sea otters before the occupation of the territory by Russia in the late 1700s" (lines 41–44). This historical fact was important to the court's reasoning as follows: First, the court held that "the reference to 'living memory'" in the FWS's definition of what constituted a traditional handicraft "imposed an excessively restrictive time frame" (lines 47–49). The court added, "The fact that Alaskan natives were prevented, by circumstances beyond their control, from exercising a tradition for a given period of time does not mean that it…has become any less a 'tradition'" (lines 49–53). Thus the testimony in question established for the court that even though circumstances had prevented Alaska Natives from making clothing from sea otter pelts "within living memory," there was historically such a traditional practice. So the passage does indicate that the court's decision was based in part on testimony establishing certain historical facts.

The Incorrect Answer Choices:

A According to the second paragraph, the 1991 case illustrates the problems that can arise in the application of the sense of "traditional" according to which tradition is based on "long-standing" practice. In its decision, the court held that it defied common sense to define "traditional" like the FWS did—namely, "in such a way that only those traditions that were exercised during a comparatively short period of history could qualify as 'traditional'" (lines 54–57). So the passage gives us reasons for concluding that the court is not basing its decision on a narrow interpretation of the term "long-standing." Rather, it is **rejecting** what it regards as an overly narrow interpretation of the term—i.e., one according to which the only "long-standing" traditions are those that have been practiced within living memory.

B The court held that the reference to living memory imposed an excessively restrictive time frame (last paragraph). It is worth noting that in making this determination, the court was interpreting "within living memory" in the same way as the FWS. More importantly, in reaching its decision, the court was in effect saying that the requirement that a handicraft be practiced "within living memory" is not a legitimate criterion for determining whether it is a traditional handicraft. Thus the court's decision was not based on a common-sense interpretation of "within living memory." Rather, the court's decision was that the phrase as commonly understood should not be used in determining what constitutes a traditional handicraft.

C The FWS regulations denied a "traditional native handicraft" exemption to clothing made from sea otter pelts (third paragraph). The 1991 case was brought by Alaska Natives from whom clothing made from sea otter pelts was seized by FWS agents, agents who were clearly acting in accordance with the intent of the regulations (fourth paragraph). Since the court ruled against the FWS, its decision was clearly not based on strict adherence to the intent of those regulations. Rather, it rejected the intent of the FWS regulations with respect to clothing made from sea otter pelts.

D The ruling in the 1991 case concerned only whether Alaska Native use of sea otter pelts should be allowed under the Alaska Native Exemption in the MMPA; the passage gives us no indication that the Fur Seal Treaty was considered in the case.

- *Difficulty Level: 4*

Question 4

The Correct Answer:

B The second paragraph tells us that a prevailing understanding of the term "tradition" in the law is based on "long-standing practice," where "long-standing" refers to "the continuity and regularity of a practice." According to the third paragraph, the FWS regulations at issue in both cases considered items made from sea otter pelts not to be traditional because they had not been produced within living memory, suggesting that the FWS regulations were based on a definition of "tradition" that emphasized the continuity and regularity of the practices. The last paragraph then says that in the 1986 case, the court upheld the FWS regulations. This indicates that the court endorsed the FWS's definition of "traditional," which emphasized the continuity and regularity of practices to which the term was applied.

The Incorrect Answer Choices:

A The passage gives us no indication that the court in the 1986 case was trying to reach a compromise between competing concerns. The passage says that the court ruled against Marina Katelnikoff, the Aleut individual who sued the FWS for seizing clothing made from sea otter pelts from her. The passage does not indicate that the court tried to accommodate her concerns at all (last paragraph).

C There is no indication in the passage that the court in the 1986 case thought that "traditional" should be defined in a way that reflects everyday usage. In fact, it was in the 1991 case that the court rejected the FWS's definition of "traditional" because it defied common sense.

D The passage gives us no indication that the court in the 1986 case thought that "tradition" should be applied to recently developed activities. The passage tells us only that the case concerned the FWS's seizure of articles of clothing made from sea otter pelts on the grounds that such articles were not made "within living memory." This tells us nothing about whether the court thought that recently developed activities should be considered traditional.

E The passage says that in the 1986 case the court ruled against an Aleut who made clothing from sea otter pelts (last paragraph). This was a case in which she was seeking to have this clothing exempted from a regulation on the grounds that it was produced by means of traditional native handicrafts. So instead of reflecting the concerns of people engaging in what they consider to be traditional activities, the court ruled **against** someone who was engaging in what she considered to be a traditional activity.

■ *Difficulty Level: 2*

Question 5

The Correct Answer:

A The third paragraph of the passage tells us that the hunting of sea otters was first prohibited by the Fur Seal Treaty of 1910. It does not mention any exception for Alaska Natives. The passage does not describe any change to this policy until the MMPA of 1972, which did include an Alaska Native exemption allowing for the hunting of protected animals for use in traditional native handicrafts. Whether the hunting of sea otters was covered by this exemption was of course the matter at issue in the two court cases discussed in the last paragraph. But in any case, the passage makes it quite clear that Alaska Natives were prohibited from hunting sea otters between 1910 and 1972.

The Incorrect Answer Choices:

B The passage says only that the MMPA allowed takings of protected animals for use in creating authentic native articles by means of traditional native handicrafts (third paragraph). It does not mention any particular protected animals that were allowed to be taken. But since the passage states that the FWS subsequently deemed that clothing made from sea otter pelts was not covered by the Alaska Native exemption of the MMPA, this suggests that items made from sea otter pelts were not specifically mentioned in the MMPA.

C The passage says that Alaska Natives had made many uses of sea otters before the territory was occupied by Russia in the late 1700s. This suggests that Alaska Native hunting of sea otters may have slowed or even stopped after Russia occupied the territory. But even assuming this to be the case, the passage gives us no indication of what might have been behind the change.

D The passage suggests that the Fur Seal Treaty was intended to protect the sea otter population. But the passage says nothing about the actual levels of the sea otter population in 1972 or at any other time. So the passage gives us no reason to think that by 1972 the sea otter population had returned to the levels that had existed prior to the late 1700s. Indeed, the fact that the MMPA continued to prohibit the hunting of sea otters suggests that the population had not recovered to those earlier levels.

E   The passage makes it clear that sea otters were commonly hunted by Alaska Natives prior to the late 1700s. But it gives no indication that sea otters were hunted more often than other marine animals.

- *Difficulty Level: 4*

Question 6

The Correct Answer:

E   The reference to the Fur Seal Treaty occurs at the beginning of the third paragraph, where the passage claims that the Fur Seal Treaty was the first legal restriction on hunting sea otters. With the passage of this law, Alaska Natives lost their legal right to hunt sea otters—and presumably other animals as well—for use in traditional handicrafts. This sets the stage for the account of the evolution of the Alaska Natives' legal rights with respect to traditional handicrafts that occupies the rest of the passage. The author next informs us that the MMPA of 1972 included an exemption that restored Alaska Natives' right to hunt certain protected animals for use in traditional handicrafts. However, the FWS issued regulations under the MMPA that specifically excluded sea otters from the exemption. This exclusion remained in place until 1991, when the court overturned it. Thus by referring to the Fur Seal Treaty, the author identifies the first step in the evolution of the Alaska Natives' legal rights with respect to traditional handicrafts, a step which serves as the reference point for all the subsequent developments.

The Incorrect Answer Choices:

A   The passage provides no reason to think that fur seals were first considered to be on the brink of extinction when the Fur Seal Treaty came into effect. It is possible, for example, that the Fur Seal treaty of 1910 included fur seals because they were considered to be endangered, but not on the brink of extinction. Or on the other hand, it may have been the case that fur seals were considered to be on the brink of extinction many years before the Treaty of 1910, but that nothing was done about it until 1910.

B   The passage provides no indication that the Fur Seal Treaty included any exemptions covering any animals; the exemption mentioned in the passage was part of the MMPA. So it is not the case that the reference to the Fur Seal Treaty serves primarily to indicate that animals in addition to sea otters were covered by regulatory exemptions.

C There is no reason to think that the author of the passage is concerned with the question of whether there is precedent for prohibitions against the hunting of protected animals. In general, an author seeks to show that there is a well-known precedent for a law in order to show that the law is justified, that it conforms to legal standards or principles that are already accepted as legitimate. But in the case of this passage, the author is not seeking to establish that prohibitions on the hunting of protected animals are justified. Instead, the author refers to the Fur Seal Treaty to show that, as a matter of basic historical fact, the hunting of certain animals was prohibited in 1910. This prohibition was in turn the starting point of the evolution described in the explanation of the correct response. So it is not accurate to say that the reference to the Fur Seal Treaty primarily serves to demonstrate that there is a well-known legal precedent for prohibiting the hunting of protected animals.

D The passage contains an indirect suggestion that Alaska Natives' hunting of sea otters may have slowed or stopped after Russia claimed the territory (lines 41–44), but it does not indicate why this might have happened, assuming it happened at all. There is no mention of Russian seal hunters and certainly no suggestion that Russian seal hunters imperiled the sea otter population.

- *Difficulty Level: 4*

Question 7

The Correct Answer:

C In the 1991 case the court ruled that something could be a traditional handicraft even if it wasn't practiced within living memory (last paragraph). The court held that the fact that Alaska Natives were prevented, by circumstances beyond their control, from exercising a tradition for a period of time does not mean that it is no longer a tradition. So the 1991 case could establish a precedent in future cases in which Alaska Natives had been prevented from exercising a tradition by circumstances beyond their control. (C) describes such a case: Alaska Natives were prevented from practicing a handicraft because the herd animals necessary for its practice had abandoned their local habitat due to industrial development. Of course, in order to answer this question correctly, it is necessary to recognize that the herd animals' abandonment of their local habitat is a circumstance beyond the Alaska Natives' control.

The Incorrect Answer Choices:

A In the 1991 case the court ruled that the reference to "living memory" imposed an excessively restrictive time frame on when an activity could be considered traditional for application of the MMPA (last paragraph). But there is no indication that the time frame should be so lax as to encompass several millennia. In fact, the court appeals to common sense in its decision, and common sense would tend to suggest that an abandoned practice that was common several millennia ago would not be called a tradition now. So there's no reason to think that the 1991 case would provide a relevant precedent for the case described in (A).

B The 1991 case, as described in the passage (last paragraph), does not consider handicrafts that involve taking the pelts of more than one species. So there's no reason to think that the 1991 case would provide a relevant precedent for deciding the case described in (B).

D (D) states that very few indigenous craftspeople were historically in possession of knowledge of the handicraft in question; it is not clear whether a handicraft practiced by so few individuals could be considered a tradition. Moreover, (D) does not provide any information about the time frame in which this handicraft was practiced. It leaves open the possibility that the handicraft has not been practiced at all for millennia, or that it has been practiced continuously to the present day. It is not clear that the 1991 ruling would be relevant as a precedent for deciding a case pertaining to either of these possibilities.

E The handicraft in (E) is still practiced by at least some elder Alaska Natives. Thus it appears to be a tradition that has been practiced in living memory, unlike the tradition of using sea otter pelts that was the focus of the 1991 case.

- *Difficulty Level: 5*

Questions 8–15

Synopsis: This passage describes the development of the literary style that Kate Chopin used in her novel *The Awakening*. Chopin grew up reading sentimental novels that were common in the mid-nineteenth century. Later, when Chopin started writing, she used as her models the work of writers known as local colorists. The local colorists wrote about regional life based on their objective, detached observations of culture and character. According to the author of the passage, they also came to mourn the demise of a domestic "women's culture" as women began to pursue higher education and to enter professions in greater numbers. Chopin did not share the local colorists' nostalgia over the disappearance of women's culture, or their choice of subject matter—she wrote instead about loneliness, isolation, and frustration. But she adopted the local colorists' detached writing style in order to express extreme psychological states without resorting to the excesses of the sentimental novels she read in her youth. Chopin was later influenced by an innovative movement called the New Women. New Women writers modified novelistic forms to include interludes of fantasy and parable, and they experimented with impressionistic methods to try to explore previously unexpressed aspects of female consciousness. In *The Awakening*, Chopin made even more extensive use of these impressionistic methods, focusing on faithfully rendering the workings of the protagonist's mind.

Question 8

The Correct Answer:

B (B) accurately summarizes the content of the passage, outlined in the "Synopsis." The passage describes the development of the literary style that Chopin used in *The Awakening*. She used the conventions of the local colorists to avoid the excesses of the sentimental novels that she read in her youth (third paragraph). She was later influenced by the innovative methods of the New Women (fourth paragraph), making extensive use of their impressionistic methods in *The Awakening*.

The Incorrect Answer Choices:

A The passage does not say or suggest that Chopin tried to recapture the atmosphere of the novels she had read in her youth. So (A) does not accurately summarize the passage.

C The passage does not say that *The Awakening* was unlike any work of fiction written during the nineteenth century. Furthermore, the first half of (C)—the only accurate part—is drawn entirely from the last sentence of the passage, so (C) cannot be regarded as an accurate summary of the entire passage.

D The passage does not say that Chopin rebelled against the stylistic restraint of the local colorists. Although she did not share their subject matter or nostalgia, Chopin actually used the detached style of the local colorists (third paragraph). Moreover, there is no indication that Chopin used elevated, romantic language. This description would characterize the sentimental novels whose excesses Chopin sought to avoid. So (D) does not accurately summarize the passage.

E The passage does not say that Chopin felt a kinship with the subject matter but not the stylistic conventions of the local colorists. In fact, it says almost the reverse (third paragraph): that she employed the stylistic conventions of the local colorists, but with differing subject matter. Furthermore, according to the passage, Chopin's turn to the New Women for models was motivated by dissatisfaction with the subject matter of the local colorists (their growing nostalgia), not by any felt lack of kinship with their stylistic conventions, which she had embraced. So (E) does not accurately summarize the passage.

- *Difficulty Level: 1*

Question 9

The Correct Answer:

A The passage says, at the beginning of the last paragraph, that Chopin did not share the local colorists' nostalgia for the past. The last sentence of the second paragraph says that the local colorists expressed their nostalgia by investing the images of domestic women's culture, such as the garden, the house, and artifacts of domesticity, with mythic significance. Since Chopin did not share that nostalgia, we can infer that she would have been likely to think that idealizing these settings and objects was misguided.

The Incorrect Answer Choices:

B In the third paragraph, the passage says that Chopin adopted the local colorists' convention of expressing character dispassionately ("in an uninflected manner") in order to tell "rather shocking or even melodramatic tales." This indicates that she would not have been likely to agree that this method in itself caused the fiction of the local colorists to lack emotional impact.

C The passage says that Chopin was influenced first by the local colorists and later by the New Women writers. But there is no indication in the passage that she thought that the local colorists inspired or otherwise influenced the New Women, or vice versa.

D The passage says in the second paragraph that after 1865 women entered higher education, the professions, and politics in greater numbers. Presumably this would have happened in many regions of the country, and the passage states (second paragraph) that the local colorists themselves moved in these new realms. So the passage provides no reason to think that the local colorists' focus on regional life prevented them from addressing the new realms opening up to women, nor does it provide any indication that Chopin would have been likely to think that it did.

E The passage says in the third paragraph that Chopin used the conventions of the local colorists to portray extreme psychological states in a detached, uninflected manner without resorting to the excesses of the sentimental novels. It is very unlikely that Chopin would have thought that the local colorists' conventions prevented them from portraying extreme psychological states with scientific detachment when she employed those conventions herself for that very purpose.

- *Difficulty Level: 5*

Question 10

The Correct Answer:

C In the third paragraph, the passage says that Chopin used the conventions of the local colorists to deal with extreme psychological states without resorting to the excesses of the sentimental novels; this enabled Chopin to tell shocking or melodramatic tales in an uninflected manner. In other words, Chopin was writing with the "almost scientific detachment" (second paragraph) characteristic of the local colorists. Since Chopin took as her model the women writers of the time who were local colorists (first paragraph), it follows that a detached narrative stance was a convention that Chopin adopted from other nineteenth-century women writers.

The Incorrect Answer Choices:

A There is no indication in the passage that Chopin used elevated, romantic language. Such language was typical of the sentimental novels Chopin read as a youth, whose excesses she sought to avoid (third paragraph).

B The passage says that the local colorists mourned the demise of women's culture by investing its images with mythic significance. Chopin did not share the local colorists' nostalgia for women's culture, so it is unlikely that she would have adopted mythic images of women's culture, or the practice of constructing them, as a convention.

D The passage says that strongly plotted short stories were the primary genre of the local colorists (last paragraph). Furthermore, it says that Chopin adopted narrative conventions of the local colorists to deal with extreme psychological states without sentimental excess by rendering narrative events dispassionately, in an uninflected manner (third paragraph). But it does not say that Chopin's fiction in the period when she was most influenced by the local colorists exhibited strong plot lines. Finally, the passage contrasts the strongly plotted short stories of the local colorists with the impressionistic methods used by the New Women writers, whose work included interludes of fantasy and parable. The passage says (last paragraph) that in *The Awakening*, Chopin adopted the impressionistic methods of the New Women writers, which does not support the idea that *The Awakening* had strong plot lines. So there is no point at which the passage suggests that Chopin adopted strong plot lines as a convention from other nineteenth-century women writers.

E The passage says that Chopin told stories of loneliness and isolation. But the passage never says that any of the other writers discussed did so. Hence the passage provides no indication that Chopin adopted lonely, isolated protagonists as a convention from other nineteenth-century women writers.

- *Difficulty Level: 4*

Question 11

The Correct Answer:

A The passage says that women's culture began to dissolve when more women entered higher education, the professions, and the political world, that is, when more women began to do things outside of domestic life. Additionally, at the end of the second paragraph, the passage refers to images of women's culture: the garden, the house, and artifacts of domesticity. So it is reasonable to infer that "women's culture" refers to something that was expressed primarily through domestic experiences.

The Incorrect Answer Choices:

B As discussed in the explanation of the correct answer, the "women's culture" mentioned in the passage was tied to domestic life. It may well have been the case that some aspects of women's culture would have been expressed to some degree through regional customs. But the passage gives us no indication to think that women's culture was expressed **primarily** through women's regional customs. The passage says that the local colorists wrote stories about regional life, but that doesn't mean that regional customs were the primary avenue of expression for women's culture.

C As discussed in the explanation of the correct answer, the "women's culture" discussed in the second paragraph was tied to domestic life. It is reasonable to presume that some aspects of women's culture would have been expressed in women's artistic productions. But nothing in the passage suggests that they were expressed primarily through artistic productions. In fact, the artistic production mentioned in the rest of the second paragraph is that of the local colorists, who moved as artists through the new worlds outside the domestic sphere that opened up to women in the 1870s and 1880s as women's culture began to dissolve. So their artistic productions were probably not the main avenue for the expression of women's culture.

D The passage says that women's culture began to dissolve when more women entered higher education. This strongly suggests that "women's culture" refers to something that was not expressed primarily through educational achievements.

E The passage says that women's culture began to dissolve when more women entered the political world. This strongly suggests that "women's culture" refers to something that was not expressed primarily through political activities.

- *Difficulty Level: 1*

Question 12

The Correct Answer:

C   The passage says that Chopin grew up with the sentimental novels of the mid-nineteenth century and that these novels formed the bulk of the fiction at that time. Since these novels formed the bulk of the fiction during the period just before Chopin began to write, and since she was quite familiar with them, it is accurate to say that they were the background against which Chopin's fiction developed. The author uses this information about Chopin's literary background later when describing Chopin's use of the conventions of the local colorists: the passage says that she did so in order to avoid the excesses of the sentimental novels. This also places Chopin's fiction against the background of those sentimental novels.

The Incorrect Answer Choices:

A   The passage never suggests that Chopin tried to mimic the style of the sentimental novels. On the contrary, it says that Chopin specifically tried to avoid the excesses of the sentimental novels (third paragraph).

B   The passage does say that Chopin selected different subject matter than the local colorists did, that she didn't share their nostalgia, and that she was later influenced by the New Women writers. However, the description of the sentimental novels is not offered as an explanation of any of this.

D   The passage does refer to Chopin's desire to avoid the excesses of the sentimental novels. However, there is no indication that Chopin thought that such excesses resulted from nostalgic tendencies. It was the local colorists, not the authors of the sentimental novels, who the passage presents as prone to nostalgic tendencies.

E   There is no indication in the passage that the author seeks to establish that women's literature was already flourishing by the time Chopin began to write. The lines mentioned allude to the sentimental novels that formed the bulk of the fiction of the mid-nineteenth-century, but that does not amount to an attempt to prove that women's literature was flourishing at that time.

- *Difficulty Level: 1*

Question 13

The Correct Answer:

C   In the last sentence, the passage says that in *The Awakening*, Chopin embraced the impressionistic approach of the New Women writers more fully. Additionally, the passage said earlier that the impressionistic methods of the New Women writers were intended to explore aspects of female consciousness. *The Awakening*, as the last sentence of the passage tells us, was characterized by a **sustained** focus on faithfully rendering the workings of the protagonist's mind (her consciousness, in other words). This indicates that a difference between *The Awakening* and the work of the New Women was that *The Awakening* employed impressionism more consistently throughout.

The Incorrect Answer Choices:

A   In the last paragraph, the passage says that the New Women writers experimented with impressionistic methods in an effort to explore aspects of female consciousness, and it says that in *The Awakening*, Chopin embraced this approach even more fully. So an attempt to explore aspects of female consciousness was not something that differentiated *The Awakening* from the work of the New Women.

B   The passage does not say, or in any way indicate, whether or not *The Awakening* describes the dream world of any female characters. The passage therefore cannot be reasonably interpreted as suggesting that *The Awakening* differed from the work of the New Women in that it described the dream world of female characters.

D   In the last paragraph, the passage says that New Women writers modified the form of the sentimental novel to make room for interludes of fantasy and parable. There is no indication in the passage that *The Awakening* relied more on fantasy than the work of the New Women did.

E   In the last sentence, the passage says that *The Awakening* had sections that were not particularly unified by their style or content. So there's no reason to think that a greater unity of style and content was something that differentiated *The Awakening* from the work of the New Women.

- *Difficulty Level: 4*

Question 14

The Correct Answer:

B The passage discusses Chopin's development as a writer. Throughout the passage, Chopin's artistic development is presented in relation to developments in nineteenth-century women's fiction. First, the passage describes the sentimental novels that Chopin read before she became a writer. (The passage later says that Chopin tried to avoid the sentimental excesses of these novels.) Next, the passage discusses the local colorists, whose detached style Chopin adopted. Finally, the passage discusses the New Women movement, whose impressionistic methods Chopin adopted. So the primary purpose of the passage is to discuss the relationship between Chopin's artistic development and developments in nineteenth-century women's fiction.

The Incorrect Answer Choices:

A The passage does not discuss any aspect of Chopin's life except those related to the development of her literary style. There is no indication that any other aspects of her life are reflected in *The Awakening*. This suggests that the primary purpose of the passage is concerned with the development of Chopin's literary style rather than aspects of Chopin's life that are reflected in *The Awakening*.

C The passage does not say or suggest that Chopin's fiction is a typical example of nineteenth-century women's fiction. So (C) does not accurately describe the purpose of the passage.

D The passage suggests that the style of Chopin's fiction was influenced by some of the literary movements of her time. Since it notes that these movements were in turn influenced by external social circumstances—such as the ongoing disappearance of domestic women's culture—the passage effectively acknowledges that Chopin's fiction was indirectly influenced by external social circumstances. So the purpose of the passage cannot be to **counter** a claim that Chopin's fiction was influenced by external social circumstances.

E The passage does not compare the value of *The Awakening* to that of other works of fiction. And it doesn't even mention any stories or other novels by Chopin. So (E) does not accurately describe the purpose of the passage.

- *Difficulty Level: 1*

Question 15

The Correct Answer:

D In the last paragraph, the passage says that the New Women writers pursued innovation in form and content. It also says that the New Women writers experimented with impressionistic methods to explore previously unrecorded aspects of female consciousness. The New Women writers, that is, developed innovations in fictional technique in an attempt to describe aspects of reality that had been neglected in previous works. So the works of the New Women provide support for the generalization that innovations in fictional technique grow out of writers' attempts to describe aspects of reality that have been neglected in previous works by serving as examples of works in which this occurred.

The Incorrect Answer Choices:

A There is no indication in the passage that the work of the New Women writers effected any changes in social custom, or even that they were intended to do so. Works by New Women writers included episodes in which women dream of a different world, but there is no indication that these works were trying to bring that world into being, much less that they succeeded. Since the works of the New Women do not present any examples of any works of fiction effecting changes in social customs, it does not support the generalization that works written in a passionate style are more apt to effect changes in social customs than works written in a detached style.

B The passage does not claim that the New Women writers advocated social change, still less that they regretted any such change once it had occurred. So the works of the New Women writers do not support the generalization that writers who advocate social change can end up regretting it.

C There is no indication in the passage that the works of the New Women writers grew out of changes in social customs or that these writers were trying to make sense of new social realities. The passage says that the New Women writers were trying to explore previously unrecorded aspects of female consciousness. But these aspects were not necessarily new; they may just have not been described before. Since the works of the New Women do not present a case of changes in social customs leading to changes in literary techniques, they do not support the generalization that changes in social customs inevitably lead to changes in literary techniques.

E The passage does not say that works of the New Women writers depicted extreme psychological states using an uninflected manner. According to the passage, this was what Chopin did using artistic conventions of the local colorists, quite apart from the influence that the New Women had on her. So the works of the New Women do not support the generalization that writers can most accurately depict extreme psychological states by using an uninflected manner.

- *Difficulty Level: 5*

Questions 16–21

Synopsis: This passage discusses how scientists developed a new theory about the geology of the ocean floor in response to two 1950s discoveries. The first paragraph describes the first discovery: the ocean floor exhibits odd magnetic variations. The passage explains that basalt, the rock that makes up much of the ocean floor, contains the magnetic mineral magnetite. The earth's magnetic polarity has reversed at various times, and magnetite retains the polarity that the earth had when the magnetite cooled. So some magnetite has the same polarity as the earth now has—that is, "normal" polarity—while other magnetite has reversed polarity.

The second paragraph describes the second discovery: a large underwater mountain range known as the global mid-ocean ridge. Several stripes of rock with alternating magnetic polarities run along each side of the ridge. Scientists developed a new theory—the theory of ocean floor spreading—to explain these phenomena. The theory says that the mid-ocean ridge formed in zones where the ocean floor is pulling apart and that magma erupting in these zones creates new oceanic crust.

The last paragraph presents evidence for the theory of ocean floor spreading. First, rocks near the ridge's crest are young and get older as you move away from the crest. Second, the youngest rocks all have normal polarity. Third, the passage notes that there is a strong correlation between the ages of earth's magnetic reversals (which were dated independently) and the striping pattern. The correlation holds if you assume, consistently with the ocean floor spreading theory, that the ocean floor is moving apart at a rate of several centimeters per year.

Question 16

The Correct Answer:

C The passage's first sentence states that, before the 1950s, most scientists thought that the geology of the ocean floor had not changed in millions of years. But we then read that their views changed dramatically in response to two discoveries during that decade. The passage describes these discoveries, presents a theory developed in response to them, and discusses evidence favoring that theory. So it's clear that in the 1950s two significant discoveries led to the transformation of scientific views about the geology of the oceans. This statement accurately expresses the passage's main idea.

The Incorrect Answer Choices:

A The passage does discuss a theory for the formation of the ocean floor, but this theory is not presented as a "refined" version of any preceding theory. In fact, the passage never mentions a theory of ocean floor formation that predates 1950. (The first sentence of the passage does mention the view, common before 1950, that the ocean floor had not changed much in several million years. But this does not address the formation of the ocean floor.) So (A) can't be the main idea of the passage.

B While the passage does describe the formulation of a new scientific theory that accounts for the ocean floor's magnetic stripes, it also indicates that this theory was developed in response to the discovery of the magnetic properties of the ocean floor, **not** basalt. (The first paragraph explains that scientists already knew about basalt's magnetic properties when those of the ocean floor were discovered.) Therefore, (B) does not express the passage's main idea.

D The passage only explicitly mentions compass readings in the first paragraph (line 11), where we read that magnetite locally distorts compass readings on land—a claim that has little connection to magma's role in forming oceanic crust. It's possible that compass distortions facilitated the discovery of the ocean floor's odd magnetic variations. But even if this is so, that was only one of the two discoveries that, according to the passage, led to the new theory. So (D) does not express the passage's main idea.

E The passage says that more of the ocean floor was mapped in the 1950s, but it doesn't say scientists were ever convinced of the need to map the **entire** ocean floor. Moreover, there is no indication that the ocean floor mapping that did occur resulted from the discovery of the ocean floor's magnetic variations. So (E) can't be the passage's main idea.

- *Difficulty Level: 4*

Question 17

The Correct Answer:

D The existence of a correlation of any kind between the dates of the earth's magnetic reversals and the ocean floor's striping pattern provides some confirmation of the ocean floor spreading theory, since that theory explains the correlation. The greater the correlation, the stronger the confirmation that the correlation provides. The passage uses the word "remarkable" to signal that the magnetic reversals and the striping pattern are very closely correlated, and hence that this correlation serves as strong confirmation of the ocean floor spreading theory.

The Incorrect Answer Choices:

A The correlation at issue does provide confirmation of the theory that the ocean floor is spreading, and the rate of spreading can be inferred from the correlation. The passage uses "remarkable" not to indicate anything about the slowness of the rate, however, but to indicate something about the degree of confirmation that the correlation provides for the theory. The use of "remarkable" does not indicate anything about the rate, since, for all we are told, it could just as well be that the rate is extremely **fast**, given geological time scales. That is, the use of "remarkable" would be consistent with the rate being either fast or slow.

B The passage suggests that the remarkable correlation supports the theory of ocean floor spreading. This theory addresses much more than just the existence of the global mid-ocean ridge, and the passage never suggests that correlation's relevance is restricted to the existence of this ridge.

C The remarkable correlation is between the ages of the earth's magnetic reversals and the ages and polarities of rock on the ocean floor. Nothing about the strength of the earth's magnetic field can be inferred from the existence of this correlation.

E The existence of the remarkable correlation does not imply that the earth's magnetic reversals have occurred at regular intervals. Even if these intervals are very irregular, the correlation could still be strong as long as the polarities of rocks on the ocean floor correspond to the earth's polarity at the time the rock was formed.

- *Difficulty Level: 2*

Question 18

The Correct Answer:

A The passage indicates that new oceanic crust is formed when magma erupts along the crest of the mid-ocean ridge and then cools to form basalt, which contains magnetite grains. It also states, in the third sentence of the last paragraph (lines 44–45), that at the ridge's crest "the youngest rocks all have normal polarity." The first paragraph defines normal polarity as polarity matching that of the earth's present magnetic field, so this is equivalent to saying that the magnetite grains in the youngest basalt are aligned with the earth's current polarity.

The Incorrect Answer Choices:

B In the first paragraph (lines 17–19), the passage says that in magma "grains of magnetite … align themselves with the earth's magnetic field." The passage doesn't qualify this statement by saying that most, but not all, magnetite grains align themselves in this way, so it never makes the claim expressed in (B).

C The passage does say that basalt contains magnetite, but it does not say anything about whether magnetite is present or absent in other kinds of rock.

D, E The passage does not say anything about the size of magnetite grains. It does say that basalt rocks contain these grains, but that alone doesn't tell us how their size compares to grains of sand or whether they can be seen with the naked eye.

- *Difficulty Level: 3*

Question 19

The Correct Answer:

C According to the passage, the ocean floor's magnetic stripes of basalt are formed from magma eruptions and retain the magnetic polarity that the earth had when the magma erupted. The longer a period of one type of polarity is, the more time there is for magma to erupt during this period, and additional magma eruptions will result in a wider stripe. So, if the time intervals between the earth's magnetic reversals fluctuate a lot, then a lot of magma will erupt during the longer periods, creating wide stripes, and little magma will erupt during the brief periods, creating narrow stripes.

The Incorrect Answer Choices:

A The passage's first paragraph indicates that distorted compass readings can result from basalt with reversed polarity. Even if the time intervals between the earth's magnetic reversals fluctuate a lot, there's no reason to think that stripes of reversed polarity are likely to be near the peaks of the mid-ocean ridge. If anything, the passage suggests that this is unlikely: the final paragraph indicates that rocks near the ridge's crest are very young and that the youngest rocks have normal polarity, not reversed polarity. So compass readings are not most likely to be distorted near the peaks.

B The passage never offers an explanation for the winding shape of the mid-ocean ridge. In particular, it doesn't say anything to suggest the presence of a connection, causal or otherwise, between this winding shape and the earth's magnetic reversals. The possibility raised by the question—that these magnetic reversals fluctuate greatly—provides no new reasons to think that such a connection exists, so (B) is not likely to be true even if this possibility is added to the information in the passage.

D The passage does say that scientists assigned ages to the earth's magnetic reversals by studying continental rocks. But that gives us no reason to think oceanic rocks are less suitable for that purpose, and it doesn't imply that the suitability of either kind of rock would be affected by fluctuations in the earth's magnetic field reversals.

E Each of the ocean floor's magnetic stripes corresponds to an interval between the earth's magnetic field reversals. During any such interval, the age of the basalt that forms the stripe is likely to vary: magma that erupted early in the interval will form older basalt, while magma that erupted late in the interval will form younger basalt. Nothing in the passage suggests that fluctuations in the earth's magnetic field reversals would interfere with this process.

- *Difficulty Level: 4*

Question 20

The Correct Answer:

B In the passage, the final piece of evidence for the ocean floor spreading theory involves comparing the ages and polarities of the stripes of rock along the mid-ocean ridge with the time periods when the earth's magnetic polarity was reversed. The earth's magnetic reversals were dated, in part, by examining the polarity of magnetite grains in continental rocks. If we could verify these dates by an additional method, as (B) suggests, then we could independently confirm the accuracy of evidence favoring the ocean floor spreading theory. This would add to the theory's support.

The Incorrect Answer Choices:

A The evidence for the ocean floor spreading theory involves comparing properties of the basalt stripes along the mid-ocean ridge to the dates of the earth's magnetic reversals. The mere possibility that types of rock other than basalt can distort compass readings does nothing to strengthen that evidence. Indeed, this possibility might even undermine that evidence if these other rocks could interfere with scientists' attempts to gather data on the basalt stripes.

C If some pieces of basalt found on the continents were similar to those found on the mid-ocean ridge, this alone would tell us little, if anything, about the ocean floor spreading theory. For example, it is consistent with the passage that the continental basalt originated in volcanic eruptions on the continents rather than eruptions at the mid-ocean ridge. In that case, the mere presence of such basalt would not support the ocean floor spreading theory, since this theory, as discussed in the passage, does not address continental eruptions.

D All of the evidence presented in the passage for the ocean floor spreading theory involves the ages and magnetic properties of basalt rocks found in the stripes along the mid-ocean ridge. Information about the ridge's height wouldn't tell us anything new about this evidence, so we have no reason to think that it would support the ocean floor spreading theory.

E The passage's evidence for the ocean floor spreading theory concerns basalt rocks found in the stripes near the mid-ocean ridge. There's no reason to think that this evidence would be undermined if rocks other than basalt were found on the ocean floor near the continents, so ruling out this possibility wouldn't help support the argument.

- *Difficulty Level: 4*

Question 21

The Correct Answer:

A The ocean floor spreading theory holds that new oceanic crust is formed by magma eruptions at the mid-ocean ridge; this process causes older oceanic crust to gradually move away from the ridge. This strongly suggests that the further oceanic crust is from the mid-ocean ridge, the older it is. (That suggestion is reinforced by the last paragraph's second sentence (lines 42–44), which says that rocks near the crest of the mid-ocean ridge become older as distance from the crest increases.) Submarine basalt near the continents is located as far away from the mid-ocean ridge as oceanic crust can be, so it is likely to be among the oldest rock on the ocean floor.

The Incorrect Answer Choices:

B The end of the first paragraph indicates that when basalt forms, its magnetic polarity becomes "locked in" (line 22). So the polarity of basalt does not change, regardless of how old the basalt is.

C The passage does say that magnetite can distort compass readings on land, but it doesn't say how common this is. It may also appear to suggest that these distorted readings played a role in scientists' research into the ocean floor's magnetic variations, which would imply that distorted compass readings have occurred at sea. Again, though, the passage gives no indication of how often these distortions occur; nor does it allow us to compare the frequency of compass distortions at sea to the frequency of those on land. So the statement made in (C) is not strongly supported by the passage.

D The passage states that the magnetic polarities of magnetite grains become "locked in" when magma cools to form solid basalt (line 22). It doesn't say anything to suggest that the magnetic fields corresponding to these polarities ever weaken.

E The first paragraph indicates that basalt exhibits the polarity that the earth had when the basalt formed. The earth's polarity has reversed at various times throughout history, so it has undergone many periods when its polarity was reversed. However, it has **also** undergone many periods when its polarity was the same as its present-day polarity, and any basalt formed during one of those periods will exhibit present-day polarity. So it's not true that all rocks exhibiting present-day polarity were formed after the latest reversal of the earth's magnetic field.

- *Difficulty Level: 5*

Questions 22–27

Synopsis: Both passages discuss the value of objectivity in historical scholarship. Both authors see this value as essential to historical scholarship, but the two authors have different takes on what constitutes objectivity for the historian.

For the author of passage A, an objective historian treats historical facts as prior to and independent of historical interpretation. An interpretation should be judged by how well it accounts for the facts. The author of passage A associates objectivity with neutrality, comparing an objective historian to a neutral judge. Like judges, historians should be guided by the facts and insulated from "political considerations"—that is, considerations that might lead them to become invested in a particular point of view.

Passage B, while agreeing that historical interpretations must be based on evidence and logic, explicitly rejects the idea that objectivity requires neutrality. The author of passage B sees objectivity as compatible with strong political commitment. Further, the passage argues that objectivity is most perfectly embodied in the ideal of the powerful argument—a non-neutral case for a particular historical interpretation. Constructing a powerful argument requires temporarily detaching from one's own point of view in order to achieve the kind of understanding of rival positions that is needed to mount a strong attack against them. The author of passage B thus values detachment, but only as a means of achieving understanding.

Question 22

The Correct Answer:

B Both passages suggest that objective historical scholarship is unbiased, and both passages discuss at length the measures that historians need to take in order to achieve this sort of objectivity. Passage A says that objective historians are like neutral judges and, like them, they need to "purge themselves of external loyalties" (last sentence of the third paragraph) (line 23) in order to avoid bias and partisanship.

Passage B says in the first paragraph that in order to avoid engaging in propaganda, historians must "abandon wishful thinking, assimilate bad news, and discard pleasing interpretations that fail elementary tests of evidence and logic" (lines 30–32). The second paragraph says that historians, in order to construct the powerful argument that is the hallmark of objectivity, must suspend their own perceptions in order to anticipate objections and alternative interpretations. So passage B, like passage A, is concerned with answering the question of how historians can avoid bias in their scholarship.

The Incorrect Answer Choices:

A Neither passage discusses specific works of recent historical scholarship, though they do each refer to approaches to historical scholarship with which they take issue (exemplified by relativist historians for passage A and those that resist taking a position in passage B). The flaws of these approaches are not specifically identified. So the passages are not concerned with answering the question of what the most serious flaws in recent historical scholarship are.

C Both passages describe the ideal of objectivity as it applies to historical scholarship, but neither passage discusses how this ideal developed.

D Passage A mentions relativist historians and rejects their position. But passage B does not mention relativist historians at all. It is concerned with a competing conception of historical objectivity, not with relativism. So it's not true that both passages are concerned with answering the question of whether scholarship produced by relativist historians is sound.

E Passage A says that successive generations of historians have ascribed different meanings to past events, but it does not attempt to explain why this has happened. Passage B does not discuss how historical interpretations have changed. So it's not true that both passages are concerned with answering the question of why interpretations change from one era to the next.

- *Difficulty Level: 2*

Question 23

The Correct Answer:

C Passage A says that historians' "primary allegiance" is to objective historical truth (last sentence of the passage) (line 24). If an interpretation is contradicted by facts, the historian should abandon it (middle of the second paragraph) (line 11). Passage B says that historians must have the "self-discipline" to "assimilate bad news, and discard pleasing interpretations that fail elementary tests of evidence and logic" (end of the first paragraph) (lines 30–32). So both passages identify the historian's willingness to relinquish interpretations in light of the discovery of facts inconsistent with them as a requirement for historical research.

The Incorrect Answer Choices:

A Passage A says that historians should have the qualities of the neutral judge. But the only field other than history that passage B mentions is television news (last sentence of the last paragraph) (line 61), and the author of the passage clearly rejects the methodology of television newscasters. So it is not true that both passages identify the historian's willingness to borrow methods of analysis from other disciplines as a requirement for historical research.

B Passage A does not say anything about the historian's willingness to employ methodologies favored by proponents of competing views. Passage B suggests that the historian should be willing to understand rival views and the objections that issue from them. But it does not say that historians should employ the methodologies favored by proponents of rival views. So neither passage identifies the historian's willingness to employ methodologies favored by proponents of competing views as a requirement for historical research.

D Passage A does not discuss the historian's willingness to answer possible objections. And while passage B says that the historian should consider objections in arguing for an interpretation, the passage gives us no reason to think that the author means that historians must consider all possible objections.

E Passage B lauds objective historical scholarship that makes a "powerful argument," respectfully considering rival interpretations along the way. But there is no indication that this is a requirement for historical research. The author appears, rather, to think that it is the "highest fruit" of objective thinking (second sentence of the final paragraph) (line 58), which some historical scholarship may fail to fully attain. Passage A says that historians should display "evenhandedness" (second sentence of the third paragraph) (line 20), but this means being unbiased and guided by the facts, not arguing for a position while respectfully dealing with "rival" interpretations. So it is not true that both passages identify the historian's willingness to accord respectful consideration to rival interpretations as a requirement for historical research.

- *Difficulty Level: 4*

Question 24

The Correct Answer:

B Passage A says that objective historians see their role as that of a neutral judge and that, as with the judiciary, historians must be insulated from political considerations. So the kind of objective historian described in passage A would think that an objective historical account cannot include strong political commitment. The author of passage B would clearly disagree. Passage B says that objectivity is perfectly compatible with strong political commitment (second sentence of the second paragraph) (lines 34–35).

The Incorrect Answer Choices:

A The objective historian, as described in passage A, thinks that detachment aids in achieving an objective view. Passage A says that objective historians see their role as that of a neutral judge, which requires insulation from political considerations and avoidance of partisanship (third paragraph). You might think that the author of passage B would reject detachment since that author thinks that objectivity is compatible with strong political commitment. However, the author of passage B does value detachment, just not as an end in itself. Passage B says that the objective thinker values detachment as an indispensable means of achieving deeper understanding (third sentence of the second paragraph) (lines 37–39). Such detachment enables the objective historian to understand alternative positions and thereby anticipate objections that issue from them. So the author of passage B and the kind of objective historian described in passage A would agree that detachment aids in achieving an objective view.

C Passage A mentions previous generations of historians at the end of the second paragraph, but does not indicate whether these historians were more objective than historians are now. Passage B does not discuss previous historians at all. So the passages give us no reason to think that the author of passage B and the kind of objective historian described in passage A would be likely to disagree over whether historians today are less objective than they were previously.

D Both the author of passage B and the kind of objective historian described in passage A take a dim view of propaganda. Passage A says that objective historians think that they should never be propagandists (first sentence of the third paragraph) (lines 17–18). Passage B explicitly distinguishes historical scholarship from propaganda (first paragraph) (lines 27–28) and describes in detail how to avoid engaging in propaganda by being objective. So the author of passage B and the kind of objective historian described in passage A would agree that propaganda is not an essential tool of historical scholarship.

E Passage A says that historians of different eras have ascribed different meanings to past events (last sentence of the second paragraph) (lines 12–13), and presumably objective historians would be aware of this. Passage B does not discuss historians of different eras, but given the discussion of rival interpretations in the second paragraph, the author clearly thinks that historians of the same era can have differing interpretations. There's no reason to think that the author of passage B wouldn't think the same could be true of historians of different eras. So the author of passage B and the kind of objective historian described in passage A would likely agree about whether historians of different eras have arrived at differing interpretations of the same events.

- *Difficulty Level: 4*

Question 25

The Correct Answer:

B Passage A explicitly says that the ideal of objectivity is central to the historian's profession and scholarship (first sentence) (lines 1–2) and rejects historical scholarship that does not embody this commitment to objectivity (last sentence of the second paragraph) (lines 11–15). Passage B says in the first paragraph (lines 27–32) that "the very possibility of historical scholarship" requires abandoning wishful thinking, relying on evidence and logic, and so on. That these are qualities of an objective thinker is apparent from the immediate reference to objectivity at the beginning of the next paragraph. So the attitude that objectivity is essential to the practice of historical scholarship is present in each passage.

The Incorrect Answer Choices:

A Neither passage gives us any indication of how many historians have managed to achieve the goal of objectivity. Both passages are devoted solely to discussing the nature of objectivity for historians and how it can be achieved. So the attitude that objectivity is a goal that few historians have achieved is not present in either passage.

C Passage A describes objective historians as being insulated from political allegiances (middle of third paragraph) (line 21). But passage B insists that, "Objectivity is perfectly compatible with strong political commitment" (second sentence of the second paragraph) (lines 34–35). So the attitude that objectivity cannot be achieved unless historians set aside political allegiances is clearly not present in both passages.

D Neither passage gives us any indication of whether historians are good judges of their own objectivity. Both passages are devoted solely to discussing the nature of objectivity for historians and how it can be achieved.

E Passage A mentions relativist historians, who presumably don't value objectivity, but the passage gives us no indication of how common such a view is or has been in the past. Passage B, while championing objectivity, provides us with no sense of how common or uncommon it is among historians, or how its popularity has changed over time.

- *Difficulty Level: 2*

Question 26

The Correct Answer:

D Both passages mention propaganda in order to help characterize the objective ideal for historical scholarship. Passage A says that objective historians see their role as that of a neutral judge (first sentence of the third paragraph) (lines 16–18). The passage contrasts a neutral judge with an advocate and a propagandist, which is held to be even worse than an advocate. The passage mentions a propagandist, therefore, to identify an extreme far away from the ideal of a neutral judge.

Passage B likewise draws a distinction between historical scholarship and propaganda, noting that historians must have the "self-discipline" to distinguish themselves from propagandists by discarding "pleasing interpretations that fail elementary tests of evidence and logic" (first paragraph) (lines 29–32). So passage B too mentions propaganda in order to identify one extreme to which historians may tend.

The Incorrect Answer Choices:

A At the end of the second paragraph, passage A discusses a claim made by relativist historians, proponents of a rival approach. Passage A asserts that the relativist historians are wrong, but the author's mention of propaganda does not occur in the context of that discussion, nor does it help to refute the claim made by relativist historians.

Passage B does not explicitly reject any claim made by proponents of a rival approach. It does assert that powerful arguments are more faithful to the complexity of historical interpretation than texts that resist taking a position. But the author's mention of propaganda is not offered as support for this assertion.

B The only field other than history mentioned in passage A is law. But in passage A, law (the judiciary, at least) is not presented as more biased than history. In fact it is held up as an ideal of the unbiased, objective approach. The only field other than history mentioned in passage B is television news. Passage B presents television news as employing a shallow notion of balance, but it does not suggest that television news is biased.

C Though it is clear that both authors find propaganda to be highly undesirable, they do not mention it merely to point out that it is discredited. (Nor is there any suggestion in either passage that propaganda has only recently been discredited.) Rather, they mention it in order to help characterize the objective ideal for historical scholarship.

E Both passages mention propaganda in order to help characterize the objective ideal for historical scholarship. The author of passage B thinks that objective historical scholarship reaches its peak when it takes the form of a persuasive "powerful argument." But no other kind of "persuasive writing" is discussed in passage B. The author of passage A is not concerned to contrast propaganda with kinds of "persuasive writing," but rather with a kind of writing that is objective, neutral, and responsive only to the facts.

- *Difficulty Level: 4*

Question 27

The Correct Answer:

E Passage A expounds an ideal of objectivity for historians. It does so in large part by identifying obstacles to objectivity. The third paragraph of the passage indicates, for example, that the objective historian must avoid being a propagandist, maintain insulation from political considerations, and avoid partisanship. This in turn requires that historians purge themselves of external loyalties.

Passage B presents the view that objectivity for the historian involves disciplined pursuit of the powerful argument. In order to construct such an argument, according to passage B, historians must understand the alternative arguments that they reject. For a historian, then, being unwilling to step outside of one's familiar intellectual space is an obstacle to achieving objectivity (end of the second paragraph) (lines 52–54). The passage also describes other obstacles in the first paragraph, e.g., wishful thinking, the inability to assimilate bad news, and the refusal to reject favored interpretations that fail tests of evidence and logic. Additionally, the third paragraph could be understood to present superficial neutrality as an obstacle to deeper objectivity. So the argument described in passage A and the one made in passage B are both advanced by identifying obstacles to objectivity.

The Incorrect Answer Choices:

A Though passage A mentions relativist historians, who reject fixed truth in historical interpretation, neither passage cites any specific historical scholarship. Both passages are written at a very general level, describing in an abstract way how objectivity should be understood and how it can be achieved.

B Neither passage claims that recent developments in historical scholarship have undermined the credibility of the profession. The author of passage A believes that relativist historians are mistaken (about one claim, at least). But there's no indication that the author believes that this is a recent development or that it has undermined the credibility of the profession as a whole. Passage B seems to be targeted at those who think that objectivity for a historian should be understood as neutrality. But, again, there's no indication that the author thinks that the adoption of this latter view is a recent development or that it has undermined the credibility of the entire profession.

C   There is nothing in passage B that could be interpreted as a summary of an opposing argument. The opposing view would be that objectivity involves neutrality, and passage B does not discuss any argument for this view. Passage A mentions and rejects one claim of relativist historians, but the passage does not identify any specific reasoning flaws associated with this claim.

D   Passage A does suggest that historians should adopt the qualities of a neutral judge. But the only field besides history that passage B discusses is television news. Passage B clearly does not suggest that historians should adopt standards used by television newscasters.

- *Difficulty Level: 4*

General Directions for the LSAT Answer Sheet

The actual testing time for this portion of the test will be 2 hours 55 minutes. There are five sections, each with a time limit of 35 minutes. The supervisor will tell you when to begin and end each section. If you finish a section before time is called, you may check your work on that section **only;** do not turn to any other section of the test book and do not work on any other section either in the test book or on the answer sheet.

There are several different types of questions on the test, and each question type has its own directions. **Be sure you understand the directions for each question type before attempting to answer any questions in that section.**

Not everyone will finish all the questions in the time allowed. Do not hurry, but work steadily and as quickly as you can without sacrificing accuracy. You are advised to use your time effectively. If a question seems too difficult, go on to the next one and return to the difficult question after completing the section. **MARK THE BEST ANSWER YOU CAN FOR EVERY QUESTION. NO DEDUCTIONS WILL BE MADE FOR WRONG ANSWERS. YOUR SCORE WILL BE BASED ONLY ON THE NUMBER OF QUESTIONS YOU ANSWER CORRECTLY.**

ALL YOUR ANSWERS MUST BE MARKED ON THE ANSWER SHEET. Answer spaces for each question are lettered to correspond with the letters of the potential answers to each question in the test book. After you have decided which of the answers is correct, blacken the corresponding space on the answer sheet. **BE SURE THAT EACH MARK IS BLACK AND COMPLETELY FILLS THE ANSWER SPACE.** Give only one answer to each question. If you change an answer, be sure that all previous marks are **erased completely.** Since the answer sheet is machine scored, incomplete erasures may be interpreted as intended answers. **ANSWERS RECORDED IN THE TEST BOOK WILL NOT BE SCORED.**

There may be more question numbers on this answer sheet than there are questions in a section. Do not be concerned, but be certain that the section and number of the question you are answering matches the answer sheet section and question number. Additional answer spaces in any answer sheet section should be left blank. Begin your next section in the number one answer space for that section.

LSAC takes various steps to ensure that answer sheets are returned from test centers in a timely manner for processing. In the unlikely event that an answer sheet is not received, LSAC will permit the examinee either to retest at no additional fee or to receive a refund of his or her LSAT fee. **THESE REMEDIES ARE THE ONLY REMEDIES AVAILABLE IN THE UNLIKELY EVENT THAT AN ANSWER SHEET IS NOT RECEIVED BY LSAC.**

Score Cancellation

Complete this section only if you are absolutely certain you want to cancel your score. **A CANCELLATION REQUEST CANNOT BE RESCINDED. IF YOU ARE AT ALL UNCERTAIN, YOU SHOULD NOT COMPLETE THIS SECTION.**

To cancel your score from this administration, you **must:**

A. fill in both ovals here ...... ○ ○
         AND
B. read the following statement. Then sign your name and enter the date.
YOUR SIGNATURE ALONE IS NOT SUFFICIENT FOR SCORE CANCELLATION. BOTH OVALS ABOVE MUST BE FILLED IN FOR SCANNING EQUIPMENT TO RECOGNIZE YOUR REQUEST FOR SCORE CANCELLATION.

I certify that I wish to cancel my test score from this administration. I understand that my request is irreversible and that my score will not be sent to me or to the law schools to which I apply.

Sign your name in full
_____

Date
_____

FOR LSAC USE ONLY   ●

HOW DID YOU PREPARE FOR THE LSAT?
(Select all that apply.)

Responses to this item are voluntary and will be used for statistical research purposes only.

○ By studying the free sample questions available on LSAC's website.
○ By taking the free sample LSAT available on LSAC's website.
○ By working through official LSAT *PrepTests, ItemWise,* and/or other LSAC test prep products.
○ By using LSAT prep books or software **not** published by LSAC.
○ By attending a commercial test preparation or coaching course.
○ By attending a test preparation or coaching course offered through an undergraduate institution.
○ Self study.
○ Other preparation.
○ No preparation.

CERTIFYING STATEMENT
Please write the following statement. Sign and date.

I certify that I am the examinee whose name appears on this answer sheet and that I am here to take the LSAT for the sole purpose of being considered for admission to law school. I further certify that I will neither assist nor receive assistance from any other candidate, and I agree not to copy, retain, or transmit examination questions in any form or discuss them with any other person.

_____

_____

_____

_____

_____

_____

_____

_____

SIGNATURE: _____   TODAY'S DATE: ___/___/___
                                                                                    MONTH DAY YEAR

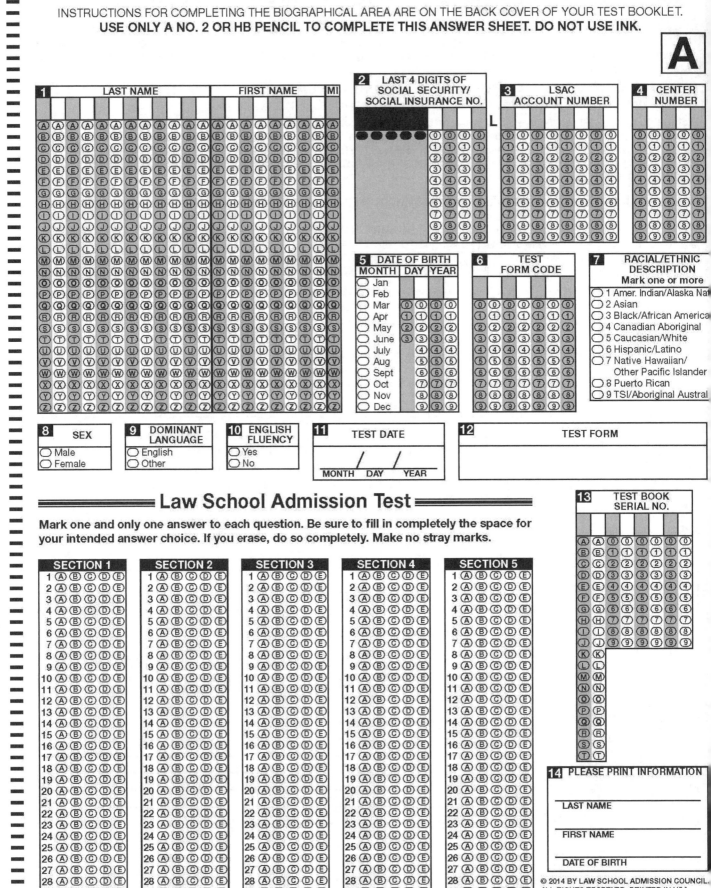

PREPTEST C, TABLE OF CONTENTS

SECTION I

Time—35 minutes

23 Questions

<u>Directions:</u> Each group of questions in this section is based on a set of conditions. In answering some of the questions, it may be useful to draw a rough diagram. Choose the response that most accurately and completely answers each question and blacken the corresponding space on your answer sheet.

<u>Questions 1–5</u>

Eight children—four girls (Nora, Oona, Petra, Sally) and four boys (Tommy, Ulysses, Wei, Xavier)—are seated in the three cars (front, middle, and rear) of a roller coaster. Each car holds a maximum of three children. The following conditions must apply:

Each car contains at least one boy.
Petra sits in the rear car.
Oona sits in the front car with two boys.
Tommy's car is immediately in front of Nora's car.
Ulysses' car is in front of Nora's car.

1. Which one of the following could be true?

(A)   Oona, Tommy, and Ulysses sit in the front car.
(B)   Oona, Tommy, and Petra sit in the front car.
(C)   Tommy, Nora, and Sally sit in the middle car.
(D)   Oona, Tommy, and Sally sit in the middle car.
(E)   Tommy, Xavier, and Petra sit in the rear car.

GO ON TO THE NEXT PAGE.

2. If Xavier and Nora sit in one of the cars with a third child, then the third child could be

   (A) Tommy
   (B) Ulysses
   (C) Wei
   (D) Oona
   (E) Sally

3. If Tommy does not sit in the front car, which one of the following must be true?

   (A) Xavier sits in the front car.
   (B) Wei sits in the front car.
   (C) Xavier sits in the middle car.
   (D) Sally sits in the middle car.
   (E) Ulysses sits in the rear car.

4. Which one of the following is a complete and accurate list of the children each of whom CANNOT sit in a car that has exactly two children in it?

   (A) Oona
   (B) Ulysses, Oona
   (C) Oona, Petra
   (D) Ulysses, Oona, Petra
   (E) Nora, Oona, Petra

5. Which one of the following must be true?

   (A) Ulysses' car is in front of Sally's car.
   (B) Sally's car is in front of Nora's car.
   (C) Oona's car is in front of Ulysses' car.
   (D) Xavier's car is in front of Wei's car.
   (E) Tommy's car is in front of Sally's car.

GO ON TO THE NEXT PAGE.

Questions 6–10

Exactly five objects—J, K, L, M, and N—are to be stacked one on top of the other. Their resulting positions are numbered from 1 through 5, from bottom to top. The resulting stack must meet the following restrictions:

L is immediately above K in the stack.

J is not in position 1.

M is not immediately below K in the stack.

N is either in position 1 or else in position 5.

6. Which one of the following could be the objects in the stack, listed from bottom to top?

(A)   J, K, L, M, N
(B)   K, L, J, N, M
(C)   L, K, J, M, N
(D)   M, K, L, J, N
(E)   N, M, J, K, L

GO ON TO THE NEXT PAGE.

7. If J is on top of the stack, which one of the following must be true?

  (A) K is in position 4.
  (B) L is in position 2.
  (C) L is in position 4.
  (D) M is in position 2.
  (E) M is in position 4.

8. If L is in position 2 in the stack, which one of the following could be true?

  (A) J is in position 3.
  (B) J is in position 5.
  (C) M is in position 1.
  (D) M is in position 5.
  (E) N is in position 1.

9. Which one of the following could be in any one of the five positions in the stack?

  (A) J
  (B) K
  (C) L
  (D) M
  (E) N

10. If M is neither directly above nor directly below J in the stack, which one of the following objects must be in position 4?

  (A) J
  (B) K
  (C) L
  (D) M
  (E) N

GO ON TO THE NEXT PAGE.

Questions 11–17

A costume designer has been asked to put together exactly three tricolored costumes, choosing among six colors— green, indigo, orange, red, white, and yellow. Each of the six colors must appear in at least one of the costumes. The costumes are to be designed according to the following requirements:

No two costumes can have the same color combination.
Any costume that has indigo in it must also have yellow in it.
Any costume that has yellow in it must also have indigo in it.
If a costume has red in it, then it can have neither indigo nor green in it.

11. Which one of the following could be the colors of each of the three costumes?

(A)   green, indigo, and orange
       green, indigo, and yellow
       orange, red, and white
(B)   green, indigo, and yellow
       green, orange, and white
       orange, red, and white
(C)   green, orange, and red
       indigo, white, and yellow
       orange, red, and white
(D)   green, orange, and white
       indigo, red, and yellow
       indigo, white, and yellow
(E)   green, white, and yellow
       indigo, white, and yellow
       orange, red, and white

GO ON TO THE NEXT PAGE.

12. Which one of the following could be true?

    (A)   All three of the costumes have green in them.
    (B)   All three of the costumes have yellow in them.
    (C)   Exactly two of the costumes have red in them.
    (D)   Exactly one of the costumes has orange in it.
    (E)   At least one of the costumes has both red and
           yellow in it.

13. If only one of the costumes has both yellow and
    orange in it, then which one of the following
    could be true?

    (A)   Exactly one of the costumes has yellow in it.
    (B)   Exactly two of the costumes have green in
           them.
    (C)   Exactly three of the costumes have white in
           them.
    (D)   At least one of the costumes has both indigo
           and white in it.
    (E)   At least two of the costumes have both green
           and white in them.

14. If one of the costumes has green, orange, and
    white in it, then which one of the following
    must be true?

    (A)   All three of the costumes have white in them.
    (B)   Exactly two of the costumes have green in
           them.
    (C)   Exactly one of the costumes has indigo in it.
    (D)   Exactly one of the costumes has orange in it.
    (E)   At least one of the costumes has both indigo
           and green in it.

15. Which one of the following, if true, completely
    determines the colors each of the three costumes has?

    (A)   All three of the costumes have white in them.
    (B)   Exactly one of the costumes has green in it.
    (C)   Exactly one of the costumes has both green and
           orange in it.
    (D)   Exactly one of the costumes has both indigo and
           white in it.
    (E)   Exactly one of the costumes has both orange
           and white in it.

16. Which one of the following must be false?

    (A)   Exactly two of the costumes have indigo in
           them.
    (B)   Exactly two of the costumes have white in
           them.
    (C)   All three of the costumes have orange in them.
    (D)   Exactly one of the costumes has both yellow
           and white in it.
    (E)   Exactly two of the costumes have both green
           and orange in them.

17. If exactly two of the costumes have yellow in
    them, then which one of the following could be
    false?

    (A)   Exactly two of the costumes have indigo in
           them.
    (B)   Exactly one of the costumes has both green and
           indigo in it.
    (C)   Exactly one of the costumes has both red and
           white in it.
    (D)   Exactly one of the costumes has green in it.
    (E)   Exactly one of the costumes has white in it.

GO ON TO THE NEXT PAGE.

Questions 18–23

A radio station is planning a program in which a total of six politicians—Fallon, Greer, Hernandez, Kim, Lewis, and Munson—will be interviewed. The program will consist of exactly four segments. At least one of the politicians will be interviewed in each segment, and none will be interviewed in more than one segment. The following constraints apply:

Hernandez must be interviewed in a segment that is earlier than any segment in which Fallon or Munson is interviewed.

Kim and Munson must be interviewed in the same segment as each other.

More of the politicians must be interviewed in the first segment than in the second segment.

18. Which one of the following is a possible matching of the politicians to the program segments in which they are interviewed?

(A)   first: Greer, Hernandez
second: Fallon
third: Kim, Lewis
fourth: Munson

(B)   first: Greer, Lewis
second: Fallon
third: Kim, Munson
fourth: Hernandez

(C)   first: Hernandez
second: Greer, Lewis
third: Fallon
fourth: Kim, Munson

(D)   first: Hernandez, Lewis
second: Greer
third: Kim, Munson
fourth: Fallon

(E)   first: Hernandez, Kim, Munson
second: Fallon
third: Greer
fourth: Lewis

GO ON TO THE NEXT PAGE.

19. Which one of the following must be true of one of the program segments?

(A) Fallon is the sole politician interviewed.
(B) Greer is the sole politician interviewed.
(C) Greer and exactly one of the other politicians are interviewed.
(D) Hernandez and exactly one of the other politicians are interviewed.
(E) Lewis and exactly one of the other politicians are interviewed.

20. How many of the politicians are there any one of whom could be the sole politician interviewed in the third segment?

(A) four
(B) three
(C) two
(D) one
(E) zero

21. If Fallon is interviewed in an earlier segment than Lewis, which one of the following could be true?

(A) Fallon is interviewed in the third segment.
(B) Greer is interviewed in the third segment.
(C) Hernandez is interviewed in the second segment.
(D) Lewis is interviewed in the second segment.
(E) Munson is interviewed in the fourth segment.

22. Greer must be interviewed in the same segment as Hernandez if which one of the following is true?

(A) Fallon is interviewed in the second segment.
(B) Greer is interviewed in the first segment.
(C) Kim is interviewed in the third segment.
(D) Lewis is interviewed in the second segment.
(E) Munson is interviewed in the fourth segment.

23. Which one of the following, if substituted for the constraint that Hernandez must be interviewed in a segment that is earlier than any segment in which Fallon or Munson is interviewed, would have the same effect in determining the program segments in which the politicians are interviewed?

(A) Hernandez must be interviewed in a segment that is earlier than any segment in which Lewis or Munson is interviewed.
(B) Hernandez must be interviewed in a segment that is earlier than any segment in which Fallon or Kim is interviewed.
(C) Neither Fallon nor Munson can be interviewed in the first segment.
(D) Fallon must be the sole politician interviewed in one of the program segments.
(E) Hernandez must be interviewed in the same segment as either Greer or Lewis.

S T O P

IF YOU FINISH BEFORE TIME IS CALLED, YOU MAY CHECK YOUR WORK ON THIS SECTION ONLY.
DO NOT WORK ON ANY OTHER SECTION IN THE TEST.

SECTION II

Time—35 minutes

25 Questions

<u>Directions:</u> The questions in this section are based on the reasoning contained in brief statements or passages. For some questions, more than one of the choices could conceivably answer the question. However, you are to choose the <u>best</u> answer; that is, the response that most accurately and completely answers the question. You should not make assumptions that are by commonsense standards implausible, superfluous, or incompatible with the passage. After you have chosen the best answer, blacken the corresponding space on your answer sheet.

1. Mysterious ancient tracks cut into limestone have recently been found on the island of Malta. The tracks wander, sometimes disappearing under modern structures. Their origin and purpose are unknown, but evidence indicates that they could have connected settlements or water sources. One archaeologist hypothesizes, based on the tracks' physical appearance and surroundings, that they were made in about 1000 B.C. by animal-drawn carts.

Which one of the following, if true, most helps to support the archaeologist's hypothesis mentioned above?

(A) Areas near the tracks have yielded relatively large amounts of fossilized animal excrement dating from approximately 1000 B.C.

(B) Some of the tracks connect areas that are sources of fresh water on Malta today.

(C) Some terrain on the island of Malta is more easily traversed on foot than are certain other types of terrain there.

(D) Historically, inhabitants of the island of Malta have not been innovative users of transportation technology.

(E) Around 1000 B.C., some settlements were abandoned in parts of Malta.

2. Book collector: The demand for out-of-print books is increasing. It has been spurred by the rise of the Internet, the search capabilities of which make it much easier to locate the out-of-print books one seeks.

The book collector's statements, if true, most strongly support which one of the following?

(A) Book collectors are now using the Internet to find book titles that they previously did not know existed.

(B) Fewer people try to find books that are in print than try to find books that are out of print.

(C) The amount of demand for out-of-print books is affected by the ease of finding such books.

(D) The Internet's search capabilities make it possible to locate most out-of-print books.

(E) Only people who have access to the Internet can locate out-of-print books.

3. Agriculture researcher: Because of its slow decomposition, paper is ineffective as a mulch to guard against soil erosion. However, a mixture of paper and manure, which decomposes faster than paper alone, is very effective. When spread over test plots, the mixture significantly decreased the amount of soil erosion. Since paper costs roughly the same as manure, farmers would be better off using this mixture than paper or manure alone.

The agriculture researcher's argument is flawed because it provides no evidence that

(A) paper by itself does not contribute to soil erosion

(B) mulch containing paper and manure works better than mulch containing only paper

(C) mulch containing paper and manure works better than mulch containing only manure

(D) mulch containing paper and manure works better than methods of preventing soil erosion that do not involve mulch

(E) mulch of pure manure provides nutrients to the soil that paper mulch does not

GO ON TO THE NEXT PAGE.

4. In the spring and fall, eastern pipistrelle bats roost deep inside caves. They feed at night on flying insects and must leave the cave to catch their prey. Flying insects are much more abundant on warm nights than on cool ones. Researchers found that many more bats leave the caves on warm nights than on cool nights, even though the temperature within the caves where the bats roost remains virtually the same from one night to the next.

Which one of the following, if true, most helps to explain the researchers' findings?

(A) The researchers studied only female bats, which tended to catch more insects on warm nights than did the male bats.

(B) Eastern pipistrelle bats can detect changes in barometric pressure within the caves that correlate closely with changes in temperature outside the caves.

(C) Eastern pipistrelle bats are incapable of long periods of sustained activity outside the roosting caves on very cool spring and fall evenings.

(D) Because of the long period of winter inactivity, eastern pipistrelle bats tend to consume more insects per day in the spring and fall than in the summer.

(E) During the periods in which the researchers studied the bats, on most evenings over half of the bats left the caves in search of food.

5. Human Resources Director: Some people dislike their jobs but still go to work every day because they feel that it is ethically wrong to miss work. Others enjoy their jobs but sometimes miss work because they genuinely believe that they are too sick to work or that they might infect others if they go to work. This makes it difficult to _____.

Which one of the following most reasonably completes the argument?

(A) determine whether employees absent from work more often than others are any less fearful of losing their jobs

(B) maintain accurate absenteeism records for all the different employees of a company

(C) draw any conclusions about an employee's job satisfaction from his or her absenteeism record

(D) assess the trustworthiness of employees who claim that they must miss work because they are ill

(E) make any reliable predictions about an employee's future behavior from his or her absenteeism record

6. The effects of technology on language and the effects of language on culture as a whole are profound and complex. The telegraph, the telephone, and the television have all changed the way people speak to one another. The best current example of such a change is the advent of electronic mail, which has effected a widespread loosening of language usage rules. This loosening has, in turn, made relationships between people more casual than ever before.

Which one of the following propositions is best illustrated by the statements above?

(A) Technology can adversely affect the nature of relationships between people.

(B) Changes in communication media can cause interpersonal relationships to change.

(C) A decrease in linguistic sophistication can lead to an increase in technological sophistication.

(D) A widespread loosening of overly rigid language-usage rules can improve communication.

(E) Changes in interpersonal relationships can cause changes in the way people speak to one another.

7. Builder: Within ten years, most of the new homes constructed in North America will have steel frameworks rather than wood ones. After all, two-by-fours and two-by-sixes—the sizes of lumber most commonly used in home construction—are deteriorating in quality and increasing in cost, while environment-friendly steel is decreasing in cost. In addition, unlike wood, steel will not warp, rot, or split.

Which one of the following, if true, most seriously weakens the builder's reasoning?

(A) Over the next ten years, labor costs in the home construction industry are expected to rise significantly.

(B) Steel-framed homes do not have to be treated with pesticides or other chemicals that can contribute to indoor air pollution.

(C) Because lumber prices have increased over the last decade, currently most new homes are built with steel frameworks.

(D) Training home construction workers to work with steel is very costly.

(E) The number of houses built each year is expected to decrease over the next decade.

GO ON TO THE NEXT PAGE.

8. Candidate: The children in our nation need a better education. My opponent maintains that our outdated school system is the major impediment to achieving this goal. In fact our school system does need reform. Nonetheless, my opponent's position places far too much blame on our schools, for it seems to equate education with schooling, yet other parts of society are at least as responsible for educating our youth as our schools are.

The statement that the school system needs reform figures in the candidate's argument in which one of the following ways?

(A) It is the main conclusion that the argument is attempting to establish about the position of the candidate's opponent.

(B) It is offered as an example of one of the social problems for which the argument proposes a solution.

(C) It is cited as establishing the candidate's contention that far too much is being blamed on schools.

(D) It is used to indicate how the failings of the school system are partially responsible for society's problems.

(E) It is a limited concession made to the candidate's opponent in the context of a broader challenge to the opponent's position.

9. A proposed amendment would allow the city council to decide that certain city elections be conducted solely by mail. But voting is a sacred right in democracies, one that has always been exercised by voting in person and not by mail. Therefore, voting by mail should not be allowed, and the proposed amendment should be rejected.

The reasoning in the argument is most vulnerable to criticism on the grounds that the argument

(A) presumes, without providing justification, that the right to vote is not violated unless elections are conducted solely by mail

(B) presumes, without providing justification, that if citizens have always had a certain legal right, they will continue to have that right in the future

(C) presents an appeal to tradition as the only reason for rejecting the proposal

(D) fails to consider the possibility that, even if it gains the power to do so, the city council might never require voting by mail

(E) has a premise that is logically incompatible with the main conclusion

10. Columnist: Raising the minimum wage to the level recently proposed will actually hurt, rather than help, workers with low incomes. As the minimum wage increases, businesses must compensate for higher wage costs by increasing prices for the goods and services that low-income workers must buy but can already barely afford.

Which one of the following is an assumption on which the columnist's argument depends?

(A) Workers who earn more than the minimum wage would not also be hurt by increased prices for goods and services.

(B) Any increase to the minimum wage smaller than the one proposed would not substantially affect prices of goods and services.

(C) The proposed minimum-wage increase would not wholly compensate low-income workers for the resulting increase in prices for goods and services.

(D) If raising the minimum wage helped low-income workers, this would be a good reason for raising it.

(E) Changes in the minimum wage are generally not as beneficial to the economy as is commonly believed.

11. A recently completed study of several hundred subjects, all of approximately the same age, showed that those who exercised regularly during the study were much less likely to die during the study. This indicates that exercise can actually increase one's life span.

Which one of the following, if true, most strengthens the argument?

(A) The subjects who did not exercise regularly during the study tended to have diets that were more unhealthy.

(B) The subjects who did not exercise regularly during the study tended to blame their lack of exercise on a lack of time.

(C) A large number of the deaths recorded were attributable to preexisting conditions or illnesses.

(D) Whether or not a given subject was to exercise during the study was determined by the researchers on a random basis.

(E) A person who exercises regularly is probably doing so out of concern for his or her own health.

GO ON TO THE NEXT PAGE.

12. Shaw: Regulatory limits on pollution emissions from power plants should be set in terms of the long-term average emissions level rather than peak emissions levels.

Levin: But short periods of high pollution emissions pose dangers to the environment. Your proposal is akin to enforcing the highway speed limit by measuring vehicles' average speed, including the time spent in traffic or at stoplights, rather than their peak speed.

Based on the analogy in Levin's argument, time that a vehicle spends at a stoplight is analogous to time that a power plant

(A) operates without any monitoring of its pollution emissions
(B) operates at peak efficiency
(C) emits pollutants at a very low level
(D) emits no pollutants at all
(E) emits pollutants at its peak level

13. Scientist: There is little doubt that the ice ages were caused by the unusually rich growth of vegetation worldwide. Since vegetation converts carbon dioxide into oxygen, excessive vegetation would have depleted the carbon dioxide in the atmosphere. Carbon dioxide helps the atmosphere retain the sun's heat. Thus, if this carbon dioxide is depleted, the earth cools significantly, thereby causing an ice age.

Which one of the following most accurately expresses the main conclusion of the scientist's argument?

(A) Excessive growth of vegetation worldwide could have caused one or more ice ages by depleting the carbon dioxide in the atmosphere.
(B) If the carbon dioxide in the atmosphere is depleted, the earth cools significantly, thereby causing an ice age.
(C) An excessive growth of vegetation causes the carbon dioxide in the atmosphere to be depleted.
(D) If unusually rich growth of vegetation caused the ice ages, it undoubtedly did so by depleting the carbon dioxide in the atmosphere.
(E) Unusually rich growth of vegetation worldwide was almost certainly the cause of the ice ages.

14. A promise is defined as any agreement that yields an obligation. It is acceptable not to keep one's promise if either the person to whom the promise is made tells the promisor not to keep it, or the promisor is unable to fulfill the obligation due to circumstances beyond the promisor's control.

Which one of the following is an application of the principle above pertaining to promising?

(A) Paul agreed to lend Tom $10. But Paul also owes Maria $10. So it is unacceptable for Paul to fulfill his promise to lend Tom $10 while he still owes Maria money.
(B) Felicia agreed to tutor Alan in mathematics on Tuesday. However, on his way to the tutorial session, Alan was injured in a car accident and was unable to attend that day. Thus, it was acceptable for Felicia not to tutor Alan in mathematics on Tuesday.
(C) Mika agreed to help Owen move on Sunday, but Owen called Mika on the Thursday before the move and asked him to help him move on Saturday instead. So it would be unacceptable for Mika not to consent to help Owen move on Saturday.
(D) Quinn agreed to water Laura's plants while Laura was out of town. But Laura had forgotten to give Quinn the keys to her place. However, it was unacceptable for Quinn to fail to fulfill his promise to Laura, since Laura did not excuse Quinn from his obligation to water her plants.
(E) Ian agreed to pick up Ali at the train station. But Ian decided to stop and return his overdue library books first. As a result, Ian was unable to pick up Ali at the train station. Thus, it was acceptable for Ian to fail to pick up Ali at the train station.

GO ON TO THE NEXT PAGE.

15. H. G. Wells's great dramatic novel *The Time Machine* is classified as science fiction simply because it takes place in the future. But this classification is inappropriate because Wells's book possesses something that great dramatic novels have and science fiction generally lacks—compelling characters that enable the reader to become absorbed in their plight and not just in the author's representation of the future of technology.

The argument's conclusion follows logically if which one of the following is assumed?

(A)   All novels that contain compelling characters are great dramatic novels.

(B)   Novels can always be clearly classified into distinct genres.

(C)   A work of science fiction cannot achieve greatness unless it contains compelling characters.

(D)   The most important determinant of a novel's quality is the strength of its characters.

(E)   A dramatic novel cannot both be great and belong to the genre of science fiction.

16. Laurel: Modern moral theories must be jettisoned, or at least greatly reworked, because they fail to provide guidance in extreme cases, which are precisely the times when people most need guidance.

Miriam: A moral theory, like an overcoat, can be quite useful even if it is not useful in every possible situation. Being useful in a wide variety of common circumstances is all we need from a moral theory.

Laurel's and Miriam's statements provide the most support for the claim that they disagree about whether

(A)   it is preferable to develop a moral theory that provides solutions to all the moral dilemmas that could arise

(B)   people abandoned earlier moral theories when they encountered dilemmas that those theories did not adequately address

(C)   a moral theory's adequacy depends on its ability to provide guidance in extreme cases

(D)   just as people need different overcoats in different climates, so too do they need different moral theories on different occasions

(E)   a moral theory developed in the light of extreme cases is unlikely to provide adequate guidance in more usual cases

17. Archaeologists excavating a Neanderthal campsite found discarded gazelle teeth there whose coloration indicated that gazelles had been hunted throughout the year. The archaeologists concluded that the Neanderthals had inhabited the campsite year-round and thus were not nomadic. In contrast, the archaeologists cite a neighboring campsite of nomadic Cro-Magnons that contained teeth from gazelles all killed during the same season.

Which one of the following, if true, most seriously weakens the archaeologists' reasoning?

(A)   Neanderthals hunted a wide variety of both migratory and nonmigratory animals.

(B)   Cro-Magnons and Neanderthals sometimes exchanged tools.

(C)   Neanderthals saved gazelle teeth for use in religious rituals and later discarded them.

(D)   Cro-Magnons usually followed the migrations of the animals they hunted.

(E)   Gazelles inhabited the area around the campsites year-round.

18. Critic: The contemporary novel is incapable of making important new contributions. The evidence is clear. Contemporary psychological novels have been failures. Contemporary action novels lack any social significance. And contemporary romance novels are stale and formulaic.

The flawed reasoning in the critic's argument is most similar to that in which one of the following?

(A)   Since no government has been able to regulate either employment or inflation very closely, it is impossible for any government to improve its nation's economy.

(B)   Because there has been substantial progress in recent years in making machines more efficient, it is only a matter of time before we invent a perpetual motion machine.

(C)   The essayist Macaulay was as widely read in his time as Dickens, but has been neglected since. Thus writers who are popular today are likely to be forgotten in the future.

(D)   This politician has not made any proposals for dealing with the problem of unemployment and thus must not think the problem is important.

(E)   In international commerce, the corporations that are best suited for success are large and multinational. Thus small corporations cannot compete at the international level.

GO ON TO THE NEXT PAGE.

19. Criminologist: According to a countrywide tabulation of all crimes reported to local police departments, the incidence of crime per 100,000 people has risen substantially over the last 20 years. However, a series of independent surveys of randomly selected citizens of the country gives the impression that the total number of crimes was less in recent years than it was 20 years ago.

Which one of the following, if true, would most help to resolve the apparent discrepancy described by the criminologist?

(A) Not all of the citizens selected for the series of independent surveys had been the victims of crime.

(B) Most crimes committed in the country are not reported to local police departments.

(C) The total annual number of crimes committed in the country has risen over the past 20 years but has fallen in proportion to the country's growing population.

(D) In the series of independent surveys, many of the respondents did not accurately describe the crimes to which they had fallen victim.

(E) Of crimes committed in the country, a much greater proportion have been reported to local police departments in recent years than were reported 20 years ago.

20. Geologist: A new method for forecasting earthquakes has reliably predicted several earthquakes. Unfortunately, this method can predict only that an earthquake will fall somewhere within a range of two and a half points on the Richter scale. Thus, since a difference of two and a half points can be the difference between a marginally perceptible shaking and a quake that causes considerable damage, the new method is unlikely to be useful.

Which one of the following, if assumed, enables the geologist's conclusion to be properly inferred?

(A) Even if an earthquake-forecasting method makes predictions within a very narrow range on the Richter scale, this method is not likely to be useful unless its predictions are reliable.

(B) An earthquake-forecasting method is unlikely to be useful unless its predictions always differentiate earthquakes that are barely noticeable from ones that result in substantial destruction.

(C) An earthquake-forecasting method has not been shown to be useful until it has been used to reliably predict a large number of earthquakes.

(D) Several well-established methods for forecasting earthquakes can predict within much narrower ranges than two and a half points on the Richter scale.

(E) An earthquake-forecasting technique, even a perfectly reliable one, will probably be of little use if its predictions never distinguish between earthquakes that are imperceptibly small and those that cause catastrophic damage.

GO ON TO THE NEXT PAGE.

21. Cultural anthropological theory tends to fall into two camps. One focuses on everyday social behavior as a system that has developed in response to human needs in a given environment. The other rejects this approach, focusing on the systems of meanings by which thoughts, rituals, and mythology in a society are structured. Cultural anthropologists, however, should employ both approaches, and also attend to a third, often neglected dimension: the view of a community as a set of individuals whose actions constitute the actual stuff of everyday life.

Which one of the following statements is most strongly supported by the information above?

(A) Patterns of social behavior have meaning only when considered from the point of view of the community.

(B) Cultural anthropologists too often rely on a conception of human needs that excludes the notion of community.

(C) Cultural anthropological theorists who focus on issues of meaning overlook the humanity of their individual subjects.

(D) Systems of behavior can be understood only by experiencing the environments to which they respond.

(E) Disagreement among cultural anthropological theorists does not necessarily imply that their approaches are incompatible.

22. Journal editor: Our treasurer advises that because of our precarious financial situation, we should change from a paper version to an online version only if doing so will not increase the cost of publication. The cost of converting from a paper version to an online version is high; however, once the conversion is made, the cost per issue is much lower for an online version. Since a benefactor has agreed to cover the costs of conversion, and since we can safely assume that our treasurer is right, we should change to an online version.

The journal editor's argument is flawed in that it

(A) treats meeting a necessary condition for changing from a paper to an online version as a sufficient reason for changing

(B) takes for granted that publishing a paper version rather than an online version is the reason the journal is in a precarious financial position

(C) overlooks the possibility that an online version would have other advantages over a paper version than cost

(D) fails to rule out the possibility that the journal will remain in a precarious financial position whether it changes to an online version or not

(E) bases its conclusion on the argument of an authority speaking outside the authority's field of expertise

23. Some people believe there is intelligent life somewhere in the universe besides Earth. But no one who believes that could also believe all planets other than Earth are devoid of life. Thus, some people do not believe all planets other than Earth are devoid of life.

The reasoning in which one of the following is most similar to the reasoning in the argument above?

(A) Some people believe computers are capable of thought. Since no one who does not believe computer chess programs sometimes beat human chess masters believes computers can think, it follows that computer chess programs do sometimes beat human chess masters.

(B) Some cat owners believe cats are incapable of feeling guilty. Since one could think that an animal is capable of feeling guilty only if one thought the animal had a conception of morality, it follows that some cat owners do not believe cats have a conception of morality.

(C) Some dog owners believe their dogs are emotionally attached to them. Since no one could believe that and also believe dogs are incapable of thought, it follows that some dog owners do not believe dogs are incapable of thought.

(D) Some people believe humans will someday colonize other planets. Since anyone who believes that probably also believes overpopulation of Earth is not a problem, it follows that some people do not believe overpopulation of Earth is not a problem.

(E) Some people believe there is life on planets other than Earth. Since anyone who believes that must also believe other planets have atmospheres that can support life, it follows that other planets do have atmospheres that can support life.

GO ON TO THE NEXT PAGE.

24. Clarissa: The natural sciences would not have made such progress but for the power of mathematics. No observation is worth serious attention unless it is stated precisely in quantitative terms.

   Myungsook: I disagree. Converting observations into numbers is the hardest and last task; it can be done only when you have thoroughly explored the observations themselves.

   Clarissa and Myungsook's statements provide the most support for claiming that they disagree about whether

   (A)   mathematics has been a highly significant factor in the advance of the natural sciences
   (B)   converting observations into quantitative terms is usually easy
   (C)   not all observations can be stated precisely in quantitative terms
   (D)   successfully doing natural science demands careful consideration of observations not stated precisely in quantitative terms
   (E)   useful scientific theories require the application of mathematics

25. Although Stillwater Pond has been polluted by farm runoff for years, several species of fish still live there. The local fishing guide says that "the most populous fish species in the pond is also the one that has adapted best to living in polluted water." So if, as recent studies suggest, the most populous fish species in the pond is the bullhead catfish, then it must be that the local fishing guide believes that the species of fish in the pond that has adapted best to living in polluted water is the bullhead catfish.

   The argument above is most vulnerable to criticism on the grounds that it

   (A)   takes for granted that the local fishing guide believes that Stillwater Pond has been polluted by farm runoff for years
   (B)   fails to take into account the possibility that the catfish in Stillwater Pond had to adapt very little to survive in polluted water
   (C)   fails to take into account the possibility that the recent studies on fish populations in Stillwater Pond are inaccurate
   (D)   fails to take into account the possibility that the local fishing guide mistakenly believes that some fish species other than the bullhead catfish is the most populous fish species in Stillwater Pond
   (E)   takes for granted that Stillwater Pond has only one species of catfish living in it

S T O P

IF YOU FINISH BEFORE TIME IS CALLED, YOU MAY CHECK YOUR WORK ON THIS SECTION ONLY.
DO NOT WORK ON ANY OTHER SECTION IN THE TEST.

SECTION III
Time—35 minutes
25 Questions

Directions: The questions in this section are based on the reasoning contained in brief statements or passages. For some questions, more than one of the choices could conceivably answer the question. However, you are to choose the best answer; that is, the response that most accurately and completely answers the question. You should not make assumptions that are by commonsense standards implausible, superfluous, or incompatible with the passage. After you have chosen the best answer, blacken the corresponding space on your answer sheet.

1. In a transportation company, a certain syndrome often attributed to stress by medical experts afflicts a significantly higher percentage of workers in Department F than in any other department. We can conclude, therefore, that the work done in Department F subjects workers to higher stress levels than does the work in the other departments in the company.

Which one of the following, if true, most helps to support the argument?

(A) Department F has more employees than any other department in the company.
(B) Some experts believe that the syndrome can be caused by various factors, only one of which is high stress.
(C) Many workers who transfer into Department F from elsewhere in the company soon begin to develop the syndrome.
(D) It is relatively common for workers in the transportation industry to suffer from the syndrome.
(E) Job-related stress has been the most frequently cited cause for dissatisfaction among workers at the company.

2. Because metallic mirrors absorb some light, they waste energy. When light strikes a metallic mirror, electrons in the mirror move, using energy and dimming the reflected image. As a result, metallic mirrors cannot be used in applications in which minimizing energy loss is important, such as high-powered lasers.

Which one of the following most accurately expresses the argument's main conclusion?

(A) Metallic mirrors reduce the effectiveness of high-powered lasers.
(B) Part of the light falling on metallic mirrors tends to be absorbed by them.
(C) High-powered lasers require mirrors that conserve energy.
(D) A tendency to waste energy is the most significant disadvantage of metallic mirrors.
(E) Metallic mirrors are unsuitable for applications where it is crucial to minimize energy loss.

3. If Patricia eats a heavy, spicy meal tonight, she will get a bad case of heartburn later. If Patricia gets a bad case of heartburn later, she will be grouchy tomorrow morning. So if Patricia eats a heavy, spicy meal tonight, she will be grouchy tomorrow morning.

Which one of the following arguments is most similar in its logical features to the argument above?

(A) If Ruth plants only daffodils, the squirrels will eat the bulbs. If the squirrels eat the bulbs, then no flowers will bloom in Ruth's garden. Since no flowers are blooming in Ruth's garden, she must have planted only daffodils.
(B) If Shawn starts gardening in early spring, he can plant tomatoes early. If Shawn can plant tomatoes early, he will have plenty of tomatoes for canning. But he does not have plenty of tomatoes for canning, so either he did not start gardening in early spring or he did not plant tomatoes early.
(C) Maria plants either petunias or geraniums in her garden. If Maria plants petunias, she plants purple ones. If Maria plants geraniums, she plants red ones. Since both petunias and geraniums are flowers, Maria will have either purple or red flowers in her garden.
(D) If Li plants old rose varieties, her garden will look beautiful. If Li's garden looks beautiful, Li's neighbors will be impressed. So if Li plants old rose varieties, her neighbors will be impressed.
(E) If Bryan's fruit trees are to produce well, he must either prune them in the fall or fertilize them in the spring. Since Bryan wants his trees to produce well but forgot to prune them last fall, Bryan is sure to fertilize his trees this spring.

GO ON TO THE NEXT PAGE.

4. Huang: Most people who commit violent crimes do not carefully consider whether or how they will be punished for these crimes. And those who don't commit violent crimes have no inclination to do so. Rather than impose harsh mandatory sentences, we should attend to the root causes of violence to reduce the rate of violent crime.

   Suarez: Would you say the same about nonviolent crimes, such as tax evasion? Surely mandatory penalties are a useful deterrent in these cases. At any rate, I am confident that mandatory sentences prevent most people who would otherwise physically harm others from doing so.

   The dialogue between Huang and Suarez most strongly supports the claim that they disagree about whether

   (A)   the best way to reduce violent crime is to address the root causes of violence
   (B)   people who commit violent crimes deserve harsh punishment
   (C)   people who commit violent crimes carefully consider how they will be punished for their crimes
   (D)   mandatory sentences will deter most people who might otherwise commit violent crimes
   (E)   severe penalties reduce the incidence of tax evasion

5. Those who participate in risky sports often do so to confront their fears. For example, rock climbers are more likely than others to have once suffered from a fear of heights. Those who participate in such risk-taking activities also have more self-confidence than others, so it is probably true that confronting one's fears increases one's self-confidence.

   Which one of the following, if true, most weakens the reasoning above?

   (A)   Often those who suffer from fears such as a fear of heights either do not know that they suffer from those fears or do not know the extent to which they suffer from them.
   (B)   In general, people who currently participate in risky sports had above-average self-confidence even before participating in any risky sport.
   (C)   Most people who refrain from engaging in risky sports refrain from doing so for reasons other than a fear of death or injury.
   (D)   Participating in risky sports is not the only way to confront one's fears.
   (E)   Most of those who do not participate in risky sports believe that they lack the capacity to excel in such activities.

6. Melchior: Some studies have linked infants' consumption of formula made from cow's milk to subsequent diabetes. Nonetheless, parents should feed cow's milk formula to their infants. After all, cow's milk is an excellent source of several nutrients important to infants' development.

   The reasoning in Melchior's argument is most vulnerable to criticism on the grounds that it

   (A)   defends a certain practice on the basis that it has a certain benefit without considering whether an alternative practice has the same benefit
   (B)   draws a conclusion that simply restates a claim that is presented in support of that conclusion
   (C)   inappropriately introduces normative claims in support of a conclusion that is entirely factual
   (D)   distorts an argument against feeding cow's milk formula to infants and then attacks this distorted argument
   (E)   confuses an absence of evidence in support of a claim with the existence of evidence against a claim

7. In an attempt to create brand loyalties, television advertisers currently target young adults, ages 18 to 25, because on average they have higher discretionary income than do consumers of other age groups. But since the average discretionary income of those over 65 will soon be greater than that of young adults, in the future television advertisers would do better to target consumers over 65 instead.

   Which one of the following, if true, would most weaken the argument above?

   (A)   Consumers over the age of 65 tend to watch different television shows than do young adults.
   (B)   The older a consumer is, the more likely he or she is to have already established brand loyalties.
   (C)   The average discretionary income of young adults is projected to rise in the near future.
   (D)   The greater a consumer's discretionary income, the more likely advertising is to encourage that consumer to buy.
   (E)   The number of consumers over the age of 65 is increasing more rapidly than is the number of young adults.

GO ON TO THE NEXT PAGE.

8. Politician: It is widely accepted that because democratic politics cannot exist without debate about political issues, and because self-governance flourishes when citizens are allowed to express their feelings verbally, a democratically governed society should refrain from interfering in individual citizens' speech. I argue that a democratically governed society should also refrain from exercising strict control over the clothing and grooming of its citizens, for this is clearly a venue of self-expression, and it can also serve to make a variety of political statements, without using words.

A logical strategy used in the politician's argument is to

(A) argue for a conclusion by suggesting that the opposite conclusion leads to an absurdity
(B) reach a general conclusion based on the absence of clear counterexamples to an empirical thesis
(C) support a conclusion by claiming that it is widely accepted
(D) reach a conclusion based on evidence that is similar to evidence commonly thought to support an analogous case
(E) reach a conclusion about what democratically governed societies actually do based on premises about what democratically governed societies should do

9. A television commercial argued as follows: both the product advertised and its competitor contain the same active ingredients, but the product advertised contains them in higher concentrations; tests show that the higher concentrations are completely safe; since a product that provides faster relief is always preferable, one should use the product advertised.

The television commercial's argument is most vulnerable to criticism on the grounds that it

(A) takes for granted that it is true in all cases that products with higher concentrations of active ingredients are more effective than their competitors
(B) attempts to establish its conclusion on the basis of evidence that is in principle impossible to disprove
(C) dismisses its competitor's claims because of their source rather than their content
(D) attempts to manipulate the emotions of potential customers of the advertised product rather than presenting logically sound reasons for preferring the product advertised
(E) takes for granted that the product with the higher concentration of active ingredients provides faster relief than its competitor

10. Biologists often announce that a certain kind of animal has been found capable of using tools; this usually refers to something like using a stick to hunt for ants in a log, or a stone to crack nuts. But such announcements are completely unsurprising, since all animals use tools. Birds build nests, fish hide in the mud to escape predators, and squirrels use buildings as shortcuts between trees. If an animal executes its purpose by means of an external physical object, then that object can reasonably be regarded as a tool.

Which one of the following most accurately describes the role played in the argument by the claim that the biologists' announcements that a certain animal has been found capable of using tools are unsurprising?

(A) It provides evidence that the animals' activities given as examples are purposeful.
(B) It is the conclusion of the argument.
(C) It is an assumption used by the argument to justify acceptance of a broader conception of what a tool is than that usually accepted by the biologists.
(D) It calls into question the basis of the biologists' conception of a tool.
(E) It addresses a weakness in the biologists' announcements that stems from their ambiguous use of the word "external."

11. Literary critic: Samuel Johnson argued that writers should refrain from attributing attractive qualities to immoral characters, since doing so increases the tendency of readers to emulate these characters. Works of fiction would be unrealistic, however, if writers were to follow Johnson's advice.

The conclusion is properly drawn in the literary critic's argument if which one of the following is assumed?

(A) One-dimensional characters are less entertaining than well-rounded characters.
(B) The attractive qualities of characters are more appealing than their immoral behavior.
(C) In reality, all bad people have some attractive qualities.
(D) In reality, it is difficult to emulate fictional characters.
(E) It is rarely evident which qualities of fictional characters are intended to be attractive qualities.

GO ON TO THE NEXT PAGE.

12. Clothes dryers manufactured by Archway Appliances, Inc. are of poor quality. Crucial bolts are missing and some sections are assembled in the wrong order, thereby creating a shock and fire hazard. Concern for safety and quality is conspicuously lacking. So Archway must use shoddy, substandard components in its clothes dryers.

The argument is most vulnerable to criticism on the grounds that it fails to consider the possibility that

(A) there is not a single known case of an Archway dryer starting a fire or electrocuting someone
(B) there are aspects of dryer construction that are more relevant to the quality of the finished product than those mentioned
(C) Archway's dryers consistently perform well and enjoy considerable customer loyalty
(D) a shoddily constructed appliance can be made of high-quality parts
(E) Archway's other product lines exhibit careful and safe assembly and use high-quality components

13. Sexual reproduction is achieved when the gamete of a male organism unites with the gamete of a female organism to form a new and genetically unique cell. Each of the two gametes contributes equally to the genetic material found in the new cell's nucleus. However, the genetic material found in the new cell's cytoplasm (the part of a cell outside the nucleus) is contributed exclusively by the female's gamete. A certain type of genetic material, referred to as GM62, is found only in cytoplasm.

Which one of the following is a conclusion that can logically be drawn from the passage above?

(A) All female organisms contribute GM62 to their offspring.
(B) Only female organisms can contribute GM62 to their offspring.
(C) Genetic material is evenly divided between the nucleus and the cytoplasm of a new cell.
(D) The role of the male gamete in sexual reproduction is less important than the role of the female gamete.
(E) It is likely that other types of genetic material that are contributed exclusively by the male gamete will be identified.

14. Forty to 60 percent of students report, in anonymous surveys, that they plagiarized at least once as undergraduates, and evidence indicates that plagiarism also occurs in our medical and business schools. Researchers have found that students who plagiarize are more likely to engage in subsequent professional misconduct such as falsified research results and fraudulent business practices. Thus, a reduction of academic plagiarism will lead to a reduction of professional misconduct.

Which one of the following most accurately describes a flaw in the reasoning in the argument?

(A) The argument relies on the accuracy of reports by people, some of whom, in the nature of the case, cannot be relied upon to provide truthful testimony.
(B) The argument introduces one subject for debate, but proceeds to give premises relevant to a different subject.
(C) The argument presumes, without providing justification, that a certain phenomenon is the only factor contributing to the incidence of a certain other phenomenon.
(D) The argument takes for granted that a certain behavior is more prevalent among members of one population than it is among members of another.
(E) The argument infers the existence of a causal connection merely on the basis of an association.

15. The number of deer living in North America has increased dramatically since the 1960s even though hunters kill no fewer deer today. Moreover, the number of natural predators of deer, such as wolves, is on the rise, and suburbs increasingly encroach on deer habitats.

Which one of the following, if true, would most help to explain the apparent discrepancy described above?

(A) Pesticides that adversely affected most wildlife living in North America have been banned since the 1970s.
(B) Recently, attempts have been made in various parts of North America to protect deer habitats from suburban development.
(C) The number of deer hunters in North America has decreased since the 1960s.
(D) Much of the increase in the population of wolves is due to wolves born in captivity and released into the wild.
(E) The greater the number of deer, the more likely they are to be afflicted with problems such as famine and disease.

GO ON TO THE NEXT PAGE.

3

16. The primary task of a university is to educate. But to teach well, professors must be informed about new developments in their disciplines, and that requires research. Yet many universities cannot afford to support faculty research adequately. So a lack of funds for research adversely affects the degree to which a university can fulfill its central mission.

Which one of the following most accurately expresses the conclusion of the argument?

(A) In order to be able to teach well, university professors must conduct research.

(B) Lack of financial support for faculty research is the root of ineffective teaching at universities.

(C) Effective teaching is the primary mission of a university.

(D) Lack of funds for research reduces the quality of education a university provides.

(E) New means of funding faculty research at universities are needed.

17. Environmentalist: The United Kingdom recently instituted a law requiring that foods containing genetically altered ingredients be labeled accordingly. Food producers, fearing that consumers would understand the labels as warnings and thus avoid their products, rushed to rid those products of genetically altered ingredients. Other countries contemplating such labeling should therefore refrain, because many crops are genetically altered to be pest resistant; loss of demand for these genetically altered crops would necessitate production alternatives, all of which are dangerous and pesticide intensive.

Which one of the following is an assumption on which the environmentalist's argument depends?

(A) In general, people interpret labels stating that some food ingredients are genetically altered as warnings.

(B) Before the United Kingdom instituted a law requiring that foods containing genetically altered ingredients be labeled as such, almost all foods sold there contained genetically altered ingredients.

(C) The reactions of food producers in other countries to laws requiring labeling of foods containing genetically altered ingredients are likely to be similar to the reactions of food producers in the United Kingdom.

(D) Warning labels on food products have proven to be effective in reducing consumption of those products.

(E) Countries that institute new food labeling regulations often experience a change in consumer eating habits.

18. Education critics' contention that the use of calculators in mathematics classes will undermine students' knowledge of the rationale underlying calculational procedures is clearly false. Every new information-handling technology has produced virtually the same accusation. Some Greek philosophers, for example, believed that the advent of written language would erode people's capacity to remember information and speak extemporaneously.

The reasoning in the argument above is most vulnerable to criticism on the grounds that the argument

(A) presents only evidence whose relevancy to the issue raised by the opponents has not been established

(B) draws a conclusion based on an ambiguous notion of knowledge

(C) takes for granted that the advantages offered by new information-handling technologies always outweigh the disadvantages

(D) takes a condition that suffices to prove its conclusion to be a condition necessary for the truth of that conclusion

(E) concludes that a hypothesis is false simply because it contradicts other beliefs held by the advocates of that hypothesis

GO ON TO THE NEXT PAGE.

19. Scott: The Hippocratic oath demands, specifically, that doctors "never divulge" information about patients. Hence the psychiatrist who released tapes of a poet's therapy sessions after the poet's death violated his oath by his actions, even though the tapes were released after the poet's death and to the poet's official biographer. It makes no difference that the poet's published works were written in a confessional manner or that she had assured the psychiatrist that he could do with the tapes as he saw fit.

   Bonara: I agree that doctors are bound not to divulge patient information and would not myself release such tapes without written permission from the patient. Nevertheless, I disagree that the circumstances were irrelevant in this case. I do not think the poet's psychiatrist violated the Hippocratic oath.

   Which one of the following principles, if established, helps most to justify Scott's evaluation of the psychiatrist's actions?

   (A) Restrictions on the release of patient information by psychiatrists are not binding after the patient's death, since after death a person can no longer suffer harm.
   (B) Once a patient has granted a psychiatrist permission to release confidential information, that information can be released to anyone at the psychiatrist's discretion.
   (C) Since a psychiatrist could influence a patient's opinions during therapy, any directives to the psychiatrist by the patient must be interpreted in the light of the patient's actions outside the therapeutic setting.
   (D) Since any psychiatrist's divulging to the public information about a patient could undermine the trust of other patients in their psychiatrists, no patient can release a psychiatrist from the obligation to keep patient information confidential.
   (E) If a patient has expressed an intention to make public information about himself or herself that is in a psychiatrist's possession, the psychiatrist is released from the obligation to keep that information confidential.

20. Professor Gandolf says that all political systems that aim at preventing conflict are legitimate. However, totalitarian political systems are usually good at preventing conflict, since those who are not in power are subject to the will of the powerful. But since all totalitarian political systems are illegitimate, Professor Gandolf's principle must be false.

   Which one of the following is an assumption required by the argument?

   (A) At least one political system that does not aim at preventing conflict is legitimate.
   (B) If a totalitarian political system prevents conflict, such prevention is only incidental to its true aims.
   (C) At least one totalitarian political system aims at preventing conflict.
   (D) No political system that fails to prevent conflict is legitimate.
   (E) Some political systems that are not totalitarian are illegitimate.

21. Musicologist: Ludwig van Beethoven began losing his hearing when he was 30. This loss continued gradually, but was not complete until late in his life. While it may seem that complete hearing loss would be a severe liability for a composer, in Beethoven's case it gave his later music a wonderfully introspective quality that his earlier music lacked.

   Which one of the following statements is most strongly supported by the musicologist's claims?

   (A) It was more difficult for Beethoven to compose his later works than his earlier ones.
   (B) Had he not lost his hearing, Beethoven's later music would have been of poorer quality than it is.
   (C) Had he not lost his hearing, Beethoven would have been less introspective than he was.
   (D) Beethoven's music became gradually more introspective as he grew older.
   (E) Had he not lost his hearing, Beethoven's later music would probably have been different than it is.

GO ON TO THE NEXT PAGE.

22. Critic: Historians purport to discover the patterns inherent in the course of events. But historians actually impose, rather than find, such patterns by choosing what to include in and exclude from their historical narratives. Thus, properly understood, histories reveal more about the presuppositions underlying different historians' attempts to understand what happened than about what actually happened.

The critic's argument depends on which one of the following assumptions?

(A) Historians have many presuppositions in common with one another.

(B) There is no way to determine with certainty whether a pattern described by a historian is actually present in and not merely imposed upon the events.

(C) Historians presuppose that certain historical patterns accurately describe many different eras.

(D) Most historians cannot become aware of the presuppositions that they bring to their narratives.

(E) Which pattern a historian imposes upon events is affected by that historian's presuppositions.

23. Councillor Miller opposes all proposals to raise taxes. Councillor Philopoulos supports increased funding for schools, which in this area are funded entirely by property taxes. It follows that Miller will oppose and Philopoulos will support Councillor Callari's proposal to increase school funding by raising property taxes.

Which one of the following exhibits flawed reasoning most similar to the flawed reasoning exhibited by the argument above?

(A) Tara finds Ms. Burke's English class, which has paper assignments but no exams, easier than Mr. Kent's English class, which has exams but no paper assignments. It follows that Tara finds it easier to write a paper than to take an exam.

(B) Jane refuses to live downtown. Denise wants to rent a penthouse apartment. It follows that Jane will not rent one of the penthouse apartments in the Joliet Towers complex downtown but Denise will rent one of those apartments.

(C) Mayor Watson promised never to support an increase in public transportation fares in Johnsonville. It follows that Mayor Watson will oppose the new proposal to improve public transportation in Johnsonville by doubling public transportation fares.

(D) Ed dislikes any food that is extremely sweet, but Bill likes most extremely sweet food. It follows that Ed will dislike these extremely sweet brownies but Bill will probably like them.

(E) In the past, the citizens of Lake County have voted down every proposal to increase property taxes. It follows that citizens of Lake County will probably vote down the new proposed increase in property taxes.

GO ON TO THE NEXT PAGE.

24. Historian: The revolutionary party has been accused of having many overambitious goals and of having caused great suffering. However, most of the party's goals were quickly achieved and the party did not have enough power to cause the suffering the critics claim it caused. So it is clear that the party was not overambitious and caused no suffering.

The reasoning in the historian's argument is flawed because the argument

(A)   gives mutually inconsistent responses to the two criticisms

(B)   fails to establish that the revolutionary party caused no suffering

(C)   fails to establish that any of the revolutionary party's critics underestimated the party's power

(D)   provides no evidence that the revolutionary party's goals were not overambitious

(E)   fails to consider other major criticisms of the revolutionary party

25. Although withholding information from someone who would find that information painful is sometimes justified, there is no such justification if the person would benefit from having the information. Therefore, even though it would be painful for Jason to learn that his supervisor is displeased with his work, his colleague Jane should nonetheless inform Jason of this fact, for knowing that his supervisor was displeased would enable Jason to improve his supervisor's opinion of his work.

Which one of the following is an assumption on which the argument relies?

(A)   If Jane does not tell Jason that his supervisor is displeased with his work, then Jason's situation will worsen.

(B)   If Jane does not tell Jason that his supervisor is displeased with his work, Jason will never find out.

(C)   If Jane tells Jason that his supervisor is displeased with his work, Jason will be grateful for the information even though it will be painful for him to learn it.

(D)   Jason might eventually improve his supervisor's opinion of his work even if he never learns that his supervisor is displeased with his work.

(E)   Jason would benefit if he were able to improve his supervisor's opinion of his work.

S T O P

IF YOU FINISH BEFORE TIME IS CALLED, YOU MAY CHECK YOUR WORK ON THIS SECTION ONLY.
DO NOT WORK ON ANY OTHER SECTION IN THE TEST.

SECTION IV

Time—35 minutes

27 Questions

<u>Directions:</u> Each set of questions in this section is based on a single passage or a pair of passages. The questions are to be answered on the basis of what is <u>stated</u> or <u>implied</u> in the passage or pair of passages. For some of the questions, more than one of the choices could conceivably answer the question. However, you are to choose the <u>best</u> answer; that is, the response that most accurately and completely answers the question, and blacken the corresponding space on your answer sheet.

The 50 million sheep of New Zealand outnumber its people 13 to 1, the highest such ratio in the world. At the wool industry's peak, in the 1950s, the wool growers of New Zealand delivered well over a third of
(5)   that country's total export revenues. Yet this figure has declined drastically, as has the industry's profitability. New Zealand is second only to Australia in total wool production and is the world's largest producer of "strong wool," a relatively coarse wool characteristic
(10) of crossbred sheep that is used mostly for carpets. But for the past 20 years, competition from synthetics has inexorably driven down the price of clean strong wool, causing annual production to drop by 65,000 tons as farmers switch land to other uses. Thus wool has fallen
(15) behind beef, lamb, milk, butter, cheese, fish, fruit, and wood and pulp as an agricultural export earner.

Rather than raising wool prices, the only reliable route to profitability lies, as in any agricultural enterprise, in improving productivity. New Zealand's
(20) commercial sheep farmers need to achieve the same kind of annual productivity gains that manufacturers of synthetic materials have recorded. This goal could readily be achieved if the industry as a whole were to adopt the management and breeding practices of the
(25) country's leading (and comfortably profitable) wool growers.

Gains on the order of those achieved by the world's cotton growers—who on average have been improving productivity at several times the rate of wool growers—
(30) can come wholly through better farm management. At present, wool growing in New Zealand, like agriculture everywhere, is deeply divided. On the one side are professional operations that exceed market returns, with 30 percent of farms achieving double the average
(35) profitability and the top 10 percent achieving 3 to 4 times the average. On the other side are family farmers willing to receive a substantially lower return to maintain their lifestyle.

To encourage increased overall productivity, the
(40) establishment of a commercial genetic research company (which would concentrate on genetic selection for crossbreeding sheep, not on the artificial manipulation of genetic material in individual sheep) is recommended. This would represent a shift in spending away from
(45) industry efforts to improve the efficiency of wool processing (for example, by lowering spinning costs) and toward efforts to cut the cost of producing a given unit of raw wool or to increase the quality of raw wool produced. Enormous gains in overall productivity

(50) could be made through genetic improvement. The best of New Zealand's sheep produce wool worth significantly more than the wool of the country's average sheep, and these superior sheep can be identified and kept as breeding stock.

1. Which one of the following most accurately expresses the main point of the passage?

    (A)   New Zealand wool growers should be encouraged to shift to other agricultural exports to maintain profitability.
    (B)   Wool growing in New Zealand parallels agricultural practices worldwide in that it is becoming deeply divided between large professional operations and smaller family farms.
    (C)   New Zealand's wool industry has been adversely affected by the development and improvement of synthetics.
    (D)   Superior farm management should be encouraged among New Zealand's wool growers to revitalize the country's wool industry.
    (E)   The wool industry in New Zealand has put too much focus on increasing the efficiency of processing and has failed to address the issue of dwindling breeding stocks.

2. Which one of the following is given in the passage as the cause of the decline in the price of clean strong wool?

    (A)   farmers' switching their land to other uses
    (B)   market competition from synthetic materials
    (C)   market competition from Australian wool growers
    (D)   competition from cotton growers for available land
    (E)   the deep division in the wool industry between large and small farms

GO ON TO THE NEXT PAGE.

3. According to the passage, which one of the following is true of New Zealand's wool industry?

   (A) It supports a strong carpet manufacturing industry in New Zealand.

   (B) It is overseen by a board that is representative of operators of both large and small farms.

   (C) It has recently begun to shift investment toward researching more-efficient wool-processing techniques.

   (D) It has followed a pattern of growth similar to that of the world's cotton industry.

   (E) It is the largest producer of strong wool in the world.

4. Approval of which one of the following is implicit in the author's argument in the passage?

   (A) competition between New Zealand's wool growers and producers of synthetics

   (B) changes in land use by New Zealand's farmers over the last several decades

   (C) the farming practices of New Zealand's family farmers who grow wool

   (D) efforts by New Zealand's wool-growing industry to increase the efficiency of wool processing

   (E) the farm management practices of the most profitable wool-growing farms in New Zealand

5. The passage most strongly suggests that which one of the following would be a function of the research company proposed for New Zealand in the final paragraph?

   (A) to develop more-productive varieties of sheep by introducing genes from other organisms into the genetic material of sheep

   (B) to concentrate on conducting basic genetic research that could have applications in various areas of agriculture

   (C) to encourage wool growers to focus on developing other wool varieties as an alternative to growing strong wool

   (D) to create a composite profile of optimal physical traits for sheep based on characteristics of the sheep that produce the most valuable wool

   (E) to oversee the distribution of funds among the various programs intended to increase the efficiency of wool processing

6. Which one of the following principles is most clearly operative in the author's reasoning in the passage?

   (A) An industry that seeks to increase its overall productivity should adopt, on an industry-wide basis, the techniques used by its most productive members.

   (B) Increasing the overall productivity of an industry ought to involve requiring the industry's leading members to give aid to the industry's less productive members.

   (C) Even if an industry has successfully increased its productivity, it should continue to explore new avenues for reducing costs.

   (D) An industry whose productivity is declining should model its business practices on those of its most successful competing industries.

   (E) If an industry's productivity is declining, then that industry should return to the practices it employed at the height of its success.

GO ON TO THE NEXT PAGE.

In filmmaker Woody Allen's *Deconstructing Harry*, the writer Harry Block is presented as extremely neurotic and narcissistic. Block uses his experiences as fodder for his work, no matter how

(5) embarrassing the result may be for the other people in his life. And while Allen exaggerates Block's narcissism for comic effect, the effect is not simply comic: the film is emblematic of Allen's career precisely because of its extravagantly exaggerated censure of a life

(10) dedicated to and obsessed with art. *Deconstructing Harry* may be the most unequivocally peevish of Allen's depictions of artists, but it is less a new direction for Allen than a concentrated reprise of a theme present throughout his career.

(15)   For instance, a film producer in *Stardust Memories*, Allen's sourest portrait of artists before *Harry*, articulates a particularly cynical view of cinematic art after a screening of a film-in-progress by *Stardust Memories'* main character, Sandy Bates. The

(20) producer says of Bates, "His insights are shallow and morbid. I've seen it all before. They try to document their private suffering and fob it off as art." The producer, like all the figures in this film, often seems less a distinct individual than a projection of Bates's

(25) personal self-recriminations. This effectively reinforces the charge of solipsism with which Bates, the unstable and demoralized artist, indicts himself. Indeed, the possibility that artists are merely "documenting their private suffering and fobbing it off

(30) as art" appears sufficiently often in Allen's films to seem an unresolved personal issue.

    In *Manhattan*, the ex-wife of a television writer and aspiring novelist offers a denigratory take on the artistic enterprise that is similar to the producer's in

(35) *Stardust Memories*. Her book documenting the collapse of her marriage punctures her ex-husband's artistic pretensions by revealing that he "longed to be an artist but balked at the necessary sacrifices. In his most private moments, he spoke of the fear of death,

(40) which he elevated to tragic heights when, in fact, it was mere narcissism."

    It is also significant that in Allen's films, the less artistic the characters, the more likely their narrative is to result in a happy ending. Thus, the filmmaker in

(45) *Crimes and Misdemeanors*, the novelist in *Husbands and Wives*, and the screenwriter in *Celebrity* all wind up desolate and solitary, largely because of the egocentric and exploitative attitudes embodied in their art and the effects of those attitudes on those around them. On the

(50) other hand, the unpretentious, thoroughly inartistic title character in *Zelig* dies an untroubled, even happy, death, only slightly compromised by his failure to finish reading *Moby-Dick*. And the title character and talent agent in *Broadway Danny Rose* is the beneficiary

(55) of the most gratifying resolution Allen has scripted, primarily due to altruistic devotion to his utterly talentless nightclub performers.

7. Which one of the following most accurately expresses the main point of the passage?

(A)   The theme of the neurotic and narcissistic nature of artists is, though most intensely presented in *Deconstructing Harry*, one that Woody Allen has explored throughout his career.

(B)   Woody Allen's films suggest, by means of their depictions of artists, that the pursuit of an artistic life leads to unhappiness and that happiness is most often achieved by the inartistic.

(C)   *Deconstructing Harry*, like many of Woody Allen's films, shows that the creation of art requires sacrifice, though many would-be artists are unable or unwilling to give up their comforts to create enduring works.

(D)   Woody Allen's career indicates that, like most artists, he uses his own experiences and neuroses to create the works for which he has received the greatest acclaim.

(E)   Woody Allen's films show that artists are unavoidably narcissistic and neurotic and that they are, because of this, able to produce works of great beauty and power.

8. It can most reasonably be inferred that which one of the following principles underlies the author's argument regarding Allen's films?

(A)   Critics should consider not only an individual film in isolation, but also its relation to the filmmaker's entire body of work, when attempting to gauge that film's artistic merit.

(B)   People who are not themselves artists should not presume to interpret films that take as their subject the artistic temperament.

(C)   The fate that a character in a movie meets can give an indication of the filmmaker's views concerning his approval or disapproval of that character.

(D)   The writer of a film's screenplay should be considered only one of many contributors to the ultimate meaning of that film.

(E)   Prior work of a film's cast members should be taken into account when assessing the artistic merits of a film.

GO ON TO THE NEXT PAGE.

In the early 1900s, most astronomers mistakenly believed that 66 percent of the sun's substance was iron. As a graduate student at Harvard University in the 1920s, Cecilia Payne—later a professor of
(5) astronomy there—argued pioneeringly that the sun is instead composed largely of hydrogen and helium. Her claim, though substantiated by the evidence and later uniformly accepted, encountered strong resistance among professional astronomers.

(10) The orthodox view that the sun was mainly iron was buttressed by the knowledge that Earth and all known asteroids contain iron. Also, the evidence from spectroscopy—a technique used to identify chemicals by the distinctive spectral properties of the light patterns
(15) they emit when heated to incandescence—was generally taken to show that iron was the predominant element in the sun. But how could a body composed largely of iron generate the huge energy output of the sun? The eminent British physicist Lord Kelvin had
(20) hypothesized that the sun was continuously contracting and that the resulting compression had raised the temperature of the sun's materials sufficiently to account for its enormous heat. But, given the usual assumptions about the sun's size and
(25) rate of contraction, it followed that the sun's age would be about 20 million years; evidence from the fossil record, however, strongly suggested that the sun had warmed Earth for billions of years. For Payne, this meant that the "iron" hypothesis had to be reexamined,
(30) together with the extensive spectroscopic data alleged to support it.

Preliminary examination of the spectroscopic data convinced Payne that they lent themselves to multiple readings. She suspected that preconceptions about the
(35) sun's makeup as being mainly iron might have led to skewed interpretations of that data, and this led her to subject the data to rigorous critical scrutiny and review. Analyzed without preconceptions, she found, the data could be consistently read as indicating that, while it
(40) does indeed contain iron (along with other elements found on Earth), 90 percent of the sun is hydrogen and most of the remainder is helium. Most astronomers at the time dismissed Payne's interpretation, and some sought to explain it away simply by claiming that what
(45) she had examined was data about the sun's outer surface rather than its interior.

Absent a generally accepted explanation of how hydrogen and helium could produce the sun's energy, Payne's findings could not easily override her
(50) contemporaries' preconceptions. We now know that the sun's heat is generated through nuclear fusion: the sun's gravitational force compresses together atoms of hydrogen, causing a nuclear reaction. This reaction produces enormous amounts of energy, while
(55) forming helium and other elements. But this process— so well charted today that even elementary physics textbooks discuss it—was inadequately understood in the 1920s. The emergence of that understanding— which relied on Einstein's equation governing the
(60) relationship between mass and energy—eventually provided strong confirmation of Payne's results.

13. Which one of the following most accurately expresses the main point of the passage?

(A) Cecilia Payne was the first scientist to describe the mechanism by which the sun generates its heat.

(B) Cecilia Payne proposed an innovative alternative to the view of the sun's composition that prevailed in her time, but, although her view was ultimately vindicated, other scientists were slow to accept her claim.

(C) Cecilia Payne's use of spectrographic data to analyze the sun, though novel and unconventional at the time, ultimately won wide acceptance in the scientific community, influencing Albert Einstein, among others.

(D) Cecilia Payne was the first scientist to demonstrate that the sun contains both hydrogen and helium, but her claim initially encountered widespread resistance in the scientific community.

(E) Cecilia Payne was the first scientist to speculate that the sun's energy might not be generated by processes involving iron, though, at the time, neither she nor others fully understood nuclear fusion.

14. The passage provides enough information to answer which one of the following questions?

(A) Does the iron content of Earth exceed 50 percent of its total mass?

(B) Who first proved that the sun generates heat from hydrogen by nuclear fusion?

(C) Do any objects in the solar system other than Earth and the sun contain iron?

(D) What percentage of the sun's mass is composed of iron?

(E) Can the fusion of atoms other than hydrogen atoms produce energy?

GO ON TO THE NEXT PAGE.

15. The passage provides the strongest support for believing that some scientists in the 1920s held which one of the following views regarding Payne's interpretation of the spectroscopic data relating to the sun?

    (A) The methodology she used in analyzing the data was outdated, and thus her findings were of doubtful validity.

    (B) Her interpretation of the data was remarkably accurate and proved the traditional interpretation of the data to be incorrect.

    (C) Her findings were generally promising and warranted serious consideration, but no definitive assessment of them could be made without verification of certain details.

    (D) Her interpretation of the data was not entirely ill founded, but the overall conclusions she drew from the data were wrong.

    (E) Her interpretation and the overall conclusions she drew from it were correct, but those conclusions were of little scientific consequence.

16. The author's discussion of nuclear fusion in the last paragraph serves primarily to

    (A) illustrate the impact of Payne's findings on a discipline related to, although distinct from, the one in which she ultimately made her mark

    (B) explain in part the reactions of Payne's fellow scientists to her interpretation of the data that she analyzed

    (C) clarify an underlying reason for Payne's rejection of the "iron" hypothesis

    (D) show how Payne's findings came ultimately to be modified in light of later scientific developments

    (E) demonstrate that Payne's reliance on incorrect data did not prevent her from reaching a sound hypothesis

17. Based on the information in the passage, it can be inferred that the author holds which one of the following views?

    (A) The fact that Payne's research findings were not found convincing by many of her contemporaries was not due to any major mistake in her scientific reasoning.

    (B) Previous to Payne, interpreters of the spectroscopic data had deliberately disregarded data that suggested the sun contained some hydrogen.

    (C) The "iron" hypothesis would not have been accepted for so long were it not for the prominence and prestige of Lord Kelvin.

    (D) The resistance to her findings that Payne encountered among professional astronomers is uncharacteristic of the way science generally operates.

    (E) The discovery of nuclear fusion might have been delayed by several decades if Payne had not determined that the sun consists mainly of hydrogen and helium.

18. Which one of the following statements about spectroscopy is most strongly supported by information in the passage?

    (A) Its use during the 1920s was generally confined to the field of astronomy.

    (B) It yielded data about the sun's composition that Payne initially doubted but ultimately came to accept.

    (C) It played a crucial, though often unacknowledged, role in the emergence of our present-day understanding of the process of nuclear fusion.

    (D) It was regarded by certain prominent scientists in the 1920s as an unproven tool that produced data of often questionable reliability.

    (E) It was a technique advanced enough by the 1920s to detect the presence in the sun of elements that constituted considerably less than 10 percent of its mass.

19. It can be inferred from information in the passage that the scientists who tried to explain away Payne's findings by claiming that she had misconstrued the relevance of her data assumed which one of the following to be true?

    (A) It is impossible to generate heat through nuclear fusion.

    (B) The inside of the sun is not of the same composition as its outer surface.

    (C) The sun contained insufficient hydrogen to have warmed Earth for billions of years.

    (D) Payne's preconceptions about the "iron" hypothesis biased her analysis of spectroscopic data.

    (E) Spectroscopy will not detect the presence of iron if the iron is in an object as far away from Earth as the sun is.

GO ON TO THE NEXT PAGE.

Passage A discusses the views of the economist and political thinker Thomas Sowell. Passage B is adapted from an article by Sowell.

Passage A

"Cosmic justice," as Sowell uses the term, refers to the perfect justice that only an omniscient being could render—rewards and punishments that are truly deserved when all relevant things are properly taken
(5)   into consideration. Inherent human limitations, however, make it impossible to achieve this type of justice through human law, even though many times it seems that people are arguing for such justice and promote policies they think will render it through our
(10)   human laws. But our human legal systems should not try to dispense cosmic justice since we do not know all the critical relevant facts or understand all the complex causal interrelationships involved or even know definitively what cosmic justice really is.
(15)   Whether somebody truly deserves something is a very difficult thing for us to determine. For one thing, we are not knowledgeable enough about the person and situation, or smart enough, even if we knew what all the critical factors were, to perform the complicated
(20)   calculus necessary to understand how the complex interrelationships among the various variables should affect our ultimate conclusions. Deservedness necessarily focuses on a consideration of inputs. An omniscient being is capable of perfectly considering
(25)   all these things, but we are not. With all the limitations that we face as mere humans, the best we can reasonably do is judge primarily based upon outputs, or consequences, rather than inputs.

Passage B

Cosmic justice is not simply a higher degree of
(30)   traditional justice; it is a fundamentally different concept. Traditionally, justice or injustice is characteristic of a *process*. A defendant in a criminal case would be said to have received justice if the trial were conducted as it should be, under fair rules and with an impartial
(35)   judge and jury. After such a trial, it could be said that "justice was done"—regardless of the outcome. Conversely, if the trial were conducted in violation of the rules and with a judge or jury showing prejudice against the defendant, this would be considered an
(40)   unfair or unjust trial—even if the prosecutor failed to convince the jury to convict an innocent person. In short, traditional justice is about impartial processes rather than either results or prospects.
        On the other hand, cosmic justice foolishly seeks
(45)   to correct, not only biased or discriminatory acts by individuals or social institutions, but unmerited disadvantages in general, from whatever source they may arise. In criminal trials, for example, before a murderer is sentenced, the law permits his traumatic
(50)   childhood to be taken into account. Seldom is there any claim that the person murdered had anything to do with that traumatic childhood. It is only from a cosmic

perspective that it could have any bearing on the crime. If punishment is meant to deter crime, then
(55)   mitigating that punishment in pursuit of cosmic justice presumably reduces that deterrence and allows more crime to take place at the expense of innocent people.

20. Which one of the following pairs of titles would be most appropriate for passage A and passage B, respectively?

(A) "Cosmic Justice Meets Human Limitations"
      "Fairness as Process versus Cosmic Fairness"
(B) "Sowell's Theory of Justice"
      "The Key to Deterrence"
(C) "Just Deserts"
      "Fair and Unfair Disadvantages"
(D) "A Critique of Sowell"
      "Traditional Justice Writ Large"
(E) "The Impossibility of Achieving Cosmic Justice"
      "Fair Trials versus Justice as Impartial Process"

21. Which one of the following is mentioned in passage B, but not in passage A?

(A) punishment
(B) trials
(C) rewards
(D) legal systems
(E) human limitations

22. Passage A differs from passage B in that passage A is more

(A) abstract
(B) inflammatory
(C) technical
(D) narrative
(E) adversarial

GO ON TO THE NEXT PAGE.

23. Which one of the following is most analogous to the kind of approach both authors criticize?

   (A) A local library charges children lower fines for overdue materials and lost books than it charges adults.
   (B) In assigning grades, a teacher takes into account not only written assignments and class performance, but also background factors unique to individual students.
   (C) In assigning employee parking spaces, management takes into account an employee's rank within, and years of service to, the company.
   (D) An employer with a proven history of age discrimination is forced by a court to hire qualified older employees.
   (E) A university admits students based not just on academic achievement, but also on documented extracurricular activities and community service.

24. In passage B, which one of the following is an example of "inputs" as that term is used in the second paragraph of passage A?

   (A) fair rules (line 34)
   (B) unjust trial (line 40)
   (C) impartial processes (line 42)
   (D) traumatic childhood (lines 49–50 and line 52)
   (E) innocent people (line 57)

25. Passage A most strongly supports which one of the following inferences regarding the example of the murderer in passage B?

   (A) From the perspective of cosmic justice, the murderer cannot be considered responsible for his crime.
   (B) Once the jury has convicted the murderer, the judge should be permitted substantial discretion in determining his punishment.
   (C) Recognition of our common human fallibility should lead us to err in the direction of leniency toward the murderer.
   (D) The extent, if any, to which the murderer's culpability is mitigated by his childhood is beyond the ability of any judge or jury to determine.
   (E) The murderer's childhood must be presumed to have been without influence upon his criminal behavior.

26. The discussion in passage A, but not the discussion in passage B, relies on which one of the following principles?

   (A) One should refrain from action when one lacks complete information.
   (B) Whether a punishment is fair matters less than whether it deters crime.
   (C) Although we should aim at perfect justice, we should recognize that we cannot attain it.
   (D) One should not pass judgment on an action unless one knows all of the factors that influenced it.
   (E) If a goal is known to be impossible, then it should not be attempted.

27. Which one of the following is a view advanced by the author of passage A with which the author of passage B would be most likely to agree?

   (A) It is sometimes possible for the legal system to take unmerited disadvantages into account in rendering judgment on people and their actions.
   (B) Whether or not cosmic justice is an attainable ideal, human law should strive for it because doing so produces more just legal outcomes.
   (C) Impartial legal processes are a better means of achieving cosmic justice than are efforts to address unmerited disadvantages directly.
   (D) Human law should be concerned with the consequences of human actions, not with the myriad of factors that influence human actions.
   (E) Human legal systems can in theory achieve cosmic justice by focusing upon factors that tend to mitigate punishment.

S T O P

IF YOU FINISH BEFORE TIME IS CALLED, YOU MAY CHECK YOUR WORK ON THIS SECTION ONLY.
DO NOT WORK ON ANY OTHER SECTION IN THE TEST.

Wait for the supervisor's instructions before you open the page to the topic.
Please print and sign your name and write the date in the designated spaces below.

Time: 35 Minutes

General Directions

You will have 35 minutes in which to plan and write an essay on the topic inside. Read the topic and the accompanying directions carefully. You will probably find it best to spend a few minutes considering the topic and organizing your thoughts before you begin writing. In your essay, be sure to develop your ideas fully, leaving time, if possible, to review what you have written. **Do not write on a topic other than the one specified. Writing on a topic of your own choice is not acceptable.**

No special knowledge is required or expected for this writing exercise. Law schools are interested in the reasoning, clarity, organization, language usage, and writing mechanics displayed in your essay. How well you write is more important than how much you write.

Confine your essay to the blocked, lined area on the front and back of the separate Writing Sample Response Sheet. Only that area will be reproduced for law schools. Be sure that your writing is legible.

Both this topic sheet and your response sheet must be turned in to the testing staff before you leave the room.

Topic Code	Print Your Full Name Here		
063781	Last	First	M.I.

Date	Sign Your Name Here
/ /	

Scratch Paper
Do not write your essay in this space.

LSAT® Writing Sample Topic

Directions: The scenario presented below describes two choices, either one of which can be supported on the basis of the information given. Your essay should consider both choices and argue for one over the other, based on the two specified criteria and the facts provided. There is no "right" or "wrong" choice: a reasonable argument can be made for either.

Richard Bollinger, who owns a small catering business, must choose either to renovate his business's kitchen or replace his business's van. Using the facts below, write an essay in which you argue for one choice over the other, based on the following two criteria:

- Bollinger wants to expand his business.
- Bollinger does not want to incur more business debt than he has currently.

Bollinger's small kitchen needs to be expanded and updated to accommodate more clients and larger events. His business might even lose existing clients unless he renovates. Bollinger can pay for the renovation without incurring any debt, assuming standard labor costs and no overtime. He cannot afford to shut down his business for more than three weeks. The contractor who would do the renovations has advised Bollinger that overtime labor costs might be necessary in order to complete construction within the three-week timeframe. Bollinger would need to incur some debt if there are any overtime labor costs.

Bollinger's ten-year-old customized delivery van is in need of several minor repairs and major repairs will probably be needed soon. Bollinger cannot conduct his business without an operating van. Any major repairs could take several weeks to complete because parts for the van are scarce. Bollinger's van is too small to accommodate the larger events he hopes to host for new clientele. Bollinger could buy a new, larger van with funds he has on hand. Customizing the new van for his catering business might require incurring some debt.

WP-O063B

Scratch Paper
Do not write your essay in this space.

Writing Sample Response Sheet

DO NOT WRITE IN THIS SPACE

Begin your essay in the lined area below.
Continue on the back if you need more space.

Directions:

1. Use the Answer Key on the next page to check your answers.

2. Use the Scoring Worksheet below to compute your raw score.

3. Use the Score Conversion Chart to convert your raw score into the 120–180 scale.

Scoring Worksheet

1. Enter the number of questions you answered correctly in each section.

	Number Correct
Section I	_____
Section II	_____
Section III	_____
Section IV	_____

2. Enter the sum here: _____
   This is your Raw Score.

Conversion Chart
For Converting Raw Score to the 120–180 LSAT Scaled Score
LSAT Form 1LSN96

Reported Score	Raw Score Lowest	Raw Score Highest
180	99	100
179	98	98
178	97	97
177	—*	—*
176	96	96
175	95	95
174	—*	—*
173	94	94
172	93	93
171	92	92
170	91	91
169	89	90
168	88	88
167	87	87
166	85	86
165	84	84
164	82	83
163	81	81
162	79	80
161	77	78
160	76	76
159	74	75
158	72	73
157	70	71
156	68	69
155	67	67
154	65	66
153	63	64
152	61	62
151	59	60
150	57	58
149	55	56
148	53	54
147	51	52
146	49	50
145	47	48
144	46	46
143	44	45
142	42	43
141	40	41
140	39	39
139	37	38
138	35	36
137	34	34
136	32	33
135	31	31
134	30	30
133	28	29
132	27	27
131	26	26
130	25	25
129	24	24
128	23	23
127	22	22
126	21	21
125	20	20
124	19	19
123	18	18
122	—*	—*
121	17	17
120	0	16

* There is no raw score that will produce this scaled score for this form.

ANSWER KEY

SECTION I

1. A	8. A	15. A	22. D
2. E	9. D	16. E	23. B
3. D	10. C	17. E	
4. B	11. B	18. D	
5. A	12. D	19. A	
6. E	13. A	20. B	
7. E	14. C	21. E	

SECTION II

1. A	8. E	15. E	22. A
2. C	9. C	16. C	23. C
3. C	10. C	17. C	24. D
4. B	11. D	18. A	25. D
5. C	12. D	19. E	
6. B	13. E	20. B	
7. D	14. B	21. E	

SECTION III

1. C	8. D	15. A	22. E
2. E	9. E	16. D	23. B
3. D	10. B	17. C	24. B
4. D	11. C	18. A	25. E
5. B	12. D	19. D	
6. A	13. B	20. C	
7. B	14. E	21. E	

SECTION IV

1. D	8. C	15. D	22. A
2. B	9. D	16. B	23. B
3. E	10. E	17. A	24. D
4. E	11. C	18. E	25. D
5. D	12. B	19. B	26. E
6. A	13. B	20. A	27. D
7. A	14. C	21. B	

Questions 1–5

What the setup tells you: This set of questions has to do with the seating arrangement of eight children—four girls and four boys—in the three cars of a roller coaster—front, middle, and rear. The setup tells you that each car holds a maximum of three children. This is an important piece of information because it allows you to deduce that in any acceptable outcome, two of the cars will contain three children and one of the cars will contain just two children. There is no other way to fit eight children into three cars when the maximum number of children per car is three. The third condition tells you that one of the cars that contains three children is the front car. According to this condition, the front car contains Oona and two of the boys.

Some things you can deduce right away: The setup conditions allow you to deduce a number of things about what an acceptable seating arrangement will look like. For example, the first condition tells you that each car contains at least one boy. You know already from the third condition that the front car contains two boys, so you can deduce that each of the other two cars contains a single boy. The second and third conditions tell you where Petra and Oona sit: Petra sits in the rear car and Oona sits in the front car. At this point, you may want to begin summarizing what you know in diagram form. Here is one way to do this, where the notation __B is used to indicate a position that must be filled by a boy, and the front car is marked "FULL" to indicate that it contains the maximum number of children allowed.

Front	Middle	Rear
O __B __B	__B	P __B
FULL		

The fourth and fifth conditions tell you something about where Tommy and Ulysses sit relative to Nora. These conditions indicate that each of these boys sits in a car that is in front of Nora's car. The fourth condition specifies that Tommy sits in the car that is "immediately in front of Nora's car." There are only three cars, so there are only two ways in which this condition can be satisfied: either Tommy sits in the front car and Nora sits in the middle car, or Tommy sits in the middle car and Nora sits in the rear car. These two scenarios are diagrammed below:

Scenario 1

Front	Middle	Rear
O T __B	N __B	P __B
FULL		

Scenario 2

Front	Middle	Rear
O __B __B	T	N P __B
FULL		FULL

The fifth condition specifies that Ulysses sits in a car "in front of Nora's car." Notice that, in contrast to the fourth condition, there is no requirement that his car be "immediately" in front of Nora's. So, as far as the fifth condition goes, Ulysses' car could be immediately in front of Nora's car or it could be somewhere further in front of it. Looking at the two scenarios diagrammed above, you will see that in Scenario 1, the only position available to Ulysses that is in front of Nora's car is in the front car. And in Scenario 2, the only position available to Ulysses that is in front of Nora's car is **also** in the front car, since there is only one position for a boy in the middle car and it is already filled by Tommy:

Scenario 1

Front	Middle	Rear
O T U	N __B	P __B
FULL		

Scenario 2

Front	Middle	Rear
O U __B	T	N P __B
FULL		FULL

What this means is that under any acceptable seating arrangement, both Oona and Ulysses must sit in the front car.

At this point, you have deduced quite a bit about what an acceptable outcome will look like: any acceptable outcome will conform to one of the two scenarios outlined above. You may find that you can make further deductions about what an acceptable seating arrangement will look like, but it may be a better use of your time to take what you've already learned and turn to a consideration of the questions.

Question 1

Overview: This question asks you to identify the answer choice that could be true. It is generally a good idea to approach a question of this type by first checking to see whether you can identify the correct answer based on what you've already deduced. In this case, you will see that answer choice (A) conforms to what you determined was an acceptable scenario in "Some things you can deduce right away," so you can safely conclude that (A) is the correct answer. There is no need to check the other answer choices.

The Correct Answer:

A It is possible that the front car contains Oona, Tommy, and Ulysses, as the following acceptable outcome demonstrates:

Front	Middle	Rear
O T U	N W	P S X

   In this outcome, each car contains at least one boy (Tommy and Ulysses in the front car, Wei in the middle car, and Xavier in the rear car), Petra sits in the rear car, Oona sits in the front car with two boys, Tommy's car is immediately in front of Nora's car, and Ulysses' car is in front of Nora's. Thus, this outcome satisfies all of the setup conditions.

The Incorrect Answer Choices:

B Petra cannot sit in the front car since the second condition requires that she sit in the rear car. In addition, the front car cannot contain two girls and a boy, since the third condition requires that this car contain Oona and two boys. So it cannot be the case that Oona, Tommy, and Petra sit in the front car.

C Tommy and Nora cannot sit in the same car together because the fourth condition requires that Tommy's car be immediately in front of Nora's car, so it cannot be the case that Tommy, Nora, and Sally all sit in the middle car.

D Oona cannot sit in the middle car because the third condition requires that she sit in the front car, so it cannot be the case that Oona, Tommy, and Sally sit in the middle car.

E Tommy cannot sit in the rear car because the fourth condition requires that Tommy's car be immediately in front of Nora's car. Moreover, as you deduced in "Some things you can deduce right away," it is impossible for the rear car to contain two boys. So it cannot be the case that Tommy, Xavier, and Petra sit in the rear car.

- *Difficulty Level: 1*

Question 2

Overview: This question tells you to suppose that Xavier and Nora sit in one of the cars with a third child, and asks you to identify which of the five children listed in the answer choices could be the third child. A generally good strategy for answering a question that introduces a supposition is to first see what you can deduce about what an acceptable outcome will look like if that supposition holds true. In this case, what can you deduce about what an acceptable seating arrangement will look like if one of the cars contains Xavier, Nora, and one other child? Well, for one thing, you know that the car that these three children sit in cannot be the front car, since you determined in "Some things you can deduce right away" that the front car must contain Oona, Ulysses, and one other boy. This means that Xavier and Nora and the third child must be seated in either the middle or the rear car. Now, recall that you also determined in "Some things you can deduce right away" that each of these two cars contains exactly one boy. So whichever of these two cars Xavier and Nora sit in, Xavier will fill the only slot available for a boy. This means that the only way that Xavier and Nora can sit in one of the cars with a third child is if that third child is a girl. Looking over the answer choices, you can thus eliminate from consideration (A), (B), and (C) since each of them is a boy. In addition, you can eliminate (D) since you know that Oona must sit in a car with Ulysses and one other boy and so cannot sit in a car with Xavier and Nora. Thus, by a process of elimination, you can safely identify the remaining answer choice, (E), as the correct answer.

The Correct Answer:

E If Xavier and Nora sit in one of the cars with a third child, then the third child could be Sally, as demonstrated by the following acceptable outcome

Front	Middle	Rear
O T U	N S X	P W

The Incorrect Answer Choices:

A, B, C As shown in the "Overview," the third child in a car that contains Xavier (a boy) and Nora (a girl) cannot be a boy. This is because only one car contains two boys and that is the front car. Nora cannot sit in the front car, since the fourth and fifth conditions require that there be at least one car in front of Nora's car. So the only way that Xavier and Nora can sit together in a car that contains a third child is if the third child is a girl. So (A), (B), and (C) can be ruled out because they are all boys.

D Oona cannot be the third child in a car that contains Xavier (a boy) and Nora (a girl) since the third condition requires that Oona sit in the front car with two boys. Another way of ruling out (D) is to observe that Oona cannot sit in a car with Nora, since Oona must sit in the front car and, as you determined in "Some things you can deduce right away," Nora **cannot** sit in the front car.

■ *Difficulty Level: 1*

Question 3

Overview: This question asks you to identify the answer choice that must be true if Tommy does not sit in the front car. You saw in "Some things you can deduce right away" that Tommy must sit in either the front or the middle car since the fourth condition requires that he sit in the car that is immediately in front of Nora's car. So if the supposition of this question holds true—that is, if Tommy does not sit in the front car—then he must sit in the middle car, with Nora in the rear car, and any acceptable outcome will conform to what was identified as Scenario 2 in "Some things you can deduce right away":

Scenario 2

Front	Middle	Rear
O U __B	T	N P __B
FULL		FULL

In this scenario, the front and rear cars each contain three children and have open positions that can be filled only by the two remaining boys, Xavier or Wei. This means that the remaining girl, Sally, can only sit in the middle car. Thus, answer choice (D), "Sally sits in the middle car," is the one that must be correct. There is no need to consider the other answer choices.

The Correct Answer:

D As shown in the "Overview," if Tommy does not sit in the front car, then it must be true that Sally sits in the middle car. This is because if Tommy does not sit in the front car, then the only car Tommy can sit in is the middle car. And if Tommy sits in the middle car, then the front and rear cars must each contain three children: the front car must contain Oona, Ulysses, and either Xavier or Wei, and the rear car must contain Nora, Petra, and either Xavier or Wei. This leaves the middle car as the only car in which Sally can sit.

The Incorrect Answer Choices:

A, B As you saw in the "Overview," if Tommy does not sit in the front car, then he must sit in the middle car, leaving one front car position and one rear car position to be filled by the boys Xavier and Wei. It doesn't matter which boy fills which position. Xavier could sit in either the front or the rear car, and so could Wei, as the following two acceptable outcomes demonstrate:

Front	Middle	Rear
O U W	S T	N P X

Front	Middle	Rear
O U X	S T	N P W

Thus, it is not true of either Xavier or Wei that he **must** sit in the front car if Tommy does not. So neither (A) nor (B) can be the correct answer.

C If Tommy does not sit in the front car, then, as you determined in the "Overview," Tommy must sit in the middle car. But since you know that exactly one boy sits in the middle car, if Tommy sits in the middle car, then Xavier cannot.

E One of the things you deduced in "Some things you can deduce right away" is that Ulysses must sit in the front car. Thus, (E) cannot be the correct answer.

- *Difficulty Level: 2*

Question 4

What you should keep in mind for this question: This question asks you to identify the complete and accurate list of children each of whom CANNOT sit in a car that has exactly two children in it. The correct answer to the question will be a list of all and only those children for whom the answer to the following question is "yes": Is this child a child who CANNOT sit in a car that has exactly two children in it? For further advice about this kind of question, see the discussion in "A Guide to Analytical Reasoning Questions" on pages 4–15.

Overview: As a first step in answering this question, it might be helpful to note that a child who **cannot** sit in a car that has exactly two children in it is a child who **must** sit in a car that has three children in it. This is because, as you determined in "Some things you can deduce right away," each car must contain either two or three children. Now, there are two children who you've already determined must sit in a car that has three children in it: Oona and Ulysses. In "Some things you can deduce right away," you determined that they must sit in the front car along with a third child. Oona and Ulysses, therefore, are both children who CANNOT sit in a car that has exactly two children in it, so you can conclude that these two children must be included in the list. A glance at the answer choices shows that the lists in (B) and (D) are the only ones that include both Oona and Ulysses, so you know that one of these answers has to be the correct answer. Answer choices (A), (C), and (E) can all be eliminated from consideration.

Answer choices (B) and (D) differ only in that (D) includes Petra in addition to Ulysses and Oona. Is Petra a child who CANNOT sit in a car that has exactly two children in it? You know from the second condition that Petra sits in the rear car. Moreover, you deduced in "Some things you can deduce right away" that the rear car must also contain exactly one boy. Can the rear car contain only Petra and one boy? The answer is yes. The rear car could, for example, contain just Petra and Wei, as illustrated by the acceptable outcome below:

Front	Middle	Rear
O T U	N S X	P W

Since this outcome demonstrates that Petra **can** sit in a car that contains exactly two children, Petra does **not** belong on a complete and accurate list of the children each of whom CANNOT sit in a car that has exactly two children in it. Thus, (D) cannot be the correct answer. The remaining answer choice, (B), must therefore be the correct answer.

The Correct Answer:

B   As discussed in the "Overview," Oona and Ulysses are both children who CANNOT sit in a car that has exactly two children in it. These two children must both sit in the front car, a car that contains three children. Each of the six other children **could** sit in a car that has exactly two children in it, as illustrated in the acceptable outcomes below:

Front	Middle	Rear
O T U	N W	P S X

Front	Middle	Rear
O T U	N S W	P X

Front	Middle	Rear
O U W	S T	N P X

Thus, none of the other six children belong on the list.

The Incorrect Answer Choices:

A, C, E   Of the eight children, the ones who cannot sit in a car that has exactly two children in it are Oona and Ulysses. As you worked out in "Some things you can deduce right away," both Oona and Ulysses must sit in the first car, and the first car has three children in it. So the lists in (A), (C), and (E) are all incomplete because they do not include Ulysses. The lists in (C) and (E) are also inaccurate because they include children who **could** sit in a car that contains exactly two children.

D   This list is inaccurate because it includes Petra. As discussed in the "Overview," Petra **can** sit in a car that has exactly two children in it, so she does not belong on the list of children who CANNOT sit in such a car.

- *Difficulty Level: 5*

Question 5

Overview: This question asks you to identify on the basis of the setup alone the answer choice that must be true. With a question like this, it is generally a good idea to first skim through the answer choices to see whether you can identify the correct answer based on what you know already or whether you can at least eliminate from consideration any of the answer choices. Notice in this case that each of the answer choices is an assertion that one child's car is in front of another child's car. One thing you saw in "Some things you can deduce right away" is that both Ulysses and Oona must sit in the front car, so (A) and (C) are likely candidates for the correct answer and worth considering first. Of these, you can see that (C) cannot be true, since Oona and Ulysses must sit in the same car. But what about (A)? Is it true that Ulysses's car must be in front of Sally's car? Yes. The front car contains three children: Oona, Ulysses, and one other boy. The front car therefore cannot contain Sally. So, whereas Ulysses must sit in the front car, Sally must sit in either the middle car or the rear car. In other words, it must be true that Ulysses's car is in front of Sally's car.

The Correct Answer:

A As you saw in the "Overview," it must be true that Ulysses's car is in front of Sally's car, since Ulysses must sit in the first car and there is no room in the first car for Sally.

The Incorrect Answer Choices:

B It is not the case that Sally's car must be in front of Nora's car. Sally and Nora could sit in the same car, as demonstrated by the following acceptable outcome:

Front	Middle	Rear
O T U	N S W	P X

Or Sally's car could be **behind** Nora's car, as demonstrated by the following acceptable outcome:

Front	Middle	Rear
O T U	N W	P S X

C It is not the case that Oona's car must be in front of Ulysses's car. As you determined in "Some things you can deduce right away," Oona and Ulysses must sit in the **same** car—the front car.

D It is not the case that Xavier's car must be in front of Wei's car. Xavier's car could be *behind* Wei's car, as shown in the acceptable outcomes given above in the discussion of answer choice (B).

E It is not the case that Tommy's car must be in front of Sally's car. Tommy and Sally could sit in the *same* car, as the following acceptable outcome shows:

Front	Middle	Rear
O U W	S T	N P X

- *Difficulty Level: 4*

Questions 6–10

What the setup tells you: In this set of questions, the task involves stacking five different objects one on top of another in such a way that the resulting order of the objects in the stack does not violate the restrictions given in the setup. The five objects are labeled J, K, L, M, and N. The five positions in the stack are numbered 1 through 5, with position 1 at the bottom of the stack and position 5 at the top of the stack. In working through the questions in this set, it will be important for you to keep in mind that the bottom of the stack corresponds to position 1 and the top of the stack corresponds to position 5. Similarly, keep in mind that an object that is above another object is somewhere **after** it in the numerical order, while an object that is below another is somewhere **before** it in the numerical order.

There are four restrictions on the order of the objects in the stack. The second and fourth restrictions give you information about particular positions that certain objects can and cannot be in. The second restriction tells you that J is not in position 1, which you might abbreviate as follows:

J not in 1

The fourth restriction tells you that N is in one of two positions—either position 1 or position 5, and no other. N cannot appear in positions 2, 3, or 4. Or, more briefly:

N in 1 or 5 only

The first and third restrictions tell you where certain objects are in relation to others. According to the first restriction, L is immediately above K in the stack. In other words, the position of L is exactly one number greater than the position of K. One way of abbreviating such a restriction is to use a notation in which the objects in the stack are listed from left to right with the bottom (position 1) toward the left and the top (position 5) toward the right. The first restriction can then be abbreviated as follows, showing L immediately above K:

... K L ...

The third restriction tells you that M is not immediately below K in the stack. Notice that M can be above or below K, just not immediately below.

not ... M K ...

Some things you can deduce right away: There is very little that you can deduce right away from the setup restrictions. One thing to notice, however, is that you can deduce from the first restriction that L cannot be in position 1 and K cannot be in position 5. This is because if L must be **above** K in the stack, you know that L cannot be at the bottom, in position 1. And if K must be **below** L in the stack, you know that K cannot be at the top, in position 5.

K not in 5
L not in 1

Question 6

What you should keep in mind for this question: Each of the answer choices in this question represents a complete stack of objects only one of which observes all of the restrictions of the setup. In each answer choice, the five objects are listed in order from position 1 (the bottom) to position 5 (the top). Objects to the left are lower in the stack and objects to the right are higher in the stack.

Overview: This question asks you to identify the answer choice that represents an acceptable order for the objects in the stack. In questions of this type, the best strategy is usually to consider each of the restrictions in turn, checking to see whether any of the answer choices violates that restriction and eliminating answer choices as you go along. By a process of elimination, you will arrive at the correct answer.

Consider the first restriction, which states that L is immediately above K in the stack. This restriction is observed by four of the answer choices—(A), (B), (D), and (E)—but not (C), where L is immediately **below** K in the stack. So (C) violates the first restriction and it can be eliminated. Since you have eliminated answer choice (C), you do not need to return to it when you consider the rest of the restrictions.

Now move on to the second restriction, which states that J is not in position 1. Answer choice (A) violates this restriction, so (A) can be eliminated. The remaining answer choices—now (B), (D), and (E)—all observe this restriction. The third restriction states that M is not immediately **below** K in the stack. Checking answer choices (B), (D), and (E), you see that this restriction is observed by (B) and (E), but not (D), where M is immediately below K in the stack. So you can eliminate (D) from consideration and move on to the fourth and final restriction, which states that N is either in position 1 or else in position 5. In considering the two answer choices that remain, you see that (B) shows N in position 4 and (E) shows N in position 1. Answer choice (B) violates the fourth restriction, so the correct answer must be (E).

The Correct Answer:

E   As discussed in the "Overview," the correct answer is (E). Answer choice (E) satisfies all of the restrictions in the setup: L is immediately above K, J is not in position 1, M is not immediately below K, and N is in position 1.

The Incorrect Answer Choices:

A   Answer choice (A) is incorrect because it violates the second restriction. The second restriction prohibits J from being in position 1, but (A) shows J in position 1.

B   Answer choice (B) is incorrect because it violates the fourth restriction. The fourth restriction requires N to be in position 1 or in position 5, but (B) shows N in position 4.

C   Answer choice (C) is incorrect because it violates the first restriction. The first restriction requires L to be immediately above K in the stack, but (C) shows K in position 2 and L immediately **below** K in position 1.

D   Answer choice (D) is incorrect because it violates the third restriction. The third restriction prohibits M from being immediately below K in the stack, but (D) shows K in position 2 and M immediately below K in position 1.

■ *Difficulty Level: 2*

Question 7

What you should keep in mind for this question: This question involves the supposition that J is on top of the stack—that is, **in position 5**. When working with the questions in this set, be careful to associate "the bottom" with position 1 and "the top" with position 5.

Overview: For this question, you are to determine what **must** be true if J is on top of the stack (that is, in position 5). All of the incorrect answer choices will be things that **cannot** be true in that case. So start with the supposition that J is in position 5:

1	2	3	4	5
				J

Because J is in position 5, the only available position for N is position 1, since the fourth restriction requires N to be in one of those two positions:

1	2	3	4	5
N				J

Notice that there are three remaining positions in the diagram above. You know from the first restriction that L is immediately above K in the stack, so this sequence of two objects can go in one of two places in the diagram above. K and L can be in positions 2 and 3, or K and L can be in positions 3 and 4:

1	2	3	4	5
N	K	L		J
N		K	L	J

Let's consider the second case first. Notice that if K and L are in positions 3 and 4, then the only remaining position for M is position 2:

1	2	3	4	5
N	M	K	L	J

But if M is in position 2, then it is immediately below K in the stack, in violation of the third restriction. So it is the first case of the two cases above that leads in the right direction: It must be that K is in position 2 and L is in position 3, with M in position 4:

1	2	3	4	5
N	K	L	M	J

Notice that you have now determined that there is just one possible order for the objects in the stack if J is in position 5: N must be in position 1, K must be in position 2, L must be in position 3, and M must be in position 4. Scanning the answer choices, you see that answer choice (E) says "M is in position 4." Since you have determined that M must be in position 4, (E) is the correct answer.

The Correct Answer:

E As discussed in the "Overview," the correct answer is (E). If J is on top of the stack (that is, in position 5), then the order of the objects in the stack must be as follows, with M in position 4:

1	2	3	4	5
N	K	L	M	J

The Incorrect Answer Choices:

A, B, C, D Answer choices (A) through (D) are incorrect because none of them describe something that must be true if J is in position 5. In fact, because the outcome under "The Correct Answer" is the only possible outcome if J is in position 5, each of these answer choices is something that must be **false** if J is in position 5: K cannot be in position 4, L cannot be in position 2, L cannot be in position 4, and M cannot be in position 2.

- *Difficulty Level: 2*

Question 8

Overview: This question asks you to first suppose that L is in position 2 and then determine what could be true in that case. The incorrect answer choices will all be things that cannot be true if L is in position 2. As with any question that asks you to suppose that something is true, you should start with the supposition of the question and see what inferences follow from that. First, you know that if L is in position 2, then K must be immediately below it in position 1, as required by the first restriction:

1	2	3	4	5
K	L			

And because K is in position 1, N must be in position 5, since according to the fourth restriction, N must be in one of those two positions:

1	2	3	4	5
K	L			N

At this point, you might turn your attention to the answer choices to see whether there are any that can be ruled out on the basis of what you have deduced so far. Since you know what positions the objects K, L, and N must be in, and you know what objects must be in positions 1, 2, and 5, you should look for any answer choices that mention K, L, N, position 1, position 2, or position 5. Answer choice (B) says that J is in position 5, which cannot be true since you know that N is in position 5. Answer choice (C) says that M is in position 1, which cannot be true since you know that K is in position 1. Answer choice (D) says that M is in position 5, which cannot be true since you know that N is in position 5. Finally, answer choice (E) says that N is in position 1, which cannot be true since you know that N is in position 5 and, further, that position 1 is occupied by K. At this point, your inspection of the answer choices has ruled out all but answer choice (A), which by process of elimination must be the correct answer. At this point, you can choose (A) as your answer and move on to the next question.

The Correct Answer:

A As you determined by process of elimination in the "Overview," the correct answer is (A). To see that indeed J could be in position 3, consider the final diagram in the "Overview." In that diagram, positions 3 and 4 are available for the two remaining objects, J and M. The question you face at this point is which of these positions J and M can be in. The only restriction on J is that it not be in position 1, and the only restriction on M is that it not be immediately below K in the stack. This means that either J or M could be in position 3, with the other in position 4. So, with M in position 4, J could be in position 3:

1	2	3	4	5
K	L	J	M	N

The Incorrect Answer Choices:

B, C, D, E As you determined in the "Overview," none of these answer choices can be true if L is in position 2 in the stack. If L is in position 2, then K must be in position 1 and N must be in position 5. With this information, you can rule out each of the answer choices (B) through (E): J cannot be in position 5, M cannot be in position 1, M cannot be in position 5, and N cannot be in position 1.

- *Difficulty Level: 2*

Question 9

What you should keep in mind for this question: This question asks you what could be true based on the setup restrictions alone. With questions like this, it is ordinarily a good strategy to see whether any of the answer choices can be ruled out on the basis of inferences you drew at the outset. For this set of questions, as pointed out in "Some things you can deduce right away," there was not a great deal that you could deduce right away from the four restrictions given in the setup. But as you will see, the observations you did make will suffice to direct you to the correct answer here.

Overview: This question asks you to identify an object that could be in any one of the five positions in the stack. If a given object is restricted from appearing in any one of the positions, then it cannot be the correct answer. Now consider what you already know. You know from the second and fourth restrictions that J cannot appear in position 1, and that N must appear in either position 1 or position 5. Moreover, you deduced in "What the setup tells you" that K cannot appear in position 5 and L cannot appear in position 1:

> J not in 1
> K not in 5
> L not in 1
> N in 1 or 5 only

Thus, as you can see, each of the four objects J, K, L, and N is prohibited from appearing in one or more positions, so none of them can be the correct answer, allowing you to rule out answer choices (A) through (D). The remaining answer choice, (E), must be the correct answer: M is an object that could be in any one of the five positions in the stack.

The Correct Answer:

E As discussed in the "Overview," (E) is the correct answer because M is an object that could be in any one of the five positions in the stack. Here are five possible outcomes that observe all of the restrictions in the setup and show M in each of the five positions:

1	2	3	4	5
M	J	K	L	N
N	**M**	J	K	L
K	L	**M**	J	N
N	K	L	**M**	J
N	K	L	J	**M**

The Incorrect Answer Choices:

A Answer choice (A) is incorrect. J is not an object that could be in any one of the five positions in the stack since, according to the second restriction, J cannot appear in position 1.

B Answer choice (B) is incorrect. K is not an object that could be in any one of the five positions in the stack since, as you noted in "Some things you can deduce right away," K cannot appear in position 5.

C Answer choice (C) is incorrect. L is not an object that could be in any one of the five positions in the stack since, as you noted in "Some things you can deduce right away," L cannot appear in position 1.

D Answer choice (D) is incorrect. N is not an object that could be in any one of the five positions in the stack since, as required by the fourth restriction, N cannot appear in positions 2, 3, or 4.

• *Difficulty Level: 1*

Question 10

What you should keep in mind for this question: This question tells you to suppose that M is neither directly above nor directly below J in the stack. In other words, you are to suppose that J and M are not adjacent to each other in the stack. This supposition places no restriction on the order of J and M relative to each other, but it does require that they be separated by at least one other object.

Overview: This question begins with the supposition that M is neither directly above nor directly below J in the stack, and then asks you to identify the object that must be in position 4 in that case. If M is neither directly above nor directly below J, then there is at least one other object separating them. Since this supposition doesn't give us much information about exactly where either J or M should be in the order, let's start by constructing possible outcomes that conform to the supposition. By the fourth restriction, you know that N is in one of two places, either position 1 or position 5:

	1	2	3	4	5
First alternative:	N				
Second alternative:					N

In both cases, there are four positions remaining. By the first restriction, you know that the sequence of K and L will take up two adjacent positions. And by the supposition of the question, you know that J and M *cannot* be in adjacent positions. These two observations together require that the sequence of K and L be in positions that allow J and M to be placed around them:

	1	2	3	4	5
First alternative:	N		K	L	
Second alternative:		K	L		N

Any other placement of K and L would cause J and M to be adjacent to each other, contrary to the supposition of the question. Now let's consider the placement of the remaining objects, J and M. In the second alternative above (the one with N in position 5), there are two possibilities for J and M: either J is placed in position 1 and M in position 4, or M is placed in position 1 and J in position 4. So the second alternative can be completed in one of two ways:

1	2	3	4	5
J	K	L	M	N
M	K	L	J	N

But notice that neither of these ways of filling out the second alternative yields an acceptable outcome. The first attempt is in violation of the second restriction, which prohibits J from being in position 1. And the other is in violation of the third restriction, which prohibits M from being immediately below K in the stack. So with this, you have ruled out the second alternative entirely, and you are left with the first alternative above, in which N is in position 1. Now that you know that the first alternative must form the basis of any acceptable outcome, you can see that under the supposition of this question, any acceptable outcome must have N in position 1, K in position 3, and L in position 4. And since the question asks you to identify an object that must be in position 4, you can choose (C) as the correct answer and move on.

The Correct Answer:

C As you determined in the "Overview," (C) is the correct answer because L must be in position 4 if M is neither directly above nor directly below J in the stack. There is, in fact, exactly one possible outcome that incorporates this supposition and observes all of the restrictions of the setup:

1	2	3	4	5
N	J	K	L	M

Of the five objects listed in the answer choices, L is the one that must be in position 4 if M is neither directly above nor directly below J in the stack. So (C) is the correct answer.

The Incorrect Answer Choices:

A, B, D, E None of these answer choices is an object that must be in position 4 if M is neither directly above nor directly below J in the stack. As discussed above in "The Correct Answer," there is exactly one acceptable outcome that observes both the supposition of this question and the setup restrictions, and in this outcome, position 4 is occupied by L.

■ *Difficulty Level: 4*

Questions 11–17

What the setup tells you: This group of questions concerns the colors a designer includes in a group of three costumes. Your task is to determine what colors each costume can have.

The setup provides a couple of general restrictions. First, each of the costumes will have exactly three of six colors: green, indigo, orange, red, white, yellow. Second, each of the six colors will appear in one or more of the three costumes.

The setup goes on to provide some additional requirements for the color selections. First is a general requirement that no two of the costumes have all three of their colors in common. Next are two requirements that are related to each other: any costume having indigo must also have yellow, and any costume having yellow must also have indigo. The last requirement specifies that any costume that has red cannot also have either green or indigo.

Some things you can deduce right away: For this particular set of questions, you can readily discover quite a bit even before you get to the questions themselves. Let's begin by setting up a table with three rows labeled with X (where each X represents a separate one of the three costumes), with each row having three slots (for the three colors in a costume):

```
X:    _     _     _
X:    _     _     _
X:    _     _     _
```

Of the requirements listed in the setup, the most obviously restrictive is the one that deals with red, so let's use red as our jumping-off point. You know that at least one of the costumes contains red, so let's put R (representing "red") in the first slot of the first row:

```
X:    R     _     _
X:    _     _     _
X:    _     _     _
```

Since the last requirement specifies that no costume having red can have either green or indigo, and any costume that has yellow must also have indigo, that leaves only orange (represented below with O) and white (represented below with W) for the two remaining colors in that costume:

```
X:    R     O     W
X:    _     _     _
X:    _     _     _
```

So now you know that any costume containing red must also contain both orange and white. And so, since the first requirement specifies that no two costumes can have all three of their colors in common, you know that there can be only one costume that has red.

Now let's see what we can deduce about the colors mentioned in the second and third requirements: indigo and yellow. There must be at least one costume that has indigo, and any costume that has indigo must have yellow, so now you can fill in your table a little more:

```
X:    R     O     W
X:    I     Y     _
X:    _     _     _
```

Remember that you'll also need green in at least one of the costumes. If you want to have a reminder about green, you might want to put a G (for "green") off to the side of your table, maybe circling it or otherwise indicating that it's something that hasn't yet been fixed:

```
X:    R     O     W
X:    I     Y     _     [G]
X:    _     _     _
```

Don't bother wasting time making further deductions at this point. You've gotten very far already and should now move on to the questions.

Question 11

Overview: This question asks for a complete acceptable distribution of colors among the three costumes. One way to approach this sort of question is to consider each of the requirements listed in the setup one at a time and then check the answer choices to see whether that choice meets that requirement. If an answer choice doesn't meet the requirement you're considering, you can eliminate that choice and not look at it again when you consider the next requirement. When you've eliminated all of the incorrect answer choices, the one remaining has to be the correct answer.

The Incorrect Answer Choices:

A Here, one of the costumes has indigo but not yellow. This fails to meet the second requirement listed in the setup, and so (A) is incorrect.

C, D In (C) one of the costumes has both red and green, and in (D) one of the costumes has both red and indigo. Both of these fail to meet the fourth requirement, and so (C) and (D) are incorrect.

E Here, one of the costumes has yellow but not indigo. This fails to meet the third requirement, and so (E) is incorrect.

The Correct Answer:

B This meets all of the general conditions and listed requirements specified in the setup, and so (B) is the correct answer.

- *Difficulty Level: 1*

Question 12

Overview: This question asks you to identify which of its answer choices could be true, given only what's specified in the setup. Since you've already made lots of deductions already, one good approach here would be to glance through the answer choices to see if there are any you can quickly eliminate or any one of the choices that you can readily recognize as something that could be true.

The Incorrect Answer Choices:

A, B, E You can eliminate (A), (B), and (E) right away because you already know from "What you can deduce right away" that one costume has red and that a costume having red must also have orange and white (and so cannot also have either green or yellow).

C You can also eliminate (C) quickly because you've already determined that there can be only one costume that has red.

The Correct Answer:

D Since you've eliminated all of the incorrect answer choices, you know that the correct answer must be (D). During the actual test, your best approach would then be to select (D) and move on to the next question. For completeness of the discussion here, though, let's check to make sure that (D) could be true. All you need to do is identify an acceptable solution in which exactly one of the costumes has orange in it. Here's such a solution:

X:	R	O	W
X:	I	Y	G
X:	I	Y	W

Here, no two costumes have the same color combination, each costume that has indigo also has yellow and each costume that has yellow also has indigo, and there's neither indigo nor green in the costume that has red.

- *Difficulty Level: 3*

Question 13

Overview: In this question you need to determine what could be true if, in addition to the general conditions and specific requirements presented in the setup, there is only one costume that has both yellow and orange in it. Let's begin by taking the results you got in "Some things you can deduce right away" and adding orange to the costume that you know has indigo and yellow:

```
X:      R       O       W
X:      I       Y       O
X:      _       _       _
```

There must be at least one costume that has green, so you know that the remaining costume must have green:

```
X:      R       O       W
X:      I       Y       O
X:      G       _       _
```

You can then examine the answer choices for this question to see if there's anything you can rule out right away or if you can identify something that could be true.

The Correct Answer:

A Suppose that there's only one costume that has yellow. That means here that the costume that has green doesn't have yellow. It also doesn't have indigo, since any costume that has indigo also has yellow. You know it can't have red, because you've already determined that only one of the costumes can have red. That leaves orange and white for the remaining two colors in the costume that has green:

```
X:      R       O       W
X:      I       Y       O
X:      G       O       W
```

This solution conforms to what's specified in the setup, and there's only one costume that has both yellow and orange in it. So (A) is the correct answer.

The Incorrect Answer Choices:

In the actual test, once you identify the correct answer you should simply select it and move on to the next question. But for completeness of the discussion here, let's examine the incorrect answer choices.

B, E Answer choices (B) and (E) can be ruled out because if orange is in the costume that you know must have yellow in it, there can be only one costume that has green in it—the other two costumes already have all three of their colors:

```
X:      R       O       W
X:      I       Y       O
X:      G       _       _
```

So (B) and (E) are incorrect.

C You can rule out (C) by similar reasoning. Since the costume that has yellow and orange must also have indigo, that costume has all three of its colors and so can't also have white. So (C) is incorrect.

D Answer choice (D) can be eliminated because the costume that has indigo, yellow, and orange has all three of its colors and so can't also have white, and if you tried to add white and indigo to the costume that has green in it, you wouldn't have room to add yellow (and the second requirement specifies that any costume with indigo must have yellow). So (D), too, is incorrect.

- *Difficulty Level: 4*

Question 14

What you should keep in mind for this question: This question asks what **must** be true. Questions like this usually include answer choices that could be true but that don't have to be true. Be sure not to mistake something that merely could be true for something that must be true.

Overview: Here you're asked what must be true if one of the costumes has green, orange, and white in it. Together with what you've determined in "Some things you can deduce right away," that gives you this:

X:	R	O	W
X:	I	Y	_
X:	G	O	W

The only color that isn't fixed at this point is the last color in the costume that contains indigo and yellow. Since that color can't be red (only one costume can have red), it could be only green, orange, or white.

The Correct Answer:

C A quick look at the answer choices reveals the correct answer: exactly one of the costumes has indigo in it. Two of the costumes have all three of their colors fixed: one has red, orange, and white; the other has green, orange, and white. Neither one of these can also have indigo, so (C) is the correct answer.

The Incorrect Answer Choices:

In the actual test, once you identify the correct answer, you shouldn't waste time ruling out the incorrect answer choices. But for completeness here, let's examine those answer choices.

A, B, E Each of these answer choices **could** be true, but none of them has to be true. So none of them is the correct answer.

D This answer choice can't be true. As you saw in the "Overview," it must be that at least two of the costumes have orange. So (D) is incorrect.

■ *Difficulty Level: 2*

Question 15

What you should keep in mind for this question: This question asks for what would completely determine an entire acceptable solution. These sorts of questions can often be intimidating. Note that in this case, though, if you've already done the work set out in "Some things you can deduce right away," you'll see that the possible solutions are pretty tightly limited. So in a case like this, even this sort of question can turn out to be quite straightforward.

Overview: Here your task is to identify what would completely determine the colors of each of the costumes. That is, you're looking for something that, if it were true, would entirely fix what all three of the colors of all three of the costumes would be.

As you saw in "Some things you can deduce right away," quite a few of the colors are already fixed from the beginning, and green must be in at least one but no more than two of the costumes:

X:	R	O	W	
X:	I	Y	_	[G]
X:	_	_	_	

With this much of the solution already in place, it's likely that going through the answer choices one at a time will be an efficient approach here. And in fact, it will turn out that this will prove to be very efficient, as you'll see when you consider answer choice (A).

Suppose that all three of the costumes have white in them, as (A) says:

X:	R	O	W
X:	I	Y	W
X:	_	_	W

At that point, there's only one costume that can have green:

X:	R	O	W
X:	I	Y	W
X:	G	_	W

That leaves only one color in one costume left. That color can't be red since as you saw in "Some things you can deduce right away," only one costume can have red. And that color can't be either indigo or yellow, since any costume that has one of those colors must also have the other, but there's no room for both those colors. That leaves only orange:

```
X:    R    O    W
X:    I    Y    W
X:    G    O    W
```

So if there are three costumes that have white in them, the colors for each of the three costumes are completely determined. You found the correct answer, (A), and can select it and go on to the next question without examining any of the other answer choices.

The Correct Answer:

A As you saw in the "Overview," if there are three costumes that have white in them, the colors for each of the three costumes are completely determined. So (A) is the correct answer.

The Incorrect Answer Choices:

When you take the actual test, whenever you hit upon the correct answer for a question you should conserve your time by selecting that answer and moving on without considering any of the remaining answer choices. But for completeness here, let's look at each of the incorrect choices for this question.

B, C, D All three of these answer choices can be ruled out. Consider this table that represents two possible solutions:

```
X:    R    O    W
X:    I    Y    O/W
X:    G    O    W
```

In one of these solutions, there is a costume that contains indigo, yellow, and orange. In the other solution, there is a costume that contains indigo, yellow, and white. Both of those solutions have exactly one costume that has green (choice (B)), exactly one costume that has both green and orange (choice (C)), and exactly one costume that has both indigo and white (choice (D)). So (B), (C), and (D) are all incorrect.

E This answer choice can also be ruled out, since there's more than one possible solution in which exactly one costume has both orange and white in it. Here's one possibility:

```
X:    R    O    W
X:    I    Y    G
X:    I    Y    O
```

And here's another:

```
X:    R    O    W
X:    I    Y    G
X:    I    Y    W
```

So answer choice (E) is incorrect.

- *Difficulty Level: 4*

Question 16

Overview: For this question, you need to determine what must be false given only what's specified in the setup. At first this might seem rather daunting, but a good approach here is to first check what you've already deduced, which in this case is rather a lot:

X:	R	O	W
X:	I	Y	_
X:	_	_	_

The next step is to glance at the answer choices to see if you can immediately identify something that must be false. If you find it, that's the correct answer. If you can't find it, you can then carefully go through each of the answer choices.

What you should keep in mind for this question: Probably the majority of analytical reasoning questions ask you to identify what could be true or what must be true. Sometimes, though, your task is to determine what could be or must be **false**. This question is such a case: you are to determine something that must be false. Be careful, because at least some of the incorrect answer choices are likely to be things that could be false but don't have to be.

The Correct Answer:

E   As you look through the answer choices, you might notice that (E) can't be true. The costume that contains red already has all three of its colors determined, and at least one of the other costumes has both indigo and yellow. That means that there can be at most one costume that has both green and orange. Answer choice (E) must therefore be false. Since you're looking for something that must be false, (E) is the correct answer.

The Incorrect Answer Choices:

A, B, D   Each of these answer choices could be true. Here's an acceptable solution that includes exactly two costumes that have indigo in them (choice (A)), exactly two costumes that have white in them (choice (B)), and exactly one costume that has both yellow and white in it (choice (D)):

X:	R	O	W
X:	I	Y	W
X:	I	Y	G

Since you're looking for something that must be false, and (A), (B), and (D) can all be true, these choices are all incorrect.

C   This answer choice could also be true. Here's an acceptable solution in which all three costumes have orange in them:

X:	R	O	W
X:	I	Y	O
X:	G	O	W

Since you're looking for something that must be false, and (C) could be true, this choice is incorrect.

- *Difficulty Level: 4*

Question 17

Overview: Here you're asked to identify something that **could** be false if exactly two of the costumes have yellow in them. Keep in mind that any costume that has yellow in it must also have indigo, which means that in addition to the costume that has red, orange, and white, there will be two costumes that have both indigo and yellow:

```
X:    R    O    W
X:    I    Y    _
X:    I    Y    _
```

One of those remaining slots must be filled in with green, since it must be the case that at least one of the costumes has green:

```
X:    R    O    W
X:    I    Y    G
X:    I    Y    _
```

Notice that the other remaining slot *can't* be filled in with green, since that would give you two costumes that have exactly the same colors, in violation of the first requirement listed in the setup. That remaining color also cannot be red since, as you saw in "What you can deduce right away," only one costume has red. So that remaining color must be either orange or white (which could be represented as "O/W"):

```
X:    R    O    W
X:    I    Y    G
X:    I    Y    O/W
```

At this point you simply need to go through each of the answer choices, looking for something that could be false.

The Incorrect Answer Choices:

A, B, C, D   Each of these answer choices can be eliminated because they're things that must be true. The table you saw in the "Overview" reveals that exactly two costumes must have indigo (choice (A)), exactly one costume must have both green and indigo (choice (B)), exactly one costume has both red and white (choice (C)), and exactly one costume has green (choice (D)). So (A), (B), (C), and (D) are all incorrect.

The Correct Answer:

Once you've eliminated all of the incorrect answer choices, you know that the remaining choice is the correct answer. In the actual test, the best way to manage your time in that case is to select the remaining answer and go on to the next question. However, for the sake of completeness, let's go over the correct answer.

E   Does it have to be true that exactly one of the costumes has white in it? No. It's possible that exactly one of the costumes has white:

```
X:    R    O    W
X:    I    Y    G
X:    I    Y    O
```

However, there's another possible solution in which two of the costumes have white:

```
X:    R    O    W
X:    I    Y    G
X:    I    Y    W
```

You're looking for something that could be false, and it could be false that there's exactly one costume having white in it. So (E) is the correct answer.

- *Difficulty Level: 5*

Questions 18–23

What the setup tells you: This group of questions has to do with a radio program in which six politicians will be interviewed. The program will be divided into four segments. Your task involves determining which politicians will be interviewed in each segment.

The setup lays out some general restrictions on the interviews. At least one politician will be interviewed in each of the four segments. Additionally, no politician will be interviewed in more than one segment.

The constraints give more specific restrictions: Hernandez must be interviewed in a segment that is earlier than any segment in which Fallon or Munson is interviewed, Kim and Munson must be interviewed in the same segment as each other, and more of the politicians must be interviewed in the first segment than in the second segment.

Some things you can deduce right away: Probably what you'll want to do first is to get a basic idea of the number of the politicians that can be interviewed in each of the segments. Keep in mind that there are four segments and six politicians. Since at least one politician will be interviewed in each segment and each of the six politicians will be interviewed exactly once, that means that four of the politicians will be matched to a different one of the four segments (leaving two others that must also be interviewed):

> first: one politician (and ?)
> second: one politician (and ?)
> third: one politician (and ?)
> fourth: one politician (and ?)

So far, this leaves two possibilities:

1. in one segment, three politicians are interviewed and in each of the other three segments, exactly one politician is interviewed (for a total of six politicians)

2. in each of two segments, two politicians are interviewed and in each of the other two segments, exactly one politician is interviewed (for a total of six politicians)

Now, the final constraint tells you that more politicians must be interviewed in the first segment than in the second segment. That means there must be at least two politicians interviewed in the first segment. Could there be three politicians interviewed in the first segment? If there were, that would mean that there'd have to be exactly one politician interviewed in each of the other three segments (for a total of six politicians):

> first: three politicians
> second: one politician
> third: one politician
> fourth: one politician

If this were the case, then two of the three politicians interviewed in the first segment would have to be Kim and Munson, in order to satisfy the second constraint. But the first constraint tells you that Hernandez must be interviewed in an earlier segment than Munson, so Munson can't be interviewed in the first segment. Therefore, it can't be that there are three politicians interviewed in the first segment.

What if there were two politicians interviewed in the first segment? In that case, there must be exactly one politician interviewed in the second segment. And as you just saw, Kim and Munson (who must be interviewed in the same segment as each other) can't be interviewed in the first segment. You also know that Kim and Munson cannot be interviewed in the second segment, since you just deduced that only one politician is interviewed in the second segment. Therefore, you know that Kim and Munson are both interviewed in either the third or fourth segment. So here's what you've determined so far:

> first: two politicians (not K & M)
> second: one politician
> third: either one politician or both K & M
> fourth: either one politician or both K & M

Additionally, you know that Hernandez must be interviewed in an earlier segment than Fallon; this means that Fallon cannot be interviewed in the first segment. Further, because Hernandez must also be interviewed in an earlier segment than Munson, and because Fallon and Munson are interviewed in different segments than each other, this means that Hernandez must be interviewed in either the first or second segment. There are no restrictions on Greer and Lewis. Both Greer and Lewis can be interviewed in any of the four segments.

Question 18

Overview: This question asks you to identify a possible matching of the politicians to the program segments. The answer choices each represent a complete matching, in that every politician is matched to a program segment. (This kind of question is described as an "Orientation Question" on pages 6–7.) An efficient way to approach this type of question is to take the constraints in turn and check the answer choices against them, eliminating any answer choice as soon as you detect a violation of a constraint. There's no need to recheck an answer choice once you've eliminated it.

The first constraint is that Hernandez must be interviewed in a segment that is earlier than any segment in which Fallon or Munson is interviewed. This constraint allows you to eliminate answer choice (B) and answer choice (E). In (B), Hernandez is interviewed in the fourth segment, later than both Fallon (second segment) and Munson (third segment). In (E), Hernandez is interviewed in the same segment as Munson (first), not in an earlier segment than Munson.

The second constraint is that Kim and Munson must be interviewed in the same segment as each other. This constraint allows you to eliminate answer choice (A), since that answer choice has Kim being interviewed in the third segment, while Munson is interviewed in the fourth segment.

The third constraint is that more of the politicians must be interviewed in the first segment than in the second segment. This constraint allows you to rule out answer choice (C), since that answer choice has one politician being interviewed in the first segment and two politicians being interviewed in the second segment.

The only answer choice that has not been eliminated is (D), so that's the correct answer.

The Correct Answer:

D The "Overview" shows by process of elimination that (D) is the correct answer.

Although during the actual test, you probably wouldn't want to spend time verifying that (D) is correct, let's take a look here. First, (D) satisfies the basic setup by having at least one politician being interviewed in each segment. (D) satisfies the first constraint since Hernandez is interviewed in the first segment, which is earlier than both Fallon (fourth) and Munson (third). (D) satisfies the second constraint since Kim and Munson are both interviewed in the same segment as each other (third). And finally, (D) satisfies the third constraint since there are two politicians interviewed in the first segment and one politician interviewed in the second segment.

The Incorrect Answer Choices:

A (A) can be eliminated since it violates the second constraint. Kim and Munson are interviewed in different segments than each other.

B, E (B) and (E) can be eliminated since each violates the first constraint. In (B), Hernandez is interviewed in a later segment (fourth) than both Fallon (second) and Munson (third). In (E), Hernandez is interviewed in the same segment as Munson (first) instead of in an earlier segment than Munson.

C (C) can be eliminated since it violates the third constraint. More of the politicians are interviewed in the second segment than in the first segment instead of the other way around.

- *Difficulty Level: 1*

Question 19

Overview: This question asks you to select the answer choice that must be true of one of the program segments. Quickly scanning the answer choices, you see that they all concern whether a given politician is the sole interview in a segment or is interviewed in the same segment as another politician. As you saw in "Some things you can deduce right away," the setup constraints entail that the number of politicians interviewed in each segment must be:

> first: two politicians
> second: one politician
> third: either one politician or both of K & M
> fourth: either one politician or both of K & M

For the purposes of this question, the important thing to remember is that there are two segments in which exactly two politicians are interviewed—the first segment and whichever segment (either the third or the fourth) Kim and Munson are interviewed in. As you found in "Some things you can deduce right away," Fallon can't be interviewed in the first segment. Since Fallon also can't be interviewed in the same segment as Kim and Munson, this means that Fallon must be interviewed in a segment in which no other politicians are interviewed. This shows that answer choice (A) is something that must be true of one of the program segments.

The Correct Answer:

A As you saw in the "Overview," answer choice (A) is something that must be true of one of the program segments. So (A) is the correct answer.

The Incorrect Answer Choices:

Once you've identified the correct answer, there's no need to eliminate the incorrect answer choices. However, for the sake of completeness, let's see why each of the remaining answer choices could be false.

B, D Must it be true that there's a program segment in which Greer is the sole politician interviewed (B) or that there's a program segment in which Hernandez and exactly one of the other politicians are interviewed (D)? No. For example, here's a possible matching of politicians to program segments that shows that answer choice (B) and answer choice (D) could be false:

> first: G, L
> second: H
> third: K, M
> fourth: F

As you saw in "Some things you can deduce right away," Greer could be interviewed in the first segment, where exactly two of the politicians are interviewed, and you know that Hernandez could be interviewed in the second segment, where only one politician is interviewed. So both (B) and (D) are incorrect.

C Must it be true that there's a program segment in which Greer and exactly one of the other politicians are interviewed? No. For example, here's a possible matching of politicians to program segments that shows that answer choice (C) could be false:

> first: H, L
> second: G
> third: K, M
> fourth: F

As you saw in "Some things you can deduce right away," Greer could be interviewed in any segment, and thus does not have to be interviewed in the first segment. So (C) is incorrect.

E Must it be true that there's a program segment in which Lewis and exactly one of the other politicians are interviewed? No. For example, here's a possible matching of politicians to program segments that shows that answer choice (E) could be false:

> first: G, H
> second: L
> third: K, M
> fourth: F

As you saw in "Some things you can deduce right away," Lewis could be interviewed in any segment, and thus does not have to be interviewed in the first segment. So (E) is incorrect.

- *Difficulty Level: 5*

Question 20

Overview: This question asks: "How many of the politicians are there any one of whom could be the sole politician interviewed in the third segment?" The simplest way to answer this question is to eliminate, one by one, each politician that could not be the sole politician interviewed in the third segment and find out how many politicians remain.

You can quickly eliminate Kim and Munson, since you know that they must be interviewed in the same segment as each other. You can also eliminate Hernandez. In "Some things you can deduce right away," you found that Hernandez must be interviewed in either the first or second segments. This leaves three politicians: Fallon, Greer, and Lewis. As you found in "Some things you can deduce right away," any of those three politicians could be interviewed in the third segment. Further, if any of them were to be interviewed in the third segment, that politician would be the sole politician interviewed in that segment, since you know that Kim and Munson both must be interviewed in the same segment as each other and that two politicians will be interviewed in the first segment. Thus, answer choice (B) is correct: There are three politicians any one of whom could be the sole politician interviewed in the third segment.

The Correct Answer:

B Using the process of elimination described in the "Overview," you can see that there are three politicians—Fallon, Greer, and Lewis—any one of whom could be the sole politician interviewed in the third segment.

Although in the actual test, you wouldn't need to verify that (B) is correct once you've eliminated all of the other answer choices, for the sake of completeness here, let's check that the politicians listed in (B) are all politicians that could be interviewed in the third segment. Consider these three different possible matchings of politicians to program segments:

first: G, H
second: L
third: F
fourth: K, M

first: H, L
second: F
third: G
fourth: K, M

first: G, H
second: F
third: L
fourth: K, M

The first shows that Fallon could be the sole politician interviewed in the third segment, the second shows that Greer could be the sole politician interviewed in the third segment, and the third shows that Lewis could be the sole politician interviewed in the third segment.

The Incorrect Answer Choices:

A, C, D, E As you saw in the "Overview," there are exactly three politicians—Fallon, Greer, and Lewis—any one of whom could be the sole politician interviewed in the third segment. Thus, all of the answer choices other than (B) are incorrect.

- *Difficulty Level: 4*

Question 21

Overview: For this question, you're looking for something that could be true if Fallon is interviewed in an earlier segment than Lewis. So you can start with that supposition and use the setup constraints to draw further inferences.

As you found in "Some things you can deduce right away," Fallon cannot be interviewed in the first segment. You also know that Kim and Munson must both be interviewed in either the third or fourth segment. Thus, if you suppose that Fallon is interviewed in an earlier segment than Lewis, this means that Fallon must be interviewed in the second segment, and Lewis must be interviewed in either the third or fourth segment— whichever one Kim and Munson are not interviewed in. This in turn means that the politicians that haven't yet been mentioned—Greer and Hernandez—must both be interviewed in the first segment.

In terms of the simple table described in "Some things you can deduce right away," you can see that there are two possibilities:

first: G, H
second: F
third: L
fourth: K, M

first: G, H
second: F
third: K, M
fourth: L

Quickly scanning the answer choices, you can find that (E)—Munson is interviewed in the fourth segment—is the only answer choice that could be true.

The Correct Answer:

E As you saw in the "Overview," there are only two possibilities under which Fallon is interviewed in an earlier segment than Lewis. In one of those (the first table in the "Overview") Munson is interviewed in the fourth segment. Thus answer choice (E) is something that could be true if Fallon is interviewed in an earlier segment than Lewis. So (E) is the correct answer.

The Incorrect Answer Choices:

Once you've identified the correct answer, there's no need to eliminate the incorrect answer choices. However, for the sake of completeness, let's see why each of the other answer choices is incorrect, using the inferences made in the "Overview":

A In order for Fallon to be interviewed in an earlier segment than Lewis, Fallon must be interviewed in the second segment. So (A) is not the correct answer.

B In order for Fallon to be interviewed in an earlier segment than Lewis, Greer must be interviewed in the first segment. So (B) is not the correct answer.

C In order for Fallon to be interviewed in an earlier segment than Lewis, Hernandez must be interviewed in the first segment. So (C) is not the correct answer.

D In order for Fallon to be interviewed in an earlier segment than Lewis, Lewis must be interviewed in either the third segment or the fourth segment—whichever one Kim and Munson are not interviewed in. So (D) is not the correct answer.

■ *Difficulty Level: 4*

Question 22

Overview: In this question, you're asked to identify the answer choice that would guarantee that Greer must be interviewed in the same segment as Hernandez. As you saw in "Some things you can deduce right away," the first segment is the only segment that could contain an interview with both Greer and Hernandez. So in effect, you're looking for the answer choice that guarantees that both Greer and Hernandez are interviewed in the first segment.

One method of solving such a question would be to use a process of elimination. You could take each answer choice and see what follows if you suppose that it were true. This process would work on this question. However, in this case, there's a more direct way to arrive at the correct answer.

Notice that there are only three politicians—Greer, Hernandez, and Lewis—who could be interviewed in the first segment. As you saw in "Some things you can deduce right away," the other three politicians—Fallon, Kim, and Munson—cannot be interviewed in the first segment. This means that the two politicians interviewed in the first segment must be some pair of Greer, Hernandez, and Lewis. Thus, any answer choice that claims Lewis is interviewed in a segment other than the first will guarantee that both Greer and Hernandez are interviewed in the first segment.

A quick scan of the answer choices reveals that (D) is just such an option. If it were true that Lewis is interviewed in the second segment, then both Greer and Hernandez would have to be interviewed in the first segment.

The Correct Answer:

D The "Overview" describes one method for determining that answer choice (D) is something that would guarantee that Greer must be interviewed in the same segment as Hernandez. Here's an independent demonstration that answer choice (D) is correct.

Suppose that answer choice (D) is true, and that Lewis is interviewed in the second segment. As you saw in "Some things you can deduce right away," this means that Lewis must be the sole politician interviewed in the second segment. You know that Kim and Munson must both be interviewed in either the third segment or the fourth segment. You also know that Fallon cannot be interviewed in the first segment. This means that Fallon must be interviewed in either the third or fourth segment—whichever segment Kim and Munson are not interviewed in. Since two politicians need to be interviewed in the first segment, this means that the two

politicians not yet mentioned—Greer and Hernandez—must be interviewed in the first segment. This shows that Greer must be interviewed in the same segment as Hernandez if answer choice (D) is true.

The Incorrect Answer Choices:

Once you've identified the correct answer, there's no need during the actual test to eliminate the incorrect answer choices. However, for the sake of completeness, let's see why each of the other answer choices is incorrect.

A, C Must it be the case that Greer is interviewed in the same segment as Hernandez if it were true that (as in answer choice (A)) Fallon is interviewed in the second segment, or if it were true that (as in answer choice (C)) Kim is interviewed in the third segment? No. Here's a possible matching of politicians to program segments where both (A) and (C) are true, but where Greer and Hernandez are interviewed in different segments than each other:

first: H, L
second: F
third: K, M
fourth: G

So neither (A) nor (C) is correct.

B, E Consider this following possible matching of politicians to program segments in which Greer is interviewed in the first segment (B) and Munson is interviewed in the fourth segment (E):

first: G, L
second: H
third: F
fourth: K, M

Here Greer and Hernandez are not interviewed in the same segment as each other. So neither (B) nor (E) is correct.

■ *Difficulty Level: 5*

Question 23

Overview: In this question, you're asked to identify a constraint that could replace the first setup constraint in a way that would have the same effect in determining the program segments in which the politicians are interviewed. Your task is to identify an alternative constraint that would not change which possible matchings of politicians to program segments are deemed acceptable. That is, the alternative constraint cannot rule out possibilities that were originally deemed acceptable, nor can it allow possibilities that were originally deemed unacceptable.

The Correct Answer:

B In order to answer this kind of question, it is sometimes possible to determine fairly straightforwardly which of the answer choices is correct. And that is the case here. Consider the new constraint offered in (B)—namely, that Hernandez must be interviewed in a segment that is earlier than any segment in which Fallon or Kim is interviewed. The original constraint was that Hernandez must be interviewed in a segment that is earlier than any segment in which Fallon or Munson is interviewed. The only difference between the original constraint and this proposed alternative is that Munson has been replaced with Kim. In many settings, this would completely change the effect of this constraint. However, an additional constraint in this scenario is that Kim and Munson must be interviewed in the same segment as each other. Thus, for this scenario, the proposed alternative constraint will have exactly the same effect as the original first constraint. The original constraint, when combined with the rest of the setup, determined that Hernandez will be interviewed before Fallon, Kim, and Munson. The constraint stated in answer choice (B) has precisely the same effect.

The Incorrect Answer Choices:

Once you've identified the correct answer, there's no need to eliminate the incorrect answer choices. However, for the sake of completeness, let's see why each of the other answer choices is incorrect. To do so, it will help to say a bit more about what it would take for an answer choice to fail to be correct for this type of question.

You're looking for an alternative constraint that would yield precisely the same possible outcomes as the original constraint. So one strategy for checking whether an answer choice provides such a constraint is to ask two questions:

- Does the new constraint rule out possibilities that the original constraint allows?

- Does the new constraint allow possibilities that the original constraint rules out?

If the answer to either of these questions is yes, then the new constraint offered in the answer choice cannot be correct.

A To see that answer choice (A) is incorrect, consider the first bulleted question above: does the constraint offered in (A) rule out any possibilities that the original constraint allows? The answer is yes. Here's a possible matching of politicians to program segments that satisfies all of the original setup constraints, but which would violate the constraint stated in (A):

first: G, L
second: H
third: F
fourth: K, M

C To see that answer choice (C) is incorrect, consider the second bulleted question above: does the constraint offered in (C) allow any possibilities that the original constraint rules out? The answer is yes. Consider the following matching of politicians to program segments:

first: G, L
second: F
third: K, M
fourth: H

This possibility satisfies the constraint stated in (C) as well as the second and third setup constraints. However, it violates the original first constraint, since Hernandez is interviewed later than both Fallon and Munson.

D To see that answer choice (D) is incorrect, consider the second bulleted question above: does the constraint offered in (D) allow any possibilities that the original constraint rules out? The answer is yes. Consider the matching of politicians to program segments described in the explanation of answer choice (C) above. That possibility satisfies the constraint stated in (D) as well as the second and third setup constraints. However, it violates the original first constraint, since Hernandez is interviewed later than both Fallon and Munson.

E To see that answer choice (E) is incorrect, consider the first bulleted question above: does the constraint offered in (E) rule out any possibilities that the original constraint allows? The answer is yes. The possible matching of politicians to program segments described in the explanation of answer choice (A) satisfies all of the original setup constraints, but would violate the constraint stated in (E).

- *Difficulty Level: 4*

Question 1

Overview: You are asked to identify the answer choice that most helps to support an archaeologist's hypothesis about ancient tracks, discovered in Malta, that may have connected settlements or water sources. This hypothesis, which is based on the appearance and surroundings of the tracks, holds that they were made by animal-drawn carts around 1000 B.C.

The Correct Answer:

A The presence of relatively large amounts of fossilized animal excrement in areas near the tracks strongly suggests that animals were once kept in these areas. This is just what we would expect if, as the archaeologist hypothesizes, the tracks were made by animal-drawn carts. Moreover, the timing is right: the excrement dates from around 1000 B.C., which matches the hypothesized age of the tracks. (A), then, provides significant support for the archaeologist's hypothesis.

The Incorrect Answer Choices:

B The statement that some of the tracks currently connect sources of fresh water does support the claim that they originally connected settlements or water sources. But this claim is not part of the archaeologist's hypothesis, which asserts that the tracks were made around 1000 B.C. by animal-drawn carts. (B) provides no information about the age of the tracks or the way in which they were created, so it fails to support that hypothesis.

C (C) tells us that some terrain in Malta is easier to cross on foot than other terrain there, but it does not tell us which kind of terrain is found near the ancient tracks. Consequently, (C) does not give us information relevant to the archaeologist's hypothesis.

D According to (D), people in Malta historically did not use transportation technology in an innovative way. But we are not told whether the use of animal-drawn carts would have been innovative around 1000 B.C. And if the use of such carts is considered innovative for that time, then (D) would count against, rather than support, the hypothesis that the tracks were made with animal-drawn carts.

E (E) indicates that some settlements in Malta were abandoned around 1000 B.C., but it does not tell us whether any of these settlements were located near the tracks. Nor does it provide any information relevant to whether the tracks were made by animal-drawn carts. Therefore, (E) adds no support for the researcher's hypothesis.

- *Difficulty Level: 1*

Question 2

Overview: The book collector states that demand for out-of-print books is increasing. The collector attributes this increase to the rise of the Internet, which has made it much easier for people to find the out-of-print books they are seeking. The question asks you to identify the statement that is most strongly supported by these claims.

The Correct Answer:

C The collector indicates both that the Internet makes it easier to locate out-of-print books and that the increase in demand for such books was "spurred" by the rise of the Internet. This strongly suggests that the Internet's rise caused the increase in demand for out-of-print books, and did so by making them easier to find—which is to say that the amount of demand for out-of-print books was affected by the ease of finding those books.

The Incorrect Answer Choices:

A The book collector doesn't say anything about whether people are using the Internet to find books that they previously did not know existed. The collector does say that the Internet makes it easier for people to find the out-of-print books they seek, but that is compatible with the possibility that these people are seeking only books that they already knew about.

B Even if the demand for out-of-print books is increasing, it could still be that the demand for books that are in print is much higher than the demand for out-of-print books. So (B) is not supported by the book collector's statements.

D The book collector does say that the Internet makes it easier to locate out-of-print books. But this might mean simply that out-of-print books that used to be difficult to find have now become easier to find, not that people are now able to locate more out-of-print books than they could previously. The collector's statements don't tell us anything about how many out-of-print books there are, or how many of those books can be located on the Internet, so they don't support the claim that the Internet makes it possible to find most out-of-print books.

E The collector does say that the Internet makes it easier to locate out-of-print books, but that does not imply that only those with Internet access can locate these books. It may be that finding out-of-print books without the Internet is more difficult, but not impossible.

- *Difficulty Level: 1*

Question 3

Overview: The researcher indicates that, while mulches containing paper alone are not effective against soil erosion, a mixture of paper and manure effectively decreased soil erosion in test plots. Moreover, paper and manure cost roughly the same amount. On the basis of these claims, the researcher concludes that farmers should use mulches containing a mixture of paper and manure, rather than either paper or manure alone. The question tells you that the researcher's argument is flawed because it provides no evidence for a certain claim. Your task is to identify that claim.

The Correct Answer:

C The agriculture researcher's conclusion has two parts: first, farmers should use a mixture of paper and manure rather than paper alone, and second, farmers should use this mixture rather than manure alone. The first of these claims is strongly supported: a mixture of paper and manure costs about as much as paper alone, but is more effective against soil erosion. The second claim, however, lacks support. In particular, the researcher does not provide any evidence that a mixture of paper and manure combats soil erosion better than manure alone, which leaves open the possibility that manure alone is the better choice. The failure to provide evidence for this claim constitutes a significant flaw in the researcher's argument.

The Incorrect Answer Choices:

A If paper alone contributed to soil erosion, this would be evidence that it is less effective at combating soil erosion than a mixture of paper and manure. But the researcher's argument already supports this claim, since it indicates that paper alone is ineffective against soil erosion while a mixture of paper and manure is very effective for this purpose. So the researcher need not provide evidence for the claim in (A).

B The researcher does provide evidence that mulch containing paper and manure works better than mulch containing only paper—a mixture of paper and manure is said to be "very effective" while paper mulch is said to be "ineffective." So the flaw described in (B) does not apply to the researcher's argument.

D The researcher compares mulches containing a mixture of paper and manure only to mulches containing either paper alone or manure alone. The researcher never suggests that this mixture works better than methods of preventing soil erosion that do not involve mulch, so there is no need to provide evidence for that claim.

E If mulch of pure manure provides soil nutrients that paper mulch does not, this would be a reason for farmers to prefer mulches composed of manure alone. But the researcher never suggests that farmers should prefer mulches composed of manure alone, so the failure to provide evidence supporting that claim is not a flaw in the researcher's argument.

- *Difficulty Level: 1*

Question 4

Overview: Eastern pipistrelle bats often leave their caves at night to hunt for flying insects. Researchers studying these bats found that the temperature inside the bats' caves remains constant, but that more bats leave the caves on warm nights—when insects are more abundant—than on cool nights. These findings are interesting: if the bats' caves don't vary in temperature, what causes the bats' behavior to change on warm nights as opposed to cool nights? You are asked to select the answer choice that most helps to explain these findings.

The Correct Answer:

B If (B) is true, it identifies a factor—changes in barometric pressure—that the bats can detect, and that is closely associated with temperature changes. This helps to account for why the bats' behavior varies with temperature: while the bats cannot detect temperature changes directly, they can detect and respond to something that closely correlates with these changes. By identifying a mechanism that allows the bats to respond to changes in the temperature outside their caves, (B) goes a long way toward explaining the researchers' findings.

The Incorrect Answer Choices:

A Even if the researchers studied only female bats, the finding that more female bats leave the caves on warm nights would still stand in need of explanation. Thus, (A) does not help us to account for the researchers' findings.

C (C)'s claim that the bats cannot engage in sustained activity on very cool evenings gives us a reason why bats might not want to leave their caves on very cool evenings, but it doesn't help at all to explain why they are less likely to leave their caves on evenings that are merely cool. Moreover, (C) tells us nothing about why the bats' behavior varies with temperature even though temperature changes cannot be detected from within the bats' caves.

D If the bats consume more insects during the spring and fall than during the summer, then they might leave their caves more often during the spring and fall than during the summer. If anything, this would make the researchers' findings harder to explain, since it would suggest that more bats leave the caves during relatively cool seasons, but also during relatively warm nights.

E The statement that over half of the bats leave the caves on most nights does not change the researchers' observation that more bats leave on warm nights than on cool nights, nor does it explain why this is the case. Consequently, that statement does not help us to account for the researchers' findings.

■ *Difficulty Level: 1*

Question 5

Overview: According to the human resources director, some people who dislike their jobs do not miss work (because they believe it would be wrong to do so), while some people who like their jobs are occasionally absent (because they genuinely believe they are too sick or might infect others). The director concludes that this makes it difficult to do something, but we are not told what it is. The question asks you to choose the response that completes the argument in the most reasonable way. The correct answer will identify something that it would be difficult to do if the director's statements are accurate.

The Correct Answer:

C It might seem like people who are rarely absent from work are likely to have higher levels of job satisfaction, while those who are frequently absent are likely to be less satisfied. The director, however, suggests that this is not always the case: some people who rarely miss work nonetheless have low job satisfaction, while others are absent more frequently despite being very satisfied with their jobs. This makes it difficult to conclude anything about job satisfaction from absenteeism records, so (C) is a very reasonable way to complete the director's argument.

The Incorrect Answer Choices:

A The director never says anything about people who are afraid of losing their jobs. So the director's comments do not allow us to draw any conclusions about these people; in particular, those comments do not suggest that it is difficult to determine whether employees who are absent from work more frequently are any less fearful of losing their jobs.

B The director's comments do not suggest that it would be difficult to maintain accurate absenteeism records for all of a company's employees. They do suggest that some employees miss work more often than others, but that is compatible with the possibility that it is relatively easy to keep track of these absences.

D While the director does mention employees who miss work because they are ill, these employees are said to "genuinely believe" that they are too sick or might infect others. This suggests that these people are being trustworthy when they claim that they must miss work. The director never discusses the trustworthiness of any other employees, so the claim that it is difficult to assess such trustworthiness is not a reasonable way to complete the director's argument.

E The director's argument never bears on the issue of whether absenteeism, or anything else in the employee's record, is a useful predictor of an employee's future behavior. The possibility that past absenteeism rates are reliable predictors of future absenteeism rates is entirely compatible with the director's argument, so (E) is not a reasonable way to complete that argument.

- *Difficulty Level: 1*

Question 6

Overview: The passage begins with a broad pronouncement about the effects of technology on language and, consequently, on culture. It gives several examples of technologies that affect language, but focuses on email. We are told that the introduction of email has caused a loosening of language usage rules. This has in turn caused relationships between people to become more casual. You are asked to identify the proposition that is best illustrated by these statements.

The Correct Answer:

B The passage claims that the introduction of a new communication medium, email, has caused a loosening of language usage rules, which has in turn made interpersonal relationships more casual. This series of claims illustrates the proposition that changes in communication media can cause interpersonal relationships to change.

The Incorrect Answer Choices:

A The passage provides an example of how the development of new technology can affect the nature of relationships between people, by making those relationships more casual. However, there's no reason to think that this effect was adverse. Nothing in the passage suggests that there is anything bad about interpersonal relationships becoming more casual.

C The passage says that the advent of email, which could be considered an increase in technological sophistication, has led to a loosening of language usage rules. This loosening of rules could be interpreted as a decrease in linguistic sophistication. But even under this interpretation, the passage would still not illustrate (C), since (C) goes in the opposite direction. It talks about a decrease in linguistic sophistication leading to an increase in technological sophistication.

D The passage says that email has caused a loosening of language usage rules, but it does not say that this loosening has led to **improved** communication. So the passage could not illustrate any proposition about how a loosening of language usage rules can improve communication.

E The passage says that a loosening of language usage rules (which would entail changes in the way people speak to one another) has caused a change in interpersonal relationships (they have become more casual). This does not illustrate (E) because (E) goes in the opposite direction. It talks about changes in interpersonal relationships causing changes in how people speak to one another.

- *Difficulty Level: 1*

Question 7

Overview: The builder concludes that within ten years, most new homes constructed in North America will have frames made of steel rather than wood. One premise offered to support this conclusion is that lumber is deteriorating in quality and increasing in cost, while steel is decreasing in cost. Steel is also said to have other advantages over wood: it is environmentally friendly and will not warp, rot, or split. You are asked to find the statement that most weakens the builder's reasoning.

The Correct Answer:

D (D) says that it's very expensive to train home construction workers to use steel. This weakens the argument because it indicates that any advantages that steel offers in terms of cost or quality could be offset by the high cost of training construction workers. Even if steel becomes less expensive than wood over the next ten years, home builders might not be able to afford the cost of retraining their workers to use steel. Thus (D) weakens the builder's reasoning considerably.

The Incorrect Answer Choices:

A If labor costs are expected to rise significantly over the next ten years, this has no discernable impact on the builder's reasoning. Regardless of the cost of labor, builders would still have an incentive to use less expensive, higher quality materials.

B (B) cites another advantage of steel—one that would make steel frame houses more attractive to buyers. So (B) would strengthen the builder's reasoning by giving us another reason to think that home builders will switch to steel within ten years.

C (C) says that most new homes are already built with steel frames. This makes it certain that most new homes will have steel frames within ten years, which is the argument's conclusion. So if (C) is true, you might say that there is no longer any need for the builder's argument, but this would do nothing to weaken the reasoning in the builder's argument.

E If the number of houses built is expected to decrease over the next decade, this has no discernable impact on the builder's reasoning. Regardless of how many houses they are building, builders would still have an incentive to use less expensive, higher quality materials.

- *Difficulty Level: 1*

Question 8

Overview: The candidate presents a criticism of a political opponent's view about education. According to the candidate, the opponent's position is that the outdated school system is the major impediment to a better education for the nation's children. The candidate grants that the school system needs reform, but argues that the opponent's position places too much blame on schools. The candidate contends that it's not appropriate to single out schools as the major impediment because other parts of society are at least as responsible for educating children as schools are. The question asks you to identify the role played in the candidate's argument by the statement that the school system needs reform.

The Correct Answer:

E By stating that the school system needs reform, the candidate is expressing a certain amount of agreement with the opponent's views; as such, this statement is a concession to the candidate's opponent. But it is a limited concession; the candidate goes on to argue that the opponent's position goes too far, by placing too much blame on schools. Thus it is accurate to say that this concession occurs in the context of a broader challenge to the opponent's position.

The Incorrect Answer Choices:

A The main conclusion of the candidate's argument is that the opponent's position places too much blame on schools. The candidate makes other statements in support of that conclusion, but the statement that the school system needs reform actually runs counter to that conclusion. That statement is a concession that the candidate grants; it is not the main conclusion.

B The candidate does not propose a solution to any social problems. The candidate discusses the need to better educate children and admits that the school system has problems, but the candidate does not offer any solution for problems in education.

C The candidate does contend that far too much is being blamed on schools. But the candidate's argument does not cite the statement that the school system needs reform as establishing that contention. The candidate wouldn't do this because that claim provides no support for the view that too much blame is being placed on schools; that claim actually implies that there's something wrong with the school system.

D The statement that the school system needs reform is not used to indicate how the failings of the school system are partially responsible for society's problems. The candidate never claims that the failings of the school system are responsible for society's problems. The candidate instead claims that parts of society outside the school system are partially responsible for problems with children's education.

- *Difficulty Level: 2*

Question 9

Overview: The passage says that a proposed amendment would let the city council designate some elections to be conducted solely by mail. The premises of the argument are that voting is a sacred right and that voting has always been done in person. The argument concludes that voting by mail should not be allowed. You are asked to identify grounds on which the argument is vulnerable to criticism.

The Correct Answer:

C The first premise, that voting is a sacred right, doesn't imply anything about how voting should be conducted. So the only reason that the argument gives for its conclusion is that voting has always been done in person. In doing this, the argument makes an appeal to tradition. But the fact that something has traditionally been done a certain way is not by itself a good reason to keep doing it that way. So the argument is vulnerable to criticism on the grounds that it presents an appeal to tradition as the only reason for rejecting the proposed amendment.

The Incorrect Answer Choices:

A The argument does not establish a connection between voting by mail and the right to vote; it just says that voting by mail should not be allowed because it's never been done before. In particular, it doesn't rule out the possibility that the right to vote could be violated even if elections are not conducted solely by mail.

B No part of the argument makes a claim about whether citizens will continue to have the right to vote. The focus of the argument is whether voting by mail should be allowed. The argument indicates that voting by mail has not been allowed before, so when the argument concludes that voting by mail should not be allowed, the issue of whether citizens will continue to have a certain legal right that they've always had doesn't even arise.

D The possibility raised in (D)—that the city council might never require voting by mail even if it gained the power to do so—is not relevant to the issues that the argument is concerned with. In particular, the case for the argument's conclusion that the city council should not have the power to require voting by mail does not depend on how often that power would be used, or even whether it would be used at all.

E Neither of the premises is incompatible with the conclusion of the argument. Holding that voting is a sacred right is logically consistent with the argument's rejection of voting by mail and its rejection of the proposed amendment that would require voting by mail. And holding that voting has always been done in person is also logically consistent with what the argument concludes.

- *Difficulty Level: 1*

Question 10

Overview: The columnist's argument concludes that raising the minimum wage to the level recently proposed will hurt low-income workers. The premise offered to support this conclusion is that when the minimum wage is increased, businesses compensate for higher wage costs by increasing prices for goods and services that low-income workers need. You are asked to identify an assumption that this argument depends on.

The Correct Answer:

C The only premise of the argument is that businesses would increase prices to compensate for higher labor costs. However, low-income workers would also have higher incomes if the minimum wage were increased. It's possible that low-income workers' incomes would increase by just as much as, or even more than, the prices for the goods and services they buy. In that case, raising the minimum wage would not hurt low-income workers. So in order to conclude that raising the minimum wage would hurt low-income workers, the argument needs to assume that the minimum-wage increase would not completely compensate low-income workers for the price increases.

The Incorrect Answer Choices:

A The argument's conclusion is only about the effect of an increase in the minimum wage on low-income workers. Information about the effect of a minimum wage increase on higher-income workers has no bearing on this argument.

B The argument's conclusion is only about the effect that "[r]aising the minimum wage to the level recently proposed" would have on low-income workers. So the argument does not need to assume anything about the effect of an increase in the minimum wage smaller than the one proposed.

D The argument draws a conclusion about the effect of an increase in the minimum wage on low-income workers. The argument does not bring up the issue of what would be a good reason to raise the minimum wage, so it doesn't need to assume anything about that issue.

E The argument draws a narrow conclusion that is only about the effect of an increase in the minimum wage on low-income workers. So the argument does not need to assume anything about the extent to which raising the minimum wage would be beneficial to the entire economy. If changes in the minimum wage are as beneficial to the economy as is commonly believed, this would not affect the support for the narrow conclusion that the argument draws.

- *Difficulty Level: 1*

Question 11

Overview: The argument concludes that exercise can increase a person's life span. This conclusion is based on the results of a study in which subjects were much less likely to die during the study if they exercised regularly. The question asks you to select the answer choice that most strengthens this argument.

The Correct Answer:

D If the study's subjects decided for themselves whether or not to exercise regularly, then it is possible that the regular exercisers had other things in common that could explain the study's results. For example, people who choose to exercise regularly might also tend to eat nutritiously, or refrain from smoking, and either of these characteristics might account for why they were less likely to die during the study. But if researchers randomly determined which subjects would exercise regularly during the study, then it is much less likely that these subjects shared such a characteristic. By diminishing the likelihood that these alternative explanations account for the observed results, (D) strengthens the argument considerably.

The Incorrect Answer Choices:

A If subjects who did not exercise regularly during the study tended to eat less healthy diets, then the regular exercisers tended to eat healthier diets. In that case, it could well be their healthier diets, not regular exercise, that explain why these subjects were less likely to die during the study. Thus, (A) actually weakens the argument rather than strengthening it.

B Even if subjects who did not exercise regularly tended to claim that this was due to a lack of time, that does not provide any additional reason to think that those who did exercise regularly during the study lived longer as a result of their exercise. So (B) does not help to strengthen the argument.

C (C) doesn't tell us whether deaths due to preexisting conditions were more common among those who exercised regularly or among those who did not. Consequently, it does not affect the strength of the argument.

E   If, as (E) claims, someone who exercises regularly probably does so because of health concerns, then that person may be more likely to also do other things for health reasons—for example, he or she might eat nutritiously or refrain from smoking. This could increase the probability that one of these other behaviors, rather than regular exercise, accounts for the study's results. If anything, then, (E) weakens the argument rather than strengthening it.

- *Difficulty Level: 3*

Question 12

Overview: Levin uses an analogy to argue against Shaw's contention that limits on power plant emissions should be set in terms of average emissions rather than peak (maximum) emissions. According to Levin, implementing this proposal would be like enforcing speed limits by measuring average speed, rather than maximum speed. Levin's point is that, just as enforcing speed limits by measuring average speed would allow people to drive dangerously fast sometimes, enforcing emissions limits by measuring average emissions would allow power plants to emit dangerous levels of pollutants sometimes. Your task is to identify the aspect of the power plant case that, based on Levin's analogy, is most like time spent at stoplights in the speed limit case.

The Correct Answer:

D   Emissions limits regulate acceptable pollutant emissions, whereas speed limits regulate acceptable vehicle speeds. The speed of a vehicle at a stoplight is zero—it is not moving. This is most analogous, in the emissions case, to a power plant that is emitting no pollutants at all.

The Incorrect Answer Choices:

A   A power plant that operates without any monitoring of its pollution emissions would be most analogous, in the speed limit case, to a vehicle that operates without any monitoring of its speed. Such a power plant is not analogous to a vehicle at a stoplight, since many vehicles at stoplights do have their speed monitored by speedometers.

B   Levin's analogy compares speed limits to limits on pollution emissions. Since it isn't clear what level of emissions occurs when a power plant is operating at "peak efficiency," such a power plant isn't clearly analogous to any case concerning speed limits, including those that involve vehicles at stoplights.

C   A power plant that emits pollutants at a very low level would be most analogous, in the speed limit case, to a vehicle that travels very slowly. Such a power plant might be analogous to a vehicle that is in traffic, but it is not analogous to a vehicle at a stoplight, which is not traveling at all.

E A power plant that emits pollutants at its peak level would be most analogous, in the speed limit case, to a vehicle that travels at its maximum speed. Such a power plant is not analogous to a vehicle at a stoplight, since vehicles at stoplights are not traveling at all.

- *Difficulty Level: 4*

Question 13

Overview: You are asked to select the answer choice that most accurately expresses the main conclusion of the scientist's argument. To do this, you'll need to recognize the argument's premises and how they work together to support the main conclusion. One premise is the scientist's claim that excessive vegetation would have depleted carbon dioxide in the atmosphere (because vegetation converts carbon dioxide into oxygen). Another premise is the statement that depleting the earth's carbon dioxide results in ice ages (because carbon dioxide helps the atmosphere to retain heat). Bringing these two premises together, we can infer that when there is excessive vegetation, an ice age will result.

The Correct Answer:

E As noted in the "Overview," the scientist's premises work together to support the claim that when the earth has excessive vegetation, an ice age will result. This strongly supports the scientist's initial statement that the ice ages were caused by the unusually rich growth of vegetation worldwide. Since every other part of the scientist's argument contributes to supporting this statement, it is clearly the main conclusion of that argument. (E) is a close paraphrase of that statement, so it is the answer choice that most accurately expresses the main conclusion.

The Incorrect Answer Choices:

A The scientist's premises do support (A)'s claim that excessive vegetation could have caused an ice age by depleting atmospheric carbon dioxide. However, the scientist makes the stronger claim that "there is little doubt" that such vegetation caused the ice ages. This goes well beyond (A)'s claim, and it also accords with the argument's premises: as noted in the "Overview," the premises establish that excessive vegetation will cause an ice age, not merely that it could have done so. Thus, (A) is too weak to represent the main conclusion of the scientist's argument.

B The scientist does indicate that if atmospheric carbon dioxide is depleted, the earth cools significantly, thereby causing an ice age. But, as suggested by the "Overview," the scientist indicates this in order to establish a statement about the connection between excessive vegetation and ice ages. (B)'s claim functions as support for that statement, so it is a premise of the scientist's argument rather than its main conclusion.

C The scientist does indicate that excessive vegetation growth causes atmospheric carbon dioxide to be depleted. But, as suggested by the "Overview," the scientist indicates this in order to establish a statement about the connection between excessive vegetation and ice ages. (C)'s claim functions as support for that statement, so it is a premise of the scientist's argument rather than its main conclusion.

D The scientist's argument addresses the question of whether excessive vegetation caused the ice ages. But (D) addresses a different question: whether, assuming that excessive vegetation caused the ice ages, it did so by depleting atmospheric carbon dioxide. So (D) does not accurately express the scientist's main conclusion.

- *Difficulty Level: 5*

Question 14

Overview: For this question, you are given a principle and asked to identify a case in which that principle is applied. The principle holds that it is acceptable not to keep one's promise if either of two conditions applies: first, the person one made the promise to tells the promisor not to keep it; second, the promisor cannot keep the promise due to circumstances beyond the promisor's control. Note that both conditions concern situations in which, according to the principle, it is **acceptable** not to keep a promise. The principle never says what would count as unacceptable, so any answer choice that says something is unacceptable could not be an application of this principle.

The Correct Answer:

B According to (B), it was acceptable for Felicia not to keep her promise to tutor Alan because Alan was injured in a car accident and could not attend the tutoring session. This is an application of the principle's second condition: Felicia was unable to keep her promise due to circumstances beyond her control, so her failure to keep her promise is acceptable.

The Incorrect Answer Choices

A (A) indicates that since Paul already owes Maria money, it is unacceptable for Paul to keep his promise to loan Tom money. But, as discussed in the "Overview," the principle never says what would count as unacceptable. Moreover, (A) concerns keeping a promise, whereas the principle concerns failing to do so.

C According to (C), it would be unacceptable for Mika not to help Owen move on Saturday, since Mika promised to help him move on Sunday and he now needs help Saturday instead. But, as discussed in the "Overview," the principle never says what would count as unacceptable. Moreover, Mika never promised to help Owen move on Saturday, so he would not be failing to keep any promises if he did not help.

D (D) says that it was unacceptable for Quinn to fail to keep his promise to water Laura's plants while she was out of town, because even though Laura forgot to give Owen her keys, she never excused him from his promise. But, as discussed in the "Overview," the principle never says what would count as unacceptable. Moreover, the principle actually implies that Quinn's failure to keep his promise **is** acceptable, since it was due to circumstances beyond his control.

E (E) indicates that it was acceptable for Ian not to keep his promise to pick up Ali, since Ian decided to return his library books first, which made him unable to keep his promise. This does not satisfy either of the principle's two conditions. (E) does say that Ian was unable to keep his promise, but that was due to a decision that was entirely within his control. So (E) is not an application of the principle.

- *Difficulty Level: 2*

Question 15

Overview: We are told that, because it is set in the future, the great dramatic novel *The Time Machine* is classified as science fiction. The argument concludes, though, that this classification is inappropriate. It supports this conclusion with the statement that, like other great dramatic novels, *The Time Machine* has a feature that science fiction generally does not—its compelling characters. The conclusion of this argument follows logically if an assumption is added to the argument; your task is to identify that assumption.

The Correct Answer:

E The argument states that *The Time Machine* is a great dramatic novel, while (E) indicates that dramatic novels cannot be both great and science fiction. From these claims, it follows logically that *The Time Machine* is not science fiction. Therefore, as the argument's conclusion indicates, it is not appropriate to classify it as such.

The Incorrect Answer Choices:

A Since the argument does state that *The Time Machine* contains compelling characters, (A) allows us to infer that it is a great dramatic novel. But the argument already says that *The Time Machine* is a great dramatic novel. Moreover, the statement that *The Time Machine* is a great dramatic novel is compatible with the possibility that it is **also** science fiction. So the argument's conclusion does not follow logically when (A) is assumed.

B Even if all novels can be clearly classified into distinct genres, it could be that *The Time Machine* can be clearly classified as **both** science fiction **and** a dramatic novel. And even if (B) is interpreted as the stricter claim that all novels can be classified into **one** distinct genre, that genre could be science fiction. So assuming (B) does not suffice to establish the argument's conclusion.

C (C) makes a claim about science fiction works: they cannot be great unless their characters are compelling. Since the argument indicates both that *The Time Machine* has compelling characters and that it is a great dramatic novel, (C) is compatible with the possibility that *The Time Machine* is science fiction. So (C) does not help establish the argument's conclusion.

D The argument tells us that *The Time Machine* has compelling characters, so (D) might be taken to suggest that this novel is of high quality. But this does not help us address the question of whether it is appropriate to classify *The Time Machine* as science fiction, so the argument's conclusion does not follow logically when (D) is assumed.

- *Difficulty Level: 4*

Question 16

Overview: Laurel says that modern moral theories must be rejected or reworked because they provide no guidance in extreme cases. She contends that extreme cases are where people need guidance the most. Miriam says that a moral theory can be useful overall even if it's not useful in every possible situation; being useful in many common circumstances is good enough. You are asked to identify a claim that Laurel and Miriam disagree about.

The Correct Answer:

C Laurel indicates that a moral theory must be rejected or reworked if it does not provide guidance in extreme cases. So she clearly believes that a moral theory's adequacy depends on its ability to provide guidance in extreme cases. Miriam says that all we need from a moral theory is that it be useful in a wide variety of common circumstances. Extreme cases are uncommon, so Miriam would hold that a moral theory's adequacy does not depend on its ability to provide guidance in extreme cases.

The Incorrect Answer Choices:

A As far as we can tell from the dialogue, Laurel and Miriam might both think that (A) is true. Laurel's statements imply that she thinks that a moral theory must provide guidance in extreme cases, and it seems likely that Laurel would think of the situations in which moral dilemmas arise as being extreme cases. So for Laurel, it would probably be important (and not just preferable) that a moral theory provides solutions to moral dilemmas. Miriam says that all we need from a moral theory is that it be useful in a wide variety of common circumstances, so she seems to believe that a moral theory doesn't have to provide solutions to all moral dilemmas. But that doesn't mean that she wouldn't deem a moral theory that provided solutions to be preferable.

B The passage does not provide enough information to determine whether either Laurel or Miriam would accept or reject (B). The discussion between Laurel and Miriam is limited to the question of when we should accept or rework a moral theory. They never discuss the actual history of people's abandonment of moral theories.

D Laurel never suggests that we need different moral theories on different occasions. In fact, she would probably reject (D) since she seems to assume that moral theories need to be applicable to every occasion—if they weren't, they would not have to be rejected for failing to give guidance with extreme cases. And Miriam might reject (D) too. Miriam makes a comparison between moral theories and overcoats in order to make a point about usefulness not requiring being suitable for every possible situation. She does not use that comparison to draw a conclusion about employing different moral theories on different occasions. The view that she presents is consistent with the view that there are extreme cases in which moral theories should not be employed.

E It's not clear whether Laurel would agree with (E) or disagree with it. She believes that moral theories need to provide guidance in extreme cases, but we don't know that she thinks that moral theories should be developed in light of extreme cases, and we don't know her views on whether moral theories developed in light of extreme cases are likely to provide adequate guidance in more usual cases. As for Miriam, she is concerned with the circumstances under which moral theories are useful, and offers no opinion about the circumstances under which moral theories are developed. So, again, we don't have enough information to infer her views about what (E) says.

- *Difficulty Level: 2*

Question 17

Overview: The passage says that archaeologists found, at a Neanderthal campsite, discarded gazelle teeth whose coloration indicated the gazelles had been hunted throughout the year. The archaeologists concluded that the Neanderthals lived at the campsite year-round and were thus not nomadic. You are asked to identify a statement that weakens the archaeologists' reasoning.

The Correct Answer:

C If, as (C) says, Neanderthals saved gazelle teeth and later discarded them, then the teeth found at the campsite may have been collected at various widely separated locations over the course of a year or more and then discarded at the campsite. This possibility leaves little reason to conclude that the Neanderthals lived at the campsite year-round. So (C) seriously weakens the archaeologists' reasoning.

The Incorrect Answer Choices:

A (A) does not have any impact on the archaeologists' reasoning. As long as gazelles could be hunted from near the campsite year-round—which (A) doesn't give us reason to doubt—the gazelle teeth could have all come from the area near the campsite.

B The archaeologists' reasoning doesn't make use of any evidence about tools, and we are given no reason to believe that Neanderthals or Cro-Magnons used gazelle teeth as tools. So (B) has no impact on the archaeologists' reasoning.

D The archaeologists cite the Cro-Magnons to show that the gazelle teeth discarded by a nomadic group were different than those left by the Neanderthals. (D) doesn't really change this. It merely gives more detail about the Cro-Magnons' nomadic lifestyle and has no bearing on the archaeologists' reasoning.

E (E) actually strengthens the archaeologists' reasoning. The archaeologists inferred that the Neanderthals lived at the campsite year-round from evidence that gazelles had been hunted throughout the year. For this inference to work, the gazelles would have to inhabit the area around the campsite year-round. Otherwise, the archaeologists would have to explain how Neanderthals living year-round at the campsite could have come to possess teeth from gazelles hunted throughout the year.

- *Difficulty Level: 4*

Question 18

Overview: The critic concludes that the contemporary novel cannot make important new contributions. The premises that the critic offers in support of this conclusion concern three categories of novels: psychological, action, and romance. We are told that within each of these categories, there are no individual novels that have made important contributions.

This argument would establish that the contemporary novel has made no important new contributions if it convinced us that these three categories encompass all contemporary novels, but it doesn't even address that issue. So the reasoning in the argument is clearly flawed. The question asks you to identify another argument that is similar in its flawed reasoning.

The Correct Answer:

A The conclusion of (A) is that it is impossible for any government to improve its nation's economy. But the premises consider only two ways of improving the economy—regulating employment and regulating inflation—without establishing that those are the only ways of improving the economy. This flawed reasoning is very similar to the flawed reasoning in the critic's argument, which is analyzed in the "Overview."

The Incorrect Answer Choices:

B The argument in (B) infers from a claim that machines have become more efficient that they will someday be perfectly efficient. The flaw in this case is that of failing to consider that there might be a limit to technological progress. This flaw is different from the kind of failed reasoning that we see in the critic's argument.

C The argument in (C) provides one example of how things have changed over time. (Macaulay was a writer popular in his time but has been neglected since.) Its conclusion is a generalization about how things will probably change in the future. (Writers popular now will one day be forgotten.) One flaw here is that of generalizing from a single instance. Another flaw is that the argument presents a second instance (that of Dickens) with an outcome that actually runs contrary to the generalization that the argument draws. Neither of these flaws is present in the critic's argument.

D The argument in (D) concludes that a politician does not think a problem is important from the claim that the politician has not made a proposal for dealing with it. Drawing a conclusion about people's thoughts from inferences about their actions is shaky at the best of times, but it is even more questionable when you consider that we are talking about someone whose actions might be determined by any number of political considerations, and not merely by their own sense of what's important. This instance of flawed reasoning bears no resemblance to the critic's reasoning.

E The argument in (E) concludes that small corporations can't compete at all in international commerce based on the premise that large multinational corporations are best suited for success. The flaw in this case is concluding that something won't work at all from a premise that merely establishes that it is not among the best. This is a very different flaw from that in the critic's argument.

- *Difficulty Level: 3*

Question 19

Overview: The criminologist indicates that the incidence of crime, as reported to local police departments, has increased over the last 20 years. Surveys of citizens, however, give the impression that crime has been lower in recent years than it was 20 years ago. You are asked to identify information that resolves this apparent discrepancy—that most helps to explain how these two divergent claims could both be true.

The Correct Answer:

E   (E) says that the proportion of crimes reported to local police departments has gone up quite significantly over the last 20 years. This implies that relatively fewer crimes go unreported today than in the past. This provides an explanation of how the incidence of crime, as reported to local police, could have gone up even if citizens' perception of reduced crime is accurate.

The Incorrect Answer Choices:

A   The only plausible way in which (A) could resolve the discrepancy is by making a case for some sort of bias in the samples used for the citizen surveys. But if, as (A) says, not all of the survey participants had been victims of crime, this does not establish that the survey samples are biased. (A) gives us no reason to think that the proportion of victims among survey participants differs from the proportion of victims within the overall population.

B   (B) says that most crimes are not reported to local police departments. But since it doesn't say that there's been any change in the proportion of crimes that were reported over the past 20 years, (B) can't help to explain the change in the incidence of crime, as reported.

C   (C) does not help to resolve the discrepancy; it actually conflicts with both sides of the discrepancy. It indicates that the number of crimes has fallen in proportion to the population, which conflicts with the statistics indicating that the incidence of crime per 100,000 people has risen substantially. And by indicating that the total number of crimes has risen, it conflicts with the citizen surveys suggesting that "the total number of crimes was less in recent years." So if (C) were true, that would only make things more puzzling.

D   The only plausible way in which (D) could resolve the discrepancy is by making a case for some sort of bias in the samples used for the citizen surveys. But (D) doesn't give us reason to think that those samples were biased. We don't know how many of the respondents had been victims of crime in their lives, so it might be true that only a small percentage of respondents did not give accurate descriptions of the crimes to which they've fallen victim. And we don't even know that it is unusual for victims of crime to be unable to accurately describe the crimes. So if (D) is true, the respondents to the citizen surveys might still be representative of the general population.

- *Difficulty Level: 5*

Question 20

Overview: The geologist talks about a new method for forecasting earthquakes that has reliably predicted several earthquakes. The premises of the geologist's argument are that the method can predict only that an earthquake will fall within a range of 2.5 points on the Richter scale and that 2.5 points can be the difference between a marginally perceptible shaking and a quake that causes considerable damage. The geologist concludes that the new method is unlikely to be useful.

You are asked to identify an assumption that will enable this conclusion to be properly drawn from the premises. Notice that it follows from the two premises that the new method cannot pin down the severity of a quake well at all: its prediction for the severity of a given quake might range from being just marginally perceptible shaking to causing considerable damage.

The Correct Answer:

B (B) lays out a standard for identifying earthquake prediction methods that are unlikely to be useful. If the method does not always differentiate quakes that are barely noticeable from ones that cause substantial destruction, it is unlikely to be useful. As noted in the "Overview," it follows from the premises of the argument that when the new forecasting method predicts a quake, the forecast for its severity might range from being just marginally perceptible to causing considerable damage. Since there's no real difference in meaning between "barely noticeable" and "marginally perceptible," or between "considerable damage" and "substantial destruction," the new method is unlikely to be useful according to the standard in (B). Thus the conclusion of the argument follows logically once (B) is assumed.

The Incorrect Answer Choices:

A (A) lays out a standard for identifying earthquake prediction methods that are unlikely to be useful, but the crucial part of that standard is reliability: a method is not likely to be useful unless its predictions are reliable. There is some indication that the new method is a reliable predictor in that it is said to have reliably predicted several earthquakes. On the other hand, there is no basis for considering the new method to be unreliable, and if the new method is not shown to be unreliable, then the standard in (A) does not allow us to conclude that the method is unlikely to be useful.

C The conclusion of the argument is that the new method is unlikely to be useful. (C) says that a method won't be shown to be useful until it has a long and reliable track record. But (C) gives us no reason to think that the new method won't one day have a long and reliable track record. So assuming (C) does not establish that the new method is unlikely to be useful.

D (D) says there are well-established methods that can predict earthquakes within narrower ranges than 2.5 points on the Richter scale. But it's possible that the new method is more reliable than these well-established methods, or that it has some other advantage. So assuming (D) does not establish that the new method is unlikely to be useful.

E (E) lays out a standard for identifying earthquake prediction methods that are unlikely to be useful. Even if a method is perfectly reliable, if it does not distinguish quakes that are **imperceptibly small** from ones that **cause catastrophic damage**, it is unlikely to be useful. As noted in the "Overview," it follows from the premises of the argument that when the new forecasting method predicts a quake, the forecast for its severity might range from being just **marginally perceptible** to **causing considerable damage**. But notice that the standard in (E) is not strict enough to allow us to draw the conclusion that the new method is unlikely to be useful. (E) invokes a very wide range of earthquake severity, and the new method, as portrayed by the premises of the argument, is capable of distinguishing some quakes within that range.

■ *Difficulty Level: 5*

Question 21

Overview: Two approaches to cultural anthropology are described: the "behavior as a system" approach, which treats social behavior as a response to human needs, and the "meaning" approach, which emphasizes systems of meanings. Even though proponents of the "meaning" approach reject the "behavior as a system" approach, it is said that cultural anthropologists should employ both approaches, as well as a third, "community" approach. You are asked to select the answer choice that is most strongly supported by these statements.

The Correct Answer:

E Proponents of the "meaning" approach reject the "behavior as a system" approach, so it's clear that they disagree with those who favor that approach. But the view being advocated is that cultural anthropologists should employ both approaches, which strongly suggests that they are compatible. This establishes (E)'s claim that disagreement among cultural anthropologists does not necessarily imply the incompatibility of their approaches.

The Incorrect Answer Choices:

A (A)'s claim that patterns of social behavior have meaning only from the community's point of view combines aspects of the "behavior as a system," "meaning," and "community" approaches. But we are told only that these three approaches should all be used, not that they should be combined in any particular way. So this claim is not strongly supported by the statements in the passage.

B While it's true that the "community" approach is said to be "often neglected," the specific aspects of cultural anthropology that would benefit from this approach are never identified. In particular, we are never given reason to think that the notion of community should be included in anthropologists' conceptions of human needs. Moreover, it's entirely consistent with the passage that every anthropologist's conception of human needs already includes the notion of community. Thus, (B)'s claim is not strongly supported by the statements in the passage.

C (C) indicates that cultural anthropologists who focus on issues of meaning—which includes proponents of the "meaning" approach—overlook their individual subject's humanity. But the passage never raises the issue of the humanity of individual subjects, either in connection with the "meaning" approach or any other approach, so it does not strongly support this claim.

D (D) indicates that systems of behavior—which are the focus of the "behavior as a system" approach—are understandable only by experiencing the environments to which they respond. But the passage never considers any need to experience an environment, either in connection with the "behavior as a system" approach or any other approach, so it does not strongly support this claim.

- *Difficulty Level: 5*

Question 22

Overview: The journal's editor accepts some advice from its treasurer: due to its financial situation, the journal should be changed from a paper to an online version only if doing so won't increase publication costs. The editor then gives two reasons that publication costs will not increase: an online version would have a much lower cost per issue and the costs of converting to an online version would be paid by a benefactor. On this basis, the editor concludes that the journal should change to an online version. You are asked to identify a flaw in the editor's argument.

The Correct Answer:

A The treasurer's advice is that the journal should change to an online version only if costs will not increase. This treats the absence of any increase in publication costs as a necessary condition for changing; it is consistent with the possibility that the journal should not change even if publication costs do not increase. But the editor infers, from evidence suggesting that costs will not increase, that the journal should change to an online version. This inference is not legitimate. The editor's argument makes this flawed inference because it treats meeting the treasurer's necessary condition as sufficient reason to change.

The Incorrect Answer Choices:

B The editor accepts the view that, because of its financial situation, the journal should be changed from a paper to an online version only if its costs do not increase. That suggests that the journal's present financial situation is a reason for considering its future costs, but it doesn't indicate anything about the reasons for that financial situation. The editor's argument doesn't address those reasons, so it doesn't take anything about them for granted.

C The editor's argument that the journal should change to an online version is based entirely on financial considerations. These considerations could strongly support the editor's conclusion even if there are also nonfinancial advantages associated with changing, which is the possibility raised by (C). So the editor's argument need not address this possibility.

D As (D) suggests, the editor never rules out the possibility that the journal will remain in a precarious financial position whether it changes to an online version or not. But the editor doesn't need to rule out this possibility, because even if the journal's financial situation does remain precarious, this need not affect the editor's reasoning. For example, changing the journal to an online version merely might make the journal's financial situation less precarious; in that event, the editor's premises could still support the conclusion that the journal should change.

E It's true that the editor's conclusion is based partly on the argument of an authority, the journal's treasurer. The treasurer's argument, however, concerns the journal's finances, and there's no reason to think that those finances are outside the treasurer's field of expertise. So (E) doesn't describe a flaw in the editor's argument.

- *Difficulty Level: 5*

Question 23

Overview: The argument indicates that some people have a certain belief (that there is intelligent life somewhere other than Earth) and that no one who has that belief could also have a second belief (that all planets other than Earth are devoid of life). It concludes from these premises that some people do not have the second belief. The question asks you to identify the answer choice that employs reasoning most similar to that in this argument. Note that the conclusion of this argument follows logically from its premises: if no one could have both of two beliefs, and some people have one of them, then it must be that those people don't have the other one.

The Correct Answer:

C   Like the reasoning in the passage, (C) indicates that some people have a certain belief (that their dogs are emotionally attached to them) and that no one who has that belief could also have a second belief (that dogs are incapable of thought). (C) also concludes from these premises that some people do not have the second belief. This follows the same basic reasoning pattern as the argument in the passage, and as with that argument, the conclusion of the argument in (C) follows logically from its premises.

The Incorrect Answer Choices:

A   (A)'s conclusion indicates that a certain belief is true: computer chess programs really do sometimes beat human chess masters. The reasoning in the passage, in contrast, does not address whether the beliefs it considers are true. Moreover, (A)'s conclusion does not follow logically from its premises (which concern whether people have certain beliefs, not whether those beliefs are true). Compare this with the Overview's discussion of the reasoning in the passage.

B   (B)'s first premise, like that in the passage, indicates that some people have a certain belief: cats are not capable of guilt. Unlike the reasoning in the passage, though, (B)'s second premise doesn't say anything about those people; instead, it is about a requirement for thinking that an animal is capable of guilt. Moreover, because this premise doesn't tell us anything about people who have the first belief, (B)'s conclusion doesn't follow logically from its premises. This is another way in which the reasoning in (B) is not similar to the reasoning in the passage.

D   (D)'s premises say that some people have a certain belief and that anyone who has that belief "probably" also has a second belief. The reasoning in the passage, in contrast, does not concern probabilities. Moreover, (D) concludes that some people **do not** have the second belief. That conclusion doesn't follow logically from (D)'s premises, which instead suggest that some people probably **do** have the second belief. This is another way in which the reasoning in (D) is not similar to the reasoning in the passage.

E   (E)'s conclusion indicates that a certain belief is true: other planets really do have atmospheres that can support life. The reasoning in the passage, in contrast, does not address whether the beliefs it considers are true. Moreover, (E)'s conclusion does not follow logically from its premises (which concern whether people have certain beliefs, not whether those beliefs are true). Compare this with the Overview's discussion of the reasoning in the passage.

■ *Difficulty Level: 4*

Question 24

Overview: Clarissa makes two related statements about the role of mathematics in the natural sciences. Myungsook says she disagrees with Clarissa and goes on to express the basis of her disagreement. You are asked to identify a claim that Clarissa and Myungsook disagree about. Myungsook indicates that in natural science, observations must be explored thoroughly before they can be converted into numbers, which suggests that she is disagreeing with Clarissa's statement that no observation merits serious attention unless it is stated quantitatively. Myungsook's comments do not take issue with Clarissa's statement that the natural sciences would not have made such progress without mathematics.

The Correct Answer:

D Myungsook says that it's necessary in natural science to thoroughly explore observations **before** you can convert those observations into numbers. She's thereby calling for careful consideration of certain observations that are not stated precisely in quantitative terms. Hence Myungsook would agree with (D). Since Clarissa indicates that observations in natural science that are not stated quantitatively never merit "serious attention," she rejects (D)'s claim that natural science demands careful consideration of observations not stated precisely in quantitative terms.

The Incorrect Answer Choices:

A Clarissa states that the natural sciences would not have made such progress without mathematics, so she would clearly agree with (A). But Myungsook would probably agree with it as well: she clearly thinks that converting observations into numbers is an important part of the natural sciences, which suggests that she thinks that mathematics also plays an important role.

B Myungsook says that converting observations into numbers is the hardest task, so she would reject (B). But Clarissa might reject it as well: she says that observations are not worth serious attention unless they are stated quantitatively, but that does not mean that she thinks it is usually easy to state them in this way.

C The dialogue does not indicate whether either Clarissa or Myungsook would agree with (C). Clarissa says that observations are not worth serious attention unless they are stated quantitatively. But she might also think there are observations that can't be stated in this way; she would just think those observations aren't worth serious attention in the natural sciences. Myungsook, for her part, suggests that the hardest part of natural science is converting observations into numbers, but this doesn't indicate whether she also thinks that it is always possible to convert observations into numbers.

E (E) says that the use of mathematics is a requirement of "useful scientific theories," but it's not clear that either Clarissa or Myungsook are making claims that apply to scientific theories outside the natural sciences. Moreover, while Clarissa would agree that useful theories in natural science require mathematics, Myungsook might agree with that as well. She clearly thinks that converting observations into numbers is an important part of the natural sciences, which is consistent with the view that mathematics is a requirement of theories in natural science.

- *Difficulty Level: 4*

Question 25

Overview: The central premise of the argument is the statement that a local fishing guide has claimed that the most populous fish species in Stillwater Pond is the one best adapted to polluted water. The argument concludes that if, as studies suggest, the most populous fish species in that pond is the bullhead catfish, then the guide must believe that the bullhead catfish is best adapted to polluted water. You are asked to identify the grounds on which this argument is most vulnerable to criticism.

The Correct Answer:

D Nothing in the argument indicates that the fishing guide is aware of the studies, so the guide might well mistakenly believe that some species other than the bullhead catfish is the most populous fish in Stillwater Pond. In that case, the guide's claim would express the belief that this other species is the one best adapted to polluted water (even though, unbeknownst to the guide, it is not actually the most populous). This possibility exposes a significant flaw in the argument, so the argument is vulnerable to criticism for failing to take it into account.

The Incorrect Answer Choices:

A Although we are told that Stillwater Pond has been polluted by farm runoff for years, nothing in the argument addresses whether the guide believes this is the case. Moreover, the guide might believe that a species is best adapted to polluted water even if the guide doesn't believe that the water it lives in is actually polluted. So the argument isn't vulnerable to (A)'s criticism.

B The argument does not address how much any species of fish has had to adapt to survive in polluted water. It does address the guide's beliefs about which species is **best** adapted to doing so, but a species could be best adapted to living in polluted water even if it did not have to adapt very much. So the argument does not need to account for the possibility raised in (B).

C If the recent studies on fish populations in Stillwater Pond are inaccurate, then it could well be that a species other than the bullhead catfish is the most populous. But the argument concludes merely that **if** the bullhead catfish is the most populous, then the fishing guide believes that it is best adapted to polluted water. That conclusion could be strongly supported even if the studies are inaccurate, so the argument need not account for the possibility described in (C).

E The bullhead catfish might be the most populous species in Stillwater Pond, and the fishing guide might believe that it is best adapted to polluted water, even if that pond contains other species of catfish. Since the presence of other catfish species wouldn't affect the argument, there's no reason to think that it takes for granted that the pond contains only a single catfish species.

- *Difficulty Level: 5*

Question 1

Overview: The argument has one premise: a syndrome often attributed to stress is more common in Department F than in other departments in a transportation company. The argument concludes that the work done in Department F is more stressful than the work done in other departments. The question asks you to identify a statement that helps to support this argument.

The Correct Answer:

C By revealing an association between transferring into Department F and developing the syndrome, (C) provides evidence that it is something about Department F—such as the nature of the work there—that causes people to develop the syndrome. So (C) helps to support the argument that the work in Department F is more stressful than the work in other departments.

The Incorrect Answer Choices:

A (A) does not help to support the argument. (A) points out a difference between Department F and the other departments: F is larger. This would help to explain why **more** workers from Department F develop the syndrome than in any other department, but it does not help to explain why a **higher percentage** of workers in Department F develop the syndrome.

B (B) does not help to support the argument; if anything, it weakens it. If the syndrome can be caused by factors besides stress, then the high incidence of the syndrome among workers in Department F might be caused by something other than stress.

D (D) applies to all workers in the transportation industry. Therefore, it cannot help us draw any conclusion about the workers in a particular department of one company in that industry relative to other departments in that company.

E (E) applies to the entire company. Therefore, like (D), it cannot help us draw any conclusion about the workers in a particular department of the company relative to other departments in that company.

- *Difficulty Level: 1*

Question 2

Overview: The question asks you to identify the main conclusion of the argument in the passage. The passage begins with the claim that metallic mirrors absorb some light, which causes them to waste energy. The next statement elaborates on the first claim by explaining why light hitting a metallic mirror wastes energy. Finally, the passage says that metallic mirrors cannot be used where it's important to minimize energy loss. This statement is supported most directly by the first claim, which points out that metallic mirrors waste energy.

The Correct Answer:

E (E) expresses the last claim made in the passage. As discussed in the "Overview," that claim is supported directly by the first claim made in the passage, but isn't used to support any other part of the argument. It is therefore the main conclusion.

The Incorrect Answer Choices:

A Not only does (A) not express the argument's main conclusion, it doesn't even express any claim made in the passage. While the passage might suggest that (A) is true, it does not say so directly or mention the effectiveness of high-powered lasers at all. Rather, lasers are only discussed as an example of an application where minimizing energy loss is important.

B The claim that some of the light falling on metallic mirrors is absorbed by them is part of the first claim in the passage. As discussed in the "Overview," that claim is used to support the last claim made in the passage. Therefore, the claim expressed by (B) can't be the main conclusion.

C The passage does say that minimizing energy loss is important in high-powered lasers. However, this is not the main conclusion, nor is the similar claim in (C) that high-powered lasers require energy-conserving mirrors. High-powered lasers are only discussed as an example of an application where metallic mirrors are unsuitable because of energy loss. The main conclusion is the more general statement that metallic mirrors can't be used in applications where it's important to minimize energy loss.

D The passage never indicates that the most significant disadvantage of metallic mirrors is their tendency to waste energy. Consequently, (D) can't be the main conclusion.

- *Difficulty Level: 1*

Question 3

Overview: The question presents an argument and asks you to identify which other argument is most similar in its logical features. The argument in the passage chains together two if/then statements to infer a third if/then statement. More specifically, the structure of the argument in the passage is the following: If a certain event (Patricia eats a heavy, spicy meal) occurs, then a second event (Patricia will get heartburn) will inevitably follow. If that second event occurs, then a third event (Patricia will be grouchy) will inevitably follow the second. From this, the argument concludes that if the first event occurs, then the third will also occur.

The Correct Answer:

D (D) has the same logical structure as the argument in the passage, which is analyzed in the "Overview." The first event is Li planting old rose varieties. The second event, which will follow from this, is that Li's garden will look beautiful. The third event, which will follow from the second event, is that Li's neighbors will be impressed. Finally, (D) concludes that if the first event occurs, then the third event will also occur.

The Incorrect Answer Choices:

A The argument in (A) says that if one event (Ruth plants only daffodils) occurs, then a second event will follow (squirrels will eat the bulbs). If the second event occurs, then a third event will follow the second (no flowers will bloom). It then says that since the third event occurred, the first event must also have occurred. This is different in several respects from the passage's argument. Most importantly, (A)'s argument is logically flawed, whereas the passage's argument is not logically flawed. Even if all the premises in (A) are true, and there are no flowers blooming in Ruth's garden, this might be because Ruth planted some other kind of flowers that squirrels eat.

B The argument in (B) says that if one event occurs (Shawn starts gardening in early spring), then a second event will be possible (Shawn can plant tomatoes early). If that second event occurs, then a certain outcome will result (Shawn will have plenty of tomatoes for canning). It then points out that this result has not occurred (Shawn does not have plenty of tomatoes for canning). It concludes that one of the two events has not occurred. This argument has several logical features that are different than the passage's argument. One of (B)'s premises (that Shawn does not have plenty of tomatoes for canning) claims that a previously mentioned event has not occurred. The passage's argument has no premise like that. Also, (B) concludes that one of two alternatives must be true. The conclusion of the passage's argument does not do that.

C The argument in (C) differs substantially in its logical features from the passage's argument. (C) begins with a statement about two alternatives and uses other premises to draw inferences from each alternative. The passage's argument does not do anything like that. In addition, the conclusion of (C) is that one of two things will happen, while the conclusion of the argument in the passage is that if one thing happens then something else will happen.

E The logical features of (E)'s argument are quite different from those of the passage's argument. For one thing, (E) draws a conclusion about what a person will do from a premise about what that person wants. Moreover, the conclusion that (E) draws requires an additional assumption that Bryan will do what it takes to get what he wants. The passage's argument does not have these features.

- *Difficulty Level: 1*

Question 4

Overview: This question presents a dialogue about criminal punishment and asks what the two speakers disagree about. Huang's view is that those who don't commit violent crimes would not commit violent crimes regardless of the punishment, while most people who do commit violent crimes don't consider punishment, so they can't be deterred. Therefore, harsh punishments do not deter violent crimes.

Suarez thinks that in most cases in which a person would commit a violent crime, they are deterred from doing so by the presence of a mandatory punishment.

The Correct Answer:

D Suarez says that mandatory sentences prevent most people who would otherwise physically harm others (i.e., commit violent crimes) from doing so. So Suarez would clearly accept (D). As discussed in the "Overview," Huang says that most people who do commit violent crimes don't consider the threat of punishment and that those who don't commit violent crimes have no inclination to commit violent crimes. It follows that most people who are inclined to commit violent crimes are not deterred by mandatory sentences. So Huang would not accept (D).

The Incorrect Answer Choices:

A Suarez sees value in mandatory sentences but gives no indication of believing that mandatory sentences are the **best** way to reduce violent crime. Given what we are told, Suarez could agree or disagree with (A)'s statement that addressing the root causes of violence is the best way to reduce violent crime. So the claim that Suarez disagrees with Huang about (A) is not strongly supported, regardless of what Huang thinks about (A).

B Huang and Suarez discuss only whether punishment works as a deterrent. Neither of them say anything about what violent criminals **deserve**. So we can't infer anything from the dialogue about whether Huang and Suarez would disagree over (B).

C Huang says that most people who commit violent crimes do not carefully consider whether or how they will be punished. So Huang would not accept (C). Suarez says that most people who are inclined to commit violent crimes (in that they would do so if mandatory sentences weren't in place) are deterred by mandatory sentences from doing so. Suarez says nothing about those who would commit violent crimes despite mandatory sentences. So for all we know, Suarez would not accept (C) either.

E Suarez is the only one who discusses tax evasion. Huang says nothing about nonviolent crimes. So we can't infer anything from the dialogue about whether Huang and Suarez would disagree over (E).

- *Difficulty Level: 2*

Question 5

Overview: The argument states that people who participate in risky sports often do so to confront their fears. It also states that people who participate in risky sports have more self-confidence. The argument concludes that confronting fears probably increases self-confidence. The question asks what most weakens this reasoning.

Note that the argument concludes that confronting fears produces a change in self-confidence. Therefore, in order to reach the conclusion, it must be true that the self-confidence of those who participate in risky sports changed after they began participating in them.

The Correct Answer:

B As discussed in the "Overview," in order for the conclusion to be true, it must be true that the self-confidence of people who participate in risky sports has changed. But the only evidence offered for this change is that they have above-average self-confidence after participating in risky sports. So (B), which says that most of them already had above-average self-confidence even before participating in the sports, seriously undermines the impact of this evidence.

The Incorrect Answer Choices:

A Even if those who participate in risky sports to confront their fears don't know that they suffer from those fears or know the extent of them, they might still have more self-confidence than people who don't confront their fears. So the claim in (A), even if true, is not relevant to the argument.

C The argument's reasoning is based on an inference about how participating in risky sports changes the people who do participate. So information about why people do not participate is not relevant to the argument.

D One of the argument's premises is that many people participate in risky sports in order to confront their fears. But the argument does not depend on the claim that participating in risky sports is the only way to confront fears; the argument only needs to establish that participating in risky sports is one way to confront fears.

E The argument's reasoning is based on an inference about how participating in risky sports changes the people who do participate. So information about the beliefs of people who do not participate is not relevant to the argument.

- *Difficulty Level: 2*

Question 6

Overview: The passage states that infants' consumption of cow's milk formula has been linked to diabetes. The argument concludes that parents should feed cow's milk formula to their infants anyway, based on the premise that cow's milk is an excellent source of important nutrients. The question asks you to identify a criticism that the argument is vulnerable to.

The Correct Answer:

A The only reason given for the conclusion is that cow's milk formula has a benefit: it provides important nutrients. But the argument doesn't consider whether any alternative sources of infant nutrition (such as breast milk or infant formula made from something other than cow's milk) might have those same nutrients. Moreover, it doesn't consider whether any such alternatives lack the drawback of being linked to diabetes. So the argument is vulnerable to the criticism that it defends a practice because it has a certain benefit without considering whether an alternative practice has the same benefit.

The Incorrect Answer Choices:

B The argument has only one premise, that cow's milk is an excellent source of important nutrients. The conclusion that parents should feed cow's milk formula to their infants is not a restatement of that premise, but rather a prescription about what parents should do.

C The argument's conclusion is not merely a statement of fact; it makes a claim about what **should** be done. The conclusion is thus normative and not entirely factual. Additionally, the support for the conclusion is of a factual nature; it purports to state a fact about the nutritional value of cow's milk without making any claims about what people should do.

D An argument against feeding cow's milk formula to infants could be constructed using the first claim in the passage, namely, that infants' consumption of cow's milk formula has been linked to diabetes. But the argument does not explicitly consider such an argument. Moreover, the argument does not even directly address the issue of diabetes; it just draws its conclusion based on the claim that cow's milk formula has important nutrients.

E   For (E) to be a reasonable criticism, the argument would need to explicitly reject a claim because of an absence of evidence in support of it. But the argument doesn't do this; instead it advances the positive claim that parents should feed cow's milk formula to their infants. This implicitly rejects the claim that parents should not feed cow's milk formula to infants because of its link to diabetes, but the basis for implicitly rejecting that claim is not an absence of evidence for it; it is the existence of evidence for the benefits of cow's milk formula.

- *Difficulty Level: 2*

Question 7

Overview: The argument states that advertisers target young adults in an attempt to create brand loyalties and that they choose young adults because they have higher discretionary income. The passage also says that people over age 65 will soon have higher discretionary income than young adults. The argument concludes that in the future, advertisers would do better to target adults over 65. You are asked to identify a statement that weakens the argument.

The Correct Answer:

B   We are told that advertisers currently target young adults in order to create brand loyalties. Given that this is the purpose for targeting a particular age group, an important factor in choosing which group to target is whether they already have established brand loyalties. If, as (B) says, older consumers are more likely to already have established brand loyalties, this makes them a less promising target for television advertising. This tends to offset the fact that they will have higher discretionary income than young adults in the future. Thus, if (B) is true, it weakens the argument that advertisers would do better to target those over age 65.

The Incorrect Answer Choices:

A   (A) implies that advertisers should place advertisements on a particular set of shows if they want their advertisements to reach people over age 65. But that doesn't imply anything about whether targeting people over 65 is a better advertising strategy than targeting young adults.

C   The argument states that those over 65 will soon have more discretionary income than young adults. (C) doesn't change that. If the discretionary income of young adults is projected to rise, then—assuming the argument's premise is true—the discretionary income of those over 65 will rise even more. So whatever support the premise provides for the conclusion will still be there. Thus, (C) does not weaken the argument.

D   The argument concludes that advertisers would do better in the future to target those over 65, based on the premise that they will have higher discretionary income than younger adults. (D) provides additional reason to think that advertisers should target consumers based on discretionary income and therefore, if anything, (D) strengthens this argument.

E If we add (E)'s statement about an increase in the number of consumers over 65 to the premise that these consumers will soon have higher average discretionary income than young adults, this gives advertisers even more reason to target people over 65. So, if anything, (E) would strengthen the argument.

- *Difficulty Level: 1*

Question 8

Overview: The politician's argument claims that it is a widely accepted view that a democratic society should not interfere in citizens' speech because a democracy can't exist without debate and because self-governance flourishes when citizens can express their feelings verbally. The argument then concludes that a democratic society should not strictly control its citizens' clothing and grooming based on the premises that clothing and grooming can be used to express feelings nonverbally and that they can be used to make political statements. Those premises support the claim that clothing and grooming are nonverbal analogues of speech: like speech, clothing and grooming choices can be used for self-expression and to make political statements.

The question asks you to identify a logical strategy used in the argument.

The Correct Answer:

D The argument's conclusion is that democratic societies should not strictly control their citizens' clothing and grooming. As discussed in the "Overview," the argument provides evidence that clothing and grooming are nonverbal analogues of speech and can be used to make political statements. So the conclusion that democracies should not control citizens' clothing and grooming is analogous to the claim that democratic societies should not interfere with citizens' speech and it is supported by similar evidence.

The Incorrect Answer Choices:

A The opposite conclusion to the one drawn in the argument would be that a democratic society should exercise strict control over the clothing and grooming of its citizens. The argument does not consider this claim, and, specifically, does not suggest that it leads to absurdity.

B The argument does not make any claims about the absence of counterexamples to any thesis or consider any empirical thesis. It reaches its conclusion by considering an analogous case.

C The argument's conclusion is that democratic societies should not exercise strict control over their citizens' clothing and grooming. The argument does not claim that this conclusion is widely accepted. The statement that the argument does claim is widely accepted is, as mentioned in the "Overview," the analogous claim that democratic societies should not interfere in their citizens' speech.

E The argument's conclusion is that democratically governed societies **should** refrain from exercising strict control over their citizens' clothing and grooming. The argument does not draw a conclusion about what democratic societies actually do.

- *Difficulty Level: 3*

Question 9

Overview: The television commercial's argument begins with the claim that a product advertised contains the same active ingredients as its competitor, but in higher concentrations. It also claims that the higher concentrations are safe and that a product that provides faster relief is always preferable. The argument concludes that the product advertised is preferable. The question asks you to identify the grounds on which this argument is vulnerable to criticism.

The Correct Answer:

E The commercial claims that a product that provides faster relief is always preferable to others. And the only difference between the two products that is stated is that the advertised product has higher concentrations of the active ingredients. So in concluding that we should use the advertised product, the argument takes for granted that the product with the higher concentration of active ingredients provides faster relief. But this shouldn't be taken for granted. It could well be that once the concentration of active ingredients reaches a certain level, relief will not come any faster.

The Incorrect Answer Choices:

A (A) is similar to the correct answer (E), but it is different in two important respects. For one thing, (A) charges that the argument takes for granted that products with higher concentrations of active ingredients are **more effective** than their competitors. But the commercial didn't argue for its product in terms of overall effectiveness; it merely argued that the product that gives faster relief is always preferable. The second way in which (A) misses the mark is by indicating that the argument makes an assumption about what is true in **all** cases of products with higher concentrations of active ingredients. In order to reach its conclusion, the argument just needs to make an assumption about the product advertised and its competitor.

B There's no reason to think that any of the evidence presented in the argument is, in principle, impossible to disprove. Chemical analysis can reveal the ingredients and their concentrations. There are also established procedures for evaluating the safety of different concentrations of ingredients in products. The claim that a product that provides faster relief is always preferable could be evaluated by surveying consumers to determine their preferences.

C The argument in the commercial does not consider any claims made by the competitor, so it could not possibly do what (C) suggests.

D Nothing suggests that the commercial is trying to manipulate the emotions of potential customers. The only thing that could possibly suggest this is that the commercial appeals to customers' desire for a product that works fast. But there's no reason to think that this is not a sound reason for preferring the product advertised.

- *Difficulty Level: 2*

Question 10

Overview: The argument notes that biologists often announce that a certain kind of animal has been found capable of using tools. It states that these announcements are unsurprising since all animals use tools. It then provides several examples in which animals use external physical objects to their advantage, such as fish hiding in mud to escape predators. The argument ends by stating a principle, that any use of a physical object to achieve an animal's purpose can reasonably be regarded as an instance of tool use.

The question asks you to identify the role played in the argument by the claim that the biologists' announcements are unsurprising.

The Correct Answer:

B In the second half of the passage, the examples of animals using physical objects to their advantage, such as fish hiding in mud to escape predators, are not prototypical examples of tool use, such as using a stick to hunt for ants, but they are understood to be widespread, and by the principle stated at the end of the passage, they count as tool use also. So the second half of the passage is presented as support for the claim that all animals use tools. The claim that all animals use tools is, in turn, the basis of the claim that biologists' announcements of newly discovered instances of tool use are unsurprising. Since everything else in the passage is presented in support of the claim that biologists' announcements of newly discovered instances of animal tool use are unsurprising, that claim is most accurately regarded as the conclusion of the argument.

The Incorrect Answer Choices:

A All of the animal activities discussed in the passage are presented as purposeful, including the prototypical examples of tool use of the sort announced by biologists, and the use of physical objects to an animal's advantage that are presented as less prototypical cases of tool use. The claim that biologists' announcements of tool use are unsurprising is not presented as evidence that the animal's behavior is purposeful in any of these examples.

C Assumptions are unstated. The claim that biologists' announcements of tool use are unsurprising, on the other hand, is explicitly stated in the passage. Moreover, that claim does not, in itself, contain any information about what qualifies as a tool. So it cannot be used to justify the broader conception of a tool that is described in the last sentence of the passage.

D The passage does not provide any characterization of the biologists' conception of a tool. So the claim in question cannot be used to call that conception into question.

E The biologists' announcements, as characterized in the passage, do not use the word "external." So the argument cannot be attributing to the biologists' announcements any weakness stemming from their use of the word "external."

- *Difficulty Level: 5*

Question 11

Overview: The literary critic's argument concludes that works of fiction would be unrealistic if writers were to follow Johnson's advice to refrain from attributing attractive qualities to immoral characters. The question asks you to identify an assumption that would enable the conclusion to be properly drawn.

The Correct Answer:

C If all actual bad people have some attractive qualities, and if fiction writers refrained from attributing any attractive qualities to immoral characters, then the immoral characters portrayed in fiction would not be like real-life immoral people. Works of fiction would therefore be unrealistic in their portrayal of immoral characters. So the conclusion is properly drawn if (C) is assumed.

The Incorrect Answer Choices:

A The conclusion of the literary critic's argument has nothing to do with the entertainment value of fiction. So (A) does not enable the conclusion to be properly drawn.

B (B) is relevant to Johnson's argument: if (B) were false, then it seems doubtful that attributing attractive qualities to immoral characters would make them more appealing to readers. But the question asks you for an assumption that enables the literary critic's argument to be properly drawn. (B) is not relevant to the argument that the literary critic makes.

D The conclusion of the literary critic's argument has nothing to do with how difficult it is to emulate fictional characters. So (D) does not enable the conclusion to be properly drawn.

E The conclusion of the literary critic's argument has nothing to do with how difficult it is to determine which qualities of fictional characters are intended to be attractive qualities. So (E) does not enable the conclusion to be properly drawn.

- *Difficulty Level: 3*

Question 12

Overview: The argument lists a number of assembly-related defects found in dryers manufactured by Archway. The argument then concludes from this that Archway's dryers must have another sort of defect: using substandard parts. You are asked to identify a possibility the argument has failed to consider that makes the argument vulnerable to criticism.

The Correct Answer:

D The argument concludes that Archway uses low-quality parts based only on information about the way that the parts are assembled. So if a shoddily constructed appliance can be made of high-quality parts, then the information about how the dryers are assembled provides no support for the conclusion. Since there is no reason to think that high-quality parts can't be shoddily assembled, the argument is vulnerable to the criticism that it fails to consider (D).

The Incorrect Answer Choices:

A Given the argument's premise that the assembled dryers create a fire and shock hazard, the possibility in (A) does not seem to be a very likely one. Furthermore, (A) has no bearing on the argument's inference that the dryer components are substandard. So failing to consider (A) is not grounds for criticizing the argument.

B The possibility presented in (B), if true, might be grounds for qualifying the claim that the assembled dryers are of poor quality. But it wouldn't affect the evidence for assembly defects. So (B) would not seriously call into question the claims on which the argument's conclusion is based. Furthermore, (B) has no bearing on the inference to the argument's overall conclusion, that the dryer components are substandard.

C While (C), if true, might provide an independent reason to think that the components in Archway dryers are not substandard, the argument in the passage is based on other types of defects found in the assembly of Archway dryers. Since the possibility in (C) does not bear on the support that the argument's premises provide for its conclusion, it cannot be said that the argument should have considered that possibility.

E The conclusion is about the components of Archway's dryers only. So the company's other product lines are not relevant to the quality of the argument.

- *Difficulty Level: 2*

Question 13

Overview: The passage states various facts about sexual reproduction and asks what can be logically inferred from those facts. The facts that are relevant to inferring the correct answer are the following: (1) only the female gamete supplies genetic material to the new cell's cytoplasm; (2) GM62, a type of genetic material, is found only in cytoplasm.

The Correct Answer:

B The passage says that GM62 is found only in cytoplasm. So any GM62 in the new cell (the offspring) is going to have to be in the cytoplasm. The passage also says that only the female gamete supplies genetic material to the new cell's cytoplasm. This implies that only female organisms can contribute GM62 to their offspring.

The Incorrect Answer Choices:

A The only thing the passage says about GM62 is that it is found only in cytoplasm. The passage does not say that GM62 is found in all species that reproduce sexually. Therefore, we cannot conclude that all female organisms contribute GM62 to their offspring.

C The passage makes it clear that both the nucleus and the cytoplasm contain genetic material. But the passage says nothing about the distribution of genetic material between the nucleus and the cytoplasm.

D The passage says that only the female gamete contributes genetic material to the new cell's cytoplasm and that the male and female gametes contribute equally to the genetic material in the nucleus. This might lead us to think that the role of the female gamete is more important. However, the passage does not rule out the possibility that the male gamete makes important contributions that are not matched by the female gamete. Consequently, the information in the passage does not allow us to logically conclude that the role of the male gamete in sexual reproduction is less important than the role of the female gamete.

E The passage says that one type of genetic material is contributed only by the female gamete, and it says nothing to suggest that this is in some way counterbalanced by a contribution from the male gamete. So we cannot conclude that it is likely that some kind of genetic material contributed only by the male gamete will be identified.

- *Difficulty Level: 1*

Question 14

Overview: The argument cites evidence that plagiarism by university students is common. Additionally, the argument cites a research finding that students who plagiarize are more likely to engage in subsequent professional misconduct. The argument concludes that reducing academic plagiarism will cause a reduction in professional misconduct. You are asked to identify a reasoning flaw in the argument.

Note that the argument has not established that plagiarizing while a university student is what causes the subsequent professional misconduct. It has established only that the same people tend to do both.

The Correct Answer:

E As discussed in the "Overview," the argument establishes only that the people who plagiarize as university students tend to be the same ones who later commit professional misconduct. That is, it establishes only that there is an association between plagiarizing and professional misconduct. But it concludes that reducing plagiarism will cause a reduction in professional misconduct. In other words, the argument infers the existence of a causal connection merely on the basis of an association.

The Incorrect Answer Choices:

A The argument cites anonymous surveys in which students report that they had plagiarized as undergraduates. This, along with unspecified evidence for plagiarism in medical and business schools, is presented as evidence that plagiarism is widespread in universities. It is plausible that some of the students surveyed cannot be relied upon to be truthful. But no reason is given to doubt the mentioned evidence for plagiarism in medical and business schools, and given the magnitude of the plagiarism by undergraduates, (A) does not seriously call into question the inference that academic plagiarism is widespread. The rest of the argument is based on the research finding that students who plagiarize are more likely to engage in professional misconduct later. There is no indication that this finding relies on the accuracy of reports by any people who cannot be relied upon to provide truthful testimony.

B The subject being debated is whether reducing plagiarism will lead to a reduction in professional misconduct. All of the premises mention either plagiarism or professional misconduct, or both. So the premises are relevant to the subject being debated.

C The argument does not presume, or need to presume, that plagiarism is the only factor contributing to the incidence of professional misconduct. Even if plagiarism is not the only contributor to professional misconduct, this is not enough by itself to show that it's wrong to conclude that reducing plagiarism will reduce professional misconduct. So the argument does not have the flaw described in (C).

D The argument doesn't say anything specific about the prevalence of any behavior among members of any population other than undergraduates. Moreover, no facts about the prevalence of any behavior among other populations would provide any support in drawing the conclusion. So there's no reason to think that it takes for granted that a behavior is more prevalent among members of one population than among members of another.

- *Difficulty Level: 4*

Question 15

Overview: The passage says that the deer population has increased dramatically since the 1960s despite several factors that would make us think that the deer population would have either remained stable or decreased.

The question asks you to identify a fact that would most help to explain how the population of deer could have increased in spite of these factors.

The Correct Answer:

A Deer are wildlife, so if pesticides that adversely affect most wildlife have been banned since the 1970s, that could explain why the deer population has increased since then. An adverse condition that may have prevented the deer population from growing has been removed, which could outweigh the factors that tend to limit population growth.

The Incorrect Answer Choices:

B We want to find something that could help to explain why the deer population has increased. The passage says that the suburbs are increasingly encroaching on deer habitats, so some habitat loss has occurred. Therefore, the attempts to protect deer habitats from suburban development described in (B) have, if anything, merely prevented that habitat loss from being worse than it was. But the fact that the habitat loss could have been worse does not help to explain why the deer population has dramatically increased.

C The passage says that hunters kill as many deer now as they used to, so (C) just implies that the average hunter now kills more deer than before. This does not help explain why deer populations have increased.

D (D) does not do anything to neutralize the fact that wolf populations have increased. Even if the increase in the wolf population is the result of wolves raised in captivity and released into the wild, the predation by wolves would not be expected to decrease with an increase in the wolf population, so (D) would provide no help in explaining why the deer population has increased.

E (E) does not help to explain why the deer population has increased. It suggests that population increases might be self-limiting or even cyclical. If anything, this would indicate another adverse condition that we would expect to prevent the deer population from increasing.

■ *Difficulty Level: 5*

Question 16

Overview: The argument begins with statements (in the first two sentences) that imply that having professors doing research contributes to universities accomplishing their primary task (which is to educate). This implication, together with the third sentence's claim that many universities cannot adequately support faculty research due to a lack of funds, supports the argument's last claim that a lack of funds for research adversely affects the degree to which a university can fulfill its central mission.

The Correct Answer:

D As discussed in the "Overview," the argument supports the claim that a lack of funds for research adversely affects the degree to which a university can fulfill its central mission. Its central mission (or primary task) is elsewhere identified as providing education. So (D) accurately expresses the argument's conclusion.

The Incorrect Answer Choices:

A The claim expressed in (A) is implied by what's stated in the second sentence. As outlined in the "Overview," that statement is ultimately used to support the claim that a lack of funds for research adversely affects the extent to which a university can fulfill its primary mission. So the statement expressed by (A) is not the argument's conclusion.

B The argument concludes that a lack of financial support for faculty research is a cause of universities' not fulfilling their central mission of educating students, which suggests that it is a cause of ineffective teaching at universities. However, the argument leaves open the possibility that other factors may contribute to ineffective teaching and could even be more significant causes of it than lack of financial support for research. So (B) is not a claim that the argument makes.

C The argument is basically claiming, in the first sentence, that effective teaching is the primary mission of a university, but it doesn't offer any support for this claim. Therefore, this claim is not the conclusion of the argument.

E The argument concludes only that a lack of funding adversely affects the extent to which a university can fulfill its central mission. It doesn't take the additional step of concluding that new means of funding are needed.

- *Difficulty Level: 2*

Question 17

Overview: The environmentalist's argument begins by describing how, when the UK began requiring that foods with genetically altered ingredients be labeled as such, food producers got rid of genetically altered ingredients. The argument then concludes that other countries should not require labeling of genetically altered ingredients, since many crops are genetically altered to resist pests and if genetically altered crops aren't used, then dangerous and pesticide-intensive crops will have to be grown instead. You are asked to identify an assumption that the argument depends on.

The Correct Answer:

C The environmentalist's argument is based on the idea that if other countries do what the UK did, the results will be the same. If food producers in other countries wouldn't react the same way as food producers in the UK did, then there is no reason to expect food producers in other countries to get rid of genetically altered ingredients. There is then no reason to think that dangerous and pesticide-intensive crops will be grown instead of genetically altered crops in those other countries, so we lose the grounds on which the argument concluded that other countries should not require labeling of genetically altered ingredients.

The Incorrect Answer Choices:

A The argument says that food producers in the UK worried that consumers would interpret the genetically altered ingredient labels as warnings. But this is a claim about how food producers expected consumers to interpret the labels, whereas (A) is about how consumers actually do interpret labels. The way in which consumers actually interpret labels plays no role in the argument. (The argument doesn't even tell us how UK consumers actually interpreted the labels.)

B The argument states that, after the labeling law was instituted in the UK, food producers rushed to eliminate genetically altered ingredients from those foods containing them. So evidently, some foods sold in the UK prior to the labeling law contained genetically altered ingredients. But the reasoning in the argument would still be sound even if most foods in the UK did not contain genetically altered ingredients.

D The argument does not claim that the labels indicating genetically altered ingredients are warning labels; it just says that food producers worried that consumers would interpret them as warnings. Since (D) is about something that the argument never discusses, there is no reason to think that the argument depends on (D).

E The argument needs to assume that food **producers** in other countries would react to a specific food labeling regulation in the same way UK food producers did. But it doesn't need to assume anything about actual changes in consumer eating habits; in particular, it doesn't need to assume that a change in consumer eating habits often results from new food labeling regulations.

- *Difficulty Level: 3*

Question 18

Overview: The argument in the passage rejects the contention that the use of calculators in mathematics classes will undermine students' knowledge of the rationale underlying calculational procedures. To support this conclusion, it is claimed that every new information-handling technology has produced virtually the same accusation. An example is given: some Greek philosophers believed that written language would undermine people's ability to remember information and to speak extemporaneously. You are asked to identify the grounds on which this argument is most vulnerable to criticism.

The Correct Answer:

A The only support offered for the argument's conclusion that calculators will not undermine knowledge of underlying mathematical rationales is that people have in the past believed similar things about other new information-handling technologies (and those beliefs have presumably turned out to be false). However, since the argument does not establish that those past information-handling technologies are similar in their impact to the effect of introducing calculators in mathematics classes, the argument does not establish the relevance of the evidence it presents to the issue it discusses.

The Incorrect Answer Choices:

B The argument suggests that every new information-handling technology in the past was accused of undermining a form of knowledge acquired by people who handled that information before the technology was introduced. The notion of knowledge required by the argument is thus a broad one that potentially includes diverse types of knowledge. There is no reason to think that this notion of knowledge is ambiguous; it is merely broad.

C The argument does not discuss the balance of advantages and disadvantages of any information-handling technologies that it discusses. The discussion is limited to whether using such technologies will undermine people's knowledge or abilities.

D If the argument takes anything as sufficient to prove its conclusion, it is the analogy with previous criticisms of information-handling technology. But it is not at all clear that this analogy is actually sufficient for this purpose. Moreover, the argument never considers whether such an analogy might be necessary to support that conclusion. So the argument is not vulnerable to criticism on the grounds described in (D).

E The only hypothesis that the argument concludes to be false is the hypothesis that the use of calculators will undermine students' knowledge of mathematical rationales. But the argument never discusses any other beliefs held by the education critics who advocate that hypothesis. So it does not infer that the hypothesis is false simply because it contradicts other beliefs held by advocates of that hypothesis.

- *Difficulty Level: 5*

Question 19

Overview: The passage presents a dialogue about the requirement that doctors never divulge information about their patients. The first speaker, Scott, argues that a psychiatrist who released tapes of a patient's sessions violated that requirement even though the tapes were released only after the patient's death and the patient had told the psychiatrist that he could do with the tapes as he saw fit.

The question asks which principle would most help to justify Scott's evaluation of the psychiatrist's release of the tapes. Note that the question does not ask anything about what the second speaker, Bonara, says. Also, note that Scott argues that the psychiatrist should not have released the tapes. So you're looking for an answer choice that restricts conditions under which information can be divulged. Answer choices that present circumstances in which it is acceptable to divulge information can be ruled out.

The Correct Answer:

D We might question Scott's conclusion that the psychiatrist violated the requirement not to disclose information given that the patient herself gave the psychiatrist permission to release the tapes. But (D) says that a patient cannot release a psychiatrist from the confidentiality requirement. This means that the fact that the patient gave permission to release the tapes does not imply that it was acceptable to release them. (D) thus helps to justify Scott's evaluation by removing one reason to question it.

The Incorrect Answer Choices:

A (A) eases restrictions on divulging information about patients (it's acceptable after the patient's death). As discussed in the "Overview," this cannot help to justify Scott's conclusion that the psychiatrist should not have released the tapes.

B (B) eases restrictions on divulging information about patients. As discussed in the "Overview," this cannot help to justify Scott's conclusion that it was not acceptable to release the tapes.

C (C) says that a patient's directives to a psychiatrist must be interpreted in the light of the patient's actions outside the therapeutic setting. But (C) gives no specific guidance about **how** we should interpret those directives, and the dialogue doesn't give us enough information about the patient's activities outside of therapy to allow us to properly interpret the patient's directive in this situation. So (C) doesn't help to justify Scott's conclusion that the psychiatrist shouldn't have released the tapes.

E (E) eases restrictions on divulging information about patients. As discussed in the "Overview," this cannot help to justify Scott's conclusion that it was not acceptable to release the tapes.

■ *Difficulty Level: 3*

Question 20

Overview: The argument begins with a statement of Gandolf's principle: all political systems that aim at preventing conflict are legitimate. Next it says that totalitarian systems are usually good at preventing conflict (and explains why this is so). It then says that all totalitarian political systems are illegitimate. The argument concludes that Gandolf's principle is false.

The question asks you to identify an assumption that the argument requires. In order to show that Gandolf's principle is false, the argument needs to establish at least one case of a political system that does aim at preventing conflict but is not legitimate.

The Correct Answer:

C As discussed in the "Overview," the argument needs to establish at least one case of a political system that aims at preventing conflict but is not legitimate. One of the argument's premises is that totalitarian systems are not legitimate. However, the argument has not established that any totalitarian systems **aim** at preventing conflict, only that they usually happen to be good at preventing conflict. So in order to have at least one case of a political system that aims at preventing conflict but is not legitimate, the argument needs to assume that at least one totalitarian system aims at preventing conflict.

The Incorrect Answer Choices:

A The argument does not need to assume (A). If (A) were false, that would mean that no political system that **does not** aim at preventing conflict is legitimate. This would not have implications for Gandolf's principle, which concerns only political systems that **do** aim at preventing conflict.

B (B) amounts to the statement that preventing conflict is not the true aim of any totalitarian system. But, as discussed in the explanation of "The Correct Answer," the argument needs to assume that at least one totalitarian system aims at preventing conflict. So (B) is the opposite of one thing that the argument needs to assume.

D The argument does not need to assume (D). (D) is an assumption about the legitimacy of political systems that **fail to** prevent conflict. As such, it could play no part in the argument against Gandolf's principle, which concerns political systems that **aim at** preventing conflict.

E The argument does not need to assume (E). If (E) is false, then only totalitarian political systems are illegitimate. This is consistent with the premise that all totalitarian political systems are illegitimate and with the rest of the argument against Gandolf's principle.

- *Difficulty Level: 5*

Question 21

Overview: The musicologist claims that Beethoven began losing his hearing when he was 30, that the loss continued gradually, that the loss was complete late in his life, and that this hearing loss gave Beethoven's later music a wonderfully introspective quality that his earlier music lacked. You are asked to determine which statement is most strongly supported by the musicologist's claims.

Note that you are asked only what is supported by the musicologist's claims, not what is likely to be true in general.

The Correct Answer:

E The musicologist claims that Beethoven's complete hearing loss gave his later music a wonderfully introspective quality that his earlier music lacked. The word "gave" indicates causality; the hearing loss caused Beethoven's later music to be different than his earlier music. Consequently, if Beethoven had not lost his hearing, this cause would have been absent and there is a good chance the effect would be absent as well. This means that Beethoven's music probably would have been different if he hadn't lost his hearing. (E) is therefore strongly supported by the passage.

The Incorrect Answer Choices:

A It seems reasonable to expect that it would have been more difficult for Beethoven to compose after losing his hearing. However, none of the musicologist's claims directly concern how difficult it was for Beethoven to compose his works. Moreover, it remains possible, given the musicologist's claims, that some aspects of musical composition became easier for Beethoven as he gained experience. So the musicologist's claims do not support (A).

B As indicated in the discussion of "The Correct Answer," the musicologist's claims support the view that, had Beethoven not lost his hearing, his music would have lacked the introspective quality that it had. However, the statement in (B) uses "quality" in a different sense of the word. The statement in (B) is about whether Beethoven's music attained a higher level of quality overall because Beethoven lost his hearing. The musicologist makes no claims about the overall quality of Beethoven's music in this sense and so (B) is not supported by the musicologist's claims.

C While the musicologist's claims imply that Beethoven's **music** would not have had a certain introspective quality if he had not lost his hearing, the musicologist makes no claims about Beethoven himself. Beethoven may have been just as introspective overall. It's just that his music wouldn't have been introspective in the same way. So (C) is not supported by the musicologist's claims.

D While the musicologist claims that Beethoven gradually lost his hearing and that the complete hearing loss gave his later music a wonderfully introspective quality, the musicologist makes no claims about how or when Beethoven's music changed. It's possible, given just the musicologist's claims, that Beethoven's hearing loss was complete before it had this effect on his music. The change in Beethoven's music could have been abrupt rather than gradual. So (D) is not supported by the musicologist's claims.

- *Difficulty Level: 5*

Question 22

Overview: The critic's argument is built on the premise that historians impose patterns on the events they study rather than finding such patterns. The critic concludes that histories reveal more about historians' presuppositions than about what actually happened. In arguing this way, the critic is evidently making a connection between historians' presuppositions and the patterns they impose on events. You are asked to identify an assumption that the critic's argument depends on.

The Correct Answer:

E If the patterns that historians impose on events are not affected by those historians' presuppositions then those patterns would reveal nothing about the presuppositions of the historians who imposed them. Therefore, since the critic's only premise is that historians impose patterns on the events they study, the critic's argument depends on (E) in order to reach its conclusion.

The Incorrect Answer Choices:

A The critic's argument concludes that histories reveal something about historians' presuppositions. But the critic's argument is not committed to the view that different historians produce similar historical narratives. So the critic's argument doesn't need to assume anything about whether different historians share presuppositions.

B The critic's argument is based on the premise that historians impose patterns on the events they study rather than finding those patterns. So the critic's argument is committed to the view that the patterns described by historians are merely imposed on events. (B), on the other hand, states a skeptical position with regard to this view. So the argument clearly does not depend on assuming (B).

C The critic's conclusion concerns the presuppositions that historians bring to their attempts to understand the course of historical events. The critic reaches that conclusion on the basis of the view that historians impose patterns on historical events rather than discover those patterns. The idea that there are commonalities between different historical eras—that certain historical patterns describe different eras—is unnecessary for the critic's argument.

D The critic says that historians purport to discover patterns in events. However, this does not mean that they can't be aware of their presuppositions. Moreover, if historians could become aware of the presuppositions they bring, that would have no effect on the critic's inference that histories reveal more about historians' presuppositions than about what actually happened. So the critic's argument does not depend on assuming (D).

- *Difficulty Level: 4*

Question 23

Overview: The question asks you to identify an argument that exhibits flawed reasoning that is most similar to the flawed reasoning in the passage. The argument in the passage is based on general claims about two people: Miller is said to oppose all proposals to raise taxes and Philopoulos is said to generally support increased funding for schools. The argument describes a proposal by Callari to increase school funding by raising taxes and concludes that Miller will oppose the proposal and Philopoulos will support it.

The first part of the conclusion, that Miller will oppose the proposal, is reasonably well supported since Miller opposes **all** proposals to raise taxes, and the specific proposal would raise taxes. However, the second part of the conclusion, that Philopoulos will support the proposal, is not well supported. While we know Philopoulos generally supports increased funding for schools, there is no reason to think that Philopoulos supports Callari's proposal in particular.

The Correct Answer:

B (B) has the features described in the "Overview." The conclusion of the argument in (B) has two parts: that Jane will not rent one of the penthouse apartments in Joliet Towers and that Denise will rent one. The first part is reasonably well supported since (B) says that Jane will not live downtown and that the Joliet Towers are downtown. The other claim is not well supported: Denise wants to rent a penthouse apartment, but she may not want one in the Joliet Towers. While Denise has the general goal of renting a penthouse apartment, it would be unreasonable to think that she will achieve that goal by renting in one particular building complex.

The Incorrect Answer Choices:

A (A) is not very similar to the argument in the passage. While the passage's argument uses two general claims to support the two parts of its conclusion, (A) does not infer any part of its conclusion from general claims. Instead, (A)'s conclusion is based on information about two specific classes.

C (C) supports its conclusion that a particular person will not take a certain action by claiming that that person promised never to take an action of that general type. The argument in the passage concerns two separate actions and it never appeals to any promises that anyone made.

D While the conclusion in (D), like the conclusion in the passage, has two claims, both of the claims in (D)'s conclusion are well supported. The claim that Ed will dislike the extremely sweet brownies is well supported since Ed dislikes all extremely sweet food and the claim that Bill will **probably** like them is well supported since Bill likes most extremely sweet food.

E The argument in (E) draws a conclusion about what people will do in the future based on information about what people have done in the past. The argument in the passage is not based on any claims about what people have done in the past. Rather, it is based on general statements about what two people support.

- *Difficulty Level: 5*

Question 24

Overview: The historian's argument has two premises: most of the revolutionary party's goals were quickly achieved and the party did not have enough power to cause great suffering. The argument concludes that the party was not overambitious and caused no suffering. You are asked to identify a flaw in this argument.

The Correct Answer:

B The historian's argument concludes that the party caused no suffering. But the support provided for this is just that the party did not have enough power to cause the great suffering alleged by its critics. This is not sufficient to establish that the party caused no suffering at all.

The Incorrect Answer Choices:

A The historian's responses to the two criticisms are (1) that most of the party's goals were quickly achieved and (2) that the party did not have enough power to cause great suffering. (1) and (2) are consistent with each other. It's possible for a party to quickly achieve most of its goals despite being weak, for example, if its goals were easy to achieve or if it got outside help.

C To refute the second accusation against the revolutionary party, that the party caused great suffering, the historian states that the party did not have enough power to cause the suffering its critics claim it caused. This indicates that the historian thinks that the party's critics overestimated its strength, so it would not help the historian's argument to establish that the party had **more** power than some of its critics thought it had.

D If the revolutionary party's goals were overambitious, it is likely that the party's goals would be difficult to achieve. But the argument says that most of the party's goals were quickly achieved. Since it is reasonable to think that overambitious goals cannot be quickly achieved, this is evidence that the party's goals were not overambitious. Thus, (D) is false.

E The historian's argument is limited to addressing the two stated criticisms of the party. The fact that the argument doesn't consider other criticisms doesn't affect the quality of the historian's argument against the two stated criticisms.

- *Difficulty Level: 5*

Question 25

Overview: The argument states the principle that withholding information from someone who would find that information painful is not justified if the person would benefit from having the information. The argument then applies this principle to a particular case, concluding that Jane should inform Jason that his supervisor is displeased with his work, even though Jason would find this information painful, since knowing this information would enable Jason to improve his supervisor's opinion of his work. You are asked to identify an assumption that the argument relies on.

The Correct Answer:

E The argument states an exception to the view that it is sometimes justified to withhold painful information; when the information would benefit the recipient, withholding it is never justified. The argument doesn't tell us that Jason would benefit if he were informed of what Jane knows, that his supervisor is displeased with his work; it only tells us that this information would enable Jason to improve his supervisor's opinion of his work. To conclude that Jane should convey what she knows to Jason, we need to fill this gap by assuming that Jason would benefit if he were able to improve his supervisor's opinion of his work.

The Incorrect Answer Choices:

A In order to reach its conclusion, the argument does not need to assume that Jason's situation will worsen if Jane does not tell him that his supervisor is displeased. Jason might benefit from having this information even if his situation would remain unchanged if he were not to receive it, since Jason's supervisor would still be displeased with his work if the situation doesn't change.

B Even if Jason will eventually find out that his supervisor is displeased, it could benefit Jason to find out earlier (by being told by Jane). And the exception to the principle stated in the passage only requires that the person benefit from receiving the information. It does not require that the person would never have the information if it were withheld.

C In order to reach its conclusion, the argument needs to establish that having the information that his supervisor is displeased would benefit Jason. But even if having that information would benefit Jason, he won't necessarily feel grateful for it. He might be unaware of the benefit, or he might simply find the information too painful. So the argument does not need to assume that Jason will be grateful for the information.

D The argument does not need to assume that Jason might eventually improve his supervisor's opinion even if he never learns that his supervisor is displeased. Indeed, if (D) were true, it might indicate that Jason would not benefit from having the information. If that were true, the conclusion would not be supported.

- *Difficulty Level: 4*

Questions 1–6

Synopsis: The passage discusses New Zealand's wool industry. As described in the passage, the price of wool has been driven down by competition from synthetic fibers. This has caused both the production of wool and the revenues generated from wool to decline drastically. The passage asserts that the only reliable way to increase profitability in this industry is to improve productivity, and that this can be achieved through better farm management. Specifically, productivity can be improved if the entire industry adopts the management and breeding practices of the country's professional wool growers, who are much more productive and profitable than the country's family farmers. As a related measure, the passage recommends establishing a genetic research company that would focus on genetic selection for crossbreeding sheep, since the country's best sheep produce wool that is worth much more than that produced by average sheep.

Question 1

The Correct Answer:

D   As discussed in the "Synopsis," the passage as a whole advocates a particular solution to the decline of New Zealand's wool industry. The passage asserts that the only reliable route to profitability lies in improving productivity. The passage argues that greatly improved productivity could be achieved through superior farm management—namely, by adopting the farm management practices of the country's leading wool-growing farms and establishing a commercial genetic research company. Thus, an accurate statement of the main point is that superior farm management should be encouraged in order to revitalize the wool industry.

The Incorrect Answer Choices:

A   While the passage does indicate that wool has fallen behind other agricultural exports in New Zealand, it does not encourage a further shift in this direction. Instead, the passage attempts to find a way to improve the productivity and profitability of the wool industry.

B   The passage does claim that wool growing in New Zealand is deeply divided in a way that mirrors agriculture worldwide. However, the passage uses this claim in order to offer a solution to the decline of New Zealand's wool industry: the entire industry should adopt the farm management practices of the country's leading wool-growing farms. So (B) does not express the passage's main point; it instead expresses a claim that helps to establish the main point.

C   While the passage does assert that competition from synthetics has driven down the price of wool and caused wool production to fall, this is not the main point of the passage. Instead, it is stated as a simple matter of fact to frame the problem to which the passage offers a particular solution. The bulk of the passage focuses on how, even given this fact about the competition from synthetics, the profitability of the wool industry can be improved.

E   Answer choice (E) does not express the main point of the passage. The passage is not presenting an argument for the claim that New Zealand's wool industry has put too much focus on increasing the efficiency of processing. While the final paragraph does include a comment about shifting spending away from efforts to improve processing efficiency, this is merely stated as a side effect of a course of action advocated by the author. It is also worth noting that the passage does not say that dwindling breeding stocks are an issue for New Zealand's wool industry. There is no indication that breeding stocks are declining in number. Instead, the passage says that the breeding stock could be improved in terms of the value of wool produced.

- *Difficulty Level: 2*

Question 2

The Correct Answer:

B The fifth sentence of the first paragraph says that "competition from synthetics has inexorably driven down the price of clean strong wool." So the passage points to market competition from synthetic materials as the cause of the decline in the price of clean strong wool.

The Incorrect Answer Choices:

A The passage says that farmers switching their land to other uses has caused wool production to fall. It does not say that this change in land use was the cause of the decline in the price of clean strong wool. Instead, the clear suggestion is that this change in land use was caused by the falling wool prices.

C The passage does say that Australia is the leading wool producer. However, there is no indication that Australia's wool production has caused price declines for clean strong wool.

D The passage does not indicate that cotton growers are competing with wool growers for available land, much less that such competition is the cause of the decline in the price of clean strong wool.

E The passage notes a deep division between professional wool-farming operations and family farmers. Even though it is natural to regard this as a contrast between "large" and "small" farms, notice that the passage itself never presents this as an issue regarding the size of the farms. More importantly for the purposes of this question, nothing in the passage indicates that the division between farms is the cause of the decline in the price of clean strong wool.

- *Difficulty Level: 1*

Question 3

The Correct Answer:

E According to the passage, answer choice (E) is true of New Zealand's wool industry. The fourth sentence of the first paragraph says that "New Zealand...is the world's largest producer of 'strong wool.'"

The Incorrect Answer Choices:

A The first paragraph of the passage says that New Zealand is the largest producer of a type of wool that is used mostly for carpets. However, there is no indication that the manufacture of carpets using this wool occurs in New Zealand. In fact, the passage talks about wool's contribution to New Zealand's export revenues, suggesting that the wool is likely exported for use in carpet manufacturing in other countries.

B The discussion (in the last paragraph) of industry efforts to improve the efficiency of wool processing suggests that there might be some sort of organization representing the wool industry. However, the passage says nothing about the particulars of such an organization, such as the composition of the board.

C The last paragraph of the passage says that the proposed research company would represent a shift in spending away from industry efforts to improve the efficiency of wool processing. This indicates that the wool industry is currently focused on improving the efficiency of wool processing, but it does not indicate that there was a shift, much less a recent shift, in investment toward researching more efficient wool-processing techniques.

D The third paragraph of the passage says that the world's cotton growers have been improving productivity at several times the rate of wool growers. So the wool industry has clearly not followed a pattern of growth similar to that of the world's cotton industry.

- *Difficulty Level: 3*

Question 4

The Correct Answer:

E As discussed in the "Synopsis," the passage presents an argument about how New Zealand's wool industry can return to profitability. As a centerpiece of this argument, the author puts forward certain farms—namely, those professional farms that are the most productive and profitable—whose management and breeding practices should be emulated. Implicit in this argument is the author's approval of those practices as a means of achieving the desired goal. Nowhere in the passage does the author express any reservations about these practices. Instead, the author's references to them all trumpet their profitability and potential for revitalizing the country's wool industry as a whole.

The Incorrect Answer Choices:

A In the first paragraph, the author says that competition from synthetics has driven down the price of strong wool. However, there is no approval or disapproval implicit in this discussion. Instead, the price declines caused by competition from synthetics are simply treated as a fact that the wool industry needs to deal with.

B The first paragraph states that there have been changes in land use by New Zealand's farmers as the price of wool has fallen over the last 20 years. However, there is no value judgment implicit in the discussion of these changes. If anything, the author is probably dismayed by these changes, given that the author is advocating policies to reverse the decline of New Zealand's wool industry.

C Approval of the farming practices of New Zealand's family wool farmers is not implicit in the author's argument. The author's argument is about how to revitalize New Zealand's wool industry. In the course of this argument, the author explicitly contrasts professional farming operations with those of family farmers. The author argues that the practices of the professional operations, not the family farmers, should be adopted throughout the country. Thus, with respect to the goal of revitalizing the country's wool industry, the author clearly favors the practices of professional operations over the practices of New Zealand's family wool farmers.

D In the last paragraph, the passage recommends a shift in spending away from efforts to improve the efficiency of wool processing. So the author evidently thinks that such a shift is a good thing for revitalizing New Zealand's wool industry. The author may think that efforts to increase the efficiency of wool processing are generally worthwhile but are relatively less important than efforts to increase production. Or the author may think that efforts to increase processing efficiency are entirely misguided. Regardless, there is no approval of such efforts implicit in the author's argument.

- *Difficulty Level: 5*

Question 5

The Correct Answer:

D The research company proposed for New Zealand in the final paragraph is described as one that would concentrate on genetic selection for crossbreeding sheep. The passage claims that such a research company could produce massive gains in productivity. In support of this claim, the passage states that the best New Zealand sheep produce wool worth significantly more than average and that these sheep can be identified and kept as breeding stock. So we can infer that the research company would need to identify these superior sheep. This identification would undoubtedly involve identifying specific physical traits and characteristics of these superior sheep. Thus, it seems clear that one function of the research company would be to create a profile of optimal traits for sheep based on characteristics of the sheep that produce the most valuable wool.

The Incorrect Answer Choices:

A In the first sentence of the last paragraph, the passage explicitly says that the research company would not concentrate on the artificial manipulation of genetic material in individual sheep. So the passage does not suggest that the research company would try to develop more productive varieties of sheep by introducing genes from other organisms.

B The passage says that the research company would concentrate on genetic selection for crossbreeding sheep. There is nothing in the passage to indicate that the research company would concentrate on basic research that could have applications in areas of agriculture other than sheep.

C There is no indication that the research company would try to encourage New Zealand's wool growers to shift their focus away from strong wool. In fact, there is a mild suggestion that the research company might represent an ongoing commitment to strong wool. The passage says that the research company would concentrate on genetic selection for crossbreeding sheep, and that strong wool is characteristic of crossbred sheep.

E In the second sentence of the last paragraph, the passage says that the research company would represent a shift in spending away from efforts to improve the efficiency of wool processing. So there's no reason to think that the research company would oversee the distribution of funds among programs intended to increase the efficiency of wool processing.

- *Difficulty Level: 1*

Question 6

The Correct Answer:

A As discussed in the "Synopsis," the passage argues that in order to increase profitability, the New Zealand wool industry needs to increase its overall productivity. To do so, the passage advocates adopting the management and breeding practices of the most profitable and productive wool-growing farms. The principle stated in (A) is therefore operative in the author's reasoning: in order for New Zealand's wool industry to increase its overall productivity, it should adopt, on an industry-wide basis, the techniques (management and breeding practices) of its most productive members.

The Incorrect Answer Choices:

B The passage does not state or imply that the New Zealand wool industry's leading members should give aid to the less productive members. So the principle stated in (B) is not operative in the author's reasoning.

C Although it seems very reasonable that an industry that has successfully increased its productivity should continue to try to reduce costs, this principle plays no role in the reasoning in the passage. After all, the reasoning is premised on the fact that New Zealand's wool industry has not yet successfully increased its productivity. Therefore, no principle regarding what the industry should do once it has made productivity gains is relevant to the author's reasoning.

D In discussing how to revitalize the New Zealand wool industry, the author is entirely focused on business practices **internal** to that industry. Nowhere in the passage does the author look outside the industry to the practices of the New Zealand wool industry's most successful competitors. The author mentions competition from synthetics, but this is only to explain the New Zealand wool industry's decline, not to discuss any particular business practices in the synthetics industry for the New Zealand wool industry to follow. The passage also refers to the cotton industry (although cotton is not put forward as one of the New Zealand wool industry's most successful competing industries). Here again, however, the author is not advocating using any specific business practices of that industry as a model. Instead, the claim is just that the author thinks the New Zealand wool industry can achieve productivity gains of a magnitude comparable to those seen by the world's cotton growers.

E The passage does not state or imply that the New Zealand wool industry should try to return to the practices it employed at the height of its success. In fact, given the increased competition from synthetics, the practices that the wool industry employed at the height of its success would probably no longer be adequate. So the principle stated in (E) is not operative in the reasoning in the passage.

- *Difficulty Level: 3*

Questions 7–12

Synopsis: The passage discusses a theme that it claims is present in many of Woody Allen's films: that artists, and those who aspire to be artists, are neurotic, narcissistic, and essentially exploitative of those around them. The first paragraph discusses *Deconstructing Harry*, which the author thinks presents the most extreme example of this theme. But the author argues that the theme runs through Allen's earlier career as well. The next two paragraphs give several examples from Allen's earlier works in which artists are portrayed in keeping with this theme. The final paragraph describes a consequence of the nature of artists, as depicted in Allen's films: that the less artistic a character is, the more likely that character is to have a happy outcome at the end of the narrative. Artistic characters eventually suffer because of their neurotic, egocentric, and exploitative approach to art and to their lives as artists.

Question 7

The Correct Answer:

A The main point of the passage is that the theme of the neurotic and narcissistic artist, presented most intensely in *Deconstructing Harry*, is one that Allen has explored throughout his career. We can see that this is the main point because the rest of the passage is dedicated to illustrating, expanding upon, and arguing for it. As discussed in the "Synopsis," the first paragraph discusses *Deconstructing Harry* as the most extreme example of this theme. The second and third paragraphs provide examples from Allen's earlier films of the neurotic and narcissistic nature of artists. The final paragraph discusses a closely related point, namely, Allen's portrayal of artists' lives as ending in misery as a result of their narcissism.

The Incorrect Answer Choices:

B As discussed in the "Synopsis" and the explanation of (A), the passage is about the depiction of artists in Allen's films. Contrary to what (B) states, the passage does not claim that Allen's films suggest for us any conclusion about the pursuit of an artistic life in reality. While the last paragraph of the passage does discuss the differential fates of artistic and inartistic characters in Allen's films, this is best understood as a consequence of the nature of artists as depicted in Allen's films.

C The passage's discussion of *Deconstructing Harry* does not mention the idea that art requires sacrifice. This idea occurs later, in the discussion of *Manhattan*, and it is not a view endorsed by the author, but one that is merely attributed to a character in *Manhattan*. So (C) does not accurately express any point made by the author of the passage, much less the main point.

D The passage does not make any mention of Allen's own experiences or neuroses, and whether they informed his work in any way. It does briefly mention in the last sentence of the second paragraph that the possibility that artists are merely "documenting their private suffering and fobbing it off as art" appears often enough in Allen's works to suggest that it is an unresolved personal issue for Allen. But that does not amount to an assertion that Allen had neuroses or that he used them and other aspects of his personal experience as a basis for the creation of any of his works.

E The passage never claims that Allen's films show us anything about the nature of artists, and it never claims that Allen thinks that artists' narcissism and neuroses enable them to produce beautiful and powerful works. Actually, the second and third paragraphs suggest that Allen thinks narcissism and neuroses don't even lead to real art, but just to private suffering that is fobbed off as art. So (E) does not accurately express any point made in the passage, much less the main point.

■ *Difficulty Level: 4*

Question 8

The Correct Answer:

C The first three paragraphs of the passage, discussing Allen's portrayal of artists as neurotic and narcissistic, make it clear that Allen disapproves of characters in his films who are artists. The last paragraph opens by stating that it is significant, in relation to this issue, that characters in Allen's films are happier at the end of the narrative the less artistic they are, and examples of this are presented. The discussion of these examples in the last paragraph is meant to support the author's thesis that Allen has an unfavorable view of those characters in his films who are artists, and in order to do so it must rely on the underlying principle stated in (C).

The Incorrect Answer Choices:

A Although the passage talks about the persistence of a certain theme in Allen's films, it does not attempt to gauge the artistic merit of Allen's films. So we have no grounds on which to infer that the principle stated in (A), which is about how to gauge a film's artistic merit, underlies any argument in the passage. Furthermore, although the passage makes a claim about Allen's entire career, there is no indication that the author's argument requires such a general principle as that stated in (A), that critics must always consider a filmmaker's entire body of work in making critical claims.

B The argument of the passage, that Allen's films embody a certain view of the artistic temperament, does not involve denying or rejecting the prerogative of any individual, whether fictional or real, to interpret films about the artistic temperament. The passage itself does engage in such interpretation, but does not say whether or not its author is an artist. So there are no grounds on which to think that the principle in (B) underlies the argument of the passage.

D The passage never discusses who should be considered responsible for the meaning of a film. Allen is said to be the "filmmaker," but the passage doesn't actually specify that he wrote the screenplay for any of the films under discussion except *Broadway Danny Rose*. Additionally, the passage never mentions anyone other than the filmmaker, such as actors, contributing to the meaning of a film.

E The passage does not discuss anything about the issue of the prior work of cast members of any films. Also, it does not discuss the artistic merit of any film, or the process of assessing the artistic merit of any film.

- *Difficulty Level: 5*

Question 9

The Correct Answer:

D In the last sentence of the second paragraph, the passage says that the possibility that artists are merely documenting their private suffering and fobbing it off as art appears often enough in Allen's films that it seems like an unresolved personal issue. The third paragraph is devoted to providing additional support for the claim that this idea appears often in Allen's films by discussing how the idea figures in Allen's film *Manhattan*, which features a character who packages personal experiences as art in a way that is dismissed as mere narcissism. So the main function of the third paragraph is to provide additional support for a contention made in the second paragraph.

The Incorrect Answer Choices:

A The third paragraph does not present an exception to anything stated in the first paragraph. The general thesis stated in the first paragraph is that the theme of the neurotic and narcissistic artist was present throughout Allen's career, and presented in its most concentrated form in *Deconstructing Harry*. The third paragraph further exemplifies that thesis by discussing another Allen movie that deals with the theme of neurotic and narcissistic artists.

B The third paragraph does not qualify any assertion made in the first paragraph. The first paragraph mainly asserts that *Deconstructing Harry* provides an extreme example of a theme present throughout Allen's career, that of the neurotic and narcissistic artist; it makes a few minor assertions associated with that point. The third paragraph supports the main assertion of the first paragraph by providing an additional example of an Allen film that portrays an artist as neurotic and narcissistic. It does not qualify that assertion, or any other made in the first paragraph.

C The illustration in the third paragraph does not stand in contrast to the illustration in the second paragraph. In each of these paragraphs, an Allen film is used to illustrate his repeated use of the theme of the neurotic and narcissistic artist. The illustrations differ only in their details.

E As discussed in the explanation of "The Correct Answer," the third paragraph cites details from the film *Manhattan* to support the contention that Allen's films depict artists as narcissistic in fobbing off their personal suffering as art. It makes no claims pertaining to the argument of the last paragraph, which, as discussed in the "Synopsis," is concerned with the different fates of artistic and inartistic characters in Allen's films.

- *Difficulty Level: 2*

Question 10

The Correct Answer:

E The word "peevish" is used in line 11 to characterize Allen's depiction of artists, particularly the writer Harry Block in *Deconstructing Harry.* Note that "peevish" is not used to describe artists as Allen depicts them, that is, it does not say that Allen depicts artists as peevish. Rather, it is used to describe something about the depiction itself. Looking elsewhere in the passage, the first sentence of the second paragraph describes Allen's depiction of Block and other artists as "sour." Both of these descriptors, "peevish" and "sour," characterize Allen's negative depiction of artists as neurotic and narcissistic, a depiction that, as the synopsis explains, is supported by the rest of the passage. So "sour" accurately captures the meaning of "peevish" in line 11.

The Incorrect Answer Choices:

A At no point does the passage claim that Allen's depiction of artists should be regarded as an offensive depiction. In particular, the passage does not in any way make this claim where "peevish" is used in line 11.

B The passage says that Allen depicts artists as neurotic. But there's no evidence that the passage claims that the depiction should be considered a neurotic depiction, rather than just a depiction of artists **as** neurotic. As discussed in the explanation of "The Correct Answer," describing artists as they are depicted in Allen's films is not the same thing as describing something about the depiction itself.

C At no point does the passage claim that Allen's depiction of artists should be regarded as a stubborn depiction. In particular, the passage does not in any way make this claim where "peevish" is used in line 11.

D The passage claims that Allen portrays artists as egocentric (since they are narcissistic and disregard the effect they have on other people in their lives). But there's no evidence that the passage claims that the depiction should be regarded as an egocentric depiction, rather than just a depiction of artists **as** egocentric. As discussed in the explanation of "The Correct Answer," describing artists as they are depicted in Allen's films is not the same thing as describing something about the depiction itself.

- *Difficulty Level: 5*

Question 11

The Correct Answer:

C The last paragraph, where Zelig is discussed, begins with the claim that in Allen's films, the less artistic the characters are, the more likely they are to wind up happy in the end. It mentions three artistic characters, the filmmaker in *Crimes and Misdemeanors*, the novelist in *Husbands and Wives*, and the screenwriter in *Celebrity*, who end up desolate and solitary. Marking a contrast through use of the phrase "on the other hand" (lines 49–50), the author notes that Allen presents Zelig as a "thoroughly inartistic" character who dies an untroubled, happy death. Thus, the author mentions Zelig primarily to serve as a contrast to the fate of artistic characters in Allen's films.

The Incorrect Answer Choices:

A The passage does not discuss any critical view of Allen's films except the one it advocates. It does not suggest that the view it is advocating is the prevailing one or counter to the prevailing one. So there's no reason to think that the author mentions Zelig in order to counter a prevailing critical view.

B The passage discusses only one preoccupation of Allen's works: the neurotic and narcissistic nature of artists. It is not clear how Zelig, a character described as thoroughly inartistic, could be intended to exemplify that preoccupation.

D The passage says that Zelig is thoroughly inartistic. So it's not clear how mentioning Zelig could be intended to demonstrate that artistic characters have always been important in Allen's films.

E As discussed in the explanation of the correct answer, the purpose of the reference to Zelig in the last paragraph of the passage is to serve as a contrast to the fate of artistic characters in Allen's films. In particular, the passage states that Zelig's life is happy in the end and suggests that this is generally true of inartistic characters in Allen's films. But we cannot infer from this that the primary purpose of the reference to Zelig is to illustrate Allen's obvious affection for Zelig or similarly inartistic characters. The argument in the passage as a whole concerns Allen's negative portrayal of artists; the reference to Zelig illustrates this point by contrast.

■ *Difficulty Level: 1*

Question 12

The Correct Answer:

B The last sentence of the second paragraph says that the possibility that artists are just documenting their private suffering and fobbing it off as art is a topic that appears often enough in Allen's movies that it seems like an unresolved personal issue for Allen. This is the view expressed in (B), applied to Allen. The third paragraph cites another instance in which this topic appears in Allen's work, indicating that the author does think that this is a continuing topic in Allen's work.

The Incorrect Answer Choices:

A The passage states (end of second paragraph) that Allen might be personally concerned with the possibility that at least some artists are "documenting their private suffering and fobbing it off as art." But there is no indication that the author holds the view that most people who consider themselves artists are merely documenting their personal suffering and fobbing it off as art.

C The passage makes it clear that the author believes that Allen regularly features unhappy, narcissistic artists as protagonists in his movies. However, there is nothing in the passage to suggest that the author thinks that Allen is unique in doing this.

D The author of the passage makes no claim about whether or not artists must use their personal experiences as a source of inspiration for their work. The passage mentions characters in Allen's films who try to produce art out of their personal suffering, but these characters are represented in the films as failing to be truly artistic. But even if they succeeded, there is no indication that the author would draw any implications from them about real-life artists outside Allen's films.

E The passage says that Allen generally portrays inartistic individuals as happier than artists. But there's nothing in the passage to indicate that the author thinks this portrayal accurately reflects real life.

■ *Difficulty Level: 3*

Questions 13–19

Synopsis: The passage describes the research of Cecilia Payne, an astronomer who theorized that the sun was composed primarily of hydrogen and helium. Payne's theory, which ran counter to the views of most of her contemporaries, was widely rejected when she first proposed it in the 1920s. However, later scientific developments supported her account, which eventually gained general acceptance.

The first paragraph of the passage indicates that in Payne's day, the prevailing view of the sun's composition was that it was mostly iron. The second paragraph expands on this claim, noting that supporters of this view cited as evidence both data from a technique known as spectroscopy and the fact that other objects in the solar system, including Earth and all known asteroids, were known to contain iron. But there was a problem with the prevailing view: it had some difficulty explaining how an iron-rich sun could produce so much energy. Lord Kelvin, a British physicist, had proposed an explanation for this phenomenon, but Kelvin's hypothesis had implications that conflicted with other scientific data. Payne took this conflict to show that the "iron" hypothesis should be revisited.

The passage's third and fourth paragraphs detail the results of Payne's work and the reaction to this work in the scientific community. According to the third paragraph, Payne found that the spectroscopic data that had previously been taken as evidence for the "iron" hypothesis was actually consistent with the possibility that the sun was mostly hydrogen and helium. This possibility met with skepticism among Payne's scientific contemporaries. The fourth paragraph explains one reason for their skepticism: scientific knowledge at the time was not advanced enough to explain how a sun composed almost entirely of hydrogen and helium could produce its energy. The process underlying the sun's energy production was later understood to be nuclear fusion, a phenomenon that was ill-understood at the time of Payne's research. This phenomenon is now very well-understood, and, according to the passage, this understanding eventually provided strong confirmation of Payne's view.

Question 13

The Correct Answer:

B The first paragraph indicates that the prevailing view in Payne's time was that the sun was composed mostly of iron, and that Payne "argued pioneeringly" (line 5) for an alternative to this view. The next two paragraphs expand on these claims, explaining why Payne rejected the prevailing view in favor of her innovative alternative. We are also told in the first paragraph that Payne's proposal, while "later uniformly accepted," initially "encountered strong resistance among professional astronomers" (lines 8–9); the fourth paragraph elaborates on these points. Each of these elements of the passage is reflected in answer choice (B), making it a very accurate statement of the passage's main point.

The Incorrect Answer Choices:

A The passage indicates that Payne's research focused on the sun's chemical composition, not the mechanism by which the sun generates its heat. Moreover, the fourth paragraph states that this mechanism—nuclear fusion—was "inadequately understood" at the time of Payne's research (line 57). Thus, (A) does not express the passage's main point.

C The passage does suggest that Payne's theory of the sun's composition was novel and unconventional. However, it does not make any similar claims about Payne's use of data to analyze the sun. In fact, the passage indicates at lines 12–17 that such data was already used to analyze the sun before Payne began her research. Nor does it ever indicate that Payne's use of data influenced Einstein. So (C) does not express a claim made in the passage.

D According to the passage, Payne's view was not just that the sun contains (some) hydrogen and helium, but that **almost all** of the sun is hydrogen and helium. The passage also says that, at the time, most scientists believed that 66 percent of the sun was iron. That could be true even if the remaining 34 percent included hydrogen and helium. So the passage leaves open the possibility that other scientists had shown that the sun contains (some) hydrogen and helium before Payne developed her theory.

E The passage does not attribute to Payne any specific theory about how the sun generates energy, nor does it rule out the possibility that other scientists had already speculated that this energy might be produced by processes that did not involve iron. Instead, the passage focuses primarily on Payne's account of the sun's composition. Therefore, (E) does not express the passage's main point.

- *Difficulty Level: 4*

Question 14

The Correct Answer:

C In the second paragraph, the passage states that "Earth and all known asteroids contain iron" (lines 11–12). So the passage provides enough information to answer the question posed by (C): there are objects in the solar system other than Earth and the sun that contain iron—namely, asteroids.

The Incorrect Answer Choices:

A The passage does state that Earth contains iron, but it does not indicate the proportion of Earth's mass that is composed of this element. Thus, it does not provide enough information to answer (A)'s question.

B According to the passage, Payne's theory concerned the composition of the sun, not the mechanism by which it generates heat. And while the passage does indicate that our understanding of nuclear fusion relied on the work of Einstein, that does not imply that Einstein himself proved that the sun generates heat from nuclear fusion. So the question posed in (B) cannot be answered on the basis of the passage.

D According to the passage, the theory that 66 percent of the sun is iron was ultimately disproved. It was replaced by Payne's theory, which states that, while the sun contains iron, 90 percent of the sun is hydrogen and most of the remaining 10 percent is helium. This information does not tell us what percentage of the sun's mass is composed of iron—it could be almost 0 percent, or possibly even close to 5 percent.

E The passage indicates that the fusion of hydrogen atoms produces the sun's energy, but it does not indicate whether energy can be produced by the fusion of any atoms other than hydrogen atoms. So it does not provide information sufficient to answer (E)'s question.

- *Difficulty Level: 4*

Question 15

The Correct Answer:

D   At the end of the third paragraph, the passage states that some astronomers sought to account for Payne's theory by claiming that "what she had examined was data about the sun's outer surface rather than its interior" (lines 44–46). So these astronomers were granting that Payne's analysis was correct for the outer layer of the sun, but denying Payne's claim that her theory applied to the sun as a whole. This strongly suggests that they thought Payne's interpretation of the spectroscopic data was not entirely ill-founded, but that her overall conclusions were wrong.

The Incorrect Answer Choices:

A   The passage gives no indication that any of Payne's contemporaries thought that the methodology she used was outdated. It does indicate that many of them questioned her findings, but it suggests that this was due to their preconceptions about the sun, together with the absence of an explanation of how hydrogen and helium could produce the sun's energy.

B   The passage never suggests that any scientists in the 1920s thought Payne had disproved the traditional interpretation of the data. In fact, it states that most of Payne's fellow astronomers dismissed her theory, while others thought she had examined data relevant only to the sun's outer surface (which allows that the traditional interpretation might still be true of the sun as a whole).

C   The passage does not allow us to conclude that any of Payne's contemporaries thought her findings were generally promising. It does indicate that some of them thought these findings might be correct for the outer layer of the sun, but this amounts, at best, to allowing that her theory might have merit when applied to a very limited domain. Moreover, the passage never mentions any "details" that, according to Payne's fellow scientists, needed to be verified in order to definitively assess her account.

E   The passage does not indicate that any of Payne's contemporaries thought her overall conclusions were correct. Instead, it indicates that most astronomers dismissed these conclusions, and that others thought they applied only to the outer layer of the sun (and not, as Payne intended, to the sun as a whole). Moreover, the passage suggests that Payne's contemporaries recognized that her overall conclusions, if correct, were scientifically significant. Conclusions of little scientific consequence generally do not matter enough to inspire "strong resistance" (lines 8–9) among scientists.

- *Difficulty Level: 3*

Question 16

The Correct Answer:

B The last paragraph begins by saying that Payne's contemporaries were not convinced by her findings because, at the time, there was no generally accepted account of how hydrogen and helium could produce the sun's energy. The ensuing discussion of nuclear fusion provides such an account. However, it also explains that this account was not available to Payne's contemporaries; this was because the process through which nuclear fusion produces the sun's heat "was inadequately understood in the 1920s" (lines 57–58). Thus, the discussion of nuclear fusion partly explains the reactions of Payne's contemporaries to her interpretation of the data: they reacted with skepticism because the scientific knowledge that would have enabled them to account for the sun's heat on that interpretation was not yet available.

The Incorrect Answer Choices:

A The last paragraph indicates that nuclear fusion "provided strong confirmation of Payne's results" (line 61)—that is, it produced evidence that supported those results. This shows that nuclear fusion had an impact on the scientific community's view of Payne's findings (by supporting them), but it does not show that Payne's findings had any impact on nuclear fusion, let alone physics or any other disciplines. Thus, the discussion in the last paragraph does not serve to illustrate (A)'s claim.

C The discussion of nuclear fusion in the last paragraph provides an explanation of how hydrogen could produce the sun's energy. But this explanation "was inadequately understood in the 1920s" (lines 57–58), when Payne's research was conducted, so there is no reason to think that it played any role in Payne's rejection of the "iron" hypothesis. So the discussion of nuclear fusion in the last paragraph bears little connection to the claim indicated by (C).

D The last paragraph never suggests that Payne's findings came to be modified in light of nuclear fusion (or any other scientific developments). It does say that nuclear fusion provided a way to explain how the sun's energy could be produced if it had the composition hypothesized by Payne. But nothing in the passage indicates that Payne ever tried to explain the phenomenon of the sun's heat, so the explanation provided by nuclear fusion need not have modified any aspect of Payne's findings.

E Nothing in the last paragraph suggests that Payne relied on incorrect data. Instead, that paragraph indicates that our understanding of nuclear fusion helped to confirm Payne's interpretation of the data she used. Thus, this discussion does not serve to establish the point made in (E).

- *Difficulty Level: 5*

Question 17

The Correct Answer:

A The author of the passage gives multiple reasons why Payne's contemporaries were not convinced by her research findings, including their preconceptions about the sun's composition, their (mistaken) claim that her data applied only to the sun's outer surface, and the lack of a generally accepted explanation of how hydrogen and helium could produce the sun's energy. None of these involved a major mistake in Payne's reasoning, so the fact that the author identifies them as the source of other scientists' attitudes toward Payne's findings strongly suggests that, in the author's view, these attitudes did not result from such a mistake.

The Incorrect Answer Choices:

B The passage does say that, in Payne's view, other astronomers' preconceptions may have resulted in "skewed interpretations" (line 36) of spectroscopic data. But this does not imply that these astronomers deliberately disregarded any data; they may, for example, have accounted for all of the data, but done so in a manner that fit their preconceptions. Moreover, the passage states that the prevailing view of the sun's composition at the time was that the sun was 66 percent iron. So there is no reason to think that any scientists disregarded data suggesting that the sun contained (some) hydrogen, because such data might well have been consistent with the prevailing view.

C The passage says that Lord Kelvin was an "eminent" physicist (line 19), but it doesn't give us any reason to think that his eminence contributed in any way to scientists' ongoing acceptance of the "iron" hypothesis. Instead, it identifies several other factors that could have contributed to this ongoing acceptance, such as the lack of a viable explanation of how a sun composed almost entirely of hydrogen and helium could produce its heat.

D The passage is limited to a discussion of Payne, her research, and the reactions of other scientists to this research. It never discusses the way that science generally operates, nor does it provide any hint regarding whether the reception of Payne's work was typical or atypical. So it offers no grounds for concluding anything about the author's views on this topic.

E The passage indicates that scientists' understanding of nuclear fusion provided evidence for Payne's view. This could be true even if the discovery of nuclear fusion was not impacted in any way by Payne's research; nuclear fusion might simply have been applied to this research after being discovered independently. So we have no reason to think that the passage's author holds the view that the discovery of nuclear fusion would have been delayed in the absence of Payne's work.

- *Difficulty Level: 2*

Question 18

The Correct Answer:

E The third paragraph indicates that, according to Payne's 1920s analysis of spectroscopic data, 90 percent of the sun is hydrogen; the remaining 10 percent, while mostly helium, also includes iron and other elements. On this analysis, then, helium constitutes less than 10 percent of the sun, and iron and other elements constitute significantly less than this amount. Since the presence of these elements was nonetheless indicated by spectroscopic data, (E)'s claim that by the 1920s spectroscopy was advanced enough to detect the presence of elements in these amounts is strongly supported by the information in the passage.

The Incorrect Answer Choices:

A While the passage never mentions spectroscopy in connection with any other fields, this is simply because it focuses only on the relevance of this technique to Payne's theory. Consequently, we cannot know whether or not spectroscopy was applied in other fields on the basis of the information in the passage.

B The passage does not indicate that Payne ever doubted the **data** yielded by spectroscopy. Rather, it suggests that she doubted other scientists' **interpretations** of that data, believing instead that the data supported her own theory of the sun's composition.

C The passage does suggest that spectroscopy played an important role in the development of Payne's theory of the sun's composition, and that our understanding of nuclear fusion helped to confirm this theory. This shows that spectroscopy and nuclear fusion are both sources of evidence for Payne's view, but that does not imply that the former played any role, unacknowledged or otherwise, in the emergence of our understanding of the latter.

D The passage never mentions any 1920s scientists who thought either that spectroscopy was unproven or that it produced questionable data. In fact, the second paragraph suggests that many 1920s scientists used spectroscopic data to support the prevailing view of the sun's composition, which suggests that these scientists thought such data to be generally reliable. Thus, (D) is not strongly supported by the information in the passage.

- *Difficulty Level: 4*

Question 19

The Correct Answer:

B The last sentence of the third paragraph says that some astronomers tried to explain away Payne's findings (line 44)—that is, they tried to show that accepting these findings would not challenge the prevailing view that the sun was mostly iron. By claiming that Payne's data applied only to the sun's surface, then, the astronomers were suggesting that the sun's surface was mostly hydrogen and helium, as Payne hypothesized, but that iron still composed most of the sun. This could only be the case if the composition of the sun's interior differed from that of its surface. Thus, the passage supports the inference that the scientists who tried to explain away Payne's findings were assuming the claim indicated in (B).

The Incorrect Answer Choices:

A The passage gives no indication that Payne made any claims about nuclear fusion, nor does it suggest that she proposed any explanation for how the sun generates heat. This indicates that astronomers seeking to explain away Payne's findings would not have needed to make any assumptions about nuclear fusion.

C The passage indicates that during Payne's time, there was no generally accepted explanation of how **any** amount of hydrogen could produce the sun's energy. So the astronomers who tried to explain away Payne's findings would not have assumed that the amount of hydrogen in the sun was insufficient to produce the sun's energy, because for them, it would have been unclear how additional amounts of hydrogen would have helped to do so.

D There are no grounds in the passage for inferring that anyone believed Payne's analysis of spectroscopic data to be biased by her preconceptions. Rather, the passage suggests that **Payne** thought this may have been true of other scientists. Moreover, the scientists who tried to explain away Payne's findings did so by granting that, with respect to the sun's surface, these findings were accurate, not biased.

E Payne's findings, which were based on spectroscopic data, indicated that the sun did contain a small amount of iron, which suggests that spectroscopy **can** detect the presence of iron in objects as far from Earth as the sun is. The astronomers who tried to explain away Payne's findings did so by claiming that her data were correct when applied to the sun's surface (but not its interior). Assuming (E) would actually challenge this claim, so there is no reason to think that these astronomers made such an assumption.

- *Difficulty Level: 1*

Questions 20–27

Synopsis: Both passages discuss Thomas Sowell's concept of "cosmic justice" and why he thinks it should not be pursued. As noted in the italicized statement before the two passages, passage A is adapted from an article that discusses Sowell's views on cosmic justice, while passage B is adapted from an article actually written by Sowell himself. (It may be worth noting here that some Reading Comprehension passages will discuss the work or views of individuals who are members of a minority group without identifying them as such. That is the case with this passage: Sowell is a well-known economist and political thinker who is African American. Note, however, that you do not need to be familiar with particular people discussed in RC passages in order to answer the questions associated with such passages. All of the information needed for answering the questions is contained in the passages.)

According to passage A, then, what Sowell calls cosmic justice is a kind of perfect justice that requires knowing and taking into account all possible relevant factors. It is, therefore, the kind of justice that only an omniscient being could render. It is impossible for human beings to achieve cosmic justice through law because we can never know all the relevant facts and how they are causally interrelated. For this reason, according to Sowell's views, a legal system should not even try to dispense cosmic justice. The best that a legal system can do is to judge primarily based on outputs (consequences).

Passage B, on the other hand, contrasts cosmic justice with traditional justice. Traditional justice is concerned with justice defined as a fair process. Thus, whether a criminal defendant is found to be innocent or guilty, the defendant is said to have received justice if the trial was conducted under fair rules and with an impartial judge and/or jury. Cosmic justice, in contrast, tries to correct all unmerited disadvantages, even if they are not the result of anything unfair in the process, such as bias on the part of a judge or jury. As an example of the effort to correct an unmerited disadvantage, the passage discusses taking into account a convicted murderer's traumatic childhood before sentencing. According to passage B, because this is unrelated to the fairness of the trial process, it matters only from the perspective of cosmic justice.

Question 20

Overview: The first question in a Reading Comprehension set will typically ask about the main point, central idea, or primary purpose of the passage or pair of passages. This question, on the other hand, asks you to identify the two titles that would be most appropriate for the two passages. But while this question looks different on the surface, it nonetheless gets at the same general idea as main point or primary purpose-type questions. This is because the most appropriate titles will be those that accurately reflect the central ideas of the two passages.

The Correct Answer:

A The first title fits passage A very well, since passage A does indeed focus on Sowell's concept of cosmic justice. As discussed in the "Synopsis," passage A characterizes cosmic justice as a type of justice that only an omniscient being could render, and a major focus of that passage is that human limitations make it impossible for us to render cosmic justice. At the same time, passage B contrasts cosmic justice with "traditional justice," the latter being described in terms of the fairness of a process. So the second title, which sets fairness as a process in opposition to fairness conceived of as justice from the cosmic perspective, is very appropriate for passage B.

The Incorrect Answer Choices:

B The first title is an adequate one for passage A, since the passage does in fact discuss Sowell's concept of cosmic justice, and Sowell's account of cosmic justice might fairly be characterized as a theory of justice. The second title, however, presents a misleading picture of passage B. Deterrence is by no means the focus of passage B. It discusses deterrence only at the very end and only in the context of pointing out a disadvantage of striving for cosmic justice. Thus the second title fails to capture the focus of passage B.

C The first title is not a particularly appropriate one for passage A. It suggests that passage A is primarily about punishments and rewards. It thus fails to give any hint about the central focus of passage A—cosmic justice and the impossibility of attaining it. Moreover, the second title is not at all appropriate for passage B, since passage B does not focus primarily on fair and unfair disadvantages. The second paragraph does mention "unmerited disadvantages," but only in the context of explaining the difference between cosmic justice and traditional justice. The title fails to capture what the passage is really about—cosmic justice as compared to traditional justice.

D The first title is not appropriate for passage A at all. There is nothing in the passage that is critical of Sowell or his views. In fact, though the author is primarily concerned with explicating Sowell's views about cosmic justice, there are indications that the author is sympathetic toward those views. The second title is not appropriate for passage B either. The expression "writ large" is used to describe something that is similar to something else, though larger or more obvious. Thus, if the passage were to present traditional justice writ large, it would talk about something that was similar to traditional justice, but larger or more obvious. It does not do that.

E The first title is a fairly accurate one for passage A. The second title, however, is completely inaccurate with respect to passage B. The second title sets fair trials in opposition to justice as an impartial process, but passage B presents fair trials (trials conducted under fair rules) as the process by which traditional justice is actually achieved. In other words, rather than setting fair trials and impartial processes in opposition to each other, passage B argues that they are crucially linked.

- *Difficulty Level: 3*

Question 21

The Correct Answer:

B Passage B talks about trials in several places, the first of which is the third sentence of the passage. The passage says that under traditional justice, a defendant has received justice if the trial was conducted as it should be. Passage A, on the other hand, does not ever mention trials. Passage A uses the terms "human law" and "human legal systems," but its discussion of law and justice does not get specific enough to include any mention of trials.

The Incorrect Answer Choices:

A, C Passage A does mention punishment and rewards. In the first sentence, it says that cosmic justice refers to rewards and punishments that are truly deserved when everything relevant is properly considered.

D Passage A does mention legal systems. The last sentence of the first paragraph explicitly claims that our human legal systems should not try to dispense cosmic justice.

E Passage A does mention human limitations. For example, the second sentence says that inherent human limitations make it impossible to achieve cosmic justice through human law.

- *Difficulty Level: 2*

Question 22

The Correct Answer:

A Both passages are fairly abstract; however, passage A is more abstract than passage B. There is nothing concrete in passage A: there are no examples at all, and everything is stated in completely general terms. Passage B, on the other hand, does have examples. A criminal trial conducted under fair rules with an impartial judge and jury is presented as an example of traditional justice. Also, consideration at trial of a convicted murderer's childhood is presented as an example of something that is relevant only to the effort to achieve cosmic justice. The presence of these examples makes passage B more concrete than passage A.

The Incorrect Answer Choices:

B Neither passage seems especially inflammatory overall, though perhaps passage B's use of "foolishly" in the first sentence of the second paragraph might be considered a bit inflammatory. So passage A is not more inflammatory than passage B; if anything, a case might be made that it's the other way around.

C The two passages are roughly equal in their use of technical language, i.e., terminology that is introduced by the author or specific to a field of study. The main technical term used is Sowell's term "cosmic justice," which is used in both passages.

D Passage A is not narrative at all. It does not tell any story; it just describes a theory. Passage B may be considered a little bit narrative in that it has examples, which could be understood as telling stories. For example, consider the last sentence of passage B, where it is claimed that mitigating punishment reduces deterrence and results in more crime taking place at the expense of innocent people. Loosely speaking, this might be considered a mini-narrative about causes and effects. If anything, then, passage B contains more narrative than passage A.

E Neither passage seems to be particularly adversarial. While there most likely are opponents of the view under discussion, the passages don't address such opponents, nor do they attempt to respond to or anticipate any criticism. At the same time, while it is true that both passages express opposition toward the notion that human institutions should pursue cosmic justice, passage A cannot be said to be more adversarial than passage B on this front. In fact, given that passage B characterizes efforts toward cosmic justice as foolish (line 44), a case might be made that passage B is the more adversarial passage.

- *Difficulty Level: 3*

Question 23

The Correct Answer:

B To answer this question correctly, you first have to identify the approach criticized by both authors. Recall that in the synopsis of the passages, we noted how both authors criticize an approach that seeks to achieve cosmic justice by taking all of the factors affecting an individual's actions into account when assessing what that individual deserves. Overall, then, the scenario in the correct response must be analogous to this approach. Now let's look at how (B) compares to the two passages on a more specific level.

In making its argument, passage A says that we should judge based not on inputs but only on outputs, or consequences (lines 25–28). Written assignments and class performance are outputs; they are the result of efforts made by the students. In contrast, background factors that are unique to each student are the kind of thing that the author would consider to be inputs. They are factors that each student carries with him or her, and that might conceivably affect their class performance and assignments. Taking these factors into account, evidently as part of an effort to determine what grade each student deserves, is analogous to the goal of achieving cosmic justice by taking into account personal and situational factors that affect a person's actions. Thus response (B) is analogous to the kind of approach the author of passage A criticizes.

Passage B says that cosmic justice seeks to correct unmerited disadvantages in general. The example given is taking a murderer's traumatic childhood into account before sentencing—in other words, taking a person's background into account in determining what that person deserves. Response (B) says that the teacher is grading based in part on background factors unique to individual students. So (B) is most analogous to the kind of approach the author of passage B criticizes.

The Incorrect Answer Choices:

A The scenario in (A) involves adjusting the extent of a penalty (the fine) that is assigned to an infraction (late or lost books) based on whether the individual in question belongs to one of two possible categories: children or adults. This involves no attempt to take into account any "inputs" that are unique to any of the individuals, or to correct unmerited disadvantages. Thus the scenario described in (A) is not analogous to an effort to determine what an individual person truly deserves by taking that person's background and other "inputs" into account.

C The scenario in (C) involves the assignment of a benefit (a parking space) based on criteria that are defined in advance (an employee's rank and years of service) and are intentionally part of the policy of assigning parking spaces. In contrast, the background factors discussed in the passages are factors extrinsic to criminal law that are used to modify what criminal law would normally require. In addition, note that in assigning parking spaces to employees in accordance with what could be described as a fair process, management at the company is acting in a way that is actually more closely analogous to traditional, procedural justice described in passage B. Thus the assignment of parking spaces described in (C) is not analogous to an effort to determine what an individual truly deserves by taking that person's unique background and other "inputs" into account.

D The scenario in (D) bears some resemblance to the approach criticized in passage B in one particular respect: it involves an unmerited disadvantage. In response (D), the unmerited disadvantage is age discrimination. But in spite of this similarity, the scenario in (D) is not at all analogous to the approach criticized in the passages in one crucial respect. In this scenario, the entity being judged by the court—the employer—is not the victim of the unmerited disadvantage. It is instead the perpetrator, the agent that creates an unmerited disadvantage endured by others. Consequently, the ruling handed down by the court is not mitigated because of the disadvantage in question; instead, the ruling is directed at the creator of the unmerited disadvantage, and it is meant to eliminate the practice that inflicts that damage on others. Thus the scenario described in (D) is not analogous to an effort to determine what a person truly deserves by taking into account that person's background, including possible unmerited disadvantages suffered by the person.

E The scenario in (E) resembles the one criticized in both passages in that the university in this scenario takes into account factors that could be interpreted as being part of individual applicants' background in a broad sense—namely, extracurricular activities and community service. However, this scenario differs from that criticized in the passages because the background factors and other such inputs described in the passages are factors extrinsic to criminal law that are used to modify what criminal law would normally require. In contrast, extracurricular activities and community service are intentional elements of the university admissions process. They are accomplishments in the same way that academic achievements are, rather than factors that are extrinsic to the admissions process. In addition, note that in admitting students in accordance with what could be described as a fair process using criteria set out in advance by rules, the university is acting in a way that is actually more closely analogous to the traditional, procedural justice described in passage B.

- *Difficulty Level: 2*

Question 24

Overview: This question asks you to identify something from passage B that is an example of the term "inputs," as that term is used in passage A. Notice, however, that the author of passage A never explicitly says what inputs are. The author assumes that the reader will be able to figure out what is meant by "inputs" from context. Answering this question correctly therefore involves two steps: you have to infer from the information given in passage A what the author means by "inputs," and then you have to identify the thing mentioned in passage B that corresponds to this sense of "inputs."

Here are the indications found in passage A that can enable us to figure out what the author means by "inputs." First off, we can obviously conclude from the last sentence in passage A (and from the general sense of the words in question) that inputs are different than outputs, i.e., consequences. We are also told that determining what a person truly deserves (and thus what is cosmically just) requires considering inputs. But, the author says, determining what a person truly deserves is very difficult because "we are not knowledgeable enough about the person and situation, or smart enough, even if we knew what all the critical factors were," to grasp "how the complex interrelationships among the various variables should affect our ultimate conclusions" (lines 17–22). Taken together, these indications can give us a fuller sense of what the author means by "inputs": personal and situational factors that are critical to understanding what a person truly deserves from the perspective of cosmic justice. Inputs are also the opposite of outputs in the sense that they are not consequences; instead, they are factors that can play a causal role in an individual's actions.

The Correct Answer:

D Notice first that passage B says that it is only from a cosmic perspective that a convicted murderer's traumatic childhood could have any bearing on the crime, and, by implication, on what the murderer truly deserves. In other words, a traumatic childhood is something that would need to be considered to determine what is just from the cosmic perspective. Moreover, a traumatic childhood is clearly not an output, or consequence of a crime; it is something that exists prior to the murder, and that the murderer brings to the crime, providing further evidence that it is an input. This strongly suggests that a traumatic childhood is an input in the sense in which that term is used in passage A.

The Incorrect Answer Choices:

A   Passage B says that fair rules are characteristic of court trials that produce traditional justice, which is fundamentally different than cosmic justice. Inputs are relevant for determining cosmic justice, but not traditional justice. Moreover, inputs are factors that can play a causal role in a crime. Fair rules, in contrast, are part of the trial that takes place after a crime in order to establish what is just in the sense of traditional justice.

B   The term "unjust trial" occurs in passage B's discussion of traditional justice. Passage B asserts that an unjust trial is one that involves a violation of the rules and processes that guarantee a fair trial—for example, one in which there was prejudice on the part of the judge or jury. As noted in the explanation for response (A), however, inputs are factors that can play a causal role in a crime. In contrast, the trial, whether just or unjust, takes place after the crime. So an unjust trial would not be an input.

C   Passage B says that impartial processes are characteristic of fair trials, which are in turn characteristic of traditional justice. As noted in the explanation for response (A), however, inputs are factors that can play a causal role in a crime. So impartial processes would not be an input.

E   Passage B asserts that mitigating punishment in pursuit of cosmic justice will harm innocent people; this harm, if it occurs, would result after a criminal trial, and after the sentence is handed down. As noted in the explanation for response (A), however, inputs are factors that can play a causal role in a crime. So the innocent people referred to in passage B cannot be an input.

- *Difficulty Level: 2*

Question 25

The Correct Answer:

D   Passage B says that it is only from a cosmic perspective that a murderer's childhood could have any bearing on the crime. This suggests that determining the cosmically just punishment for the murderer would require determining the extent to which the murderer's culpability is mitigated by his childhood. Passage A says that inherent human limitations make it impossible to achieve cosmic justice through human law, suggesting that these limitations would make it impossible for a judge or jury to determine the extent to which the murderer's culpability is mitigated by his childhood.

Passage A also provides additional support for this claim. The end of the first paragraph says that in general, human beings do not know all the critical relevant facts (about a murderer's childhood, for example) or understand all the complex causal interrelationships involved (such as how that childhood affected the murderer). The second paragraph adds that we are not knowledgeable enough about the person (the murderer in this case) and his situation to accurately gauge what that person truly deserves. And even if we knew what all the critical factors were, we're not smart enough to perform the complicated reasoning necessary to understand how the complex interrelationships among the various variables should affect our ultimate conclusions. This means that a judge or jury would not be able to understand how all the many facts about the murderer's history, including his childhood, should affect their conclusion about his culpability. It would, therefore, be beyond their ability to determine the extent to which the murderer's culpability is mitigated by his childhood.

The Incorrect Answer Choices:

A   Passage A says that human beings are unable to determine what is cosmically just. So that passage cannot support any claim about whether or not a particular murderer would be responsible for his crime from the perspective of cosmic justice.

B   The only thing passage A says that is relevant to how punishment should be determined is that we should judge based on consequences. This does not imply anything about how much discretion judges should be given in determining punishment.

C   Passage A makes it very clear that humans are fallible. But the only thing it says about how this should affect our judgment is that we should judge based on outputs, or consequences, rather than inputs. That doesn't imply anything about whether or not we should err in the direction of leniency.

E   Passage A says that we can never understand all the complex interrelationships involved in an evaluation of the critical factors—including personal and situational factors—that bear on cosmic justice (second paragraph). This suggests that a person's childhood may very well influence his or her behavior, even if the precise nature and extent of that influence is beyond our ability to understand.

- *Difficulty Level: 3*

Question 26

The Correct Answer:

E   As discussed in the "Synopsis," passage A asserts that it is impossible for human law to achieve cosmic justice. The author then concludes that human legal systems should not even try to dispense cosmic justice (last sentence of the first paragraph). So from the premise that cosmic justice is impossible to achieve, passage A infers that cosmic justice should not be attempted; this inference is justified by the implicit principle that if a goal is known to be impossible, it should not be attempted. In contrast, there is no inference in passage B that makes use of this principle. The argument regarding cosmic justice in passage B is that trying to achieve cosmic justice involves a foolish effort to correct all disadvantages, and that such an effort will ultimately lead to more innocent people being victims of crime. This argument's success or failure is unaffected by the principle expressed in (E), so it is not the case that the argument in passage B relies on this principle.

The Incorrect Answer Choices:

A   According to passage A, we always lack complete information regarding the factors that bear on what a person truly deserves. But passage A doesn't say that we should never take action. Instead, the last sentence suggests that we should sometimes take action; legal actions based on consequences can be reasonable. So the author of passage A would evidently reject the principle expressed in (A).

B   Passage A never mentions deterrence; only passage B mentions it. So there's no reason to think that passage A would rely on a principle that compares fairness to deterrence.

C The discussion in passage A clearly does not rely on the principle expressed in (C). It is true that passage A asserts that we should recognize that we cannot attain perfect justice—in the first sentence, the author of passage A says that cosmic justice is "the perfect justice that **only** an omniscient being could render" (emphasis added). However, passage A never asserts or suggests that we should nevertheless aim for perfect justice; in fact, the author asserts just the opposite. At the end of the first paragraph, the author writes, "But our human legal systems should not try to dispense cosmic justice since we do not know all the critical relevant facts or understand all the complex causal interrelationships involved or even know definitively what cosmic justice really is."

D Passage A makes it clear that we cannot know all of the factors that influenced an action. Yet passage A does not say that we should never pass judgment on an action. Instead, it suggests in the last sentence that we can reasonably judge actions based on their consequences. So the author of passage A would evidently reject the principle expressed in (D).

- *Difficulty Level: 5*

Question 27

The Correct Answer:

D The view expressed in (D) is clearly advanced by the author of passage A. Much of passage A is occupied with the argument that we cannot know all of the factors that influence human action and that are thus critical to the determination of cosmic justice. Nor, according to passage A, could we understand the complex causal interrelationships among those factors even if we did have knowledge of all of them. Thus, the last sentence of the passage states, the best that we can reasonably do is judge based primarily on consequences.

The discussion in passage B of mitigating punishment based on a convicted murderer's traumatic childhood suggests that its author would agree with the view expressed in (D). The murderer's childhood is presumably a factor that influenced the murder; it is clearly not a consequence of the murder. Yet passage B asserts that the effort to correct all unmerited disadvantages (such as a traumatic childhood) is foolish. Moreover, passage B argues that we should not mitigate punishment based on the murderer's childhood because doing so would reduce deterrence, allowing more crime to occur at the expense of innocent people. The harm suffered by innocent victims of crime is clearly a consequence of human behavior, which strengthens the suggestion that the author of passage B believes that human law should be concerned with the consequences of human actions.

The Incorrect Answer Choices:

A The view expressed in (A) is not advanced by the author of passage A. In fact, since the kinds of unmerited disadvantages alluded to in passage B could reasonably be classified as what passage A calls "inputs," it is fair to conclude that the author of passage A would disagree with the view expressed in (A).

B The view expressed in (B) is not advanced by the author of passage A. In fact, passage A clearly states that human legal systems should not try to dispense cosmic justice (last sentence of the first paragraph).

C There is no indication in passage A that its author advances the view expressed in (C). Passage A clearly states that it is impossible for human law to achieve cosmic justice (second sentence). This means that impartial legal processes cannot achieve cosmic justice at all, so they certainly can't be a better means of achieving it than something else.

E There is no indication in passage A that its author advances the view expressed in (E). Passage A clearly states that it is impossible for human law to achieve cosmic justice (second sentence).

- *Difficulty Level: 4*